The ATLAS *of* SHIP WRECKS & TREASURE

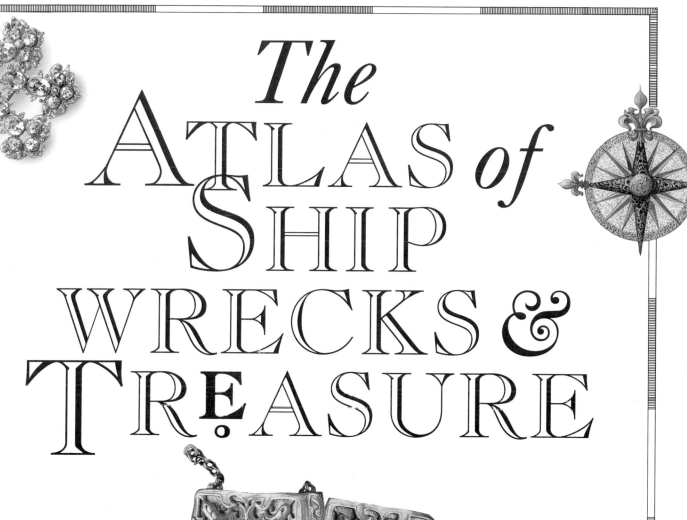

The
Atlas of
Ship
Wrecks &
Treasure

The History, Location,
and Treasures of Ships Lost at Sea

Nigel Pickford

DORLING KINDERSLEY
LONDON • NEW YORK • STUTTGART

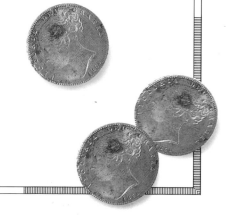

To my father Thomas Pickford

A DORLING KINDERSLEY BOOK

SENIOR EDITOR
Valerie Buckingham

ART EDITOR
Luise Roberts

EDITOR
Lisa Minsky

MANAGING EDITORS
Jemima Dunne and Carolyn Ryden

MANAGING ART EDITORS
Tina Vaughan and Gaye Allen

US EDITOR
Jill Hamilton

PRODUCTION
Maryann Rogers

CARTOGRAPHERS
Claire Ellam, Roger Bullen
James Mills-Hicks

MAP ARTIST
Peter Morter

PICTURE RESEARCH
Christine Rista, Pippa Ward

This book is not intended as an invitation or prospectus
to members of the public or other interested parties to locate,
dive on, or carry out recoveries from any of the wrecks that are
mentioned in the text, and anyone intending to do so should
take appropriate advice with regard to the safety, viability,
and legality of their proposed actions.

First American Edition, 1994
2 4 6 8 10 9 7 5 3

Published in the United States by
Dorling Kindersley Publishing, Inc.,
95 Madison Avenue,
New York, New York 10016

Copyright © 1994
Dorling Kindersley Limited, London
Text copyright © 1994 Nigel A. Pickford
Maps copyright © 1994 Dorling Kindersley Limited

Published in Great Britain by Dorling Kindersley Limited.
Distributed by Houghton Mifflin Company, Boston

Library of Congress Cataloging–in–Publication Data
Pickford, Nigel
    The atlas of shipwrecks and treasure / by Nigel Pickford. – – 1st
American ed.
        p.   cm
    Includes index.
    ISBN 1–56458–599–9
    1. Treasure-trove.   2. Shipwrecks.   I. Title.
G525.P49   1994
910.4'5'03 – – dc20   93–48856
                                                          CIP

Color reproduction by Colourscan, Singapore

Printed and bound in Italy
by Arnoldo Mondadori Editore, Verona

Contents

INTRODUCTION 6

Moorish astrolabe

PART ONE: SHIPWRECKS 11

BRONZE AGE TO BYZANTIUM 12
The Antikythera Wreck 14
The Serçe Limani Wreck 16

THE VIKINGS 18
Sutton Hoo Burial Ship 20
Oseberg Burial Ship 22

CHINESE JUNKS 24
The Sinan Wreck 26
The Vung Tau Wreck 28

LEVANTINE TRADE 30
The Wreck of Ulbo Island 32
The Tobie 34

PORTUGUESE CARRACKS 36
The Flor de la Mar 38   The São Paulo 40
The Madre de Deus 42
The Dourado 44

THE ARMADA 46
The Tobermory Galleon 48
The Girona 50

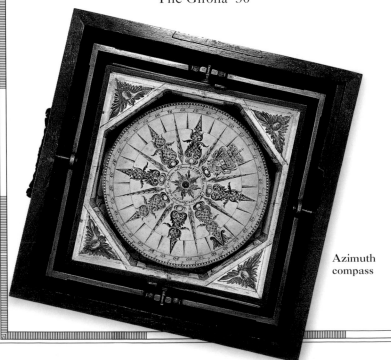

Azimuth compass

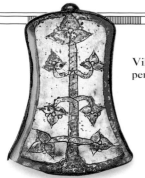

Viking
pendant

Marine telescope

SPANISH PLATE FLEETS 52
The Tortugas Wreck 54
Nuestra Señora de la Concepción 56
The Vigo Bay Wrecks 58
The Guadalupe and Tolosa 60

PIRATES AND PRIVATEERS 62
Las Cinque Chagas 64
The Reinera e Soderina 66
The Whydah 68

EAST INDIAMEN 70
The Batavia 72   The Geldermalsen 74
The Hartwell 76

Turquoise
ornament

Lapis
necklace

MAIL SHIPS AND LINERS 100
The Prins Frederik 102
The Titanic 104
The Egypt 106
The Andrea Doria 108

THE SECOND WORLD WAR 110
HMS Edinburgh 112
The City of Cairo 114
The I-52 116
The John Barry 118

PART TWO:
GAZETTEER 121

THE GAZETTEER MAPS 124
THE SHIPWRECK LISTINGS 160
GLOSSARY 194
BIBLIOGRAPHY 195
INDEX 196
ACKNOWLEDGMENTS 200

THE AGE OF REVOLUTION 78
The Bonhomme Richard 80
The Orient 82

THE GREAT COLLECTORS 84
The Vrouw Maria 86
The Mentor 88
The Fame 90

THE RUSH FOR GOLD 92
The Central America 94
The General Grant 96
The Royal Charter 98

Introduction

WHAT IS A TREASURE SHIP? For most people the word conjures up images of gold- and silver-laden Spanish galleons returning to Europe from the Americas. But treasure cargoes have been a feature of many different historical periods, traversing a wide variety of ocean routes. The East–West axis between the Orient and Europe has been just as important in the history of bullion flows as the Spanish–Caribbean connection. One of the aims of this book is to illustrate the diversity and richness of both ships and their routes in the trade of precious commodities throughout the ages.

The broad definition of treasure ship I have used in the following pages is any ship used to transport a high-value cargo of precious metals or artifacts that do not lose their value when immersed for long periods in salt water. It therefore applies as much to a Second World War cruiser with a bomb room full of gold as to an East Indiaman with a cargo of Chinese porcelain. However, for many underwater explorers, a plum stone, the leather sole of a shoe, a wooden block and pulley, or a section of keel are all greater treasures than gold doubloons because they tell us about life lived by the seamen of the time, and about the technical development of the ships themselves.

Traveling by Sea

The transportation of valuables by boat has a long history stretching back at least 2,500 years and most probably considerably longer. For successive generations, water was the favored method of travel. Greco–Roman civilization, for instance, was centered around the Mediterranean Sea not by accident but because the sea was the unifying factor. It was the mountain ranges of the hinterland that presented a far more serious obstacle to the development of commerce.

ROSARY
Western explorers brought Catholicism to the East, as well as valuable trade.

Ships were the fastest and the safest mode of transport. The risk of robbery when traveling by land posed a greater threat than the perils of the sea. Not that the ocean wasn't a dangerous place. Inadequate maps and primitive methods of navigation contributed to many of the earlier shipwrecks. Perhaps surprisingly, the vast majority of all shipwrecks have occurred in relatively shallow water within sight of the shore, entering and leaving port being one of the most dangerous parts of a ship's voyage.

My Early Influences

The fascination of shipwrecks works on people at different levels. My interest was first stimulated when, as a small child, I removed moldering leather-bound volumes, such as *The Mariner's Chronicle* by Archibald Duncan, from my father's study and read the contents with avidity and horror. My attention was then focused on the tragic stories: heart-rending accounts of poor emigrant families crossing to America, or of young servants of the East India Company on their way from Europe to Fort St. George, India. What stood out most was the extraordinary courage that certain individuals displayed at moments of crisis, and the amazing tenacity with which shipwreck survivors so often clung to life. In many cases it was several years before sailors or passengers found their way back to their native land, undertaking arduous journeys which frequently involved weeks at sea in an open boat, or months trekking across vast and hostile terrain, or long periods in captivity to some foreign potentate. For a child who was growing up in suburban London, stories such as these were highly exotic.

At the time of these youthful readings, my father was working for Risdon Beazley Ltd, an English "cargo recovery" company – one of the most successful and also one

CHINESE PORCELAIN
This sixteenth-century plate was made in China to a design specified by Portuguese traders. At the top of the plate is a Portuguese galleon in full sail.

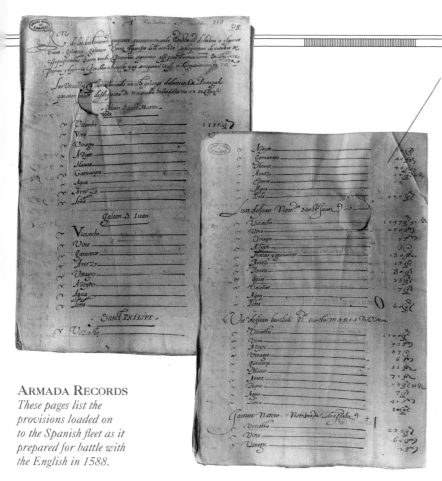

Spanish logbook
Goods loaded on board
the "galleons, galleasses,
naves and patches of the
Armada" included wine,
water, oil, and vinegar.

ARMADA RECORDS
*These pages list the
provisions loaded on
to the Spanish fleet as it
prepared for battle with
the English in 1588.*

of the most secretive that has ever existed. For over 40 years he assiduously researched thousands of high-value wrecks throughout the world, and was involved in nearly 100 successful salvage operations. Seventy percent of the ships he targeted were found with the cargo as predicted, an enviable track record with which few modern-day researchers can compete. From the perspective of a child, his work appeared somewhat dull and tedious, involving, as it did, long hours poring over dusty archival material. It was difficult to connect this dark-suited and bowler-hatted person with the glamorous world of treasure hunting. Indeed, my father would never have used the phrase "treasure hunter" about himself. His business was cargo recovery, a much more mundane activity.

Detective Work

Later on, my interest in shipwrecks shifted away from the human story to focus more on the intellectual problems posed by each story, and I feel that I now understand rather better the compulsion that drove my father. Researching a shipwreck is best compared to an elaborate piece of historical detective work. Logbooks, letters, ships' plans, survivors' accounts, newspaper reports, official enquiries, court actions, insurance records, old

charts, weather reports, tidal movements, fishermen's gossip, sandbank migrations, and the direction of currents all need to be carefully studied and assessed in order to try to come to a conclusion about the truth of where a ship went down, where on that ship the cargo might be stowed, and exactly what cargo it was carrying. Not all accounts of fabulous fortunes on board are necessarily true – far from it. The shipwreck researcher's job is to sift the truth from the myth, to chip away at the accretions of lies that attach themselves to sunken hulls like so many barnacles. Success in this field depends on a painstaking and meticulous tracking down of clues, combined with a continuous and very necessary skepticism about the veracity of all statements.

Locating the widely dispersed repositories of information is an arcane and frustrating activity. Sadly, many potentially rich sources have been destroyed. Much Portuguese material, for instance, was lost in the Lisbon earthquake of 1755, and a fire at the Royal Exchange Building, London, in 1838 caused another major loss. Yet, information on shipwrecks may turn up in the most unlikely of places. I once discovered some fascinating details about a shipwreck in the diary of a seventeenth-century astrologer who had developed a reputation for finding lost treasure, including some that was lost at sea.

Obviously, no book on this subject could pretend to be totally comprehensive, not least because, for most of the centuries under consideration and for most areas of the world, records are simply not available. Moreover, the archive material that does exist is too scattered and too vast for any one person to do more than scratch at the surface, even in a lifetime of research. However, I hope that this book will give some idea of the wealth of information on shipwrecks and treasure that is available.

PARALLEL RULERS
*Ships' navigators used these on
charts to plot their course along
a given compass bearing.*

TERRESTRIAL GLOBE
*This globe was made in 1745
and, in addition to the land
masses of the world, shows
trade winds encountered
in the oceans.*

COPPER DIVING HELMET
This was invented in 1819, and enabled divers to work at depths of 200 feet (60 meters) using air pumped down a long pipe from the surface.

Graves or Commercial Targets?

Treasure hunters or cargo recoverers, call them what you will, do, of course, have their fair share of critics. Some believe that all shipwrecks should be left alone as graves and not violated for commercial purposes. Such arguments carry force, particularly when applied to recent losses. However, the response is often more emotional than logical. First, not all shipwrecks involve loss of life. Second, where there is loss of life, it is the exception rather than the rule for bodies to be trapped inside a hull. Only when the sinking is very quick, and the hull is very large and constructed from iron or steel, are people likely to be trapped on board. The vast majority of people unfortunate enough to be lost at sea float free from the ship itself. The "graves" issue has recently been debated once again with the discovery and exploration of the *Titanic* in 1987 and in 1993. The New York-based company RMS Titanic Inc. has been accused of desecration for lifting a selection of artifacts. Interestingly, far less criticism has been leveled at the American team that photographed and filmed the wreck. This is not entirely logical. If one accepts that the *Titanic* is a grave, then surely it must be equally unacceptable to penetrate and film the site of the wreck as it is to remove artifacts from it.

The idea of the sanctity of a shipwreck is, in fact, a culturally relative concept. The Japanese certainly do not regard them as graves. In recent years they have paid large sums of money for Second World War losses to be salvaged specifically for the purpose of recovering the bodies so that they may be properly buried. The Western position tends to be more muddled. The British government, for instance, designated Royal Navy ships as war graves but did not extend the same dignity to the thousands of merchant ships that were lost in the two world wars. In reality, Royal Navy ships are not necessarily protected from salvage attempts when the Government perceives a commercial interest. The gold on the *HMS Edinburgh*, for example, was salvaged in 1981 (see pages 112–13).

To my mind, a shipwreck is not a grave in any meaningful sense of the word. It is the result of an accident or an act of war. But that is not to say that its salvage should not be handled sensitively, particularly if there is a likelihood of bodies being trapped inside, and if the disaster was recent enough for there still to be people alive who lost close relatives on board.

Archaeological Arguments

Another criticism directed at treasure hunters comes from the archaeological community. The underwater archaeologist is something of a newcomer to the oceans. The traditions of the treasure hunter, by contrast, go back thousands of years. The ancient Greeks have illustrations of divers working on shipwrecks, and one somehow doubts that they were busy laying grids and plotting the position of every pottery shard on the seabed. The archaeologist, however, has a legitimate argument, being concerned that an uncontrolled plundering of historic wrecks will destroy unique examples of an irreplaceable maritime heritage. My difficulty with this argument lies in the more extreme positions adopted by some archaeologists. These purists, for instance, believe that no artifacts should be lifted from the seabed, and that archaeologists must confine themselves to measurement and plotting.

It is unfortunate that archaeologists and commercial salvors have not been able to work more successfully together more often, since they have much to offer each other. The commercial salvor certainly benefits from the expertise of the archaeologist in identifying artifacts, and understanding ship construction and the decomposition of materials. The archaeologist, in turn, benefits from the entrepreneurial skills and financial resources of the commercial salvor. There have been some outstandingly successful

ORIENTAL JADE
Green jade from China (above) and paler nephrite from India (right) were prized by Western merchants.

CLYSTER PUMP
This pewter instrument for administering enemas was found on a Spanish shipwreck dating from 1733.

cases, such as the investigation of the Whydah wreck (see pages 68–69), where salvors and archaeologists have collaborated, and perhaps this will form the pattern for the future.

GOLD MEDALLION
This portrait of the Virgin Mary was salvaged from a Spanish ship that wrecked in 1724 in the Caribbean. The Latin inscription reads "Mother of the Savior."

The Allure of Treasure Ships

The motivation of the treasure hunter has often been caricatured as being one of simple greed. It would be silly to deny that the desire to make a profit is not present among many would-be salvors. But there are also those who have spent large amounts of their own money on project after project, certainly not with the view of any instant financial reward, but out of a passionate and disinterested love of shipwrecks. As with most things human, the psychology tends to be rather more complex than it first appears. If profit is the overriding motive, there are much more sensible routes to making quick money. So, in addition

COMPASS
Nineteenth-century traveling compass.

to greed, there has to be a love of gambling, a strong tendency to dream, a boundless optimism, a passion for quests, an enjoyment of physical risks, and a perverse desire to attempt that which is inherently difficult.

The ultimate attraction of exploring a treasure ship is that it offers the individual an immediate and very powerful way of entering into a different historical period. A shipwreck is a perfectly preserved time capsule. This journey backward in time, as in all the best science-fiction movies, is made possible only through the deployment of state-of-the-art technology, remote-operated vehicles, fiber-optic cameras, and computer-controlled side-scan sonars. In the exploration of a sunken wreck, the future and the past meet. I hope this book will provide something of that unique experience.

NIGEL A. PICKFORD

LEGAL COMPLEXITIES OF SALVAGE

It is a common misconception that anything lost at sea is there for the taking. This is not the case: the legal situation regarding shipwrecks is extremely complex, and anyone contemplating the excavation of a shipwreck must investigate the legal situation very thoroughly.

Establishing Ownership

First, it is necessary to distinguish between the owners of the hull and the owners of the cargo. In most cases the two parties are quite separate. For example, East Indiamen (the ships that belonged to the English East India Company, see pages 70–77) tended to be owned by groups of private financiers, but the bulk of the cargo was owned by the English East India Company. Since the winding-up of the Company, legal title to the cargo of an English East Indiaman has passed to Her Majesty's Government in the guise of the Treasury Solicitor, with whom would-be salvors have to negotiate.

If an insurance claim for a loss has been paid out, then the ownership passes to the insurance company. In London, the Salvage Association handles the interests of underwriters including the War Risk Insurance Office, a government body that insured risks during the two world wars. In the United States, MARAD (the US Department of Maritime Administration) carries out a similar function. If ownership can be properly established, it is possible for a would-be salvor to enter into a contract with the owner. Usually, all costs are paid by the salvor, who then pays the owner a negotiated percentage of what (if anything) is recovered.

Territorial and International Waters

The legal situation is complicated further by the existence of territorial waters. Some countries, such as China and the Philippines, claim exclusive rights over all wrecks lost within what they deem to be their waters (even if it is possible to prove ownership), provided those wrecks have been lying on the seabed for a number of years. On the other hand, most Western European and English-speaking countries continue to recognize an owner's rights, even if the loss occurred hundreds of years earlier. Furthermore, every country has its own ideas on the extent of its territorial waters. For most countries this is 12 miles (19.3 kilometers), but some, for example Thailand, claim much farther.

If the owner is not known and the ship lies in territorial waters, most nations consider that the cargo belongs to the relevant state. However, many countries make a generous salvage award to the salvor in order to deter illicit salvage. In British waters these awards often amount to 75 percent or more of the value of the recovered cargo. When a shipwreck lies in international waters there is an additional complication of determining whose law the wreck comes under. There are international agreements regarding the sea, such as the United Nations' Convention on the Law of the Sea, but not all countries subscribe to them. Usually, each example has to be decided on an individual basis.

Questions of Cultural Heritage

An already confusing legal situation becomes still more opaque when the question of preserving a nation's cultural heritage is introduced. Some countries allow no commercial salvage of historic wrecks, although the definition of historic is open to different interpretations. Australia, for instance, operates one of the strictest underwater archaeological policies in the world, and the government claims all rights to wrecks over 50 years old. It does, however, combine this with a generous policy of awards to divers who locate wrecks and declare their finds to the state body concerned.

France, Spain, Greece, and Portugal also have very restrictive policies on historic wrecks located in their territorial waters. Britain, the United States, and many of the African, South American, and Far Eastern countries take a more *laissez-faire* attitude that tries to reconcile the interests of the salvor with the need to protect important underwater sites of cultural significance. So far, the protection of historic wrecks extends only to wrecks found within territorial waters.

PART ONE

SHIPWRECKS

Full fathom five thy father lies;
Of his bones are coral made;
Those are pearls that were his eyes:
Nothing of him that doth fade,
But doth suffer a sea-change
Into something rich and strange.

ACT 1, SCENE 2, THE TEMPEST BY WILLIAM SHAKESPEARE

From Roman ships laden with classical sculptures to gold-carrying blockade runners of the Second World War, *Shipwrecks* tells the stories of 40 of the most significant wrecks of all time. Spanning many different eras of seafaring, it presents a compelling picture of treasure ships through the ages, illustrating the enormous variety of ships that transported treasure, the magnificent diversity of artifacts carried, and the changing technology of salvaging. Hand-drawn maps illustrate the different historical periods featured, highlighting the main trade routes, the type of ships that sailed them, and the goods that they carried.

SHIPS TRADING IN THE EAST BY
HENDRIK CORNELISZ VROOM
Painted in 1614 by a Dutch artist, this harbor scene shows large
European cargo-carrying ships moored out at sea, while goods are
being unloaded and loaded at the wharfside.

BRONZE AGE TO BYZANTIUM

The Mediterranean Sea has been a focus of international trade for many centuries and contains an exceptionally rich collection of shipwrecks. These wreck sites have provided archaeologists with fascinating and valuable insights into ancient civilizations dating back to the Bronze Age. Between 200 B.C. and A.D. 600 the Roman state was a great trading empire, as well as a military and naval power. Its full-bellied, square-rigged merchant ships, weighing up to 300 tons, sailed from the ports of Brundisium (Brindisi) and Ostia in Italy, across the Mediterranean to entrepôt markets such as Alexandria in Egypt, Hormuz in Persia (Iran), and Aden on the Arabian peninsula. Here they acquired precious stones, exotic animals, spices, silks, steel, and iron, originating from India, Ceylon (Sri Lanka), and China. The raw materials were used to supply the Roman Empire's manufacturing industries. Gems were cut and worked into magnificent jewelry, and textiles were transformed into clothing. These were often reexported, but manufactured exports were not sufficient to create a balance of trade so the Roman Empire had a constant need for precious metals. For this purpose, gold was obtained from Africa and the hinterland of Europe, silver from Spain, and copper from Cyprus.

NORTHERN TRADE
Many traders, including the Phoeniceans, explored well beyond the Mediterranean. Some went as far as Britain; others explored the Baltic Sea.

ILLYRIA

Aquileia

ADRIATIC SEA

SAN PIETRO SHIP ①
A Roman ship that was lost off southern Italy around A.D 200–250, carrying black marble sarcophagi probably from Asia Minor.

Narbo
(Narbonne)

Massilia
(Marseille)

ITALY

Ancona

② Piombino

CORSICA

Rome
Ostia

GIGLIO SHIP ②
A bronze helmet, pottery, and musical instruments have been salvaged from this Greek ship that traded between Tuscany and Greece in 750–500 B.C.

Puteoli
(Pozzuoli)

③

TYRRHENIAN SEA

Brundisium
(Brindisi)

Tarentum
(Taranto)

①

Tarraco
(Tarragona)

BALEARES
(BALEARIC ISLANDS)

SARDINIA

LYSIPPOS SHIP ③
A Greek ship that wrecked off Italy, with a cargo of sculptures now in the Paul Getty Museum, California.

LIPARI
ISLANDS

MEDITERRANEAN SEA

HISPANIA
(SPAIN)

Panormus
(Palermo)

SICILY

Gades
(Cadiz)

Carthage
(Tunis)

④

MAHDIA SHIP ④
This Roman merchant ship was found in 1907 near Tunis, and contained marble columns and statues.

ROMAN GOLD NECKLACE
This intricate Roman necklace with a crescent-shaped pendant would have been designed for a wealthy Roman woman. It was made from plaited gold wire, probably using gold that had been obtained from Africa.

Leptis Magna
(Al Khums)

AFRICA

Significant Mediterranean Traders

Extensive trading in high-value goods carried out by the Egyptians, Phoenicians, Phocaeans, and Greeks had begun many centuries before, and continued throughout the height of Roman dominance. For example, the Egyptians brought gold, incense, and myrrh from Punt in southern Arabia; the Phoenicians pursued the valuable trade in shellfish murex (which produced the imperial purple dye), and traded gold from Leptis Magna and Ophir – thought to be the Somali coast of east Africa; the Phocaeans sought raw materials from as far away as Britain; and the Greeks traded with India for precious stones.

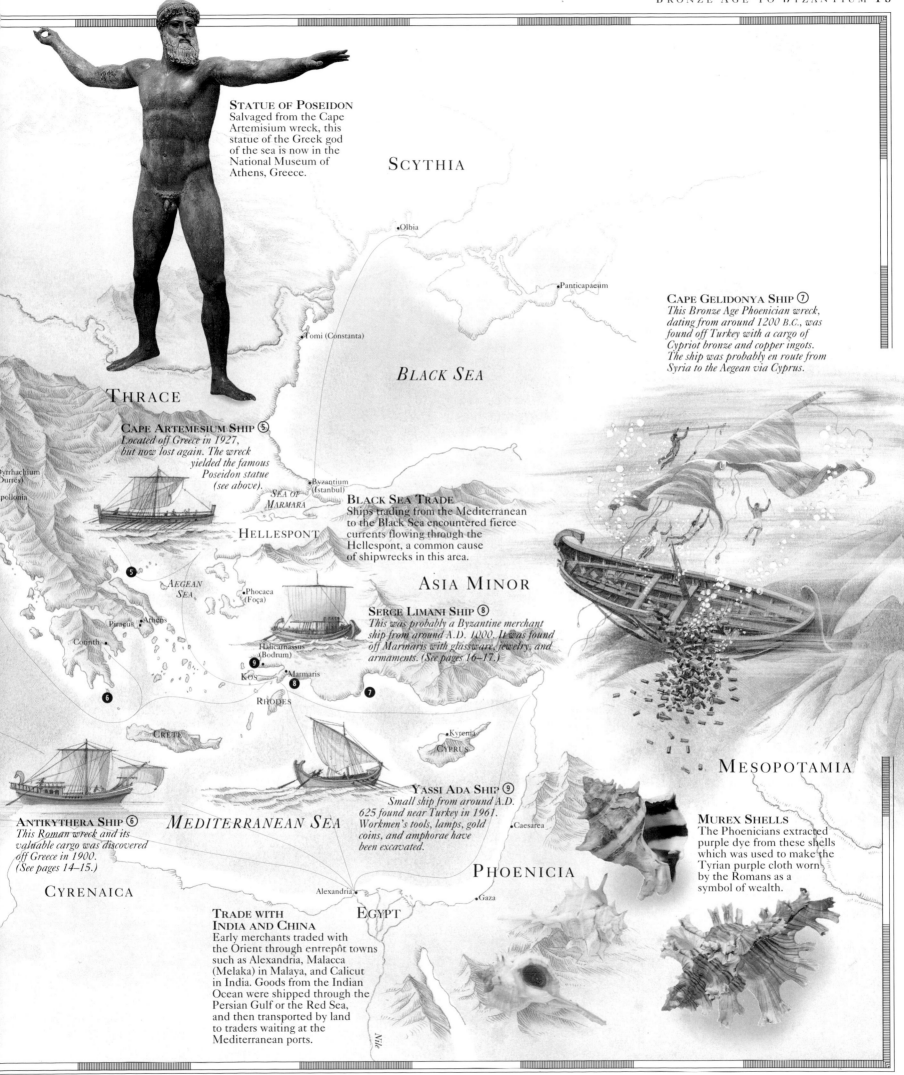

STATUE OF POSEIDON
Salvaged from the Cape Artemisium wreck, this statue of the Greek god of the sea is now in the National Museum of Athens, Greece.

SCYTHIA

•Olbia

•Panticapaeum

CAPE GELIDONYA SHIP ⑦
This Bronze Age Phoenician wreck, dating from around 1200 B.C., was found off Turkey with a cargo of Cypriot bronze and copper ingots. The ship was probably en route from Syria to the Aegean via Cyprus.

•Tomi (Constanta)

BLACK SEA

THRACE

CAPE ARTEMESIUM SHIP ⑤
Located off Greece in 1927, but now lost again. The wreck yielded the famous Poseidon statue (see above).

Dyrrhachium (Durrës)

Apollonia

Byzantium (Istanbul)

SEA OF MARMARA

BLACK SEA TRADE
Ships trading from the Mediterranean to the Black Sea encountered fierce currents flowing through the Hellespont, a common cause of shipwrecks in this area.

HELLESPONT

ASIA MINOR

AEGEAN SEA

⑤

Phocaca (Foça)

SERÇE LIMANI SHIP ⑧
This was probably a Byzantine merchant ship from around A.D. 1000. It was found off Marmaris with glassware, jewelry, and armaments. (See pages 16–17.)

Piraeus •Athens

Corinth

Halicarnassus (Bodrum)

⑨

Kos

⑧ Marmaris

⑦

⑥

RHODES

CRETE

Kyrenia

CYPRUS

MESOPOTAMIA

YASSI ADA SHIP ⑨
Small ship from around A.D. 625 found near Turkey in 1961. Workmen's tools, lamps, gold coins, and amphorae have been excavated.

ANTIKYTHERA SHIP ⑥
This Roman wreck and its valuable cargo was discovered off Greece in 1900. (See pages 14–15.)

MEDITERRANEAN SEA

•Caesarea

MUREX SHELLS
The Phoenicians extracted purple dye from these shells which was used to make the Tyrian purple cloth worn by the Romans as a symbol of wealth.

CYRENAICA

Alexandria•

EGYPT

•Gaza

PHOENICIA

TRADE WITH INDIA AND CHINA
Early merchants traded with the Orient through entrepôt towns such as Alexandria, Malacca (Melaka) in Malaya, and Calicut in India. Goods from the Indian Ocean were shipped through the Persian Gulf or the Red Sea, and then transported by land to traders waiting at the Mediterranean ports.

Nile

THE
ANTIKYTHERA WRECK

In October 1900 Captain Dimitrios Kondos and his team of sponge divers were working off the north coast of Antikythera, a tiny Greek island between Crete and the mainland of Greece at the entrance to the Aegean Sea. This island, by virtue of its location in the center of a busy Mediterranean shipping route and with its inhospitable coastline of perpendicular cliffs dropping steeply into the sea, has been a natural hazard to shipping for thousands of years, and so home to many wrecks. However, Captain Kondos and his team were not looking for shipwrecks but for sponges.

Early sponge diving in the Mediterranean was carried out by naked skindivers. By the 1870s copper helmets and canvas suits were in use, which enabled divers to work at 200 feet (60 meters) for up to five minutes, and it was this kind of equipment that was used by Captain Kondos. The job was still dangerous, perhaps even more so with an increased risk of carbon-dioxide-induced narcosis, and the danger of the "bends" from too sudden a decompression of nitrogen in the bloodstream as the diver surfaced.

When one of Kondos's divers, Elias Stadiatos, signaled to return to the surface before his five minutes were up, Kondos assumed something was wrong. This was reinforced when Stadiatos started raving about seeing heaps of rotting naked corpses and horses on the seabed. It was only after Kondos dived and returned with the arm of a bronze statue that it became clear a wreck had been found.

Together with the Greek Education Ministry, and supported by the Greek Navy, Kondos and his divers were engaged to salvage the wreck. By the end of 1901, an amazing haul of artifacts had been recovered in an operation that was a triumph of early underwater archaeology. Finds included statues of a philosopher's head and a young boy (see opposite), a discus thrower, Hercules, a marble bull, and a bronze lyre.

ROMAN MERCHANT SHIP
The Antikythera ship is thought to have been very similar to this model in design and construction, except that its hull was sheathed in lead below the waterline to protect against the corrosive effects of marine life. Note the swan's head carving on the stern post, a common decorative motif on Roman ships.

Main sail
Decorated with mythological beasts

Steering oar
One oar on each side of the ship, both worked by one man on deck

Wooden hull
Probably would have been caulked with a tar and flax mixture

STATUE OF A YOUTH
This bronze sculpture has been preserved in remarkably good condition, considering that it was underwater for almost 2,000 years. The statue is now held at the National Museum of Athens, Greece.

Identifying the Wreck

The age of the wreck was a source of controversy for years. The bronze statues date from the fourth century B.C., but the marble statues were thought to be, for the most part, first-century B.C. copies of earlier classical originals. The amphorae carried had originated from diverse sources such as Rhodes, Kos, and southern Italy; the pottery plates probably came from Asia Minor, and glassware from Alexandria. Detailed analysis of all the more humble domestic items suggests a shipwreck date of around 70–80 B.C., and a trading route linking the Aegean with Rome. Various evidence points to this wreck being a Roman ship. It was made of elm, which was often used by Romans. It has been suggested that it might have been carrying part of the loot captured by General Sulla from Athens in 86 B.C. Sulla was well known for shipping vast quantities of plundered antiques back to Rome. After his victory against Athens, Sulla was in Asia Minor where it is likely that this ship called. Also, there is an inconclusive but fascinating reference by the Greek writer Lucian to one of Sulla's ships carrying plunder and sinking off Malea, which happens to be in the vicinity of Antikythera. Excavation work still continues because several items such as lead anchor stocks or smaller bronze items, which one might have expected to have been found nearby, have not yet been located.

PHILOSOPHER'S HEAD
This was found in 1901 during the exploration of the Antikythera wreck.

Forestay
Linking the two masts, giving strength

FACTS AND FEATURES

Treasure	Bronze and marble statues
Discovered	Off Greece in 1900
Capacity of ship	300 tons
Route	Greece to Italy

SPONGE DIVERS

In classical literature, the tiny port of Simi, Greece, was famed for producing the best sponge divers in the world, and the tradition of sponge diving went back to at least the fifth century B.C.

The Antikythera wreck was found by sponge divers from Simi. The salvage work was tough and dangerous, and involved working at the very limits of the technological development of the day.

Artemon (foresail)
Flew from forward-leaning mast, forerunner of a bowsprit

DIVING FROM A BOAT
Detail from an early Greek vase.

Rounded hull
Merchant ships were designed for carrying bulk cargoes

THE
SERCE LIMANI WRECK

By the year A.D. 1000 the Mediterranean was almost entirely a Muslim lake. Southern Spain in the west, the entire north African coast, Syria in the east, and many of the strategically crucial islands such as Sicily were all under Islamic influence.

There was no single unified Muslim political structure in the same way that there had been a single Roman empire before it. Despite this, there was a strong coherent Muslim culture, as well as highly developed trading links. The only other significant power in the Mediterranean at this time was the Christian Byzantine empire centered on what is now Turkey and Greece, with Istanbul (Constantinople) at its hub.

In 1973 the American archaeologist George Bass discovered a wreck from about A.D. 1000 in the bay of Serçe Limani on the southern Turkish coast. It is hardly surprising that he was eager to excavate it, because so little was known about the ships and the maritime trade of this period of world history.

Hybrid Design

Excavations began in 1977 and work still continues on this fascinating underwater project. Knowledge gleaned from this work has altered thinking about Byzantine ship-building techniques, and also Islamic glass manufacture at a crucial stage in its history.

The Serçe Limani ship was built in a style that showed an interesting mix of the old Greco–Roman tradition of shipbuilding (which involved constructing the shell first using intricately jointed planking), and the gradually emerging new method (which meant building the frame first and then attaching the planking to the frame). As a result, the ship's frame was of a stronger construction than those found in earlier ships.

Muslim and Christian Influences

One of the greatest puzzles posed by the investigation of the Serçe Limani wreck has been the disentanglement of the Christian and Arabic influences, and the enigma of where the ship originated and what trade it was engaged in when it was wrecked.

At the beginning of the excavation work, experts thought the ship was Muslim-owned. More recent evidence has led George Bass to conclude that it was more probably Christian-owned, with a crew from the Black Sea area, but quite clearly engaged in trade with the Arab world. It is clear that, although the Serçe Limani wreck occurred only 50 years before the Crusades began, there was much commercial and social integration between Christian and Islamic cultures.

The evidence of Muslim culture is both pervasive and diverse. Ceramics recovered from the cargo hold show Egyptian and Syrian influences. A number of gold coins of Islamic origin have been found. Chessmen and a beautiful gold earring, both of which show Arabian design, have been recovered.

On the other hand, many salvaged items show a strong Christian tradition. Lead fish net weights are decorated with Christian crosses and, in one instance, with the name of Jesus. A number of weapons appear to have originated from the Christian-dominated Balkans. The amphorae that have been recovered are thought to have come from the related area of the Sea of Marmara. Some have pitch-lined interiors, which suggests they were used for wine, the consumption of which was forbidden in the Muslim world. Bones from pigs, also prohibited by Muslims, were found at the ship's stern, where officers and merchants would have lived.

Floating Bottle Bank

During the excavation of the Serçe Limani, significant quantities of glass were found at the site. All the glass recovered shows traces of lead from northwest Iran. This evidence is consistent with the suggestion that the ship was embarked somewhere along the coast of modern-day Israel. This area was a major center for Islamic glass manufacture around A.D. 1000. The ship's final point of call was probably Caesarea or another nearby port.

The main cargo that has survived underwater consists of three tons of broken glass, which was contained in the ship's hold.

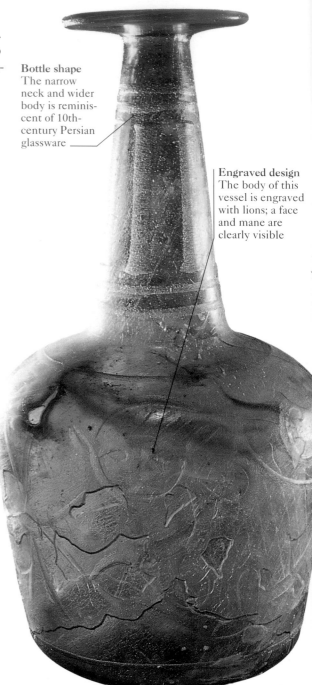

Bottle shape
The narrow neck and wider body is reminiscent of 10th-century Persian glassware

Engraved design
The body of this vessel is engraved with lions; a face and mane are clearly visible

GLASS VESSEL FROM THE SERCE LIMANI WRECK SITE
Arab manufacturers were famous for their glass products during this period, being both technically and artistically far in advance of any producers in western Europe. Over 80 unbroken glass vessels, such as this one, were found in the living quarters of the wreck. All these vessels were engraved, usually quite simply although this one has a sophisticated design. The thickness of the vessels ranged from less than 0.04–1 inch (1 mm to 2–3 cm). Most of the glass was clear, but some was tinted green or blue.

EARLY TRADING ROUTES

The main Mediterranean current flows eastward through the Strait of Gibraltar, along the north African coast, then splits: part of it flows up along the west coast of Italy and around to France; the other part continues around Lebanon and Turkey, finally expending itself in the Aegean Sea. Trading routes within the Mediterranean followed these currents for speedier sailing.

Trading with India and China involved transshipment at various entrepôt towns such as Alexandria, Hormuz, Aden, Calicut, and Melaka. The Indian Ocean, Persian Gulf, and Red Sea transport was dominated by Arab and Indian shipping. Beyond Melaka the dominant form of shipping was the Indonesian proa or sampan, and beyond southern Cambodia the Chinese junk was preeminent. However, these areas were not exclusive. Up to the 10th century A.D., Arab shipping traded directly with China, only in later centuries confining itself to the limits of the Indian Ocean.

GLASS WEIGHTS
These weights were used for weighing coins. Glass was a favored material for this because it was tamperproof. These examples from the Serçe Limani wreck are worn by seawater but inscriptions on others date the wreck to around 1024.

It is most unlikely that this glass represents finished glassware that was smashed when the ship wrecked. First, although the cause of the ship's loss remains unknown, there is no evidence that its end was very violent. This can be deduced because a large part of the hull is still relatively intact where it has been well preserved beneath mud and sand. Secondly, though all the items of glassware that have been recovered from the cargo hold were broken, some intact glassware was found in the living areas. And thirdly, the broken glass has a quantity of glassworks waste mixed in with it. So it seems that the Serçe Limani wreck was an early form of bottle bank: used and broken glass were probably being returned to a factory for remelting.

Other Cargo and its Distribution

In addition to glass, it is likely that the vessel had quantities of raisins and the spice sumac on board (however, these were subsequently washed away), because small traces of these items have been found. Without a considerable weight of a bulk cargo like these food products, the ship would have been seriously unstable.

Intriguingly, for such a small ship, two separate living quarters have been identified. The smaller area was in the bow of the ship, and yielded kitchen utensils such as cooking pots blackened with use, along with glassware, ceramics, and wooden combs. The larger area was near the stern, where the items recovered included glazed ceramics, bronze and copper vessels such as buckets and pitchers, sets of weights, silver and gold jewelry, and a large quantity of weaponry consisting of swords, an ax, 11 spears, and 52 javelins.

Most of the weapons were likely to have been carried for self-defense rather than for trading, because they appear to have been issued to the people on board in sets of one spear and five javelins, each set individually wrapped in a burlaplike cloth.

THE SHIP'S CONSTRUCTION

The Serçe Limani wreck was a small merchant trader about 50 feet (15 meters) in length, capable of carrying approximately 30 tons of cargo, and was probably built on the Black Sea.

The ship had a flattish-shaped bottom and was relatively broad for its length, having a width to length ratio of roughly one to three. It would have had a single mainmast with two triangular (lateen) sails. Both iron and wooden nails had been used in attaching the planking to the frame. There is no evidence of the planks having been fastened with the coir ropes, made from coconut fiber, that were traditionally used to stitch together the planking of Arab dhows built for sailing the Indian Ocean. So, in this respect, the Arab influence upon the shipbuilding methods used for the Serçe Limani was perhaps less significant than the Mediterranean influence.

OUTLINE OF THE SERÇE LIMANI WRECK
The ship was built entirely of pine, except for the elm keel. Its remains are displayed in the Bodrum Museum in Turkey, and a reconstruction shows clearly where the amphorae were found, closely packed together.

Eastern Goods

Not all the goods salvaged from this wreck came from around the Mediterranean. One of the items recovered was a bronze sword hilt that seems to have an Eastern influence on its design. This has an unusual, Indian-style decorative motif of the two-headed Hansa bird, and so is a reminder that Arabian shipping looked out toward the Indian Ocean as well as across the Mediterranean.

THE VIKINGS

From the ninth century onward there occurred a period of massive Scandinavian expansion and enterprise. This resulted in incredible sea voyages that were of a varied nature and purpose: in part trading, in part plundering, and in part colonizing. The Swedes sailed east as far as the Black Sea and Caspian Sea; the Norwegians and Danes ventured south to the shores of Ireland, England, France, and Spain, and on into the Mediterranean as far as Italy. There was also a westerly migration to Iceland, Greenland, and the shores of America, which the Vikings reached in the eleventh century.

Much of our knowledge of Viking ships comes from the longships (known also as langskips) found in the burial sites of Oseberg and Gokstad in Norway. These ships were oar-powered, double-ended with high stem and stern posts, had a shallow draft, and one large square sail. They were constructed for speed and lightness, often being carried overland. A recently built replica of the Gokstad boat has crossed the Atlantic using sails and oars in 28 days.

The longships are unlikely to have been used to reach America, or for the great trading voyages between Scandinavia, Iceland, Greenland, and Britain that are written about so frequently in the sagas. Instead, Vikings are thought to have used ships similar to a merchant ship that was discovered at Skuldelev, Denmark. This was a hafskip, or knarr (knorr) ship as it is called in the sagas, and was 66 feet (20 meters) long. Hafskips depended mainly on sailpower rather than oars, had a side rudder, and were broader and deeper than the langskip, with a higher freeboard. They were very brightly painted, with red and blue striped sails. The cargo was stowed amidships in an open hold, and covered with an ox skin. Each ship could carry between 50 and 100 passengers and crew, and its average life was 30 years.

Extraordinary Navigation Skills

Viking navigators did not have the benefit of the compass, nor were they able to determine their latitude by means of the quadrant or sextant, and yet they navigated the oceans far out of sight of any land. Their main aids were a lead sounding device, a form of dead reckoning, and a wide knowledge of the sun and stars. Despite their obvious skills of seamanship, however, Viking sailors frequently found themselves lost, hardly surprising in the thick fogs of their northern waters. They even had a special word to describe this condition of being lost at sea: *hafvilla*.

Davis Strait

DANGEROUS ICE
The approach to the east coast of Greenland was hazardous because of the proximity of the ice fields.

TRADING GOODS
Greenlanders traded walrus ivory, hides from narwhal and walrus, and the occasional more exotic item such as a live polar bear, for foodstuffs, household utensils, and cash.

GREENLAND

SHIPS OF ERIK RAUDI ①
Traveling from Iceland to Greenland on an early colonizing voyage, a fleet of ships was lost in 986 on the southwest coast of Greenland.

Brattahlid

LABRADOR SEA

Cape Farewell

MARKLAND

STANGARFOLI ②
This ship was wrecked in 1189 on the coast of Greenland, carrying money and artifacts from Iceland.

SHIP OF ARNBJORN ③
A Viking ship that was lost in 1125 on the east coast of Greenland. A large sum of money was found near the site soon after.

ATLANTIC OCEAN

Gulf of St. Lawrence

VINLAND (NEWFOUNDLAND)

SEAQUAKES
Vikings dreaded the phenomenon of "sea hedges" when the ocean waves appeared to hem the ship in on three sides, as if with impenetrable walls.

GUARD FOR A VIKING SWORD, C. 1100
Cast in brass, and engraved with animal motifs, this sword guard displays the sophistication that is typical of Viking craftsmanship. It was found off the Smalls reef, near the coast of Wales in 1991.

SARGASSO SEA

VIKING SWORD, C. 900–1000
The blade was double-edged, with a slightly blunted tip. The metal handgrip would probably have been covered with leather.

STRANDIR COAST
The northwest coast of Iceland
was notoriously dangerous,
and many Viking vessels
were wrecked there.

ICELANDIC TRADE
Iceland exported woolen
cloth, skins, fish, and
falcons in exchange
for wine, foodstuffs,
copper, iron,
and tin.

SHIP OF BISHOP OLAF ④
This vessel wrecked at Hitarnes,
Iceland, with a rich lading of walrus,
ivory, and other valuables.

SHIP OF CECILIA ⑥
Cecilia, the daughter of King
Hakon, was returning home
to Bergen, Norway, in 1248
after marrying King Harald of
the Hebrides, when her ship was
lost south of the Shetlands. Many
important dignitaries were on board
when the ship sank, and wreckage
was later washed up on the shore.

FIFA AND HJALP ⑧
Lost off the Shetlands in
1151, these were carrying artifacts
from Bergen,
Norway.

OSEBERG SHIP ⑪
This ninth-century royal
burial ship was excavated
in Norway in 1904.
(See pages 22–23.)

GOKSTAD SHIP ⑫
Ninth-century burial
ship containing
wooden artifacts

VIKING DRINKING CUP
Its style of decoration is
characteristic of glass from
eighth- or ninth-century
western Europe.

SILVER CUP
Dating from the eleventh
century, this highly decorated
Viking cup displays
Byzantine influences.

SHIP OF FLOSSI ⑤
Twelfth- or thirteenth-century
ship that sank, because of
overloading, while sailing
from Norway to Iceland.

SMALLS WRECK ⑥
This ship was wrecked off
the Welsh coast around
1100. A sword guard was
recovered (see opposite).

SUTTON HOO ⑨
Burial ship from about
625, excavated in 1939.
(See pages 20–21.)

MERCHANT SHIP ⑩
Hafskip from about 1000,
excavated at Skuldelev,
Denmark (see opposite).

INLAND ROUTES
Vikings sailed up rivers
such as the Loire, the
Garonne, and the Meuse.
Churches and monasteries
were particular targets for
plundering en route.

ROUTE TO THE
BLACK SEA
The Dnieper provided
access to Istanbul, an
important entrepôt port
linking East with West.

TRADE WITH
THE ORIENT
Vikings navigated
down the Volga to
the Caspian Sea to
trade furs, gold, and
silver for Eastern
jewels, spices,
and silks.

BARENTS
SEA

NORWEGIAN
SEA

WHITE
SEA

Gulf of
Bothnia

NOVGOROD

Trondheim

RUSSIA

FAEROE
ISLANDS

Shetlands

NORWAY
Bergen

Gokstad

Gulf of
Finland

Pentland
Firth

Skagerrak

SWEDEN

Gotland

Gulf of
Riga

Volga

SCOTLAND

NORTH
SEA

DENMARK

Skuldelev

Roskilde

BALTIC
SEA

IRELAND

IRISH
SEA

NORMAN
ENGLAND

English
Channel

WALES

Kiev

Dnieper

Volga

Rhine

Meuse

Paris

Loire

FRANCE

Rhône

Garonne

Bay of
Biscay

Gulf of
Genoa

ITALY

Danube

BLACK SEA

CASPIAN
SEA

Gulf of
Lions

ADRIATIC
SEA

Constantinople
(Istanbul)

BYZANTINE EMPIRE

Euphrates

Tigris

SPAIN

TYRRHENIAN
SEA

IONIAN
SEA

AEGEAN
SEA

Strait of
Gibraltar

MEDITERRANEAN SEA

Baghdad

MUSLIM
CALIPHATES

Persian
Gulf

SUTTON HOO

BURIAL SHIP

One of the most spectacular treasure ship finds of all time began in a rather low-key manner. In 1938 Mrs. Pretty, who had a passionate interest in things archaeological, employed an archaeologist, Basil Brown, to excavate three burial mounds on her land at Sutton Hoo, Suffolk, England. The findings encouraged them to excavate another mound a year later. The mound was approximately 100 feet (30 meters) across, and its excavation unearthed an extraordinary collection of ornate gold, bronze, and jeweled items of the Viking period.

The ship that was discovered at Sutton Hoo is not a treasure ship in the usual sense of the word. It was not lost at sea through accident or war but was deliberately buried on land as part of an Anglo–Saxon funeral ritual. Indeed, there was no ship as such found at all: every last scrap of wood had decomposed and disappeared.

Ghostly Impressions

Damp conditions combined with highly acidic soil had eroded all organic material, but left behind there was the most amazing ghost of a ship. The shape of each individual plank had become impressed in the sand; and the iron rivets used to nail the planks still lay in the exact pattern of their original positions. The sand had compacted around the ship but was none the less extremely fragile, and the gradual disclosure of the ship's structure was a triumph of patient, careful excavation.

Along the gunwale was a series of oarlocks or "tholepins," which would have been used by the ship's rowers. If rowers had sat along the entire length of both sides, there would have been room for about 40 of them. However, the oarlocks were missing from the central part of the ship. This could have been because it was the area of the burial chamber within which the body and treasure were placed and so the oarlocks were removed. It is also possible that there never had been any oarlocks along this section either because there was a mast and sail there or because the area was exclusively for passengers and their belongings. If this was so, then the number of

EXCAVATION SITE IN 1939
Looking along the full length of the ship toward the bow, the outlines of the planks and the rivets are clearly visible. The stern is rounder than the bow, which is unusual in a longship and may have been caused by damage during burial.

rowers deployed would have been somewhat less than 40. There is evidence of a steering oar having been lashed onto the starboard side in front of the stern post, indicated by the doubling up of lateral framework timbers at this point and the thickening of the ends of these timbers on the starboard side.

The mound had been visited by robbers in the sixteenth or seventeenth century, who had driven a shaft 10 feet (3 meters) deep into it. By extraordinary good fortune they stopped just short of the burial chamber. Maybe they were disturbed, or grew nervous about the shaft's sandy walls collapsing.

Viking Treasure

The treasures of Sutton Hoo fall into many categories showing different aspects of the man who was buried there. An awesome bronze helmet, a brutal ax hammer, and a beautifully decorated sword and shield show that he was a soldier. An extraordinary whetstone crested with a bronze stag and decorated with carved faces has been identified as a form of scepter, which suggests a king or powerful ruler. The lavish silver bowls and exquisite jewelry, buckles, and clasps clearly indicate a man of great wealth.

The more intimate and domestic side of his life is represented by drinking vessels of horn, burwood cups, a lyre, buckets, and a cauldron. A number of the items, such as a bronze hanging bowl with fish on a pedestal that would twist freely in the water when the bowl was filled, suggest a level of elegance and sophistication that has not always been attributed to these so-called "dark ages." Although no actual textiles such as rugs or wall hangings have survived, their presence can be deduced from the outlines of fibers found, preserved in rusted iron, wherever the fabric had originally been placed against it.

THE MISSING BODY

Sutton Hoo is not only a burial ship without a ship, it is also lacking a body. Just as there are no remains of any timber, there are no remains of any bones, not even the teeth of a skeleton. Archaeologists presume that the acidity of the soil has completely destroyed any organic substances. Significantly, recent comparison of the soil inside the burial chamber with the soil outside shows a higher phosphate level inside, which strongly suggests that there had at one time been bones within the burial chamber.

Among the many finds was a purse full of gold coins, all from different mints across Gaul. They had, no doubt, been included to provide sufficient funds for the dead person's passage into the next world. The coins date the burial at around A.D. 625, which is also the year in which the Anglo-Saxon King Raedwald is known to have died, so it has been suggested that the Sutton Hoo burial ship might well have been Raedwald's grave.

Exotic Influences

The items in the burial ship suggest a cosmopolitan range of inspirations that are not immediately associated with the quiet backwater of the River Debden, on the edge of which Sutton Hoo is situated. Some of the patterns on the silver bowls indicate a Middle Eastern origin combined with the influence of Roman culture, while intricate Celtic designs relate more to the artistic traditions of Sweden or Germany. These designs suggest that the River Debden was at the hub of Anglo-Saxon economic activity in the seventh century.

Decorative panels
Interlocking designs are enclosed by a border, and studded with circular garnets

DRAGON
This gilt-bronze shield mount is 8–10 in (20–25 cm) long, with a polished garnet eye, and ferocious fangs. It would have decorated a shield around 3 feet (90 cm) in diameter.

Man and two beasts
May depict the myth of Odin being swallowed by the wolf Fenrir

Mythological bird
A bird of prey clasps a smaller bird in its claws. The image is reversed to the left.

BONE OR IVORY PURSE LID
Fine lines of gold contain an intricate design of garnets and colored glass. The leather purse was found face down in the sand, and contained 37 gold coins.

CHOICE OF SITE

The Viking burial ship positioned as it was, in a prominent position high above a river, would no doubt have been seen from a great distance. To move the huge ship up from the river to the chosen location, it would have been hauled a mile (nearly two kilometers) over land, on an upward slope. This prodigious logistical feat was probably achieved by moving the ship on timber rollers.

The choice of site was clearly not one of simple convenience or even the result of a random accident but a carefully considered choice executed with immense skill.

UNEARTHING THE SHAPE OF THE SHIP

The ship that emerged from the excavated site at Sutton Hoo was over 90 feet (27 meters) long, with a beam of nearly 16 feet (5 meters) amidships. It has been estimated that the stem and stern posts would have risen to a height of 13 feet (4 meters) above the keel, although there was no physical evidence for this.

Impressions left in the sand revealed that the ship had nine main planks or "strakes" on either side of the keel, each strake consisting of several pieces of timber to achieve the full ship's length. The planks were riveted together in an overlapping pattern ("clinker-style"), and internally there were 26 lateral frames to which the planks were attached with pins of oak, except for the top plank, which was attached by iron bolts.

So amazingly detailed were the outlines of the ship that were left in the sandy soil, that it was even possible for the archaeologists to tell where the ship had been repaired. They located three separate places that had an increased frequency of rivets where the framework had been patched. These repairs suggest that the Sutton Hoo ship had seen long and active service, and had perhaps only been used for burial purposes toward the end of its natural life.

OSEBERG
BURIAL SHIP

I n 1904 archaeologists excavated a burial ship site at Oseberg on the Oslo Fjord in Norway, and uncovered a miraculously well-preserved ship dating from approximately A.D. 800, which has since been fully restored and can now be seen on display in the Viking Ship Museum in Oslo. The find is important because it is both a fascinating example of Viking shipbuilding methods and styles of this period, and also a unique work of art, with its elaborately carved stern and stem posts depicting an intricate maze of mythological beasts.

The ship's structure was largely intact because it had been buried in blue clay, which has exceptional hermetic properties, and the burial chamber had been further sealed beneath a mound of sod. The ship had a very shallow freeboard, so it would not have been sea-worthy on open seas, although it would have been suited to the more protected coastal waters of a fjord. The exceedingly high stern and prow would also have made it vulnerable to strong winds at sea.

The Oseberg ship is one of the very earliest that has been found to show evidence of a mast. Interestingly, the "mast partner," which supports the mast on deck, had been cracked at some stage, and had been repaired by two iron bands. The damage is not surprising because the support structure for the mast is fairly flimsy. This might have been caused by inadequate knowledge of the new technology of sail at this period, but equally likely is that the mast partner was deliberately kept small to maximize deck space, with emphasis placed upon personal convenience rather than upon commercial needs. Other features lend weight to this theory, for example, the fact that the deck planking was nailed down for most of the length of the ship rather than kept loose for convenient cargo stowage.

QUEEN AASA

The royal personage in the Oseberg grave may have been Queen Aasa, daughter of Harald Granraude, King of Agder. In the sagas, Gudrod the Hunter asked Harald for his daughter's hand in marriage, but Harald refused. Gudrod's response, in classic Viking style, was to take her by force, first killing her father and brother. Aasa, under-standably objecting to this manner of courtship, persuaded a servant to kill Gudrod while he was drunk one night. The servant was himself killed the following morning, but Aasa appears to have survived this particular episode of domestic fracas.

Square sail
The Oseberg is one of the first ships found in northern waters known to have used a sail

Carved stern
Serpent head to frighten the enemy

WEATHERVANE
Made from gilt copper with a pierced center panel, a solid carved border, and an animal crest. Vikings had an intimate understanding of the signs of the sea and nature, and how to use them for navigation.

Rudder for steering
Attached by a rope made from pine roots

OSEBERG SHIP MODEL
The unsuitability of this ship for sailing in open seas suggests it might have been a royal leisure boat rather than a warship or merchant ship.

Stowage crutch
For storing oars when not in use

Central mast
With flimsy support structure

Two Occupants of the Burial Site

Two bodies were discovered in the grave, and both were women. One was in her late twenties, while the other was an older woman suffering from severe arthritis. The young woman was clearly an important member of a powerful family, probably royalty, and the old woman was most likely her slave. Arab travelers to Norway during this period recorded how it was the custom for a slave to be sacrificed at the burial of his or her master, in order to continue to serve them in the next world. The remains of horses, dogs, and cattle were also found in the burial mound, along with supplies of apples, wheat, and nuts to ensure that they were well fed on their final journey.

In addition to these possessions, the Oseberg burial mound yielded a selection of more humble domestic items, such as a bucket of yew wood and an iron cauldron with tripod, no doubt also vital for the journey to the next world.

SILVER DANISH DISK BROOCH
Tenth-century, with a curved and twisting beast. Viking designs often featured real or mythological beasts: many were found on the carvings from the Oseberg burial ship.

ANIMAL POSTS
Five carved wooden posts, in the shape of animal heads, were found at Oseberg, four in the burial chamber itself. Their use is still unknown, but the workmanship is very sophisticated.

Elaborate Wood Carvings

Although the domestic goods discovered reveal much about life of the period, the real treasure of the Oseberg ship lies in its wonderfully intricate and animated wood carvings. These are found on the ship itself and also on various other artifacts that were recovered from the burial mound, a four-wheeled carriage, a royal bed and chair, and a sledge. Monster heads on the finials of the sledge were no doubt meant to ward off evil spirits. They reveal a sophisticated artistic tradition with a creative sense of design and pattern.

Bronze figure
Thought to be Buddha, showing Vikings had some contact with the East

FACTS AND FEATURES

Treasure	Carved artifacts
Date of burial	A.D. 800
Discovered	1904
Location	Norway

Stem post
With decorative scroll work

WOODEN BUCKET
Found on the Oseberg ship, this was probably used for storing or serving liquid.

Wooden planking
Constructed mainly from oak, with small sections at either end in beech

Freeboard
The distance between the ship's gunwale and the waterline was very shallow

Pine oars
Newly made before burial

CHINESE JUNKS

Chinese merchants have been accomplished seamen since the thirteenth century, and navigated vast distances to trade their wares. Exports from China remained remarkably consistent throughout hundreds of years. On the outward journeys, Chinese merchant junks carried gold, silver, porcelain, specialty teas, lacquerware, silks, ginseng, rhubarb, saddles, and sabres. These were traded for precious items such as ebony, ivory, and camphor wood from Champa (south Vietnam); coral and rhinoceros horn from Sumatra; gems and pearls from Ceylon (Sri Lanka); betel nuts, tin, sago, tigers, and crocodiles from Malacca (Melaka) in Malaysia; ambergris, cowrie shells, and coconuts from the Maldives; and opium and rosewater from Aden on the Arabian peninsula.

Cheng Ho's Voyages

The great period of Chinese maritime history was the first 30 years of the fifteenth century. At that time the navy of the ruling Ming Dynasty had a fleet of several thousand warships that controlled the oceans westward as far as the east coast of Africa, eastward to Japan, and southward throughout Indonesia.

Nothing exemplifies this Chinese supremacy and strength more dramatically than the seven expeditions made between 1405 and 1433 by the Grand Eunuch Cheng Ho, on behalf of the Emperor Yung Lo. The voyages were intended to impress foreign countries with Chinese greatness and power, to reimpose in some places the system of paying tribute to China, to gather new species of animals and plants for natural and medical science, and to further trade. The size and scope of the expeditions were prodigious: the first voyage, for example, had over 30,000 men in 300 ships, 62 of which carried treasure. Most of the men were soldiers, but there were also interpreters, meteorologists, businessmen, clerks, cooks, doctors, naturalists, specialist caulkers to repair the ships on the long voyage, and steersmen to navigate in unfamiliar waters. It is unclear quite how large Cheng Ho's treasure ships were, but some sources put them as big as 453 feet in length and 184 feet in width (138 by 56 meters). They could achieve 6 to 8 knots per hour, but the average speed was nearer 3 knots. A typical round trip took nearly two years, covering 15,000 miles (24,000 kilometers).

LODESTONE
The Chinese were the first to discover the naturally occurring magnetic properties of lodestone (iron oxide), about 2,000 years ago. This led to the development of magnetic compasses.

TRADING ON THE INDIAN WEST COAST
The ports of Quilon, Cochin, and Calicut supplied the Chinese with pepper, ginger, and cinnamon, as well as more exotic items such as elephants and parakeets.

ADEN
The Chinese called here for glassware and artistic ornaments. Cheng Ho's seventh expedition proceeded even farther from here, up to Jedda on the Red Sea.

EAST AFRICAN TRADE
The Chinese had traded with Africa since the eleventh and twelfth centuries, as has been borne out by the dates of the Chinese coins that were found along the coasts of Somalia and Mozambique.

MID-19TH-CENTURY JUNK ①
Shap'ng Tsai, a notorious Vietnamese pirate, operated throughout the Gulf of Tongking. He lost several ships, including this Chinese junk, which sank in battle in 1850 with treasure on board.

ARAL SEA

PERSIA

Ormuz (Hormuz)

Persian Gulf

Gulf of Oman

Dhofar

Aden

Gulf of Aden

ARABIAN SEA

SOMALILAND

INDIAN OCEAN

Malindi

MADAGASCAR

INDIA

Calicut

Cochin

Quilon

CEYLON (SRI LANKA)

MALDIVES

Ganges

Indus

CHINESE COMPASS
Chinese navigators used compasses such as these when sailing the oceans. Other aids used by Chinese sailors were the cross staff for calculating latitude, stellar charts, and navigational charts known as water mirrors.

BENGAL
The Chinese traded their goods for Indian silks, cloths, sugar, and steel from this area.

14TH-CENTURY CHINESE JUNK ②
Its cargo of Chinese porcelain was salvaged in 1992 by Michael Hatcher. Claiming ownership, the Thai government arrested the salvage ship and seized the cargo.

PORCELAIN FACTORIES
The town of Fowliang (Jingdezhen) was a center for Chinese porcelain production in the seventeenth century. Cargo from the *Vung Tau* and the *Sinan* ship originated here.

CHINESE JUNK ④
This ship was lost in 1611. It was carrying gold and porcelain from Macao to Japan.

VUNG TAU ⑤
A Chinese junk that sank around 1690, and was salvaged in the 1990s. (See pages 28–29.)

SHIP OF TU YUAN ③
This was lost around 1400 off Sumatra, and may well have been part of Cheng Ho's first expedition: a fleet of over 300 ships that included 62 treasure ships and nearly 30,000 men.

ADMIRAL STELLINGWERF REEF WRECK ⑥
This junk was lost in 1643 carrying porcelain from China to Java. Its cargo was salvaged by Michael Hatcher in the 1980s and was auctioned by Christie's, fetching several million dollars.

SINAN SHIP ⑦
This junk wrecked in the early fourteenth century, carrying a large quantity of copper coins and ceramics. (See pages 26–27.)

T'AI PING ⑧
A Chines junk that was lost in 1056 at T'ai Ping, near the mouth of the Min River. On board was an ambassador to the Chinese court who was bringing gifts for the emperor.

MANDARIN'S CAP WRECK ⑨
This junk sank about 1200 with a cargo of silver ingots and porcelain. It was partly salvaged in the 1980s.

ROYAL CAPTAIN SHOAL WRECK ⑩
A small trading junk that was shipping ceramics, glass beads, and bronze from Manila to Borneo when it ran onto a sandbank around 1600.

GINSENG ROOT
China has exported ginseng for centuries. It is still much valued for its medicinal properties.

Trade Routes

Cheng Ho's Voyages

Map labels: SEA OF JAPAN, YELLOW SEA, KOREA, JAPAN, NORTH PACIFIC OCEAN, Yellow River, MING CHINA, Nanking (Nanjing), Wusong, EAST CHINA SEA, Yangtse, Fowliang (Jingdezhen), Min River, FUKIEN (FUJIAN), Amoy (Xiamen), Canton (Guangzhou), Pearl River (Hongshui), Macao, SOUTH CHINA SEA, HAINAN, Gulf of Tongking, ANNAM, Mekong, CHAMPA (SOUTH VIETNAM), Qui Nhon, SIAM (THAILAND), Gulf of Siam, Manila, PHILIPPINES, KEDAH, Malacca (Melaka), Singapore, SUMATRA, SRIVIJAYAN EMPIRE, Palembang, Bangka Strait, Batavia (Jakarta), JAVA, BORNEO, NEW GUINEA, AUSTRALIA, TIBET, BENGAL, BURMA, Bay of Bengal, Irrawaddy

THE SINAN WRECK

CHINESE TRADING JUNK
This model dates from 1938 but it retains many of the features found in junks of the fourteenth century. Junks were based on the rough shape of a duck, unlike Western ships which were streamlined like fish. The Sinan ship was not flat-bottomed like this model but had a keel, and just two masts.

During 1975 a fisherman, trawling off the southwest coast of the Republic of Korea, discovered a wreck loaded with porcelain artifacts. The porcelain was dismissed as imitation at first but was later confirmed as genuine fourteenth-century ceramics. The Korean Ministry of Culture and the Navy subsequently recovered a quantity of well-preserved artifacts, including copper coins, celadon stoneware (pottery with a gray-green glaze), and other items such as silver and iron ingots, bronze and iron cooking utensils, and red sandalwood. The ship was buried in thick mud, which limited visibility for the salvors although it had preserved the cargo and the ship's timbers. More than 200,000 copper coins, weighing over 28 tons, have been salvaged, the most recent dated 1310.

Copper coins were used by the Chinese in what was termed the Nanhai trade, to buy foreign goods such as spices, glassware, horses, ivory, pearls, and medicinal herbs. China exported silks, lacquerware, gold, silver, celadon, and other ceramics. Individual merchants would rent some space in a ship for their own personal trade, although the trade as a whole was under the control of the government, which also benefited from the revenue. A Chinese proverb says that one lucky voyage would make a man rich, another lucky voyage would make him extremely rich, and a third lucky voyage would make him rich beyond imagination. It would appear, however, that the voyage of the Sinan ship was not a lucky one.

Topsail
Only the main mast carried more than one sail

Mizzen mast
Most masts were made from pine

Cargo hold
Junks had transverse bulkheads, which made them less vulnerable to sinking, and helped protect the cargo. The Sinan ship had eight bulkheads.

Rudder post
Often made from elm or oak

膠1510

Second mast
Placed toward the
front of the ship

Bamboo sail
Sails revolved
around the mast so
that Chinese ships
could sail very close
to the wind

CHINESE PORCELAIN

The porcelain ceramics found on the wreck probably came from the kilns of Fowliang (Jingdezhen), a city with about a million people working in its pottery industry by the early eighteenth century.

Celadon porcelain was prized both for its color and its reputed life-preserving, magical powers: if food was poisoned, the celadon dish in which it was served was said to change color or to shatter.

CELADON CARGO
These original wooden crates helped the cargo survive in almost perfect condition for over 600 years. The Chinese characters on the crate mean "great luck."

FACTS AND FEATURES

Length	105 feet (32 meters)
Breadth	33 feet (10 meters)
Depth	11 feet (3.5 meters)
Burden	200 tons
Crew	Over 300 men

Staggered masts
Junks had up to nine
fixed masts set at
varying angles

Spare sails
Furled up and stored
on the open deck

Wooden hull
Made from
fir and pine

Iron anchor
Four-clawed,
grapnel-type

TRADING ROUTES

The Sinan ship was probably trading from south China to Japan, and a bronze weight that was recovered from the wreck was inscribed with the name of Yinxian (Ningbo), so this was a possible port of call. The three most important ports and shipbuilding centers along the south China coast in this period were Guangzhou (Canton), which dealt with trade to southeast Asia; and Quanzhou and Mingzhou, centers for trade to Japan, Korea, and the Philippines.

Ships sailing for Korea would tend to leave China in the summer and return in the winter, while those sailing to Japan would make use of the southwesterly winds of the early summer, and wait to catch the northeasterly winds to return in the following spring.

Ceramics of the Yuan Dynasty

The wrecking of the Sinan ship is thought to have taken place around 1323, which places it in the period of the Yuan dynasty (1279-1368), after Kublai Khan's Mongol invasion of China from the north. By this time the basic technology used in producing ceramic wares had already been established for some time, but potters started to use cobalt blue beneath a clear glaze to produce the very distinctive blue and white porcelain that was to become so widely prized in later centuries. Developments took place in styles of decoration as well as in glazing techniques, and the ceramics of this era are notable for being bolder and more imaginative than those of the immediately preceding Sung period. This perhaps reflected Mongol taste, or the new regime may have allowed greater freedom to the artists involved.

Structure of the Sinan Ship

In addition to the valuable cargo salvaged, the timbers of the hull of the ship itself have also been brought up from the seabed, and are undergoing preservation treatment before reconstruction. The ship had eight transverse bulkheads and only two masts. The mainmast would have been about 100 feet (30.5 meters) high, and the foremast was about 80 feet (24.5 meters). Anchors were likely to have been of the four-clawed iron type, although none has been recovered.

The Sinan ship was almost certainly built in south China, since it was constructed from species of red pine and fir that grow only in that region. Scientific analysis and the size of the timbers indicate the trees were about 100 years old when felled for shipbuilding.

THE
VUNG TAU WRECK

During the mid-1980s a Vietnamese fisherman discovered a good area for catching red snapper off the tiny island of Hon Bay Canh, one of the Con Dao group of islands, about 100 nautical miles from Vung Tau, Vietnam. He presumed that he had found a particularly productive coral reef, the favorite haunt of red snapper, and took a detailed sighting of his position, which was approximately six nautical miles east-southeast of the island, so that he could re-turn to the spot in the future.

The fishing was so plentiful that the man came back repeatedly. One day he hooked something rather different on his line: a concreted lump of iron containing several porcelain items. He had clearly been fishing over a wreck, which accounted for the good haul, since fish congregate over wrecks.

The fisherman took the porcelain to a Vietnamese antiques dealer, who offered to buy more of the same, and before very long the antique shops from Ho Chi Minh City to Singapore and Hong Kong began to fill up with great quantities of blue and white china.

UNDERWATER DISCOVERY
Working in the darkness under the sea, Sverker Hallstrom's team of salvage divers shone spot-lights upon the neatly stacked piles of cargo. Raising the treasure was a delicate task because layers of sand and mud covered the china. Much of the cargo was found to be in the same position in which it had first been stowed for the voyage.

Eventually, the Vietnamese authorities heard what was happening and appointed the state-owned salvage company Visal to carry out more systematic salvage operations. After only a few months, however, it was clear to Visal that it needed an outside company with specialized equipment to complete a proper excavation of the site. A Swedish salvage

expert based in Singapore, Sverker Hall-strom, was selected and he began recovery operations at the wreck site in the fall of 1990.

Unconventional Ship Design

The wreck turned out to be the remains of a Chinese ship of an unusual kind because its structure combined elements of both the traditional Chinese junk and the westernized tradition of shipbuilding as typified by the Portuguese-influenced lorcha. The keel, the sternpost, and the relatively streamlined shape of the hull implied Western influence; whereas the bulkheads, the stepping of the masts, and the caulking materials (tung oil and lime mixed with shredded jute or bam-boo fiber) were more traditionally Chinese. The ship was approximately 110 feet long and 33 feet wide (33.5 meters by 10 meters).

Fire at Sea

Charred beams were discovered down to the waterline, making it clear that the ship had sunk because of fire. Whether this was caused by lightning or other accident, or maybe following an attack by pirates, is not known. The wreck has been dated at around 1690.

The few coins that were found at the site were from the reign of the Chinese Emperor Kangxi (1662-1722), and a small Chinese inkstick that was also recovered had a relief-molded date on it that corresponded to 1690.

Cups

Soup spoons

Saucer dishes

Beaker vase

Oviform vase
With panels of stylized wisteria and pine

Bowls
All with glazed rims

White-glazed dishes

CATEGORIZING THE TREASURE
After it was recovered, the cargo was sorted into piles on the deck of the salvage ship. A detailed inventory of each item was then made by the salvors before the pieces were sent for auction.

DISPLAY OF CARGO FOR CHRISTIE'S AUCTION CATALOG
Designer Nina Campbell created a special arrangement of some of the Vung Tau blue and white porcelain for Christie's. This formal and symmetrical scene reflects the way collections of china were displayed over 300 years ago. This is a relatively small arrangement: there were 800 items displayed in Kensington Palace, London, in the 1680s.

AUCTION FEVER

In one of the best-publicized auctions of recent years, part of the recovered porcelain cargo was sold in Amsterdam by Christie's, the auction house, in April 1992. The auction attracted much attention, particularly from Europe, North America, and the Far East. There were over 1,000 multiple lots selling the coveted blue and white goblets, teapots, mustard pots, pillboxes, and teabowls; as well as small *blanc-de-chine* figures, bowls, and soup spoons. The auction was a great success and raised over $7 million.

Ceramic Treasures

An enormous wealth of artifacts was found in and around the remains of the hull. Most important, both in value and volume, were the famed blue and white porcelain and the *blanc-de-chine* porcelain. Both were probably destined for Europe, after transshipment at Jakarta (Batavia). The porcelain kilns at Fowliang (Jingdezhen) had only just started production again in the 1680s, after decades of disruption caused by the Manchu invasion from the north of the Ming Empire.

One of the more interesting features of the pieces that were salvaged is the extent to which they reveal Western influence in the choice of design and shape. Some of the larger vases, for instance, depict gabled buildings that closely resemble Dutch canal houses of the period. This suggests that Western merchants were already sending out patterns to their Chinese business partners stipulating the exact styles required.

Trade Goods and Personal Items

The Vung Tau ship also carried some fine examples of the more utilitarian ware known as "Kitchen Qing," probably destined for the Chinese merchant community in the trading port of Jakarta. In addition, there were stoneware and earthenware vessels that may have been containers for a variety of oils, pastes, drugs, and delicacies. Walnuts, areca nuts (now known as betelnuts), lychees, rice, and persimmons were among the remains of foodstuffs that have been identified. Very few personal items have been recovered but they include a set of weighing scales, a pocket sundial of Western origin, and a mirror. Other miscellaneous items carried included iron cooking pots and woks, earthenware flooring tiles, ear picks, alloy buttons, tweezers, bamboo combs for removing lice, small brass chests, dice, and inkstands. All were found in large enough quantities to suggest they had been trade goods. The ship was probably following the customary trading route from Xiamen (Amoy), China, down the Vietnamese coast, on to the island of Tioman near the Singapore Strait, then along the east coast of Sumatra, and finally on to Jakarta.

CHINAMANIA

In the late seventeenth century, Europe had become gripped by what was known as "Chinamania." To have whole rooms dedicated to the display of oriental porcelain was the height of fashion. The writer Daniel Defoe referred somewhat scathingly to this craze as "the Custom or humour, as I may call it, of furnishing houses with China-ware which increased to a strange degree afterwards, piling China upon the tops of cabinets, scrutores, and every Chymney-Piece, to the tops of the Ceilings, and even setting up Shelves for their China-ware, where they wanted such Places."

LEVANTINE TRADE

Venice in Italy was ideally positioned to conduct trade between the land-oriented empires of German Europe (the Holy Roman Empire) and the Muslim Levant or East (the Ottoman Empire). By the year 1000, Venice had emerged as a powerful city state whose wealth was based almost entirely upon shipping and commerce. Venice's Navy dominated the Adriatic Sea, exporting timber and slaves from Dalmatia, importing gold from north Africa, and supplying the European hinterland with silks and spices from the Orient. Venetian traders used the ports of Alexandria in Egypt, Acre in what is now Israel, and Constantinople (Istanbul) in Turkey to import coveted Oriental goods. By the fifteenth century, Venice had expanded its influence west and north to trade with Spain, France, England, and the Netherlands.

VIDALA ①
A Venetian ship that sank while at anchor in a cove off the Dalmatian coast in 1592, en route to the Orient. Its cargo of wool, silks, and other goods was valued at 130,000 ducats, and was plundered by pirates.

ANNA MARIA ④
This 400-ton galleon and its cargo of silver, brimstone, and rice was lost off Portland Beach, England, in 1682. The ship was en route from Venice to the Netherlands.

SANTO CRISTO DE CASTELLO ②
A Genoese ship lost in a Cornish cove in 1666, while carrying silver coins from Genoa.

TOBIE ③
In 1593 this English merchant ship was wrecked on the Moroccan coast en route to Italy and the eastern Mediterranean. (See pages 34–35.)

Trade and Navigation Developments

Venetian merchants exported silver and gold coins, and gold bullion to purchase Oriental spices and other Eastern goods including silks, indigo, pearls, precious stones, and porcelain.

As well as trading with the Levant, Venice traded within the Mediterranean, importing Cretan wine and dried fruits, Sicilian wheat, raw gold from the north African ports of Tunis and Tripoli, and woolens, olive oil, coral, and copper from Languedoc and Spain.

Venice was one of the first Western seafaring nations to use charts, compasses, and sandglasses. These thirteenth-century navigational systems enabled ships to sail without depending upon the stars. They were therefore able to sail in winter, when stars were often not visible, and also to sail directly across the oceans rather than hug the coast. The favored ships were oar- and sail-powered galleys and the larger round ships, which were powered by sail alone.

Map labels: NORTH S[EA], ENGLAND, London, Bruges, NETHERL[ANDS], Portsmouth, ISLE OF WIGHT, English Channel, FRANCE, Seine, Loire, Bay of Biscay, Garonne, LANGUEDOC, Andorra, NAVARRE, CATALONIA, Gulf of L[ion], Ma[rseille], Barcelona, ARAGON, Duero, PORTUGAL, Tagus, CASTILE (SPAIN), Valencia, BALEARIC ISLANDS, Lisbon, Guadalquivir, MEDITERRANEAN SEA, Cape St. Vincent, Cadiz, KINGDOM OF GRANADA, Strait of Gibraltar, Cape Spartel, Ceuta, Fez (Fes), MOROCCO, AFRICA

SCENE FROM VENICE IN 1338
Fourteenth-century Venice was a thriving center of commerce. This view shows Venetian galleys and round ships trading in the busy routeway from the Adriatic Sea to St. Mark's Square.

SPICES FROM THE ORIENT
In return for Eastern spices, such as pepper, nutmeg, tamarind, mace, cloves, ginger, and cinnamon, Venetian merchants traded falcons and furs from northern Europe, saffron and honey from Catalonia, and Venetian manufactured products including glass, metalwork, jewelry, woolen and silk textiles, mirrors, and soap.

Tamarind

Nutmeg with mace

SILK ROUTE
The overland trading route to China via Tana was highly vulnerable because of political instability.

ULBO ISLAND WRECK ⑤
A Venetian trading ship that was lost off the Dalmatian coast while sailing at night through treacherous seas in 1417. (See pages 32–33.)

RAGUSA
This trading center was a source of silver, wax, and hides for Venetian merchants. Ragusa was so important that it threatened to become a serious commercial rival to Venice.

CONSTANTINOPLE
Fought over for centuries because its position was strategically invaluable, the city fell to the Venetians in 1204. As a result, Venice dominated the highly vulnerable Eastern spice trade, and sent two trading convoys a year to the city. The round trip took about two months.

VENETIAN SHIP ⑨
Attacked by the military leader Mehmed II, this ship sank near Constantinople (Istanbul) in 1452 with a cargo of valuables.

THE ORIENT TO CONSTANTINOPLE
Oriental goods reached the trading center of Constantinople (Istanbul) via the Persian Gulf, Trebizon, and the Black Sea.

RHODES
Particularly used by traders from the Catalan coast, this was an important center for trade to the Ottoman Empire.

PIRATE SHIP ⑩
This ship sank in battle in 1607 while attacking a Venetian ship at Saline, Cyprus.

GUIDOTTA E SIMONA ⑥
This Venetian ship was attacked in 1613, near the island of Zante (Zákinthos) in Greece, by Barbary pirates seeking its cargo of gold and jewelry destined for Alexandria, Egypt.

SAN MICHELE ⑧
This ship belonged to the King of Naples and was carrying valuables when it was lost near Alexandria, Egypt, in 1479.

ABU QIR WRECK ⑦
This Catalan cog was carrying saffron, almonds, olive oil, coral, and cloth to Egypt, when it was wrecked in 1418.

ALEXANDRIA
Site of many shipwrecks because prevailing northwesterly winds made this Egyptian port hard to depart from when heading back to Venice, except in late autumn and early spring. To minimize the risk, returning Venetian ships often sailed NNE to Cyprus first.

THE RED SEA ROUTE
Goods from the Orient were shipped up the Red Sea to Mecca and then overland by camel either to Acre or Damascus, or they were taken as far as Suez and then carried by camel to Cairo. The latter route was disliked because there were many reefs in the northern reaches of the Red Sea, and Suez was an inadequate port.

CRUSADING KNIGHT
This plaque from a tomb shows a heavily armored knight on horseback. During the eleventh century, Venice participated in the Crusades and shipped pilgrims to the Holy Land. As a result, many trading posts were established, and the Fourth Crusade in 1202 led to the seizure of part of Constantinople by the Venetian fleet.

RUSSIA

KHANATE OF THE GOLDEN HORDE

POLAND-LITHUANIA

MOLDAVIA

WALLACHIA

KHANATE

CRIMEA
Kaffa

BLACK SEA

Vistula

Dnieper

HOLY ROMAN EMPIRE (Germany)

Venice

Pisa
Livorno

LIGURIAN SEA

VENETIAN EMPIRE

CORSICA

APULIA

Rome

ITALY

SARDINIA

TYRRHENIAN SEA

KINGDOM OF NAPLES

Naples

Palermo

SICILY

Tunis

Tripoli

DALMATIA

Ragusa (Dubrovnik)

ADRIATIC SEA

CORFU

Strait of Messina

IONIAN SEA

AEGEAN SEA

MOREA

CYCLADES

Cape Matapan

CRETE

RHODES

OTTOMAN EMPIRE

TURKEY

Constantinople (Istanbul)

CYPRUS

MEDITERRANEAN SEA

EGYPT

Cairo

Suez

MAMELUKE EMPIRE

RED SEA

Nile

THE WRECK OF
ULBO ISLAND

VENETIAN EMBASSY IN THE EAST, SCHOOL OF BELLINI
As a result of the crusades of the twelfth century and the victory at Istanbul (Constantinople) in 1204, Venice established several strategic trading posts and naval bases throughout the eastern Mediterranean. It dominated the valuable Eastern spice trade and imported other key products, such as cotton from Syria and wines from Crete.

Nicolo Barbarigo was the commander in charge of a fleet of great merchant galleys returning to Venice, Italy, from Alexandria, Egypt, in December 1417, when one of the fleet was wrecked. It is probable that Barbarigo's fleet was hurrying to be back for the Christmas Fair, an opportune occasion for selling the valuable cargo of spices, precious stones, and porcelain on board.

As with all Venetian galleys, the galleys of this fleet would have been built and owned by the state of Venice and hired out to individual merchants for a voyage. Usually these merchants would, in turn, sublet some of the available space to lesser traders.

Oarsmen and Oarpower

Venetian galleys, which are thought to date from the end of the ninth century, were not wholly dependent on sailpower, but also used oarsmen for maneuvering in and out of ports and moving away from coasts when there was a lack of wind. On early galleys, the oarsmen were usually independent Venetian wage-earners. But by the time Barbarigo had become a commander, this had begun to change. Venice was chronically short of manpower, partly because of the ravages of the plague and partly because of recent wars with Genoa, so foreign workers were increasingly used.

Sailing by oarpower was particularly labor-intensive, and at least 200 men were required for a typical Venetian galley. The oarsmen usually worked in three shifts, with two men (a "bireme" galley) or three (a "trireme" galley) to a bench, each with their own oar.

ITALIAN FINANCIERS
Venice was one of the first cities to develop advanced systems of commerce, including double-entry bookkeeping, insurance, banks, and bills of exchange. In the thirteenth century, Venice and Florence issued gold coins, called ducats or sequins in Venice and florins in Florence.

GINGER
Grown in Asia, ginger was one of the first spices to reach the West.

GOLDEN RAISINS
Dried fruits were imported from Syria.

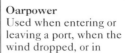

VENETIAN CARGOES

Venetian galleys sailed to Alexandria, Acre, and Istanbul (Constantinople) to connect with the trading routes to the East (see pages 30–31). They were used to transport high-value cargoes due to their speed, even though they could only hold one ton per crew member. On outward journeys, galleys carried gold and silver coins, and gold bullion to buy oriental wares. Venetian traders also exported glass, metalwork, jewelry, silk and woolen textiles, mirrors, and soap. On homeward voyages, they carried valuable spices, dried fruits, cottons, wax, indigo, pearls, precious stones, and porcelain. These goods were mainly for re-export to England, the German-Hungarian hinterland, Spain, France, and the Netherlands.

Oarpower
Used when entering or leaving a port, when the wind dropped, or in battle for extra speed

Pilgrim quarters
Galleys were sometimes used to ship pilgrims, who would be housed in darkness in the hold

Living Conditions on Board

Most of the crew lived, ate, and slept on deck, next to their rowing benches. At the stern or poop end of the ship would have been a raised, tiered section. The lowest tier was used for storing treasure and ammunition; the more important passengers and ship's officers slept in the middle tier and Mass was also said there; the top tier formed the captain's quarters and housed the compass. Projecting from behind this area were the rudder controls. The kitchen was on deck in front of the poop.

The Fateful Night

As Barbarigo's fleet neared the coast of Italy, it seems likely that it was behind schedule. At the time of the shipwreck, it was sailing at night through the most treacherous section of the Adriatic Sea, which was strictly against the rules. One of the galleys hit rocks off Ulbo, an island near the Dalmatian coast, and foundered.

Nicolo Barbarigo did not stop to assist, but took the rest of the fleet on to the nearest port. This was probably not callousness on his part, but a decision based on the adverse weather conditions or the dangerous currents. However, the Venetian ruling body for maritime affairs clearly held him responsible for the loss because he was tried, found guilty, and fined 10,000 ducats – a considerable sum of money.

APPROACHING ALEXANDRIA
St. Mark's boat nears the Pharos, the great lighthouse of Alexandria, which was one of the Seven Wonders of the Ancient World. Alexandria was a significant trading post, hence the depiction of its celebrated lighthouse in this mosaic. Now in the Chapel of Zeno in St. Mark's Cathedral in Venice, the mosaic dates from around 1200.

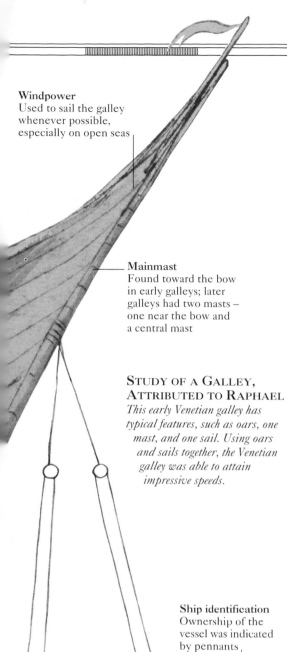

Windpower
Used to sail the galley whenever possible, especially on open seas

Mainmast
Found toward the bow in early galleys; later galleys had two masts – one near the bow and a central mast

STUDY OF A GALLEY, ATTRIBUTED TO RAPHAEL
This early Venetian galley has typical features, such as oars, one mast, and one sail. Using oars and sails together, the Venetian galley was able to attain impressive speeds.

Ship identification
Ownership of the vessel was indicated by pennants

Battle strategy
Raised section at the very prow of the ship was used for deploying bowmen during hostilities

Accommodation
Seamen who worked in the fore part lived and slept in the area beneath the prow

DESIGN OF VENETIAN ROUND SHIPS

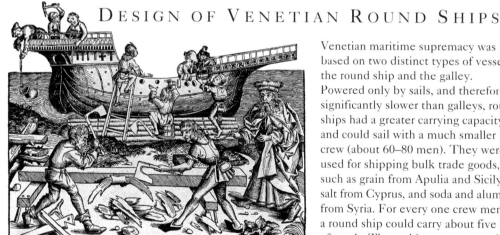

SHIPBUILDERS AT WORK
On the raised deck of the stern, two carpenters make adjustments to the structure, while a third raises water from the sea. In the foreground, under the supervision of the shipwright, a length of timber is planed to form a beam.

Venetian maritime supremacy was based on two distinct types of vessel: the round ship and the galley. Powered only by sails, and therefore significantly slower than galleys, round ships had a greater carrying capacity and could sail with a much smaller crew (about 60–80 men). They were used for shipping bulk trade goods, such as grain from Apulia and Sicily, salt from Cyprus, and soda and alum from Syria. For every one crew member, a round ship could carry about five tons of goods. These ships were generally around 200 tons burden, with square sails and a rudder attached to a stern post, although some could be as large as 500 tons burden, and could carry as many as 20 anchors.

FACTS AND FEATURES

Average Venetian galleys were:

120 feet (36.5 meters) in length

15 feet (4.5 meters) in width

250 tons in capacity

THE
TOBIE

The *Tobie* was an English merchant ship, of 250 tons burden, from the port of London. When it left London on August 16, 1593, bound for Livorno in Italy and Zákinthos and Patras in Greece, it was carrying a very valuable cargo estimated to be worth $18,000. This probably included tin, wool, and specie (coins). Its master, George Goodlay, was on his first voyage as master on the Levant route. He was described by a contemporary chronicler and geographer, Richard Hakluyt, as being pigheaded and incompetent, and was largely blamed for the disaster that occurred.

After leaving the River Thames, the *Tobie* sailed down the Channel and called at Portsmouth to load wheat. It finally set sail from the nearby Isle of Wight on October 6. On October 18, the ship neared the entrance to the Strait of Gibraltar, but the weather deteriorated and, to prevent running onto land, the crew had to sail back out to sea. When the wind improved, they again tried

THE THAMES FLOWING THROUGH LONDON
The river leads out to sea to the right, toward Europe. It was a busy thoroughfare both for merchant ships, helped by its strong tides, and for smaller boats carrying passengers through the heart of the city.

to approach the mouth of the Strait, but the captain miscalculated the ship's position and ran it aground during the night of the 19th, an hour and a half before dawn. At the time of wrecking, the *Tobie* was carrying sail, always a dangerous option at night on an unknown coast. The position where the ship struck was estimated to be four leagues (approximately 12 miles or 19 kilometers) to the south of Cape Spartel, Morocco.

Fatal Indecision

Faced with this dire situation, the master admitted that he alone was entirely responsible. In the ensuing crisis he lost his self-confidence and decisiveness. When the

Rowing boat
The Thames was often the most direct route through the city for people as well as goods

Four-story warehouse
Steps led right down to water's edge, and cargoes could also be winched up through the windows

ELIZABETHAN TRADE

The *Tobie*'s voyage took place when England was trading strongly with the Levant. About ten years before, England had sent an experienced merchant as a commercial ambassador to the court at Istanbul (Constantinople), and had also set up a new company (the Turkey or Levant Company) to trade with the East. England traded cloth, tin, and pewter for silks, cottons, currants, indigo, and spices. Gradually, England began to compete with Venice for the valuable spice trade (until then, Portugal had been Venice's main rival).

The *Tobie* is thought to have been carrying tin and wool, two of the most common English exports of that time.

The Elizabethan Wool Trade
Wool played a significant role in England's economy. The country's mild climate ensured that sheep could be successfully reared in most areas and, about 50 years before the *Tobie*'s journey, great areas of land had been enclosed to aid larger-scale farming. The rural economy

ENGLISH SHEPHERD
The wool industry was a mainstay of England's economy. Much of the wool was exported, but sheep were also farmed for their milk and meat, which were sold locally.

TIN ORE
This was one of England's chief exports.

dominated, and nine out of ten men worked on the land. However, the wool industry was not organized on a large scale. Shepherds brought fleeces to market to sell to spinners. The spinners brought the spun yarn back to market to sell to weavers who would, in turn, sell the cloth to clothiers or dyers. The finished cloth would then be sold directly to London merchants for export in the lucrative Levant trade.

The Tin Trade
England had plentiful deposits of tin, iron, and coal, all of which were mined successfully. Tin mines were concentrated in the southwest, and Cornwall supplied most of the raw ore for export. During Elizabethan times, England was the largest exporter of tin.

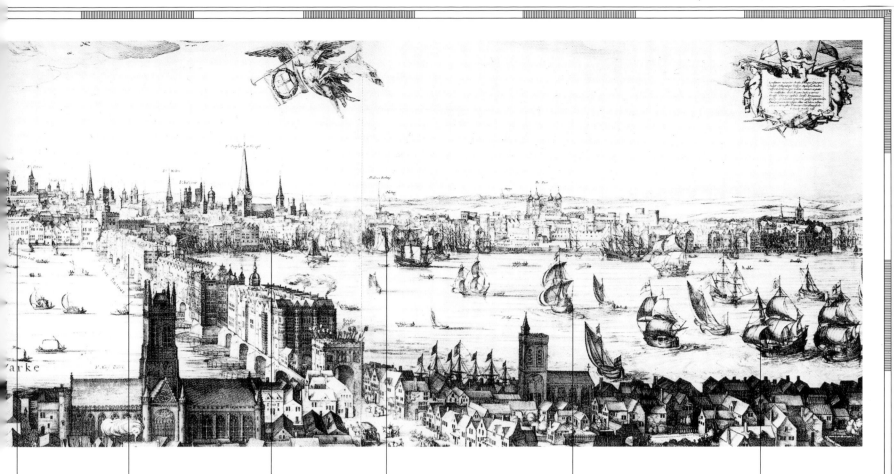

Fishmongers' Hall
Fishing was a valuable trade because fish had religious importance in the Elizabethan diet

London Bridge
Built with one drawbridge for large ocean-going vessels, and 19 small arches for local river traffic

Billingsgate wharf
Main wharf for landing fish; used by ocean ships to avoid navigating London Bridge

Cargo ship
Partly rigged English ship, moored facing seaward in preparation for its outward journey

Changing tack
Unusually, this ship is placed broadside onto river currents, and in a busy shipping lane

Incoming ships
Making their way upstream from the sea at the end of their voyage to London

crew suggested that the mainmast should be cut away to reduce the strain on the ship's timbers, and perhaps also to form a raft on which to reach the shore, he disagreed and suggested instead that they hoist out the boat. Then, when the height of the water in the holds was pointed out, he changed his mind and agreed to cut down the mast. Before anything could be achieved, however, the ship broke in two and the crew was forced to seek safety by climbing into the shrouds of the foremast.

Anticipating Death

Having abandoned all hope of survival, the crew began to sing Psalm 12, "Help Lord for good and godly men." Before they had reached the end of the fourth verse, the foremast collapsed and they were thrown into the water. Out of the crew of 50 men, 38 drowned before reaching shore, which was about a quarter of a mile (400 meters) away.

Those sailors who survived did so either by swimming or by clinging to wooden chests or pieces of the wreckage. Both the master and his mate, William Palmer, were drowned.

The 12 survivors looked for some sign of habitation, but found only wild beasts and burned-out houses, which had been destroyed by the Portuguese. They had only water to drink and wild date roots to eat, and that night they climbed into olive trees to rest and to avoid the danger from lions and other marauding animals.

Late on the following day, the survivors came across a battle between Moorish and Spanish/Portuguese forces. The sailors decided to give themselves up to the victors, who were Moors, but, as they approached, several hundred soldiers rushed at them with javelins. It looked as if they intended to kill the sailors, but at the last moment they only struck them with the flat of their weapons. At first the Moors presumed their captives were Spanish, but the sailors explained through an interpreter that they were English merchants en route to the Levant, and that their ship had been wrecked not far from that place.

The leader of the Moors ordered the sailors to be stripped and searched. He took about $300 in gold and pearls, and gave them bread and water. The next day, the sailors were taken back to the shipwreck, about 16 miles

(26 kilometers) away. During the journey, they were ill-treated by the Moors, who beat them if they went too slowly and forced them to carry their captors' equipment. The Moors salvaged what they could from the wreck, and then took the sailors to Ksar el Kebir (Cassuri) in the heart of Morocco.

Hostages for Ransom

The sailors were imprisoned at Ksar el Kebir, together with Spanish captives and French victims of another shipwreck. One week later, the sailors were taken to the capital of Morocco by 900 soldiers, via Fes and Salé. They were provided with tents on the journey and managed to find running water wherever they camped even though they passed through country without any habitation. Eventually they appeared before the court in Morocco, which committed them to jail for 15 days while a ransom was arranged. The money was paid by the community of English merchants in Morocco, and the sailors were released. Of the 12 shipwreck survivors, only 10 returned to London: one died in captivity and the other died on the journey home.

PORTUGUESE CARRACKS

In 1498 the Portuguese navigator Vasco da Gama reached India via the Cape of Good Hope. He was the first European to reach the East using a direct sea route and, in so doing, reoriented the trade of the entire world. Until then Venice had dominated trade with the East, using a combination of land and sea routes to bring coveted oriental wares back to Europe (see pages 30–35).

Over the next 20 years, Portugal set about consolidating its trade advantage by establishing fortified trading posts in strategically placed ports such as Ormuz in Persia (Iran), Goa in India, and Malacca (Melaka) in the Far East.

During the early sixteenth century the ships used for Portuguese exploration and trade were lightly built caravels of about 100 tons, which sailed in fleets of 7 to 14 ships. By the end of the century, ship design had evolved from caravels to giant-sized carracks weighing 1,500 tons or more, and the number of ships in each fleet grew smaller. The round trip to Goa took about 18 months including a 3- or 4-month stay in India to refit ships and load goods. The route, known as the Carreira da India, was very tough, and only four out of every five ships survived it.

JULES ①
A carrack lost in 1673 on treacherous shoals near Lisbon, returning from Goa, with a cargo of amber and pearls.

LAGOS
One of the main departure points for Portuguese ships voyaging to the East was Lagos, on the Algarve coast.

CAPE BOJADOR
This psychological boundary was broken in 1434 by Captain Gil Eannes, opening up the African coast for trade. Until then, seafarers believed that sea-serpents lurked beyond, ready to devour any intrepid explorers.

TRADE WITH AFRICA
From the 1440s, Portugal imported slaves, gold, and ivory from west Africa. Large quantities of the gold came from the upper regions of the rivers Niger, Volta, and Senegal.

SANTA ROSA ②
In 1726 this ship foundered near Recife, with its cargo of South American gold.

DOLDRUMS
The outward route from Portugal to the East veered toward Brazil to avoid being trapped in the doldrums, an area of such calm that it could add months to a voyage.

MONOMATAPA
The east African gold mines of Monomatapa supplied gold to the Portuguese. This gold was picked up by Portuguese on their way out to the East, then minted into São Tomé coins in Goa, and used to buy spices and pepper from the pepper traders of the Malabar coast in India.

FRAMENGO ④
Returning from India in 1559, the ship wrecked on São Tomé, after weathering storms off the Cape of Good Hope.

MINAS GERAIS
The Portuguese had a presence in Brazil from 1500, but it was only after the discovery of gold in the Minas Gerais area, central Brazil, in 1690, and diamonds in 1720, that the journey between Brazil and Portugal became a trade route.

SACRAMENTO ③
This East Indiaman sank off Brazil in 1688. Brass cannons, majolica plates, and religious items have been recovered.

SANTO ALBERTO ⑤
This overloaded East Indiaman set out from Cochin, India, in 1593. It wrecked near land so its gold, silver, and crystal rosaries were salvaged.

Map labels: BRITAIN, HOLY ROMAN EMPIRE, FRANCE, OTTOMAN EMPIRE, Oporto, PORTUGAL, SPAIN, Lisbon, Lagos, AZORES, MADEIRA, CANARY ISLANDS, Cape Bojador, MAMELUKES EMPIRE, Arguim, CAPE VERDE, AFRICA, ABYSS, Senegal, GUINEA, Niger, AKAN, Volta, São Tomé, ATLANTIC OCEAN, Axim, Elmina, Congo, Pernambuco (Recife), BRAZIL, Bahia (Salvador), MONOMATAPA, Rio de Janeiro, Cape of Good Hope

LISBON HARBOR SCENE
One of the busiest ports on the Portuguese coast, Lisbon was an important commercial center for Portugal until its capture by Spain in 1580. In this engraving, a large Portuguese carrack with a high forecastle can be seen in the center, along with smaller caravels on the left. Other ships have been drawn up on the shore for repairs and refitting.

MADRE DE DEUS ⑭
To avoid capture in Nagasaki Bay, the captain blew up his ship in 1609. *(See pages 42–43.)*

BACAIM WRECK ⑥
Returning from Persia (Iran), this ship sank in 1618 with a cargo of gold and perfumes.

FLOR DE LA MAR ⑨
This galleon was part of a fleet returning to India in 1511, with goods seized from Malacca (Melaka), when it sank. (See pages 38–39.)

PRATAS REEF WRECK ⑮
Traveling from Manila to Macao, this ship foundered with a cargo of amber, musk, pearls, and precious stones.

KUANTUNG WRECK ⑫
In 1601 a ship carrying silver coins was lost off the Kuantung coast between Goa and Macao.

CEYLON ⑧
A Portuguese register ship lost off Mangalore, India, in 1808. It was carrying coins worth 600,000 rupees.

SAO PAULO ⑩
Hit by storms, this East Indiaman wrecked off Sumatra in 1561. (See pages 40–41.)

SERRAO'S SHIP ⑯
This trading ship was lost in 1512 carrying coins from Malacca (Melaka) to the Spice Islands (Moluccas).

BOM JESUS ⑦
An East Indiaman was wrecked on reefs in 1590, en route from Lisbon to Goa with a rich cargo of coins.

STRONG WINDS AND CURRENTS
Instead of sailing the shortest distance to India, the outward route followed the prevailing ocean currents eastward before turning up toward India.

DOURADO ⑬
This brig foundered on rocks in 1829, losing priceless antiquities. (See pages 44–45.)

AUSTRALIA
Although it was not discovered by Europeans until the eighteenth century, early maps showed landmasses here, to balance the weight of those in the Northern Hemisphere.

SAO THOME ⑪
On its return from Cochin, India, in 1589, this ship leaked badly, and wrecked. Some people escaped on a longboat but several hundred drowned when the main ship broke up.

PERSIA

ARABIA

MUGHAL INDIA

Damão

Mangalore

GOA

Calicut

Cochin

MING CHINA

Canton

Macao

FORMOSA

Manila

SIAM (THAILAND)

Tengah Reef

SOUTH CHINA SEA

Malacca (Melaka)

Singapore

SUMATRA

BORNEO

SPICE ISLANDS (MOLUCCAS)

Bantam (Banten)

JAVA

PACIFIC OCEAN

INDIAN OCEAN

Sea of Japan

JAPAN

Nagasaki

LISBONA.

THE
FLOR DE LA MAR

In 1511, Alfonso de Albuquerque, a Portuguese governor based in Goa, India, set out to conquer the rich seaport of Melaka (Malacca) in Malaysia. After taking the town, Albuquerque constructed a fortress and set up a mint: a revealing combination that neatly sums up the military and commercial motives of his expedition. He decided to return to India and loaded some of the captured booty onto four ships, one of which was the *Flor de la Mar*. The treasure included palanquins plated with gold, a table with golden feet, and the Queen of Malacca's throne encrusted with precious stones, valued at the time at 300,000 cruzados. Probably the most fabulous items were four lion sculptures, which may have been a present from the King of China to the King of Malacca, or possibly taken from the ancient sepulchres of the kings of Malacca. They were supposedly made of gold, with jewels used for their eyes, tongues, teeth, and claws. Also on board was a special gold bracelet set with bones from an animal called the cabal, native to the mountains of Thailand (Siam). The bones were reputed to have magical properties: as long as the bracelet was worn, blood would not flow from any wounds. The last cargo stowed on board was a human one of pretty young Malay girls and youths.

Wrecked on Reefs

On the return journey the fleet ran into a storm near the coast of eastern Sumatra. The *Flor de la Mar* anchored but, as night fell, the storm worsened and the ship ran onto reefs. The hull rapidly broke in two, the stern part wedged on the rock and the forepart floating free. A raft was constructed and most Portuguese were rescued. One of the uglier aspects of this wrecking is that Albuquerque allowed only white Europeans to board the raft. Others were pushed away with pikes and left to drown. Presumably this was the fate of the slave girls and youths.

FACTS AND FEATURES

Cargo	Exotic treasure and slaves
Salvage	Under investigation but no treasure recovered so far
Route	Melaka–Goa

PORTUGUESE CARAVEL
A small merchant ship and forerunner of the larger carracks of the sixteenth century, the lightly built, lateen-rigged caravel was used for trading and voyages of exploration.

Yard or spar
Characteristically as long as the ship: up to 100 feet (30 meters)

CARRACKS IN FULL SAIL
Painted in the early sixteenth century, near the time of the shipwreck of the Flor de la Mar, *this scene shows the very high forecastles and sterns of the large Portuguese carracks, which made them unwieldy and not very seaworthy.*

ALFONSO DE ALBUQUERQUE

One of the first colonial governors sent abroad from the Portuguese court, the Great Alfonso de Albuquerque (as he was usually referred to in Portuguese chronicles) was instrumental in establishing Portugal's control over the sea routes to the East. In 1510 he seized Goa in India, as part of the Portuguese strategy of establishing outposts to help develop the valuable Eastern trade in spices. After a year ruthlessly putting down local opposition in Goa, he turned his attention to other military objectives, and set sail to conquer Melaka.

MELAKA

In the early sixteenth century, Melaka (then spelled Malacca or Malaca) was acknowledged as one of the principal seaports of the world. It was where East met West, and so benefited from the opening up of trade routes between Europe and the Far East. Merchants from China and the Moluccas (Spice Islands) traded goods with Gujerati traders from west India, who then carried the transshipped goods back to India and on to the Middle East.

Melaka was an immensely valuable port, both strategically and commercially, and the Portuguese ruled there for 130 years until it was seized in 1641 by the new rising power in the East, the Dutch.

Foremast
Has a topmast with a foretop sail

Square sail
Ideal for running before the wind; triangular sails were better suited to light winds or sudden gusts

COAST OF MELAKA
Portuguese illustrations of coastal profiles showed sailors how the outline of the land would appear to ships two leagues (6 miles/10 kilometers) out to sea.

Place labels
Individual places on the coast were labeled, together with the direction from which the illustrated view was seen

Bowsprit
To stay the sails on the foremast

Forecastle
Lower on caravels than on carracks

Oak or pine hull
Needed frequent waterproofing. The Portuguese did this partly in the water (Italian careening) but it was inefficient, and several ships developed leaks and sank.

RECENT SALVAGE

In 1991 the Indonesian company PT Jayatama Istikacipta claimed to have located the remains of the *Flor de la Mar* in about 120 feet (36.5 meters) of water, under mud, near the Tengah reef, north of Tanjong Jambuair or Diamond Point. This is much farther north than documentary evidence had suggested was likely, but then documents may often be misleading. The company states that its search so far has cost $20 million. The current value of the cargo has been estimated at anything between $1 billion and $8 billion, although quite how such estimates are made is difficult to understand. So far, only tin coins, knives, and wood have been recovered. In the meantime, the Malayan government has laid claim to the wreck on the basis that the cargo was stolen from Malaysia. The Indonesian government claims ownership of the wreck because it lies in Indonesian waters.

THE
SAO PAULO

The *São Paulo* left the Portuguese port of Belem, just outside Lisbon, on April 20, 1560 along with five more Portuguese East Indiamen. It was a large, strong ship, probably over 400 tons, and built out of Indian teak. Late April was well after the recommended time for departure, which was February or March, and the *São Paulo* was soon in difficulties. After surviving storms in the North Atlantic, it was becalmed off west Africa and took two months to sail from 7°N to 5°N, during which time a number of those on board fell ill and became delirious. Following

DETOUR TO BRAZIL

The usual route from Portugal to India was to sail to west Africa, and then to head southwest across the Atlantic towards the coast of Brazil before sailing back to the foot of Africa and rounding the Cape of Good Hope. This apparent detour was to avoid the doldrums that were frequently experienced off the coast of Guinea, where a ship could be trapped for months without making any progress. The *São Paulo* was caught in this trap for two months but eventually reached Salvador for repairs and rest before setting sail for the Cape.

a good rest in Salvador (known then as the Bay of All Saints) in Brazil, the *São Paulo* set sail for the Cape of Good Hope. Having rounded this, it took the outer course east of Madagascar rather than beat up through the Mozambique Channel. However, the weather turned stormy and the *São Paulo* was driven before a violent westerly wind until it was finally wrecked off the west coast of Sumatra. The luckless pilot took much of the blame for this disaster, one contemporary account describing him as a fool obsessed with "decorated charts and gilded astrolabes."

The *São Paulo* drifted onto a small uninhabited island near the equator on January 21, 1561. The landscape was marshy, steaming, thickly wooded, and terrifying.

Marooned on an Island

To begin with everything went well. The castaways ate and drank whatever was washed ashore or could be salvaged, their fare including the best muscatel wines, cheeses, and olives. They reconnoitered the island, which was about three miles (five kilometers) in circumference, and close to the Sumatran mainland. They built a camp and a chapel,

and roofed their huts with palm leaves, which proved more effective against the rain than the Arras tapestries and Flanders cloth they had saved from the shipwreck. They used these instead to decorate the chapel.

The island proved to be full of apes that stole their food. The shipwrecked sailors shot a few but their flesh was very unpalatable. The apes, however, were a minor problem. Before long, some of the Portuguese fell sick and died, while others were captured and eaten by natives from a larger island nearby, who had rejected friendly gestures and gifts.

Escape Plans

The survivors set about building a large boat from the remains of the ship's longboat, enlarging the skiff, and constructing another small boat. The large boat was meant to carry about 260 people, and the other two boats were to carry the remaining 70. They showed great ingenuity in making these boats, building a smithy and creating saws out of swords.

Two months later the boats were ready, but it became clear on the voyage to Sumatra that the longboat was overcrowded, mainly because some merchants had stowed large quantities of goods aboard. When it reached Sumatra, over half the occupants were tricked by the captain into disembarking, leaving 172 people, including children and many of the sick, to make their way on land. The abandoned people set out along the Sumatran west coast, carrying a banner of holy relics at the front, and priests bringing up the rear with a crucifix.

SICKNESS AT SEA

Portuguese ships that underwent the round trip from Lisbon to India and back again traveled on what was considered the toughest and most grueling route of the time. Conditions on the ships were often overcrowded and unhygienic, with up to 800 people aboard on the outward-bound route. Disease was rife, particularly typhus and dysentery. Food and drink were of poor quality and frequently in limited supply. It was not unusual for half the crew and passengers to have died before reaching their destination.

Conditions Aboard the São Paulo
Those unlucky men who were afflicted by disease while becalmed off Africa received the most primitive of medical treatment. The sick men, mostly delirious soldiers and novice sailors, were left on deck, exposed to the extremes of sun and rain. They were repeatedly bled, which

was a common-enough medical practice but one which would have left them further weakened. They were also tied together to prevent them throwing themselves overboard. At one point 350 out of a total of 500 on board were ill.

Life for those not afflicted by disease was little better. Falling from masts was a regular hazard. During one particularly severe storm an apprentice seaman (a grummet) fell from the main topmast into the sea, leaving a portion of his brains on one of the yardarms.

PORTABLE MEDICINE CHEST
This seventeenth-century chest was suitable for sea voyages, and held basic drugs such as emetics to induce vomiting, antispasmodics, and opium for painkilling, all probably carried on the São Paulo.

Walnut case
Hardwood to withstand rigors of travel

Metal canisters
For storing drugs affected by light

Airtight containers
Glass bottles with pewter screwtops kept contents fresh

NOVA & ACVRATA TOTIVS ASIÆ TABVLA, auct. G. BLAE

Mark of the Blaues
The Blaues had a famous map-making firm in Amsterdam

Arctic Circle
Inset detail added context to main map

Local shipping
Small ship with eastern-style design

Mythical sea monsters
For map decoration

Ocean-going ship
Western-style cargo ship, similar to *São Paulo*

Portrait of Muscovites
Dressed in furs and bright woolens

A Change of Fortune

Meanwhile, those in the boats had surprised a large junk on the seas, which they managed to capture after a fierce struggle. Now that the Portuguese had a boat large enough to take all of the survivors, they returned to fetch those who were still trekking along the coast. The latter had recently had the good fortune to kill a crocodile over 15 feet (4 meters) long, the roasted flesh of which was claimed to be very good. The reunited group set off, sailing in a westerly direction until they came to the Menencabo River, about three degrees below the equator, where they met some apparently friendly natives who persuaded them to go up the river to meet

DONA FRANCISCA

One of the most distinguished passengers on board, Doña Francisca was widely regarded as one of the great beauties of her age. She survived the wreck and the arduous trek along the Sumatran coast only to be captured in the raid by armed natives on the night of April 17. She was never seen or heard of again. The Portuguese presumed she had been taken to join the king's harem, and that this had been a prime motive for the attack.

WALL MAP OF ASIA, 1673
This ornate chart produced by mapmaker G. Blaue is titled "A new and accurate map of the whole of Asia." It includes 16 scenes of national dress along both sides, including Sumatran people at the bottom left; and views of 12 important eastern trading posts, such as Banten, Kandy, and Calcutta, in the medallions along the foot. The detail shows some of the places featured in the tale of the São Paulo *shipwreck.*

the local king. When the king arrived, he was presented with textiles, crystal glass goblets, and a very valuable mirror.

The *São Paulo* survivors appear to have been remarkably careless of their own safety at this point. Not only did they allow themselves to be trapped up the entrance to the river, they also ignored the large number of armed natives who were continually arriving in canoes, as well as the covetous attitude of the king toward their armaments. Instead, they indulged themselves in eating and drinking. They fell victim to a surprise night attack on April 17, in which over 70 were killed.

Those who escaped set sail for Banten, Java, where they were warmly greeted and looked after by the local Portuguese; rather too well perhaps, because about a dozen of them died through overeating. After staying there for nearly a month, the remaining 250 survivors set out for Melaka (Malacca), where they arrived on July 25, 1561, over six months after being shipwrecked.

Landing point
Islet half a league from the Sumatran west coast, onto which the *São Paulo* was blown

Menencabo River
Scene of ambush and massacre

Melaka, place of safety
Final destination of shipwrecked sailors

THE
MADRE DE DEUS

Andre Pessoa was appointed captain major of the *Madre de Deus*, a Portuguese carrack that sailed from China to Nagasaki, Japan, in 1609. This was the first ship to sail that route for two years and so carried an exceptionally rich cargo reportedly worth 8 million cruzados. The ship had over 200 merchants on board, each of whom planned to spend substantial amounts in Nagasaki, buying goods to bring back for trade in China. The *Madre de Deus* left Macao on May 10 and, after encountering typhoons en route, arrived in Nagasaki Bay on June 29.

A quarrel promptly broke out between Pessoa and the governor of Nagasaki, Hasegawa. It is unclear precisely what the quarrel was about but Hasegawa plotted with the king of neighboring Arima to persuade the Shogun Iyeyasu to attack the Portuguese. Iyeyasu had his own motives for disliking the Portuguese: the presence of so many Jesuits in his kingdom, causing a rapidly increasing Japanese Christian following, had become a threat to his power. Iyeyasu granted permission for the king of Arima to confiscate the *Madre de Deus* and its cargo, and to capture Pessoa, dead or alive.

Poop deck
Short, raised deck at rear of ship

Under Attack at Night

Realizing the danger of attack, Pessoa ordered all the Portuguese merchants back on board to make a hasty departure. Many were not ready, so Pessoa moved the ship a little way off Nagasaki and anchored in Fakunda harbor, awaiting the tardy merchants, and a wind by which he could return to Macao. Meanwhile, the king of Arima arrived at Nagasaki and entreated Pessoa to meet peacefully on land. Pessoa did not trust him and refused to leave his ship, so the king changed tactics, embarked 1,200 troops in 33 small rowing boats, and sailed out at night to attack the *Madre de Deus* with muskets and arrows. They were met with gunfire and the Japanese retired without having boarded. This happened for three nights until, on July 9, the Japanese attacked with a large, floating tower that enabled them to set fire to the *Madre de Deus*. Pessoa, realizing that his ship was lost, ordered the powder magazine to be blown up and threw himself into the sea. There were apparently no Portuguese suvivors.

Relay boat
Smaller boats for transporting trade goods from the main ship to shore

Steering to shore
Paddles were used to take boats from ocean waters to the shallower harbor

Inlaid chests
Wooden trunks held cargo for trading

SILK CARGO

Raw Chinese silk (ready for dyeing or embroidering in Japan) formed part of the cargo carried on the *Madre de Deus* for trading in Nagasaki. Raw silk is the fabric spun from silkworm larvae cocoons. After silkworms lay their eggs on leaves of white mulberry trees, the larvae hatch and spin a cocoon of silk thread. Cocoons are harvested, and their thread unraveled for spinning into fabric.

SILK SPINNING IN SEVENTEENTH-CENTURY CHINA
A new basket of cocoons is presented to the spinner, who is spinning the first batch. She is working over a gentle heat, to kill the worms in their cocoons. The unbroken thread is then carefully wound over the rack in front of the spinner and her helper, ready for weaving into lengths of raw silk.

Main topcastle
Large enough to
hold a lookout

Mainmast
Placed toward
middle of ship

Forecastle
Characteristically
high, making the
ship unstable

Black hull
The Japanese called
Portuguese vessels
"Black Ships"

Diving for Treasure

According to contemporary accounts, the Japanese attackers were able to salvage some packages of silk and three boxes of silver at the time of the explosion. It was reported by a Dutch merchant in Japan that 200,000 ducats' worth of silks and silver were recovered. The fact that raw silk (an export product from China used to trade for Japanese goods) was still on board adds weight to the theory that the merchants had not had time to complete their business in Nagasaki.

Diving operations continued throughout the seventeenth century. One account states that there were 150 chests of silver on board at the time of loss, of which 70 were recovered in 1617. More than 30 years later, in 1653, a further salvage attempt brought up three silver bars, along with a few miscellaneous artifacts. Since the wreck was said to lie at a depth of 33 fathoms (about 200 feet or 60 meters), this salvage is most impressive for the period, and it must have been a fascinating and difficult salvage operation. Certainly, the loss of the *Madre de Deus* and its reputed riches has passed into Japanese folklore, and the wreck still continues to hold its allure for would-be salvors. There were extensive salvage efforts in the late 1920s and, as recently as the 1980s, the Japanese Maritime Development Company was reported to be carrying out recovery work at the site.

JAPANESE IMAGES OF PORTUGUESE
These scenes of traders from a large carrack are taken from an early seventeenth-century folding screen. They show how the Japanese saw the foreign merchants, exaggerating their Western physical features such as large noses, mustaches, and height.

An Eastern perspective
Japanese artists accentuated height differences between locals and Europeans

ANDRE PESSOA

In the year before the *Madre de Deus* episode, Pessoa held office in Macao when fighting broke out between the Japanese and Portuguese. Pessoa quelled the disturbance and imprisoned a Japanese sailor, who was then strangled, while the remaining Japanese hid in two houses. Pessoa ordered one of these houses to be burned and the fleeing Japanese to be shot. He also forced the surviving Japanese to sign confessions taking the blame. As a result, Pessoa was hated in Japan, which would have fueled the *Madre de Deus* conflict.

Trading completed
Merchants wait on
wharfside to return
to their main ship

THE
DOURADO

By the mid-seventeenth century the great days of the Portuguese maritime empire were already numbered. Even so, Portuguese shipping played an important role in the trade from Macao to India, right into the nineteenth century, as shown by the tale of the *Dourado*, a Portuguese brig.

The *Dourado* left Macao for Bombay, India, on January 18, 1829, and was reported to have struck rocks east of Point Romania a week later, on January 25. In the impact, the ship lost its rudder and so became ungovernable. The crew tried to steer the ship by using canvas sail but without success, and it drifted south and south-southeast, filling with water at such a rate that the pumps could not cope. At midnight the captain decided to abandon ship. The passengers and crew were taken off in the longboat and a smaller boat, and headed for the safety of Singapore. Only one person drowned. So far, all this was very much routine for the period.

Reports of a Fortune

What made the *Dourado* special, and created considerable excitement at the time, was that it was said to have $500,000 on board when it foundered. As soon as the larger of the two boats arrived at Singapore, the captain of the *Dourado* reported that his vessel had been lost on a rock known as Mount Formosa and requested that an armed guard be sent immediately to protect it while he made preparations for the recovery of the cargo. The British authorities responded speedily and dispatched a team of divers to salvage the *Dourado*, along with a detachment of soldiers in three ships to guard the wreck against local Malay pirates. But it was feared that the ship had sunk in deep water and that the expedition would prove to be a wild-goose chase. This skepticism appeared to have been justified, and the three ships returned very shortly without finding the wreck.

Meanwhile, excitement mounted about the value of the *Dourado*'s cargo, following the arrival of Monsieur le Chevalier Louis Domenic de Rienzi in Singapore, on the smaller of the *Dourado*'s two boats, a couple of days after the longboat.

SINGAPORE IN 1830
The busyness of this crowded harbor scene demonstrates Singapore's maritime importance. Its position on the shortest route between the Indian Ocean and the South China Sea ensured heavy use by merchant shipping.

Fully rigged ship
Three-masted European ship, each mast carrying three square sails

Sampan panjangs
Small, shallow-drafted boats ferried passengers as well as goods

British settlement
Built in the Palladian style by town planner George Coleman

Footsoldiers
Troops maintained the British presence in newly acquired Singapore

SINGAPORE

Positioned right at the southern tip of the Malay Peninsula, Singapore was perfectly situated to develop into a focal point for trade to and from southeast Asia. In 1819 Sir Thomas Stamford Raffles (see also pages 90–91) had established a British settlement on Singapore Island, and described it as

... a child of my own.... It is impossible to conceive a place combining more advantages; it is within a week's sail of China, still closer to Siam, Cochin China, etc., in the very heart of the Archipelago or, as Malays call it, "The Navel of the Malay countries."

Raffles's fledgling colony proved to be an instant success and, by the time he left the East in 1824, Singapore had become a thriving commercial center and port.

Rienzi the Explorer

After long and wide-ranging travels, Rienzi had gone to Macao to erect a monument to his hero Camoens, the sixteenth-century Portuguese author of *The Lusiads*, in the grotto of Patane. Rienzi had then embarked with the accumulated treasures of his wanderings on the *Dourado*, anticipating a triumphant return to his French homeland.

Events did not go as planned. Rienzi later claimed to have lost his entire life's work in the wreck of the *Dourado*. Among the items lost were a vast and valuable collection of the most precious medals, cameos, statues, inscriptions, and other antiquities, objects of natural history, scarce books, Egyptian and

oriental manuscripts, arms, and astronomical instruments. The greatest loss, however, was that of the remains brought by Monsieur Rienzi from the ruins of Petra in Arabia, and from Syre and Assab in Abyssinia. Rienzi claimed to have been the first to have rediscovered the sites of all these ancient towns.

Monsieur Rienzi took every opportunity to write at length in several publications of the immensity of his personal loss, and of the heroic manner in which he had conducted himself during the shipwreck. He talked of saving his best friend, who was unable to swim, as well as rescuing his pet dog. Rienzi also described in grandiloquent language his sufferings from thirst and heat during the voyage back to Singapore. If Rienzi is to be

Cargo-carrying ships
Western trading ships moored in deep water just outside the harbor

Docks
Small ships tied up in sheltered waters at the mouth of the harbor

believed, it was only his intervention that prevented some of the ship's crew putting off early in the last remaining boat, which would have left several passengers still stranded on board the *Dourado*.

Unfortunately, no other source survives either to corroborate or to refute these highly extravagant stories of heroism and valor. Modesty was clearly not a dominant character trait of Monsieur Rienzi.

Discovery and Salvage

The three ships first sent out from Singapore might not have been able to locate the wreck of the *Dourado*, but the wreck very shortly turned up off the island of Bintan. Colonel

Elout, the local Dutch commander, promptly wrote a letter on February 1 to the British Governor in Singapore, K. Murchison, in which he referred to the discovery of the wreck and requested further information about the cargo. On February 3 Murchison answered,

> *I have the honour to state in reply that the treasure on board the* Dourado *has been represented to amount to $500,000 and there can be no doubt that the Captain of the* Dourado *will gladly reimburse you for any expenses incurred in the attempt to save his property.*

Subsequent salvage operations apparently met with no success. Three months later Rienzi had given up hope of salvaging a significant amount of his property. All that the divers had managed to retrieve were a few trifling items, a silver statue, a bronze inscription, a box with some papers, and one

or two other miscellaneous objects. As for the $500,000 belonging to the captain, there is no mention of any of this being recovered.

From the various accounts of the wreck, it appears that the *Dourado* was probably not wrecked off Point Romania after all, but had hit the rocks of Pedra Branca, and then drifted south and south-southeast to end up on the coast of Bintan. In late January the northeast monsoon would have been at its strongest and accidents of this nature on Pedra Branca were common.

Pedra Branca was so called because it appeared perfectly white, owing to the droppings of the seabirds that frequented it. In 1847 the Horsbrough Lighthouse (named after the English East India Company's hydrographer, James Horsbrough) was built on these rocks in an attempt to reduce the colossal loss of shipping in this area.

MONSIEUR RIENZI

Rienzi was a self-styled explorer, revolutionary, soldier, poet, tragedian, archaeologist, and intellectual polymath, very much in the Byronic style. Indeed, he claimed that his epic poem, *Barde Voyageur*, was an influence upon Byron's *Childe Harold*. He also claimed to be the only living descendant of Cola Gabrino di Rienzi, who had been a Roman tribune (an official in the ancient Roman empire) and a revolutionary.

Rienzi was born in the momentous year of 1789 (the start of the French Revolution). He fought at Wagram in 1809, became mixed up in the Conspiracy of Malet in 1812 and fled to the United States, traveling in Mexico and the Caribbean. After Rienzi returned to France, he fought at the Battle of Waterloo in 1815, then supported the Greeks in their struggle against the Turks and traveled around the Caspian Sea, the Caucasus, and Asia Minor, before going to Colombia to assist Simón Bolívar in 1819. In 1821 he returned to Italy to fight in the ranks of the Carbonari, only to be wounded at Marathon. Explorations of Egypt, Abyssinia, and the Sudan preceded his ill-fated travels in China and the Far East.

After the shipwreck, Rienzi returned to France where he published many books, including *Océanie* in 1835, and *Dictionnaire usuel et scientifique de géographie* in 1840. Melodramatic to the end, Rienzi killed himself at Versailles in 1843.

ANCIENT RUINS OF PETRA
Rienzi had collected antiquities from Petra, Arabia, which were all lost when the Dourado *wrecked.*

OCÉANIE
OU
CINQUIÈME PARTIE DU MONDE.

REVUE GÉOGRAPHIQUE ET ETHNOGRAPHIQUE
DE LA MALAISIE, DE LA MICRONÉSIE, DE LA POLYNÉSIE ET DE LA
MÉLANÉSIE;
OFFRANT LES RÉSULTATS DES VOYAGES ET DES DÉCOUVERTES DE L'AUTEUR
ET DE SES DEVANCIERS, AINSI QUE SES NOUVELLES CLASSIFICATIONS ET DIVISIONS
DE CES CONTRÉES,

PAR

M. G. L. DOMENY DE RIENZI,
VOYAGEUR EN OCÉANIE, EN ORIENT, ETC., ETC., MEMBRE DE
PLUSIEURS ACADÉMIES DE FRANCE ET D'ITALIE, DE LA SOCIÉTÉ DE GÉOGRAPHIE,
DES SOCIÉTÉS ASIATIQUES DE PARIS ET DE BOMBAY (INDE), ETC., ETC.

« Cherchez la science et la vérité, dussiez-vous ne les trouver
« qu'à l'extrémité du monde. »
MOHAMMED.

TOME PREMIER.

PARIS,
FIRMIN DIDOT FRÈRES, ÉDITEURS,
IMPRIMEURS-LIBRAIRES DE L'INSTITUT DE FRANCE,
RUE JACOB, N° 24.

M DCCC XXXVI.

FRONTISPIECE FROM *OCEANIE* **BY RIENZI**
Published six years after Rienzi survived the shipwreck, Océanie was his account of the people and scenery he had encountered during his travels in the East.

THE ARMADA

In 1588 King Philip II of Spain launched a naval attack upon Queen Elizabeth I of England. The organization and mobilization of the fleet that formed the Spanish Armada was on a scale and at a cost never before undertaken by a European monarch, and many ships were requisitioned from as far as Venice and Rostock, and gathered together in Lisbon. In all, 130 ships were assembled, including 22 Spanish and Portuguese galleons which were the most important battleships of the fleet. The Armada was a formidable offensive force with nearly 30,000 men, over half of them infantry soldiers.

Philip's motives were a familiar mixture of religious and strategic. He styled himself as the crusading Catholic King, intent upon establishing freedom of worship for English Catholics suffering under Protestant rule. Equally important was his desire to curtail Elizabeth's support for the Dutch rebels in the Netherlands, with whom Spain was at war. Philip planned to send a fleet, captained by the Duke of Medina Sidonia, to Dunkirk, where it would rendezvous with the Duke of Parma's troops, who were stationed in the Netherlands. Together, they would invade England.

The Spanish fleet left Lisbon on May 28, 1588, but it encountered storms and regrouped at Corunna (La Coruña) in Spain, reaching Plymouth on July 30. There was a series of skirmishes with the English, lasting nearly a week, as the Spanish progressed up the Channel to meet the troops at Dunkirk.

MINERVA MEDAL, 1602
Cast to commemorate England's naval victory over Spain, this medal depicts Queen Elizabeth I as Minerva, the goddess of wisdom. She is shown, below, triumphant over a dragon and a snail (symbolizing her enemies), and the inscription translates as "For the chaste, an eternal crown."

The Vanquished Armada

The Armada reached Calais on August 6, but the harbor was too shallow for the large galleons so the ships anchored at sea, exposing them to attack. That night, the English sent in fireships (unmanned floating ships packed with explosives, designed to cause panic among the enemy), and the Spanish ships broke formation and scattered. The ensuing Battle of Gravelines on August 8 was the fiercest of the campaign and the Spanish lost four ships. The Spanish Armada was far from defeated, but the Duke of Parma's troops were not ready to embark, so invasion was impossible. Then, because of fierce gales from the south, the Armada could not retreat along the Channel and instead had to return to Spain by taking the long northern route via Scotland and Ireland.

During August and September the fleet encountered an appalling series of storms in the Atlantic, which dispersed them over a wide area and destroyed nearly half of the ships. Most were lost on rocks off Ireland, although many escaped this fate and eventually reached the haven of the northern Spanish ports. Thousands of the original invasion force died during the return journey.

LA GIRONA ⑥
This galleass struck rocks off Ireland and sank, along with over 1,000 men and a very rich cargo. (See pages 50–51.)

ATLANTIC OCEAN

LA TRINIDAD VALENCERA ⑦
This converted grain ship lies in shallow water.

LA RATA ENCORONADA ⑧
Lost off western Ireland, it had many wealthy passengers on board, and was pillaged by locals at the time of loss.

SANTA MARIA DE LA ROSA ⑨
A galleon wrecked on a reef, with Prince D'Ascoli, son of Philip II, on board.

LA URCA DONCELLA ①
Foundered in Santander harbor, Spain, after weathering storms in the Atlantic.

THE ARMADA UNDER ATTACK
Spanish strength lay in the superiority of its infantry, so the Armada's plan was to board the enemy ships and overwhelm the crew. The English fleet had greater gun power, and could reload faster, and so wisely kept its distance, firing from afar.

Corunna (La Coruña)

GALICIA

PORTUGAL

Duero · Simancas

SPAIN

Tagus Madrid

POINT OF DEPARTURE
In 1580 Philip II of Spain conquered Portugal, and so, eight years later, was able to use Lisbon as his initial base for assembling ships from afar to make up his great Spanish Armada.

Guadalquivir ANDALUCIA
Cadiz

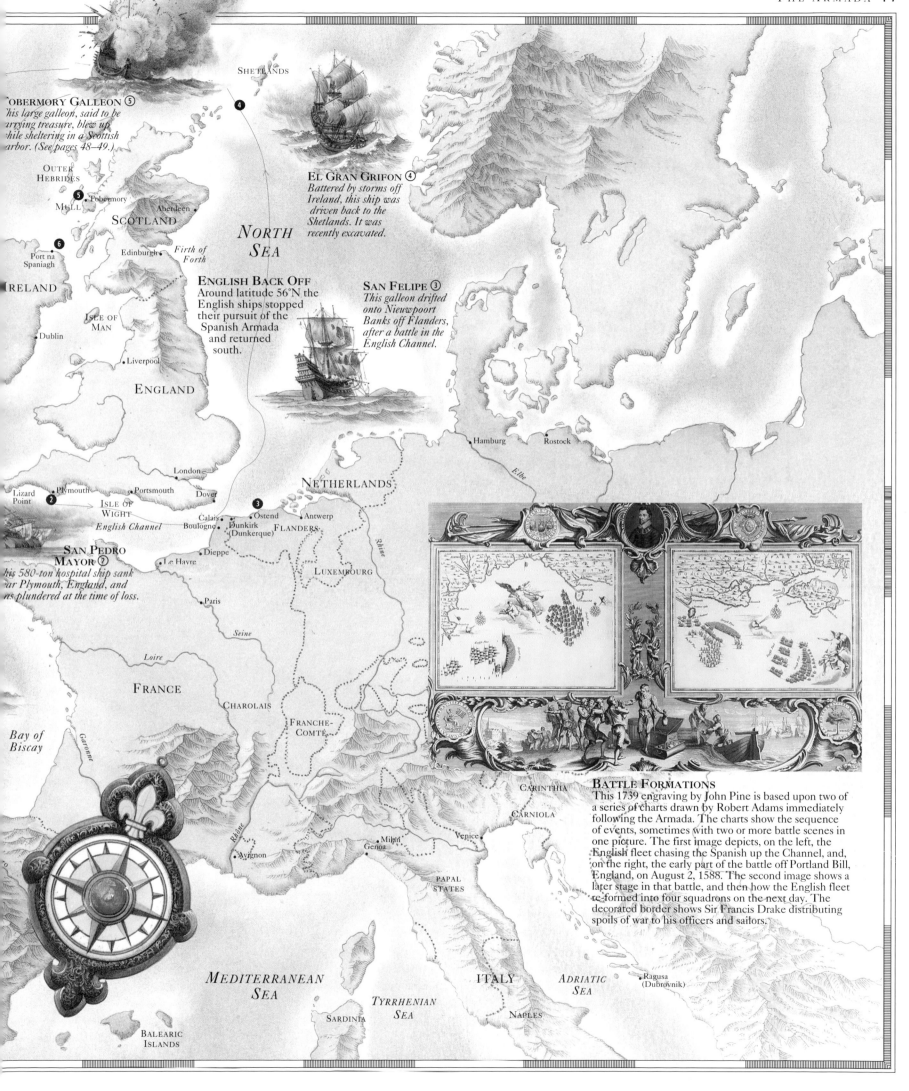

OBERMORY GALLEON ⑤
*his large galleon, said to be
arrying treasure, blew up
hile sheltering in a Scottish
arbor. (See pages 48–49.)*

SHETLANDS

EL GRAN GRIFON ④
*Battered by storms off
Ireland, this ship was
driven back to the
Shetlands. It was
recently excavated.*

OUTER
HEBRIDES

MULL
Tobermory

Aberdeen

SCOTLAND

*NORTH
SEA*

Port na
Spaniagh

Edinburgh   *Firth of
Forth*

IRELAND

Dublin

ISLE OF
MAN

Liverpool

ENGLAND

ENGLISH BACK OFF
Around latitude 56°N the
English ships stopped
their pursuit of the
Spanish Armada
and returned
south.

SAN FELIPE ③
*This galleon drifted
onto Nieuwpoort
Banks off Flanders,
after a battle in the
English Channel.*

Hamburg   Rostock

London

Elbe

Lizard
Point   Plymouth   Portsmouth   Dover

NETHERLANDS

ISLE OF
WIGHT

English Channel   Calais   Ostend   Antwerp

Boulogne   Dunkirk
(Dunkerque)   **FLANDERS**

**SAN PEDRO
MAYOR** ⑦
*his 580-ton hospital ship sank
ar Plymouth, England, and
s plundered at the time of loss.*

Dieppe   Le Havre   *Rhine*

LUXEMBOURG

Paris

Seine

FRANCE

CHAROLAIS

Loire

FRANCHE-
COMTÉ

*Bay of
Biscay*

Garonne

CARINTHIA

CARNIOLA

Rhône

Milan
Avignon   Genoa   Venice

BATTLE FORMATIONS
This 1739 engraving by John Pine is based upon two of
a series of charts drawn by Robert Adams immediately
following the Armada. The charts show the sequence
of events, sometimes with two or more battle scenes in
one picture. The first image depicts, on the left, the
English fleet chasing the Spanish up the Channel, and,
on the right, the early part of the battle off Portland Bill,
England, on August 2, 1588. The second image shows a
later stage in that battle, and then how the English fleet
re-formed into four squadrons on the next day. The
decorated border shows Sir Francis Drake distributing
spoils of war to his officers and sailors.

PAPAL
STATES

Ragusa
(Dubrovnik)

*MEDITERRANEAN
SEA*   ITALY   *ADRIATIC
SEA*

*TYRRHENIAN
SEA*   NAPLES

SARDINIA

BALEARIC
ISLANDS

THE
TOBERMORY GALLEON

One of the most tantalizing treasure ships of all time lies beneath the sheltered waters of Tobermory Bay, on the west coast of Scotland. For over four centuries kings have quarreled with earls, protracted legal cases have been fought, lives have been lost, and bankruptcies have been filed, all in pursuit of the gold and jewels worth $45 million rumored to be on board a ship sunk in the bay. And yet, until recent research in King Philip II's archives in the castle at Simancas in northern Spain, not even the ship's true name was known.

Arrival of a Mysterious Galleon

Some facts have been established beyond dispute. In September 1588, a large and well-armed Spanish galleon put in at the Isle of Mull, driven there through bad weather. It was one of the stragglers from the defeated and scattered Spanish Armada that was slowly making its painful way back to Spain via the northern route around the top of Scotland and to the west of Ireland. The sight of this great Spanish warship in the unfrequented waters of a remote Scottish island clearly made a great impact on the locals. It was reported as weighing 1,400 tons, carrying 800 soldiers and 80 pieces of brass ordnance. A deal was made between the Spaniards and the local Scottish chieftain, Maclean of Duart Castle, in which the Spanish supplied Maclean with soldiers to enable him to wreak bloody revenge on some of his traditional local enemies in return for food and water, as well as supplies of wood for repairs. For six weeks, this arrangement held and then, totally unexpectedly, the refitted galleon blew up and sank.

The possible explanations are many and various. Legend has it that Maclean's wife was taking revenge upon her husband for his adultery with a beautiful Spanish princess who was on board. Alternatively, a grocer called Smallet, who was a self-proclaimed English spy, claimed to be responsible, no doubt hoping for promotion. As so often happens, the most prosaic explanation is also the most likely one: there was probably an accident with the powderkegs on board.

Engine cover
Screwed into position where marked *d*

Leather sleeve
Made exactly to fit the arms of each diver

Porthole
Glass plate for diver to see through

Metal body
Knees were bent at the point marked /

Lifeline
Passed through a ring up to the diver's arms, so he could summon help by tugging

JACOB ROWE'S DIVING ENGINE
This ingenious diving suit was excruciatingly uncomfortable. Divers lay on their stomachs inside a horn-shaped contraption made of copper. Their arms poked out of holes into leather sleeves, while their bodies were braced against the floor to stop the pressure of water forcing them back against the roof.

Fight for Salvage Rights

Soon after the sinking, rumors began to circulate of the fabulous wealth that had gone to the bottom. The seventh earl of Argyll, as admiral of the Western Isles, had the legal right to any wreck in those waters, but for the next 100 years the luckless earls of Argyll wrangled with the Stuart kings for the rights to the Tobermory treasure. Throughout the disputes a succession of salvage attempts was made by leading experts of the period. The large timbers of the hull had concreted, making penetration inside the wreck difficult. Several brass cannons had been raised from the muddy bottom of Tobermory Bay but nothing of the fabled treasure had turned up.

It was not until 1729 that a real breakthrough came with the use of new technology developed by Jacob Rowe, who had already successfully recovered a vast fortune in bullion from a wreck in the Shetlands in Scotland. Rowe was clearly something of an inventor: in addition to a diving engine, he had developed the art of underwater explosions, and designed a loaded dart (like a primitive road drill) for breaking up concreted structures. Using this, he managed to penetrate inside the hull but two years of painstaking timber removal work produced no sign of treasure. Jacob Rowe packed up his gear and took himself off to more favorable climes. After this calamitous failure there was rather a lull of enthusiasm for further salvage efforts.

From Dredgers to Diviners

With the dawn of the twentieth century, interest in the Tobermory galleon revived once more. In 1903, the West of Scotland Syndicate carried out an excavation using suction pumps. After two years nothing more interesting than a set of brass dividers and a broken sword had been recovered, so the team turned to dredging and salvaged more items, including a silver candlestick holder, but still no treasure. They even called in a diviner but without success. By 1909 the syndicate had exhausted its funds, at which point the enigmatic Colonel Foss appeared. His efforts (see right) yielded little but the ship was not left in peace.

After the Second World War, the eleventh duke of Argyll took personal control of yet another attempt to locate the treasure. He employed a British admiralty survey team to pinpoint the wreck, and a swashbuckling wartime hero, Commander Crabb, to supervise the salvage. But apart from the skull of a cabin boy, very little was recovered.

The Answer Buried in the Archives

One would have thought that these repeated failures would finally have discouraged the most optimistic of treasure hunters. Perhaps what is most remarkable about this lengthy catalog of failure and frustration is that would-be salvors have made so little effort to examine the copious and highly detailed Spanish archives. Spanish records provide a far cheaper and more reliable route to the truth than physical excavation of the site. Research has now established beyond doubt that the legendary Tobermory galleon was the *San Juan de Sicilia* from Ragusa. Still more galling for those who have lost fortunes searching for royal treasure is that there had never been any significant quantity on board. Philip II sent only around 150,000 escudos with the Armada, distributed between four or five carefully selected ships – of which the *San Juan de Sicilia* was not one.

COLONEL FOSS AND CREW

For 25 years Colonel Foss pursued his personal obsession with finding the Tobermory treasure, and formed one syndicate after another to fund his attempts. His talents as a salvor were somewhat questionable, although he was undeniably skillful at persuading people to part with their money. The area of the supposed wreck was dredged and redredged, in the manner of a modern archaeologist's worst nightmare. Pewter plates and other items were recovered – but not the promised treasure. By the early 1930s, Foss's backers had finally become disillusioned with him and, amid accusations of fraud and corruption, Foss lost control of the salvage operations, although he never abandoned his faith in the reality of treasure to be found just below the next cubic yard of mud.

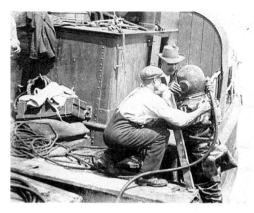

ONE OF COLONEL FOSS'S DIVING TEAM
A diver for Foss's Pieces of Eight Syndicate has his faceplate adjusted before diving, in 1910 or 1911.

THE CURSE OF THE CABIN BOY'S SKULL

Among the scattering of human remains found in 1954 was a skull, thought to belong to a cabin boy. It was given to a local hotelier who tried to bore a hole in it to hang it on the bar wall. Immediately, he suffered blinding headaches and, believing he was under a terrible curse, he hid the skull at the back of a cupboard. There it remained until 1985 when a new hotel owner laid the dreaded object to rest in the depths of the Sound of Mull.

GALLEONS, GALLEASSES, AND CARRACKS

The Tobermory wreck was a Spanish galleon, and so had been one of the frontline ships of the Armada. Galleons and galleasses were the most important fighting ships, specially built for this purpose, with 40 to 50 cannons on board.

Galleons: Spanish galleons were larger and grander than English ones and sat higher in the water. The very large galleons were difficult to maneuver and sometimes had to be towed into position by small row boats. The English galleons had a lower superstructure, so they benefited from reduced wind resistance and better maneuverability.

Galleasses: These were longer and narrower than galleons, and were equipped with oars as well as sails, which made them easier to maneuver even when there was no wind at all.

Spanish galleon
Sitting high in the water

Spanish galleass
Firing on the English fleet

English galleon
Lookout men in main topcastle

Defending forces
Footsoldiers and cavalry lined up on shore

Carracks and caravels (merchant ships): These formed the second line and were adapted for battle by being fitted with extra guns. A caravel was a lighter version of the larger carrack.

THE RIVAL FLEETS IN ACTION
Apart from galleons and galleasses, there was an assortment of smaller boats used for dispatching messages and negotiating shallow waters.

THE
GIRONA

For almost 400 years the wreck of the *Girona*, a Spanish galleass, remained untouched off the coast of Ireland where it met its fate in the autumn of 1588. It was salvaged in the late 1960s by a team of divers led by Robert Stenuit. His extensive researches had revealed that when the *Girona* sank it had on board the crews, soldiers, passengers, and valuables of not just one Armada ship but of three, and included many leading figures from Spain's aristocracy.

One of the most popular of Spanish commanders, Don Alonso de Leiva was the very emblem of courtly chivalry, brave in battle and generous to his soldiers. He was second in command of the entire Armada and sailed upon the *Santa Maria Encoronada*, a cumbersome broad-beamed carrack, difficult to maneuver in adverse winds. This ship, along with many others of the defeated Armada, sought shelter from the gales on the treacherous Irish coast. On September 17 it anchored in Blacksod Bay and sent a landing party of 14 men in search of water. These were promptly captured by a local terrorist, Richard Burke, nicknamed Devil's Hook, but were rescued shortly afterward. Then the *Santa Maria* ran aground. Don Alonso led his men to land, took off what stores he could from the wreck, and set fire to the remains.

They soon heard reports that another Spanish ship had put in to shore only a short distance away. This was the *Duquesa Santa Ana*, a 900-ton Andalusian hulk with 23 guns, 280 soldiers, and 77 sailors. A Spanish sailor from the *Duquesa*, later captured by the English, stated: "After she [*Santa Maria*] perished, Don Alonso and all his company were received into the hulk of *St. Ann* with all the goods they had in the ship of any value, as plate, apparel, money, jewels, weapons, and armor."

The wreck of the *Girona* lay undiscovered until 1967, when an enterprising Belgian diver, Robert Stenuit, made a remarkable find. He had spent 600 hours working in archives throughout the world, studying contemporary evidence and charts of the area where the *Girona* was known to have sunk.

Along the wild Irish coastline was a small bay called Port na Spaniagh. Stenuit realized that locals must have named it for a reason. Convinced he had located the right area, Stenuit made his first dive. After only one hour's search, he discovered lead ingots, which had been used as ballast by the Spanish, two bronze cannons, and a copper coin of the right period. He knew immediately that he had found his treasure ship.

FACTS AND FEATURES

Treasure	Valuables from three ships
Date of wreck	October 28, 1588
Depth	20–30 feet (6–9 meters)

Identification flag
Indicates the ship's Spanish origin

ARMED SPANISH GALLEASS
Although equipped with cannons for inflicting damage at a distance, the Spanish relied more heavily on grappling and superior numbers of soldiers when boarding enemy ships.

NAVIGATIONAL DIVIDERS
Used to chart courses, the Girona's dividers still function after 400 years on the seabed.

Cannon firing
Spanish cannons were difficult to reload, requiring men to hang over the edge of the ship

Calamitous Sequence of Misfortune

Don Alonso was to fare no better on the *Duquesa* than he had done on the *Santa Maria*: the hulk was driven northward by the winds and currents, and was also wrecked. Once again Don Alonso led the majority of his people to safety and brought the valuables ashore. The Spanish were befriended by a local Irish chieftain and, as before, soon learned of yet another Spanish ship that had put into harbor for essential repairs.

This third ship was the *Girona*, which had originally left Spain with 121 sailors, 186 soldiers, 50 bronze cannons, and 224 rowers, many of whom were convicts or slaves. On its final journey, the *Girona* carried over 1,000 men, with the accumulated treasure from all three ships, including some of the finest Renaissance jewelry.

Don Alonso set out once more but, instead of attempting to return to Spain, headed for Scotland, which was politically neutral in the Anglo–Spanish war. It did not prove to be third-time lucky. The *Girona* struck "the rock of Bunboys ... hard by Sorley Boy's House," and sank without a trace, with a horrifying loss of life. Of the 1,000 or more people on board, only five came safely to land.

Foremast
Flying a small flag, decorative pennants, and two sails

Catholic priest on board
Spain had religious, as well as political and economic, motives for attacking Protestant England

Bowsprit
Foremast's sails were attached here

A bank of oars
The *Girona* was fitted with 18 great oars on each side, giving extra maneuverability

THE TREASURE

Divers spent two years salvaging more than 12,000 artifacts from the *Girona*, which included 405 gold coins minted in six different countries, 12 gold rings, and eight gold chains. As part of both a proud invasion force and a crusading army, the *Girona* carried on board some exquisite jewelry, intricately worked gold chains, and religious items, such as crucifixes and a set of altar plate. The Cross of a Knight of Santiago – a beautifully made gold ornament that had belonged to the commander Don Alonso de Leiva himself – was recovered from the wreck, together with other badges of the Orders of Chivalry. Other, more personal, artifacts have a special poignancy, including a gold ring with the setting of a heart clasped by a hand and the inscription "*No tengo mas que darte*" (I have nothing more to give thee).

It has been suggested that this was the parting gift of a lady to her lover as he joined the Armada.

Clues to everyday life at sea were provided by the discovery of items such as leather soles for shoes, and even a plum stone. Pieces of navigational equipment and ordnance were also found, including swivel guns, lead shot, and several sounding leads. The *Girona* had been very heavily armed for battle against the English, with 50 bronze cannons mounted on walkways above the rowing benches.

Maltese cross

Ruby-studded salamander pendant

Gold escudo

AFTER THE DEFEAT
This contemporary map shows the route taken by the Armada around the coasts of Scotland and Ireland, before heading back to Spain. The defeated ships negotiated unfamiliar and treacherous waters with inaccurate maps, and encountered appalling storms. Some completed the journey, but up to 11,000 men and over 30 ships perished before the fleet reached Spain.

SPANISH PLATE FLEETS

The great Spanish galleons plied their trade between Spain and the Americas. They carried clothes, armaments, and household goods from Europe to the Spanish settlers in the New World who had colonized the area in search of gold and silver. An equally important cargo on outward-bound ships was mercury from the mines in southern Castille, which was essential to the production processes of the South American silver industry. These goods were traded for gold and silver bullion. By the end of the sixteenth century the fleets were bringing back over 3 million pesos on behalf of the cash-hungry Spanish monarchy, as well as several times that amount for private merchants. To prevent tax evasion and to control the trade, bullion was assayed and stamped by Spanish authorities in the Americas, and the amount carried on each fleet was limited to minimize potential loss if ships sank or were captured. As well as gold and silver plate, the fleets brought back cocoa, pearls, emeralds, leather, and tallow.

The trading galleons traveled in convoys of between 10 and 40 ships. Any captain who let his ship stray away from the fleet could be punished by death. The fleet was protected by two to four armed galleons, paid for by taxes levied on merchants. During international conflicts, up to eight warships would accompany the fleet.

JAPAN

CHINA

Amoy
(Xiamen)

Canton
(Guangzhou)

PHILIPPINES
Manila

SPICE ISLANDS
(MOLUCCAS)

NORTHERN
MARIANA
ISLANDS

SAN FELIPE ①
A ship lost in 1596 on the return journey from Manila to Acapulco with its cargo of gold and porcelain.

FERROLENA ②
In 1802 this ship and over 1 million pesos in silver sank on the China coast en route from Manila.

ROUTE TO ACAPULCO
After leaving the Philippines, Spanish fleets headed in a northeast direction until they reached a latitude of about 35°N, where westerly winds took them to Acapulco, Mexico.

PACIFIC OCEAN

HAWAIIAN
ISLANDS

SANTA MARGARITA ③
This recently located ship was en route to Acapulco when it went down in 1603. It was heavily looted at the time of loss.

ROUTE TO MANILA
Fleets usually departed from Acapulco, Mexico, in December, and took only 8–10 weeks to reach Manila in the Philippines, making direct use of the easterly trade winds.

NS DE LA CONCEPCION ④
Caught in storms in 1638 while traveling the Manila–Acapulco route, this ship ran aground on a reef and was lost.
(See pages 56–57.)

Routes between Acapulco and Manila

Manila was founded in 1571 and was developed as a Spanish colonial outpost in the Philippines. By the end of this century, 3 to 5 million pesos of silver a year were sent from the mines of South America to Manila to buy silks, porcelain, and other Eastern goods. Spanish authorities tried to limit this trade because they preferred the silver to be sent to Spain, but the commercial attractions were very strong for traders, who could expect a sixfold return on their investment in the Philippines trade. Officially, annual trade was limited to two ships of up to 300 tons each, carrying no more than 200,000 pesos between them. In reality, the lure of profit was so strong that each ship carried up to 2 million pesos. So lucrative was this trade that the command of a galleon sailing from Acapulco, Mexico, to the Philippines was worth 40,000 pesos to the ship's captain in commissions, gifts, and bribes – even though he himself was not allowed to trade. The galleons used on this route were often built in the Philippines out of local teak, a wood known for its endurance, which was essential since the round trip could take four to seven months.

Silver and
wooden crucifix

Gold and
pearl earring

SPANISH JEWELRY
These personal possessions were salvaged from a Spanish ship that wrecked in 1715.

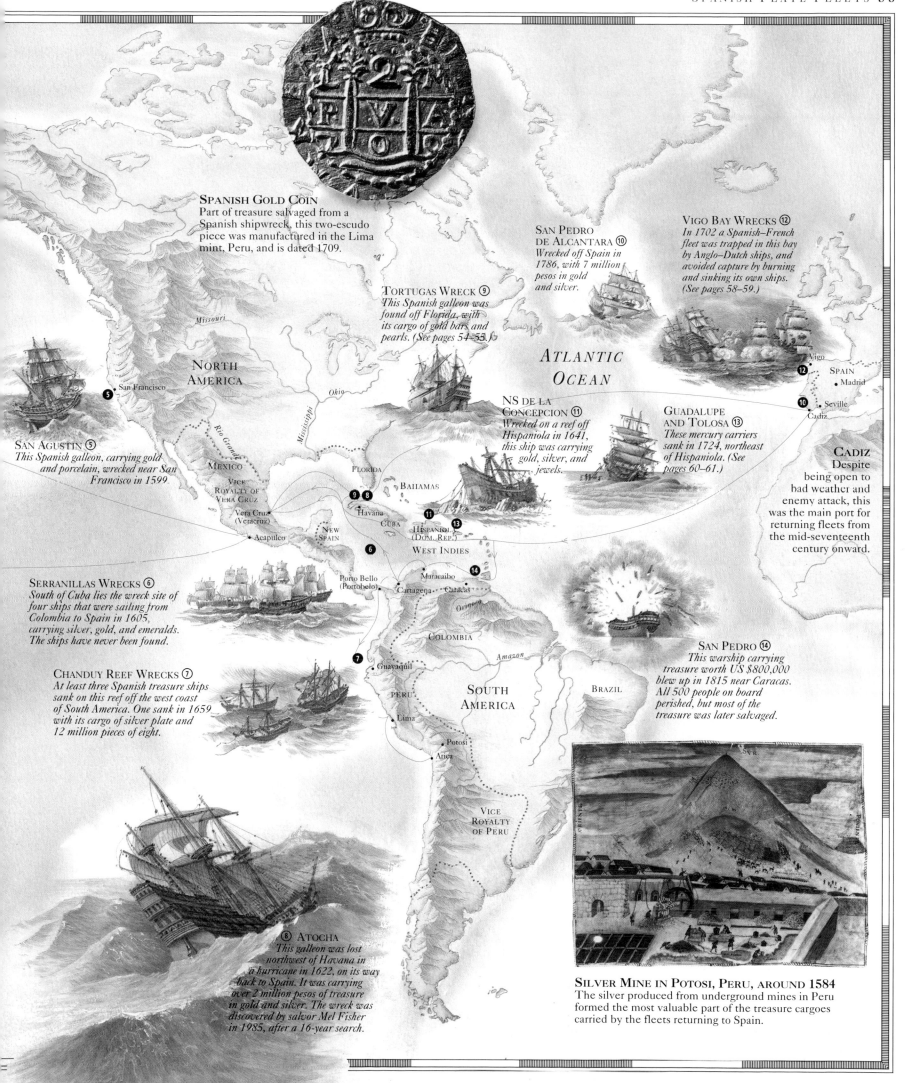

SPANISH GOLD COIN
Part of treasure salvaged from a Spanish shipwreck, this two-escudo piece was manufactured in the Lima mint, Peru, and is dated 1709.

SAN PEDRO DE ALCANTARA ⑩
Wrecked off Spain in 1786, with 7 million pesos in gold and silver.

VIGO BAY WRECKS ⑫
In 1702 a Spanish–French fleet was trapped in this bay by Anglo–Dutch ships, and avoided capture by burning and sinking its own ships. (See pages 58–59.)

TORTUGAS WRECK ⑨
This Spanish galleon was found off Florida, with its cargo of gold bars and pearls. (See pages 54–55.)

NS DE LA CONCEPCION ⑪
Wrecked on a reef off Hispaniola in 1641, this ship was carrying gold, silver, and jewels.

GUADALUPE AND TOLOSA ⑬
These mercury carriers sank in 1724, northeast of Hispaniola. (See pages 60–61.)

SAN AGUSTIN ⑤
This Spanish galleon, carrying gold and porcelain, wrecked near San Francisco in 1599.

CADIZ
Despite being open to bad weather and enemy attack, this was the main port for returning fleets from the mid-seventeenth century onward.

SERRANILLAS WRECKS ⑥
South of Cuba lies the wreck site of four ships that were sailing from Colombia to Spain in 1605, carrying silver, gold, and emeralds. The ships have never been found.

CHANDUY REEF WRECKS ⑦
At least three Spanish treasure ships sank on this reef off the west coast of South America. One sank in 1659 with its cargo of silver plate and 12 million pieces of eight.

SAN PEDRO ⑭
This warship carrying treasure worth US $800,000 blew up in 1815 near Caracas. All 500 people on board perished, but most of the treasure was later salvaged.

⑧ **ATOCHA**
This galleon was lost northwest of Havana in a hurricane in 1622, on its way back to Spain. It was carrying over 2 million pesos of treasure in gold and silver. The wreck was discovered by salvor Mel Fisher in 1985, after a 16-year search.

SILVER MINE IN POTOSI, PERU, AROUND 1584
The silver produced from underground mines in Peru formed the most valuable part of the treasure cargoes carried by the fleets returning to Spain.

Missouri

NORTH AMERICA

San Francisco

ATLANTIC OCEAN

Ohio

Mississippi

Rio Grande

MEXICO

VICE ROYALTY OF VERA CRUZ

Vera Cruz (Veracruz)

Acapulco

FLORIDA

BAHAMAS

Havana

CUBA

HISPANIOLA (DOM. REP.)

WEST INDIES

NEW SPAIN

Porto Bello (Portobelo)

Maracaibo

Cartagena

Caracas

COLOMBIA

Orinoco

Amazon

Guayaquil

PERU

SOUTH AMERICA

BRAZIL

Lima

Potosi

Arica

VICE ROYALTY OF PERU

Vigo

SPAIN

Madrid

Seville

Cadiz

THE
TORTUGAS WRECK

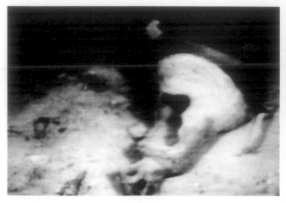

BRONZE BELL AT TORTUGAS WRECK SITE
The image of a bronze bell on the seabed was recorded by video cameras attached to the remote-operated vehicle, Phantom, during its initial survey of the wreck site.

In the 1960s, a shrimp fisherman working off the Florida coast, southwest of the Dry Tortugas, brought up an olive jar in his net. The jar was later identified as being of the kind used to carry wine and oils on Spanish ships in the early colonial period. The place where the jar had been found was far too deep to make an investigation into the presence of a shipwreck a commercially practical proposition at that time.

Location Survey and Recovery

By the late 1980s, technology had become advanced enough to make this project feasible, and an American salvage company, Seahawk Deep Ocean Technology Inc., took on the operation. An initial survey was carried out using a remote-operated vehicle (ROV), known as Phantom DHD2. This was equipped with video cameras and articulated arms, and was operated from the surface by means of a joystick and a television monitor. Images of the wreck site, showing wooden beams, a pile of ballast stones, and many ceramics and olive jars, were recorded on the video camera and transmitted to the television monitor.

By using this advanced technology, Seahawk was able to recover a bronze bell from the seabed. As a result, the company was considered "salvor in possession" under US admiralty law and could therefore obtain salvage rights to the wreck. This law establishes the right of a salvor, once he has found a wreck, to salvage it without any interference from other parties.

Identifying the Wreck

The wreck itself has yet to be identified, but there is considerable evidence to suggest that it is one of the ships from the Spanish fleet of 1622 that was caught in a hurricane and lost in deep water, as opposed to others from the same fleet that piled up on the Florida reefs.

The Spanish fleet that year, once it had unloaded its cargo at Havana, Cuba, and loaded the return cargo, did not leave

WOODEN CARAVEL
The size of the wreck site suggests the ship was a small caravel like this model. Caravels were used by the Spanish and Portuguese in the sixteenth century.

Rear lantern
Lit at night to enable the fleet to keep together

Tops
Vantage point for gunners during conflicts, and lookout post for land or other shipping

FACTS AND FEATURES

Site length	82 feet (25 meters)
Site depth	1,300 feet (400 meters)
Ship weight	180 tons
Ship route	Cuba to Spain

Bowsprit
Used for attaching the sprit sail

Forecastle
Smaller and lighter than those of earlier carracks

Beakhead
Mainly used for handling rigging; later versions had carved figureheads

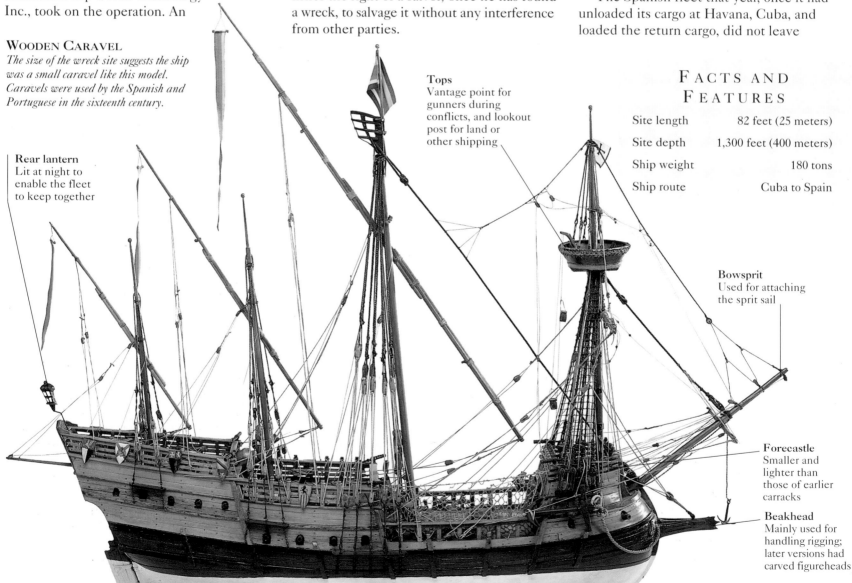

MERLIN ON DECK OF THE RECOVERY SHIP
This sophisticated remote-operated vehicle, known as Merlin, is ready to be winched up and over the side of the ship. One of its two manipulators can be seen at the bottom center.

RECORDING THE TREASURE
Before any treasure was recovered from the wreck, it was photographed through a grid to record its position accurately.

MANIPULATOR IN ACTION
Merlin's manipulator is capable of lifting both heavy weights (up to 250 lbs/113 kg) and delicate objects such as this ceramic olive jar. It works by using suction pads.

Havana to return to Spain until September 4. This was much later than recommended and well into the stormy season. One day out from port, the fleet ran into a fierce hurricane. Out of the 28 ships in the fleet, 11 or 12 are known to have been lost. If this wreck is one of those, it is possibly the *Nuestra Señora de los Reyes*, the *Jesus y Nuestra Señora del Rosario*, or the *Nuestra Señora de la Consolación*, all of which were observed to fall behind.

Sophisticated Salvage

Once Seahawk had established salvage rights to the Tortugas wreck, it brought in a larger recovery ship with a deep-water anchoring system, and a much more sophisticated ROV known as Merlin. One of the most versatile and advanced ROVs available, Merlin has two manipulators for retrieving heavy objects (up to 250 lbs/113 kg) and very fragile ones – the manipulators have the delicacy of touch to handle an egg without breaking it. Merlin also has a suction dredge, equally capable of handling items of extreme fragility, with which it retrieves small objects. The specification for the suction dredge was that it should be possible to pass a wine glass through it without the glass breaking. Merlin carried an array of video and still cameras, relaying the pictures by optical fibers from the wreck site to the ship. These cameras also ensured that Merlin's position was displayed on a video screen.

Over 17,000 artifacts have been recovered from the wreck site, and the salvors paid equal attention to the archaeological importance of the site and to its commercial value. All the items, which include gold bars, astrolabes, pearls, and an emerald ring, were logged into a database at the moment of recovery so that there is a record of which part of the site they were extracted from. Most of the gold bars and astrolabes have been recovered from the northwest end of the wreck where there is the greatest exposure of wooden beams as opposed to ballast stones, which were used at the front of the ship to balance the cargo at the rear. This suggests that the northwest end was the aft (rear) of the ship, since gold and navigational equipment were traditionally situated here, near the officers' quarters.

NUESTRA SENORA DE LA
CONCEPCION

The voyage from Acapulco, Mexico, to Manila, Philippines, was relatively straightforward; the large cargo-carrying galleons running before the dominant easterly winds could complete the 9,000-mile (15,000-kilometer) journey in around four months.

The route from Manila to Acapulco, which the *Concepción* was following on what proved to be its final voyage, was much more arduous. After negotiating the treacherous San Bernardino Strait, it was necessary to head in a northeasterly direction past the Northern Mariana Islands to a latitude of about 35°N, in order to pick up the westerly winds to carry the ship across to the American west coast. From here ships headed south to Acapulco.

The *Nuestra Señora de la Concepción* was one of the largest Spanish galleons to trade on the Manila–Acapulco route. When it left Manila in the Philippines, for Acapulco, Mexico, in 1638, the *Concepción* was also one of the richest and most heavily laden ships that had ever set out on that journey. The Spanish Crown had issued repeated regulations limiting the size of ships and restricting the quantity of cargo in order to minimize losses, but little notice had been taken of these bureaucratic dictates, and ships regularly sailed carrying more than their safe capacity.

Manila had been established by the Spanish in 1571 as a colonial outpost crucial for securing the trade from Acapulco to the East. Consequently, the sailing of ships such as the *Concepción* was one of the most important events of the year. Its departure was marked by the firing of cannons, the ringing of bells, ceremonial blessings, and parades through the streets; the success of the voyage was vital to the prosperity of the Spanish community in the Philippines.

The Wrecking of the Concepción

The *Concepción* never reached Acapulco. As the ship approached the Northern Marianas, a group of islands in the Pacific Ocean, it ran into a fierce storm. The pilot, officers, and captain disagreed on the best course of action to take, and meanwhile the storm worsened. The *Concepción*'s masts broke, the ship became ungovernable, and it went aground on September 20, 1638, on a reef off the southwest corner of Saipan, in the Northern Mariana Islands. There were over 400 people on the ship, but only a handful survived. Most of those who did not drown were killed by natives. Six Spaniards escaped to Guam, near the Northern Mariana Islands, and they eventually made their way back to the Philippines. Their journey took nearly a year.

During the following years, local islanders recovered much of the cargo from the sunken *Concepción* and, 46 years after the wrecking, the Spanish government salvaged 35 of the 36 cannons on board. Despite these extensive operations, there was still a wealth of jewelry and artifacts awaiting the excavation and salvage operations that took place in 1987 and 1988.

Artifacts that were recovered included a gold filigree box, a gold comb (see opposite); a gold shoe pendant studded with diamonds, thought to have been used as a perfume bottle; yards of gold chain; and several pottery storage jars.

PERFUME VIAL
This sword-shaped vial, worn around the neck, is from a Spanish ship wrecked in 1715.

SILVER PLATE
Ornate plates like this one salvaged from the San José wrecked in 1733 were common Spanish cargo.

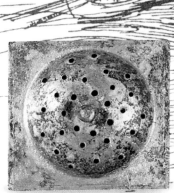

Inkwell holder

Sander

INKWELL AND SANDER
Pewter inkwell holders (far left) and sanders (left) were carried in the officers' quarters on most ships. These are from a Spanish ship that sank in 1733.

SPANISH GALLEON
The Concepción, *a large Spanish galleon, was similar to the galleon pictured here. The galleons that sailed from Manila, Philippines, to Acapulco, Mexico, were generally built in the Philippines and would have been made from a local teak that was considered to be the most enduring for this particular route.*

Mainmast
The breaking of the *Concepción's* mast contributed to the sinking of the ship

Sails
Spanish galleons used square-rigged sails

Deep holds
Enormous amounts of cargo, including silks, porcelain, spices, and copper and iron utensils were stored here

SALVAGED BOX
This crushed filigree gold box recovered from the Concepción *was originally oval.*

GOLDEN COMB
This was salvaged from the Concepción *and was embossed with the name of Doña Catalina de Guzman, a widow in Manila.*

RICH CARGO

The *NS de la Concepción* was transporting one of the most valuable cargoes ever carried en route from Manila, Philippines, to Acapulco, Mexico. It included beautiful, wrought-gold filigree jewelry and hundreds of yards of gold chain, as well as more mundane items, such as pottery storage jars used to hold the supplies of wine, vinegar, salt, and dried meats.

Most of the cargo consisted of transshipments from other countries. Silks and porcelain would have come mainly from China, together with copper and iron utensils, lacquered boxes, and carved figures. From India and Sri Lanka (Ceylon) came precious stones, wood carvings, and cotton textiles. Swords, knives, and gunpowder were imported from Japan, and mace, cinnamon, cloves, and pepper came from the Moluccas (Spice Islands).

FACTS AND FEATURES

Length	150 feet (45 meters)
Capacity	1,500 tons
Route	Manila to Acapulco
Cargo	Gold, silver, and jewels

THE
VIGO BAY WRECKS

The Spanish plate fleet of 1702 left the port of Havana, Cuba, on July 24 to return home to Cadiz in Spain with a particularly large remittance of silver, part of which was destined for the perennially empty coffers of King Philip V of Spain. The fleet was provided with the usual protection of the *Armada de Barlovento*, which was a fleet of warships created specifically for this purpose. The treasure ships also had the extra support of several French warships, commanded by François Louis de Rousselet Châteaurenault.

As the combined fleet neared the end of its journey and approached Spanish waters, Manuel de Velasco, the Spanish commander, sent a small, fast boat to Seville to inform the authorities of the fleet's approach.

War Breaks Out

Shortly afterward, news came back that hostilities had been declared between France and Spain on the one hand, and Britain and the Netherlands on the other, and that Cadiz itself was under attack by the Anglo–Dutch fleet commanded by Admiral Rooke. The Spanish plate fleet had sailed right into the middle of the War of the Spanish Succession. There was no question of the French and Spanish taking on the Anglo–Dutch in a major action at sea. Admiral Rooke's fleet was considered far too powerful, and the silver cargo too valuable to risk losing in combat. Instead, Châteaurenault and Velasco decided to divert north to Vigo, Spain.

The Battle of Vigo Bay

On September 23 Châteaurenault and Velasco entered Vigo Bay, where they barricaded the small harbor of Redondela, and prepared the forts for action. Admiral Rooke's fleet then arrived on October 22, in pursuit of the Spanish plate fleet, and began a vigorous attack (see below). It quickly became obvious that the French–Spanish fleet stood no chance, so Châteaurenault, the French commander, took the last option left to him, which was to order the French and Spanish ships to be fired and sunk, to prevent their capture. In the event, five Spanish and six French ships were taken captive by the Anglo–Dutch fleet and all the rest were either sunk or burned. The eminent nineteenth-century naval historian, W. L. Clowes, wrote,

The treasure and booty taken were of enormous value, the flotilla of galleons having been the richest that had ever reached Europe from the West Indies. Some of the lading had been removed before the action; but it was estimated that gold and silver & cargo to the value of 13 million pieces of eight, fell into the hands of the victors or were destroyed.

The legends surrounding the treasure lost at Vigo Bay sprang up almost immediately. On January 19, 1703, the *Postboy*, an English journal, reported that a single captured Spanish ship, the *Tauro*, was brought back to England, where it was said to have "an abundance of wrought plate, pieces of eight and other valuable commodities and so much that it is computed that the whole cargo is worth £200,000."

Salvage Failures

Under the circumstances, it is hardly surprising that for the past 250 years, almost without a break, one consortium of treasure hunters after another has attempted to salvage the spectacular fortune that supposedly lies beneath the muddy waters of Vigo Bay.

In 1720, the first salvage attempt took place, by a Swede. Since then, Italian, French, British, and Dutch salvors have also tried their luck. The most recent major effort was probably that of an American, John Potter, and the Atlantic Salvage Company in the late 1950s. None of these expeditions was successful in recovering the hoped-for treasure.

Missing Treasure

A careful examination of documentary evidence explains why the salvors achieved so little. Most of the silver, over 13.6 million pesos, had been unloaded and taken inland before the Anglo–Dutch fleet arrived. The fact that the ships were largely empty of

ADMIRAL SIR GEORGE ROOKE AND THE BATTLE OF VIGO BAY

Admiral Rooke played a key part in commanding the English Navy during the War of the Spanish Succession, in which England and Holland joined forces against France and Spain.

A large Anglo–Dutch fleet, under Rooke's command, attacked the Spanish port of Cadiz, and reports of this battle had persuaded the Spanish plate fleet to sail instead to one of the more northern ports, Vigo, which they felt would be safer than Cadiz. Rooke's attack on Cadiz turned out to be a dismal failure but, by a lucky turn of events, he called into the neutral port of Lagos for water on his way back to England and heard that the wealthy Spanish plate fleet was anchored in Vigo Bay. Rooke sailed straight there and found 16 to 17 Spanish ships, protected by a similar number of French ships, with a boom laid across the harbor entrance. The next day, the British warship, *Mary*, sailed bow on at the boom, and broke through it with surprising ease. Shortly afterward, the hill forts were overrun by Anglo–Dutch soldiers, and it was obvious that the French–Spanish fleet was lost.

Admiral Sir George Rooke, 1650–1709

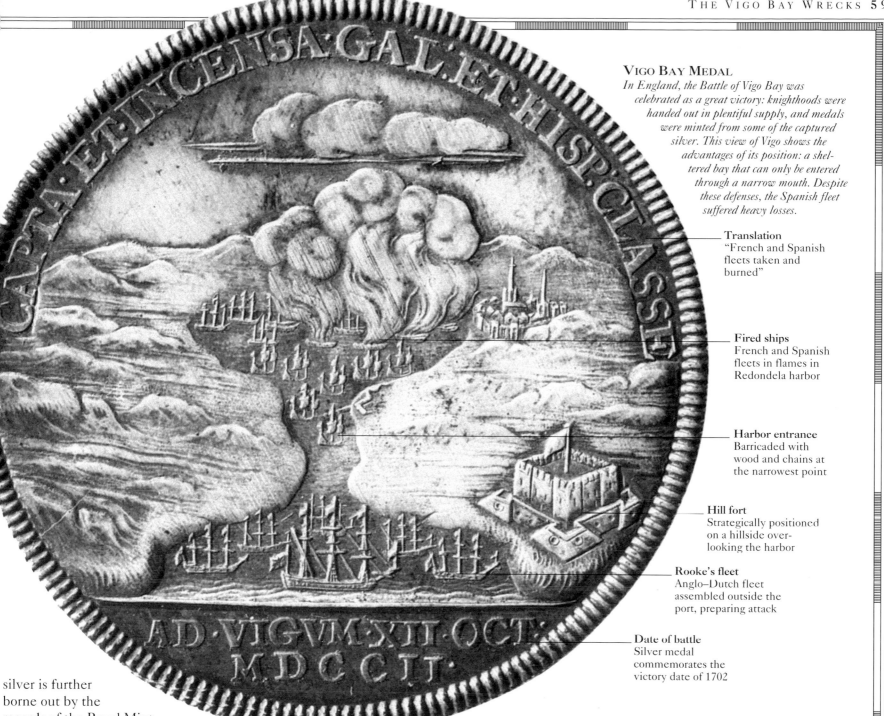

CAP̄A·ET·INCENSA·GAL·ET·HISP·CLASSE

AD·VIGVM·XII·OCT·MDCCII·

VIGO BAY MEDAL
In England, the Battle of Vigo Bay was celebrated as a great victory: knighthoods were handed out in plentiful supply, and medals were minted from some of the captured silver. This view of Vigo shows the advantages of its position: a sheltered bay that can only be entered through a narrow mouth. Despite these defenses, the Spanish fleet suffered heavy losses.

Translation
"French and Spanish fleets taken and burned"

Fired ships
French and Spanish fleets in flames in Redondela harbor

Harbor entrance
Barricaded with wood and chains at the narrowest point

Hill fort
Strategically positioned on a hillside over-looking the harbor

Rooke's fleet
Anglo–Dutch fleet assembled outside the port, preparing attack

Date of battle
Silver medal commemorates the victory date of 1702

silver is further borne out by the records of the Royal Mint in England. Isaac Newton, the keeper of the Mint at the time, stated that the total amount of silver retrieved from the battle was 4,504 lbs and 2 oz (2,043 kilograms). Even allowing for some plundering en route, this was hardly the fabulous loot of press reports that launched over 30 expeditions.

There is still one undiscovered Vigo wreck that continues to lure today's would-be salvors, and that is the *Santo Cristo de Maracaibo*. This ship, which was captured by the English, was being escorted back to England when it struck a rock just after leaving Vigo, and sank in water more than 200 feet (60 meters) deep. The depth of water has, so far, prevented any expedition from salvaging the ship. It is unlikely that it contains a vast quantity of silver, but the artifacts on board would be of immense historical interest.

JULES VERNE

In the late 1860s, Jules Verne wrote *Twenty Thousand Leagues Under the Sea*, a tale featuring the exploits of Captain Nemo and his travels and adventures under the sea. These included the hunt for treasure at Vigo, and one scene describes men "clearing away half-rotted barrels, burst-opened chests, among still blackened wrecks. From these chests and barrels escaped ingots of gold and silver, cascades of piasters and jewels."

UNDERWATER SEARCH FOR TREASURE
This atmospheric image from Twenty Thousand Leagues Under the Sea *owes much to the imagination of Jules Verne, who anticipated future developments in diving technology and incorporated them in his writing.*

THE
GUADALUPE AND TOLOSA

The *Nuestra Señora de Guadalupe* and the *Conde de Tolosa*, galleons from the Spanish fleet of 1724, were en route from Cadiz, Spain, to Havana, Cuba, and then to Veracruz (then known as Vera Cruz), Mexico. Between them the ships carried over 1,200 passengers and crew, approximately 250 tons of mercury, and 144 cannons, as well as gunpowder, commercial merchandise, personal goods, and food, water, and wine.

Mercury Carriers

The *Guadalupe* and *Tolosa* were classified as azogues, the Spanish term for ships carrying mercury. The *Tolosa*, unlike the smaller *Guadalupe*, was not designed to carry mercury, however, and was not as strongly constructed.

Mercury was used to extract pure silver from the mined ore during the manufacturing process and was indispensable to the functioning of silver mines. Silver mines in Mexico were dependent on supplies of mercury that were shipped in from Spain. The packaging of mercury to be shipped was very complicated: half a quintal of mercury (18 quintals weighing about one ton) was poured into a tightly sewn leather bag and placed in a watertight cask. Two or three of these were then enclosed in a wooden box, which was nailed shut, bound with twine, and wrapped in a special protective matting.

Hit by Hurricane

The two Spanish galleons successfully crossed the Atlantic and, having run along the south coast of Puerto Rico, they called at Aguadilla (Aguada), on the northwest point of the island, to take on board badly needed supplies of fresh food and water. On the night of August 24, when the ships were a few days out from Aguadilla, near Samaná Bay, Dominican Republic (Hispaniola), they were hit by a hurricane. Both the *Guadalupe* and the *Tolosa* anchored to try to weather the storm.

NEW WORLD SILVER
Mercury was shipped to the New World because it was essential for extracting silver from ore.

DIVING ON THE TOLOSA
Captain Tracy Bowden, President of Caribe Salvage and the captain of the salvage ship, Hickory, pours mercury recovered from the Tolosa. It was this discovery of mercury that confirmed the identity of the Tolosa. *Before mercury was found, five divers had spent several weeks exploring the site.*

Fate of Tolosa and Survivors

The *Tolosa*, which was separated from the *Guadalupe* early on in the storm, managed to anchor at the mouth of Samaná Bay and ride out the storm until dawn. The wind was too fierce for the anchors to hold, however, and the *Tolosa* was swept into the bay, some three miles (five kilometers) away from shore, where it was beaten against rocks and wrecked on a massive coral reef. Because it sank in relatively deep water and against a protective reef, most of the treasure remained intact.

Fewer than 40 people out of the 600 crew and passengers on board survived. Eight of the survivors had the presence of mind and stamina to climb up into the tops of the mainmast, and seven of them were still alive some 32 days later when the salvage boats finally reached them from Santo Domingo in the Dominican Republic. It is thought that the survivors who were taking refuge in the mast were able to stay alive by securing supplies of food and freshwater from the barrels that floated upward from the holds.

Fate of Guadalupe and Survivors

The *Guadalupe* grounded on a sandbank, and about 550 of the 650 passengers and crew managed to reach the shore. The cargo of mercury on board probably provided the *Guadalupe* with extra stability and prevented it from keeling over.

Once the survivors of the *Guadalupe* had reached land, their troubles were by no means over. In order to reach the city of Santo Domingo, they were faced with a grueling 200-mile (320-kilometer) trek along the coast.

Punishing Trek to Safety

The initial part of the expedition was not too difficult because the land was flat and there were a number of rivers to drink from. After several days, however, as the survivors were approaching Cape San Raphael, the coast became very rocky and irregular, with high cliffs and no beach to follow. At this stage, several survivors had to be left behind and many others died from starvation or physical exhaustion en route from Cape San Raphael to Santo Domingo.

As the survivors neared their destination, they were noticed by fishermen. These summoned help from Santo Domingo, and boats were sent to rescue the remaining shipwreck survivors.

VIEW OF HAVANA, CUBA, 1683
This Cuban port was the main assembly place for Spanish fleets delivering European goods to the new colonies in South and Central America. Havana also had large shipbuilding yards at this time and Spain built many of its ships there.

Twentieth-century salvors

In 1976, a North American salvage company, Caribe Salvage SA, signed a contract with the Dominican Government to excavate both the *Tolosa* and the *Guadalupe*. Work on the *Guadalupe* started in 1976 and lasted for about a year. It was followed, in 1977, by the search for the *Tolosa*, and its subsequent excavation.

The salvors found evidence of the mercury cargo at the *Guadalupe* site, but were not able to recover the mercury in any significant quantity because access to the lower part of the hold, where the mercury was probably stowed, was blocked by a mound of iron fittings. These were being exported for use in the shipbuilding industry in Havana.

THE TREASURE

GOLD CROSS
Found on the Tolosa, *this very rare cross belonged to the Order of the Knights of Santiago.*

The salvors had considerable success on the wreck sites of both the *Guadalupe* and the *Tolosa* when it came to recovering some of the European manufactured goods being exported for use by the increasingly cultivated colonists.

Officially, only Spanish goods were allowed to be exported but, as with so many aspects of Spanish life, there was a wide gap between the bureaucratic regulations and the day-to-day practice.

Salvaged Goods

Fine wheel-engraved soda glassware from Germany and elegant British clocks were recovered from the *Guadalupe* and the *Tolosa*, suggesting a keen demand in Mexico for high-quality items. More characteristically Spanish were the large quantities of religious icons carried on board both ships. Other items that were recovered from the seabed included pearls, surprisingly undamaged by their immersion in salt water, brass swivel guns, iron hand grenades, silver, porcelain, and pewter tableware, glass decanters, jugs that had been used for storing drinking water, brass lanterns, and several pieces of personal jewelry.

PRECIOUS JEWELS
Among the treasure found on the Tolosa *were 1,000 intact pearls and four pieces of diamond-studded gold jewelry.*

GOD OF WINE
This glass and gold leaf medallion of Bacchus from the Tolosa *was once fixed to a glass.*

PIRATES AND PRIVATEERS

For as long as goods have been transported by sea, there have also been pirates and privateers who have made it their business to seize those goods. Pirates acted entirely on their own behalf whereas privateers were sponsored by others, sometimes issued with letters of marque (see opposite). The ships used by pirates and privateers have been varied in type, but the requirements have always been universal: speed and maneuverability are prized above all else. For example, in the sixteenth and seventeenth centuries, oared galleys were favored by the Muslims and other pirates based along the north coast of Africa; lateen-rigged xebecs by the Salé pirates off the Atlantic coast of Africa; caravels by Sir Francis Drake and his associates. Oarpower was mostly employed in the Mediterranean because it can provide an extra turn of speed in light winds. Larger sailing ships, however, were needed in the rough seas of the Atlantic Ocean.

HENRY ④
To avoid capture by French privateers in 1695, Captain Hudson ran this English East Indiaman ashore and set fire to it on the coast of Ireland. The ship was en route from India to Britain, carrying diamonds worth £75,000 sterling.

ALS EFFERNE WRECK ⑤
In 1589, while carrying a cargo worth £100,000 sterling, this ship was captured by the Duke of Cumberland but sank against cliffs in Cornwall, England.

NS DE GUIA ⑥
A Spanish ship laden with gold, silver, and pearls worth 200,000 ducats was sunk by English pirates as it neared the Azores.

WHYDAH ②
This ship belonged to the pirate Sam Bellamy, and was lost in 1717 off Cape Cod with a rich cargo of silver and gold. (See pages 68–69.)

OXFORD ③
The flagship of the notorious pirate Henry Morgan, the Oxford blew up and sank in 1669, while Morgan was planning an attack on Cartagena, Colombia.

LAS CINQUE CHAGAS ⑦
Reputedly one of the richest ships that ever sailed from the East, it was attacked and sunk by English pirates in 1594. (See pages 64–65.)

ROSARIO ①
This ship was en route from Lima, Peru, to Panama when it was taken by English pirates in 1681. They set it adrift with its cargo of silver, which they had supposed to be tin.

MAGDALENA ⑧
Sunk by the pirate Henry Morgan in 1669 off Venezuela, this ship carried 40,000 pieces of eight, silver plate, and swords. Morgan salvaged about 15,000 pieces of eight at the time.

ATLANTIC OCEAN

Cape Cod
FLORIDA
Gulf of Mexico
BAHAMAS
Havana
CUBA (Spanish)
JAMAICA (BRITISH)
ST. DOMINGUE (FRENCH)
PORTO RICO (SPANISH)
PORT-LOUIS
GUADELOUPE (FRENCH)
CARIBBEAN SEA
Maracaibo
Porto Bello (Portobelo)
PANAMA
DUTCH
FRENCH
VICE ROYALTY OF NEW SPAIN
VICE ROYALTY OF PERU
BRAZIL (PORTUGESE)
Amazon
AZORES
PORTUGAL
CANARY ISLANDS
Arguin (French)
St. Louis (French)
Cacheu (Portuguese)
Freetown (British)
Baltimore ENG
Bahia (Salvador)
ASCENSION ISLAND

PORT ROYAL ON THE SOUTH COAST OF JAMAICA
The English drove out the Spanish settlers in 1655, and encouraged pirates to base their operations at Port Royal, believing they would prevent the Spanish from returning. The port was well placed for attacking Spanish ships carrying gold and silver back to Europe from the Caribbean, and became a haven for pirates.

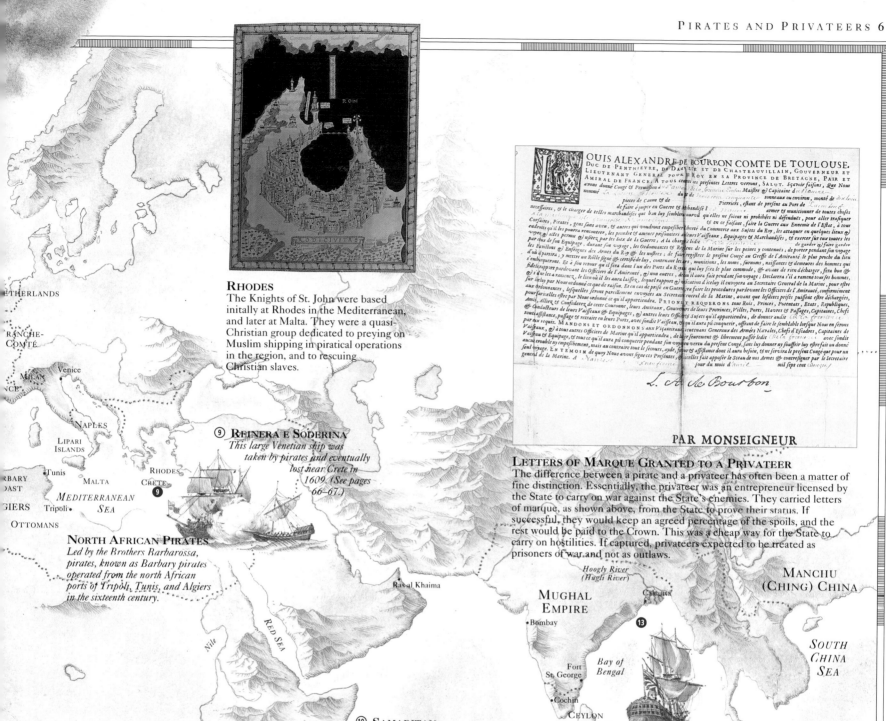

RHODES
The Knights of St. John were based initally at Rhodes in the Mediterranean, and later at Malta. They were a quasi-Christian group dedicated to preying on Muslim shipping in piratical operations in the region, and to rescuing Christian slaves.

⑨ REINERA E SODERINA
This large Venetian ship was taken by pirates and eventually lost near Crete in 1609. (See pages 66–67.)

NORTH AFRICAN PIRATES
Led by the Brothers Barbarossa, pirates, known as Barbary pirates operated from the north African ports of Tripoli, Tunis, and Algiers in the sixteenth century.

QUIS ALEXANDRE DE BOURBON COMTE DE TOULOUSE, Duc de Penthievre, de Damvile et de Chasteauvillain, Gouverneur et Lieutenant General pour le Roy en sa Province de Bretagne, Pair et Amiral de France, A tous ceux ces presentes Lettres verront, Salut. Sçavoir faisons, Que Nous avons donné Congé & Permission

PAR MONSEIGNEUR

LETTERS OF MARQUE GRANTED TO A PRIVATEER
The difference between a pirate and a privateer has often been a matter of fine distinction. Essentially, the privateer was an entrepreneur licensed by the State to carry on war against the State's enemies. They carried letters of marque, as shown above, from the State to prove their status. If successful, they would keep an agreed percentage of the spoils, and the rest would be paid to the Crown. This was a cheap way for the State to carry on hostilities. If captured, privateers expected to be treated as prisoners of war and not as outlaws.

⑩ SAMARITAN
Part of a privateering expedition to the Indian Ocean in 1635, this ship was lost in the Comoros islands.

⑬ KENT
In October 1800, this English East Indiaman was boarded by French privateer Surcouf and captured south of Calcutta. Although the Kent did not actually sink, Surcouf threw the gold it was carrying into the sea after an argument with the French authorities.

⑪ HERBERT
This East Indiaman was attacked and blown up by French privateers in 1689. It was carrying a cargo of silver specie and silver bars.

MADAGASCAR
This island was a well-known haunt of pirates, such as James Plantain "King of Ranter's Bay," who preyed on shipping in the Indian Ocean in the eighteenth century.

⑫ SPEAKER
John Bowen's pirate ship was lost off Mauritius in 1702. The surviving pirates paid the Dutch governor 2,100 pieces of eight to ensure his goodwill.

⑭ SHIP OF CH'EN TSU-I
One of a fleet of ships that was attacked by the Chinese explorer Cheng Ho in 1407, this ship sank at Palembang, Sumatra.

MANCHU (CHING) CHINA

SOUTH CHINA SEA

MUGHAL EMPIRE

MEDITERRANEAN SEA

OTTOMANS

RED SEA

Nile

Congo

Zambezi

ANGOLA

Luanda (Portuguese)

Benguela (Portuguese)

Quelimane (Portuguese)

Mozambique (Portuguese)

Sofala (Portuguese)

MADAGASCAR

MAURITIUS

Cape Colony (Dutch)

Cape Town

Cape of Good Hope

Bombay

Fort St. George

Cochin

CEYLON (SRI LANKA)

Bay of Bengal

Calcutta

Hoogly River (Hugli River)

Ras al Khaima

JAVA

SUMATRA

NETHERLANDS

FRANCHE-COMTÉ

MILAN

Venice

NAPLES

LIPARI ISLANDS

Tunis

MALTA

RHODES

CRETE

Tripoli

ALGIERS

BARBARY COAST

LAS CINQUE CHAGAS

One of the most flamboyant amateur English privateers (government-sponsored pirates) of the late Elizabethan period was George Clifford, the third earl of Cumberland. An accomplished courtier who possessed one of the largest estates in the kingdom, Cumberland was addicted to gambling and seriously in debt. A contemporary described him as having "an extreme love for horse races, tiltings, bowling matches ... and all such expensive sports did contribute the more to the wasting of his estate." It is not altogether surprising that he was attracted to privateering, a risky venture with the highest potential rewards. His motives were not entirely mercenary. He also had in mind the honor of the nation: his projected targets were exclusively Spanish or Portuguese (Portugal was then under Spanish rule, and Spain was at war with England).

Capture of the Madre de Dios

Cumberland's first five ventures achieved little in the way of profit. In 1592, however, his luck changed. A fleet that he had helped to finance took possession of the *Madre de Dios* off the Azores. This was a Portuguese carrack returning from the East carrying a very valuable cargo that included jewels and porcelain, as well as spices. It was the first time that such a large ship had been taken by English ships and, when it arrived at Dartmouth in England, its size caused a sensation.

The *Madre de Dios* cargo was valued at $750,000 but, by the time the ship was brought into port, it had already been heavily pillaged. Even so, the cargo that remained was valued at $225,000.

Cumberland's New Fleet

Two years later, in 1594, Cumberland teamed up with a group of wealthy London merchants and between them they fitted out three ships of about 300 tons each, the *Sampson*, the *Royal Exchange*, and the *Mayflower*, together with a pinnace (a small vessel with two masts) called the *Violet*. The ships left the port of Plymouth, England, on April 6, and later that same month, near Berlenga, an island off Portugal, they captured a small sailing ship (a bark), although there was nothing of value on board. But on June 13, while cruising to the south of Faial, an island in the Azores, they spied a great Portuguese carrack, *Las Cinque Chagas*, which was making its way back from the East Indies. This was the opportunity they had been waiting for.

The Cargo of Las Cinque Chagas

The *Chagas* was even larger and more valuable than the *Madre de Dios*. Apart from its official cargo, it carried on board many Portuguese and Italian merchants, all with their own private merchandise. It had also taken on passengers and cargo from two other ships: the *Santo Alberto*, a ship that had wrecked on the east African coast, and another ship that had wrecked off the coast of Mozambique.

The *Chagas* had wintered in Mozambique, experienced a difficult passage around the Cape of Good Hope, South Africa, and called in to Angola on Africa's east coast to replenish

VALUABLE JEWELS
Passengers on both Las Cinque Chagas *and the* Madre de Dios *were carrying their personal jewelry with them. Any jewels left on the* Madre de Dios *were plundered before it reached England and passengers who were rescued when the* Chagas *sank had to bargain for their lives with jewels.*

SILVER CROSS
Decorative crosses, such as this, were worn in sixteenth-century Europe.

GEMSTONES
Very fashionable for personal adornment in the sixteenth century. Wealthy passsengers on the Madre de Dios *and* Las Cinque Chagas *would have owned clothes studded with valuable jewels like these.*

MADRE DE DIOS

Captured by a fleet of privateers (see pages 62–63) that the third earl of Cumberland had helped to finance, the *Madre de Dios* was the largest ship ever to have been taken by English. It was 165 feet (50 meters) long and almost 47 feet (15 meters) wide, with a mainmast that was 106 feet (32 meters) in length.

Returning to Portugal from the East, the *Madre de Dios* was carrying spices such as mace, cinnamon, and nutmeg; drugs; silks; calico; quilts; carpets; Chinese porcelain; and jewels – although the jewels had been plundered before the *Madre de Dios* reached England.

supplies. Angola was also a source of slaves, and the *Chagas* loaded some 400 slaves, which added to the overcrowding.

As a port of call, Angola suffered from two serious drawbacks. First, there was a great danger of picking up disease. Second, there was the strong likelihood of becoming stuck in the doldrums – areas off west Africa that were notorious for lack of winds. The *Chagas* fell victim to both.

By the time the *Chagas* approached the latitude of the Azores, its captain, Don Francisco de Mello, was under pressure from his crew and passengers to put into the islands for fresh supplies. Many of those on board had already died from fever, and others were close to starvation. Aware of the danger the ship would face from pirates if it came too close to the Azores, de Mello held a vote among his more important officers and passengers. The vote was fairly inconclusive but he agreed to put into port, at the same time extracting a promise that if the *Chagas* should be attacked, those on board would fight to the death.

Capture of Las Cinque Chagas

De Mello's fears were realized and the *Chagas* came under attack from Cumberland's English fleet. The battle continued until midnight, and at ten o'clock the following morning, the three English privateer ships approached again. The *Mayflower* fell off from

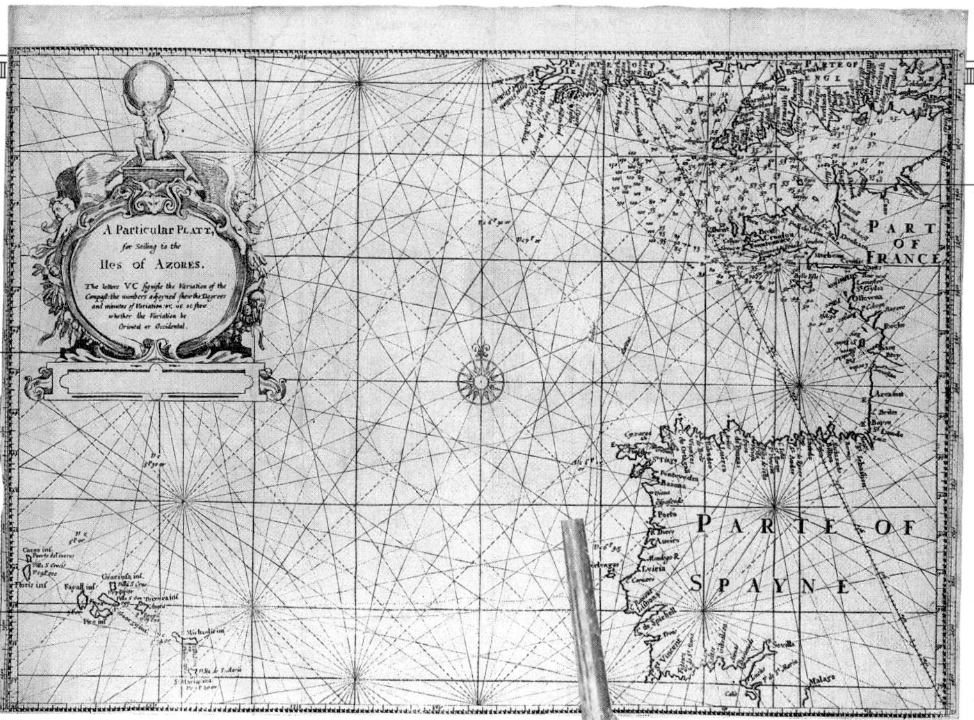

Cartouche
Contains the key to
the numbers and
letters used
on the map

MAP OF THE AZORES
*Drawn by cartographer Edward Wright in 1657, this map
shows the voyage of the English fleet, partly financed by the
earl of Cumberland, which resulted in the attack and wrecking of the Portuguese carrack* Las Cinque Chagas *in 1594.*

Faial
The English fleet
fell in with the
Chagas south
of this island
in the Azores

Plymouth, England
Where Cumberland's fleet
began its journey to the
Azores on April 6, 1592

Queen's glove
Wearing one
of Elizabeth I's
gloves in his
hat symbolized
the earl of
Cumberland's
honored status

the fight, but the *Royal Exchange* and the
Sampson continued the attack on the *Chagas*.
Eventually, the *Chagas*'s bowsprit went up
in flames, and the fire rapidly spread. At the
sight of this, some Portuguese considered
surrendering and put up a white flag, but
they were overruled. The English ships were
lucky to disengage themselves from the
conflagration, and the crew doused the
decks to prevent them from catching fire.

Death by Fire or Water

The Portuguese had the choice of burning
alive on the *Chagas* or throwing themselves
into the water. Most chose the latter option,
but only 13 of these were rescued
by the English boats. According
to some Portuguese accounts, the
English saved only those who
flashed handfuls of jewels in their
faces, ruthlessly killing the rest
with pikes. English accounts of
the scene, hardly surprisingly,
make no mention of this behavior.

The *Chagas* drifted blazing
for the rest of the day and the
following night. On the next
morning it blew up, taking its
valuable cargo with it to the
seabed. No manifest for that
cargo survives, but it was no
doubt similar to the cargo that
had been found on the *Madre de
Dios* (see box, opposite).

EARL OF CUMBERLAND
*Part of a miniature by Nicholas
Hilliard that portrays George
Clifford, the third earl
of Cumberland, as Queen
Elizabeth I's Champion, 1590.*

Lance
Used for jousting and
in battles, this lance is
decorated with stars to
match Cumberland's suit

Bejeweled cloth
Richly decorated
with sapphires
and diamonds

DONA LOUISA DE MELO

One of the women on board the
Chagas, Dona Louisa de Melo,
suffered a perverse fate. Saved from
the wreck of the *Santo Alberto*, and
forced to trail about 650 miles
(1,050 kilometers) across the African
wilderness, she was eventually
rescued by the *Chagas*, only to be
wrecked once more. However, her
sense of decorum apparently
prevailed over her instinct for
survival. She refused to remove her
heavy clothes before plunging into
the sea and her body was later
washed up on the shores of Faial
in the Azores.

Star suit
Cumberland's suit
of armor, made
in the royal
workshop in
Greenwich,
England

THE
REINERA E SODERINA

John Ward was one of many Elizabethan seamen who had enjoyed the swashbuckling life of a privateer captain (see pages 62–63) while England was at war with Spain in the latter part of the sixteenth century. However, he found himself without work when James I came to the English throne in 1603 and more peaceful relations existed between the two countries. His response, like that of other privateers no longer supported by the Crown, was to turn pirate.

The main center of operations for piracy at the beginning of the seventeenth century was along the north coast of Africa, using the Muslim-controlled ports of Tunis, Algiers, and Tripoli – an area known as the Barbary coast – as a base to prey on rich Mediterranean shipping en route to and from the East. It was only possible to do this with the cooperation of the local Muslim rulers in those ports.

The Barbary Pirates

The pirates based in this area had been a threat to Christian shipping since the early sixteenth century, when the Brothers Barbarossa (see opposite) had controlled large fleets of galleys, operating under the protection of Ottoman Emperor Sultan Selim I and the Dey of Tunis. What was new in the early seventeenth century was the involvement of Christian renegades, such as Ward, and their introduction of Atlantic-based ships, which had square rigs and a greater cannon capacity. To obtain the benefits of this

PIRATE SHIP
Oared galleys, similar to this seventeenth-century French galley, were popular with pirates operating off the north African coast. Pirates favored ships with oars because they were fast and easily maneuverable.

Lateen sails
One of two triangular sails used for long-distance travel

Ram
For decorative purposes, not strong enough for use in battle

Raised deck
Fighting platform from which guns were fired; cannons were mounted below

FACTS
AND
FEATURES

Type	Venetian
No. of cannons	55
Route	Cyprus to Italy

Decorative pennant
Pirates would remove any identifying pennants from captured ships

THE BROTHERS BARBAROSSA
From the early sixteenth century, when they came to north Africa, Aruj and Khair-ed-Din Barbarossa, also known as Redbeard, controlled a powerful and feared pirate fleet that targeted Christian shipping in the Mediterranean Sea.

advanced technology, the Muslim rulers were prepared to welcome unruly and disaffected seamen from the western European maritime nations, such as England, France, and the Netherlands. These men, and Ward in particular, were notorious for their licentiousness, drunkenness, and violence, but were tolerated by the Muslims because of their useful fighting qualities.

Capture of the Reinera e Soderina

In 1607, John Ward captured a Venetian trading ship (argosy), *Reinera e Soderina*, en route from Cyprus to Venice, Italy. It was carrying indigo, salt, spices, and other oriental produce, and the cargo was valued at 500,000 crowns. Ward took the ship into Tunis where he sold the cargo. This was said to have made Ward's fortune and the sailors received as much as £80 sterling each as their share of the proceeds.

The capture of the *Reinera e Soderina* caused a diplomatic incident that continued for years. The cargo was sold on through a number of intermediaries in Tunis until merchants from an English ship bought some of it, with a view to shipping it for sale to Flanders, Belgium. The Venetian ambassador induced the English Lord High Admiral to intercept the English ship and take the cargo. This was done, much to the chagrin of the English merchants who claimed that the cargo was a bona fide purchase from Turkish merchants. A lengthy court case ensued with appeals and counter-appeals. The final decision was in favor of the Venetians.

Ward, meanwhile, retained possession of the *Reinera e Soderina* and embarked on another voyage looking for new victims. After making several further captures, the *Reinera e Soderina* is said to have sunk in 1609, 100 miles (160 kilometers) off the Greek island of Kithira (Cerigo) because it was leaking, and it went down with considerable loss of life. Ward, however, had previously transferred to another of his ships or, according to some accounts, escaped in a small boat. It is not known how much of his ill-gotten gains also went down in the *Reinera e Soderina*.

Ward lived out the rest of his years in a castle in Tunis. In his old age, he is said to have adopted the Muslim religion and style of dress, and taken to raising chicks in incubators. He died in 1622 from the plague.

WATER BOTTLE
Belonging to the Order of the Knights of St. John, a group that preyed on Muslim shipping and rescued Christian slaves.

Small boats
For getting to and from the shore

Oarpower
Provided the ship with extra speed, helping pirates to come up behind their victims

CAPTURED CHRISTIANS
In the sixteenth century, before Christian pirates were accepted by the Muslims, the Turks doled out horrific punishments to Christians. It is likely that Christian engravings, as shown above, exaggerated tortures for propaganda purposes.

THE
WHYDAH

(see pages 52–53)

On July 24, 1715, a Spanish treasure fleet of 11 ships (see pages 52–53) set out for Spain from Havana, Cuba. One week later, 10 of the 11 ships had been wrecked on the Florida coast. The Spanish authorities quickly launched a massive salvage effort and, within a few months, over 4 million pesos were recovered.

News of the disaster attracted many Caribbean treasure hunters to the scene, including an American, Paul Williams, and an Englishman, Sam Bellamy, who hoped to make their fortune. They set out from Rhode Island early in 1716 but by the time they reached the Bahamas in the West Indies, any accessible treasure had already been lifted and so, rapidly disillusioned with treasure-hunting as a way of making quick money, they decided to turn pirate. Williams and Bellamy soon joined forces with two other pirates, Benjamin Hornigold and Louis Lebous. Between them, they had two single-masted sailing vessels (sloops) and 140 men.

International Fleet

A few months later, after the capture of several valuable cargoes, an interesting moral dispute arose about the legitimacy of taking English ships. Hornigold was firmly against seizing ships flying the English flag, but Bellamy had no reservations about attacking ships of any nation. As a result, Hornigold went his own way and Bellamy pursued any vessel that took his fancy, including Spanish, French, English, and Dutch ships. Many seamen from the captured vessels joined the pirates, some willingly and some because they were forced to. The nationality of the pirates was as mixed as that of the ships they attacked. Most were English, but there were also French, Dutch, and Caribbean-Indian pirates.

Capture of the Whydah

In February 1717, Bellamy's pirating spree culminated in the capture of the *Whydah*. This English galley weighed about 300 tons and was carrying 18 guns. It was engaged in the standard triangular Atlantic trade of the early eighteenth century: England to Africa,

from Africa to Jamaica, and back to England. It was en route from Jamaica to England with a cargo that included sugar, indigo, gold, silver, and ivory, having just completed a slaving trip from west Africa to the Caribbean.

Bellamy first saw the ship in the Windward Passage between Cuba and Puerto Rico, and there began a three-day chase that ended with the *Whydah* surrendering off Long Island in the Bahamas. There was no loss of life and, as was Bellamy's habit, he treated his victims relatively well. The captain was sent off with some unwanted cargo in another ship that had been captured by the pirates, and was given $30 in gold coins (specie). The rest of the gold and silver

CAROUSING PIRATES
This is the popular image of the high life lived by pirates on the open seas. Drink played its part in the story of the Whydah: *the pirates sampled a cargo of Madeira wine that they had captured and, while they were suffering under its influence, a storm blew up and their ship was wrecked.*

SPANISH GOLD COINS
Salvaged from a ship that wrecked in 1715, these coins are similar to those that drew Williams and Bellamy to the hunt for treasure in the Caribbean.

MODERN SALVAGE

In 1984, Barry Clifford of Maritime Explorations, North America, located the remains of the *Whydah* in depths of water of about 25 feet (7.5 meters) and beneath a deep layer of sand, making excavation difficult and expensive. Newspaper reports estimated the value of the cargo at $400 million but, from the artifacts recovered, it seems that this was too optimistic.

Some 8,000 coins have been salvaged so far, together with a fascinating collection of artifacts. These include a beautiful dueling pistol, fashioned from black walnut, with an iron barrel and brass decorations, and a silk sock suggesting a pirate with a dandified taste in foot apparel. Anchors, cannons, the ship's bell, and sailor's clay pipes have all been salvaged and expertly conserved in a very professional operation costing around $6 million.

taken by the pirates was valued at about $30,000. Each pirate received a $75 bag as his share of the booty.

Bellamy transferred his own quarters to the *Whydah* and more ships were plundered as the pirates headed northward. In April, Paul Williams separated from the rest of the pirates, although it is not known why, but agreed to reunite with them off Block Island, south of Rhode Island.

Capture of the Mary Ann

On April 26, 1717, the remaining pirate ships, the *Whydah*, a two-masted merchant ship (a snow), and a sloop, captured the *Mary Ann*. This vessel was a small, square-rigged, three-masted ship (a pink) en route from Dublin to New York with a cargo that consisted entirely of Madeira wine. The combination of wine and bad weather proved to be the pirates' undoing. They took over the *Mary Ann* and proceeded to become riotously drunk.

Unfortunately, their partying coincided with a fierce storm blowing up from the east and the *Mary Ann* was driven onto a sandy beach close to Sluttsbush, Massachusetts. Fearing the worst, the pirates went below deck and one of the captured Irishmen was asked to read a prayer book out loud for an hour. The boat did not break up, however, and the following day the small crew were taken off by two local sailors in their sailing canoe, some of the pirates still in a fairly drunken state. The original crew members of the *Mary Ann*, who had not been transferred to the *Whydah*, quickly denounced some of those who had been rescued, as pirates. As a result, the pirates were arrested and sent to jail.

Wrecking and Salvage of the Whydah

Meanwhile the *Whydah* struck the outer bar of Cape Cod, about 10 miles (16 kilometers) to the north of the *Mary Ann*'s position, only considerably farther out to sea and with far more disastrous results. Only 2 of the 146 people on board survived: a man named John Julian, and the ship's carpenter, Thomas Davis. Davis went to the nearest house, which belonged to a Samuel Harding, and the two of them started to salvage what they could from the wreck. Before long, the entire Cape Cod community was on the sandbanks looting whatever came ashore. During this time, Paul Williams's ship was seen standing off from the shore, and he sent a boat to the wreck site in an attempt to salvage any lost silver and gold.

When the governor of the Massachusetts colony heard about the wreck, he sent Captain Southack to the scene to take charge. Southack had a reputation as a cartographer and artist, and his chart of Cape Cod, with annotated references to the wreck of the *Whydah*, has since become a classic document for future generations of treasure hunters. When Southack arrived at the scene, it was almost a week since the wreck had occurred. Many goods had been removed and the locals refused to disclose their whereabouts, much to Southack's annoyance; he recorded in his journal, "Pepol very Stife and will not [surrender] one thing of what they Gott on the Rack."

Southack recorded the wreck site as 3.5 miles (5.6 kilometers) from Billingsgate, Massachusetts, and stated that it had turned upside down, which no doubt made the recovery of any treasure much more difficult. He stayed for some weeks, but managed to salvage only approximately $300 worth of miscellaneous goods and ship's tackle. He clearly suspected Samuel Harding and Thomas Davis of having secreted the bulk of the treasure before he arrived, but it is difficult to conceive that they managed to salvage any of it, given their limited resources and the difficulties of the task.

This was the usual method of executing men convicted of piracy in England and North America. It would generally take place on an execution dock and attracted crowds of onlookers who gathered on the dock and on boats or ships moored nearby. This nineteenth-century engraving shows a pirate about to be hanged at a dock in Wapping, England.

In the meantime, a row had broken out over who should take responsibility for burying the bodies that were washing ashore. Southack did not see why the state should pay for this out of the meager quantity of goods that he had managed to salvage from the wreck of the *Whydah*, but the local coroner placed a sequestration order on the salvaged goods, and Southack reluctantly concurred.

Fate of the Pirates

In October 1717, eight of the pirates were brought to trial in Boston, Massachusetts. Davis, the carpenter, and Thomas South, one of the crew who had been on board the *Mary Ann*, were acquitted as unwilling accomplices. The other six pirates were hanged for piracy at Charlestown Ferry, Boston.

EAST INDIAMEN

The East India Companies were formed in the early part of the seventeenth century to develop the valuable trade opening up between Europe and the Orient. The two main companies were the English Company (EEI), founded in 1600, and the Dutch Company (VOC), founded in 1602. Later on, French, Swedish, Portuguese, and Danish companies also started trading. The East India Company traders used large ships known as East Indiamen to carry their wares.

East Indiamen carried immensely rich cargoes. On their outward journey, the most valuable part of the cargo was gold and silver, usually shipped from the home ports but occasionally picked up at Lisbon in Portugal, Bahia (Salvador) in Brazil, or Persia (Iran). Other goods carried for trading were metals such as lead, copper, tin, and iron – usually carried as ballast; textiles such as woolens; and manufactured goods such as hats, pens, watches, and firearms.

The main attraction of the East, particularly in the early years, was its spices: pepper from Sumatra and India; cinnamon from Ceylon (Sri Lanka); cloves from the aptly named Spice Islands (Moluccas); and balsam from Java. Other attractions included precious stones, crystal, and carpets from Surat, India; Persian silks and perfumes; Chinese porcelain and, later, tea. Not all these items were carried back to Europe, but were used instead to trade for other goods en route. For instance, textiles from Bengal were widely sold throughout Indonesia; the Dutch also bought Persian goods with Japanese silver. By about 1700 the Dutch and the British were firmly established in the Far East, and the British Company also had a strong base in Mughal India.

VENDELA ①
This Danish East Indiaman was wrecked off the Shetland Islands in 1737. It was carrying silver coins and bullion.

PRINCE DE CONTY ②
In December 1746 this French East Indiaman was lost on the cliffs of Belle Île, France. It was carrying porcelain and gold ingots as well as oriental goods.

SANDBANKS
Often the most dangerous part of a journey was entering and leaving port; many ships foundered on sandbanks off the Netherlands.

TRADE ROUTES
The outward route took advantage of the northeast trade winds; on their return the ships followed the southeast trade winds up the Atlantic.

HARTWELL ③
This ship was heading for the Cape Verde islands in 1798 to disembark mutineers. (See pages 76–77.)

BRITANNIA ④
When sailing in a convoy in 1805, the Britannia struck reefs off Brazil. All but one sailor survived – he clung to treasure determined to die rich.

QUEEN ⑤
Along with money and silver plate, this ship carried a cargo of gunpowder and blew up in Bahia (Salvador) harbor, Brazil, in 1800.

WITTE LEEUW ⑥
In 1613 on its homeward journey, carrying diamonds, Ming pottery, and spices, the Witte Leeuw was blown up by Portuguese carracks.

JOHANNA ⑦
En route to the Bay of Bengal with 70 treasure chests, the Johanna was wrecked off the Cape of Good Hope, South Africa.

To Bahia (South America)

NORWAY
SWEDEN
SHETLANDS
DENMARK • Copenhagen
BRITAIN
London • • Amsterdam
Plymouth •
Lorient
FRANCE
PORTUGAL SPAIN
Lisbon •
Azores
ATLANTIC OCEAN
MEDITERRANEA
CANARY ISLANDS
CAPE VERDE
AFRICA
GOLD COAST SLAVE COAST
Gulf of Guinea
SOUTH ATLANTIC OCEAN
CAPE COLON
Cape Town
Cape of Good Hope
OTTO
OTTO

General trading routes
————— Dutch routes
- - - - - English routes

PEPPER
This formed a bulky, but much prized, trade cargo on returning East Indiamen.

CLOVES
Native to the Spice Islands (Moluccas), this valuable commodity was used in the East for centuries before it reached Europe.

PEPPER GATHERING
Pepper was highly sought after in Europe, and traders bought it from Sumatra, and Malabar on the west coast of India.

TRADE WITH CHINA
The East India companies later purchased tea from China in exchange for goods acquired on outward voyages.

THE GANGES
The shifting sands of the Ganges leading up to Calcutta made this a treacherous place for shipping.

MANCHU CHINA

JAPAN

Nagasaki

Nanjing (Nanking)

FORMOSA (TAIWAN)

Canton (Guangzhou)

PERSIA (IRAN)

Gombroon (Bandar 'Abbas)

ARABIA

MUGHAL INDIA

BENGAL

Calcutta

BURMA

Surat   Masulipatnam (Machilipatnam)

Bombay

Bay of Bengal

SOUTHWEST TRADE WINDS
The English navigators used the southwest trades to take them up the Indian Ocean.

FREDRICK ADOLPHUS ⑬
In 1791 this Swedish East Indiaman wrecked in the South China Sea. It was carrying 39 boxes of silver.

⑯

⑬

Manila

PHILIPPINES

RYNSBURGH ⑯
During a typhoon in 1772, the Rynsburgh foundered off China. Eight Chinese divers were eaten by sharks but the cargo of silver was recovered.

RAVENSTEIN ⑨
This ship ran onto a reef off the Maldives in 1725. Nine chests of the cargo were recovered.

MALDIVES

CEYLON (SRI LANKA)

⑨

INDIAN OCEAN

Saigon (Ho Chi Minh City)

Pinang

MALAYA

SUMATRA

Singapore

⑭

SOUTH CHINA SEA

BORNEO

SPICE ISLANDS (MOLUCCAS)

NEW GUINEA

Bencoolen (Bengkulu)

Strait of Sunda

JAVA

Makassar (Ujung Pandang)

GELDERMALSEN ⑭
This ship sank in 1752 and its recently salvaged cargo of Chinese porcelain sold for over $15 million. (See pages 74–75.)

BOMBAY-STRUNG PEARLS
Pearls from the Orient were taken to Bombay, India, where they were drilled and strung onto silk, then finished with silver tassels.

WINTERTON ⑩
This hit a reef off Madagascar in 1792, traveling too fast with a following monsoon wind.

MADAGASCAR

⑩

⑫

Tulear

⑪

MAURITIUS

SAINT GERAN ⑫
This French East Indiaman was wrecked on August 17, 1744, just off Port Louis, Mauritius, with 18 cases and one barrel of money on board. The ship broke up before the money could be saved. Some of it was later looted by locals.

HOUTMAN ABROLHOS ISLANDS

⑮

WESTERN AUSTRALIA

...OSVENOR ⑧
...wn to have been carrying ...monds and the treasure of ...t India officer, William ...a, the Grosvenor sank off ...a on August 4, 1782.

SOLEIL D'ORIENT ⑪
Wrecked off Madagascar in 1681, the Soleil d'Orient's priceless cargo of gifts from the King of Bantam to Louis XIV of France was lost.

THE DUTCH ROUTE
This alternative outward route followed the "Roaring Forties," sailing a course along the latitude 40°S across the Southern Ocean to the East.

BATAVIA ⑮
When carrying silverware and a valuable collection of jewels, the Batavia was blown off course and dashed against rocks in Australian waters in 1629. (See pages 72–73.)

THE
BATAVIA

The *Batavia* sailed from Amsterdam, in the Netherlands, on October 27, 1628, en route to the town in Java after which it was named, which is now known as Jakarta. The ship had been newly built by the Dutch East India Company (VOC).

The *Batavia* carried a rich cargo: 250,000 guilders of silver, a valuable collection of jewels and silver plate, and trade goods, such as cloth, lead, and cochineal. It also contained a more unusual cargo: sandstone for a gateway (see below).

There were 316 people on board, including a detachment of soldiers, and women and children. Among the women was Lucretia van der Mylen, who was on her way to join her husband in the East. During the voyage, she attracted rather more than her fair share of attention. Some suggestion has been made that the captain, Pelsaert, had an affair with her and that the navigator, Jacobsz, would have liked to supplant him in her affections. There is no concrete evidence to support this, although there was apparently much ill-feeling between the two men.

After stopping at the Cape of Good Hope, South Africa, for fresh supplies, the *Batavia* took a southerly route to make best use of the westerly winds. One of the dangers of this route was the risk of

SALVAGE

Divers sent from Jakarta (Batavia) salvaged 10 chests of silver from the *Batavia* shortly after the events of 1629. After that, the wreck lay undisturbed until 1963, when it was located and several cannons and coins were recovered from the site. The Dutch government transferred rights over the wreck to the Australian government and, in 1972, the Western Australian Museum began intensive archaeological and recovery operations. It salvaged enormous quantities of treasure, personal items, ship's fittings, and supplies, now on public display.

SILVER SALVAGED FROM THE BATAVIA
A variety of finely engraved Dutch silverware was found at the wreck site. Pelsaert was exporting this to the East to trade for other goods.

SANDSTONE PORTICO
The Batavia *carried pre-shaped building blocks to create an impressive gateway, probably destined for the castle in Jakarta (then named Batavia). These sank with the ship in 1629 but were salvaged in the 1970s.*

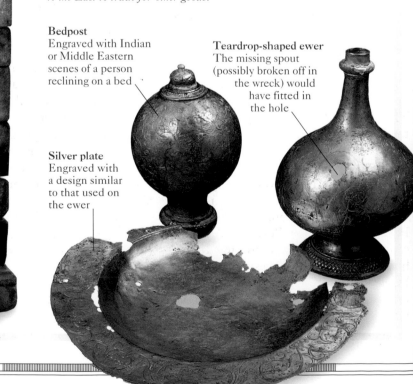

Bedpost
Engraved with Indian or Middle Eastern scenes of a person reclining on a bed

Teardrop-shaped ewer
The missing spout (possibly broken off in the wreck) would have fitted in the hole

Silver plate
Engraved with a design similar to that used on the ewer

SAILING INTO DANGER
This contemporary engraving shows how the Batavia *was under full sail on the night of June 4, 1629 (left), and was negotiating the shallow water around the Houtman Abrolhos Islands, off Australia, when it ran aground on a reef.*

ATTEMPTS TO SAVE THE BATAVIA
The crew cut down the mainmast to lighten the ship, hoping to float it off the reef, but it heeled over on its port side (below) and the crew and passengers had to abandon ship.

because this made it easier to put into action his plan of seizing power and the *Batavia* treasure. Most of the silver was still trapped on the wreck, but the jewels had been taken off and were in his possession. Cornelisz's subsequent behavior, however, does not suggest a coherent plan of action, but rather the deranged fantasies of a psychopath with considerable charisma.

During the next few weeks, 125 survivors, including women and children, were killed by Cornelisz and his close supporters, in a systematic orgy of terror. He dressed himself in scarlet robes that he fashioned from cloth recovered from the wreck, and assumed violent and autocratic control, also making the hapless Lucretia his mistress.

There was one source of opposition to Cornelisz: a man called Hayes who, along with about 40 soldiers, refused to submit to his orders. Hayes's group constructed handmade weapons and managed to repulse two attacks from Cornelisz's henchmen. Then Hayes made a surprise attack, killed the leaders of Cornelisz's group, and took Cornelisz prisoner.

Pelsaert Rescues Survivors

On July 2, 1629, Pelsaert, Jacobsz and their two boats were picked up by the *Sardam* and taken to Jakarta. Pelsaert was interviewed by the Governor General, and sent to fetch the survivors. Jacobsz was imprisoned.

Pelsaert had difficulty finding the islands where the *Batavia* had been lost but, on September 16, the ship was found. Hayes managed to warn Pelsaert of what had been happening in his absence. The mutineers gave themselves up and were duly punished (see box below). Pelsaert never recovered from the trauma, and died the following year.

miscalculating how far east the ship had sailed before it turned north. During the night of June 4, 1629, the *Batavia* struck Morning Reef, part of East Wallabi Island, which is one of the Houtman Abrolhos group of islands about 40 miles (65 kilometers) off the coast of Western Australia.

The *Batavia* became lodged on the reef, and most of its passengers disembarked in longboats and reached the small and barren islands to the north. About 80 people remained on board, getting drunk in the time-honored manner of sailors when their ship is wrecked. They also broke open and plundered one of the chests of silver.

The most critical concern for those who reached the islands was a lack of freshwater. Some barrels of water were washed ashore from the wreck, but at first the islands seemed to have no natural supplies of freshwater. In this dire situation, Pelsaert, Jacobsz, and 45 others seized the only two remaining boats and made off. This sudden alliance of Jacobsz with Pelsaert, who had been enemies for over a year, suggests that in this new crisis both men saw their only chance of survival through a temporary truce.

In the first few days some of those on the islands died of thirst, but then supplies of water were discovered. Luckily, there was also a plentiful supply of food in the form of seal meat, birds' eggs, and fish.

Cornelisz's Reign of Fear

One of those remaining on the wreck was Cornelisz, an Amsterdam apothecary, who was the merchant in charge of the trading aspects of the voyage (the "supercargo"). He turned out to be the real evil genius of the disaster. Already, during the latter part of the voyage, Cornelisz and Jacobsz, in collusion with a small group of sailors, had been plotting to seize the *Batavia*, drown all non-conspirators, and make off with the ship and its treasure; but the ship had wrecked before they could carry out their plans.

It was ten days before Cornelisz left the wreck of the *Batavia*. He was the last to leave the ship, but when he reached land he assumed overall command as the most senior member of the VOC remaining. He divided people between the various islands. This was ostensibly to avoid overcrowding, but also

MURDERERS' FATE

After the wreck of the *Batavia*, the castaways split up between small islands. Their ordeal was not over because Cornelisz and his close supporters massacred 125 of them. When the survivors were eventually rescued by Pelsaert over two months later, the ringleaders, dispirited by this stage, quickly surrendered.

Seven were hanged, including Cornelisz. Under Dutch law at that time, a man could not be hanged until he had confessed to his crime and not retracted that confession for a period of 24 hours. However, in order to extract a confession, water torture could be used. It took nearly two weeks before a confession could be extracted from Cornelisz.

THE
GELDERMALSEN

The *Geldermalsen*, a typical Dutch East Indiaman, arrived in Guangzhou (Canton), China, in July 1751 with a cargo of tin and cotton from Jakarta (Batavia), together with the gifts that were necessary to smooth the paths of business between Dutch traders and the Chinese authorities.

The five-year-old ship belonged to the Zeeland chamber of the Dutch East India Company (VOC), and was approximately 150 feet (45 meters) in length. It was captained by Jan Morel.

After it had unloaded its cargo from Jakarta, the *Geldermalsen* took on board a cargo of tea, silks, ginger, rhubarb, lacquerware, and around 200,000 pieces of porcelain, for which it was to become famous over 200 years later when the porcelain was auctioned in Amsterdam in April 1986.

The Geldermalsen's Porcelain

The porcelain was known in the common parlance of the time as Nanking porcelain, after the town where it was mistakenly thought to have been made. It was produced specifically to the VOC designs sent out from the Netherlands and was commissioned by local VOC agents in Guangzhou. However, because of the slowness of communications and possible shortages of supply, there were significant differences between what had been requested and some of the items that were eventually salvaged from the wreck of the *Geldermalsen*. There was, for instance, no recorded order for vomit pots, yet around 500 of these were salvaged. Conversely, a request for coffee pots appears to have been ignored.

The porcelain was not of the finest quality nor was it aimed at the fastidious collector. It was mass-produced in the potteries at Fowliang (Jingdezhen) for the expanding Dutch middle-class market who, in the preceding few decades, had enthusiastically taken to drinking tea from porcelain tea services. From Fowliang, the porcelain was taken to Nanjing (Nanking), and was then shipped to Guangzhou for onward shipping to Europe. It was stowed in over 200 crates in the lower part of the ship's hold.

TEA CULTIVATION AND TRADE
This engraving of a Chinese tea factory reflects the popularity of tea-drinking in China, which is reputed to date back to 2750 B.C. It was not until the seventeenth century, however, that tea was introduced to Europe. The Geldermalsen's main cargo of green and black tea was being shipped from China to the Netherlands.

Drying of tea leaves
After a short period of fermentation, the harvested leaves are dried over hot ovens

GREEN AND BLACK TEA
The Geldermalsen carried Chinese green and black tea stored in chests. These tea chests would have been tightly packed into the ship's hold for the rough journey to Europe.

Supervising production
Chinese merchants oversaw tea production and then sold the tea to Europeans

Cargo of Tea

Although it was the porcelain that caused such a sensation when it was auctioned by Christie's in 1986, it actually represented only about five percent of the original value of the cargo. The main bulk of the cargo from China, both in value and in volume, was green and black leaf teas, huge quantities of which were carefully loaded above the porcelain in the ship's hold.

After loading its valuable cargo of Chinese tea and porcelain, the *Geldermalsen* left the port of Guangzhou in late December 1751. The ship made good use of the northwest monsoon to sail southward across the South China Sea on the first part of its lengthy return journey to the Netherlands.

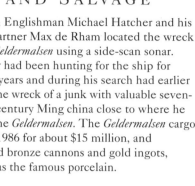

Tea from the fields
Leaves were picked and brought to a processing center, located near the shore for easy transport

Dignitary
Wearing an official hat

LOCATION AND SALVAGE

In 1985, Englishman Michael Hatcher and his Swiss partner Max de Rham located the wreck of the *Geldermalsen* using a side-scan sonar. Hatcher had been hunting for the ship for several years and during his search had earlier found the wreck of a junk with valuable seventeenth-century Ming china close to where he found the *Geldermalsen*. The *Geldermalsen* cargo sold in 1986 for about $15 million, and included bronze cannons and gold ingots, as well as the famous porcelain.

Mother and baby
About 6 in (16 cm) high

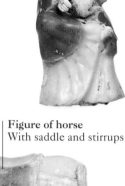

Figure of horse
With saddle and stirrups

Woman
With rose spray on shoulder

fresher and also had been better packaged. In order to compete, the Dutch were compelled to allow their ships to return straight from Guangzhou to Europe via the Strait of Sunda, without first calling at Jakarta. This caused problems for the important Guangzhou–Jakarta gold trade.

Gold was traditionally cheaper in China than in most other trading centers and so it made commercial sense for the Dutch to buy it at Guangzhou and then resell in Jakarta. Once the Dutch began regularly using the direct route to Europe, they transshipped the gold ingots directly onto small ships that were waiting for them at Noord Island, in the Strait of Sunda, and stopped calling in at Jakarta.

SALVAGED PORCELAIN FIGURES
These Chinese figures were being exported to the Netherlands on the Geldermalsen *when it sank in 1751. The figures are glazed in soft blues, white, and beige, and signs of wear from 200 years of immersion in the sea can be seen. They were salvaged in 1985 and auctioned in Amsterdam in 1986.*

The Wrecking of the Geldermalsen

When the *Geldermalsen* set sail on its final journey from Guangzhou, there were 112 people on board. The majority of them were Dutch, but there was a fair proportion of English. On the evening of January 3, 1752, while sailing in good weather, the ship struck the Admiral Stellingwerf Reef, even though the boatswain, Van Dijk, had claimed earlier in the day that the reef had already been sighted and that the ship was safely past it.

The crew cut down the *Geldermalsen*'s mainmast to help stability, and the ship eventually came off the reef. Later that night, however, the *Geldermalsen* sank, and approximately two-thirds of its crew drowned.

During the subsequent enquiry into the disaster, which was held in Jakarta, Van Dijk was cross-questioned on his faulty statement. He must have been found at least partially responsible for the loss of the *Geldermalsen* because he was demoted.

GOLD INGOTS

In total, 126 gold ingots were found near the *Geldermalsen* wreck and were auctioned at Christie's, Amsterdam. Each ingot weighed about 12.8 oz (365 grams); 0.035 oz (one gram) of gold was worth about one Dutch guilder in 1750. Some of the ingots were shoe-shaped, and the first of these sold realized 20 times its bullion value. The more conventionally shaped gold bars, however, fetched only three times their bullion value.

The ingots were found outside the hull, not far from the wreck. This suggests that there had possibly been a failed attempt at salvaging the box containing the ingots at the time of sinking.

SHOE-SHAPED INGOTS
The shoe-shape of these gold ingots is a Chinese symbol of wealth.

Dutch Trade in the Far East

During the seventeenth century, VOC ships making the journey back to Europe from Guangzhou sailed first to the port of Jakarta, where they made their final cargo loadings. When tea began to grow in popularity in the West the Dutch continued to allow Jakarta to dominate the trade. Tea was shipped to Jakarta by Chinese junk, where it was transshipped onto an East Indiaman that was returning to Amsterdam.

However, the Dutch rapidly began to lose out against their competitors, particularly the English who shipped tea directly back from China to Europe. As a result, the tea arrived

THE HARTWELL

The *Hartwell* was, according to its proud owner, John Fiott, the biggest ship of its kind in the service of the English East India Company (EEI Co.). Launched amid much celebration, the *Hartwell* began its ambitious maiden voyage to China in February 1787. It set out from England with an immensely rich cargo, which included 209,280 oz (5,933 kilograms) of fine silver carried on the Company's account. Other merchandise, such as clocks, jewelry, textiles, and lead, was sent by private traders. John Fiott's brother was the captain, and other family members were shareholders.

From the start the *Hartwell* ran into trouble. Gales put the ship behind schedule and, on May 20, a mutiny broke out (see box opposite). After three successive nights without sleep, owing to the disturbances, the ship's officers accidentally ran the ship onto a reef northeast of the island of Boa Vista, in the Cape Verde islands off west Africa. It rapidly broke up and the entire cargo was lost, although all the crew were saved.

Back in England, Captain Fiott and his chief mate were convicted by the English East India Company Court for carrying too many sails during darkness and making navigational errors. The EEI Co. then turned its attention to salvaging its property.

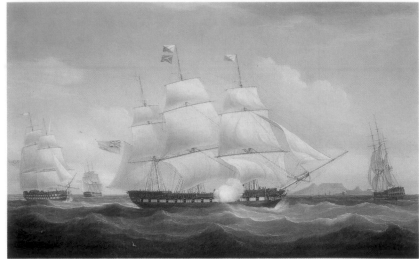

EAST INDIAMEN UNDER SAIL, 1820
In this painting, the English trading ships Minerva, Scaleby Castle, *and* Charles Grant *are shown passing Cape Town, South Africa, en route to the East. The ships were built in 1798, eleven years after the* Hartwell *which would have been of a similar design.*

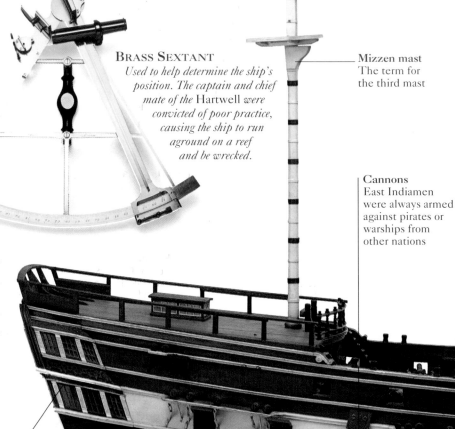

BRASS SEXTANT
Used to help determine the ship's position. The captain and chief mate of the Hartwell *were convicted of poor practice, causing the ship to run aground on a reef and be wrecked.*

Mizzen mast
The term for the third mast

Cannons
East Indiamen were always armed against pirates or warships from other nations

EAST INDIAMAN MODEL
The Hartwell *was a cargo-carrying ship built to withstand the rigors of the long journey to the East. A round trip to China or Japan might take three years, and ships usually lasted for four voyages. This model shows the* Scaleby Castle, *which was built in 1798, and was similar to the* Hartwell.

Captain's quarters
Where valuable private goods were stored for safety

Breadroom
Where the *Hartwell's* chests of silver were locked away

Cargo hold
Lead was loaded first onto the *Hartwell* for ballast

THE HARTWELL LOG BOOK
Rescued from the wreck by Captain Fiott, this logbook describes in its last entry the mutineers "defying all orders ... and tending to risk the lives of officers." The ringleaders of this "Dangerous Mutiny" were punished by two dozen lashes each.

First Attempt at Salvaging the Wreck

The English East India Company employed the most successful salvagers of the period, William and John Braithwaite, to salvage the silver. The Braithwaite brothers entered into an agreement by which they would be paid their expenses plus 12.5 percent of the sum they recovered. This appears to be a good deal, but it was a highly dangerous and skilled job. For the first two years of operations they had only limited success. The treasure chests had all been broken up by the action of the waves, and the valuable coins were scattered across the reef where the wreck lay. The brothers were also beset by continual skirmishes with marauding pirates from the Caribbean. In one raid William was badly wounded, two of his divers were killed, and the pirates made off with recovered treasure worth 11,000 Spanish dollars. After this setback, John Braithwaite returned to England to adapt the diving bell and to obtain better armaments for their defense.

Second Successful Salvage

John Braithwaite returned to his brother in the Cape Verde islands in 1790 and they started up salvage operations once more, using their new equipment. This time they met with considerably more success. When they finally decided they could achieve no more, and suspended operations in 1791, their records showed that an impressive 97,650 silver dollars had been recovered.

This amounted to a handsome profit for the Braithwaites, but it still leaves a large quantity of dollars remaining near the wreck for adventurous and enterprising modern-day treasure hunters. Silver dollars of this period, in good condition, can fetch a considerable amount, which suggests there could still be $3,750,000 of treasure waiting to be recovered on the *Hartwell* reef, as it is now known.

Hatch in deck
For loading cargo through

Tender
Used by the *Hartwell*'s crew to escape on after the wreck

Flat deck
Built with a flush deck, unlike the raised forecastles found on earlier East Indiamen

MUTINY ON BOARD THE HARTWELL

Mutiny broke out among the crew of the *Hartwell* on its maiden voyage, causing the captain to change direction and, ultimately, to wreck the ship. The immediate cause of the rebellion was a refusal to put lights out. Knives were drawn, abusive language used and, after a struggle, three men were secured and clapped in irons. Disorder, however, continued to spread and before long 50 of the crew were "singing very daring songs and defying all orders from the officers." After three days the mutiny was put down and the captain changed course for the Cape Verde islands, to hand the mutineers to the Governor. But the ship was wrecked before reaching its destination.

Air supply
Lowered in weighted barrel

Escaping air
Used air was expelled here

DIVING BELL AND DIVER
The diving bell is similar to that used by the Braithwaite brothers in the 1790s when they salvaged the Hartwell *wreck. The design of the rigid diving suit was primitive and dangerous but the salvage operations were none the less successful, netting the brothers 12,206 Spanish silver dollars.*

Ax
For breaking through the ship's hull when salvaging

Lead weight
Enabled the diver to stay underwater

Wooden hull
Made of oak planks 6 in (15 cm) thick

FACTS AND FEATURES

Hartwell's weight	938 tons
Cost	$17 per ton
Shipyard	Itchenor, England

AGE OF REVOLUTION

The United Kingdom was in a state of conflict with its American colonies by 1775 as it struggled to maintain a power base on the Eastern seaboard. After the American Declaration of Independence in 1776 a major international war across the Atlantic became inevitable. The role of the British Royal Navy, acknowledged as the dominant seapower throughout the world at this period, was critical. It acted as a blockading force, disrupting American trade, and also played a vital part in keeping the besieged British Army on the American mainland supplied. The American Navy was no match for the British but responded by fitting out privateers (see page 63) to prey on British commerce.

In 1778 France entered the war in support of the American rebels, and the naval war took on a more global aspect. Control of the valuable Caribbean sugar and tobacco trade was vital to both British and French economies, and both nations dispatched fleets for this purpose, although the result was something of a stalemate.

The Peace of Versailles was signed in 1783 and the United States was born. There followed a decade of peace but in 1793 war broke out again, this time between Britain and revolutionary France, a war that was to continue for the next 22 years and witnessed a loss of shipping and men on a scale that had never been seen before. Attacks on British merchant shipping were made by French privateers in most parts of the globe. The British developed a protective convoy system for its trading ships, and fleets of up to 600 would cross the Atlantic together.

In 1799 Napoleon Bonaparte overthrew the French Government and became first consul of France, making himself Emperor in 1804. With the growth of his military dominance, Dutch and Spanish fleets came under French control. Despite his successes, Britain strengthened its control of the seas through a series of brilliant naval victories. By 1812, when the United States entered the war on the side of France, the real threat to Britain was already over.

Ships of the Line

The fundamental component of the naval wars of this period was the ship of the line. The strategic concept of the battle line in which the ships maintained a strict bow to stern position, facing the enemy with their broadsides, had been introduced some 150 years earlier but it was during the French Revolutionary and Napoleonic wars that it reached its final stage of development.

Warships were categorized into rates from 1st rate to 6th rate but only the first four rates were normally used as ships of the line in the main battle fleet, the 5th and 6th rates being lightly gunned frigates used more often for special and independent missions. Typical 1st rate ships would be around 2,500 tons, carry 120 guns on three decks, and be about 200 feet (60 meters) long. They were substantially larger than any merchant ships of their day, the most important factor being the amount of firepower that they could bring to bear on their enemy.

CANADA

FRENCH SHIP-BUILDING BASE
Because of a shortage of wood in Europe, France built many of its ships abroad, particularly at Québec.

NEWFOUNDLAND

Québec

Halifax

New York

Philadelphia

DELAWARE

Cape Henlopen

BLUNDERBUSS
Many different types of weapons were used in eighteenth-century conflict. The flintlock blunderbuss, which could fire a number of small shots, was most effective when fired at close range.

HUSSAR ①
This 627-ton, 28-gun British frigate was becalmed off the coast near New York in 1763. It became ungovernable, struck a rock, and drifted to the shore where it sank.

HMS DE BRAAK ②
In 1798 this 255-ton, 14-gun sailing sloop sank off the Delaware coast with great loss of life.

THE CARIBBEAN
A number of inconclusive sea battles were fought between the British and the French, struggling to dominate valuable trade. The Battle of Saints in 1782 secured Jamaica for the British, although the French Navy remained a force to be reckoned with.

ATLANTIC OCEAN

BAHAMAS (UK)

CUBA

JAMAICA
Port Royal

CARIBBEAN SEA

ANTIGUA

DOMINICA
MARTINIQUE
ST. LUCIA
BARBADOS

SOUTH AMERICA

Orinoco

VICE ROYALTY OF NEW GRANADA

Amazon

VICE ROYALTY OF BRAZIL

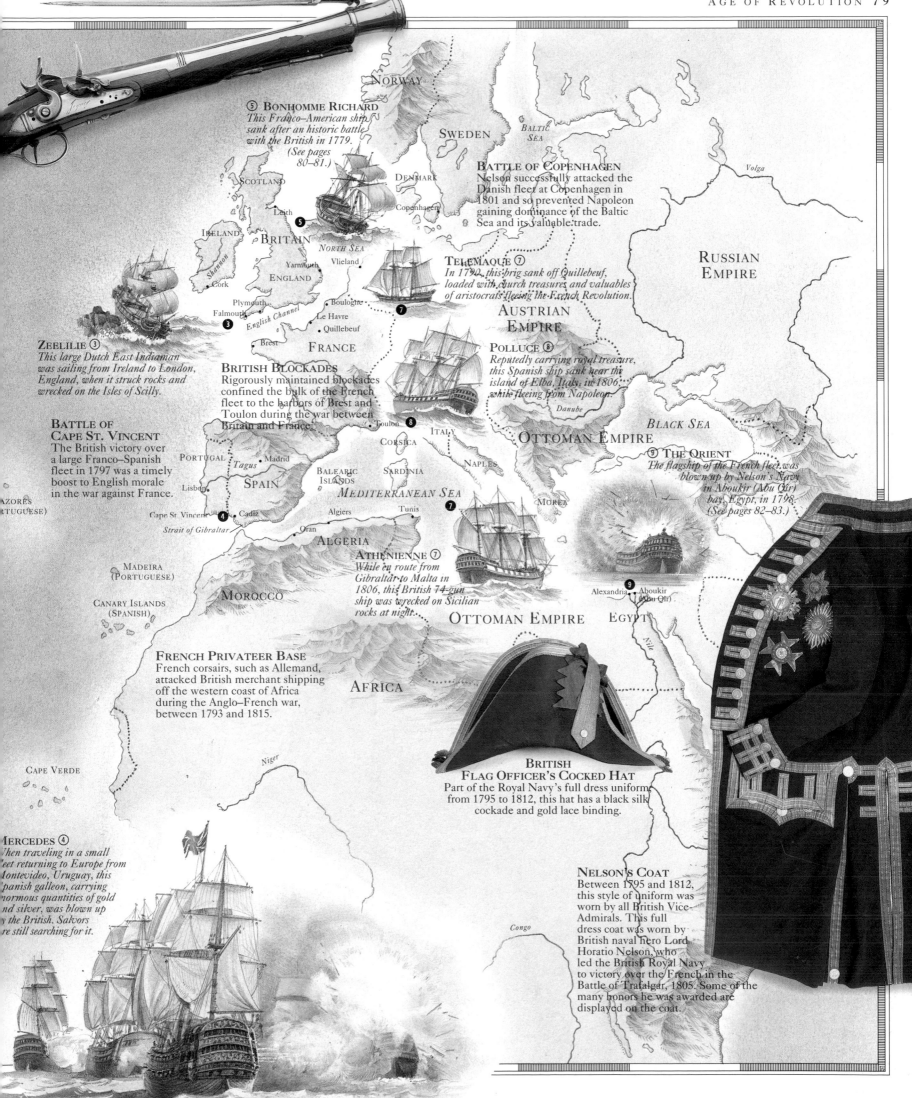

⑤ BONHOMME RICHARD
This Franco–American ship sank after an historic battle with the British in 1779. (See pages 80–81.)

BATTLE OF COPENHAGEN
Nelson successfully attacked the Danish fleet at Copenhagen in 1801 and so prevented Napoleon gaining dominance of the Baltic Sea and its valuable trade.

TÉLÉMAQUE ⑦
In 1790, this brig sank off Quilleboeuf, loaded with church treasures and valuables of aristocrats fleeing the French Revolution.

POLLUCE ⑧
Reputedly carrying royal treasure, this Spanish ship sank near the island of Elba, Italy, in 1806, while fleeing from Napoleon.

ZEELILIE ③
This large Dutch East Indiaman was sailing from Ireland to London, England, when it struck rocks and wrecked on the Isles of Scilly.

BRITISH BLOCKADES
Rigorously maintained blockades confined the bulk of the French fleet to the harbors of Brest and Toulon during the war between Britain and France.

BATTLE OF CAPE ST. VINCENT
The British victory over a large Franco–Spanish fleet in 1797 was a timely boost to English morale in the war against France.

⑨ THE ORIENT
The flagship of the French fleet was blown up by Nelson's Navy in Aboukir (Abu Qir) bay, Egypt, in 1798. (See pages 82–83.)

ATHÉNIENNE ⑦
While en route from Gibraltar to Malta in 1806, this British 74-gun ship was wrecked on Sicilian rocks at night.

FRENCH PRIVATEER BASE
French corsairs, such as Allemand, attacked British merchant shipping off the western coast of Africa during the Anglo–French war, between 1793 and 1815.

BRITISH FLAG OFFICER'S COCKED HAT
Part of the Royal Navy's full dress uniform from 1795 to 1812, this hat has a black silk cockade and gold lace binding.

MERCEDES ④
When traveling in a small fleet returning to Europe from Montevideo, Uruguay, this Spanish galleon, carrying enormous quantities of gold and silver, was blown up by the British. Salvors are still searching for it.

NELSON'S COAT
Between 1795 and 1812, this style of uniform was worn by all British Vice-Admirals. This full dress coat was worn by British naval hero Lord Horatio Nelson, who led the British Royal Navy to victory over the French in the Battle of Trafalgar, 1805. Some of the many honors he was awarded are displayed on the coat.

Map labels: NORWAY, SWEDEN, BALTIC SEA, DENMARK, Copenhagen, Volga, SCOTLAND, Leith, IRELAND, BRITAIN, NORTH SEA, RUSSIAN EMPIRE, Shannon, Cork, ENGLAND, Yarmouth, Vlieland, Plymouth, Boulogne, AUSTRIAN EMPIRE, Falmouth, English Channel, Le Havre, Quilleboeuf, Brest, FRANCE, Danube, BLACK SEA, Toulon, ITALY, OTTOMAN EMPIRE, CORSICA, PORTUGAL, Tagus, Madrid, NAPLES, Lisbon, SPAIN, BALEARIC ISLANDS, SARDINIA, MOREA, AZORES (PORTUGUESE), Cape St. Vincent, Cadiz, MEDITERRANEAN SEA, Algiers, Tunis, Strait of Gibraltar, Oran, ALGERIA, Alexandria, Aboukir (Abu Qir), EGYPT, MADEIRA (PORTUGUESE), MOROCCO, OTTOMAN EMPIRE, Nile, CANARY ISLANDS (SPANISH), AFRICA, CAPE VERDE, Niger, Congo

THE
BONHOMME RICHARD

The *Bonhomme Richard* was not a treasure ship in the conventional sense of carrying large quantities of gold and silver or artifacts of great intrinsic value when it sank. However, it was a ship of immense historical importance, lost in a battle that saw America's first major naval victory, the Battle of Flamborough Head; and was commanded by the very first American naval hero, John Paul Jones. As such, its contents would have great associative value. Many attempts have been made to locate it, but so far without success.

Toward the end of 1778, John Paul Jones was in Lorient on the west coast of France, anxiously negotiating with the government in France, which was an ally of the rebel Americans (see pages 78–79), for a ship with which he could harry British merchant shipping. An old French East Indiaman was converted to a warship (see box below), and renamed the *Bonhomme Richard*.

Bonhomme Richard Sets Sail

By August 1779, the 40-gun *Bonhomme Richard* and a small accompanying fleet were ready to sail. They were under instruction to attack British ships and also to divert attention from the much larger Franco–Spanish invasion fleet that planned to attack the south coast of England.

Jones's fleet sailed to the west of Ireland, around the top of Scotland, and back down into the North Sea. It was sailing southward, along the east coast of England, when it sighted the British Baltic fleet. The fleet carried supplies for the Navy and was convoyed by two warships: the 20-gun sloop-of-war *Countess of Scarborough*, under Captain Piercy, and the 50-gun *Serapis*, under Captain Pearson.

The British warships positioned themselves between Jones's fleet and the British merchant ships, which quickly escaped back up the coast. By 6 p.m. on September 23, the *Serapis* and the *Bonhomme Richard* were within firing range.

CONVERSION OF
BONHOMME RICHARD

John Paul Jones, the American commander, wanted a fast ship with a powerful battery of guns, large enough to carry a substantial crew and boarding troops. The only ship available was the *Duc de Duras*, a French East Indiaman built in 1766 that had already made four trips to the East and so was near the end of its life.

Jones renamed it the *Bonhomme Richard* and converted it to a gun-carrying warship. Fitting it out took six months and included cutting ports on the gun deck to house six extra 18-pounder cannons, although these newly cut ports were dangerously close to the waterline.

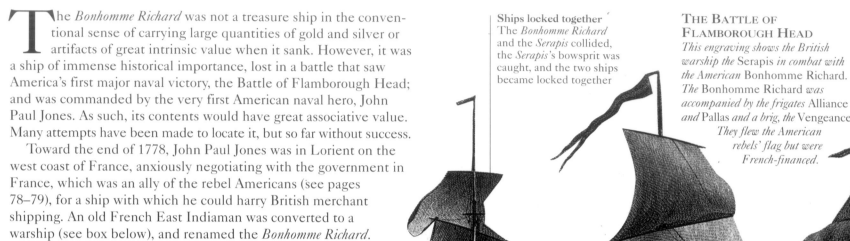

Ships locked together
The *Bonhomme Richard* and the *Serapis* collided, the *Serapis*'s bowsprit was caught, and the two ships became locked together

THE BATTLE OF FLAMBOROUGH HEAD
This engraving shows the British warship the Serapis *in combat with the American* Bonhomme Richard. *The* Bonhomme Richard *was accompanied by the frigates* Alliance *and* Pallas *and a brig, the* Vengeance. *They flew the American rebels' flag but were French-financed.*

FACTS AND
FEATURES

Length	145 feet (44 meters)
Capacity	900 tons
Route	France to England

The *Serapis* had the advantage with regard to gun power, and this superiority increased when some of the 18-pounder cannons that Jones had had installed on the *Bonhomme Richard*'s gun deck exploded when fired, causing considerable carnage. After this, Jones gave orders for them not to be used.

If the *Serapis* had kept its distance from the *Bonhomme Richard* it would most probably have emerged as the victor, being faster, better armed, and better constructed, but the two ships became locked together, three miles (five kilometers) southeast of Flamborough Head, and an extremely bloody battle took place, with considerable loss of life on both sides. Jones's marksmen dominated the on-deck fighting, but the *Serapis*'s cannons continued to blast holes in the hull of the *Bonhomme Richard* below the waterline so that the holds steadily filled with water. Toward dusk, one of Jones's men lobbed a grenade through a hatch in the *Serapis*, causing an explosion in the gunpowder store, and killing many of the *Serapis*'s crew. Captain Pearson surrendered shortly afterward, just before the *Serapis*'s mainmast collapsed. The battle ended at about 10:30 that night but, even though the *Bonhomme Richard* was severely hit, Jones did not abandon it. His carpenters began to patch the leaks, as well as repair the captured *Serapis*.

By the evening of the next day, it was clear that the *Bonhomme Richard* was beyond repair and would have to be abandoned. On the second night, all those on board were transferred to other ships. The last man left at 10 a.m. on September 25; half an hour later the warship had sunk.

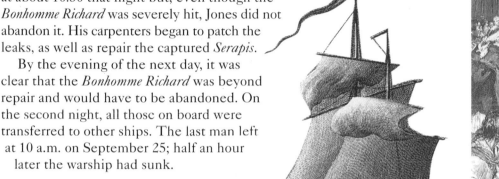

JOHN PAUL JONES
Commander of the Bonhomme
Richard, *Jones was a legend
in America for his victories.*

SALVAGE ATTEMPTS

In 1975, the Atlantic Charter Maritime Archaeological Foundation was formed in order to locate, excavate, and restore the remains of the *Bonhomme Richard*. In September 1976, in conjunction with Decca Recorder and the National Ocean Industries Association of Washington DC, a sophisticated search was carried out. A side-scan sonar survey found a wreck that could have been the *Bonhomme Richard* in 180 feet (55 meters) of water. It was approximately the right length and breadth, and was in roughly the same position from which a local fisherman had retrieved an iron gun dated 1775. But, to date, nothing more definite seems to have been accomplished.

SURRENDER OF SERAPIS
*Depicted in this engraving
is the surrender of Captain
Pearson on the deck of the
Franco–American warship,
the* Bonhomme Richard.
*Captain Pearson had been
the commander of the British
ship* Serapis, *which lost at
the Battle of Flamborough
Head, in September 1779.*

The Alliance
An American 36-gun frigate commanded by Captain Landais, who had refused to acknowledge Jones's command and take his orders

THE
ORIENT

Anchored frigate
Other ships besides the
main battle fleet sheltered
in the Bay of Naples

Ships of the line
The British fleet
consisted of
thirteen 74-gun
warships and
one 50-gun ship

Sixth-rate frigate
Lightly armed with
28 guns, so this was
used for special
missions rather than
in the main battle

BRITISH FLEET AT NAPLES
This painting by Giacomo Guardi shows Nelson's fleet on June 17, 1798 waiting at the Bay of Naples, Italy, for news of Napoleon's fleet. The British ambassador to the court of Naples, Sir William Hamilton, told Nelson the French fleet was off Sardinia, and began a naval hunt throughout the Mediterranean.

Early in 1798, after Napoleon's victories in Italy, the British heard that a new French fleet was being fitted out in Toulon, France, together with several troop ships (transports). The British did not know, however, where this new fleet was going. In London, the favored theories were either that Napoleon was planning a campaign through Spain toward Portugal, or that the fleet was to pass through the Strait of Gibraltar and launch an invasion of Ireland.

British Fleet

On May 2, 1798, Rear Admiral Horatio Nelson was detached from the Earl of St. Vincent's fleet, stationed off Cadiz, Spain. He sailed in the *Vanguard*, accompanied by two other ships of the line (see pages 78–79), two frigates, and a sloop. His aim was to discover the movements and intentions of the French fleet.

On June 7, Nelson's small spy fleet was reinforced by a detachment from the fleet off Cadiz, which had itself been reinforced by a fleet from England. Nelson's fleet now comprised thirteen 74-gun ships and one 50-gun ship. He was instructed to "take, sink, burn, or destroy" the French fleet, and there began one of the great naval hunts of all time.

French Fleet

Napoleon's fleet consisted of 72 warships, including gunships and frigates, and some 200 to 400 transports carrying more than 36,000 soldiers. The flagship of the fleet was the 118-gun *Orient*, in which Napoleon sailed. The fleet left Toulon and sailed via Sicily towards Malta where, on June 9, it joined up with more transports that had been sent from Civitavecchia, Italy.

Napoleon's fleet invaded Malta with little resistance from the Maltese. Some valuable spoils were taken, including 30,000 muskets, and treasure including the silver plate from the Church of St. John, valued in total at about three million French francs. Later reports of questionable authenticity also mentioned the disappearance of 12 enormous solid silver statues of the apostles, and the silver gates of the Valletta Cathedral in Malta.

British Hunt for the French

On June 17, the British entered the Bay of Naples, Italy, and were informed by the British ambassador that the French had been seen off the island of Sardinia, heading southward, probably toward Malta. Nelson's fleet sailed off in this direction, but on June 20, at Messina, Sicily, Nelson learned that the French had already seized Malta. Then, on June 22, 12 leagues (36 miles/19 km) southeast of Cape Passero, Sicily, Nelson's fleet was informed by a passing merchant ship that the French had left Malta four days before and were heading toward the port of Alexandria in Egypt. The British arrived at Alexandria on June 28, but there were no French ships in the area so they headed northward and arrived at Syracuse, Italy, on July 19 to obtain some fresh supplies.

Napoleon had indeed left Malta when the intercepted merchant ship stated, and was heading toward Alexandria. It took the French considerably longer than the British to reach Egypt, however, and Napoleon's fleet arrived in Alexandria on July 1, two days after Nelson's British fleet had left. The French troops disembarked from the transports and Alexandria was taken.

It was very difficult for large ships to enter the harbor at Alexandria, so Napoleon ordered Vice Admiral Brueys, captain of the *Orient*, to anchor all 13 ships of the line and four frigates in the Bay of Abu Qîr (Aboukir), about 20 miles (32 kilometers) east-northeast of Alexandria. Napoleon and his army then marched across the Egyptian desert to launch an assault upon Cairo.

ORIENT'S NAME

The flagship of the French fleet, in which Napoleon sailed, was the 118-gun *Orient*, built in 1790 as the *Dauphin Royal*. In 1792, its name had been changed to the *Sans Culotte* but, for his new campaign, Napoleon renamed it the *Orient*. If the British had realized it, this name gave a clear clue to Napoleon's real intentions – which were to conquer the East and seize power over India from the British.

The British fleet left Syracuse on July 25. Knowing that Napoleon's fleet was still in the eastern Mediterranean, Nelson sailed for Morea, Greece, and was informed en route that the French fleet had been sighted four weeks earlier off the coast of Candia, Crete, sailing southeast toward Alexandria. The British fleet set out once more for Alexandria.

The Battle of the Nile

Toward evening on August 1, Nelson finally tracked down Brueys's fleet, which was in line formation and anchored in the shallow waters of the Bay of Abu Qîr, with a long and treacherous sandbank at its immediate rear. Brueys thought that Nelson would not risk making an attack until the following day because of the considerable dangers of trying to navigate the bay in the dark. However, this kind of situation, which called for expert seamanship and unconventional tactics, was exactly what Nelson excelled at and most relished. His ships immediately went in on both sides of the anchored French fleet but

THE DESTRUCTION OF THE ORIENT AT THE BATTLE OF THE NILE, AUGUST 1, 1798
This oil painting by George Arnauld shows the explosion of Napoleon's flagship, the Orient, *during the Battle of the Nile. Under attack from the British, the* Orient *caught fire; this spread to the magazine, where gunpowder was stored, and the ship blew up, resulting in huge loss of life.*

stopped short halfway down the line, which ensured that half the French ships could not join the action because they were to leeward. The French fleet had the greater firepower: one 118-gun ship, three 80-gun ships, nine 74-gun ships, and four frigates, against thirteen British 74-gun ships and one 50-gun ship. However, Nelson's surprise attack gave the British the tactical advantage. The British lost no ships but the French fleet suffered very heavy losses – all but two of its ships were either captured or wrecked, including the *Orient*, which caught fire and blew up during the battle. Vice Admiral Brueys died from wounds on the *Orient*'s quarterdeck. He gallantly insisted on being carried there rather than being taken below for treatment.

Salvage Attempts

Since its loss, the *Orient* has been the target of many treasure hunters. The first recorded attempt at salvage was in 1814, but the divers were unable to relocate the wreck's remains. Failure has consistently dogged the project

ever since. In the 1930s, for instance, Egypt offered the salvage rights for auction. The French government was outraged. It claimed that the *Orient* wreck belonged to the French state and that nothing could be salvaged without French permission. The issue was a legal quagmire and the Second World War broke out before it was resolved.

In the 1950s, King Farouk of Egypt organized a new salvage attempt, but the results do not appear to have been significant and it is unclear whether any salvage ever took place. It is also not certain that the treasures seized in Malta were actually on the *Orient* when it blew up. Some of them had certainly been shipped back to France on the frigate, *Sensible*, which was captured en route by the British.

NELSON'S REWARD

The British victory over the French in 1798, which prevented Napoleon from conquering the East, brought Nelson a great variety of honors, and presents from grateful foreign potentates. He was made Baron Nelson of the Nile and was awarded annual pensions by both the English and Irish parliaments. He was also given $15,000 by the English East India Company.

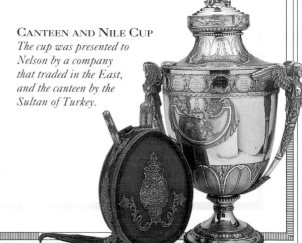

CANTEEN AND NILE CUP
The cup was presented to Nelson by a company that traded in the East, and the canteen by the Sultan of Turkey.

THE GREAT COLLECTORS

The eighteenth century is generally regarded as the period that witnessed the triumph of reason. This was the age of Diderot, the great French encyclopedist and philosopher, and Voltaire, the French sage. It did not seem to matter that wars were as bloody as ever, disease just as virulent, and poverty just as ubiquitous. There was a new and widely dispersed sense of confidence among cultured circles, and a belief that rational thought would eventually triumph over all these ugly manifestations of disorder.

One way in which this concern with the so-called civilized values revealed itself was the growth of interest in collecting antiquities and art as appropriate activities for the cultured person. In the second half of the eighteenth century this became something of a mania in aristocratic circles; it is not a coincidence that the British Museum in London was founded in 1753. Particular interest was expressed in the sculptures and buildings of the classical age, as well as the sites of ancient Egypt.

The Royal Collections

Royal courts had always attracted poets, musicians, and painters, but the emphasis had previously been placed upon contemporary forms of entertainment and the reflection of the glory of the present monarch rather than focusing upon the achievements of the past. Now, however, European rulers vied with each other to build up vast collections of works of art from previous historical periods. Catherine the Great, Empress of Russia, achieved her collection by large and diverse purchases. The methods of Napoleon, Emperor of France, were more direct. He shipped the treasures of the countries he conquered to the Musée du Louvre in Paris.

Advances in Science

Another area where the collecting mania expressed itself was in the field of science. Since the sixteenth century, explorers had brought back drawings and samples of products from the places they visited, but the focus of interest had been the relevance of these items for future trade. In the later eighteenth century, the emphasis shifted to the systematic classification of different species, plants, and minerals. Captain James Cook's great voyages of exploration between 1768 and 1779 were, of course, an expression of English empire-building but, significantly, he took with him Joseph Banks, a wealthy amateur botanist who painstakingly recorded the many new species of flora and fauna they encountered. In the 1830s Charles Darwin made similar expeditions, and later used the information he had gathered as the basis for his theory of evolution.

VROUW MARIA ④
In 1771 this small Dutch snow sank in the Baltic Sea, en route from Amsterdam to St. Petersburg. Its cargo of treasures belonging to Catherine the Great was also lost. (See pages 86–87.)

GENERAL BARKER ②
This large East Indiaman was carrying a collection of Oriental curiosities belonging to the returning governor of Madras, India, along with chests of money and plate, when it was wrecked on the Dutch coast in 1781.

ST. PETERSBURG
The Russian winter palace in St. Petersburg housed Catherine the Great's art collection, assembled from all over Europe.

MENTOR ⑤
In 1802 Lord Elgin chartered this brig to transport Greek marbles and statues to England, but the ship struck a rock outside the Greek harbor of Kithira, and the cargo went down with the ship. (See pages 88–89.)

HMS COLOSSUS ①
This 74-gun English naval storeship was driven onto a reef off the Isles of Scilly en route from Naples to London via Lisbon in 1798. It was carrying war booty seized from the French at Aboukir, Egypt, and a collection of ancient Greek vases. It was salvaged in 1974.

LISBON
During the eighteenth century English warships regularly carried specie and bullion between Lisbon and London, on behalf of private merchants. This was a profitable source of income for the British Royal Navy.

ARLES WRECK ③
This ship sank in the Rhône River, France, in 1805 while carrying Napoleon's collection of Roman statues and relics to the museums of Paris. A salvage attempt in 1933 was unsuccessful.

COMMEMORATIVE MEDAL
This medal was made to commemorate Napoleon's march through the Egyptian desert to the pyramids in 1798. European fascination with ancient Egypt resulted in the temples and sites being looted, often by amateur archaeologists who then shipped their spoils home.

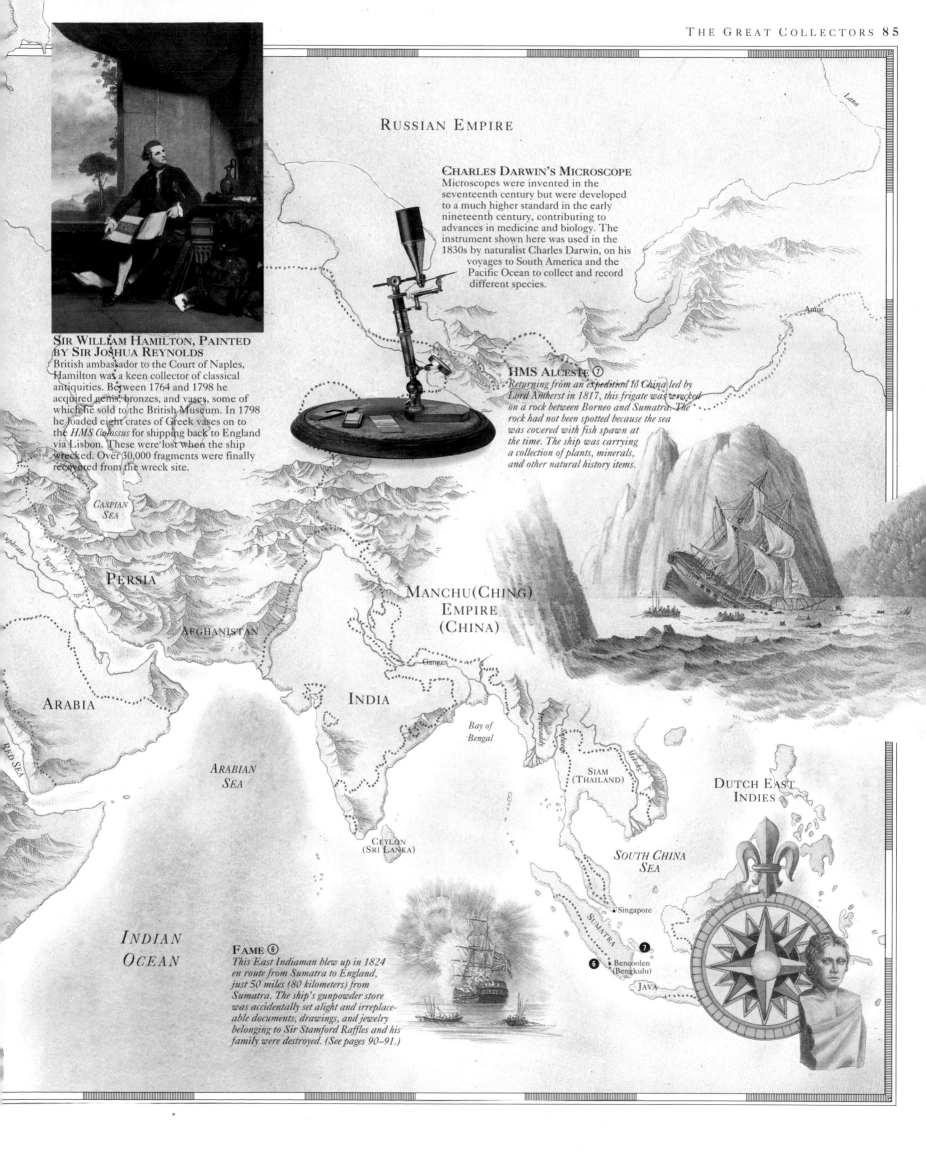

RUSSIAN EMPIRE

SIR WILLIAM HAMILTON, PAINTED BY SIR JOSHUA REYNOLDS

British ambassador to the Court of Naples, Hamilton was a keen collector of classical antiquities. Between 1764 and 1798 he acquired gems, bronzes, and vases, some of which he sold to the British Museum. In 1798 he loaded eight crates of Greek vases on to the *HMS Colossus* for shipping back to England via Lisbon. These were lost when the ship wrecked. Over 30,000 fragments were finally recovered from the wreck site.

CHARLES DARWIN'S MICROSCOPE

Microscopes were invented in the seventeenth century but were developed to a much higher standard in the early nineteenth century, contributing to advances in medicine and biology. The instrument shown here was used in the 1830s by naturalist Charles Darwin, on his voyages to South America and the Pacific Ocean to collect and record different species.

HMS ALCESTE ⑦

Returning from an expedition to China led by Lord Amherst in 1817, this frigate was wrecked on a rock between Borneo and Sumatra. The rock had not been spotted because the sea was covered with fish spawn at the time. The ship was carrying a collection of plants, minerals, and other natural history items.

CASPIAN SEA

PERSIA

AFGHANISTAN

MANCHU(CHING) EMPIRE (CHINA)

Ganges

ARABIA

INDIA

Bay of Bengal

ARABIAN SEA

SIAM (THAILAND)

DUTCH EAST INDIES

CEYLON (SRI LANKA)

SOUTH CHINA SEA

RED SEA

Singapore

SUMATRA

INDIAN OCEAN

FAME ⑥

This East Indiaman blew up in 1824 en route from Sumatra to England, just 50 miles (80 kilometers) from Sumatra. The ship's gunpowder store was accidentally set alight and irreplaceable documents, drawings, and jewelry belonging to Sir Stamford Raffles and his family were destroyed. (See pages 90–91.)

⑦

⑥ Bencoolen (Bengkulu)

JAVA

THE
VROUW MARIA

On July 31, 1771, Catherine the Great, Empress of Russia, bought through her agents in the Netherlands several magnificent works of art from a collection in Amsterdam (see box opposite). Some of these were transported to her palace in St. Petersburg, Russia, by land but most were embarked on board a fairly small two-masted Dutch snow, the *Vrouw Maria*. Sadly for all those involved, and for future art connoisseurs, the *Vrouw Maria* sank in the Baltic Sea, with all its treasures still in the hold.

The master of the *Vrouw Maria* was a Dutchman called Reinhold Lorentz, and most of the crew were also Dutch. On August 12, they began loading the cargo in the port in Amsterdam and, after waiting for the right winds, they set sail on September 5. On the 18th they passed Skagen, the northern tip of Denmark, and on the 23rd they anchored at Helsingør (Elsinore) beneath the Castle of Kronborg. The captain went ashore here to pay the Sound Toll dues – these were taxes levied by Denmark on the cargoes of all ships passing in and out of the Baltic Sea. After negotiating the narrow Sound the ship turned northward again and headed up the Baltic Sea. All the while, the days were becoming increasingly darker and shorter.

On October 3, at 8:30 p.m. when the crew were at prayers, the *Vrouw Maria* ran onto rocks. The ship was badly damaged and the rudder was lost. With some difficulty the crew of the *Vrouw Maria* anchored in 13 fathoms of water, and manned the pumps. At dawn, they decided to abandon ship. They loaded two small boats with food and bedding, and managed to reach another rock nearby that was safer.

CATHERINE THE GREAT
Some acquisitions of Catherine, a keen collector of works of art, were shipped on the Vrouw Maria *to her palace in Russia.*

FULLY RIGGED SNOW IN OPEN SEA
Snows are two-masted European merchant vessels, in use between the sixteenth and nineteenth centuries. In addition to its large square sails on both masts, a snow carried a small trysail mast behind the mainmast. The largest snows would be up to 1,000 tons, but the Vrouw Maria *was reputedly much smaller and similar to the one illustrated here.*

National flag
Shows the Dutch ownership of this vessel

U-shaped hull
To maximize the cargo-carrying capacity

FACTS AND FEATURES

Burden	Around 150 tons
Cargo	Valuable art treasures
Route	Amsterdam to St. Petersburg

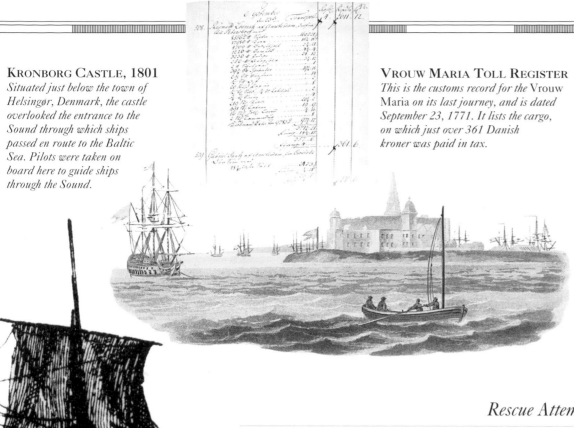

KRONBORG CASTLE, 1801
Situated just below the town of Helsingør, Denmark, the castle overlooked the entrance to the Sound through which ships passed en route to the Baltic Sea. Pilots were taken on board here to guide ships through the Sound.

VROUW MARIA TOLL REGISTER
This is the customs record for the Vrouw Maria *on its last journey, and is dated September 23, 1771. It lists the cargo, on which just over 361 Danish kroner was paid in tax.*

ART TREASURES
On July 31, 1771, Catherine the Great, the Empress of Russia, purchased a number of works of art from the Braamcamp collection. Braamcamp was a successful businessman in the wine and lumber trades, and had built up one of the most admired art collections in Europe. After his death the collection was sold. Catherine bought sculptures, porcelain, glass, and gold and silver ornaments. Among the paintings also acquired by Catherine were works by Coedyk, Metsu, Dou, Wouverman, and Ostade. These were intended to enhance the fabulous collection already assembled in the Winter Palace in St. Petersburg, Russia. Part of the Braamcamp purchase was sent from Amsterdam to St. Petersburg by land, but the bulk was embarked upon the *Vrouw Maria* and so was lost when the ship wrecked on rocks.

Rescue Attempts

In the evening the crew hailed a passing boat and its captain promised to come back with help. The wind calmed down and the crew returned to the *Vrouw Maria* and salvaged 10 barrels and a chest. Next day, the promised help arrived and everyone went back to the *Vrouw Maria*. They pumped all day but the water level went down only fractionally, and they sent for further help. By October 7, 34 men were involved in the rescue attempt but with no success. The pumps were clogged with coffee beans and the water was swilling with sugar, both of which had formed part of the cargo. On the morning of the 9th, the ship disappeared beneath the sea, which ended all hope of more salvage. The Russian Court heard about the disaster and high-level diplomats were rapidly engaged to find out what could be done. Such diplomatic activity was extremely unusual for the wreck of a small Dutch snow that had involved no loss of life. It transpired that not only had Catherine the Great lost valuable goods on the *Vrouw Maria*, but so also had the Russian Foreign Minister, Count Panin, and some other members of the Russian aristocracy.

Early the following year a fisherman thought he had found the wreck of the *Vrouw Maria* but it turned out to be an empty promise. To date, that is the last that has been heard of both ship and cargo.

COPY BY LAQUI OF A SCENE BY GERARD DOU
The original painting was on its way to Catherine the Great's palace, but was lost when the Vrouw Maria *sank.*

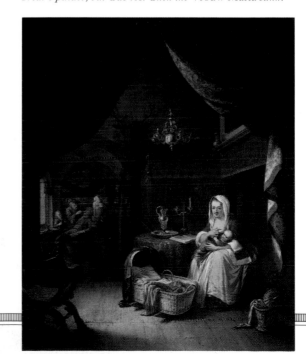

"Snout-shaped" bow
The term snow derives from the Dutch word *snaauw*, meaning snout, and refers to the shape of the bows

THE MENTOR

FULLY RIGGED BRIG
A brig is a two-masted ship that is square-rigged on the foremast and mainmast. Brigs were often used for short voyages or coastal journeys. Lord Elgin originally bought his brig, the Mentor, for a cruise around the Greek islands but diverted it to Piraeus to take the sculptures that had accumulated there to England.

Toward the end of the eighteenth century, wealthy European aristocrats took an increasing interest in Roman and Greek art. Architecture and interior design reflected this fashion. When Lord Elgin was discussing the plans for his new mansion at Broom Hall, Fifeshire, in Scotland, his architect suggested that they base the building upon drawings and casts of the ancient remains at Athens, Greece. Elgin was enthusiastic, and went even further, bringing back a large part of the Parthenon itself.

In 1799, Elgin's representative in Athens, Lord Hunt, obtained a grant, or firman, allowing him to excavate, erect scaffolding, and even to take away stone sculptures. Before very long Elgin was employing 300 to 400 men to dismantle and crate up the treasures of Athens. In Elgin's defense, it has to be said that the sculptures were in a deplorable state of neglect. For hundreds of years local people had systematically broken them up and burned them in order to produce lime. Also, Elgin was not the first to remove parts of the original temples, but no one had before embarked on the task on quite such a scale and in such a systematic manner.

Elgin was shortly faced with a shipping problem. The crates piled up at the Greek port of Piraeus faster than they could be transported to England. Two ships from the English Navy, *HMS La Diane* and *HMS Mutine*, were pressed into service. Elgin also had his own brig, called the *Mentor*, and chartered another brig, the *Dorinda*.

The *Mentor* was loaded with 17 cases, which included 14 pieces from the Parthenon Frieze, four pieces from the Frieze of the Temple of Athena Nike, and other items such as an ancient throne. The *Mentor* left Piraeus on September 16, 1802. Two days later, during a storm, it struck a rock at the entrance to the harbor of the nearby island of Kithira (Cerigo) and sank. The crew reached shore, but the valuable cargo went down with the ship to the seabed.

Studding sails
These extra sails were set in light winds to give more power

Figurehead
Believed to give symbolic protection to ships

CLASSICAL GALLERY
Fashionable aristocrats and collectors decorated their houses with choice Roman and Greek statues and urns. This painting by Zoffany shows a room in a London house filled with a private collection of classical statues and friezes.

Hull
Divers smashed the *Mentor*'s hull underwater to find the treasure

FACTS AND FEATURES

Treasure	Greek antiquities
Depth of site	72 feet (22 meters)
Route	Greece to England

Horizontal yards
These supported the square sails, and were able to move around the mast to make the best use of the wind

Cargo hold
Elgin had asked for the hatches leading to the cargo hold to be enlarged to load sculptures, but this was ignored

Salvage Operations

Salvage attempts began immediately and, with the aid of local sponge divers, four of the 17 cases were recovered. Elgin issued characteristically lordly instructions that any English Navy ship in the area should go to Kithira immediately to help with the salvage. He also made an agreement with a Greek shipowner, Basilio Menachini, promising him that he would be made British Vice-Consul at La Spezia, Italy, in return for providing ships and equipment to help in the emergency. *HMS La Victorieuse* arrived at Kithira first, and waited for Menachini's ships. After two weeks the crew became impatient and decided not to wait any longer before trying to raise the entire hull from the bottom of the sea by themselves. The predictable happened. The cables snapped when the *Mentor* was halfway up and it crashed back to the seabed. *La Victorieuse* abandoned the salvage project and continued on Navy business.

Within hours of *La Victorieuse*'s departure, Menachini's ships arrived at Kithira. These ships were also incapable of raising the *Mentor* by themselves. Winter storms were beginning, and the salvage project was therefore abandoned until the following year.

In the summer of 1803, sponge divers cut open the *Mentor*'s hull on the seabed. This made it easier to reach the cargo, and five more cases were recovered. In 1804 the balance of the treasure was brought up and, at Elgin's request, Admiral Nelson sent a ship to Kithira to bring the items back to England. The salvage project cost Elgin £5,000 sterling.

FRIEZE FROM THE MENTOR
Four pieces from the Temple of Athena Nike, one of the monuments on the Acropolis overlooking Athens, sank with the Mentor. *This salvaged section of the frieze shows clear signs of wear by seawater.*

CONTROVERSIAL ACQUISITION

The dismantling of the Parthenon by the English continued after the loss of the *Mentor* until 1807, when the French took control of Athens. Eighty crates of marbles were captured by the French, but the English Navy still dominated the Mediterranean so they were unable to ship their spoils back to France. Eventually, England regained power and the marbles reached London in 1812. Ever since, Greece and England have argued over their ownership.

LORD ELGIN
Famous for taking vast quantities of antiquities from Greece. He sold some to the British Museum in 1816.

THE
FAME

At the beginning of the year 1824, Sir Thomas Stamford Raffles, the British Resident in Bengkulu (Bencoolen), Sumatra, was anxiously awaiting the arrival of the *Fame*. This was the East Indiaman (see pages 70–71) upon which he had booked passage for himself and his second wife, Sophia, to return to England. Raffles's dynamic administration on behalf of the Court of Directors of the English East India Company had come to a close. By 1824, Raffles was exhausted, partly from his administrative burdens and partly from family loss – four of his five children by Sophia had died during his residency. Raffles had ambitions to farm and perhaps to enter Parliament on his return.

Delays in Departure

The arrival of the *Fame* was held up, and Raffles and Sophia could barely conceal their impatience at this delay to their departure:

You can hardly imagine to yourself the serious disappointment to all our hopes and plans which this occasions. We begin to think we are doomed to end our days here, and there is something like a spell upon our movements.

While they waited for the *Fame* to arrive, a ship called the *Borneo* arrived at Bengkulu to load a cargo of pepper to take to England. Raffles was just in the process of chartering this ship for his own return, even though it was far too small and inconvenient for the enormous quantity of possessions he was taking with him, when the *Fame* at last appeared over the horizon, and he reverted to his original plan.

Cargo Carried

Raffles loaded 122 packing cases onto the *Fame*. These contained his collection of documents, books (many of them extremely rare or in manuscript form), maps, drawings, and other miscellaneous objects of scientific curiosity. They were stowed in the ship's hold, taking up about a third of the total cargo space. Included was Raffles's map of Sumatra, of which he was particularly proud, a 1,000-page history of Borneo, and similar-sized histories of Celebes and the Moluccas (Spice Islands).

In addition, there were several cases that Raffles wished to keep in his cabin beside him so he could consult them more easily during the voyage. As if this were not enough, there was:

... scarce an unknown animal, bird, beast, or fish, or an interesting species of plant, which we had not on board: a living tapir, a new species of tiger, splendid pheasants, etc., domesticated for the voyage; we were, in short, in this respect, a perfect Noah's ark.

LOSS OF TREASURE

Raffles lost a fortune in the flames of the *Fame*. He estimated his personal financial setback from the fire at between £20,000 and £30,000 sterling. This sum included only the known cost value of the items he had lost, and so would not have allowed for gifts made to him. None of this property had been insured. Yet Raffles was not of a temperament to be unduly downcast by setback. The morning after the disaster, he recommenced work on his map of Sumatra, set his draftsmen to making new drawings of natural history specimens, and sent his servants to collect animals to replace those that were lost in the fire.

In addition to his own possessions, Raffles also embarked a large number of personal presents that he had received during the years of his governorship, such as a specially inscribed silver plate service from the people of Java; a collection of diamonds that had been presented to him by the British captors of Jakarta (Batavia); and a diamond ring given to him by Charlotte, Queen of Great Britain. Raffles's wife, Sophia, also carried a valuable collection of personal jewelry with her.

Fire Breaks Out

The *Fame* sailed at dawn on February 2, with 41 crew and passengers on board. Raffles described the day as one of the happiest of his life. However, this happiness was to be short-lived. In a letter written two days after the fire, Raffles graphically described the calamity.

Sophia had just gone to bed, and I had thrown off half my clothes, when a cry of fire, fire! roused us from our calm content, and in five minutes the whole ship was in flames! I ran to examine whence the flames principally issued, and found that the fire had its origin immediately under our cabin. Down with the boats. Where is Sophia? – Here. A rope to the side. Lower Lady Raffles. Give her to me, says one; I'll take her, says the Captain. Throw the gunpowder overboard. It cannot be got at; it is in the magazine close to the fire. Stand clear of the powder. Scuttle the water casks. Water! Water!

The fire had apparently begun in the store room and had been caused by a steward carelessly drawing off brandy from a cask by

JAVA, 1812
Government House, Bogor, painted after the British occupied Java. This sketch was an early addition to Raffles's collection, and was not part of the consignment for the Fame. Raffles ruled Java from 1811 to 1816.

LOSS OF THE FAME
*Ten minutes after the ship caught fire, all the passengers
and crew had escaped in two open boats. Just ten minutes
later the* Fame *was a mass of flames.*

LADY SOPHIA RAFFLES
*Replica of a miniature portrait that was
lost when the* Fame *was
burned in 1824.*

the light of a naked candle. The alarm was
given at 8:20 p.m., and within 20 minutes the
Fame was on fire from end to end. It burned
steadily until midnight, when the gunpowder
store caught fire "... and sent up one of the
most splendid and brilliant flames that ever
was seen, illuminating the horizon in every
direction, to an extent of not less than fifty
miles [80 kilometers]."

All the passengers and crew left the *Fame*
and transferred safely into two small boats.
Even a man called Johnson who was ill in his
cot was saved, although the small boats had
to go back for him when they heard his cries.
They were about 50 miles (80 kilometers)
southwest of Bengkulu, and had no supplies
of food or water, and no covering to shelter
them from the sun. Sophia was wearing only
a wrapper and was without stockings or

shoes. The boat carrying Raffles and Sophia
had a missing plug and a member of the crew
had to keep his finger in the hole. Even so,
the boat needed to be bailed out continually.

Land Reached

They set off rowing in a north-northeasterly
direction, using the captain's compass and
calculating for the strong currents that would
sweep them southward. At dawn, they could
see the Sumatran coast and they reached land
that morning. Shortly afterward, rescue boats
came along the coast from Bengkulu to pick
them up. They arrived at Bengkulu in the
afternoon, by which time Sophia was said to
have "fallen into a succession of fainting fits."

Final Return Voyage

Raffles found another ship, the *Wellington*, to
charter for their journey to England but, just
as they were about to embark, the captain
went mad and so once again they were
delayed. Eventually, on April 10, they sailed
in the *Mariner*, a ship on its way from Botany
Bay, Australia, to England. They arrived on
August 22, after an uneventful journey.

RAFFLES

Sir Thomas Stamford Raffles (1781–1826)
played an important role in the establishment
of British power in the East at the beginning
of the nineteenth century. He was the
Lieutenant-Governor of Java between 1811
and 1816, and Resident of Bengkulu, southwest Sumatra, from 1818 to 1824. During
this time, he also laid the foundations for the
British colony of Singapore (see page 44).

SIR THOMAS STAMFORD RAFFLES, 1817

THE RUSH FOR GOLD

In January 1848 gold was found at Sutter's Mill, California, and within a few months the first of the great nineteenth-century gold rushes had begun. California's population grew from 26,000 to 115,000 in the space of a year. A lucky prospector could make $16,000 in a week although it was more usual to make $25. So great was the attraction that shopkeepers, teachers, bakers, carpenters, manual laborers, and, in some cases, entire ships' crews deserted their occupations to try their luck. It rapidly became very difficult to find anyone to perform the usual simple tasks: everyone in California had gone prospecting.

Similar finds in Australia, New Zealand, South Africa, Mexico, and Alaska led to further gold rushes throughout the century. Gold finds coincided with a massive population explosion among emigrant nations and so there was a large and willing workforce prepared to risk everything and set off on the gold trail. This was the heyday of liberal individualism, and the concept of the lone prospector venturing into the mountains to make his fortune was encouraged by the public and the state authorities alike.

Diverse Ships Pressed Into Service

With the development of the goldfields, the demand for shipping increased dramatically and many ships that transported hopeful emigrants were unseaworthy or overcrowded, which led to several tragedies. Various types of ship were used to transport raw gold. Sailing clippers left San Francisco for Canton (Guangzhou) in China to trade gold for tea, and iron steamships journeyed from Australia to Britain. The ship that is most associated with transporting gold in this era is the American-built, wooden sidewheel paddlesteamer. (See Mail Ships and Liners, pages 100–101.)

THE LAST OF ENGLAND, 1852–1855, BY FORD MADOX BROWN
This painting was originally called *The Emigrants* and was inspired by the emigration of Pre-Raphaelite sculptor Thomas Woolner, who journeyed to Australia to join the gold diggings. The painting depicts Madox Brown and his wife Emma on a boat that was sailing from England.

ROYAL CHARTER ①
This British screw-propelled iron steamship en route from Australia to England, wrecked in 1859 on rocks off the Welsh coast hours from its destination. (See pages 98–99.)

DIAMONDS AND GOLD
In 1868 diamonds were found at Cape Colony, and within a year a single stone worth $37,500 had been discovered at Kimberley. The Rand goldfields were discovered around 1886, and were worked by industrial companies rather than individuals.

QUEEN OF THE THAMES ②
This ship sank in 1871 en route from Melbourne to London having mistaken a bush fire for a lighthouse. It was carrying gold dust worth $10,000.

GOLD MINERS TREK INLAND
Digging for gold was hard work because the miners had to carry every piece of equipment with them into inhospitable terrain. Despite this, many miners made the trek, lured by the potentially high profits for little outlay.

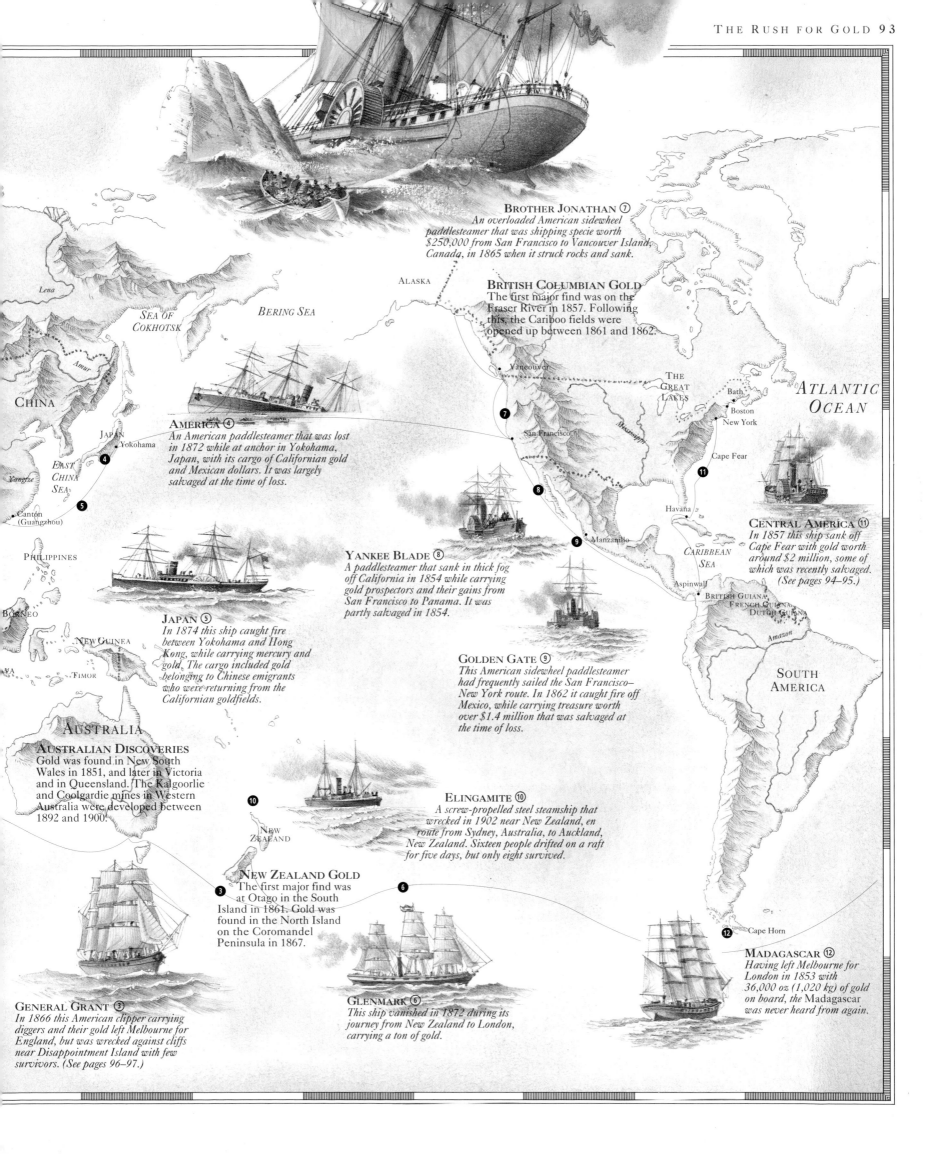

BROTHER JONATHAN ⑦
An overloaded American sidewheel paddlesteamer that was shipping specie worth $250,000 from San Francisco to Vancouver Island, Canada, in 1865 when it struck rocks and sank.

BRITISH COLUMBIAN GOLD
The first major find was on the Fraser River in 1857. Following this, the Cariboo fields were opened up between 1861 and 1862.

AMERICA ④
An American paddlesteamer that was lost in 1872 while at anchor in Yokohama, Japan, with its cargo of Californian gold and Mexican dollars. It was largely salvaged at the time of loss.

YANKEE BLADE ⑧
A paddlesteamer that sank in thick fog off California in 1854 while carrying gold prospectors and their gains from San Francisco to Panama. It was partly salvaged in 1854.

JAPAN ⑤
In 1874 this ship caught fire between Yokohama and Hong Kong, while carrying mercury and gold. The cargo included gold belonging to Chinese emigrants who were returning from the Californian goldfields.

GOLDEN GATE ⑨
This American sidewheel paddlesteamer had frequently sailed the San Francisco–New York route. In 1862 it caught fire off Mexico, while carrying treasure worth over $1.4 million that was salvaged at the time of loss.

CENTRAL AMERICA ⑪
In 1857 this ship sank off Cape Fear with gold worth around $2 million, some of which was recently salvaged. (See pages 94–95.)

AUSTRALIA

AUSTRALIAN DISCOVERIES
Gold was found in New South Wales in 1851, and later in Victoria and in Queensland. The Kalgoorlie and Coolgardie mines in Western Australia were developed between 1892 and 1900.

ELINGAMITE ⑩
A screw-propelled steel steamship that wrecked in 1902 near New Zealand, en route from Sydney, Australia, to Auckland, New Zealand. Sixteen people drifted on a raft for five days, but only eight survived.

NEW ZEALAND GOLD
The first major find was at Otago in the South Island in 1861. Gold was found in the North Island on the Coromandel Peninsula in 1867.

GENERAL GRANT ③
In 1866 this American clipper carrying diggers and their gold left Melbourne for England, but was wrecked against cliffs near Disappointment Island with few survivors. (See pages 96–97.)

GLENMARK ⑥
This ship vanished in 1872 during its journey from New Zealand to London, carrying a ton of gold.

MADAGASCAR ⑫
Having left Melbourne for London in 1853 with 36,000 oz (1,020 kg) of gold on board, the Madagascar was never heard from again.

THE CENTRAL AMERICA

In August 1857, at Aspinwall on the Caribbean side of Panama, the *Central America* loaded a substantial consignment of gold bars and coins worth $1,219,179, the largest part of which belonged to the Wells Fargo American Exchange Bank. This had been transported from the gold fields near San Francisco to Aspinwall by another ship, the *John L. Stephens*, and was transferred onto the *Central America* for the final part of its journey to New York. In addition, the ship carried a large number of gold miners who were returning from California.

The *Central America* was a wooden side-wheel paddlesteamer (see pages 100–101) with three decks, three masts, and a gross tonnage of 2,141 tons. It was 278 feet (85 meters) long and 40 feet (12 meters) broad, with a depth of 32 feet (9.75 meters).

The *Central America* called into Havana, Cuba, to take on more passengers and gold. It set sail again on September 8 with 575 people on board, and gold estimated at the time to be worth around $2 million. For the first two days the weather was fine and the *Central America* covered more than 500 miles (800 kilometers), giving an average speed of 10 knots per hour.

Sailing into the Path of a Hurricane

Toward the evening of September 10 the weather began to deteriorate as a strong wind blew up. By morning the *Central America* was caught in a fierce hurricane, considerable quantities of water were leaking into the engine room, and the ship was listing heavily to starboard. By evening all the engines had stopped and the *Central America* could no longer keep its head to the wind. It became helpless, rolling in the troughs of the sea. A desperate attempt to set sail on the masts in order to bring the ship's head into the wind and so to regain power and control proved to be unsuccessful.

Soon after midday on September 12 the *Marine*, a brig from Boston, sighted the stricken vessel. Boats were lowered from the *Central America* and 148 passengers, including all the women and children, were rescued. The *Central America* finally sank around 8 p.m.

SAILING TO CALIFORNIA IN SEARCH OF GOLD
The gold rush began in 1848, and attracted prospectors from around the world, particularly Europe. Several miners returning from San Francisco with their gold were aboard the Central America *when it sank in 1857.*

WHY THE CENTRAL AMERICA SANK

The loss of the *Central America* in fierce storms caused a public furor at the time. Paddle-steamers were inherently unstable, but some claimed that the *Central America* was particularly vulnerable because it carried insufficient ballast. On the outward voyage from New York it habitually carried a full cargo of coal but on this fated return journey the bunkers were not refilled, which caused the ship to be lighter and less stable. Much criticism was also made of the facts that no qualified carpenter was on board to stop the initial leaks or repair the pumps that had been swamped by water, the number of crew was inadequate, and there were lifeboats for only 300 people.

Salvage Searches and Disputes

The cargo aboard the *Central America* is now valued at between one-half and one billion dollars. In weight alone, the gold amounts to only 3 tons, with a bullion value of about $35 million, but some of the coins on the wreck had been newly minted with a double eagle emblem and are extremely rare, now possibly being worth as much as $8,000 each. Also on board were pioneer coins, which were privately minted coins used as legal tender during the gold rush era.

Converted ship
Abandoned ships like this were drawn up on shore and used as buildings

SHIPS AT SAN FRANCISCO, 1849
Before the gold rush San Francisco was a minor port, but after gold was discovered in California the town became a center for ships of all types bringing miners to search for gold, and cargo-carrying ships taking raw gold on to other trade centers. The number of ships arriving at the port increased from 4 to 400 within two years.

In 1987 an American-based salvage team, Columbus America Discovery Group, located the remains of the *Central America* in over 7,000 feet (2,000 meters) of water, and used a remote-operated vehicle to recover gold bars and coins. As often happens where treasure is concerned, the salvors soon found themselves in a court of law. Rival claimants to the gold included Columbia University, New York; Capuchin monks; Harry John, an eccentric treasure-hunting millionaire; and the veteran

Supplies for the voyages
Dry goods stored on the wharf waiting to be loaded

Sidewheel paddlesteamer
Gold was most often transported in this type of ship during the Californian gold rush

Abandoned ship
Ships deserted by crew members in pursuit of gold waited in the harbor to be reclaimed

Drying the sails in port
This ship, called the *Vicar of Bray*, was a trading vessel making journeys around Cape Horn

Loading the supplies
Goods for the journey being taken on board

salvor, Jack Grimm. John and Grimm claimed that Columbus America had found the wreck only with the assistance of research data from Columbia University, which Grimm and John had commissioned. The Capuchin monks claimed that the salvage rights had been given to them by John. The London Salvage Association also claimed part of the proceeds because it represented the original insurers.

Columbus America argued that the wreck and the gold had been abandoned and so as "salvors in possession" it had the sole title to the treasure. The first judge to hear

the case found in favor of Columbus America, but a court of appeal overruled this, and the US Supreme Court let the latter ruling stand. In view of the legal uncertainties, Columbus America has declined to return to the wreck, and so the salvage operation remains incomplete.

REINFORCED TREASURE BOX
Gold bars and coins were carried in boxes like this one, especially designed for the Wells Fargo Bank. Most of the cargo on the Central America belonged to this bank.

THE GENERAL GRANT

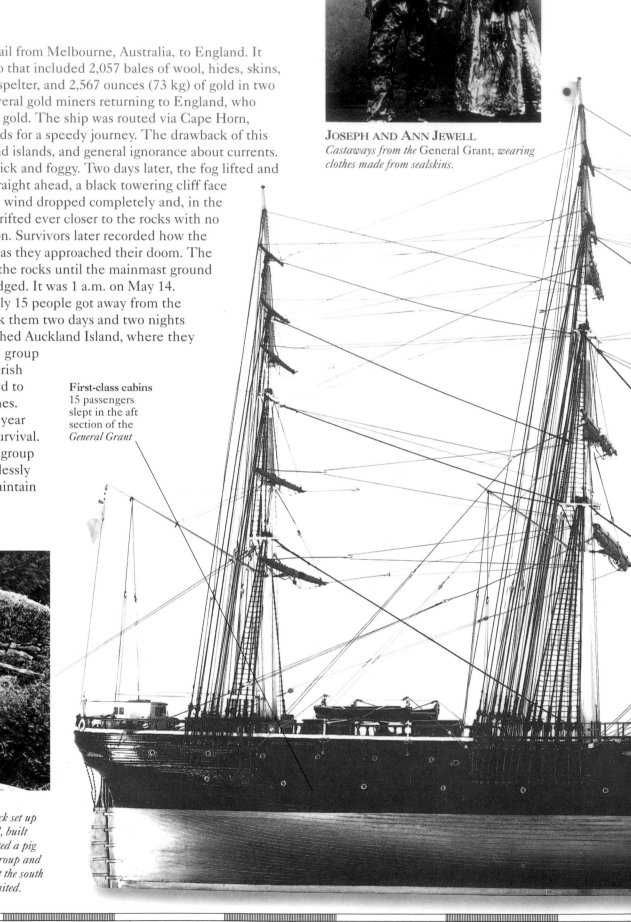

In May 1866 the *General Grant* set sail from Melbourne, Australia, to England. It was carrying a mixed general cargo that included 2,057 bales of wool, hides, skins, bark and timber, 9 tons of zinc or spelter, and 2,567 ounces (73 kg) of gold in two iron-bound chests. On board were several gold miners returning to England, who were probably also carrying their own gold. The ship was routed via Cape Horn, which made good use of westerly winds for a speedy journey. The drawback of this route was the poor charting of reefs and islands, and general ignorance about currents.

On May 11 the weather became thick and foggy. Two days later, the fog lifted and it became clear that there was land straight ahead, a black towering cliff face of 400 feet (120 meters) or more. The wind dropped completely and, in the eerie calm that descended, the ship drifted ever closer to the rocks with no way of avoiding the inevitable collision. Survivors later recorded how the cliffs seemed to open up before them as they approached their doom. The *General Grant* drifted into a cavern in the rocks until the mainmast ground against the cave roof and the ship wedged. It was 1 a.m. on May 14.

The ship sank before dawn and only 15 people got away from the barren rocks in the small boats. It took them two days and two nights of continuous rowing before they reached Auckland Island, where they made camp. Leadership of the small group fell naturally to James Teer, a large Irish gold digger. It was Teer who managed to light a fire with the last of their matches. They kept the fire going for the next year and a half and it was crucial to their survival. Teer kept strict discipline among the group and, leading by example, worked tirelessly to procure food and shelter, and to maintain constant watch for any sail that might rescue the castaways.

JOSEPH AND ANN JEWELL
Castaways from the General Grant, *wearing clothes made from sealskins.*

First-class cabins
15 passengers slept in the aft section of the *General Grant*

CASTAWAYS' SECOND CAMPSITE
The 15 survivors of the General Grant *shipwreck set up camp on an island, where they gathered firewood, built huts, sewed clothes from sealskins, and even started a pig farm. There were inevitable tensions within the group and a small party set up a temporary second camp at the south of the island, although eventually the groups reunited.*

The Rescue of the Castaways

CLIPPER SHIP MODEL
This is similar to the General Grant, *which was built in 1863 at a cost of $81,166 by Jacob Morse, on the Kennebec River in Maine. Clippers were sturdy, cargo-carrying, sailing ships suitable for long-distance journeys.*

A group of four men decided to take a chance and sail to freedom even though they did not know the seas and had no navigation charts. They set off in a small boat with enough supplies for three weeks. Unwittingly, they sailed on a course that took them into the emptiness of the Pacific Ocean, and they were never seen again.

Morale reached a low point after the departure of the breakaway group and the death of one of the other castaways from blood poisoning, but on November 21, 1867 their patience was finally rewarded. A sail was sighted and the castaways promptly launched a small boat to intercept the ship. This was the *Amherst*, which was carrying out a seal-killing expedition. The captain of this ship offered to take the castaways straight to New Zealand, but James Teer and his companions chose to remain a further six weeks on the island helping to catch seals.

DAVID ASHWORTH
He survived the initial wreck in 1866 but lost his life in a salvage attempt in 1870, searching for gold.

Many Salvage Bids Made

Between 1860 and 1876 three separate attempts were made by different survivors to salvage the *General Grant*'s gold. It must have taken considerable courage to return to the scene of such a harrowing ordeal. None of these attempts proved to be successful.

By 1912 the bullion lost in the *General Grant* was stated to be worth £500,000 sterling. An expedition organized by the entrepreneur E.C. May went bankrupt. Another expedition, which he organized in 1914, ended in the wreck of the salvage ship. In 1916 salvors penetrated what they thought was the cavern where the *General Grant* was wrecked, but no sign of the ship or its gold was found.

None of this deterred would-be salvors and more schemes were floated for raising the gold, the supposed value of which had risen to £4.5 million sterling by 1934. The last known attempt was in 1969 but, again, no trace of the ship was found.

Main berths
For 41 steerage passengers and 17 crew members

Wooden hull
The *General Grant* was made from white oak and pine

Cargo hold
For carrying the mixed cargo, including gold, wool, and zinc

FACTS AND FEATURES

Length	179.5 feet (55 meters)
Burden	1,103 tons
Route	Australia to England

THE
ROYAL CHARTER

The *Royal Charter* was a steam clipper (see box right) of 2,719 tons and was about 320 feet (100 meters) long with three masts and a funnel. It was launched in 1855 and on its maiden voyage made the run from Plymouth, England, to Melbourne, Australia, in just 60 days. The return route via Cape Horn tended to take slightly longer.

When the *Royal Charter* left Melbourne on August 26, 1859 it had on board a typically mixed list of passengers. In steerage there were a number of gold diggers who were returning home to their families in England with their newly won fortunes. Traveling first class were business people such as Mrs. Foster, a hotelier who reportedly carried with her money and valuables worth approximately £5,000 sterling. Rather sinisterly, there was also an insane jeweler, Samuel Henry, who had spent the voyage locked and guarded in his cabin. In total there were 390 passengers, many of whom were women and children, and a crew of 112.

Storms Encountered near Home

The voyage to England was even faster than usual. The Old Head of Kinsale, southern Ireland, was sighted at dawn on October 24, and 14 passengers went ashore there. By early afternoon the *Royal Charter* was off Holyhead, north Wales. The weather began to deteriorate as a strong wind blew up from the southeast, but there was no indication yet of the hurricane that was to come.

At 9 p.m. the *Royal Charter* was so close to Liverpool Bay that relatives had already begun to receive telegrams announcing the safe arrival of those on board. At 10 p.m. the gale increased to a hurricane. Even this would not have been a problem, because the *Royal Charter* was a strongly built ship, if the wind direction had not suddenly shifted from the southeast to the northeast. It was this sudden change of direction and the force of the gusting wind that now exposed the *Royal Charter* to a rocky shore that was only 5 miles (8 kilometers) distant.

In desperation Captain Taylor tried to turn the ship back into the relative safety of the Irish Sea but the engines were not powerful

LUXURIOUS CLIPPER

Promoted as combining all the advantages of a steamer with those of a clipper sailing ship, the *Royal Charter* had the sleek, fast lines of a clipper, with a length seven times that of its width, but was built from iron rather than wood. This type of ship was really a hybrid between the wooden sailing ship of the past and the iron steamship of the future. Steampower was used only when there was not enough wind for the ship to make reasonable headway, but having it as an optional source of power ensured that the ship could offer almost guaranteed fast sailing times between the United Kingdom and Australia: 59 days to Melbourne was "a performance never before accomplished."

The *Royal Charter* was designed for comfort, and was advertised as having unrivaled cabins for all classes of passengers. First-class fares went up to 75 guineas and third-class fares began at 16 guineas.

SAILING BILL FOR THE ROYAL CHARTER, 1856
This ship was one of the fastest to sail the UK to Australia route and this advertisement highlighted its speed, as well as the luxurious accommodation.

enough, and the wind was too strong for carrying sail. He ordered his crew to fire distress guns and send up rockets, and blue lights were lit on the ship to signal that it was now in mortal danger. Yet there was no chance that another ship could offer assistance in such a terrible storm: during that night no fewer than 133 ships were wrecked around the coasts of England and Wales.

At around 10:30 p.m., and with the *Royal Charter* now only 3 miles (5 kilometers) from shore, Captain Taylor ordered the anchors to be put out but they were not sufficient to stop the slow drift toward the coast. At about 1:30 a.m. the port anchor cable parted and an hour later the starboard cable also snapped. There was now nothing to keep the ship off the land and everyone braced themselves for the inevitable. At around 2:30 a.m. the captain ordered the masts to be cut down to reduce wind resistance and while this operation was in progress all passengers were confined below decks so that they would not be injured by the falling timbers.

An hour later the ship struck land. Captain Taylor announced that they had grounded on a sandy beach, and that the tide was going out. He ordered everyone to wait patiently until dawn, when they would be able to walk to safety. But he was clearly wrong. The tide was coming in and, even more disastrously, there were numerous ledges of treacherous rock between the ship and the shore.

Rescue Operations

Meanwhile, the fury of the gale increased, beating the iron ship against the rocks. In this desperate crisis Joseph Rodgers, an ordinary seaman, offered to try to get a line ashore. He lowered himself over the ship's side into the boiling sea and, against all odds, managed to clamber to safety with the assistance of some local villagers who had come down to the shore to help. A "bosun's chair" was rigged up onto the line and preparations were made to evacuate the women and children using this precarious system. The first young

WRECKED ON ROCKS IN A HURRICANE
The Royal Charter *was driven onto the Welsh coast, where it grounded and broke in two. A few survivors clung to pieces of wreckage and were washed ashore.*

continued on the wreck site until 1873, but, even as recently as the 1970s and 1980s, teams of prospecting divers have continued to recover the occasional gold sovereign.

Official Inquest and Enquiry

The bodies from the *Royal Charter* were laid out in the small church of Llanallgo, Wales, and during the days after the wreck a succession of badly shocked relatives identified them. A very understandable complaint of the relatives was that the authorities concentrated on the salvage of the gold rather than the recovery of those bodies that were still missing. An inquest into the deaths was held, followed by an official inquiry into the shipwreck. In both of these, Captain Taylor was posthumously found to be blameless for the loss of his ship, despite wild accusations that he had been drunk and that the *Royal Charter* had been unseaworthy.

woman who was offered this chance to be winched to safety refused to entrust herself to the chair, and some of the crew went in her place. It was later claimed that they went because they had orders to try to set up a second line, but this line did not materialize. Before the bulk of women and children could be fetched from below decks, the ship broke in two and separated them from their only hope of survival. The ship must have broken up at around 7:00 a.m. because all the watches that were recovered from the dead people had stopped between 7:20 and 8:00.

A handful of men clinging to pieces of wreckage were thrown up by the huge waves onto rock ledges, and made their way from there to safety. Those on shore linked hands and formed chains to drag the fortunate from the sea. There were 28 villagers on the shoreline taking part in the rescue. It was a very risky operation because at any moment the rescuers could have found themselves swept out to sea. Despite these efforts, the majority of those on board the ship were pulverized against the rocks by the force of the waves.

There were only 41 survivors in total, all of them men and 18 of them crew. The captain and all the officers of the ship were lost. Most of the survivors were lucky enough to reach land by the line strung between ship and shore. The women were probably hampered by their bulkier clothing. One of the luckiest survivors was James Dean, a young goldminer from Wigan. He managed to sleep through the entire hurricane and up until the ship broke into two. He could not swim but clung frantically to a piece of wreckage and was eventually hurled onto the shore.

Recovery of the Ship's Gold

A Customs agent, Mr. Smith, was quickly on the scene, and before night fell on October 25, coastguardsmen from Liverpool had arrived to protect the wreck. Even so, it has passed into local folklore that many of the villagers became wealthy overnight on what treasure they managed to pick up among the rocks. Four people were prosecuted for looting and house-to-house searches were made, but very little was discovered.

On October 29 salvage operations were started, but these proved difficult because the strongroom had disintegrated and the gold was distributed over a large area. Nevertheless, by February 1860, a good proportion had been recovered. How much of this was part of the official consignment and how much had been privately owned was impossible to tell. Salvage operations

SOVEREIGNS FROM THE ROYAL CHARTER
Gold was found in Australia in 1851, and the Sydney mint was set up in 1853. These gold coins are from the Sydney mint.

Steam tug
The support vessel for the diving teams on the three diving boats

DIVING FOR GOLD, 1859
The first salvage operation began five days after the Royal Charter *wrecked. The strongroom had been badly damaged when the ship smashed against the rocky shore and the gold was widely scattered. Despite this, diving teams recovered gold worth around $435,000.*

MAIL SHIPS AND LINERS

The middle decades of the nineteenth century witnessed a series of innovations in shipbuilding and design that were to transform the shipping industry beyond all recognition. The fundamental features of ocean-going sailing ships had remained the same for almost 400 years, but by the end of the nineteenth century these ships were virtually obsolete.

The replacement of windpower with the far more reliable energy source of steam was the basis of this revolution. The first ocean-going steamships were wooden sidewheel paddlesteamers, associated with transporting gold in the gold rush era (see pages 92–93). Because they were difficult to dock and lacked stability in heavy seas, they were superceded, as the century progressed, by the more efficient iron-built screw-propelled steamships, with rear propellors. The change from the use of wood to iron was also significant. Iron was better suited to withstand the enormous vibrations created by the engines and enabled ships to be built on a far larger scale than would have been possible if they had been built from wood. The development of the compound engine in the 1850s was also critical to the triumph of steam because it enabled twice as much power to be produced from the same quantity of coal.

The Emergence of Shipping Lines

The introduction of the iron-built screw-propelled steamer in the 1830s coincided with an enormous increase in the demand for travel between Europe and the colonies, alongside an increased need for a means of reliable communication. At this time, the British Government was awarding lucrative mail contracts to the emergent new shipping companies such as Cunard, Royal Mail, and the Peninsular and Orient. European nations were developing passenger fleets of their own, but Britain was the dominant maritime nation throughout the nineteenth century. In 1914 nearly 50 percent of registered steam tonnage was British.

During the nineteenth century, the great shipping lines carried people to the new lands of opportunity – Australia, Canada, the United States, and South Africa. They also shipped huge quantities of specie between governments and central banks, forming a vital commercial link.

By the early twentieth century, the magnificence of the giant passenger liners was expressive of a self-confident and opulent era. These ships were associated with a style of luxurious travel that earned them the soubriquet of "traveling palaces." It is questionable, however, whether conditions for ordinary seamen improved, despite the more reliable provision of food and water.

③ EGYPT
In 1922 this P & O steamer sank after a collision with another ship in thick fog. (See pages 106–107.)

⑤ PRINS FREDERIK
This passenger liner was lost in 1890 near the Bay of Biscay, en route from Amsterdam to Java, via Genoa. (See pages 102–103.)

① ANDREA DORIA
One of the last great passenger liners, this ship collided with the Stockholm near New York, en route from Genoa, Italy, in 1956. (See pages 108–109.)

④ TITANIC
This American White Star liner sank after hitting an iceberg in 1912 while sailing from Southampton, England, to New York. Recent salvage is the subject of controversy. (See pages 104–105.)

⑥ CLEOPATRA
This ship was lost, along with its cargo of gold-dust and silver coins, in a river in Sierra Leone in 1862, after failure to allow for the strong currents.

② JOHN ELDER
This British 4,169-ton Pacific Steam Navigation Company steamship was carrying a large cargo of gold and silver from Valparaiso to Liverpool when it was lost northeast of Cape Carranza, Chile, in 1892.

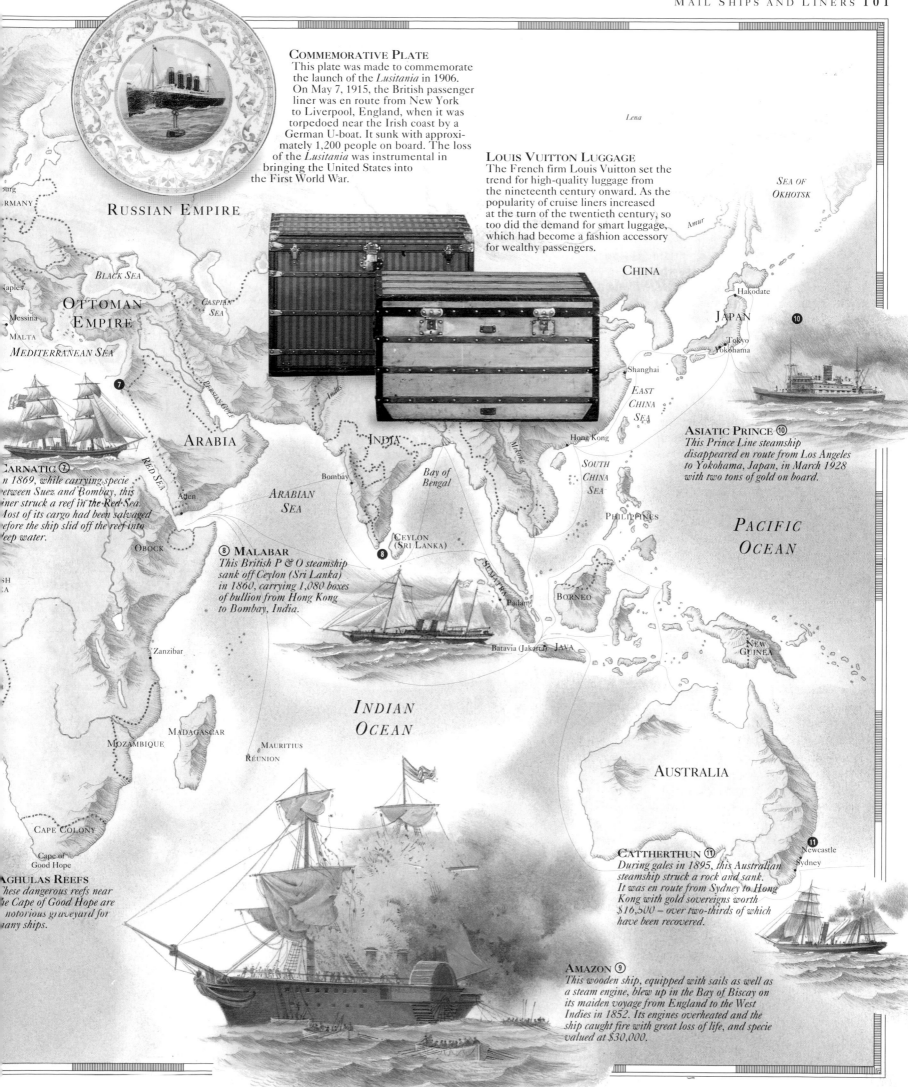

COMMEMORATIVE PLATE
This plate was made to commemorate the launch of the *Lusitania* in 1906. On May 7, 1915, the British passenger liner was en route from New York to Liverpool, England, when it was torpedoed near the Irish coast by a German U-boat. It sunk with approximately 1,200 people on board. The loss of the *Lusitania* was instrumental in bringing the United States into the First World War.

LOUIS VUITTON LUGGAGE
The French firm Louis Vuitton set the trend for high-quality luggage from the nineteenth century onward. As the popularity of cruise liners increased at the turn of the twentieth century, so too did the demand for smart luggage, which had become a fashion accessory for wealthy passengers.

ASIATIC PRINCE ⑩
This Prince Line steamship disappeared en route from Los Angeles to Yokohama, Japan, in March 1928 with two tons of gold on board.

CARNATIC ⑦
n 1869, while carrying specie etween Suez and Bombay, this iner struck a reef in the Red Sea. Most of its cargo had been salvaged efore the ship slid off the reef into eep water.

⑧ **MALABAR**
This British P & O steamship sank off Ceylon (Sri Lanka) in 1860, carrying 1,080 boxes of bullion from Hong Kong to Bombay, India.

AGHULAS REEFS
hese dangerous reefs near e Cape of Good Hope are notorious graveyard for any ships.

CATTHERTHUN ⑪
During gales in 1895, this Australian steamship struck a rock and sank. It was en route from Sydney to Hong Kong with gold sovereigns worth $16,500 – over two-thirds of which have been recovered.

AMAZON ⑨
This wooden ship, equipped with sails as well as a steam engine, blew up in the Bay of Biscay on its maiden voyage from England to the West Indies in 1852. Its engines overheated and the ship caught fire with great loss of life, and specie valued at $30,000.

THE
PRINS FREDERIK

DECK PLANS FOR THE PRINS ALEXANDER
These builders' plans show the layout of the sister ship of the Prins Frederik. *The two ships were built for the same shipping line, the Dutch company Maatschappy Nederland, one of the best shipping companies of the day. The* Prins Frederik *offered comfortable accommodations to its passengers on the long journey to the East. The ship was classified as 100-A1, the highest rating of the time.*

On June 21, 1890, the steamer *Prins Frederik* left Amsterdam, the Netherlands, en route to Java, Indonesia, with a full complement of 93 passengers on board, as well as Captain Klaus Visman and his crew. The ship was carrying a general cargo and the usual mails, but also had on board, locked in the bullion room at the stern of the ship on the starboard side, 400,000 silver rijksdaalders (coins) that were stowed in wooden casks, for the payment of the Dutch army in Batavia (Jakarta). The bullion room had been specially lined with quarter-inch (6 mm) iron plate; the fitted wooden doors were also lined with iron, and the room was secured with patented Chubb locks.

Setting the Ship's Course

The *Prins Frederik* called at Southampton, England, and left there on June 24. At 1:30 p.m. the following day the ship was just north of the Bay of Biscay. The island of Ushant was observed bearing SE quarter E, at a distance of about 10 miles (16 kilometers) and the captain ordered the ship's course to be altered to SW quarter W. At the time, the *Prins Frederik* was making full speed of about 11.5 knots. At around 6 p.m. the mist began to thicken, and so the ship reduced speed in accordance with standard marine measures.

Meanwhile, the British steamship *Marpessa*, commanded by Captain Geary, was traveling across the Bay of Biscay in the opposite direction. At 10:40 p.m. on June 25 Captain Geary calculated that his ship was in the position 47.00°N 6.30°W when he heard another ship's whistle a little in front on the port side. Later, Captain Geary claimed that the *Marpessa* was traveling at only 3 knots and that upon hearing the other ship's whistle he had quickly put the engines into reverse.

Ships' Positions at Impact

Despite these avoidance measures, the *Prins Frederik* cut right across the bows of the *Marpessa*, and the two ships collided. The bows of the *Marpessa* were stoved in, and the *Prins Frederik* received a hole around its engine rooms on the starboard side.

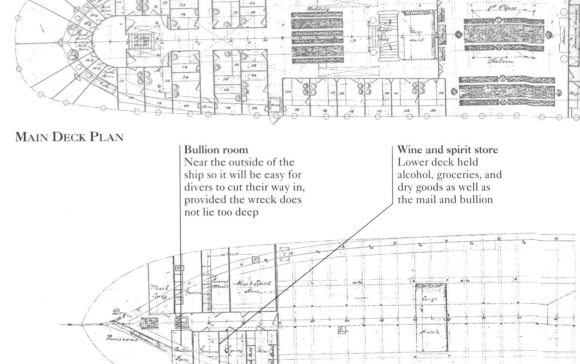

MAIN DECK PLAN

Bullion room
Near the outside of the ship so it will be easy for divers to cut their way in, provided the wreck does not lie too deep

Wine and spirit store
Lower deck held alcohol, groceries, and dry goods as well as the mail and bullion

LOWER DECK PLAN

Shortly after the collision the *Prins Frederik* sank. The *Prins Frederik*'s boats, however, had already been lowered and all passengers and crew were taken on board the *Marpessa*. The forehold of the *Marpessa* filled with water but the rest of the ship remained sound.

According to Captain Visman, the *Prins Frederik* was not traveling at full speed, as suggested by Captain Geary, but only at 2–3 knots. Like Geary, Visman claimed that as soon as the other ship's whistle was heard the *Prins Frederik*'s engines were stopped and the ship put into reverse. Visman stated that at the time of collision the ships were 70 miles (113 kilometers) SW by W of Ushant, which places it about 50 miles (80 kilometers) away from the position given by Geary.

The positions of both ships in the hours preceding the collision were critical evidence, because they were one of the few ways of establishing how fast both ships had been traveling before the accident, when foggy conditions had reduced visibility. It was in the interests of both captains to claim that they had made less progress than was actually the case, thereby minimizing the speed of the ships, and this is a possible explanation for the discrepancy in positions given.

Court Case Begins

As soon as news of the disaster reached the owners of the *Prins Frederik*, they began legal action for damages against the owners of the *Marpessa*. During the case the First Officer of the *Marpessa* was found guilty of altering the logbook after the collision to show the speed made by the *Marpessa* to be 6 knots rather than 8 knots. Geary explained this away as a mere correction of a clerical error. The judge clearly believed him because the court found in favor of the *Marpessa* and against the *Prins Frederik*. There followed something of an outcry in the Dutch press, which made accusations of nationalistic bias against the British court, but the decision stood.

Steam engines
Powered by coal, they enabled the ship to travel at up to 11.5 knots per hour

Linen area
The drying room and linen room were next to the funnel to make use of the heat

Luggage room
Because the ship was designed for long journeys, large amounts of luggage were carried

Cargo hatch
Wide opening to enable bulky goods to be loaded easily

Mast
Although primarily powered by steam, the ship also carried masts and sails

Sailmaker's cabin
The ship carried a sailmaker and a carpenter to make running repairs during the voyage

Crew's quarters
Bunks and tables for 18 seamen and 18 firemen

SCREW-PROPELLED IRON STEAMERS

The *Prins Frederik* had been built in 1882 by J. Elder & Co. of Glasgow, Scotland, and was a screw-propelled iron steamship with two decks and a spar deck, and a gross tonnage of 2,978 tons. The first steamships were made from wood but, as the nineteenth century progressed, iron was preferred because it was better suited to withstand the enormous vibrations created by the engines, and also enabled the ship to be built on a far larger scale. Size was an all-important factor because of the large amount of space taken up by the engines for the boilers, and the large bunkers needed for the coal. The development of the compound engine in the 1850s was also critical to the triumph of steam because it enabled twice as much power to be produced from the same quantity of coal.

Implications for Salvors

The difference in the positions given for the collision by the captains of the *Prins Frederik* and the *Marpessa* was important not just for the court in 1890 but also for modern-day salvors. If the position given by the captain of the *Prins Frederik* (70 miles/113 kilometers SW by W of Ushant) is right, the wreck lies in only 500 feet (152 meters) of water; but if the position given by the captain of the *Marpessa* is correct (47.00°N 6.30°W), the wreck lies off the continental shelf at a depth approaching 6,000 feet (1,830 meters).

In 1987, a French company located a wreck on the seabed that closely matched the description of the *Prins Frederik*, a

ADVERTISEMENT, 1890
This poster for the steamship Prins Alexander, *the sister ship of the* Prins Frederik, *shows some of the features found on board: the luxuriously furnished saloons, well-equipped cabins, and spacious decks.*

Passengers' saloon
Entered by a grand staircase, this wood-paneled room resembled comfortable drawing rooms of the period

Cargo derrick
For hoisting goods from the wharf onto the ship, and then lowering them through cargo hatches into the holds

Outside cabin
Three-berth bedroom with two bunk beds, and a single under the porthole

First-class saloon
With three long tables for passengers' use

three-masted, screw-propelled, iron steamship, of approximately the correct age and length, in roughly the position given by the captain of the *Prins Frederik*, in about 500 feet (150 meters) of water.

Although the wreck was videotaped it was covered in a tangle of fishing nets and it was impossible at the time of the survey to make an absolutely positive identification. Other three-masted, screw-propelled, iron

steamships are known to have sunk in the same area; for example, the *Sarpedon* sank in 1876, another treasure-carrying victim of collision. In the summer of 1994, a British Company, Marine Salvage Services, planned to return to the wreck and attempt a more definitive identification. If it is the *Prins Frederik*, then it is possible that Captain Klaus Visman's reputation will finally be restored, over 100 years after the event.

THE
TITANIC

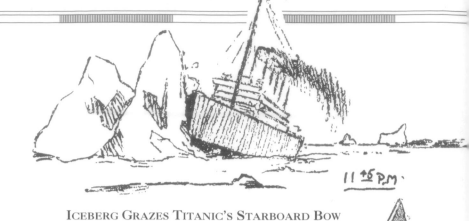

No shipwreck in history has ever attracted the same volume of public interest as has the *Titanic*. As a subject of controversy and as a source of myth it has few parallels. The ship's loss in 1912 marked a symbolic end to Edwardian self-confidence and elitist smugness. Shortly afterward, the First World War broke out and the old social order collapsed.

The *Titanic* was a passenger liner built by Harland and Wolff for the American White Star Line as part of a new program of ship-building to enable the company to compete effectively with Cunard, which had recently become a serious commercial threat. Leading technological experts of the time described the ship as "practically unsinkable."

Maiden Voyage

On April 10, 1912 the *Titanic* set off across the Atlantic Ocean on its first sea voyage, from Southampton, England, to New York, via Cherbourg, France, and Queenstown, Ireland. It was only half-full, but this was considered to be more than satisfactory from a commercial point of view. The cost of the grandest of the first-class suites, one way, was $4,350.

Iceberg Warnings

The voyage was uneventful until April 14, when the *Titanic*, which had completed about two-thirds of its journey, received several radio warnings from other ships that there were icebergs ahead. A warm winter had led to ice drifting farther south than usual. Despite the warnings no precautions were taken; on the contrary, Captain Smith gave orders for the *Titanic*'s speed to be increased. Around 10 p.m. the *SS Californian*, which had stopped in an ice field about 10 to 20 miles (15 to 30 kilometers) to the north, radioed with another ice warning, but, because the radio operator was busy with messages for passengers, it is doubtful whether this most critical warning ever reached the *Titanic*'s bridge.

ICEBERG GRAZES TITANIC'S STARBOARD BOW

THE TITANIC'S LAST MOMENTS
Despite the official view that the ship sank in one piece, eye-witnesses, including the artist who drew these pictures showing it broken in two, were proved right when the wreck was located.

At 11:40 p.m. a lookout noticed an ice floe ahead and rang the warning bell. The duty officer gave the order to turn the wheel hard to starboard, which swung the bow of the ship to port. He then had the engines put into reverse and gave the order to swing the wheel the other way to turn the bow back to starboard. These orders were an instinctive reaction but were, in fact, contrary to the accepted best practice of the day. The *Titanic* took a long time before beginning to turn and by then it was already too late. The iceberg had gouged a hole in the starboard hull.

SHIP BROKE IN TWO
The forward end sank first.

THE LAST VIEW
The Titanic *reportedly stayed like this for five minutes before plunging to the seabed.*

THE TITANIC
Built to be the ultimate in transatlantic luxury, the ship even had a swimming pool, a gymnasium, and Turkish baths. It had nine decks, and could carry 2,500 passengers.

Radio room
Several warnings about the ice floes received here

First-class staircase
Access for first-class passengers to boat and promenade decks

Dining room
Above the boilers and coal stores, for use of third-class passengers

Crow's nest
The lookout here was first to spot the fateful ice floe

Boat deck
Location of the lifeboats and the officers' quarters

Crew's quarters
There were 915 crew, half for catering and domestic duties

Aftermath of Collision

The impact of the iceberg barely disturbed the pleasures of those on board: a slight shuddering was all that was felt. However, the damage was fatal. Six compartments had been breached, and it was obvious to the ship's officers that the ship could not survive despite the closure of its watertight doors.

An SOS signal was sent from the radio room, one of the very first uses of this new emergency call sign, and arrangements for the disembarkation of the women and children in lifeboats were implemented.

The *Titanic* carried lifeboats for less than half the people on board. In addition, most of the lifeboats that were launched were only half-full. This was partly due to the inevitable confusion at the time and partly deliberate policy. Officers did not want to lower the boats fully laden with 60 people because they doubted their capacity to stand the strain during winching.

Passengers and crew generally behaved with dignity during the abandonment of the ship. Discipline was largely maintained but one officer admitted he had used a pistol to prevent the boats from being rushed.

There was much scandal at the time over the refusal of those in the half-filled lifeboats to pick up others in the water. Those in the relative safety of the boats were reluctant to venture back for fear of being swamped by desperate survivors. Those in the freezing water did not survive long, but those in the lifeboats were rescued after about an hour and a quarter by the *Carpathia*. This had been 58 miles (93 kilometers) from the *Titanic* when it sank but had navigated at top speed to reach the stricken ship.

Who Survived?

In total, 1,490 passengers and crew died, including the captain who went down with his ship. Statistics suggest that the principle of women and children first was broadly adhered to. Of the first-class passengers, 94 percent of women survived and only 31 percent of men. But only 47 percent of the women in steerage survived, with 14 percent of men. There has been controversy over whether the steerage passengers were deliberately kept in their part of the ship until the last moment, but the higher fatality rate might reflect that their cabins were farther from the boat deck.

Locating the Wreck

It was inevitable that someone would try to locate the *Titanic* on the seabed. In 1985 Robert Ballard and a scientific team from the Woods Hole Institute, together with the salvage company Ifremer of France, launched a search. The wreck was located with a deep-towed side-scan sonar, and then investigated using a manned submersible and a remote-operated vehicle. The wreck lay in two halves on the seabed in such a manner as to suggest that it had broken in two before sinking. This confirmed eyewitnesses' accounts, which the official enquiry had not believed. Underwater photography also revealed that the physical damage to the ship was relatively slight, consisting of just a narrow, intermittent gash. This has led recent analysts to suggest that the *Titanic* was more likely to have sunk because the brittleness of its steel plates in sub-zero temperatures caused them to fracture on impact, rather than as a result of direct damage from the iceberg itself.

Salvaging the Treasure

The *Titanic* was reported to have been carrying $5 million of diamonds, as well as other precious items such as a sumptuously covered and jeweled copy of the *Rubaiyat of Omar Khayyam*, not to mention the personal possessions and jewelry of the passengers themselves. However, the real "treasure" of the *Titanic* lies in the thousands of pieces of ship's fittings and contents that would have enormous value for collectors.

There are those, such as Ballard himself, who are totally opposed to any disturbance of the wreck, insisting that it be kept as a grave, and this is also the official position of the American and Canadian governments. Yet, this policy is not entirely consistent with sending a manned submersible into the wreck's entrails and filming personal possessions. It also does not take into account the fact that the ship lies in international waters and, while Canada might claim the wreck is in its economic zone, this may not give it rights since the United Nations Convention of the Sea does not include shipwrecks in its list of rights in economic zones.

A New York-based company, RMS Titanic Inc., was clearly unimpressed by these arguments. It returned to the wreck in 1987 and salvaged several artifacts with which to mount a *Titanic* exhibition.

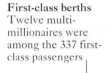

First-class berths
Twelve multi-millionaires were among the 337 first-class passengers

Engine room
Coal-fired boilers powered engines that drove propellers

Freshwater tanks
Holding supplies needed for the week's voyage

Second-class berths
Housing 271 passengers, with their own staircase to decks

Cargo hold
Refrigerated sections at rear of ship, above the shaft tunnel

Third-class cabins
For 712 steerage passengers, mainly emigrants

Docking bridge
For passengers to enter and leave ship via poop deck

THE
EGYPT

The Peninsular and Oriental liner, the *Egypt*, left London, England, on May 19, 1922, en route to Bombay, India, via the Suez Canal. It had on board 294 crew, mainly Asian, and 48 passengers. In addition to the usual general cargo of manufactured goods the *Egypt* carried gold and silver bullion and specie worth $1,625,290, about 10 tons of silver, and 5 tons of gold.

Off the island of Ushant, at the western tip of Brittany, France, the *Egypt* ran into thick fog. Captain Collyer ordered the ship's speed to be reduced and the ship's horn to be sounded continuously. Another siren, that of the French steamship the *Seine*, was heard on the port side, and then the *Seine* struck the *Egypt* amidships, causing the *Egypt* to sink within 20 minutes.

Immediately after the collision there was considerable chaos on board the *Egypt*, and some of the crew rushed the lifeboats. In all, 86 people drowned: 71 crew and 15 passengers.

Salvage Limitations

At first, salvage did not seem to be a practical proposition. Examination of sea charts showed that the *Egypt* had sunk in depths of around 400 feet (120 meters) and the technological limits of successful salvage operations at that time were 150 feet (45 meters). Moreover, the *Egypt*'s strongroom, where the gold and silver were stowed, was a long, narrow chamber 25 by 5 feet (7.5 by 1.5 meters), three decks down at the bottom of the ship, to which it would be difficult to gain access.

THE EGYPT WRECK SITE
The wreck was located on August 30, 1930, and salvaged by a Swedish engineer, Peter Sandberg, and an Indian company, Sorima. This image shows the Egypt *on the seabed after the salvors had cut through three decks to reach the bullion room. Gold was first recovered on June 22, 1932.*

FACTS AND FEATURES

Treasure	Gold and silver
Salvage	Almost complete
Recovered	Over $1,500,000

Salvage grab
For positioning the explosives to blast through the hull, and then to recover the bullion

Diver's shell
The man inside this observation chamber guided the position of the grab via a telephone link with the salvage ship above

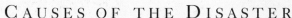
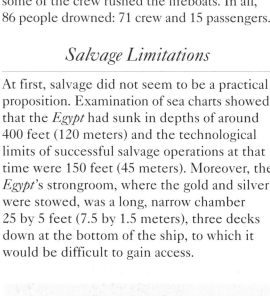

CAUSES OF THE DISASTER

The *Seine* collided with the *Egypt* in fog so thick that visibility was down to 22 yards (20 meters). Fog is a common hazard off Brittany, France, but disaster could have been prevented if the usual conventions of the sea had been followed. The *Egypt* heard the *Seine*'s horn on the port side and, since the rules stipulate that ships should move to starboard on hearing horns, this should not have been a problem. The *Seine* was following the coastal route from La Rochelle to Le Havre and would normally have been sailing close to shore, but had been taking a course farther out to give the dangerous rocks off Ushant a wide berth in the fog. This was no doubt sensible, but also confusing for other ships in the area.

During the Court of Enquiry into the accident, allegations were made that the *Egypt* had been traveling at excessive speed, but the captain and officers of the *Egypt* were acquitted of any wrongdoing.

THE SALVAGE SHIP
A heavy object being brought up from the Egypt *lying 400 feet (120 meters) below causes the ship on the surface to list severely. The salvors lost one ship and some divers while working on another wreck in 1930.*

However, a far-sighted Swedish engineer, Peter Sandberg, felt that recent advances in the design of underwater apparatus might make salvage feasible after all. Rigid steel structures capable of withstanding external water pressure at depths of up to 500 feet (150 meters) or more had already been built. Sandberg constructed a version, which he called the eye, that he intended to equip with sophisticated underwater tools to penetrate the ship and recover the cargo. First, however, he had to locate the wreck.

After two futile attempts to find the *Egypt*, Sandberg joined forces with an Italian company, Sorima, led by Commendatore Quaglia. Sorima was very much at the cutting edge of salvage technology, and had been working in the Mediterranean using recently developed Neufeldt and Kuhnke articulated diving suits that were strong enough to withstand the pressure of the sea at 400-foot (120-meter) depths. The team spent over a year searching for the wreck, using a variety of methods. These included employing a Capuchin monk to divine the presence of metals with twigs, and using a primitive magnetometer. Eventually, on August 30, 1930, it was the old-fashioned method of towing a cable suspended between two ships until it caught on an object on the seabed that proved successful in locating the *Egypt*.

Exploding a Path to the Bullion

Sorima developed a simpler manned observation chamber, somewhat like Sandberg's eye but, instead of using tools on the seabed, all the work was done by a grab lowered from winches on board the salvage ship. The grab placed explosives on the wreck, which were then remotely detonated from above. After each explosion, the grab removed any obtruding metal. By this means, Sorima slowly worked down the ship until it reached the strongroom. The first gold was not recovered until June 22, 1932, nearly two years after the wreck had been found, and over 10 years after it sank. Work continued for a year when all but $55,040 of the gold and silver was recovered. Still unaccounted for are 14,929 sovereigns, 17 gold bars, and 30 silver ingots.

Domed head
Smooth design helped to minimize water resistance

Pincer tools
Operated by hand inside the suit, and used to pick up items

Rubber joints
Allowed mobility at hip, knee, and ankle

Fragmented deck
To reach the strong-room, salvors used explosives to blast a path down through the ship

Strongroom
Gold and silver were stored in this narrow chamber three decks down into the ship

ARTICULATED SUIT
The salvage company Sorima equipped its divers with these suits, enabling them to work at great depths, essential since the Egypt *lay in deep water. But using a grab was, in the end, found to be more effective.*

The shattered hull
As the salvors worked on the ship, the hull fell outward to the sea floor

White-painted hull
Helped salvors to identify the *Egypt*; the towing cable caught on the wreck, snapped, and was marked with white paint when it came to the surface

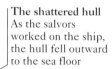

THE TRIUMPHANT SALVORS WITH SOME OF THE RECOVERED GOLD
This commemorative photograph celebrates the highly successful salvage operation. Shown at the top right is Quaglia, the leader of the project. By the time work ceased in 1933 they had recovered gold and silver worth over $1.5 million.

THE
ANDREA DORIA

The *Andrea Doria*, named after a famous sixteenth-century Genoese admiral, was one of the last of the great transatlantic passenger liners. Shortly after this ship made its final voyage in 1956, the increasing availability of airplane flights put such liners out of business.

The *Andrea Doria* left Genoa, Italy, on July 17, en route to New York via Cannes, France, and Gibraltar. All was the usual round of pleasure and enforced idleness until the evening of July 25 when, just one day's sailing from New York, it ran into fog near the Nantucket lightship. This area is notorious for fog, caused by the warm currents of the Gulf Stream coming up against the colder northern waters. The *Andrea Doria*'s captain, Piero Calamai, ordered a token reduction in speed of just over one knot. This was a reasonable decision: fogs were not unusual, liner schedules were tight, and the *Andrea Doria* was equipped with the latest radar technology.

Collision Course

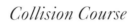

At approximately 10:20 p.m. the *Andrea Doria* altered course in order to head directly in to New York. At 10:45 p.m. a ship was spotted on the radar screen, heading toward them at a distance of about 17 miles (27 kilometers). This ship was the *Stockholm*, a Swedish–American liner. At 10:50 p.m. the *Stockholm*'s radar screen showed the *Andrea Doria* about 12 miles (19 kilometers) away. Neither ship made any significant reduction in its speed.

These ships were less than 1 mile (1.5 kilometers) apart when they finally made visual contact, a quite inadequate stopping distance for ships of this size. Still worse, they both misjudged each other's actions. The *Stockholm* turned to starboard,

THE NEWLY BUILT ANDREA DORIA, 1952
The Andrea Doria *was built in the Ansaldo shipyards in Genoa, Italy, for the Italia Line. Its layout catered to three classes, with separate swimming pools, dance halls, and dining rooms. On its final voyage there were 190 first-class passengers, 267 cabin-class, and 677 tourist-class.*

FACTS AND
FEATURES

Gross tonnage	29,083 tons
Length	656 feet (200 meters)
Top speed	23 knots per hour
Route	Genoa to New York

PASSENGERS ABOARD

Included on the passenger list for what was to be the *Andrea Doria*'s final voyage was a songwriter, Mike Stoller, who was shortly to become famous as the writer of Elvis Presley's "Hound Dog." Other passengers were drawn from both ends of the social spectrum: from the very wealthy, who preferred the comfort and luxury of a ship crossing to an airplane flight; to very poor emigrants to the New World, for whom a cabin deep in the bowels of the ship was the cheapest form of travel.

The bridge
Where a radar screen first indicated the *Stockholm*'s approach

Cargo derrick

THE ANDREA DORIA ROLLS ONTO ITS SIDE
The dramatic photograph on the left records the last moments of the Andrea Doria. *Because the ship took several hours to sink after its collision with the* Stockholm, *there was plenty of time for such photographs to be taken.*

AERIAL VIEW OF THE VANISHING SHIP
Seconds after the photograph on the left was taken, the Andrea Doria *plunged 240 feet (73 meters) to the seabed, leaving just these foaming waves and scattered debris.*

thinking the *Andrea Doria* was on its port side. But the *Andrea Doria* turned to port itself, thus ignoring one of the basic rules of the sea: a ship should turn in toward danger rather than expose its flank to the bow of an oncoming ship. The result was a horrendous collision at 11:10 p.m., with the sharp *Stockholm* bow penetrating far inside the hull of the *Andrea Doria*, killing 46 passengers. Five of the *Stockholm*'s crew also died. The collision occurred in a busy shipping lane and a number of other ships came speeding to the rescue. Although the *Andrea Doria* sank, the *Stockholm* managed to reach land.

Legends of Treasure

The *Andrea Doria* lay in very deep water but, even so, a number of dives to take photographs were made in the days after the disaster. One of the first to dive was Peter Gimbel, for whom the ship became an obsession. In the following years, rumors grew about the fabulous wealth in jewels and money that lay in the ship's vaults. In 1985, Gimbel funded an expedition that succeeded in bringing up the ship's safe but, disappointingly, it was found to contain only paper money.

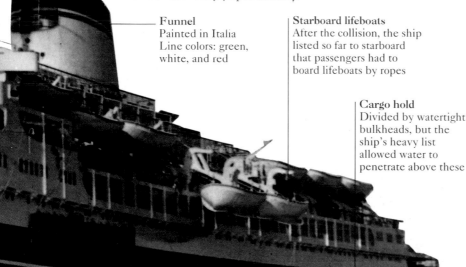

Radar mast

Funnel
Painted in Italia Line colors: green, white, and red

Starboard lifeboats
After the collision, the ship listed so far to starboard that passengers had to board lifeboats by ropes

Cargo hold
Divided by watertight bulkheads, but the ship's heavy list allowed water to penetrate above these

REASONS WHY THE ANDREA DORIA SANK

This luxurious passenger liner was claimed by its designers to be unsinkable. It had 11 watertight bulkheads, of which only one was penetrated by the *Stockholm* when it collided with the *Andrea Doria*, and so the ship should not have sunk. However, the *Andrea Doria* was near the end of its voyage and was light on ballast. It had used up most of its fuel and freshwater but the crew had not reflooded the empty tanks with seawater, presumably because this procedure would have taken up valuable time and liner captains were under pressure to adhere to tight schedules. As a result, when the *Stockholm* struck the ship on the starboard side and seawater rushed in, the *Andrea Doria* immediately took on such a heavy list that water began to penetrate above the bulkheads, rendering them useless.

ANDREA DORIA SURVIVORS IN NEW YORK
These people were picked up by the Île de France, *a French liner. As many as 1,660 passengers and crew were rescued.*

SECOND WORLD WAR

The evacuation of gold and other valuables shipped out of Europe in warships and liners at the end of 1939 and during 1940, as German armies marched into the Netherlands, Belgium, France, and Poland, was of quite staggering proportions. The amount of government-owned gold reserves transported was some 7,500 tons, or $81 trillion's worth at today's prices, mostly destined for either the United States and Canada or west Africa. Securities of a similar value were also shipped, plus an unknown quantity of private wealth. Evacuation was often so hasty that the gold was not properly boxed. Gold is an exceedingly heavy commodity and its enormous weight in a relatively small space could easily capsize ordinary deck structures unless special support was provided. This was less of a problem for liners because in general they carried smaller quantities and had properly constructed specie rooms. Warships usually put gold in the ammunition lockers or the torpedo chambers.

Success of Gold Shipments

Even more extraordinary, perhaps, than the sheer volume of this flight of wealth out of Europe is that, with only one exception, there is no recorded instance of any of this vast quantity of evacuated gold not reaching its destination in the early months of the war. And yet this gold was being shipped during a period when German U-boats were already taking an enormous toll on Allied shipping. By contrast there are a number of recorded losses during the later years of the war when the risk of loss was considerably less. One theory is that gold was indeed lost in 1940, but there was an official cover-up to preserve Allied financial credibility.

Nearly fifty percent of gold shipped was under United Kingdom control and was destined for the United States and Canada. France was the other large shipper of gold and the bulk of French gold was sent to the French colony of Dakar in west Africa. Apart from the main routes from Europe via the United Kingdom to the United States or Canada, and France to Dakar, gold and silver were shipped to safety along several other routes. German and Japanese treasure shipments were on a far smaller scale. Both are rumored to have made substantial evacuations of valuables, but details on the shipments are scarce and many of the stories of fabulous treasure hoards have never come to light.

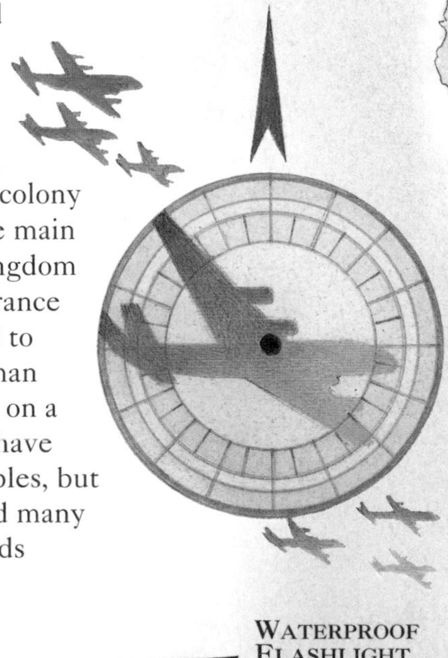

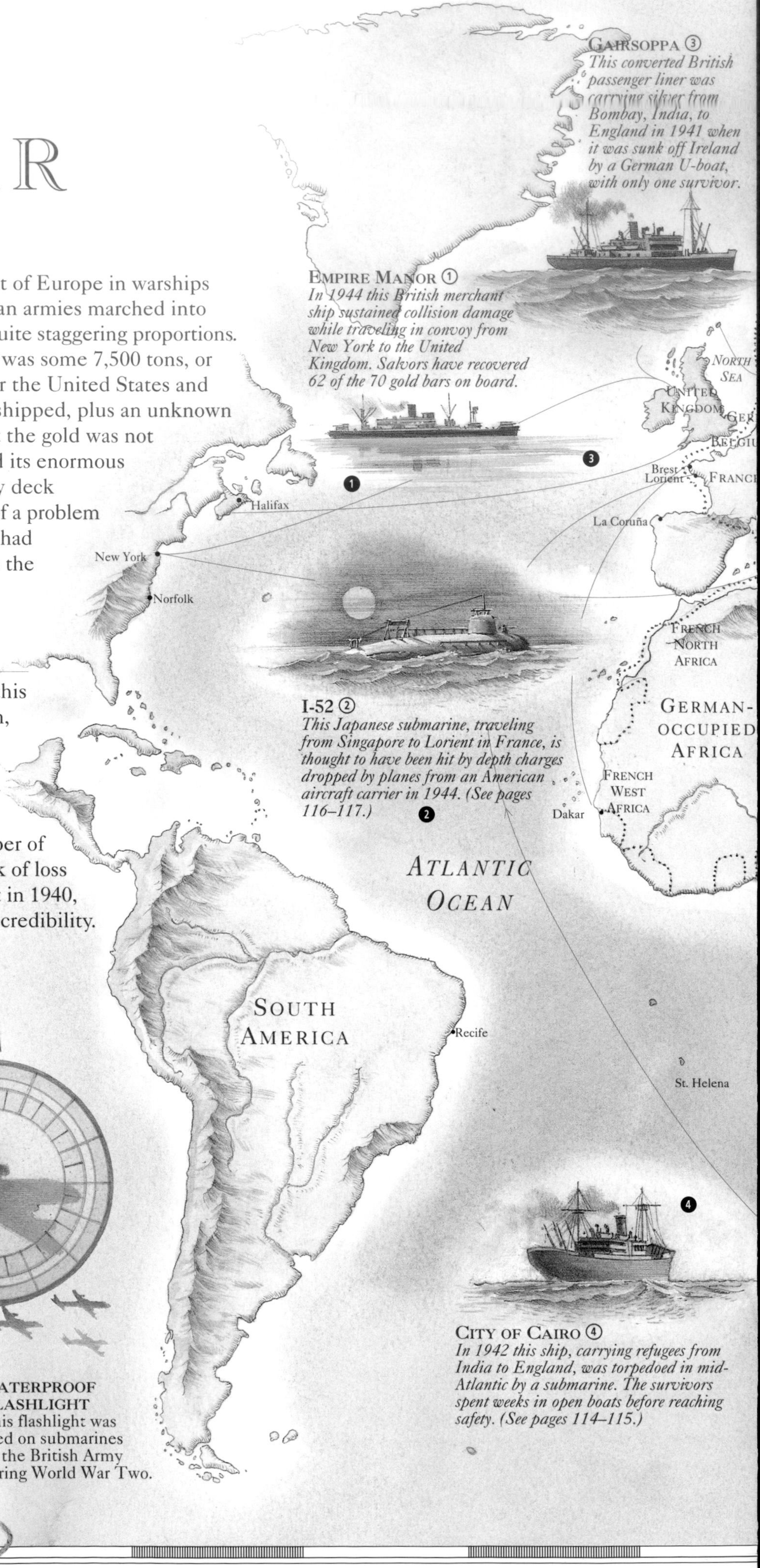

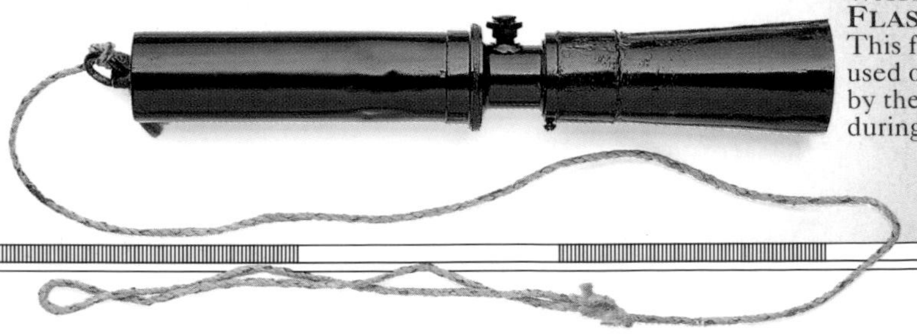

WATERPROOF FLASHLIGHT
This flashlight was used on submarines by the British Army during World War Two.

GAIRSOPPA ③
This converted British passenger liner was carrying silver from Bombay, India, to England in 1941 when it was sunk off Ireland by a German U-boat, with only one survivor.

EMPIRE MANOR ①
In 1944 this British merchant ship sustained collision damage while traveling in convoy from New York to the United Kingdom. Salvors have recovered 62 of the 70 gold bars on board.

I-52 ②
This Japanese submarine, traveling from Singapore to Lorient in France, is thought to have been hit by depth charges dropped by planes from an American aircraft carrier in 1944. (See pages 116–117.)

CITY OF CAIRO ④
In 1942 this ship, carrying refugees from India to England, was torpedoed in mid-Atlantic by a submarine. The survivors spent weeks in open boats before reaching safety. (See pages 114–115.)

ATLANTIC OCEAN

SOUTH AMERICA

NORTH SEA

UNITED KINGDOM

GERMANY

BELGIUM

FRANCE

FRENCH NORTH AFRICA

GERMAN-OCCUPIED AFRICA

FRENCH WEST AFRICA

Halifax

New York

Norfolk

La Coruña

Brest

Lorient

Dakar

Recife

St. Helena

EDINBURGH ⑤
A British Navy cruiser that was attacked and sunk en route from Russia to the United Kingdom in 1942. A spectacular salvage operation recovered most of its gold. (See pages 112–113.)

GERMAN BIBER SUBMARINE
Used in the Second World War by German forces who were trained to perform underwater naval operations, this submarine could carry one man and two full-size torpedoes. It was largely ineffective, however, because of its improvised design.

JOHN BARRY ⑥
This American Liberty ship, en route to India with a cargo of silver, was torpedoed in 1944. Attempts at salvage are now under way. (See pages 118–119.)

MANILA BAY TREASURE ⑧
In 1942, an American minelayer dumped 2,632 boxes of silver into Manila Bay to prevent them falling into Japanese hands. The bulk has been recovered but about 1 million silver pesos are still unaccounted for.

AWA MARU ⑩
This converted Japanese passenger ship was traveling as a hospital ship from Singapore to Japan in 1945 when it was struck by an American submarine. In addition to strategic supplies of tin, tungsten, and rubber, the Awa Maru is rumored to have been carrying gold, platinum, diamonds, and art treasures. So far, only tin has been recovered.

ITSUKISHIMA ⑦
A Japanese minelayer that was torpedoed by a Dutch submarine in 1944 with, according to some accounts, 2 tons of gold stowed in the captain's room.

NIAGARA ⑨
This liner, owned by the Canadian-Australian Line, was carrying 12.5 tons of gold from New Zealand to Canada in 1940 when it hit a mine and sank. Almost all the cargo has been salvaged.

HMS
EDINBURGH

Few sea routes during wartime were without their attendant risks, but the convoys of ships carrying tin, aluminum, tanks, and airplanes from England to Russia during 1942 were in for a particularly grim experience. It was vital to keep these routes open to supply equipment to Russia, which had just entered the war against Germany. There was the constant risk of attack from German U-boats and surface ships. Also, the weather conditions in the Arctic Circle were bitterly hostile: so much ice would form over a ship's superstructure that it was in real danger of becoming top-heavy. Any sailor unfortunate enough to end up in the water would have a life expectancy of no more than a few minutes.

On April 29, 1942, the large, heavily armed warship *HMS Edinburgh* left Murmansk, Russia, escorting the convoy QP11 on its return voyage to England. It had 850 men on board, and had a top speed of 32.5 knots. In one of its bomb rooms deep inside the hull it was also carrying approximately 4.5 tons of gold in 93 boxes, worth $2,320,620 at the time . This gold was part of Stalin's payment for the war supplies that Russia had been receiving.

German aerial surveillance had already observed the convoy forming in Murmansk and, on April 30, U-boat 456 fired a torpedo that struck *HMS Edinburgh* on the starboard side. The ship immediately took on a heavy list but the hatches were battened down and the seawater was contained within the area where the torpedo had struck. However, a number of men who were below deck at the time were killed outright, and there is a strong likelihood that several others were trapped, unable to escape as the water ingressed. A second torpedo struck the stern and wrecked the steering gear. *HMS Edinburgh* attempted to limp back to Murmansk but the damaged steering gear caused the stricken warship to go around in circles, so it made little progress.

On May 2, *HMS Edinburgh* was fiercely attacked by three German destroyers, and another 57 crew were lost. The ship was abandoned by the remaining crew who took refuge in one of the British destroyers that was accompanying it. The ship was then deliberately sunk by the British to prevent its cargo of gold from falling into enemy hands.

"MOON POOL" ON SALVAGE SHIP

A chamber containing divers salvaging HMS Edinburgh *was lowered through this moon pool, a hole in the bottom of the salvage support vessel. To avoid the need for time-consuming decompression procedures after each dive, the divers lived in this chamber for weeks at a time, breathing a mixture of helium and oxygen, and working in shifts.*

THE SALVAGE OPERATION

In April 1981 the salvage company Jessop Marine sent its survey ship *Dammtor* to hunt for the wreck of *HMS Edinburgh* in the Barents Sea. After a search of only 10 days the ship was found in the approximate position 72.00°N 35.00°E. A remote-operated vehicle took some detailed film of the wreck as it lay on the sea floor, which the salvage company analyzed to plan its operation. On August 30 of that same year, the dive support ship *Stephaniturm* made its way to the wreck site with a team of handpicked deep-sea divers on board. It carried the latest technological equipment.

All those involved in the salvage, including the divers, were working on a "no cure no pay" basis: if the gold was not salvaged they would receive nothing. The diving operation was a triumph of meticulous planning and physical endurance. No divers had worked at such depths for prolonged periods of time. A number of divers suffered from bad ear infections, an occupational hazard of the business, and others sustained bruised limbs or scalded feet from the hot water that circulated inside their suits to prevent them from freezing to death in the Arctic water.

SISTER SHIP OF HMS EDINBURGH

HMS Belfast *is identical in design and layout to the warship* HMS Edinburgh, *which was 613.5 feet (187 meters) long and weighed 10,000 tons. In 1942* HMS Edinburgh *was attacked by a German U-boat while carrying a consignment of Russian gold to England.*

4-in (100-mm) guns
These antiaircraft guns had a range of over 10 miles (16 km) and could also target surface vessels

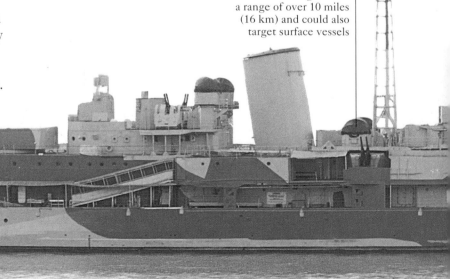

Quarterdeck
This was torn open and crumpled during a German attack

SIGHTING OF GOLD
The Russian gold ingots from HMS Edinburgh lay in wooden boxes in one of the original bomb rooms. A bomb can be seen in the top left-hand corner of this underwater photograph.

Selecting a Salvage Company

Although the gold in *HMS Edinburgh* lay off Russia, 800 feet (245 meters) below the surface, it was not altogether forgotten. In 1954, the British government gave the salvage company Risdon Beazley Ltd. permission to carry out salvage operations but, at the time, there were many other more immediately attractive targets in less politically sensitive waters, so the project was put on hold. In 1957, *HMS Edinburgh* was designated a war grave, a factor that was to prove important later, when different firms competed again for the contract in the early 1980s.

In the late 1970s, interest in the wreck stirred once more. The British government was anxious to see the gold recovered. Not only would it provide valuable revenue for the Exchequer, but there was the ever-increasing possibility that, if a contractor were not employed soon, the ship would be pirated, or the Russians might be tempted to salvage it themselves.

Identification marks
CCCP and the hammer and sickle sign show this is gold belonging to the Russian government

GOLD INGOT FROM HMS EDINBURGH
This is the first of the 431 Russian gold bars recovered by the salvage company Jessop Marine from a bomb room in the wreck. It was cast in Moscow in 1937.

TRIUMPHANT KEITH JESSOP
The salvor and some of his diving crew celebrate the recovery of the first bar of gold from HMS Edinburgh on September 15, 1981. Within three weeks a further 430 bars had been recovered from the wreck site.

Jessop Marine, a salvage company run by diver Keith Jessop, won the contract, partly because the government felt that its methods, which used cutting machinery and divers, were more appropriate to a war grave than the more explosive "smash and grab" techniques proposed by other contenders. Jessop Marine was asking for 45 percent of the proceeds, and the remainder would be split one-third to the British government and two-thirds to the Russian government, reflecting the ratio in which the original wartime insurance of the gold had been split.

On September 15, 1981, a diver penetrated the wreck and recovered a bar of gold. By October 7, when bad weather forced the suspension of the salvage, 431 out of 465 bars had been recovered, worth in excess of $64 million.

Bomb rooms
Situated on the starboard side, and used to store the gold bullion as well as bombs

Impact point
The first enemy torpedo fired by U-boat 456 landed close to the bomb rooms, crippling *HMS Edinburgh*

Director tower
Gunning operations were directed from this control tower, manned by lookouts

FACTS AND FEATURES

Treasure	93 boxes of gold
Salvage	Almost complete
Route	Russia to England

Aircraft deck
HMS Edinburgh carried two reconnaissance aircraft, launched from this deck by catapult; on return they landed on the sea and were winched aboard by a crane

6-in (152-mm) guns
For attacking enemy ships with 112 lb (50 kg) shells at a range of up to 14 miles (22.5 km)

THE
CITY OF CAIRO

Built in Hull, England, in 1915 for Ellerman Lines, the *City of Cairo* had two decks, two masts, a burden of 8,034 tons, and was 449.9 feet (137 meters) long. On October 1, 1942 it was lying in Bombay docks, India, ready to leave for England via the Cape of Good Hope, South Africa. The ship had a crew of 150 and about 150 passengers, of whom nearly a third were women and children. Most of the cargo of cotton and manganese ore had been loaded. At the last moment, heavily guarded army trucks drew up at the wharfside and some 2,000 boxes of silver coin (3 million oz/85 million grams of silver) were lowered into the hold. The exigencies of war sometimes resulted in large amounts of treasure being embarked on the most unlikely vessels, such as this passenger ship.

The first part of the journey to Cape Town was uneventful but slow, the *City of Cairo* managing a top speed of only 12 knots and its engines burning smokily, both of which factors would make it vulnerable to U-boat attack. A large fleet of U-boats was operating off South Africa, and had already taken a heavy toll on Allied shipping.

Sailing into Danger

The most perilous part of the journey was the section from Cape Town to Recife, Brazil. The *City of Cairo* left Cape Town on November 1 and followed the African coast until reaching a longitude of 23.30°S, where it turned westward across the Atlantic. It had no protective escort and was instructed to zigzag until it entered safer waters. By November 6 the passengers and crew began to relax a little, thinking the worst was over.

At this point Karl-Friedrich Merten, the commander of *U68*, which was cruising on the surface, noticed a column of smoke on the horizon. Whether this was smoke from the sulfur candle used to dislodge a stowaway cat (see right) or a reoccurrence of the dirty coal problem experienced earlier is still not known. An hour later Merten struck the *City of Cairo* with a torpedo, holing it and shattering some of the boxes of silver coin. As soon as it was clear what had happened, Captain

Rogerson gave the order to abandon ship. All the women and children left the ship safely and only six people were lost in the evacuation. Twenty minutes after the first torpedo had struck, a humane interval allowing time for those on board to make their escape, Merten fired a second torpedo and the *City of Cairo* sank, stern first, along with all of its valuable cargo.

Survivors in Lifeboats

Merten carried out the standard cross-questioning of those in the lifeboat nearest to his ship, and informed them of their position. There were six small open boats, heavily overcrowded with almost 300 survivors between them; one had a tiny engine but very little fuel. They were over 1,000 miles (1,600 kilometers) from the African coast, and twice as far from South America, with the tiny island of St. Helena 500 miles (800 kilometers) to the north. Given their very limited supplies, there was only one real choice: to make for St. Helena. The problem lay in finding such a tiny island in the middle of such a vast ocean. To navigate, the survivors had only one sextant, an Oyster Rolex watch, and several compasses between them, so it was vital that all six boats stayed together.

The survivors calculated that they should reach St. Helena in two to three weeks, and rationed the drinking water accordingly. Everyone was to be limited to 4 fl oz (110 ml) a day, even though they were mercilessly exposed to tropical heat.

CAT SANK SHIP?

A cat that stowed away on the *City of Cairo* when it left Bombay may have played a major part in the sinking of the ship. It had hidden in one of the lifeboats and an attempt was made to smoke it out using a sulfur candle. The commander of the U-boat that sank the *City of Cairo* spotted a column of smoke and homed in on the ship. The cat survived the torpedo and escaped on one of the lifeboats, but it lost its life two weeks later, after the people on its boat were rescued but the boat itself was sunk to prevent it from being a hazard to shipping.

At the beginning, the castaways were fortunate in that the weather was fine and calm. The initial good cheer did not last long: the boats were so crowded that it was impossible to move around in them; they leaked so badly that everyone was constantly sloshing around in water; and while the days were blisteringly hot, the nights were bitterly cold.

The health and the spirits of the crew and passengers began to take a turn for the worse. Arguments raged as to whether extra mouthfuls of water should be given to those who were sickest or whether any surplus rations should be kept for the fittest and strongest, on whom they all relied.

Flotilla Disintegrates

The fastest of the boats left the flotilla on November 11 to go ahead and summon help. During the night of the 12th contact was lost with a second boat. The following night there was a storm and a spar broke away from a third boat; a fourth noticed its distress signal and went to assist. By the following morning the flotilla had completely disintegrated, and Captain Rogerson's boat was the only one still in contact with the navigation boat, upon which they had all completely depended.

BREAKAWAY BOAT

The fastest boat of the six lifeboats from the torpedoed *City of Cairo* was commanded by Chief Officer Sidney Britt. He decided if it went on ahead it would reach St. Helena early and be able to arrange for help for the other boats. So on November 11 it broke away from the rest of the flotilla. Within a week it became obvious to the 54 people on board that they had missed the island. Tempers frayed and behavior deteriorated. At night someone was illicitly tapping the precious water supply. Britt died on November 20, and several people gave up the struggle and simply lowered themselves overboard. By the time the boat was picked up by the German blockade-runner *Rhakotis* on December 12, it was 500 miles (800 kilometers) to the northwest of St. Helena. There were only three survivors, and one of them died after rescue. The remaining two survivors were again shipwrecked when the *Rhakotis* was itself sunk. One of them managed to reach Britain, but the second became a prisoner of war.

Rescue of the Lifeboats

Early on the morning of November 19, the people in the boat that had lost contact on the 12th noticed a ship on the horizon. They flashed torches and sent up SOS flares. After an agonizing delay the ship, the *SS Clan Alpine*, turned toward the small boat and rescued the occupants. Most were still alive but in a severely weakened state. Amazingly, considering that for the previous week they had been sailing only by the feel of the wind and a compass, this boat was on direct course for St. Helena and only about 50 miles (80 kilometers) short of its target.

Later that same morning *SS Clan Alpine* picked up the survivors from two more boats. The people in these boats had already sighted the mountains of St. Helena but were saved the necessity of negotiating the difficult coastal waters. Of the 166 occupants in these three boats, 16 had died, and 2 more later died on St. Helena.

On the same day, by an extraordinary coincidence, those in a fourth boat, which was still straggling 200 miles (320 kilometers) behind the leading boats, were spotted by another British ship, *SS Bendoran*. Of the original 55 on board, 47 were still alive.

CITY OF CAIRO
Portrait of the ship in front of Table Mountain, South Africa. The thick black smoke belching from the funnels made the ship easy to spot at sea, and therefore vulnerable to attack. This may have contributed to its sinking.

YOUNG SURVIVORS
Some of the children who reached the safety of St. Helena. Two show clear signs of sunburn, illustrating some of the hazards they faced on their two-week voyage in lifeboats after the shipwreck.

The *Bendoran* was en route to Cape Town and before long the survivors found themselves back in the port where they had been less than a month before.

There were only 17 in the fifth boat. They had calculated that they should reach St. Helena by November 20. By the 23rd, several were already dead, no sign of the tiny island had been seen, and hope began to fall away. They were certain that they must have missed St. Helena and, rather than circle around in a vain attempt to discover it, they decided to head west to the coast of South America, which they knew to be a further

1,500 miles (2,400 kilometers) distant. It was an extraordinarily ambitious undertaking for a small group of people already at the limit of their endurance. On the night of December 27, after a voyage of 51 days, they were finally picked up by the Brazilian ship *Caravellas*. They were only 80 miles (130 kilometers) short of their target but only two were still alive. Three months later, by a particularly cruel irony, one was returning across the Atlantic from the US to Britain on a ship that was torpedoed and lost with all on board. The other, understandably, refused to cross the Atlantic until the war was over.

THE
I-52

One of Germany's greatest problems during the Second World War was a shortage of strategic supplies, in particular rubber and metals such as tungsten and tin. Its main ally, Japan, had access to these supplies in abundance, particularly after Japan's successful invasion of Malaya in 1942. However, transporting these items to German-occupied Europe was extremely hazardous, because the navies of the United States and Great Britain controlled both the North and South Atlantic.

From 1941 onward Germany made a number of attempts to ship in these supplies both on the northern route (via the Barents Sea) and on the southern route (via the Indian Ocean), but these blockade-breaking ships, as they were called, suffered a very high casualty rate. As the war progressed, the losses became unacceptably high, but Germany's need for the materials was ever more urgent. Toward the end of 1943, Germany developed the desperate strategy of using cargo-carrying submarines. The first submarine to make a successful voyage from Japan to Lorient in German-occupied France, via the Indian Ocean, was the *I-29* in 1943. Included in the delivery of strategic materials were 2 tons of gold, part-payment to Germany for supplying Japan with both technical information and war materials.

The I-52 and its Maiden Voyage

On December 18, 1943, the building of the *I-52* was completed at the Kure Navy Yard in Japan. This submarine had a displacement of 2,095 tons, and was 356.5 feet (109 meters) long. It could travel at a top speed of 17.75 knots when surfaced and 6.5 knots when submerged, and it had been specifically designed for long-range cargo-carrying. The *I-52* carried 19 torpedoes, was tested to a depth of 330 feet (100 meters), and because the submarine was equipped with extra-large fuel tanks it had a range of 27,000 nautical miles, at 12 knots.

During March 1944, the *I-52* left Kure for Singapore on its first voyage. Its commander was Kameo Uno, and the chief engineer was Lieutenant Commander Shin-ichi Matsuura.

Conning tower
Used for observation when on the surface. The *I-52* could dive to 330 feet (100 meters) in safety.

Deck-mounted gun
Antiaircraft guns provided some defense when the submarine was on the surface

Escort tug
This was used to accompany the submarine into the port

Torpedo tube
The *I-52*'s torpedo tubes are likely to have been removed to increase cargo space

JAPANESE SUBMARINE ENTERING PORT
The I-8 *enters Lorient, France, in 1943, with the crew standing to attention on the deck in front of the guns. A year later, the* I-52 *was heading for the same destination when it was sunk by American depth charges.*

Its total crew amounted to 94, and it also carried a small number of elite technical personnel. Shortly before the *I-52* left Kure it had loaded a very large quantity of gold in ingot form, which was the balance of the amount owed by Japan to Germany.

The *I-52* arrived in Singapore at the end of March and loaded on board some 230 tons of tungsten, molybdenum, and tin, 54 tons of rubber, and 5 tons of quinine. On April 23, 1944, it left for Lorient, France.

Toward the evening of June 23, the *I-52* rendezvoused with the German submarine *U530* in a position approximately 800 miles (1,290 kilometers) southwest of the Azores. Three German personnel (a liaison officer, signalman, and pilot) together with some radio equipment transferred to the Japanese submarine. Around this time, Lieutenant Commander Taylor, in an aircraft launched from the aircraft carrier *USS Bogue*, had seen a surfaced submarine that fitted the description of a Japanese cargo carrier – "very large and pointed at bow and stern." This sighting was not purely fortuitous: Allied interception and interpretation of enemy radio signals had given them detailed knowledge of the movements of the *I-52* and the German submarine.

The Allies attacked by dropping MK 24 mines into the area as well as a large number of sonar buoys. These sonar buoys were a new development and picked up vibrations from submarine propellers, enabling monitoring aircraft to calculate more or less the position of the enemy submarines. The Allies presumed that their depth charges had hit both of them (see box opposite).

The German submarine did, in fact, survive the attack but its logbook records that the

AFTERMATH OF THE SUBMARINE SINKING

After the attack on the Japanese submarine *I-52* on June 23, 1944, destroyers *USS Janssen* and *Haverfield* were despatched to the area where the submarine was thought to have been destroyed. They picked up from the sea a grisly collection of items that had floated to the surface, including sheets of crude rubber, a rubber sandal with a Japanese inscription, some wood that was thought to be Philippine mahogany, some light, black silk fishing line, and a small quantity of human flesh that was identified by laboratory analysts as probably originating from the stomach of an oriental person. There was also a considerable quantity of oil over the surface of the water. It was concluded that the attack had been successful, but later evidence threw some doubt on this.

AIRCRAFT CARRIER USS BOGUE, 1943
The USS Bogue was converted from a cargo ship to carry aircraft during the Second World War. It could house 30 airplanes, some of which can be seen in the photograph. It was one of these aircraft that dropped the MK 24 mines that are thought to have sunk the I-52 in 1944.

DEPTH CHARGE EXPLODING NEAR A SUBMARINE, 1944
Depth charges are canisters filled with explosives that are detonated by depth-sensitive pistols. In the attack on the I-52, the American commanders first launched sonar buoys to detect the position of the enemy submarines, then launched depth charges to sink the submarines.

crew heard explosions about an hour after the rendezvous had been completed, coming from the direction where the Japanese submarine was likely to have been at that time. Evidence for the loss of the *I-52* in a position approximately 15.16°N 39.55°W appeared to be fairly conclusive.

Did the I-52 Sink?

Both German and Japanese records suggest that the issue might not be quite so straightforward. German records refer to the *I-52* sending a radio signal requesting new routing instructions on July 24, a whole month after it had supposedly been sunk southwest of the Azores. Another radio signal received on July 30 gave its position as 36 hours from Lorient. Later Japanese records refer to the *I-52* being presumed lost in the Bay of Biscay, after all radio contact had ceased from August 1. If so, it is possible that the *I-52* could have been a victim of the heavy aerial bombing that was taking place at the time. Both German and Japanese sources officially recorded their own dead as being lost toward the end of July in the Bay of Biscay area.

This introduces the interesting theory that the *I-52* may have only been damaged but not sunk during the attack on June 24. The debris collected by the US destroyers after the attack (see box above) might have been a deliberate ruse on the part of the Japanese to trick the Allies into thinking that the *I-52* had sunk, and so distract them from further attacks. What is certain is that this war shipment of gold never reached its destination and, so far, the *I-52* and its cargo have not been found.

THE JOHN BARRY

The *John Barry* was one of the first Liberty ships (American mass-produced merchant vessels) to be launched (see below). It was built in Portland, Oregon, and was owned by the United States Maritime Commission. It left Hampton Roads, Norfolk, in a convoy on July 24, 1944, arriving at Port Said, Egypt, on August 19. It then sailed independently via Suez and Aden across the Arabian Sea, en route for the Saudi port of Ras Tannurah, near Bahrain in the Persian Gulf. It was following a zigzag route to make it a more difficult target for torpedoes.

On the evening of August 28 the sky was overcast with a hazy moon, and the sea was rough, with a very strong wind blowing from the west-southwest. Despite the zigzag path taken and the crew maintaining a blackout and radio silence, the ship was struck on the starboard side by a torpedo from the German U-boat 859, at 10:00 p.m. The *John Barry*'s engines were stopped and the radio officer transmitted an SOS signal. The ship's position was approximately 15.10°N and 55.18°E. The captain, Joseph Ellerwald, gave the order to abandon ship in the lifeboats, and all except two of the crew got away safely. Shortly after evacuation, a second torpedo struck the *John Barry* on the starboard side, and then a third torpedo struck on the port side. The ship

appeared to break in two, and sank with bow and stern ends up. The next day all the survivors were picked up by the American ship *Benjamin Bourne* and the Dutch ship *Sunetta*.

When the *John Barry* was torpedoed it was carrying a very mixed cargo, including auto parts for Russia and boxes of silver Saudi ryals (see opposite). This cargo, by itself, would not be a sufficiently attractive target for a salvage operation. What makes the *John Barry* one of the most controversial treasure-ships of all time and also one of the most fascinating underwater mysteries yet to be solved, is whether it also carried some 2,000 tons of silver bullion in its holds.

The evidence that such a large quantity of silver was on board, worth nearly $300 million at today's prices, is considerable. To begin with, when officially interviewed by the authorities in Aden, the purser stated that the cargo included silver bullion worth $26 million, a sum which represents about 1,200 tons of silver at 1944 prices. Nor did he just make the statement once, which might be a result of confusion caused by the trauma of sinking. He made it a second time when being interviewed in Washington.

Extra Evidence for Silver Cargo

There are other factors that support the purser's statements, such as the fact that the balance of the *John Barry*'s known cargo was approximately 1,200 tons short of the ship's capacity. It seems unlikely that it would have sailed only partially loaded, especially when it is known to have had a considerable quantity of cargo stowed

LIBERTY SHIPS

During the war the Allied merchant fleet used Liberty ships, which were cheap, functional, and efficient, to keep essential supplies flowing across the Atlantic and through the Mediterranean to Allies in the East, such as India and Russia. Nearly 3,000 Liberty ships were built in the US between 1941 and 1945, a prodigious industrial achievement, rolling out of the shipyards in the manner of a factory line assembly plant. The record for building one from the laying of the keel to launch was 4 days and 15.5 hours. It was necessary to build at this rate to compensate for the heavy losses inflicted on the Allies by German U-boats.

PROPELLED WEAPONS

TORPEDO

CIGARETTE CARD OF A TORPEDO
Contemporary illustration of the launching of a torpedo. These self-propelled underwater missiles could be fired from submarines, light craft, or airplanes. The John Barry *was struck by three torpedoes, fired from a German U-boat. The ship broke in two and sank with all its cargo.*

Cargo derrick
For winching cargo from the dockside into the holds; the *John Barry* also stowed cargo on deck

MODEL OF A LIBERTY SHIP
More than 2,750 Liberty ships were built in America during the Second World War. They were cargo carriers rather than warships. The John Barry *had two decks and five holds.*

Swiveling gun
Cargo ships carried guns for protection against the enemy

Propeller
Powered by steam engines

CARGO ON BOARD

When the *John Barry* was sunk it was carrying a mixed aid cargo to Russia, which included 11 tons of auto parts, 65 tons of trucks, 108 tons of cranes, 23 tons of tractor crawlers, as well as large quantities of steel plate and piping for use in oil-refining.

There were also on board 750 boxes that contained 3 million silver Saudi ryals. These Saudi ryals were an alloy containing about 30 percent silver and so represent only about 1 million oz (28 million grams) of silver. What makes the shipwreck much more attractive to salvors are the enticing rumors that the ship was also carrying nearly 2,000 tons of silver bullion in its holds.

on deck rather than in the holds. Also, a guard who witnessed the loading refers to trucks with silver being brought on board at night under conditions of great secrecy. However, the trucks might just have been those that formed part of the cargo for Russia, which was being loaded at night because of pressures of time rather than secrecy.

Ambiguity and confusion also surround the available statistics. Statements of silver exported from the US to India for 1944 exceed statements of imports by India, by

about the same amount that was supposed to have been on the *John Barry*. Even so, these statistics are open to misinterpretation because they were produced by different governments and calculated according to different criteria. The two sets of dates do not tally exactly, one set being for the fiscal year and the other set for the calendar year.

Evidence Against Silver Cargo

The arguments against the silver bullion ever having been on board are also weighty. First, no government has ever claimed ownership, despite approaches to the Russians, the Indians, the Americans, and the British. Second, although the loss of the much less valuable Saudi ryals is carefully documented, there is no mention of the missing bullion in the records. Third, during their lengthy interviews, neither the captain nor the first engineer make any mention of the bullion. Last, and perhaps most telling, is the question of why anyone would have risked sending so much bullion in one vulnerable ship that could achieve only 12 knots at top speed. There is no other known instance of a ship of such a lowly status as the *John Barry* carrying a silver shipment of this massive size.

Salvage Under Way

One group, however, is so convinced that the silver bullion really is on board that it has spent several million dollars on location and preliminary salvage work. This consortium, which includes Sheikh Ahmed Farid of Oman, the American Captain Shoemaker, and the British salvor Keith Jessop, who salvaged *HMS Edinburgh* (see pages 112–13), has reputedly bought the salvage rights for a sum rumored to be around $750,000. The group employed Eastport International, a company specializing in the location of objects on the seabed at great depths, to find the wreck. In 1991, Eastport succeeded in locating and photographing the remains of the *John Barry*.

A massive salvage operation has now been started, which includes a giant Dutch salvage company, Smit, working as a contractor along-side a French specialist company, Ifremer, the company that helped locate the *Titanic* (see pages 104–5). Underwater explosives are very precisely placed by remote-operated vehicles in order to penetrate the hull. A grab operated from the surface will lift the cargo, if found. After two years of operations no bullion has been brought up from the wreck, but the salvors are still confident of success.

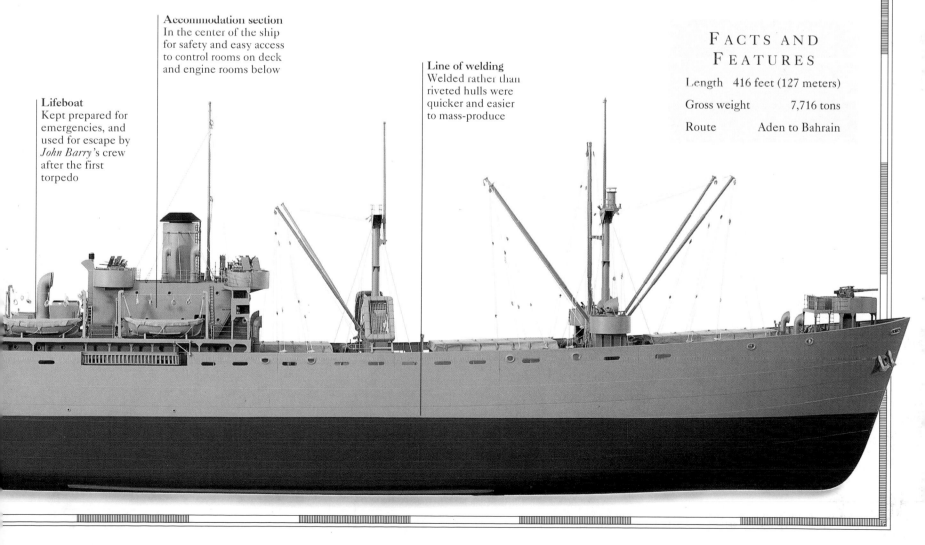

Lifeboat
Kept prepared for emergencies, and used for escape by *John Barry*'s crew after the first torpedo

Accommodation section
In the center of the ship for safety and easy access to control rooms on deck and engine rooms below

Line of welding
Welded rather than riveted hulls were quicker and easier to mass-produce

FACTS AND FEATURES

Length	416 feet (127 meters)
Gross weight	7,716 tons
Route	Aden to Bahrain

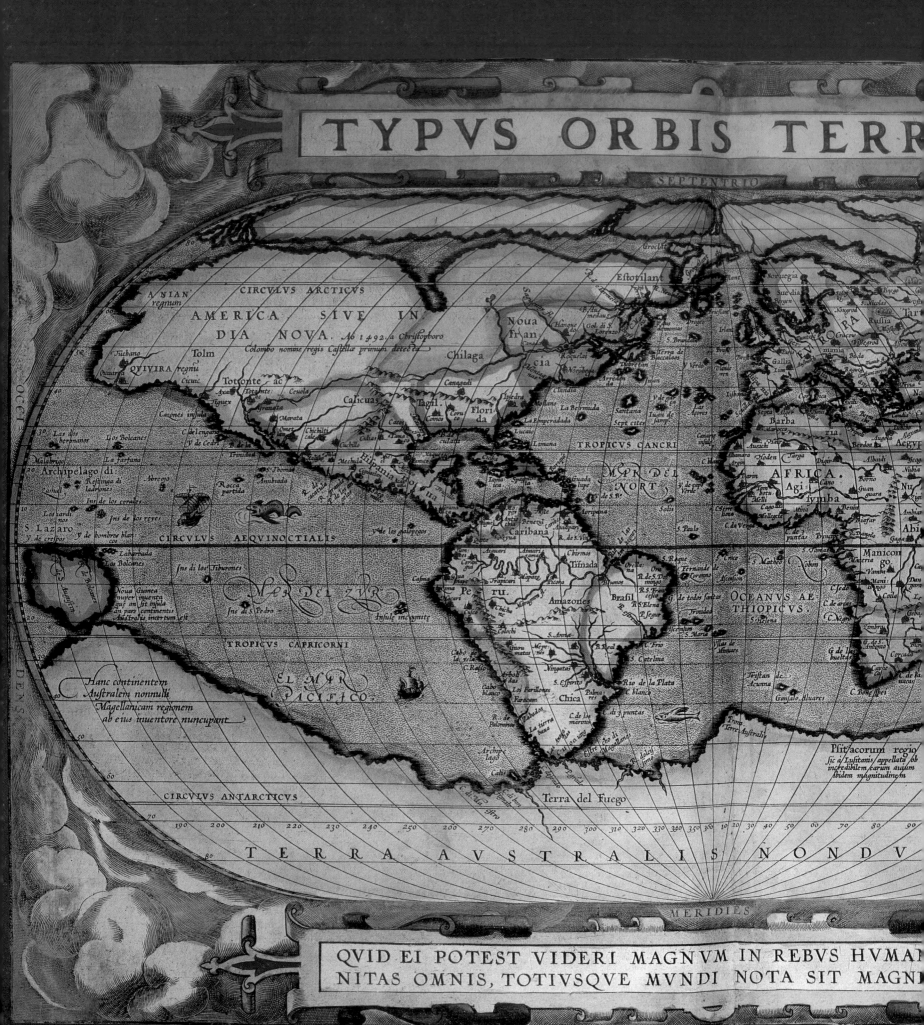

TYPVS ORBIS TERR

CIRCVLVS ARCTICVS

A NIAN regnum

AMERICA SIVE IN
DIA NOVA. Ao 1492. a Chriſtophoro
Colombo nomine regis Caſtella primum detecta

Estotilant

Noua
Fran-
cia

Tolm
Totonte
ac

Quiuira regnú
Cicuic

Chilaga

Canagadi

Florida

TROPICVS CANCRI

MAR DEL
NORT

EVROPA

AFRICA.

CIRCVLVS AEQVINOCTIALIS

MAR DEL ZVR

Caribana

Tifnada

Amazones

Brasil

Peru.

OCEANVS AE
THIOPICVS.

TROPICVS CAPRICORNI

Hanc continentem
Australem nonnulli
Magellanicam regionem
ab eius inuentore nuncupant

EL MAR
PACIFICO

Chica

Rio de la Plata

Terra del Fuego

CIRCVLVS ANTARCTICVS

190 200 210 220 230 240 250 260 270 280 290 300 310 320 330 340 350 360 10 20 30 40 50 60 70 80 90

QVID EI POTEST VIDERI MAGNVM IN REBVS HVMAN
NITAS OMNIS, TOTIVSQVE MVNDI NOTA SIT MAGNI

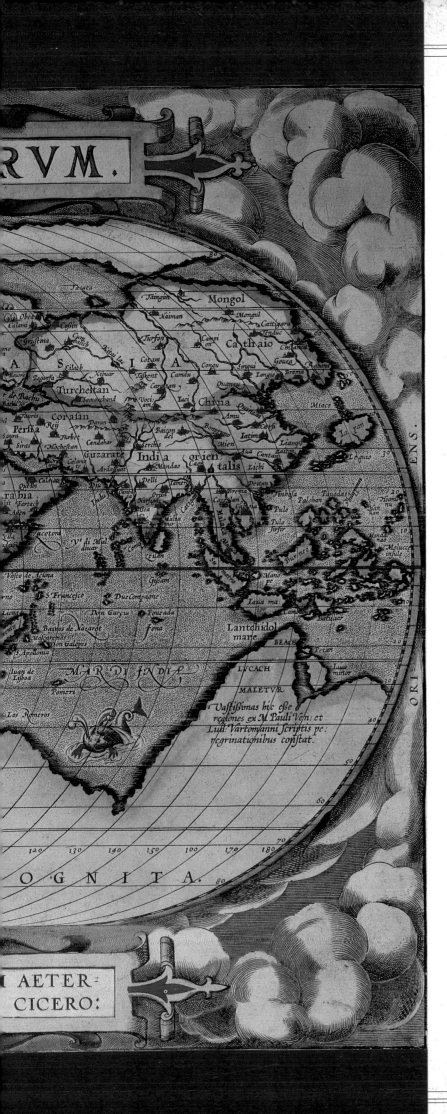

PART TWO
$\mathcal{G}$AZETTEER

The sky, it seems, would pour down stinking pitch,
But that the sea, mounting to th' welkin's cheek,
Dashes the fire out. O, I have suffered
With those that I saw suffer! a brave vessel,
(who had, no doubt, some noble creature in her,)
Dash'd all to pieces. O, the cry did knock
Against my very heart! Pour souls, they perish'd!
ACT 1, SCENE 2, THE TEMPEST BY WILLIAM SHAKESPEARE

The gazetteer section provides a comprehensive survey of more than 1,400 shipwrecks around the world. These include some of the earliest known wrecks as well as ships that sank in the twentieth century. All the wrecks are plotted on a series of specially devised maps, showing the depths at which they lie. Detailed shipwreck listings provide information about the type of ship, the route that it took, the cargo that it carried, and whether it has been salvaged.

WORLD MAP BY ABRAHAM ORTELIUS, 1598
Hand-colored engraving by Ortelius, a Flemish mapmaker. He was famed for his atlas Theatrum Orbis Terrarum *(or* Theater of the World)*, from which this illustration is taken.*

HOW TO USE THE
GAZETTEER

The gazetteer is divided into two parts: maps and shipwreck listings. First, there are 20 maps (see below) on which are plotted the sites of over 1,400 shipwrecks. These are followed by listings that give details about each of the shipwrecks plotted on the maps. Between them, the maps and listings provide detailed information about a variety of shipwrecks, from Roman times to the twentieth century, and from all around the world.

GAZETTEER MAP AREAS
This world map shows the regions covered by the 20 maps in the gazetteer, with their corresponding page numbers. Details about the wrecks plotted on each map are in the listings.

The Maps

The world map below shows the areas covered by the 20 maps in this section of the book. The box opposite gives the title of every map, and the pages on which it can be found. Each map carries the following information:

• The sites of up to 99 shipwrecks, numbered in date order.

• The historical period in which each ship was wrecked: each shipwreck plotted is color-coded according to the date the ship sank. A color key appears on each of the maps.

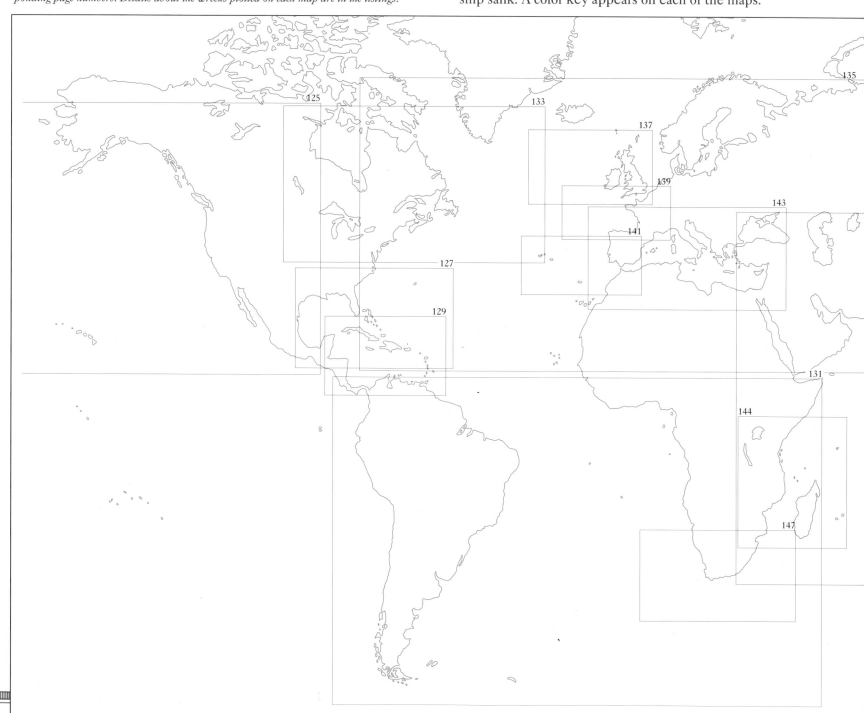

- Whether any salvage history is known about a wreck – if so, the shipwreck number appears in a square; if not, it appears in a circle.

- The approximate depth at which each wreck lies: indicated by variations in sea color. A key gives the bathymetric scales used.

Shipwreck Listings

For each of the 20 maps there is a corresponding list from which you can find out more information about any of the ships that are plotted on the maps. These listings start on page 160 and the box on the right shows the pages on which particular listings can be found. The listings give the following information for the shipwrecks:

- The name of the ship and the date on which it sank.

- A grid reference to help find the position of the wreck on the map.

- The type of ship, its location, cargo, and route (if known).

- Date and details of any known salvage attempts, plus any extra information that is available about the ship, cargo, or crew.

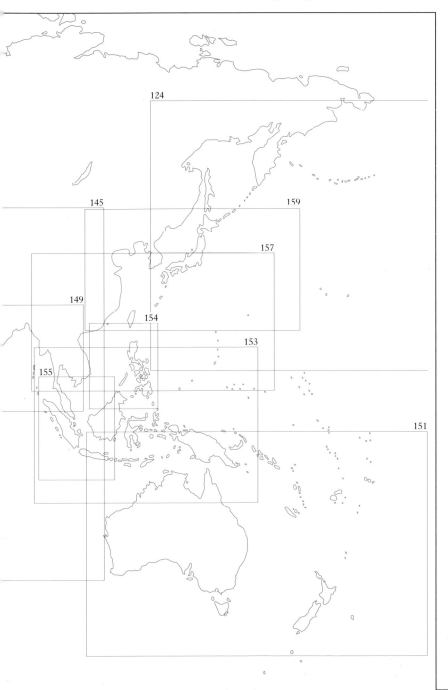

KEY TO MAPS AND LISTINGS

Map number	Map	Listings
West Coast of North America and the North Pacific	124–125	160–161
Gulf of Mexico to Bermuda	126–127	161–163
The Caribbean	128–129	163–165
South America, West Africa, and the South Atlantic	130–131	165–167
East Coast of North America	132–133	167–168
Northern Europe and the North Atlantic	134–135	168–170
The United Kingdom and Republic of Ireland	136–137	170–173
The Bay of Biscay to the Southern North Sea	138–139	173–174
Atlantic Spain, Northwest Africa, and the Azores	140–141	174–176
The Mediterranean	142–143	177–178
Madagascar and East Africa	144	178–179
The Indian Ocean, Red Sea, and Persian Gulf	145	180–181
Southern Africa	146–147	181–183
India, Sri Lanka, and the Bay of Bengal	148–149	183–185
Australia and New Zealand	150–151	185–186
Island Asia	152–153	186–187
The Philippines	154	187–188
Malaya and Sumatra	155	189–190
The South China Sea and Gulf of Thailand	156–157	190–192
Japan, Korea, and Eastern China	158–159	192–193

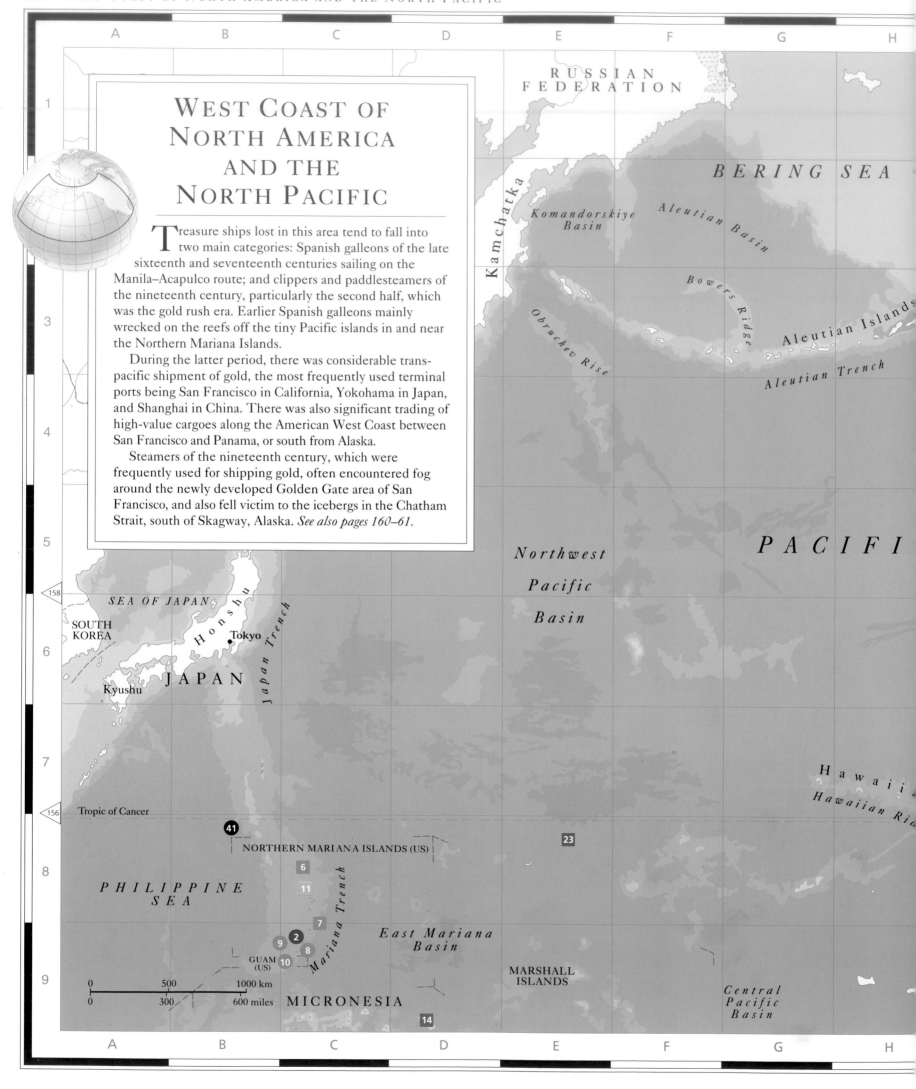

WEST COAST OF NORTH AMERICA AND THE NORTH PACIFIC

Treasure ships lost in this area tend to fall into two main categories: Spanish galleons of the late sixteenth and seventeenth centuries sailing on the Manila–Acapulco route; and clippers and paddlesteamers of the nineteenth century, particularly the second half, which was the gold rush era. Earlier Spanish galleons mainly wrecked on the reefs off the tiny Pacific islands in and near the Northern Mariana Islands.

During the latter period, there was considerable trans-pacific shipment of gold, the most frequently used terminal ports being San Francisco in California, Yokohama in Japan, and Shanghai in China. There was also significant trading of high-value cargoes along the American West Coast between San Francisco and Panama, or south from Alaska.

Steamers of the nineteenth century, which were frequently used for shipping gold, often encountered fog around the newly developed Golden Gate area of San Francisco, and also fell victim to the icebergs in the Chatham Strait, south of Skagway, Alaska. *See also pages 160–61.*

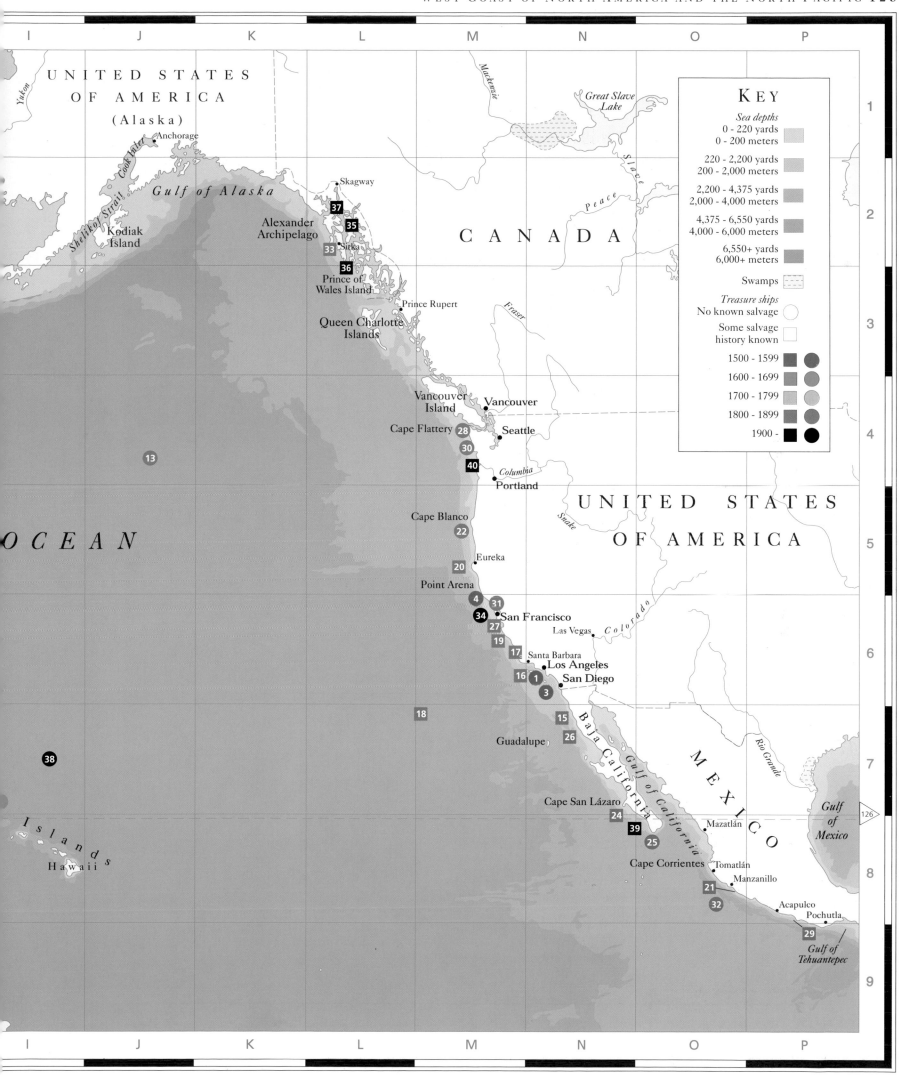

I J K L M N O P

UNITED STATES
OF AMERICA
(Alaska)

Yukon

• Anchorage

Cook Inlet

Gulf of Alaska

• Skagway

Shelikof Strait

Kodiak
Island

37

35

33 Sitka

36

Alexander
Archipelago

Prince of
Wales Island

Queen Charlotte
Islands

• Prince Rupert

CANADA

Mackenzie

*Great Slave
Lake*

Peace

Slave

Fraser

KEY

Sea depths
0 - 220 yards
0 - 200 meters

220 - 2,200 yards
200 - 2,000 meters

2,200 - 4,375 yards
2,000 - 4,000 meters

4,375 - 6,550 yards
4,000 - 6,000 meters

6,550+ yards
6,000+ meters

Swamps

Treasure ships
No known salvage

Some salvage
history known

1500 - 1599
1600 - 1699
1700 - 1799
1800 - 1899
1900 -

Vancouver
Island

Cape Flattery 28

30

40

• Vancouver

• Seattle

Columbia

• Portland

Snake

UNITED STATES

OF AMERICA

OCEAN

13

Cape Blanco
22

20 • Eureka

Point Arena

4 31

34 • San Francisco

27
19

17 • Santa Barbara
• Los Angeles

16 1 • San Diego

3

18

Colorado

• Las Vegas

15

26

Guadalupe

Baja California

Gulf of California

MEXICO

Rio Grande

*Gulf
of
Mexico*

126

38

Islands

Hawaii

Cape San Lázaro

24

39

25

• Mazatlán

Cape Corrientes

• Tomatlán

• Manzanillo

21

32

• Acapulco
• Pochutla

29

*Gulf of
Tehuantepec*

1

2

3

4

5

6

7

8

9

I J K L M N O P

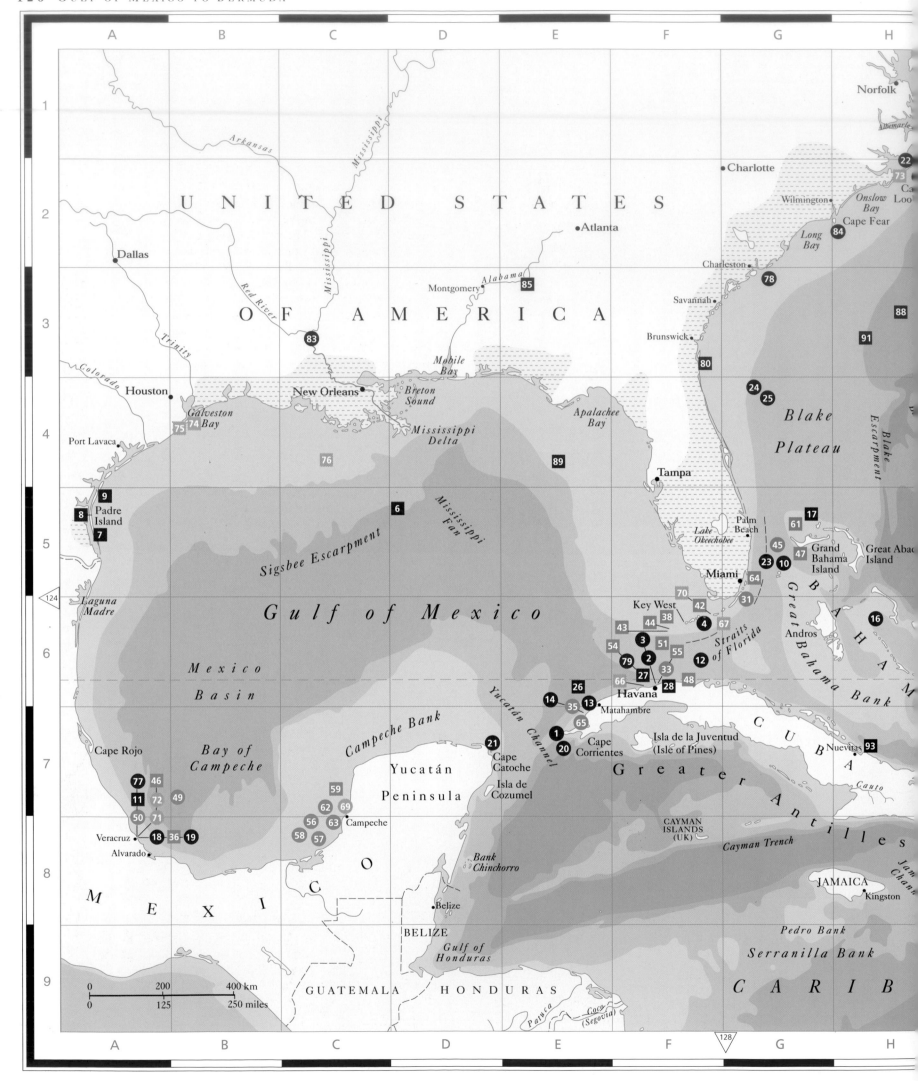

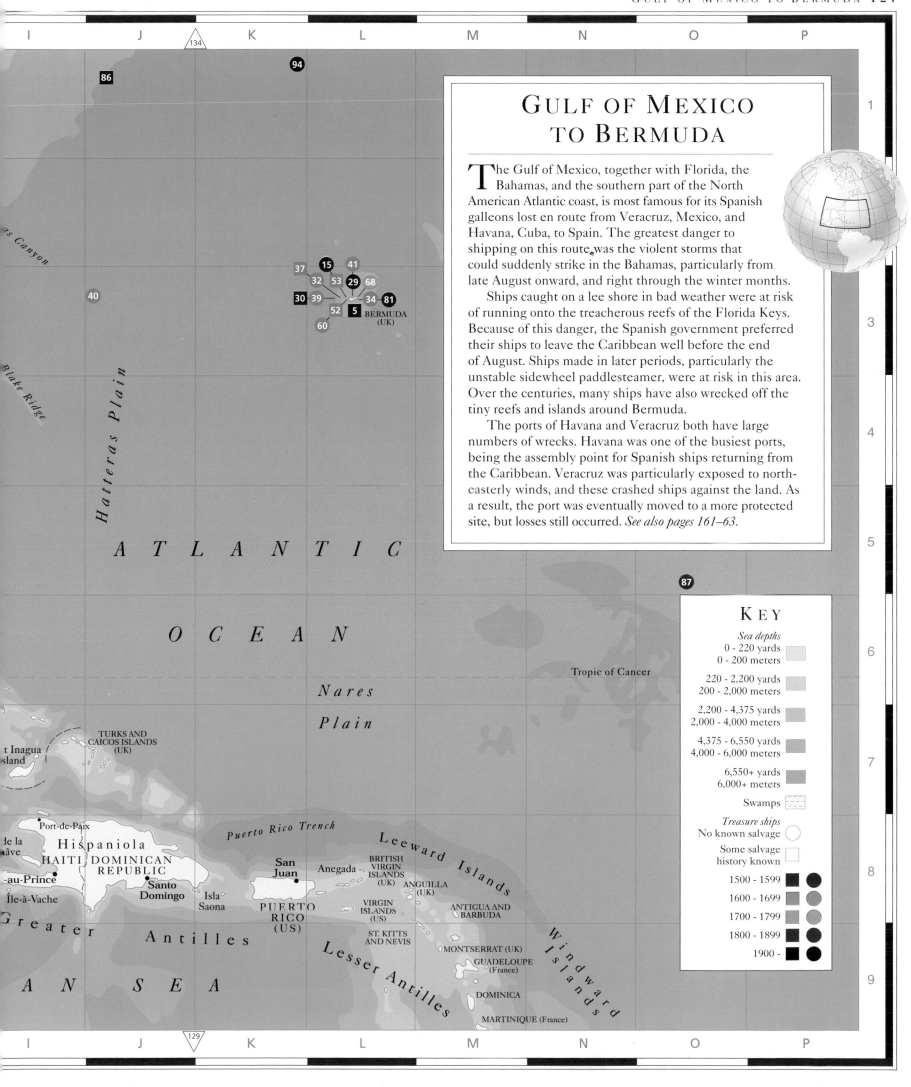

GULF OF MEXICO TO BERMUDA

The Gulf of Mexico, together with Florida, the Bahamas, and the southern part of the North American Atlantic coast, is most famous for its Spanish galleons lost en route from Veracruz, Mexico, and Havana, Cuba, to Spain. The greatest danger to shipping on this route was the violent storms that could suddenly strike in the Bahamas, particularly from late August onward, and right through the winter months.

Ships caught on a lee shore in bad weather were at risk of running onto the treacherous reefs of the Florida Keys. Because of this danger, the Spanish government preferred their ships to leave the Caribbean well before the end of August. Ships made in later periods, particularly the unstable sidewheel paddlesteamer, were at risk in this area. Over the centuries, many ships have also wrecked off the tiny reefs and islands around Bermuda.

The ports of Havana and Veracruz both have large numbers of wrecks. Havana was one of the busiest ports, being the assembly point for Spanish ships returning from the Caribbean. Veracruz was particularly exposed to north-easterly winds, and these crashed ships against the land. As a result, the port was eventually moved to a more protected site, but losses still occurred. *See also pages 161–63.*

KEY

Sea depths

0 - 220 yards / 0 - 200 meters	
220 - 2,200 yards / 200 - 2,000 meters	
2,200 - 4,375 yards / 2,000 - 4,000 meters	
4,375 - 6,550 yards / 4,000 - 6,000 meters	
6,550+ yards / 6,000+ meters	
Swamps	

Treasure ships

No known salvage ○
Some salvage history known ☐

1500 - 1599	◼	●
1600 - 1699	◼	●
1700 - 1799	◼	●
1800 - 1899	◼	●
1900 -	◼	●

Map labels

ATLANTIC OCEAN

Nares Plain

Hatteras Plain

Blake Ridge

Tropic of Cancer

Puerto Rico Trench

Hispaniola

HAITI

DOMINICAN REPUBLIC

Port-de-Paix

Santo Domingo

Isla Saona

Île-à-Vache

San Juan

Anegada

PUERTO RICO (US)

BRITISH VIRGIN ISLANDS (UK)

VIRGIN ISLANDS (US)

ANGUILLA (UK)

ANTIGUA AND BARBUDA

ST. KITTS AND NEVIS

MONTSERRAT (UK)

GUADELOUPE (France)

DOMINICA

MARTINIQUE (France)

Leeward Islands

Windward Islands

Lesser Antilles

Greater Antilles

TURKS AND CAICOS ISLANDS (UK)

Inagua Island

BERMUDA (UK)

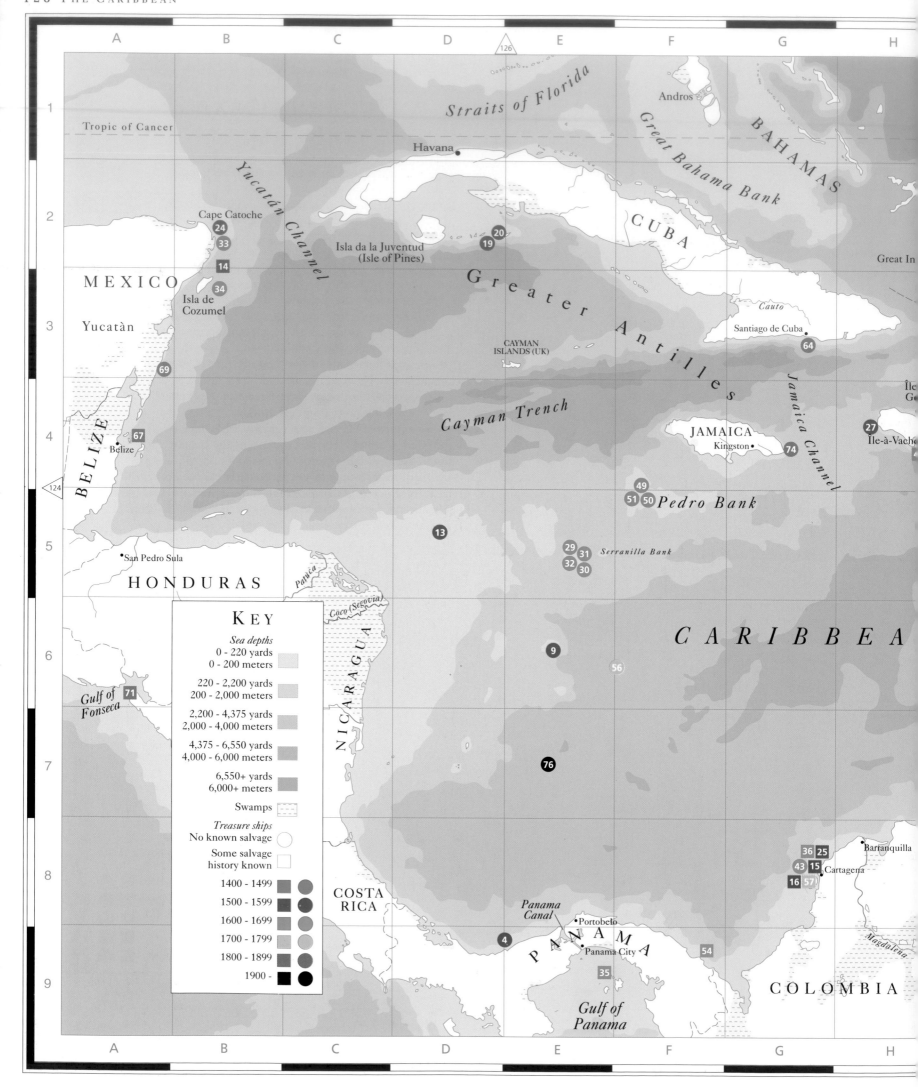

Tropic of Cancer

Straits of Florida

Andros

BAHAMAS

Great Bahama Bank

Havana

Yucatàn Channel

Cape Catoche
24
33
14
34

MEXICO

Isla de Cozumel

Yucatàn

Isla da la Juventud (Isle of Pines)

20
19

CUBA

Greater Antilles

Cauto

Santiago de Cuba
64

Great In

CAYMAN ISLANDS (UK)

Cayman Trench

Jamaica Channel

69

BELIZE

67
Belize

JAMAICA
Kingston •
74

27
Île-à-Vache
Île Go

49
51 50 *Pedro Bank*

13

San Pedro Sula •

HONDURAS

Patuca

29 31
32 30
Serranilla Bank

CARIBBEA

Coco (Segovia)

9

56

NICARAGUA

Gulf of Fonseca
71

76

KEY

Sea depths
0 - 220 yards
0 - 200 meters

220 - 2,200 yards
200 - 2,000 meters

2,200 - 4,375 yards
2,000 - 4,000 meters

4,375 - 6,550 yards
4,000 - 6,000 meters

6,550+ yards
6,000+ meters

Swamps

Treasure ships
No known salvage

Some salvage history known

1400 - 1499
1500 - 1599
1600 - 1699
1700 - 1799
1800 - 1899
1900 -

COSTA RICA

36 25
Barranquilla •

43 15
Cartagena •
16 57

Magdalena

Panama Canal
Portobelo •

4

PANAMA
Panama City •

54

35

COLOMBIA

Gulf of Panama

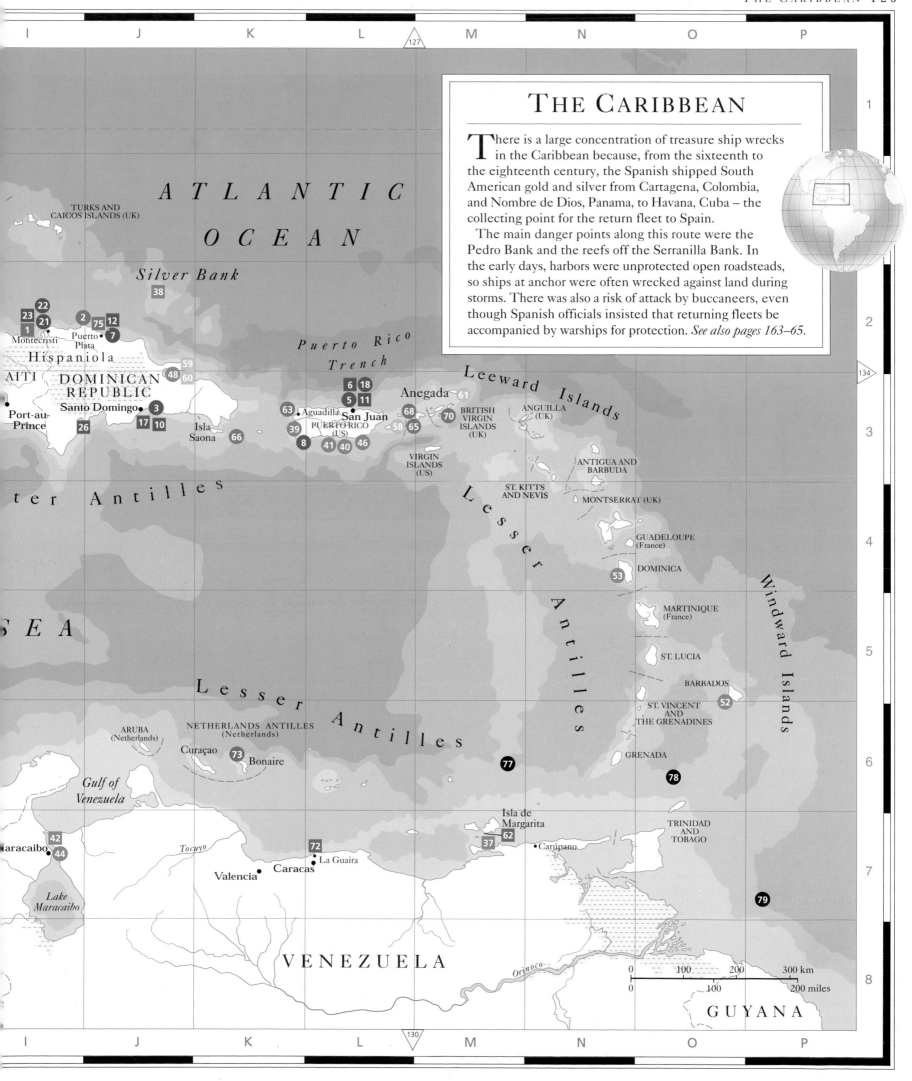

I J K L M N O P

THE CARIBBEAN

There is a large concentration of treasure ship wrecks in the Caribbean because, from the sixteenth to the eighteenth century, the Spanish shipped South American gold and silver from Cartagena, Colombia, and Nombre de Dios, Panama, to Havana, Cuba – the collecting point for the return fleet to Spain.

The main danger points along this route were the Pedro Bank and the reefs off the Serranilla Bank. In the early days, harbors were unprotected open roadsteads, so ships at anchor were often wrecked against land during storms. There was also a risk of attack by buccaneers, even though Spanish officials insisted that returning fleets be accompanied by warships for protection. *See also pages 163–65.*

ATLANTIC

OCEAN

Silver Bank

TURKS AND
CAICOS ISLANDS (UK)

38

22
23 21
1
Montecristi
2   75 12
Puerto   7
Plata

Puerto Rico

59
48 60

AITI
DOMINICAN
REPUBLIC

Trench

Leeward Islands

6 18
5 11

ANGUILLA
(UK)

134

Port-au-
Prince

Santo Domingo   3

17 10

26

Isla
Saona

66

63 Aguadilla
San Juan

39
PUERTO RICO
(US)
8

Anegada   61

68
70

58 65

41 40 46

BRITISH
VIRGIN
ISLANDS
(UK)

ANTIGUA AND
BARBUDA

er   Antilles

VIRGIN
ISLANDS
(US)

ST. KITTS
AND NEVIS

MONTSERRAT (UK)

Lesser   Antilles

GUADELOUPE
(France)

4

53   DOMINICA

SEA

MARTINIQUE
(France)

ST. LUCIA

5

BARBADOS

Windward   Islands

52

ST. VINCENT
AND
THE GRENADINES

Lesser   Antilles

GRENADA

ARUBA
(Netherlands)

NETHERLANDS ANTILLES
(Netherlands)

Curaçao
73   Bonaire

77

78

6

*Gulf of
Venezuela*

Isla de
Margarita

TRINIDAD
AND
TOBAGO

42
Maracaibo
44

Tocuyo

72

37   62
•Carúpano

•La Guaira

Valencia•   Caracas•

7

*Lake
Maracaibo*

79

VENEZUELA

Orinoco

0   100   200   300 km

0   100   200 miles

8

GUYANA

I J K L M N O P

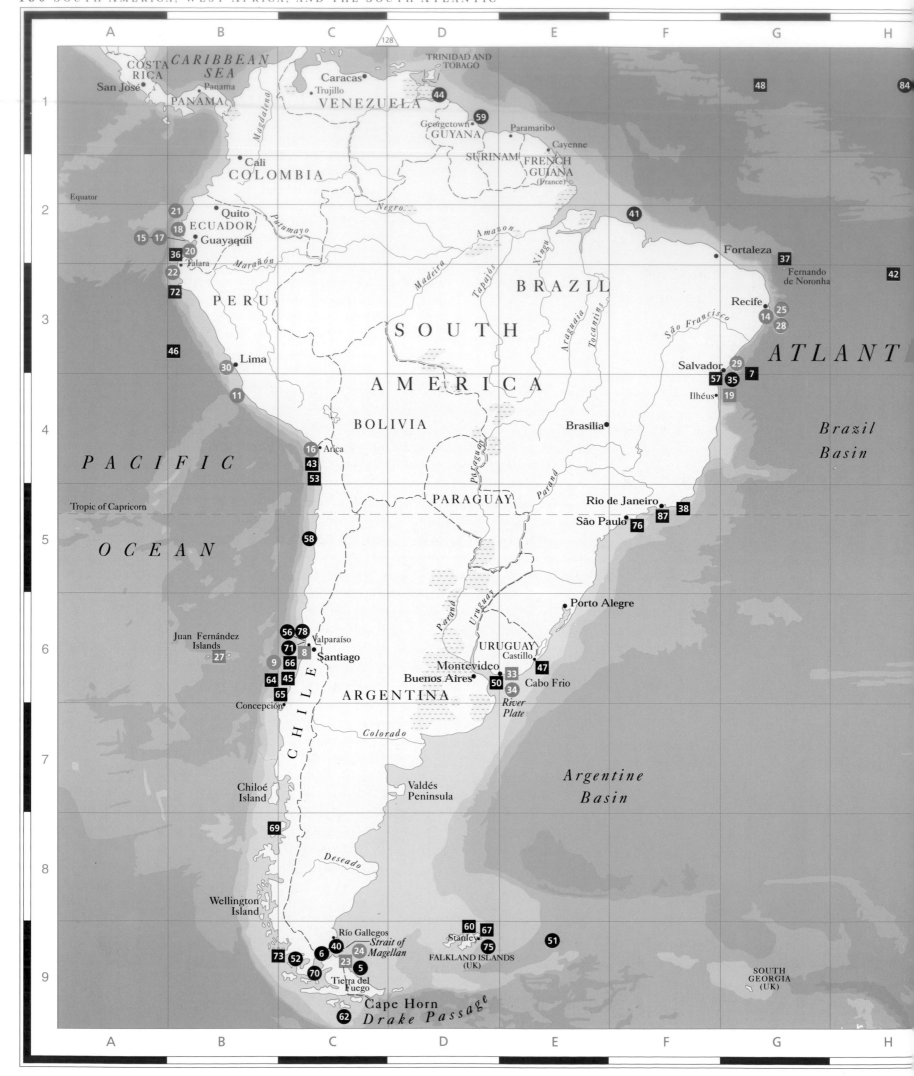

A   **B**   **C**   △   **D**   **E**   **F**   **G**   **H**

128

CARIBBEAN SEA

COSTA RICA

San José

Panama

PANAMA

Caracas

Trujillo

TRINIDAD AND TOBAGO

VENEZUELA

44

Georgetown

59

Paramaribo

Cayenne

GUYANA

SURINAM

FRENCH GUIANA (France)

Cali

COLOMBIA

Equator

Negro

21

Quito

ECUADOR

Amazon

41

18

15 17

Guayaquil

36 20

Talara

Marañón

BRAZIL

Fortaleza

37

22

Madeira

Tapajós

Xingu

SOUTH

São Francisco

Recife

42

72

PERU

AMERICA

14 25 28

ATLANT

46

30

Lima

Araguaia

Tocantins

Salvador

29

57 35 7

11

Ilhéus

19

BOLIVIA

Brasilia

Brazil Basin

16 Arica

43

53

Tropic of Capricorn

PACIFIC

PARAGUAY

Paraná

Rio de Janeiro

38

São Paulo

87

76

OCEAN

58

Porto Alegre

Paraguay

Juan Fernández Islands

56 78

Valparaíso

Paraná

Uruguay

URUGUAY

Castillo

27

71

8

47

9 66

Santiago

Montevideo

33

Cabo Frio

64 45

Buenos Aires

50

65

ARGENTINA

34

Concepción

River Plate

Argentine Basin

Colorado

Chiloé Island

Valdés Peninsula

69

Deseado

Wellington Island

Río Gallegos

60 67

Stanley

51

40

Strait of Magellan

75

73 52

6

24

FALKLAND ISLANDS (UK)

70

23 5

Tierra del Fuego

SOUTH GEORGIA (UK)

CHILE

62

Cape Horn

Drake Passage

A   **B**   **C**   **D**   **E**   **F**   **G**   **H**

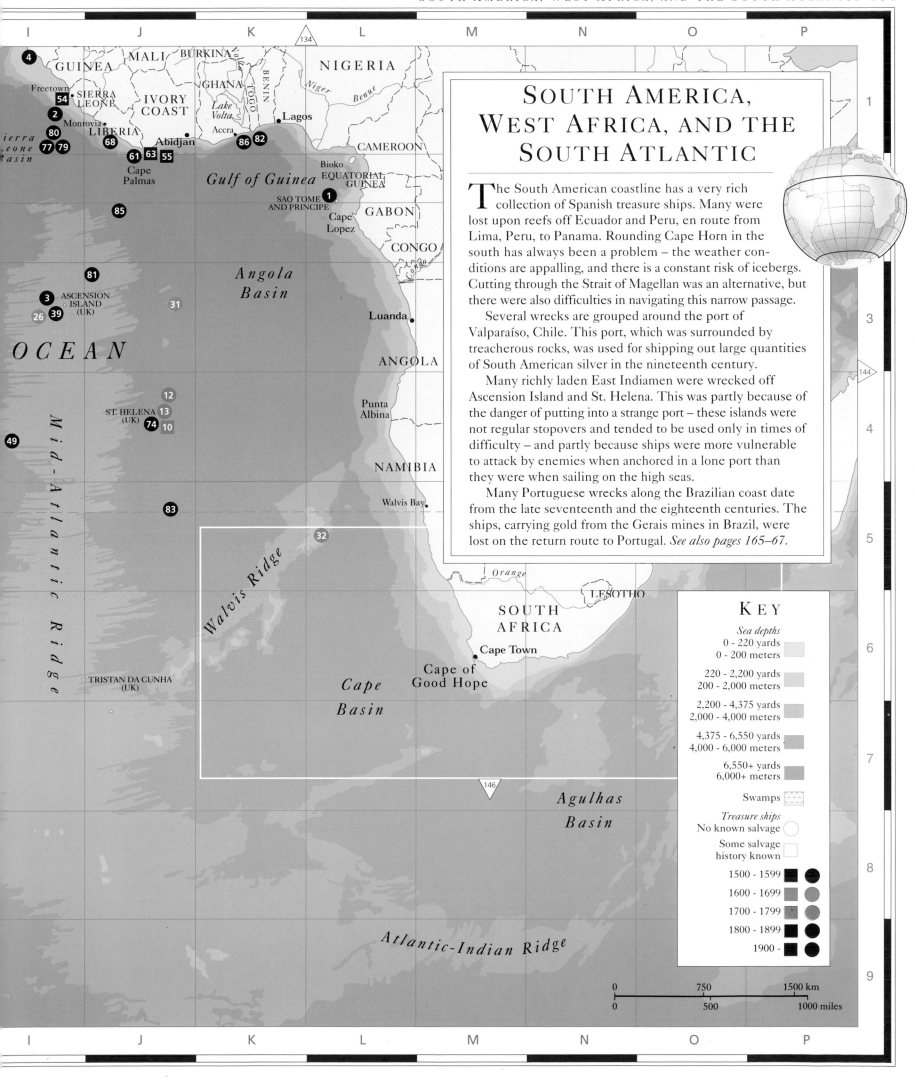

SOUTH AMERICA, WEST AFRICA, AND THE SOUTH ATLANTIC

The South American coastline has a very rich collection of Spanish treasure ships. Many were lost upon reefs off Ecuador and Peru, en route from Lima, Peru, to Panama. Rounding Cape Horn in the south has always been a problem – the weather conditions are appalling, and there is a constant risk of icebergs. Cutting through the Strait of Magellan was an alternative, but there were also difficulties in navigating this narrow passage.

Several wrecks are grouped around the port of Valparaíso, Chile. This port, which was surrounded by treacherous rocks, was used for shipping out large quantities of South American silver in the nineteenth century.

Many richly laden East Indiamen were wrecked off Ascension Island and St. Helena. This was partly because of the danger of putting into a strange port – these islands were not regular stopovers and tended to be used only in times of difficulty – and partly because ships were more vulnerable to attack by enemies when anchored in a lone port than they were when sailing on the high seas.

Many Portuguese wrecks along the Brazilian coast date from the late seventeenth and the eighteenth centuries. The ships, carrying gold from the Gerais mines in Brazil, were lost on the return route to Portugal. *See also pages 165–67.*

KEY

Sea depths

0 - 220 yards 0 - 200 meters	
220 - 2,200 yards 200 - 2,000 meters	
2,200 - 4,375 yards 2,000 - 4,000 meters	
4,375 - 6,550 yards 4,000 - 6,000 meters	
6,550+ yards 6,000+ meters	
Swamps	

Treasure ships

No known salvage ○
Some salvage history known □

1500 - 1599	■	●
1600 - 1699	■	●
1700 - 1799	■	●
1800 - 1899	■	●
1900 -	■	●

0   750   1500 km
0   500   1000 miles

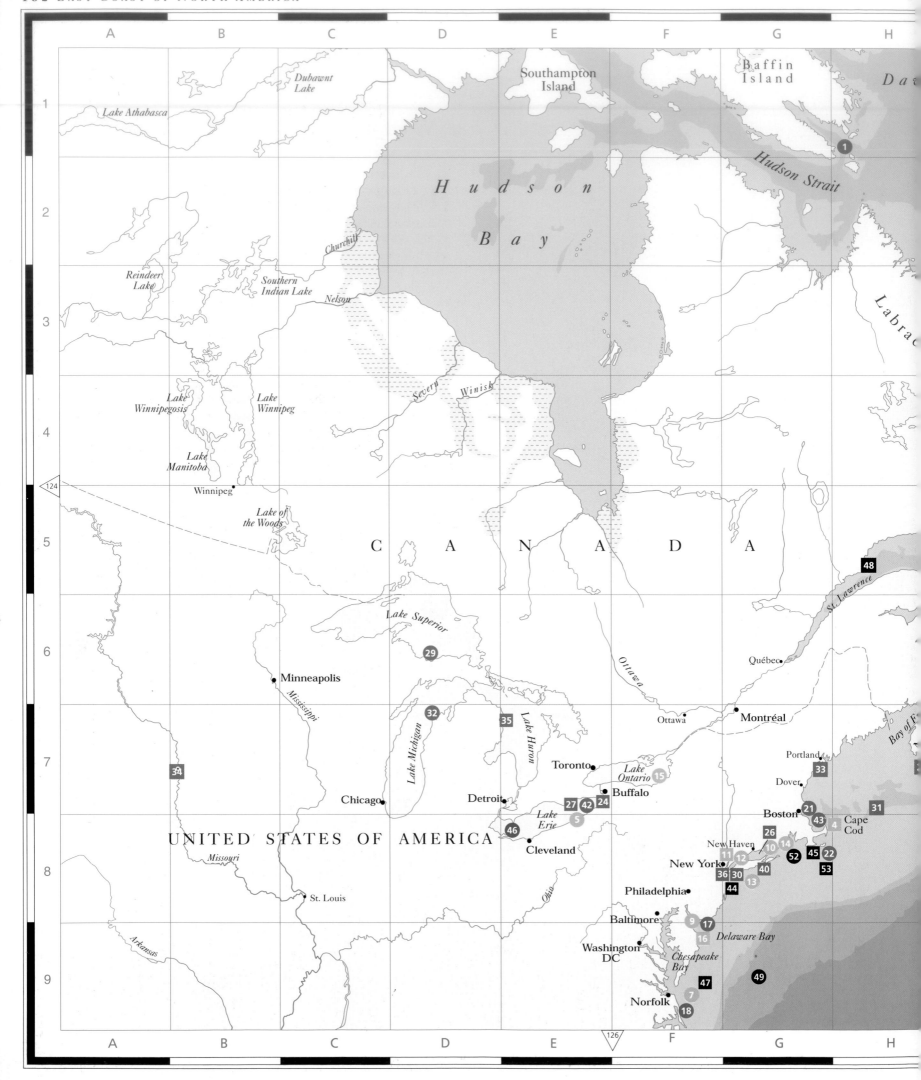

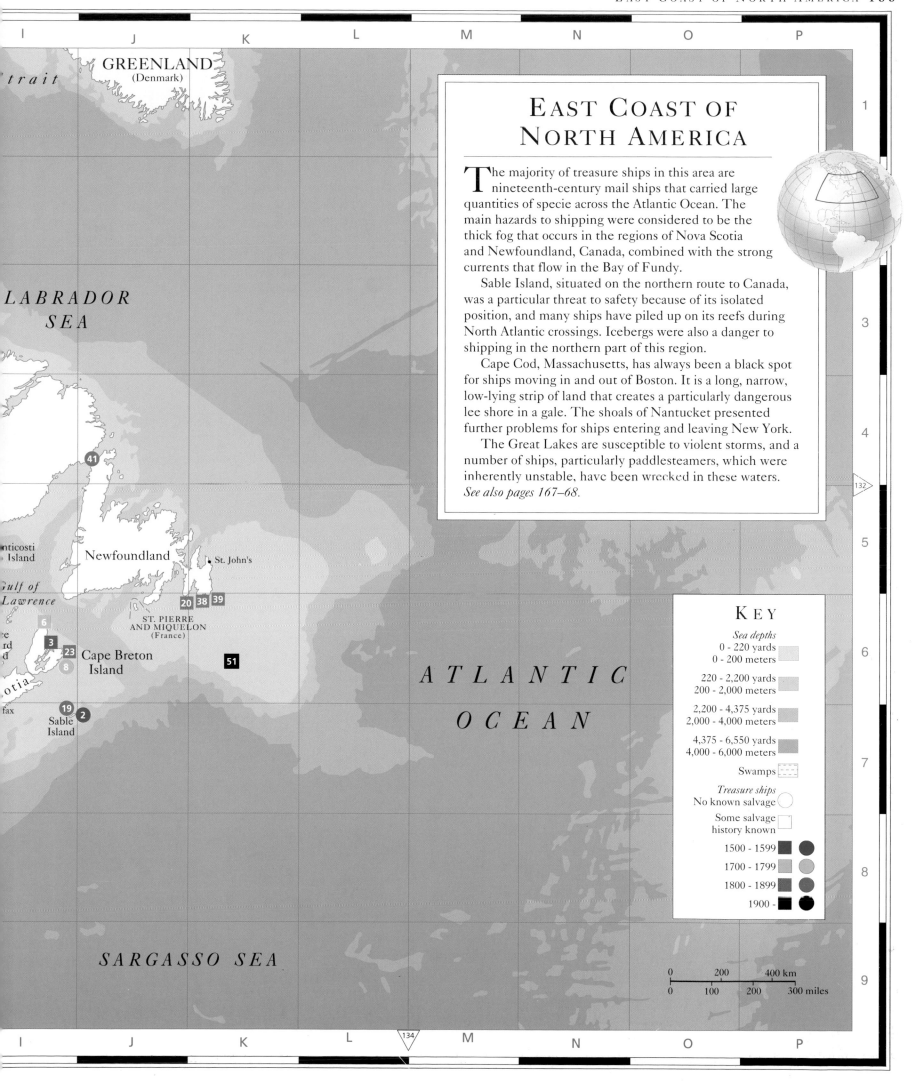

GREENLAND
(Denmark)

trait

*LABRADOR
SEA*

41

Newfoundland • St. John's

*Gulf of
Lawrence*

20 38 39

ST. PIERRE
AND MIQUELON
(France)

6

3

23

8

Cape Breton
Island

51

19 2

Sable
Island

*ticosti
Island*

otia

fax

rd

EAST COAST OF
NORTH AMERICA

The majority of treasure ships in this area are
nineteenth-century mail ships that carried large
quantities of specie across the Atlantic Ocean. The
main hazards to shipping were considered to be the
thick fog that occurs in the regions of Nova Scotia
and Newfoundland, Canada, combined with the strong
currents that flow in the Bay of Fundy.

Sable Island, situated on the northern route to Canada,
was a particular threat to safety because of its isolated
position, and many ships have piled up on its reefs during
North Atlantic crossings. Icebergs were also a danger to
shipping in the northern part of this region.

Cape Cod, Massachusetts, has always been a black spot
for ships moving in and out of Boston. It is a long, narrow,
low-lying strip of land that creates a particularly dangerous
lee shore in a gale. The shoals of Nantucket presented
further problems for ships entering and leaving New York.

The Great Lakes are susceptible to violent storms, and a
number of ships, particularly paddlesteamers, which were
inherently unstable, have been wrecked in these waters.
See also pages 167–68.

ATLANTIC

OCEAN

KEY

Sea depths

0 - 220 yards
0 - 200 meters

220 - 2,200 yards
200 - 2,000 meters

2,200 - 4,375 yards
2,000 - 4,000 meters

4,375 - 6,550 yards
4,000 - 6,000 meters

Swamps

Treasure ships
No known salvage

Some salvage
history known

1500 - 1599

1700 - 1799

1800 - 1899

1900 -

SARGASSO SEA

0		200		400 km

| 0 | 100 | 200 | 300 miles |

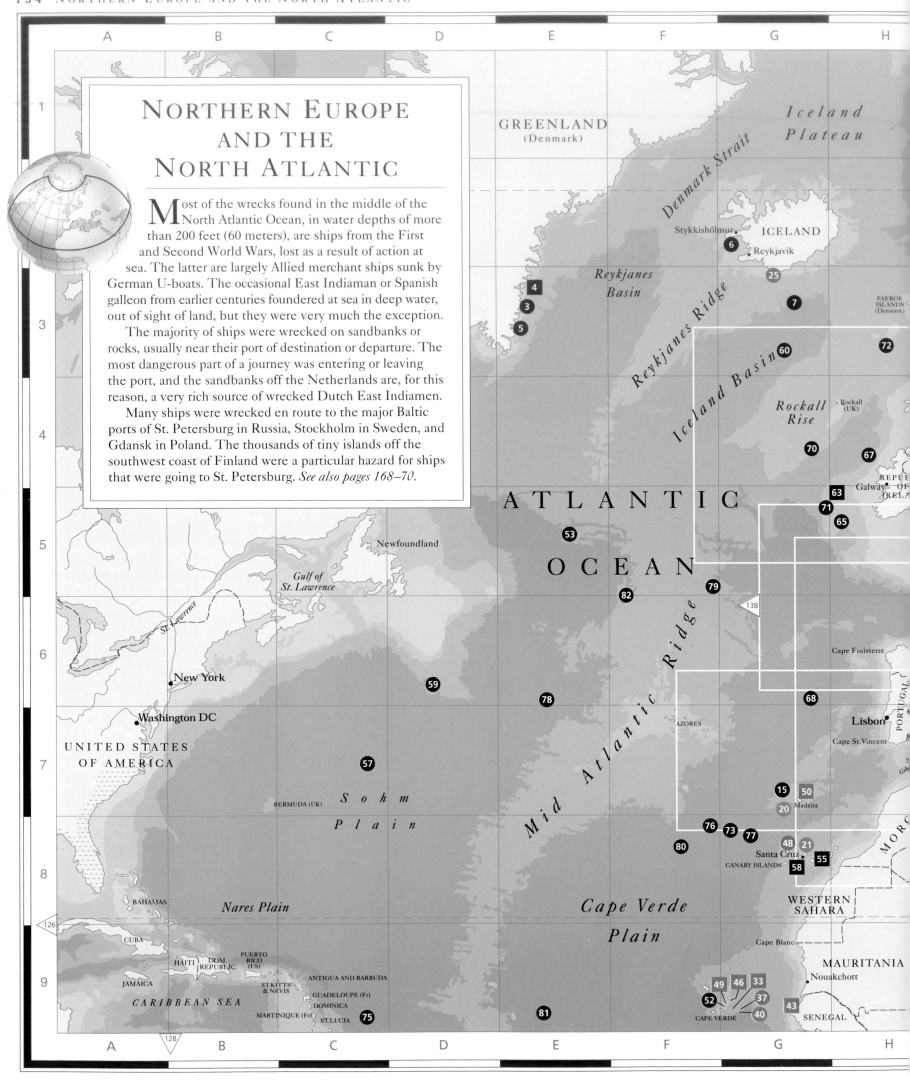

NORTHERN EUROPE AND THE NORTH ATLANTIC

Most of the wrecks found in the middle of the North Atlantic Ocean, in water depths of more than 200 feet (60 meters), are ships from the First and Second World Wars, lost as a result of action at sea. The latter are largely Allied merchant ships sunk by German U-boats. The occasional East Indiaman or Spanish galleon from earlier centuries foundered at sea in deep water, out of sight of land, but they were very much the exception.

The majority of ships were wrecked on sandbanks or rocks, usually near their port of destination or departure. The most dangerous part of a journey was entering or leaving the port, and the sandbanks off the Netherlands are, for this reason, a very rich source of wrecked Dutch East Indiamen.

Many ships were wrecked en route to the major Baltic ports of St. Petersburg in Russia, Stockholm in Sweden, and Gdansk in Poland. The thousands of tiny islands off the southwest coast of Finland were a particular hazard for ships that were going to St. Petersburg. *See also pages 168–70.*

Norwegian Basin

NORWEGIAN SEA

Brønnøysund ⑨

⑬ Trondheim

③⑤ Åndalsnes

Shetland ▷136

Oslo

③② Stavanger
②⑧

NORTH SEA

⑫

① ②
④①
Gothenburg
⑪
⑤⑥ ③⑧ ①⑩ ②③ Kalmar
Esbjerg ②② ②⑥
DENMARK
③⑧ ⑤① ④④ Copenhagen ②⑨
⑥⑥ ③⑥ ⑤④
①⑧ ⑥⑥ ⑥⑨ Hamburg
①⑥ ⑥④ ④⑤ ①⑨ Amsterdam
⑭ ⑥⑨ NETHERLANDS
BELGIUM
GERMANY
⑥② LUXEMBOURG
FRANCE

SWEDEN

FINLAND

Sundsvall

Gävle

Åland Turku Helsinki
④⑦ ④② ③④
Stockholm Tallinn
ESTONIA
Gotland
③① ⑥① *Gulf of Riga*
②⑦
BALTIC SEA
③⓪
⑰ RUSSIAN FED.
Klaipėda
LITHUANIA
Gdańsk

Vardø ⑦④
Varangerfjorden

BARENTS SEA

Arctic Circle

WHITE SEA

Lake Onega

Lake Ladoga

St.Petersburg

RUSSIAN FEDERATION

Pechora

POLAND

E U R O P E

BELORUSSIA

UKRAINE

Dniepr

Don

Volga

KAZAKHSTAN

CZECH REPUBLIC
SLOVAKIA
LIECHTENSTEIN
AUSTRIA HUNGARY
SWITZERLAND
SLOVENIA
CROATIA
BOSNIA AND HERZEGOVINA
YUGOSLAVIA
ITALY
ADRIATIC SEA
Danube
ROMANIA
MOLDAVIA

Rhine

ANDORRA
Corsica
Sardinia
BALEARIC ISLANDS
Sicily
TUNISIA

BULGARIA
MACEDONIA
ALBANIA
GREECE

BLACK SEA

GEORGIA
AZERBAIJAN
ARMENIA
TURKEY ▷142

Caspian Sea

UZBEKISTAN
TURKMENISTAN

KYRGYZSTAN

TAJIKISTAN

▷140

AEGEAN SEA
Crete
CYPRUS
MEDITERRANEAN SEA
MALTA

SYRIA
LEBANON
ISRAEL
JORDAN

Tigris
IRAQ
Euphrates

IRAN

AFGHANISTAN

Indus

PAKISTAN

INDIA

GERIA

LIBYA

EGYPT

Nile

RED SEA

SAUDI ARABIA

KUWAIT
BAHRAIN
QATAR
Persian Gulf
U.A.E.
OMAN

Tropic of Cancer ▷145

ARABIAN SEA

FRICA

NIGER

CHAD

SUDAN

ERITREA

YEMEN

OMAN

▷136 ▷140 ▷142 ▷145

KEY

Sea depths
0 - 220 yards / 0 - 200 meters
220 - 2,200 yards / 200 - 2,000 meters
2,200 - 4,375 yards / 2,000 - 4,000 meters
4,375 - 6,550 yards / 4,000 - 6,000 meters
6,550+ yards / 6,000+ meters
Swamps

Treasure ships
No known salvage
Some salvage history known

500 - 999
1100 - 1199
1200 - 1299
1300 - 1399
1400 - 1499
1500 - 1599
1600 - 1699
1700 - 1799
1800 - 1899
1900 -

0   500   1000 km
0   300   600 miles

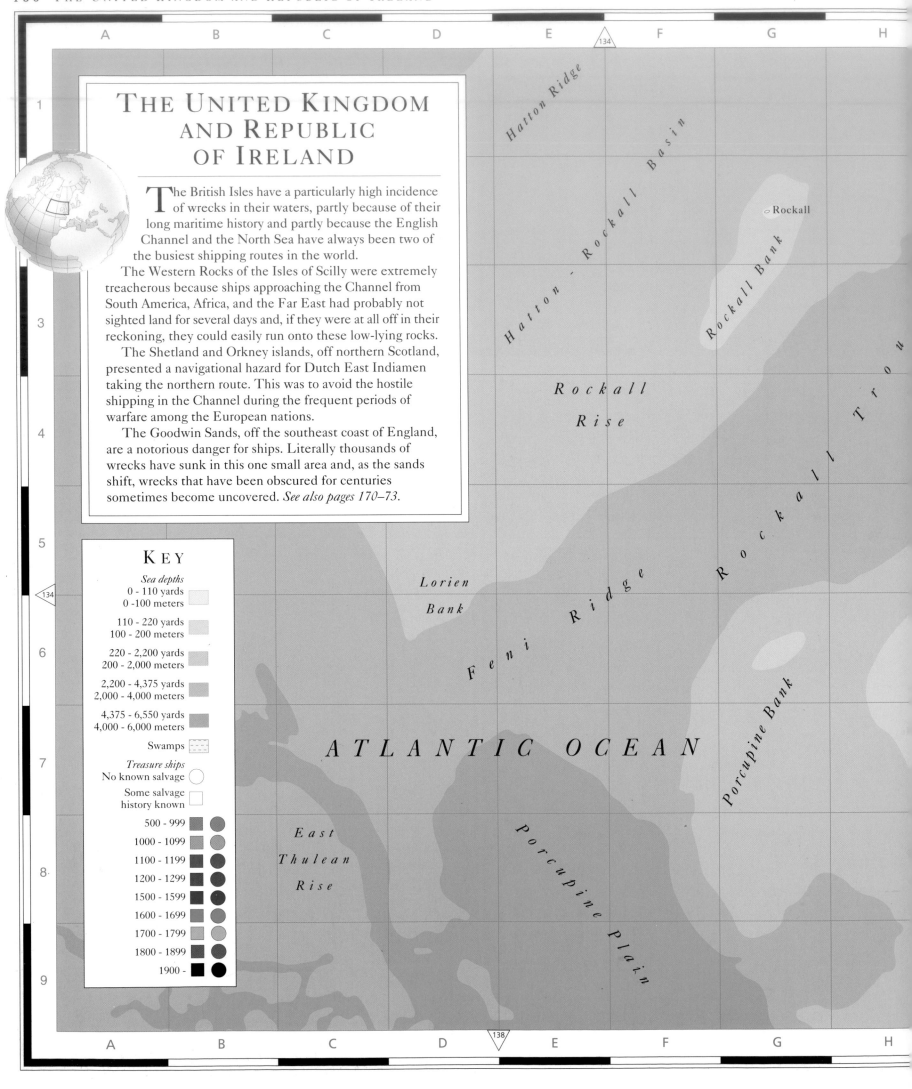

THE UNITED KINGDOM AND REPUBLIC OF IRELAND

The British Isles have a particularly high incidence of wrecks in their waters, partly because of their long maritime history and partly because the English Channel and the North Sea have always been two of the busiest shipping routes in the world.

The Western Rocks of the Isles of Scilly were extremely treacherous because ships approaching the Channel from South America, Africa, and the Far East had probably not sighted land for several days and, if they were at all off in their reckoning, they could easily run onto these low-lying rocks.

The Shetland and Orkney islands, off northern Scotland, presented a navigational hazard for Dutch East Indiamen taking the northern route. This was to avoid the hostile shipping in the Channel during the frequent periods of warfare among the European nations.

The Goodwin Sands, off the southeast coast of England, are a notorious danger for ships. Literally thousands of wrecks have sunk in this one small area and, as the sands shift, wrecks that have been obscured for centuries sometimes become uncovered. *See also pages 170–73.*

KEY

Sea depths

0 - 110 yards / 0 -100 meters	
110 - 220 yards / 100 - 200 meters	
220 - 2,200 yards / 200 - 2,000 meters	
2,200 - 4,375 yards / 2,000 - 4,000 meters	
4,375 - 6,550 yards / 4,000 - 6,000 meters	
Swamps	

Treasure ships

No known salvage ◯

Some salvage history known ▢

500 - 999		
1000 - 1099		
1100 - 1199		
1200 - 1299		
1500 - 1599		
1600 - 1699		
1700 - 1799		
1800 - 1899		
1900 -		

Hatton Ridge

Hatton - Rockall Basin

Rockall

Hatton - Rockall Basin

Rockall Bank

Rockall Rise

Rockall Trough

Lorien Bank

Feni Ridge

Porcupine Bank

ATLANTIC OCEAN

Porcupine Plain

East Thulean Rise

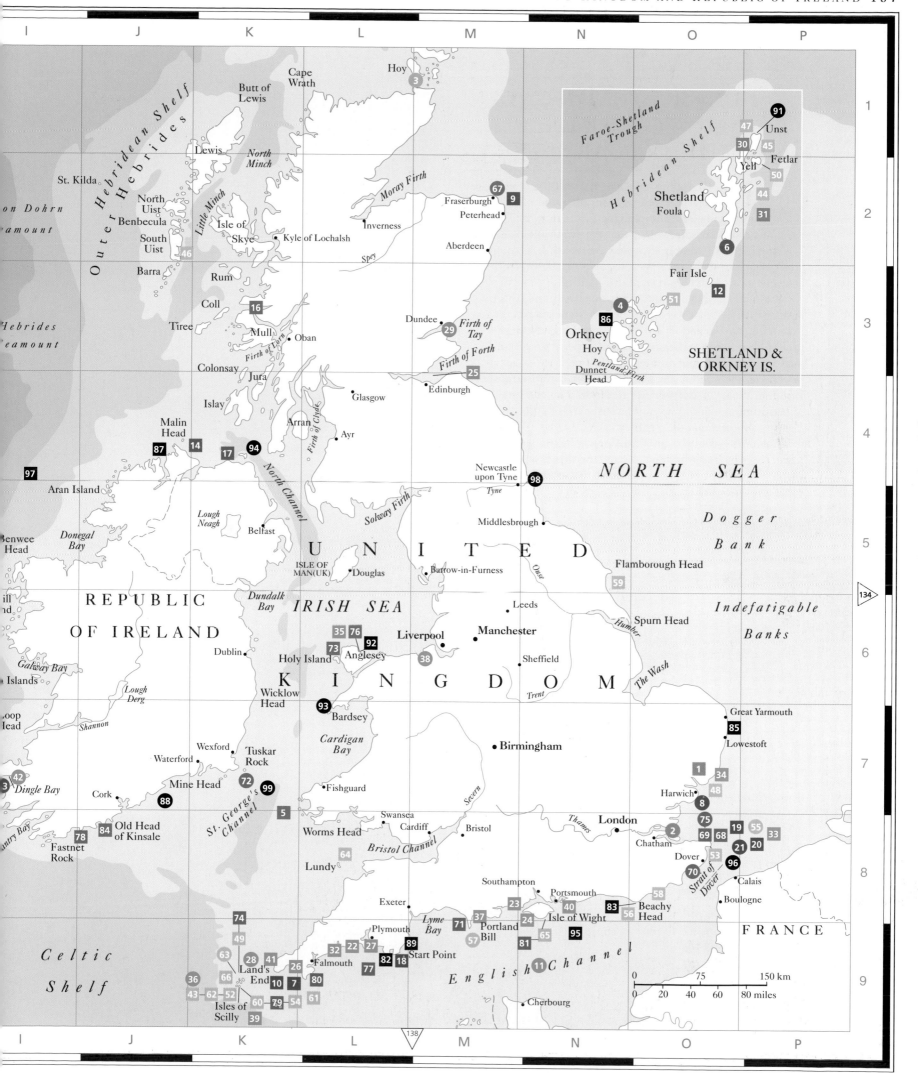

I J K L M N O P

Hoy
3

Butt of
Lewis
Cape
Wrath

Faroe-Shetland Trough

91
47
Unst
30
45
Yell
Fetlar
50
44
31

Hebridean Shelf

Lewis
North
Minch

St. Kilda

on Dohrn
eamount

North
Uist
Benbecula

Little Minch

Isle of
Skye

Moray Firth

Fraserburgh
67
Peterhead
9

Inverness

Shetland
Foula

6

South
Uist
46

Barra

Hebrides
eamount

Rum

Coll

Tiree

Mull

16

Kyle of Lochalsh

Spey

Aberdeen

Fair Isle
12

4
86
51

Oban

Firth of Lorn

Colonsay

Jura

Dundee
29
Firth of Tay

Orkney
Hoy
Dunnet
Head
Pentland Firth

SHETLAND &
ORKNEY IS.

Islay

Firth of Clyde

Glasgow

Firth of Forth
25

Edinburgh

Arran

Malin
Head
87
14
17
94

Ayr

NORTH SEA

97

North Channel

Aran Island

Newcastle
upon Tyne
98
Tyne

Dogger
Bank

Lough
Neagh

Belfast

Solway Firth

Middlesbrough

Benwee
Head

Donegal
Bay

ISLE OF
MAN (UK)
Douglas

Barrow-in-Furness

Ouse

Flamborough Head

59

Indefatigable
Banks

Spurn Head

134

REPUBLIC
OF IRELAND

Dundalk
Bay

IRISH SEA

Leeds

Humber

Galway Bay
Islands

Lough
Derg

UNITED

35 76
73 92

Liverpool

Manchester

Sheffield

KINGDOM

Dublin

Holy Island

Anglesey
38

oop
ead

Shannon

Wicklow
Head
93
Bardsey

Cardigan
Bay

Trent

The Wash

Great Yarmouth
85
Lowestoft

Wexford

Waterford

Tuskar
Rock

42

Mine Head
72
99

Birmingham

1
34
48

Dingle Bay

Cork

88

Fishguard

Harwich
8

5

Bay

78
84

Old Head
of Kinsale

St. George's Channel

London

2

75
69 68
19 55
21 20
33

Fastnet
Rock

Swansea
Cardiff

Bristol

Chatham

Dover
53
96

Worms Head

Bristol Channel

70

Strait of Dover

Calais

64

Lundy

Southampton

58

Beachy
Head
83 56

Boulogne

Celtic

74

Exeter

Lyme
Bay

23
Portsmouth
40
Isle of Wight

95

FRANCE

49

Plymouth
71
37
Portland
Bill
57
24
81
65

63
28 41
26

32 22 27
77 82 18

89
Start Point

11

English Channel

150 km

Shelf

36
66

43 62 52
60 79 54
61

Land's
End
10 7 80

Isles of
Scilly
39

Cherbourg

0   75

0 20 40 60 80 miles

I J K L M N O P

138

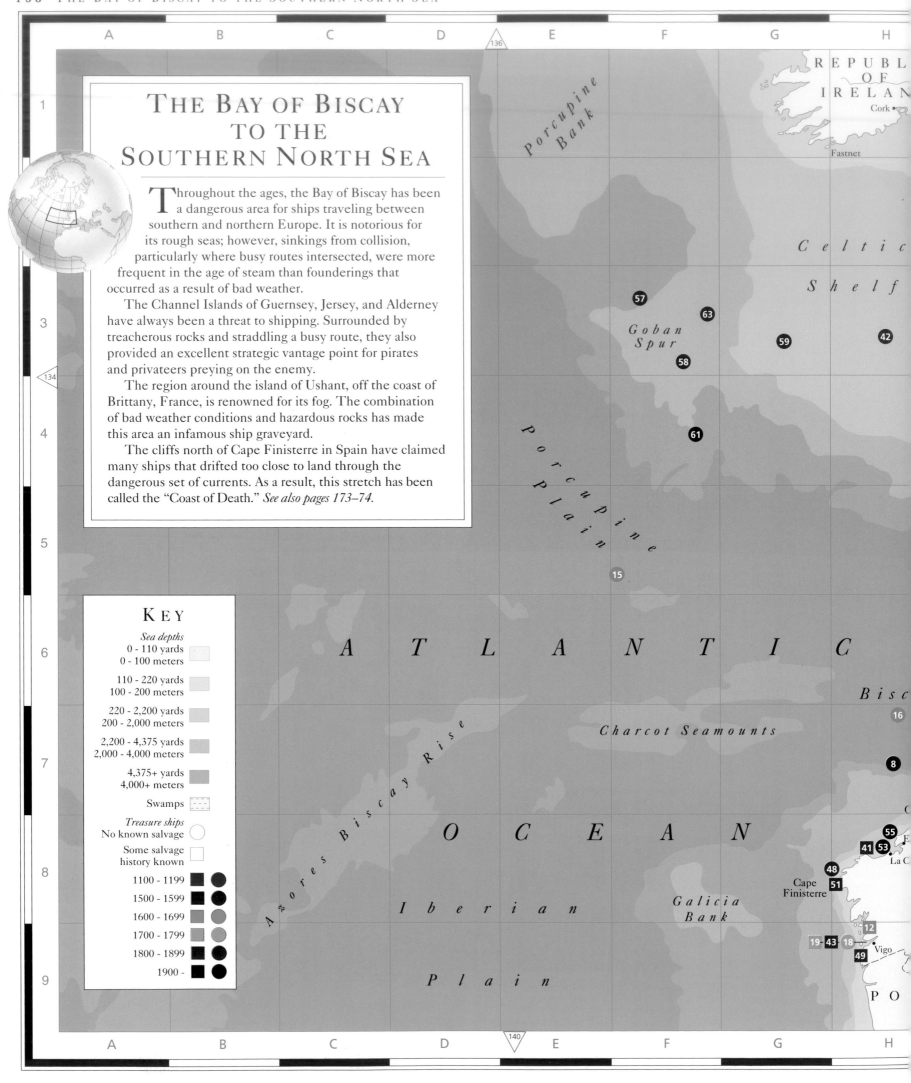

THE BAY OF BISCAY TO THE SOUTHERN NORTH SEA

Throughout the ages, the Bay of Biscay has been a dangerous area for ships traveling between southern and northern Europe. It is notorious for its rough seas; however, sinkings from collision, particularly where busy routes intersected, were more frequent in the age of steam than founderings that occurred as a result of bad weather.

The Channel Islands of Guernsey, Jersey, and Alderney have always been a threat to shipping. Surrounded by treacherous rocks and straddling a busy route, they also provided an excellent strategic vantage point for pirates and privateers preying on the enemy.

The region around the island of Ushant, off the coast of Brittany, France, is renowned for its fog. The combination of bad weather conditions and hazardous rocks has made this area an infamous ship graveyard.

The cliffs north of Cape Finisterre in Spain have claimed many ships that drifted too close to land through the dangerous set of currents. As a result, this stretch has been called the "Coast of Death." *See also pages 173–74.*

KEY

Sea depths

0 - 110 yards / 0 - 100 meters	
110 - 220 yards / 100 - 200 meters	
220 - 2,200 yards / 200 - 2,000 meters	
2,200 - 4,375 yards / 2,000 - 4,000 meters	
4,375+ yards / 4,000+ meters	

Swamps

Treasure ships
No known salvage ○
Some salvage history known ☐

1100 - 1199	■ ●
1500 - 1599	■ ●
1600 - 1699	■ ●
1700 - 1799	■ ●
1800 - 1899	■ ●
1900 -	■ ●

REPUBLIC OF IRELAND

Cork

Fastnet

Porcupine Bank

Celtic Shelf

Goban Spur

Porcupine Plain

ATLANTIC OCEAN

Azores Biscay Rise

Charcot Seamounts

Biscay

Iberian Plain

Galicia Bank

Cape Finisterre

La C

Vigo

PO

57 63 59 42 58 61 15 16 8 55 41 53 48 51 12 19 43 18 49

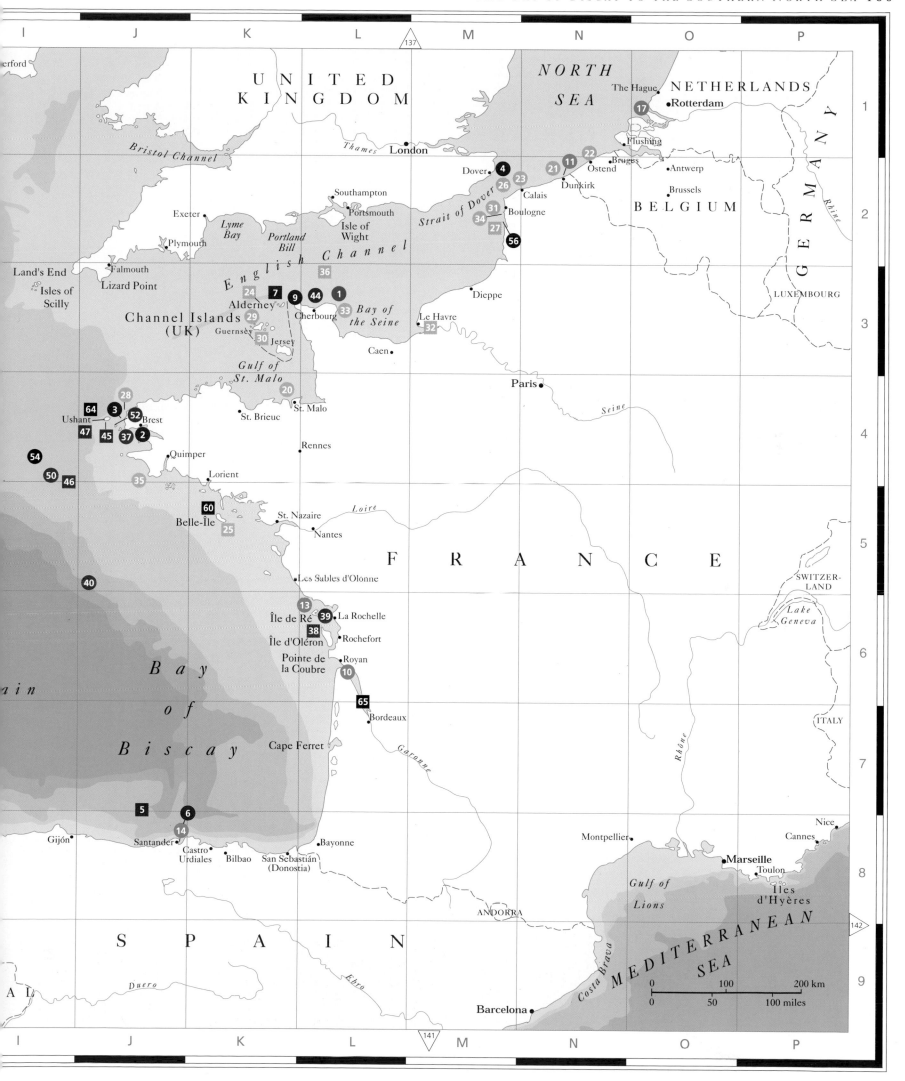

UNITED KINGDOM

NORTH SEA

NETHERLANDS

The Hague
• Rotterdam
Flushing
Bruges
Ostend
Antwerp
Dunkirk
• Brussels

BELGIUM

Bristol Channel

Thames London

Dover
Southampton
Portsmouth
Isle of Wight
Strait of Dover
Calais
Boulogne

LUXEMBOURG

Exeter
Lyme Bay
Portland Bill
Land's End
• Isles of Scilly
Lizard Point
Plymouth
Falmouth

English Channel

Dieppe

GERMANY

Rhine

Alderney
Cherbourg
Bay of the Seine
Le Havre
Caen
Paris

Channel Islands (UK)
Guernsey
Jersey

Gulf of St. Malo

St. Malo
St. Brieuc

Seine

Ushant
Brest
Quimper
Lorient

Rennes

FRANCE

Loire
St. Nazaire
Nantes

Belle-Île

SWITZER-LAND

Lake Geneva

Les Sables d'Olonne

Île de Ré
La Rochelle
Rochefort
Île d'Oléron
Pointe de la Coubre
Royan

ITALY

Bay of Biscay

Bordeaux

Cape Ferret

Garonne

Rhône

Nice
Cannes

Montpellier

Marseille
Toulon

Gijón
Santander
Castro Urdiales
Bilbao
San Sebastián (Donostia)
Bayonne

ANDORRA

Gulf of Lions

Îles d'Hyères

SPAIN

MEDITERRANEAN SEA

Costa Brava

Duero
Ebro

Barcelona

0   100   200 km
0   50   100 miles

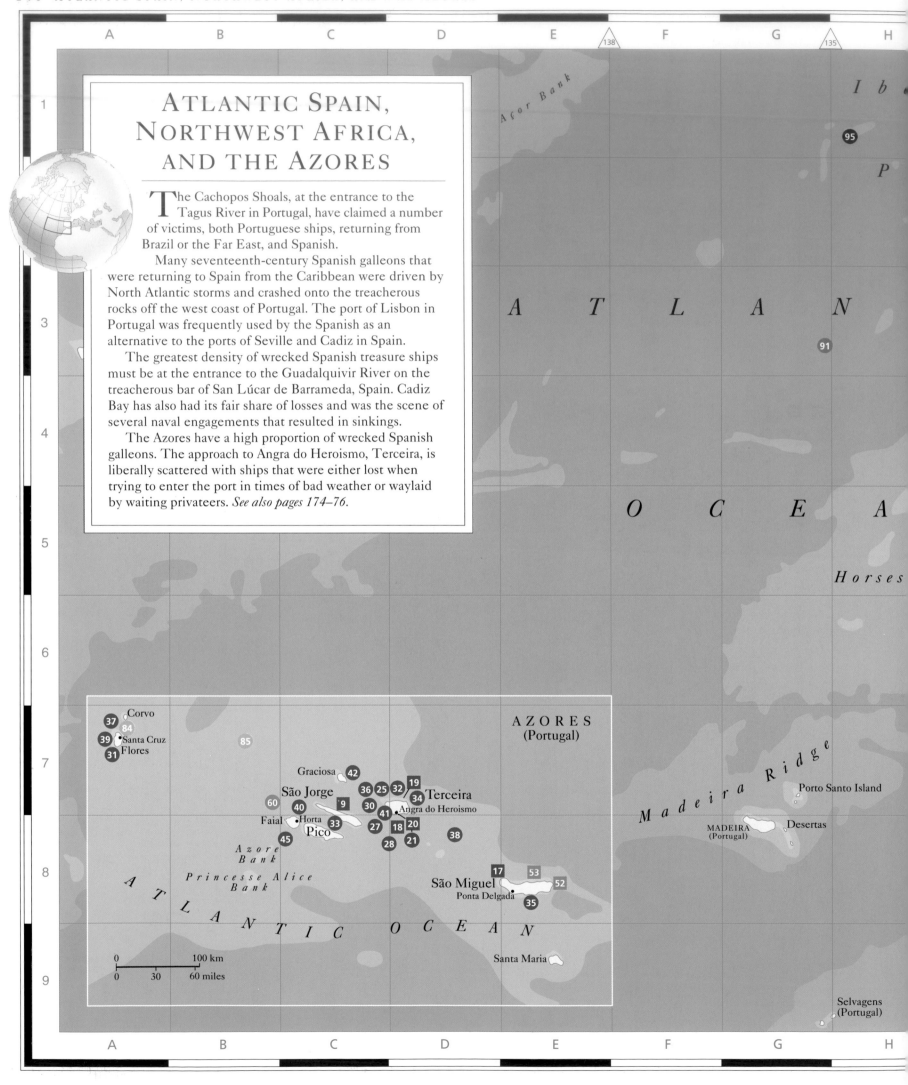

ATLANTIC SPAIN, NORTHWEST AFRICA, AND THE AZORES

The Cachopos Shoals, at the entrance to the Tagus River in Portugal, have claimed a number of victims, both Portuguese ships, returning from Brazil or the Far East, and Spanish.

Many seventeenth-century Spanish galleons that were returning to Spain from the Caribbean were driven by North Atlantic storms and crashed onto the treacherous rocks off the west coast of Portugal. The port of Lisbon in Portugal was frequently used by the Spanish as an alternative to the ports of Seville and Cadiz in Spain.

The greatest density of wrecked Spanish treasure ships must be at the entrance to the Guadalquivir River on the treacherous bar of San Lúcar de Barrameda, Spain. Cadiz Bay has also had its fair share of losses and was the scene of several naval engagements that resulted in sinkings.

The Azores have a high proportion of wrecked Spanish galleons. The approach to Angra do Heroismo, Terceira, is liberally scattered with ships that were either lost when trying to enter the port in times of bad weather or waylaid by waiting privateers. *See also pages 174–76.*

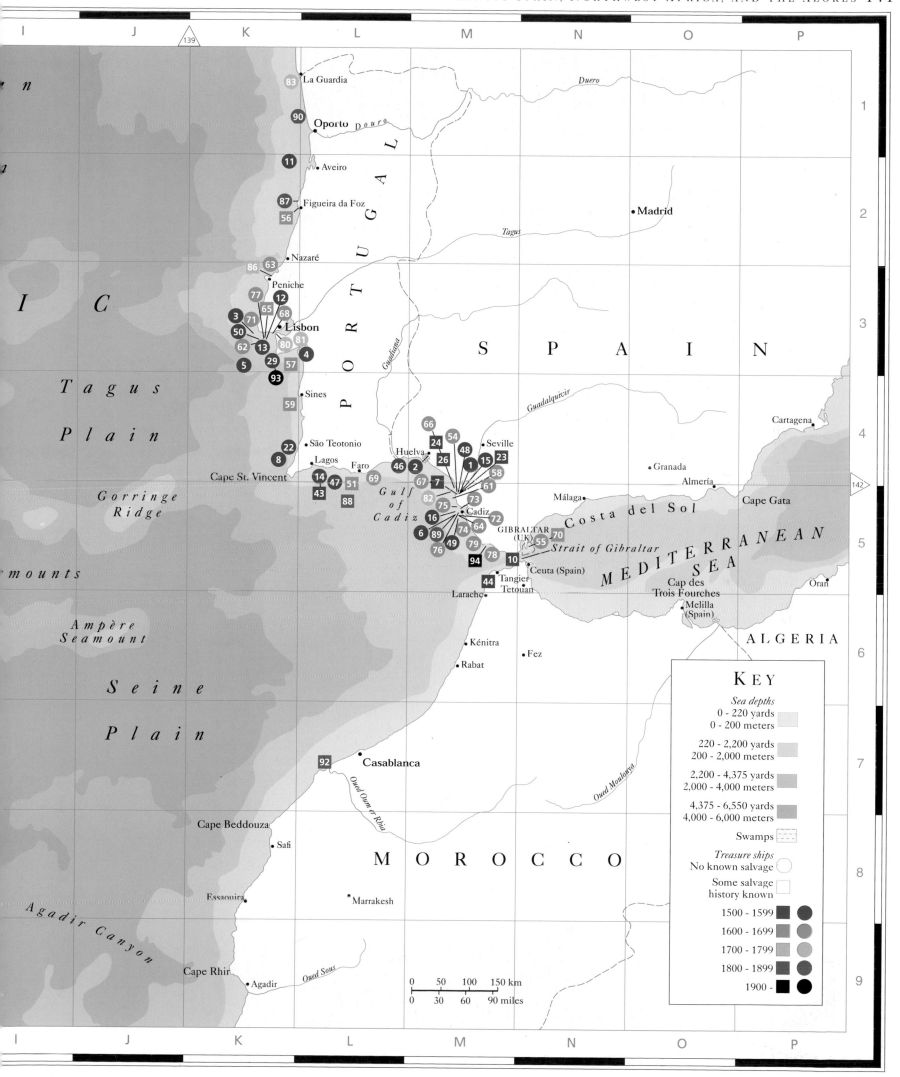

KEY

Sea depths

0 - 220 yards
0 - 200 meters

220 - 2,200 yards
200 - 2,000 meters

2,200 - 4,375 yards
2,000 - 4,000 meters

4,375 - 6,550 yards
4,000 - 6,000 meters

Swamps

Treasure ships
No known salvage

Some salvage
history known

1500 - 1599

1600 - 1699

1700 - 1799

1800 - 1899

1900 -

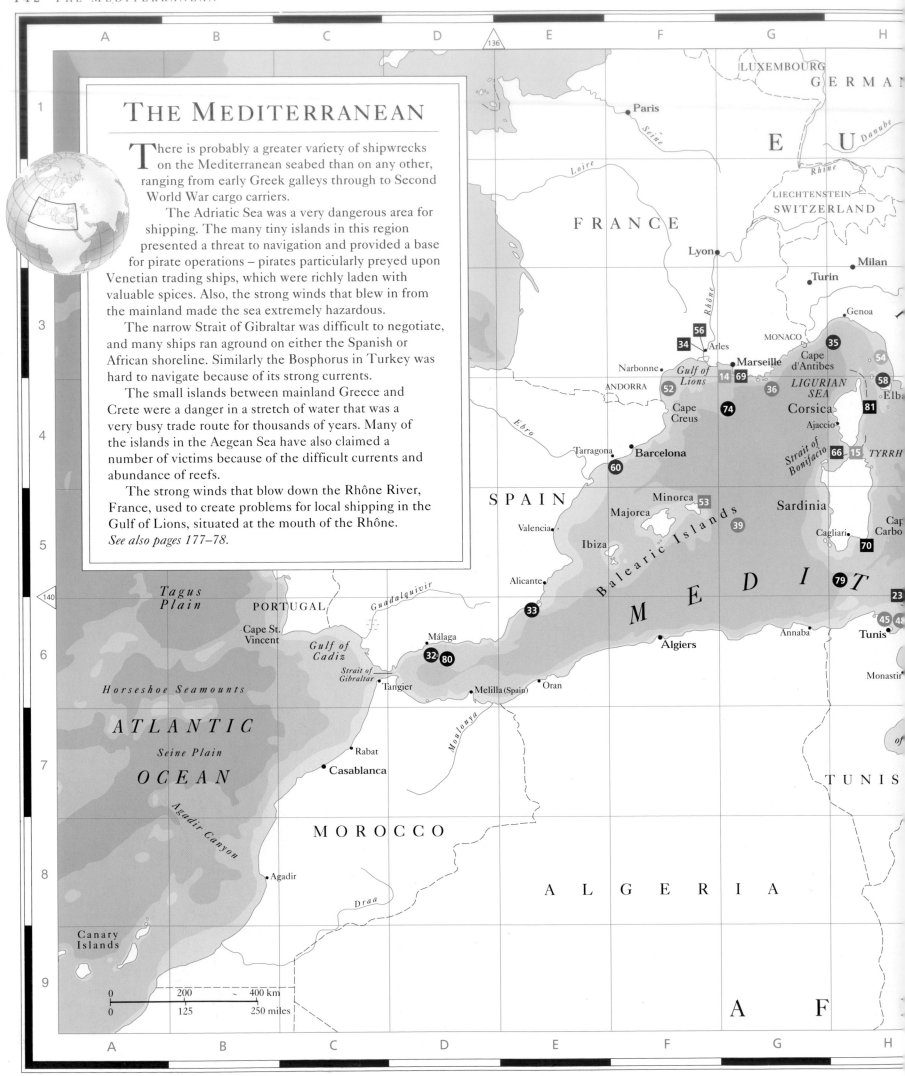

THE MEDITERRANEAN

There is probably a greater variety of shipwrecks on the Mediterranean seabed than on any other, ranging from early Greek galleys through to Second World War cargo carriers.

The Adriatic Sea was a very dangerous area for shipping. The many tiny islands in this region presented a threat to navigation and provided a base for pirate operations – pirates particularly preyed upon Venetian trading ships, which were richly laden with valuable spices. Also, the strong winds that blew in from the mainland made the sea extremely hazardous.

The narrow Strait of Gibraltar was difficult to negotiate, and many ships ran aground on either the Spanish or African shoreline. Similarly the Bosphorus in Turkey was hard to navigate because of its strong currents.

The small islands between mainland Greece and Crete were a danger in a stretch of water that was a very busy trade route for thousands of years. Many of the islands in the Aegean Sea have also claimed a number of victims because of the difficult currents and abundance of reefs.

The strong winds that blow down the Rhône River, France, used to create problems for local shipping in the Gulf of Lions, situated at the mouth of the Rhône.
See also pages 177–78.

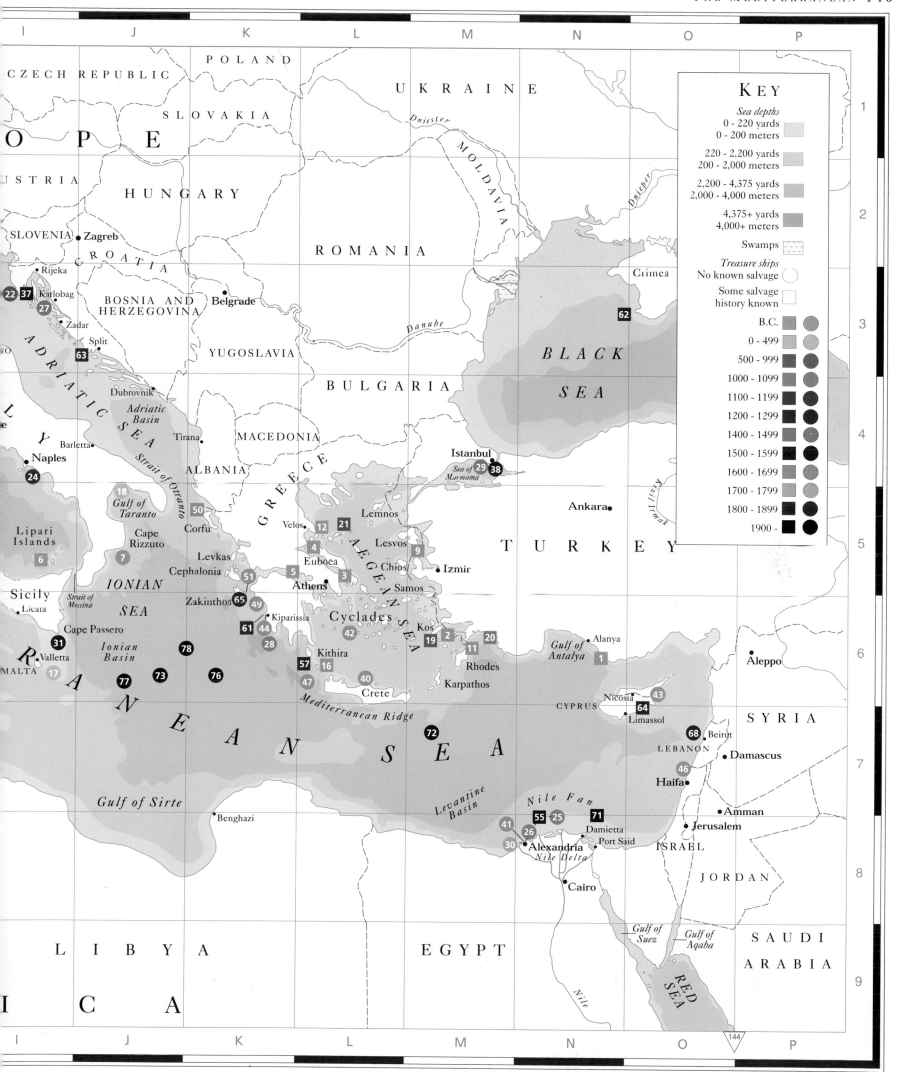

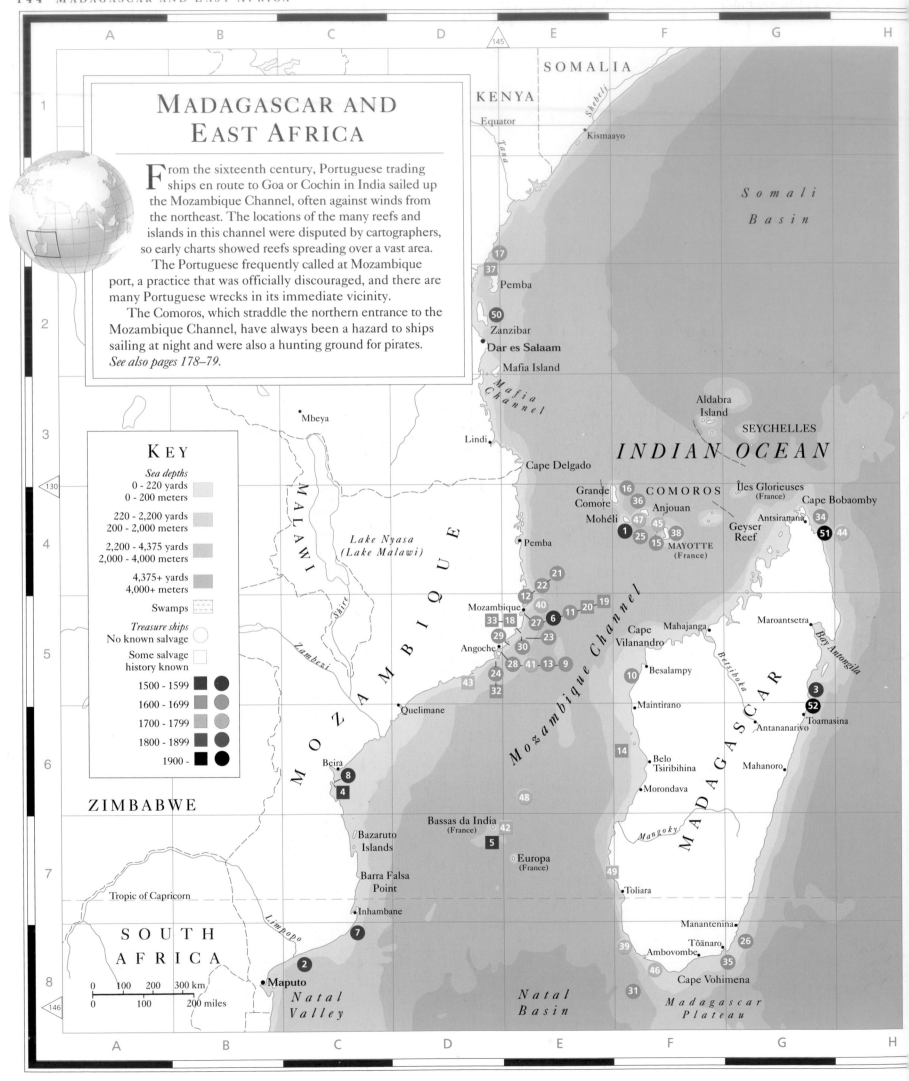

MADAGASCAR AND EAST AFRICA

From the sixteenth century, Portuguese trading ships en route to Goa or Cochin in India sailed up the Mozambique Channel, often against winds from the northeast. The locations of the many reefs and islands in this channel were disputed by cartographers, so early charts showed reefs spreading over a vast area.

The Portuguese frequently called at Mozambique port, a practice that was officially discouraged, and there are many Portuguese wrecks in its immediate vicinity.

The Comoros, which straddle the northern entrance to the Mozambique Channel, have always been a hazard to ships sailing at night and were also a hunting ground for pirates. *See also pages 178–79.*

KEY

Sea depths

0 - 220 yards / 0 - 200 meters	
220 - 2,200 yards / 200 - 2,000 meters	
2,200 - 4,375 yards / 2,000 - 4,000 meters	
4,375+ yards / 4,000+ meters	
Swamps	

Treasure ships

No known salvage

Some salvage history known

1500 - 1599	
1600 - 1699	
1700 - 1799	
1800 - 1899	
1900 -	

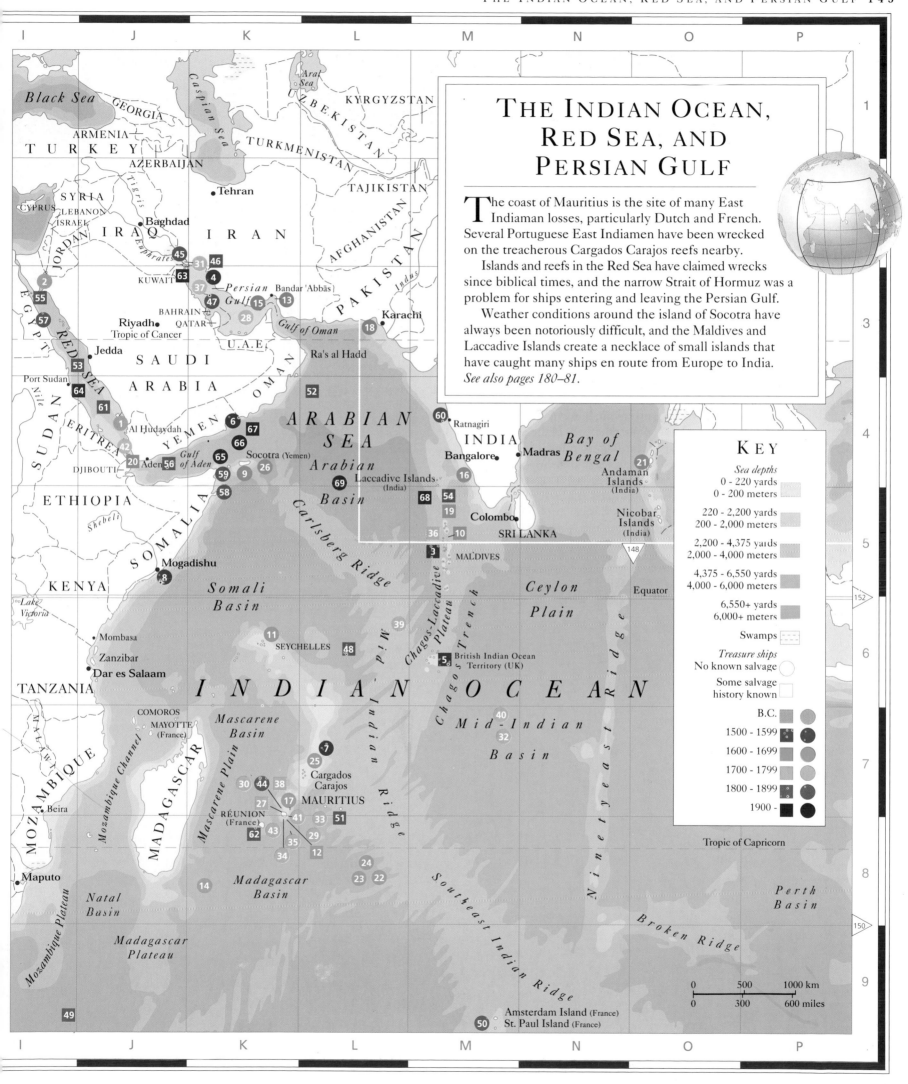

THE INDIAN OCEAN, RED SEA, AND PERSIAN GULF

The coast of Mauritius is the site of many East Indiaman losses, particularly Dutch and French. Several Portuguese East Indiamen have been wrecked on the treacherous Cargados Carajos reefs nearby.

Islands and reefs in the Red Sea have claimed wrecks since biblical times, and the narrow Strait of Hormuz was a problem for ships entering and leaving the Persian Gulf.

Weather conditions around the island of Socotra have always been notoriously difficult, and the Maldives and Laccadive Islands create a necklace of small islands that have caught many ships en route from Europe to India. *See also pages 180–81.*

KEY

Sea depths

0 - 220 yards	0 - 200 meters
220 - 2,200 yards	200 - 2,000 meters
2,200 - 4,375 yards	2,000 - 4,000 meters
4,375 - 6,550 yards	4,000 - 6,000 meters
6,550+ yards	6,000+ meters

Swamps

Treasure ships
No known salvage
Some salvage history known

	B.C.
1500 - 1599	
1600 - 1699	
1700 - 1799	
1800 - 1899	
1900 -	

Black Sea
GEORGIA
ARMENIA
TURKEY
AZERBAIJAN
CYPRUS
SYRIA
LEBANON
ISRAEL
JORDAN
IRAQ
•Baghdad
Tehran•
IRAN
Caspian Sea
UZBEKISTAN
KYRGYZSTAN
TURKMENISTAN
TAJIKISTAN
AFGHANISTAN
Aral Sea
KUWAIT
Euphrates
Tigris
EGYPT
RED SEA
Jedda
SAUDI
ARABIA
Riyadh
Tropic of Cancer
BAHRAIN
QATAR
U.A.E.
Persian Gulf
Bandar 'Abbās
PAKISTAN
Indus
•Karachi
Gulf of Oman
Ra's al Hadd
Port Sudan
SUDAN
Nile
ERITREA
Al Hudaydah
YEMEN
OMAN
DJIBOUTI
Aden
Gulf of Aden
Socotra (Yemen)
ARABIAN SEA
Laccadive Islands (India)
Arabian Basin
ETHIOPIA
Shebeli
SOMALIA
Mogadishu
KENYA
Lake Victoria
Mombasa
Zanzibar
Dar es Salaam
TANZANIA
Maputo
Beira
MOZAMBIQUE
Mozambique Channel
MALAWI
MADAGASCAR
Natal Basin
Mozambique Plateau
Madagascar Basin
Madagascar Plateau
COMOROS
MAYOTTE (France)
Mascarene Basin
Mascarene Plain
RÉUNION (France)
MAURITIUS
Cargados Carajos
SEYCHELLES
INDIAN OCEAN
Somali Basin
Carlsberg Ridge
Mid-Indian Ridge
Chagos-Laccadive Plateau
Chagos Trench
British Indian Ocean Territory (UK)
Mid-Indian Basin
Ninetyeast Ridge
Southeast Indian Ridge
Broken Ridge
Perth Basin
Tropic of Capricorn
INDIA
Bangalore
Madras•
Bay of Bengal
Ratnagiri
Andaman Islands (India)
Nicobar Islands (India)
Colombo
SRI LANKA
MALDIVES
Ceylon Plain
Equator
Amsterdam Island (France)
St. Paul Island (France)

0	500	1000 km
0	300	600 miles

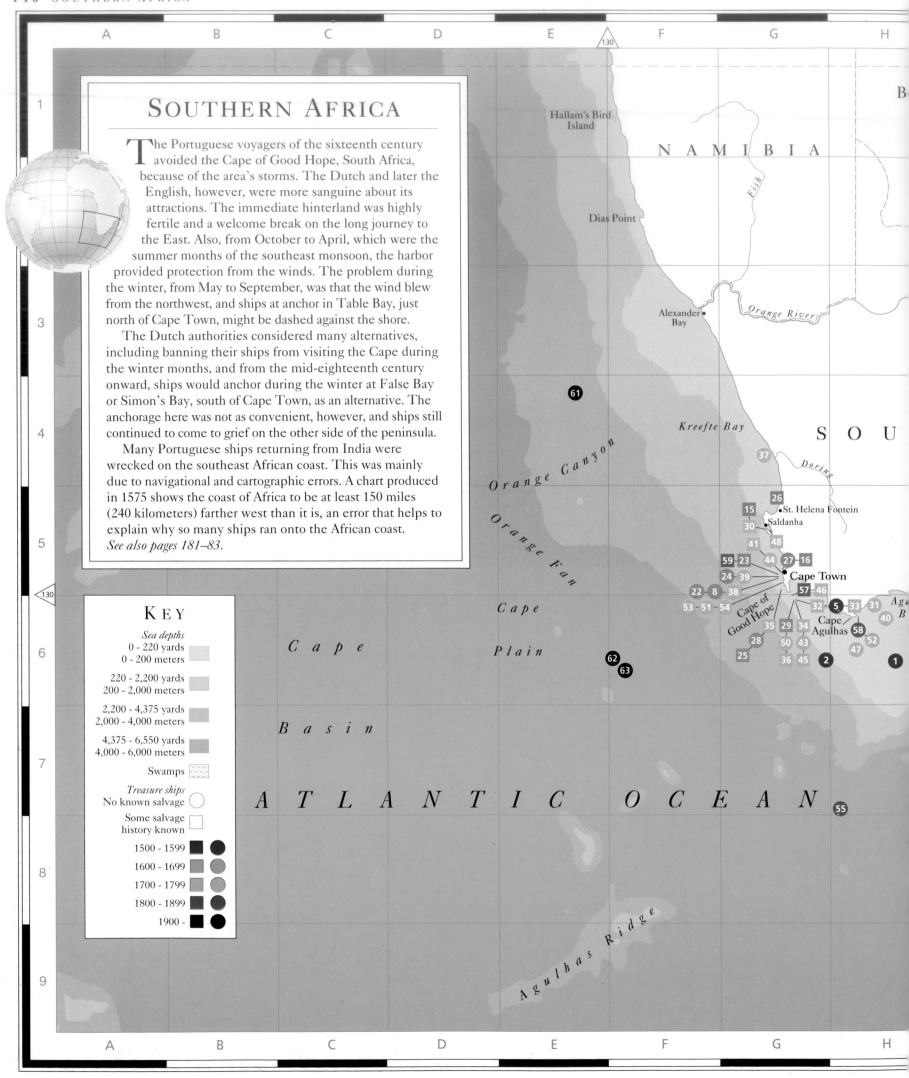

SOUTHERN AFRICA

The Portuguese voyagers of the sixteenth century avoided the Cape of Good Hope, South Africa, because of the area's storms. The Dutch and later the English, however, were more sanguine about its attractions. The immediate hinterland was highly fertile and a welcome break on the long journey to the East. Also, from October to April, which were the summer months of the southeast monsoon, the harbor provided protection from the winds. The problem during the winter, from May to September, was that the wind blew from the northwest, and ships at anchor in Table Bay, just north of Cape Town, might be dashed against the shore.

The Dutch authorities considered many alternatives, including banning their ships from visiting the Cape during the winter months, and from the mid-eighteenth century onward, ships would anchor during the winter at False Bay or Simon's Bay, south of Cape Town, as an alternative. The anchorage here was not as convenient, however, and ships still continued to come to grief on the other side of the peninsula.

Many Portuguese ships returning from India were wrecked on the southeast African coast. This was mainly due to navigational and cartographic errors. A chart produced in 1575 shows the coast of Africa to be at least 150 miles (240 kilometers) farther west than it is, an error that helps to explain why so many ships ran onto the African coast.

See also pages 181–83.

KEY

Sea depths

0 - 220 yards / 0 - 200 meters	
220 - 2,200 yards / 200 - 2,000 meters	
2,200 - 4,375 yards / 2,000 - 4,000 meters	
4,375 - 6,550 yards / 4,000 - 6,000 meters	
Swamps	

Treasure ships

No known salvage ○

Some salvage history known □

1500 - 1599	■	●
1600 - 1699		●
1700 - 1799		●
1800 - 1899		●
1900 -	■	●

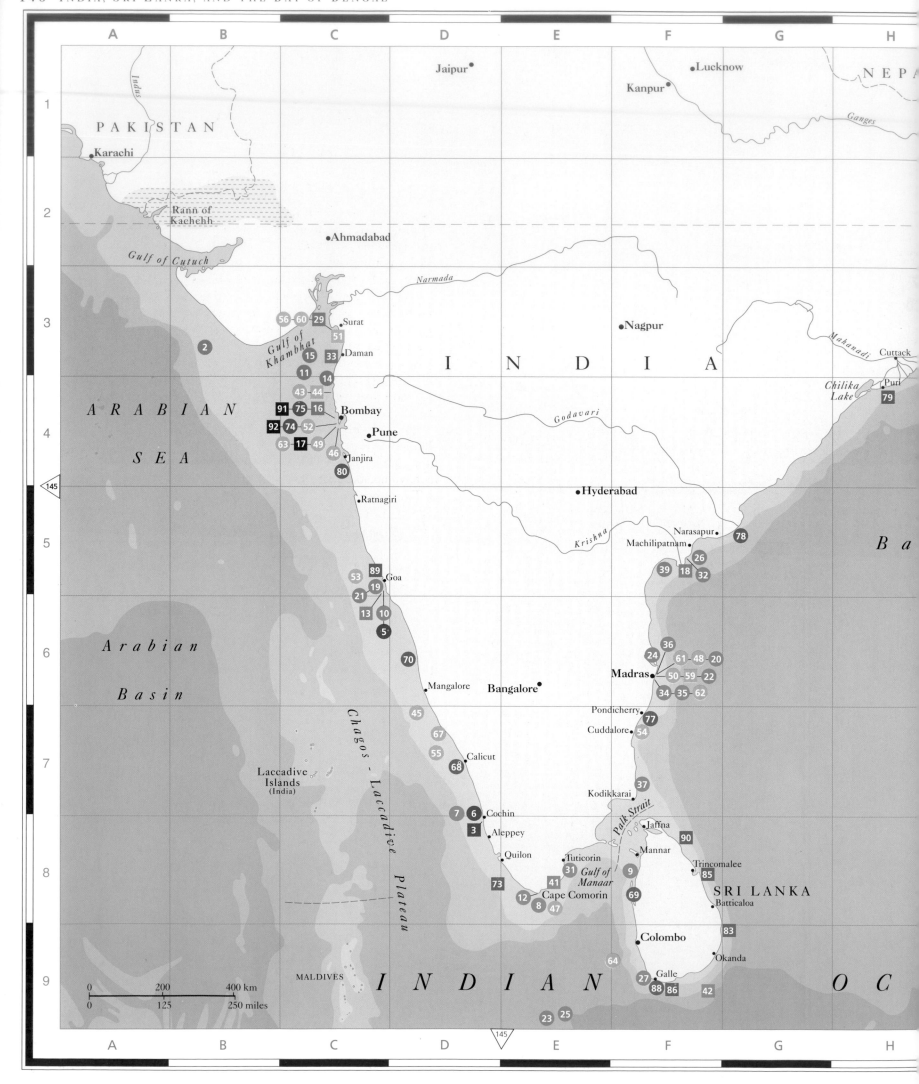

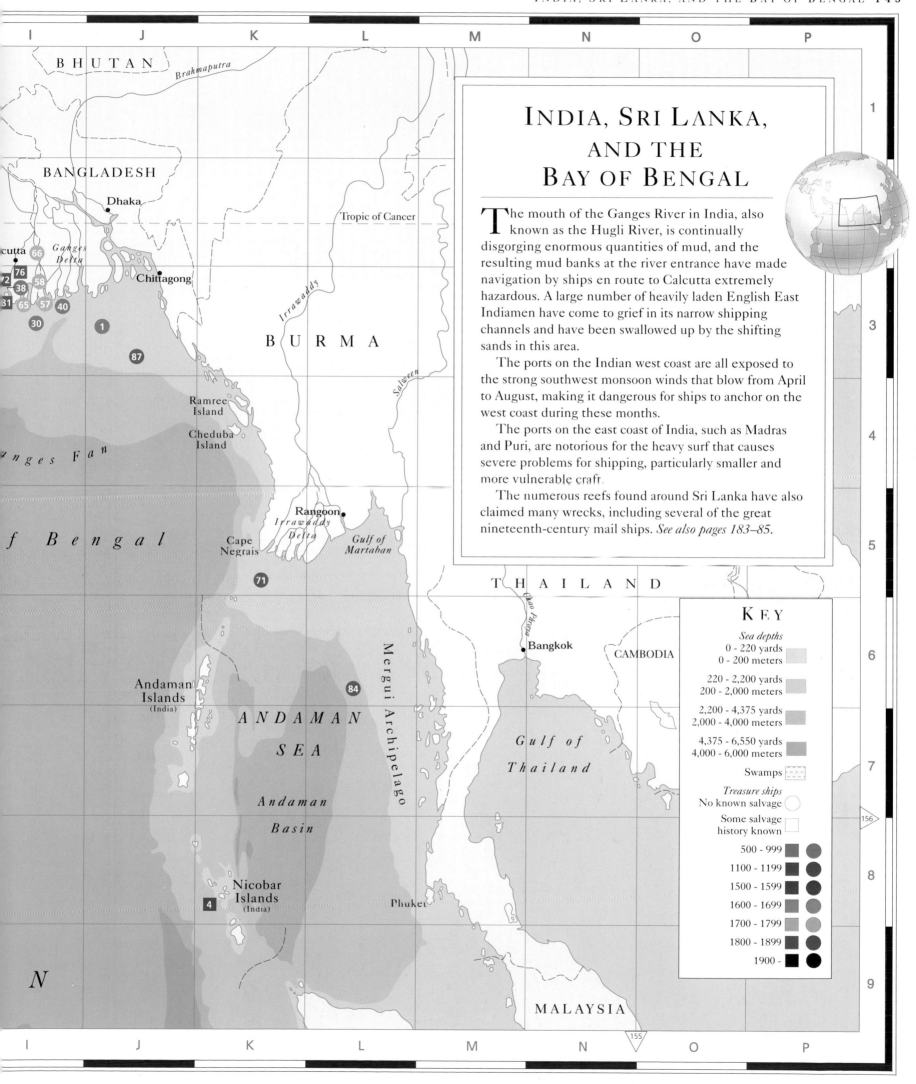

BHUTAN

Brahmaputra

BANGLADESH

Dhaka

Calcutta

66

76

2

38 58

31

65 57 40

30

1

87

Ganges Delta

Chittagong

Irrawaddy

Salween

Tropic of Cancer

BURMA

Ramree Island

Cheduba Island

Ganges Fan

of Bengal

Rangoon

Irrawaddy Delta

Cape Negrais

Gulf of Martaban

71

THAILAND

Chao Praya

Bangkok

CAMBODIA

84

Andaman Islands (India)

ANDAMAN SEA

Mergui Archipelago

Andaman Basin

Gulf of Thailand

4

Nicobar Islands (India)

Phuket

N

MALAYSIA

INDIA, SRI LANKA, AND THE BAY OF BENGAL

The mouth of the Ganges River in India, also known as the Hugli River, is continually disgorging enormous quantities of mud, and the resulting mud banks at the river entrance have made navigation by ships en route to Calcutta extremely hazardous. A large number of heavily laden English East Indiamen have come to grief in its narrow shipping channels and have been swallowed up by the shifting sands in this area.

The ports on the Indian west coast are all exposed to the strong southwest monsoon winds that blow from April to August, making it dangerous for ships to anchor on the west coast during these months.

The ports on the east coast of India, such as Madras and Puri, are notorious for the heavy surf that causes severe problems for shipping, particularly smaller and more vulnerable craft.

The numerous reefs found around Sri Lanka have also claimed many wrecks, including several of the great nineteenth-century mail ships. *See also pages 183–85.*

KEY

Sea depths
0 - 220 yards
0 - 200 meters

220 - 2,200 yards
200 - 2,000 meters

2,200 - 4,375 yards
2,000 - 4,000 meters

4,375 - 6,550 yards
4,000 - 6,000 meters

Swamps

Treasure ships
No known salvage

Some salvage history known

500 - 999
1100 - 1199
1500 - 1599
1600 - 1699
1700 - 1799
1800 - 1899
1900 -

156

155

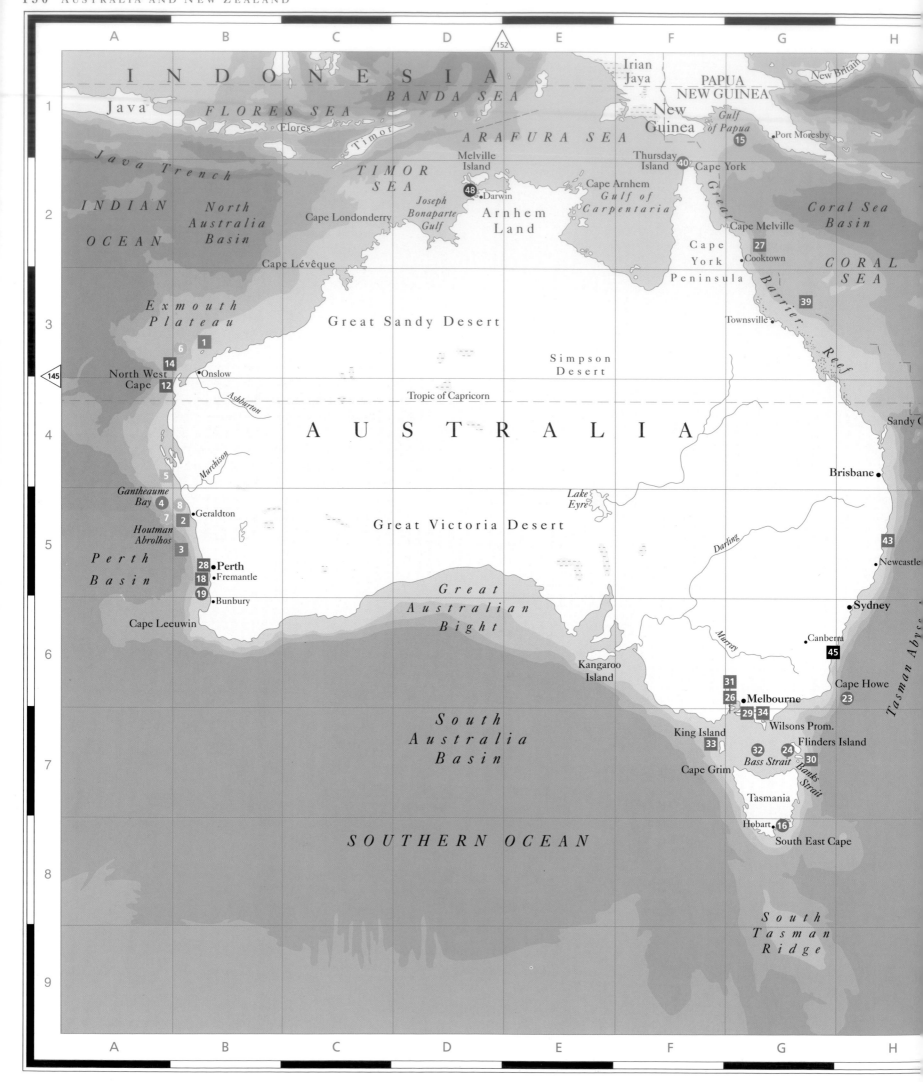

152

A B C D E F G H

I N D O N E S I A

BANDA SEA

Irian
Jaya

PAPUA
NEW GUINEA

New Britain

1

Java

FLORES SEA

Flores

Timor

ARAFURA SEA

New
Guinea

*Gulf
of Papua*

Port Moresby

15

Java Trench

*TIMOR
SEA*

Melville
Island

Thursday
Island

40 Cape York

2

INDIAN

North
Australia
Basin

Cape Londonderry

*Joseph
Bonaparte
Gulf*

48 •Darwin

Arnhem
Land

Cape Arnhem
*Gulf of
Carpentaria*

Cape
York

Cape Melville

27 •Cooktown

*Coral Sea
Basin*

C O R A L
SEA

OCEAN

Cape Lévêque

Peninsula

Great Barrier Reef

3

*Exmouth
Plateau*

6 1

North West
Cape

14

12

•Onslow

Great Sandy Desert

*Simpson
Desert*

Townsville •

39

Ashburton

Tropic of Capricorn

A U S T R A L I A

Sandy C

4

Murchison

Brisbane •

5

*Gantheaume
Bay* 4

7 8

2 •Geraldton

*Lake
Eyre*

Great Victoria Desert

43

•Newcastle

*Houtman
Abrolhos* 3

Darling

5

*Perth
Basin*

28 •Perth
18 •Fremantle
19 •Bunbury

*Great
Australian
Bight*

Sydney •

•Canberra

45

Cape Howe

6

Cape Leeuwin

Kangaroo
Island

Murray

31
26 •Melbourne
29 34

23

Tasman Abyss

*South
Australia
Basin*

King Island

Wilsons Prom.

Flinders Island

33

32 24 30

7

Bass Strait

Cape Grim

Banks Strait

Tasmania

S O U T H E R N   O C E A N

Hobart • 16

South East Cape

8

*South
Tasman
Ridge*

9

A B C D E F G H

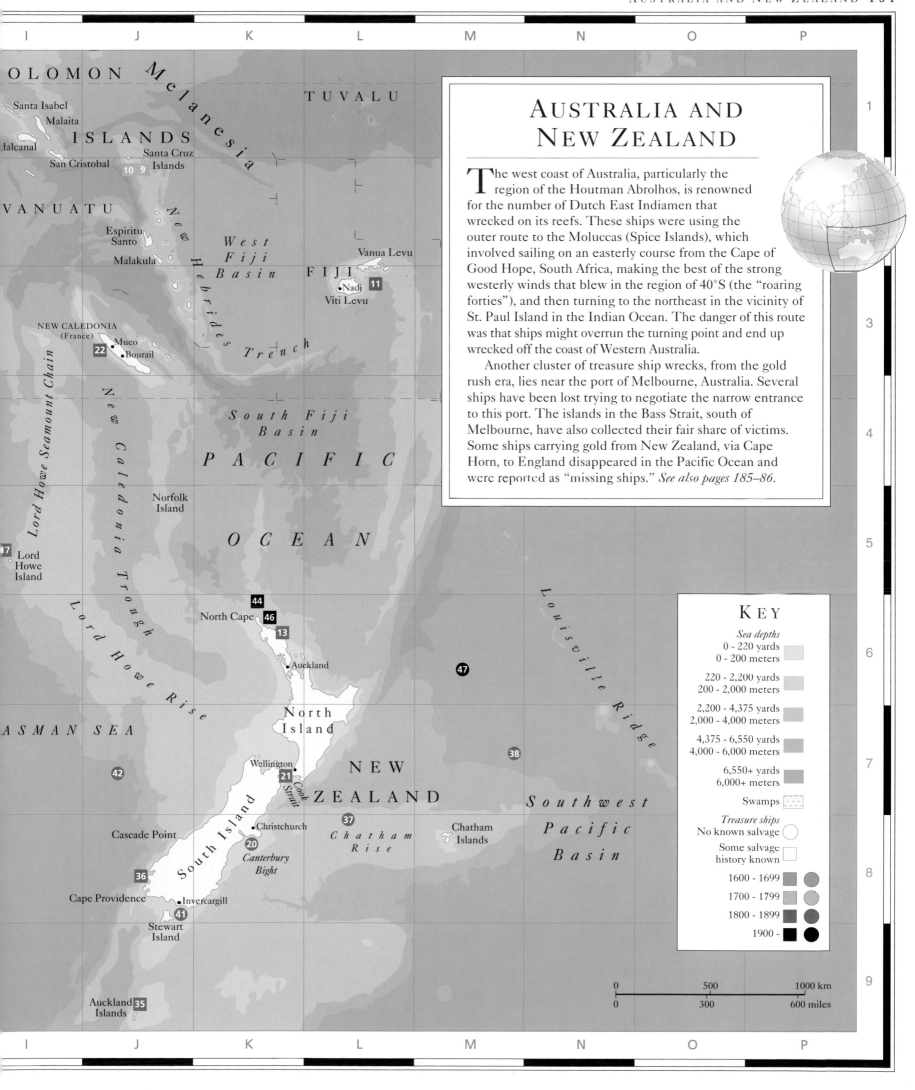

AUSTRALIA AND NEW ZEALAND

The west coast of Australia, particularly the region of the Houtman Abrolhos, is renowned for the number of Dutch East Indiamen that wrecked on its reefs. These ships were using the outer route to the Moluccas (Spice Islands), which involved sailing on an easterly course from the Cape of Good Hope, South Africa, making the best of the strong westerly winds that blew in the region of 40°S (the "roaring forties"), and then turning to the northeast in the vicinity of St. Paul Island in the Indian Ocean. The danger of this route was that ships might overrun the turning point and end up wrecked off the coast of Western Australia.

Another cluster of treasure ship wrecks, from the gold rush era, lies near the port of Melbourne, Australia. Several ships have been lost trying to negotiate the narrow entrance to this port. The islands in the Bass Strait, south of Melbourne, have also collected their fair share of victims. Some ships carrying gold from New Zealand, via Cape Horn, to England disappeared in the Pacific Ocean and were reported as "missing ships." *See also pages 185–86.*

KEY

Sea depths

0 - 220 yards 0 - 200 meters	
220 - 2,200 yards 200 - 2,000 meters	
2,200 - 4,375 yards 2,000 - 4,000 meters	
4,375 - 6,550 yards 4,000 - 6,000 meters	
6,550+ yards 6,000+ meters	
Swamps	

Treasure ships

No known salvage ○

Some salvage history known □

1600 - 1699		
1700 - 1799		
1800 - 1899		
1900 -		

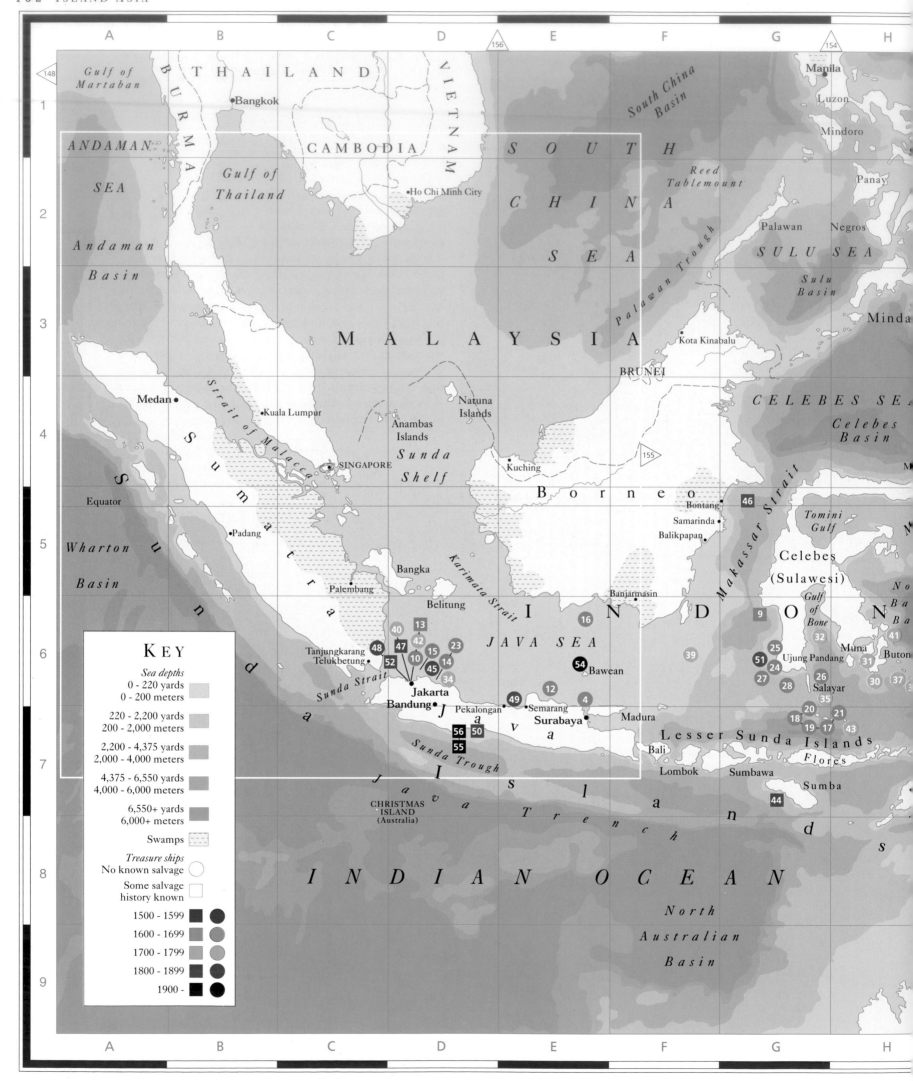

Key labels and geographic text within the map:

KEY

Sea depths
0 – 220 yards
0 – 200 meters

220 – 2,200 yards
200 – 2,000 meters

2,200 – 4,375 yards
2,000 – 4,000 meters

4,375 – 6,550 yards
4,000 – 6,000 meters

6,550+ yards
6,000+ meters

Swamps

Treasure ships
No known salvage
Some salvage history known

1500 – 1599
1600 – 1699
1700 – 1799
1800 – 1899
1900 –

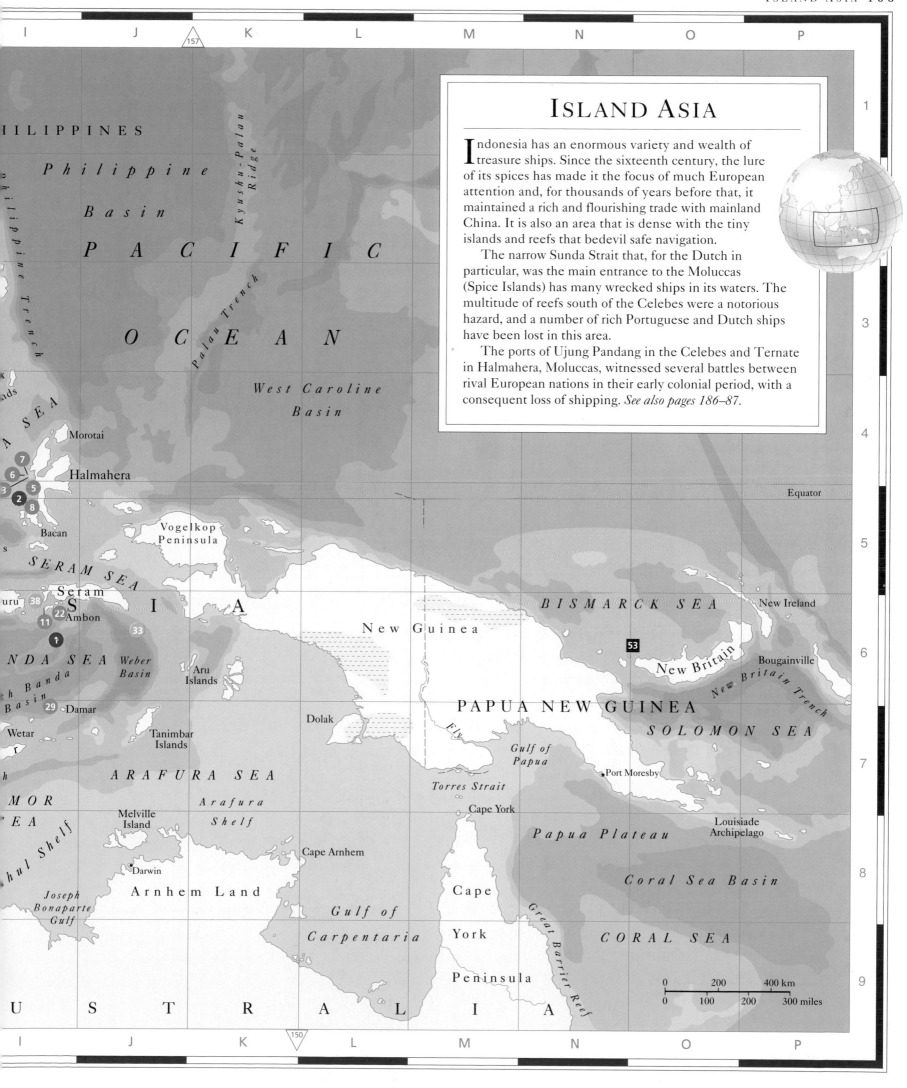

ISLAND ASIA

Indonesia has an enormous variety and wealth of treasure ships. Since the sixteenth century, the lure of its spices has made it the focus of much European attention and, for thousands of years before that, it maintained a rich and flourishing trade with mainland China. It is also an area that is dense with the tiny islands and reefs that bedevil safe navigation.

The narrow Sunda Strait that, for the Dutch in particular, was the main entrance to the Moluccas (Spice Islands) has many wrecked ships in its waters. The multitude of reefs south of the Celebes were a notorious hazard, and a number of rich Portuguese and Dutch ships have been lost in this area.

The ports of Ujung Pandang in the Celebes and Ternate in Halmahera, Moluccas, witnessed several battles between rival European nations in their early colonial period, with a consequent loss of shipping. *See also pages 186–87.*

PHILIPPINES

Philippine Basin

Kyushu-Palau Ridge

Philippine Trench

P A C I F I C

O C E A N

Palau Trench

West Caroline Basin

A SEA

Morotai

7

6

5

2

8

Halmahera

Equator

3

Bacan

Vogelkop Peninsula

s

SERAM SEA

uru

38

Seram

S   I   A

New Guinea

BISMARCK SEA

New Ireland

11

22 Ambon

33

New Britain

Bougainville

NDA SEA

Weber Basin

Aru Islands

New Britain Trench

h *Banda Basin*

29 Damar

Dolak

PAPUA NEW GUINEA

SOLOMON SEA

B a s i n

Wetar

Tanimbar Islands

Fly

Gulf of Papua

Port Moresby

r

h

ARAFURA SEA

Arafura Shelf

Torres Strait

Louisiade Archipelago

MOR

EA

Melville Island

Cape York

Papua Plateau

hul Shelf

Cape Arnhem

Darwin

Coral Sea Basin

Joseph Bonaparte Gulf

A r n h e m   L a n d

Gulf of Carpentaria

Cape

York

Peninsula

Great Barrier Reef

C O R A L   S E A

U   S   T   R   A   L   I   A

53

0		200		400 km
0	100	200	300 miles

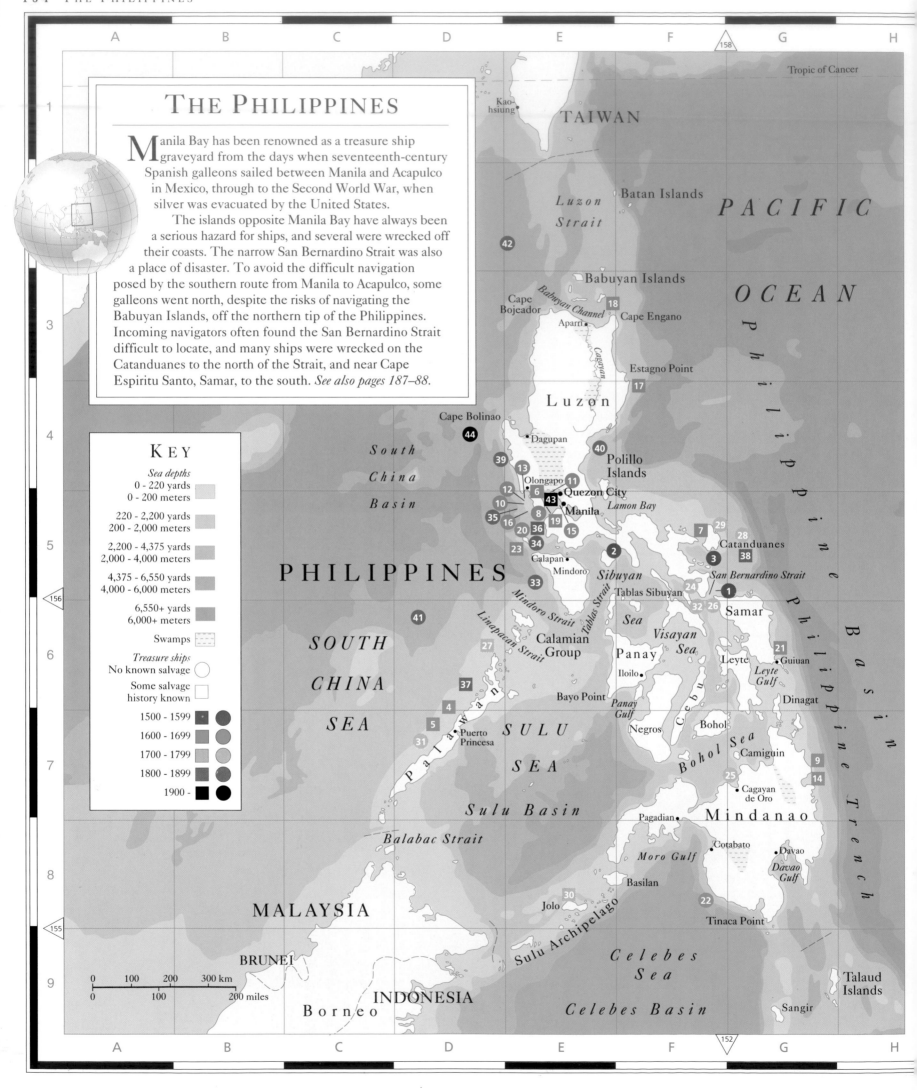

THE PHILIPPINES

Manila Bay has been renowned as a treasure ship graveyard from the days when seventeenth-century Spanish galleons sailed between Manila and Acapulco in Mexico, through to the Second World War, when silver was evacuated by the United States.

The islands opposite Manila Bay have always been a serious hazard for ships, and several were wrecked off their coasts. The narrow San Bernardino Strait was also a place of disaster. To avoid the difficult navigation posed by the southern route from Manila to Acapulco, some galleons went north, despite the risks of navigating the Babuyan Islands, off the northern tip of the Philippines. Incoming navigators often found the San Bernardino Strait difficult to locate, and many ships were wrecked on the Catanduanes to the north of the Strait, and near Cape Espiritu Santo, Samar, to the south. *See also pages 187–88.*

KEY

Sea depths

- 0 - 220 yards / 0 - 200 meters
- 220 - 2,200 yards / 200 - 2,000 meters
- 2,200 - 4,375 yards / 2,000 - 4,000 meters
- 4,375 - 6,550 yards / 4,000 - 6,000 meters
- 6,550+ yards / 6,000+ meters
- Swamps

Treasure ships

- No known salvage ○
- Some salvage history known □

- 1500 - 1599
- 1600 - 1699
- 1700 - 1799
- 1800 - 1899
- 1900 -

MALAYA AND SUMATRA

The Strait of Malacca, with its fast currents, narrow channels, reefs, pirates, and density of commercial shipping, was a main trading area for East Indiamen and has been a ship graveyard for hundreds of years.

By the nineteenth century, the improved accuracy of charts had reduced the risk of running aground. There was, however, a considerable increase in the volume of shipping in the Strait of Singapore and the Strait of Malacca, partly as a result of the establishment of Singapore as a trading post in 1819. This increase in trade led to more traffic and therefore collisions. Violent storms in the area were an additional hazard, and a number of ships were struck by lightning and blew up.

From the days of the Dutch–Portuguese conflicts in the seventeenth century up to the Second World War, several ships were lost in battle in this region. *See also pages 189–90.*

KEY

Sea depths

0 - 220 yards / 0 - 200 meters	
220 - 2,200 yards / 200 - 2,000 meters	
2,200 - 4,375 yards / 2,000 - 4,000 meters	
4,375 - 6,550 yards / 4,000 - 6,000 meters	
6,550+ yards / 6,000+ meters	

Swamps

Treasure ships

No known salvage

Some salvage history known

1400 - 1499
1500 - 1599
1600 - 1699
1700 - 1799
1800 - 1899
1900 -

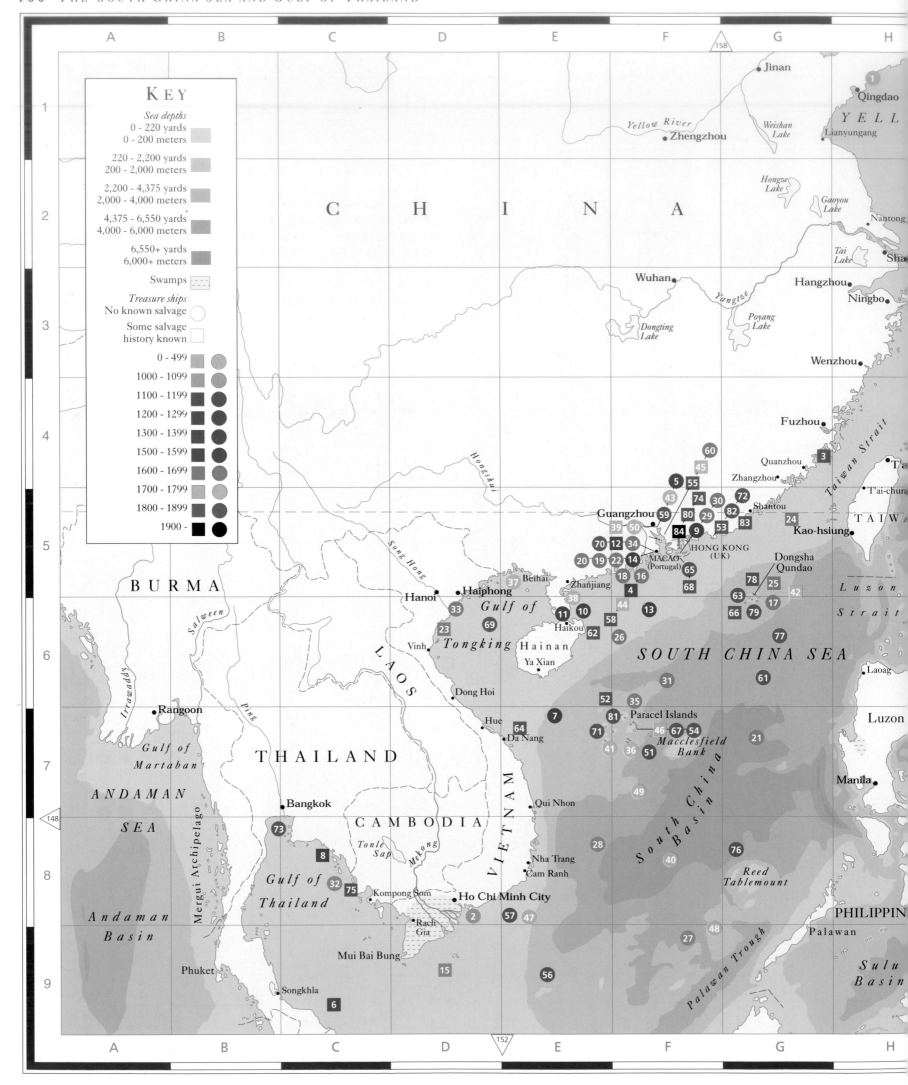

KEY

Sea depths

0 - 220 yards
0 - 200 meters

220 - 2,200 yards
200 - 2,000 meters

2,200 - 4,375 yards
2,000 - 4,000 meters

4,375 - 6,550 yards
4,000 - 6,000 meters

6,550+ yards
6,000+ meters

Swamps

Treasure ships
No known salvage

Some salvage
history known

0 - 499
1000 - 1099
1100 - 1199
1200 - 1299
1300 - 1399
1500 - 1599
1600 - 1699
1700 - 1799
1800 - 1899
1900 -

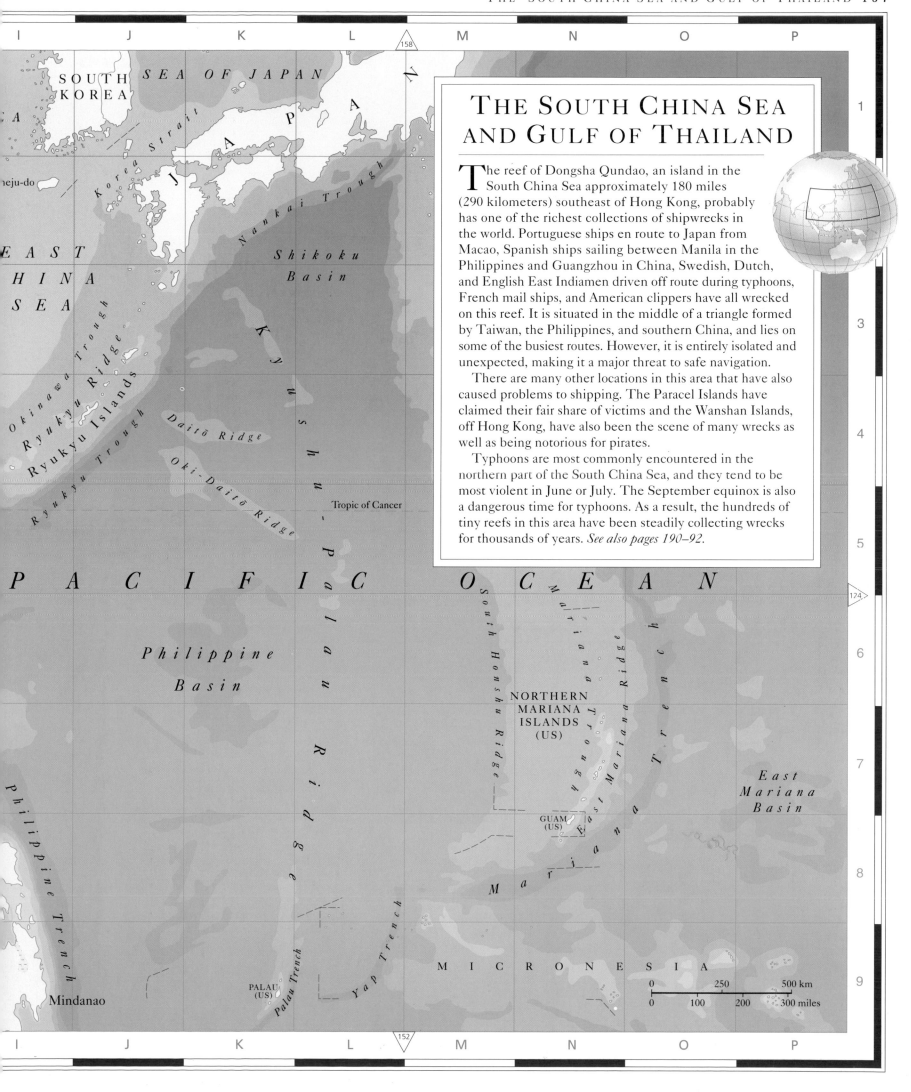

THE SOUTH CHINA SEA AND GULF OF THAILAND

The reef of Dongsha Qundao, an island in the South China Sea approximately 180 miles (290 kilometers) southeast of Hong Kong, probably has one of the richest collections of shipwrecks in the world. Portuguese ships en route to Japan from Macao, Spanish ships sailing between Manila in the Philippines and Guangzhou in China, Swedish, Dutch, and English East Indiamen driven off route during typhoons, French mail ships, and American clippers have all wrecked on this reef. It is situated in the middle of a triangle formed by Taiwan, the Philippines, and southern China, and lies on some of the busiest routes. However, it is entirely isolated and unexpected, making it a major threat to safe navigation.

There are many other locations in this area that have also caused problems to shipping. The Paracel Islands have claimed their fair share of victims and the Wanshan Islands, off Hong Kong, have also been the scene of many wrecks as well as being notorious for pirates.

Typhoons are most commonly encountered in the northern part of the South China Sea, and they tend to be most violent in June or July. The September equinox is also a dangerous time for typhoons. As a result, the hundreds of tiny reefs in this area have been steadily collecting wrecks for thousands of years. *See also pages 190–92.*

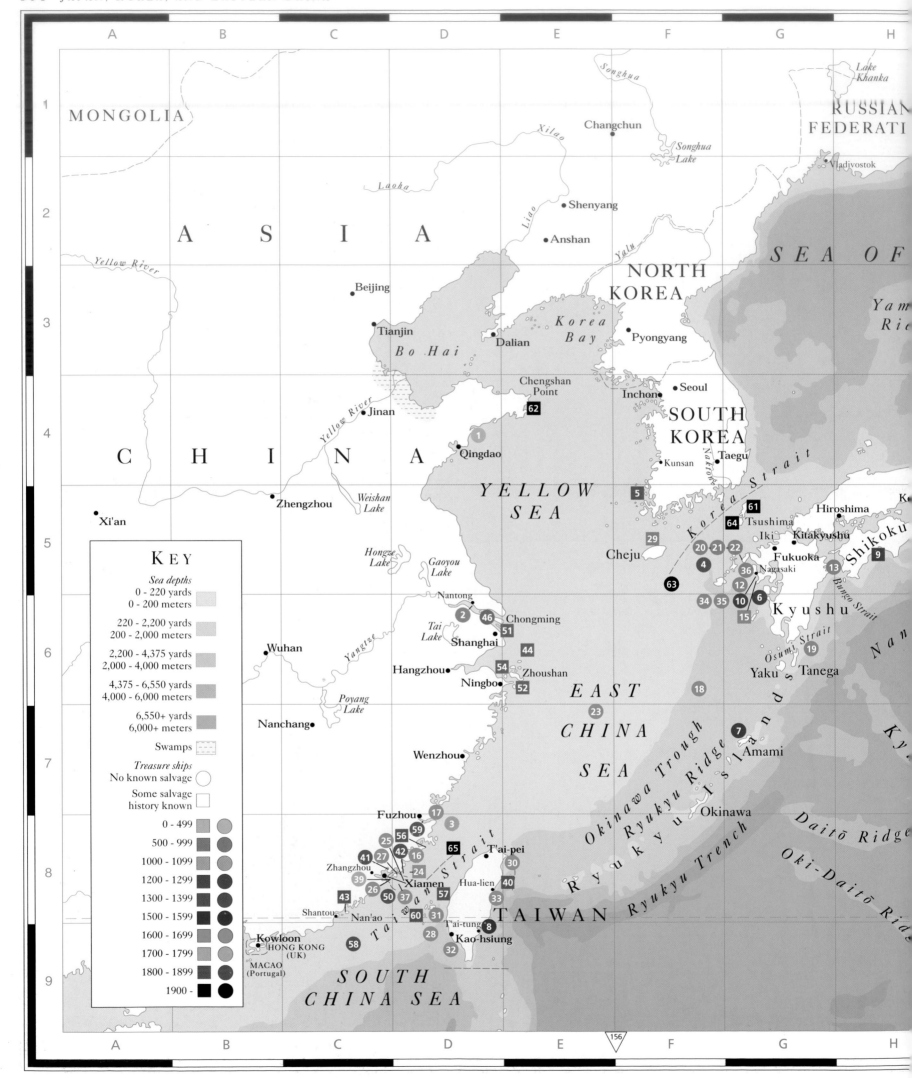

KEY

Sea depths

0 - 220 yards	
0 - 200 meters	
220 - 2,200 yards	
200 - 2,000 meters	
2,200 - 4,375 yards	
2,000 - 4,000 meters	
4,375 - 6,550 yards	
4,000 - 6,000 meters	
6,550+ yards	
6,000+ meters	

Swamps

Treasure ships

No known salvage ◯

Some salvage
history known ▢

0 - 499		
500 - 999		
1000 - 1099		
1200 - 1299		
1300 - 1399		
1500 - 1599		
1600 - 1699		
1700 - 1799		
1800 - 1899		
1900 -		

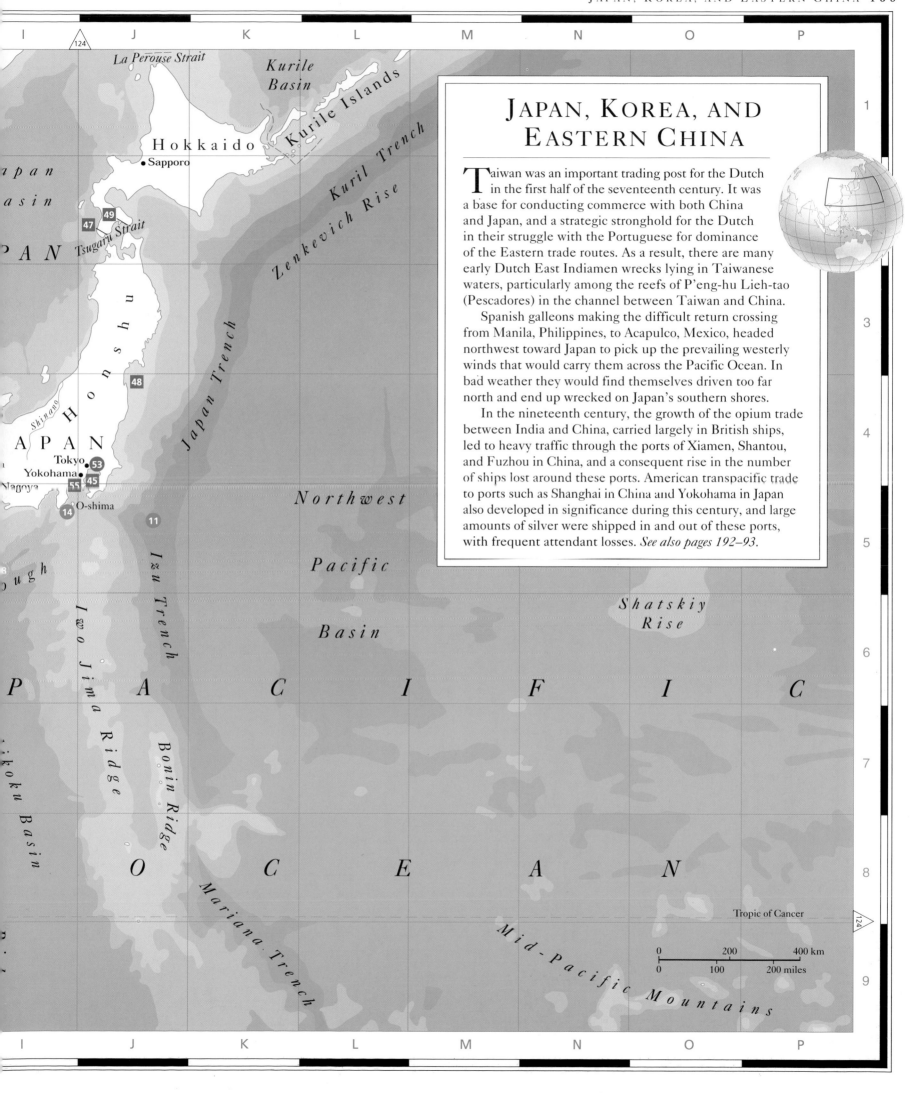

La Perouse Strait

Kurile
Basin

Kurile Islands

Hokkaido

Sapporo

Japan
Basin

Kuril Trench

Zenkevich Rise

Tsugaru Strait

47 49

Honshu

Japan Trench

48

Shinano

APAN

Tokyo
Yokohama 53
Nagoya 55 45

14 O-shima

11

Izu Trench

Northwest

Pacific

Basin

Shatskiy
Rise

ough

P A C I F I C

Iwo Jima Ridge

Bonin Ridge

O C E A N

ikoku Basin

Mariana Trench

Tropic of Cancer

Mid-Pacific Mountains

0	200		400 km
0	100	200 miles	

JAPAN, KOREA, AND EASTERN CHINA

Taiwan was an important trading post for the Dutch in the first half of the seventeenth century. It was a base for conducting commerce with both China and Japan, and a strategic stronghold for the Dutch in their struggle with the Portuguese for dominance of the Eastern trade routes. As a result, there are many early Dutch East Indiamen wrecks lying in Taiwanese waters, particularly among the reefs of P'eng-hu Lieh-tao (Pescadores) in the channel between Taiwan and China.

Spanish galleons making the difficult return crossing from Manila, Philippines, to Acapulco, Mexico, headed northwest toward Japan to pick up the prevailing westerly winds that would carry them across the Pacific Ocean. In bad weather they would find themselves driven too far north and end up wrecked on Japan's southern shores.

In the nineteenth century, the growth of the opium trade between India and China, carried largely in British ships, led to heavy traffic through the ports of Xiamen, Shantou, and Fuzhou in China, and a consequent rise in the number of ships lost around these ports. American transpacific trade to ports such as Shanghai in China and Yokohama in Japan also developed in significance during this century, and large amounts of silver were shipped in and out of these ports, with frequent attendant losses. *See also pages 192–93.*

THE
SHIPWRECK LISTINGS

The information in these shipwreck listings corresponds to the shipwrecks that are plotted on the 20 gazetteer maps. For most entries, the type of ship, its location, route, cargo, and the date that it wrecked are given. There are some ship entries, however, for which there are few historical records and the information is incomplete. Modern place-name spellings have been used where available but, if there is no direct equivalent, the historical spellings have been retained.

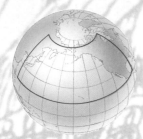

WEST COAST OF NORTH AMERICA AND THE NORTH PACIFIC

The map for these listings is on pp. 124–125.

● No known salvage
■ Some salvage history known

❶ N6 TRINIDAD 1540
SHIP Spanish
LOCATION Near Santa Ana River, California, US
CARGO Treasure

❷ B9 SAN PEDRO 1569
SHIP Spanish
LOCATION Guam
ROUTE Manila, Philippines, to Acapulco, Mexico
CARGO Porcelain and gold

❸ N6 SANTA MARTA 1582
SHIP Spanish
LOCATION Santa Catalina Island, California, US
ROUTE Manila, Philippines, to Acapulco, Mexico
CARGO Gold and porcelain

❹ M6 SAN AGUSTIN 1595
SHIP Spanish
LOCATION North of San Francisco Bay, California, US
ROUTE Manila, Philippines, to Acapulco, Mexico
CARGO Porcelain and gold

❺ F7 HOOP Sept 24, 1600
SHIP Dutch East Indiaman, 500 tons
LOCATION Region of Hawaiian islands
ROUTE Netherlands to Far East, via Strait of Magellan, Chile
CARGO Specie

❻ B8 SANTA MARGARITA 1603
SHIP Spanish
LOCATION Carpana, Northern Mariana Islands
ROUTE Manila, Philippines, to Acapulco, Mexico
CARGO Gold and porcelain
SALVAGE Looted at time of loss and recently rediscovered by Bill Mathers

❼ B8 NUESTRA SENORA DE LA CONCEPCION Sept 20, 1638
SHIP Spanish
LOCATION Saipan, Northern Mariana Islands
ROUTE Manila, Philippines, to Acapulco, Mexico
CARGO Gold, silver, and jewels
SALVAGE Looted at time of loss and recently rediscovered by Bill Mathers
See pp. 56–57

❽ B9 AGANA WRECK 1686
SHIP Spanish
LOCATION Port of Agana, Guam
ROUTE Acapulco, Mexico, to Manila, Philippines
CARGO Silver specie

❾ B9 NUESTRA SENORA DEL PILAR 1690
SHIP Spanish
LOCATION Reef off Cocos Island, near Guam
ROUTE Acapulco, Mexico to Manila, Philippines
CARGO Silver specie

❿ B9 JUAN RODRIGUEZ WRECK 1696
SHIP Spanish
LOCATION Bank of Santa Rosa, Guam
ROUTE Manila, Philippines, to Acapulco, Mexico
CARGO Gold and porcelain

⓫ B8 NUESTRA SENORA DE LA CONCEPCION 1775
SHIP Spanish
LOCATION Northern Mariana Islands
ROUTE Acapulco, Mexico, to Cavite, near Manila, Philippines
CARGO Silver
SALVAGE Salvaged at time of loss

⓬ H9 ESPERANZA 1816
SHIP Spanish
LOCATION Palmyra Island, Line Islands
CARGO Treasure
SALVAGE Probably salvaged at time of loss

⓭ J4 ROSE 1841
SHIP Schooner
LOCATION Pacific
ROUTE Far East to US
CARGO Specie valued at US $180,000

⓮ D9 GEORGE BUCKHAM June 1851
SHIP British
LOCATION Caroline Islands, 8.00N 154.00E
ROUTE Newcastle, Australia, to Hong Kong
CARGO Specie
SALVAGE Some salvage at time of loss

⓯ N7 UNION July 5, 1851
SHIP American
LOCATION 60 miles (95 km) south of San Quintin, Baja California, Mexico
ROUTE San Francisco, California, US, to Panama
CARGO Specie
SALVAGE Salvaged at time of loss

⓰ M6 WINFIELD SCOTT Dec 2, 1853
SHIP American, Pacific Mail Steamship Company
LOCATION Off Santa Barbara, California, US
ROUTE San Francisco, California, US, to Panama
CARGO Gold valued at US $1 million
SALVAGE Salvaged at time of loss

⓱ M6 YANKEE BLADE Sept 30, 1854
SHIP American paddlesteamer
LOCATION Off Point Arguello, Santa Barbara, California, US
ROUTE San Francisco, California, US, to Panama
CARGO Treasure valued at US $153,000
SALVAGE Treasure valued at US $70,000 recovered in 1854

⓲ M7 MASTIFF Sept 15, 1859
LOCATION 30.46N 128.35W
ROUTE San Francisco, California, US, to Hong Kong
CARGO Gold
SALVAGE Gold valued at US $83,000 transferred to the *Achilles*, but private gold lost

⓳ M6 SIERRA NEVADA Oct 1859
SHIP American
LOCATION 80 miles (130 km) south of Monterey, California, US
ROUTE San Francisco, California, US, to San Luis Obispo, California, US
CARGO Specie
SALVAGE Largely salvaged at time of loss

⓴ M5 NORTHERNER Jan 5, 1860
SHIP American, Pacific Mail Steamship Company
LOCATION 40.26N 124.24W
ROUTE San Francisco, California, US, to Canada
CARGO Gold
SALVAGE Mailbags washed ashore

㉑ O8 GOLDEN GATE July 27, 1862
SHIP American paddlesteamer, 2,850 tons
LOCATION Off Manzanillo, Mexico, 19.03N 104.20W
ROUTE San Francisco, California, US, to New York, US
CARGO Gold valued at US $1,400,000
SALVAGE Largely salvaged at time of loss

㉒ M5 BROTHER JONATHAN July 28, 1865
SHIP American sidewheel paddlesteamer, 1,359 tons
LOCATION St. George's Reef Lighthouse, NW Seal Rocks, California, US
ROUTE San Francisco, California, US, to Victoria, British Columbia, Canada
CARGO Specie valued at US $250,000

㉓ E8 LIBELLE July 1866
LOCATION 19.11N 166.31E
ROUTE San Francisco, California, US, to Hong Kong
CARGO Specie
SALVAGE Some salvage at time of loss

㉔ N8 GOLDEN CITY Feb 22, 1870
SHIP American paddlesteamer
LOCATION Cape San Lázaro, Baja California, Mexico
ROUTE San Francisco, California, US, to Panama
CARGO Gold valued at US $791,000
SALVAGE Salvaged at time of loss

㉕ O8 CONTINENTAL Oct 26, 1870
SHIP American
LOCATION Near Cape San Lucas, Baja California, Mexico
ROUTE Mexico to San Francisco, California, US
CARGO Specie valued at US $140,000

㉖ N7 SACRAMENTO Dec 5, 1872
SHIP American, Pacific Mail Steamship Company
LOCATION 29.10N 115.22W
ROUTE Panama to San Francisco, California, US
CARGO Specie valued at US $1.5 million
SALVAGE Partly salvaged

㉗ M6 PRINCE ALFRED June 14, 1874
SHIP American
LOCATION Duxbury Reef, 6 miles (10 km) north of San Francisco, California, US
ROUTE San Francisco, California, US, to Victoria, Vancouver Island, British Columbia, Canada
CARGO Gold
SALVAGE Salvaged at time of loss

㉘ M4 PACIFIC Nov 4, 1875
SHIP Goodall, Nelson, Perkins & Co., paddlesteamer, 875 tons
LOCATION 40 miles (65 km) south of Cape Flattery, Washington, US
ROUTE Victoria, Vancouver Island, British Columbia, Canada, to San Francisco, California, US
CARGO Treasure valued at US $79,220

㉙ P9 CITY OF SAN FRANCISCO May 16, 1877
SHIP American, Pacific Mail Steamship Company
LOCATION 16.16N 98.36W
ROUTE Panama to San Francisco, California, US
CARGO Gold
SALVAGE Several attempts at salvage, but results unknown

㉚ M4 GREAT REPUBLIC Apr 19, 1879
SHIP American paddlesteamer, Pacific Mail Steamship Company
LOCATION Off Columbia River, Oregon, US
ROUTE San Francisco, US, to Portland, Oregon, US
CARGO Specie

㉛ M6 CITY OF CHESTER Aug 22, 1888
SHIP American
LOCATION San Francisco, California, US
CARGO Possibly cargo valued at US $30 million

32 08 COLIMA May 27, 1895
SHIP American, Pacific Mail Steamship Company, 2,906 tons
LOCATION 50 miles (80 km) south of Manzanillo, Mexico
ROUTE San Francisco, California, US, to Panama
CARGO Gold

33 L2 MEXICO Aug 5, 1897
SHIP American, Pacific Mail Steamship Company, 1,797 tons
LOCATION 57.03N 135.18W
ROUTE Alaska, US, to San Francisco, California, US
CARGO Gold
SALVAGE Some cargo in the cabins was salvaged but nothing below deck level was saved

34 M6 CITY OF RIO DE JANEIRO Feb 22, 1901
SHIP American, Pacific Mail Steamship Company, 3,532 tons
LOCATION Mile Rock, Golden Gate, San Francisco, California, US
ROUTE Yokohama, Japan, to San Francisco, California, US
CARGO Gold

35 L2 ISLANDER Aug 15, 1901
SHIP Canadian, Pacific Navigation Company, 1,495 tons
LOCATION Steven's Passage, near Juneau, Alaska, US
ROUTE Alaska, US, to Vancouver, British Columbia, Canada
CARGO Gold valued at US $3 million
SALVAGE Largely salvaged in 1930s and worked again more recently

36 L3 RAMONA Nov 20, 1911
SHIP Wooden steamer, 1,061 tons
LOCATION 56.01N 134.09W
ROUTE Alaska, US, to Vancouver, British Columbia, Canada
CARGO Gold valued at £25,000 sterling
SALVAGE Some salvage at time of loss

37 L2 PRINCESS SOPHIA Oct 26, 1918
SHIP Canadian, Pacific Railway Company, 2,320 tons
LOCATION Vanderbilt Reef, Lynn Canal, Alaska, US
ROUTE Skagway, Alaska, US, to Vancouver, British Columbia, Canada
CARGO Gold valued at £200,000 sterling
SALVAGE Some salvage at time of loss

38 I7 ASIATIC PRINCE Mar 24, 1928
SHIP British, Prince Line, 5,800 tons
LOCATION 24.00N 155.00W
ROUTE New York, US, to Yokohama, Japan
CARGO Gold

39 N8 COLUMBIA Sept 13, 1931
SHIP American, Grace Line
LOCATION Point Tosca, Santa Margarita island, Baja California, Mexico
ROUTE New York, US, to San Francisco, California, US
CARGO Silver bars valued at US $700,000
SALVAGE Silver bars valued at US $600,000 recovered

40 M4 FELTRE Feb 17, 1937
SHIP Italian
LOCATION Columbia River, Oregon, US
CARGO Silver bars valued at US $185,000
SALVAGE Largely salvaged at time of loss

41 B8 FLORENTINE 1951
SHIP American
LOCATION 22.30N 140.28E
CARGO Gold

GULF OF MEXICO TO BERMUDA

The map for these listings is on pp. 126–127.
● No known salvage
■ Some salvage history known

1 E7 SHIP OF FRANCISCO PIZARRO 1510
TYPE Spanish pinnace
LOCATION Cape San Antonio, Cuba
CARGO Artifacts

2 F6 SANTA CATALINA 1537
SHIP Spanish, 200 tons
LOCATION Havana harbour, Cuba
ROUTE Havana, Cuba, to Spain
CARGO Gold and silver
Capt. Francisco Lopez

3 F6 SANTA MARIA 1544
SHIP Spanish, 180 tons
LOCATION Near Havana, Cuba
ROUTE Nombre de Dios, Panama, to Havana, Cuba
CARGO Gold and silver

4 F6 VISITACION 1550
SHIP Spanish, 200 tons
LOCATION Reefs of Los Martires, Lower Matecumbe Keys, Florida, US
ROUTE Veracruz, Mexico, to Spain
CARGO Gold and silver

5 L3 SANTA BARBOLA 1551
SHIP Spanish, 400 tons
LOCATION Bermuda
ROUTE Nombre de Dios, Panama, to Spain
CARGO Gold and silver
SALVAGE Treasure salvaged at time of loss

6 D5 SANTA MARIA DE CAMINO 1554
SHIP Spanish, 350 tons
LOCATION Gulf of Mexico
ROUTE Caribbean to Spain
CARGO Gold and silver
SALVAGE Largely salvaged at time of loss
Capt. Diego Diaz

7 A5 ESPIRITU SANTO Apr 29, 1554
SHIP Spanish
LOCATION Padre Island, Texas, US
ROUTE Veracruz, Mexico, to Havana, Cuba
CARGO Gold and silver
SALVAGE Salvaged at time of loss and recently rediscovered

8 A5 SAN ESTEBAN Apr 29, 1554
SHIP Spanish
LOCATION Padre Island, Texas, US
ROUTE Veracruz, Mexico, to Havana, Cuba
CARGO Gold and silver
SALVAGE Salvaged at time of loss and recently rediscovered

9 A5 SANTA MARIA DE YCIAR Apr 29, 1554
SHIP Spanish
LOCATION Padre Island, Texas, US
ROUTE Veracruz, Mexico, to Havana, Cuba
CARGO Silver coins, silver bullion, liquid amber, cochineal, refined sugar, wool, and cowhides
SALVAGE Salvaged at time of loss and recently rediscovered

10 G5 SANTA MARIA DEL CAMINO 1555
SHIP Spanish, 200 tons
LOCATION Bahama Canal, Bahamas
ROUTE Havana, Cuba, to Spain
CARGO Gold and silver
Capt. Alonso Martin Morejon

11 A7 SANTA MARIA LA BLANCA 1555
SHIP Spanish, 220 tons
LOCATION San Juan Ulua, Veracruz, Mexico
ROUTE Veracruz, Mexico, to Spain
CARGO Gold and silver
SALVAGE Largely salvaged
Capt. Francisco de Sanctana

12 F6 SANTA MARIA EN VILLACELAN 1556
SHIP Spanish, 220 tons
LOCATION Near Matanzas, Cuba
ROUTE Havana, Cuba, to Spain
CARGO Gold and silver

13 E6 LA CONCEPCION May 24, 1556
SHIP Spanish, 220 tons
LOCATION Between Cape San Antonio, Cuba, and Havana, Cuba
ROUTE Nombre de Dios, Panama, to Havana, Cuba
CARGO Gold and silver

14 E6 LA MAGDALENA May 24, 1556
SHIP Spanish, 220 tons
LOCATION Between Cape San Antonio, Cuba, and Havana, Cuba
ROUTE Nombre de Dios, Panama, to Havana, Cuba
CARGO Gold and silver
Capt. Vicencia Bozino

15 L2 MADALENA 1563
SHIP Spanish
LOCATION Off reefs, NW Bermuda, approximately 33.00N
ROUTE Havana, Cuba, to Spain
CARGO Gold and silver

16 H6 SAN CRISTOBAL 1563
SHIP Spanish, 120 tons
LOCATION Bahamas
ROUTE Santo Domingo, Dominican Republic, to Spain
CARGO Gold and silver
Capt. Rodrigo Alonso

17 G5 SANTA CLARA 1564
SHIP Spanish, 300 tons
LOCATION Little Bahama Bank, Bahamas
ROUTE Cartagena, Colombia, to Spain
CARGO Gold and silver
SALVAGE Largely salvaged at time of loss
Capt. Juan Diaz Bozino

18 A8 ANGEL 1568
SHIP English
LOCATION Port of San Juan Ulua, Veracruz, Mexico
CARGO Specie and artifacts
Ship of Sir John Hawkin's fleet lost in battle with the Spanish.

19 B8 JESUS OF LUBECK 1568
SHIP English warship
LOCATION Port of San Juan Ulua, Veracruz, Mexico
CARGO Specie and artifacts
Flagship of Sir Thomas Hawkins's fleet, lost in battle with Spanish. Many Spanish ships also sunk in same engagement.

20 E7 SHIP OF ERASSO 1577
SHIP Frigate
LOCATION Off west Cuba
CARGO Booty and treasure
Contained booty of pirates Barker, Coxe, and Roche

21 D7 SHIP OF ANTONIO MANRIQUE 1581
SHIP Spanish
LOCATION Off NE Yucatán, Mexico
ROUTE Nombre de Dios, Panama, to Havana, Cuba
CARGO Treasure

22 H2 TIGER June 1585
SHIP British
LOCATION Ocracoke Inlet, North Carolina, US
ROUTE UK to US
CARGO Artifacts
Flagship of Sir Richard Grenville

23 G5 SAN JUAN 1586
SHIP Spanish, 120 tons
LOCATION Bahama Canal, Bahamas
ROUTE Caribbean to Spain
CARGO Gold and silver
Capt. Martin de Irigoyan

24 G4 JESUS MARIA 1589
SHIP Spanish, 400 tons
LOCATION Bahama Canal, Bahamas, approximately 30.00N
ROUTE Veracruz, Mexico, to Spain
CARGO Gold and silver
Capt. Francisco Salvago

25 G4 SANTA CATALINA 1589
SHIP Spanish, 350 tons
LOCATION Bahama Canal, Bahamas, approximately 30.00N
ROUTE Veracruz, Mexico, to Spain
CARGO Gold and silver
Capt. Domingo Ianez Ome

26 E6 SHIP OF MIGUEL DE ACOSTA 1590
SHIP Spanish, 400 tons
LOCATION Off the Organos, towards Cape San Antonio, Cuba
ROUTE Caribbean to Spain
CARGO Gold and silver
SALVAGE Unsuccessful attempt at salvage
Part of fleet of Rodrigo de Rada. Lost with a ship belonging to Diego de Bode during action with English corsairs.

27 F6 NUESTRA SENORA DEL ROSARIO 1593
SHIP Spanish, 220 tons
LOCATION Near Havana, Cuba
ROUTE Veracruz, Mexico, to Spain
CARGO Gold and silver
SALVAGE Largely salvaged at time of loss

28 F6 SANTA MARIA DE SAN VICENTE 1593
SHIP Spanish
LOCATION Near Havana, Cuba
ROUTE Veracruz, Mexico, to Spain
CARGO Silver
SALVAGE Largely salvaged at time of loss
Capt. Miguel de Alcate

29 L3 SHIP OF BARBOTIERE Dec 17, 1593
SHIP French
LOCATION NW reef of Bermuda, 21 miles (34 km) from shore
ROUTE Hispaniola to France
CARGO Specie

30 K3 SAN PEDRO 1596
SHIP Spanish, 320 tons
LOCATION Off Somerset Island, Bermuda
ROUTE Havana, Cuba, to Spain
CARGO Treasure
SALVAGE Recently salvaged by Teddy Tucker
Capt. Hieronimo de Porras

31 G6 SHIP OF DIEGO RODRIGUEZ 1600
SHIP Spanish, 50 tons
LOCATION Florida, US
ROUTE Havana, Cuba, to Spain
CARGO Gold and silver

32 L3 SANTA ANA 1605
SHIP Spanish, 200 tons
LOCATION Western reefs of Bermuda
ROUTE Honduras to Spain
CARGO Gold and pearls
Capt. Diego Cacolin

33 F6 SAN FRANCISCO 1606
SHIP Spanish, 100 tons
LOCATION Havana, Cuba
ROUTE Havana, Cuba, to Spain
CARGO Gold and silver
Capt. Antonio Cardoso

34 L3 SEA VENTURE 1609
SHIP British
LOCATION Eastern point of Bermuda
ROUTE UK to the Americas
CARGO Specie and artifacts
Ship of Sir George Somers. Apparently used by Shakespeare as the basis for The Tempest.

35 E7 EL BUEN VIAJE 1621
SHIP Spanish, 150 tons
LOCATION Between Venezuela and Havana, Cuba
ROUTE Cartagena, Spain, to Havana, Cuba
CARGO Gold, silver, and pearls

36 B8 NUESTRA SENORA DEL ROSARIO 1621
SHIP Spanish, 370 tons
LOCATION Port of San Juan Ulua, Veracruz, Mexico
ROUTE Veracruz, Mexico, to Spain
CARGO Gold and silver
SALVAGE Largely salvaged at time of loss
Capt. Juan de Benavides y Balan

37 K3 SAN ANTONIO 1621
SHIP Spanish, 300 tons
LOCATION West of Bermuda, 10 miles (16 km) from land
ROUTE Havana, Cuba, to Spain
CARGO Treasure
SALVAGE Largely salvaged at time of loss, and salvaged recently by Teddy Tucker
English plundered cargo at time of loss

38 F6 LA MARGARITA 1622
SHIP Spanish
LOCATION Marquesas Keys, Florida, US
ROUTE Havana, Cuba, to Spain
CARGO Gold and silver
SALVAGE Largely salvaged by Nunez Melian a few years after loss
Capt. Pedro Guerrero de Espinosa. 10 or 11 ships lost in this storm and in the same area.

39 L3 NUESTRA SENORA DE LA LIMPIA CONCEPCION 1622
SHIP Spanish, 116 tons
LOCATION Bermuda
ROUTE Honduras to Spain
CARGO Gold and silver

40 J3 SAN AGUSTIN 1622
SHIP Spanish, 780 tons
LOCATION 450 miles (725 km) from Bermuda
ROUTE Havana, Cuba, to Spain
CARGO Gold and silver

41 L2 SAN IGNACIO 1622
SHIP Spanish, 750 tons
LOCATION Near Bermuda
ROUTE Havana, Cuba, to Spain
CARGO Gold and silver
Capt. Simon de Beydacar

42 F6 NUESTRA SENORA DE ATOCHA Sept 5, 1622
SHIP Spanish, 150 tons
LOCATION Off Matecumbe Keys, Florida, US
ROUTE Havana, Cuba, to Spain
CARGO Gold and silver valued in excess of 1 million pesos – cargo valued today at US $750 million
SALVAGE Relocated and worked by Mel Fisher in 1980s after a 16-year search

43 F6 NUESTRA SENORA DEL ROSARIO Sept 5, 1622
SHIP Spanish, 600 tons
LOCATION Dry Tortugas, Florida, US
ROUTE Havana, Cuba, to Spain
CARGO Gold and silver
SALVAGE Largely salvaged at time of loss

44 F6 TORTUGAS WRECK Sept 5, 1622
SHIP Spanish
LOCATION 20 miles (30 km) SW of Dry Tortugas, Florida, US
ROUTE Havana, Cuba, to Spain
CARGO Gold, silver, and artifacts
SALVAGE Salvaged by American salvage company, Seahawk, in 1990s
See pp. 54–55

45 G5 ESPIRITU SANTO 1623
SHIP Spanish
LOCATION Entrance to Bahama Canal, Bahamas
ROUTE Havana, Cuba, to Spain
CARGO Gold and silver

46 A7 LARGA 1628
SHIP Spanish
LOCATION Veracruz, Mexico
ROUTE Veracruz, Mexico, to Havana, Cuba
CARGO Treasure
SALVAGE Salvaged at time of loss
Ship sank when leaving Veracruz

47 G5 LUCAYA WRECK 1628
SHIP Spanish
LOCATION South side of Grand Bahama Island, Bahamas
ROUTE Havana, Cuba, to Spain
CARGO Gold and silver
SALVAGE Relocated by Jack Slack
One of the ships captured by Piet Heyn

48 F6 MATANZAS WRECKS 1628
SHIP Spanish
LOCATION Entrance to Matanzas River, Cuba
ROUTE Havana, Cuba, to Spain
CARGO Silver valued at 12 million florins
SALVAGE Most of the treasure was seized by the Dutch and taken to the Netherlands
15 ships lost, captured, or burned by Piet Heyn. Spanish commander, Benavides, later executed.

49 B7 NUESTRA SENORA DEL JUNCAL 1631
SHIP Spanish
LOCATION North of Veracruz, Mexico
ROUTE Veracruz, Mexico, to Havana, Cuba
CARGO Large quantity of gold and silver
Part of fleet of Manuel Serrano de Rivera

50 A8 SANTA TERESA 1631
SHIP Spanish
LOCATION Veracruz, Mexico
ROUTE Veracruz, Mexico, to Havana, Cuba
CARGO Gold and silver

51 E6 NUESTRA SENORA DE LA ANUNCIADA 1635
SHIP Spanish
LOCATION North of Havana, Cuba
ROUTE Havana, Cuba, to Spain
CARGO Silver
SALVAGE 2 silver bars saved before ship sank

52 L3 EL GALGO 1639
SHIP Spanish patache
LOCATION Bermuda reef, Bermuda, 9 miles (14 km) from land
ROUTE Havana, Cuba, to Spain
CARGO Treasure
SALVAGE Looted

53 L3 LA VIGA 1639
SHIP Spanish
LOCATION Bermuda reef, Bermuda, 9 miles (14 km) from land
ROUTE Havana, Cuba, to Spain
CARGO Treasure
SALVAGE Looted
Capt. Matthew Lorenzo

54 F6 NUESTRA SENORA DE ATOCHA Y SAN JOSEF 1641
SHIP Spanish, 400 tons
LOCATION Close to Havana, Cuba
ROUTE Veracruz, Mexico, to Havana, Cuba
CARGO Gold and silver
SALVAGE Some salvage at time of loss
Capt. Geronimo Beleno

55 F6 SAN MARCOS 1642
SHIP Spanish, 300 tons
LOCATION Havana, Cuba
ROUTE Havana, Cuba, to Spain
CARGO Gold and silver
SALVAGE Salvaged at time of loss

56 C8 MARICAO Aug 11, 1644
SHIP Pirate ship
LOCATION Lecheharos Reefs, south of Cape Catoche, Mexico
CARGO Silver plate and jewels
Ship belonged to Jackson

57 C8 SWANN Aug 11, 1644
SHIP Pirate ship
LOCATION Lecheharos Reefs, south of Cape Catoche, Mexico
CARGO Silver plate and jewels
Ship belonged to Jackson

58 C8 VALENTINE Aug 11, 1644
SHIP Pirate ship
LOCATION Lecheharos Reefs, south of Cape Catoche, Mexico
CARGO Silver plate and jewels
Ship belonged to Jackson

59 C7 SANTIAGO 1647
SHIP Spanish
LOCATION Bay of Campeche, Mexico
ROUTE Veracruz, Mexico, to Havana, Cuba
CARGO Gold and silver
SALVAGE Partly salvaged at time of loss

60 L3 SPANISH SHIP 1648
SHIP Spanish, 350 tons
LOCATION Rocks off Bermuda
ROUTE Caribbean to Spain
CARGO Large quantity of silver dollars

61 G5 NUESTRA SENORA DE LA MARAVILLAS 1656
SHIP Spanish, 650 tons
LOCATION Little Bahama Bank, Bahamas
ROUTE Havana, Cuba, to Spain
CARGO Gold and silver
SALVAGE Recently salvaged by Herbert Humphries
Capt. Matias de Orellana

62 C7 NUESTRA SENORA DE LOS REMEDIOS 1668
SHIP Spanish
LOCATION 48 miles (77 km) from port of Campeche, Mexico
ROUTE Mexico to Spain
CARGO Treasure

63 C8 NUESTRA SENORA DEL CARMEN 1669
SHIP Spanish
LOCATION Campeche, Mexico
CARGO Specie
Fleet of Espinosa

64 G5 WINCHESTER 1695
SHIP British warship
LOCATION On rocks, 12 miles (20 km) from Cape Florida, Florida, US
ROUTE West Indies to UK
CARGO Booty from the sacking of Port-de-Paix, Haiti
SALVAGE Salvaged at time of loss and relocated recently

65 E7 NUESTRA SENORA DE LAS MERCEDES 1698
SHIP Spanish almiranta
LOCATION Rock of Sibarima, Cuba
ROUTE Veracruz, Mexico, to Spain
CARGO Gold and silver

66 F6 SANTISIMA TRINIDAD 1711
SHIP Spanish
LOCATION Port of Mariel, Cuba
ROUTE Veracruz, Mexico, to Spain
CARGO Silver
SALVAGE Some salvage at time of loss

67 G6 FLEET OF UBILLA July 30, 1715
SHIP Spanish
LOCATION Coast of Florida, US
ROUTE Havana, Cuba, to Spain
CARGO Gold and silver valued at over 6 million pesos, Chinese porcelain, and silver plate
SALVAGE Cargo valued at over 5 million pesos recovered at time of loss. Recently salvaged by Kip Wagner and Real Eight Company.

68 L3 SHIP OF LORD BELHAVEN 1721
SHIP British, 50 cannon
LOCATION Bermuda
ROUTE UK to Barbados
CARGO Silver valuables
100 crew on board, but only 3 survivors

69 C7 SHIP OF ANTONIO SERRANO 1725
SHIP Spanish galleon
LOCATION Sonda of Campeche, Mexico
ROUTE Campeche, Mexico, to Havana, Cuba
CARGO Specie

70 F5 FLEET OF RODRIGO DE TORRES July 15, 1733
SHIP Spanish
LOCATION Matecumbe Keys, Florida, US
ROUTE Havana, Cuba, to Spain
CARGO Gold and silver valued at a minimum of 12 million pesos
SALVAGE Largely salvaged at time of loss. Worked more recently by Art McKee.
15 ships lost in total

71 A8 INCENDIO 1738
SHIP Spanish
LOCATION Veracruz, Mexico
ROUTE Veracruz, Mexico, to Havana, Cuba
CARGO Gold and silver

72 A8 LANFRANCO 1738
SHIP Spanish
LOCATION Veracruz, Mexico
ROUTE Veracruz, Mexico, to Havana, Cuba
CARGO Specie

73 A7 GUADALUPE Aug 1750
SHIP Spanish
LOCATION Ocracoke Inlet, North Carolina, US
ROUTE West Indies to Spain
CARGO Specie
SALVAGE Pillaged at time of loss

74 B4 EL NUEVO CONSTANTE 1766
SHIP Spanish
LOCATION Galveston Island, Texas, US
ROUTE Veracruz, Mexico, to Spain
CARGO Treasure
SALVAGE Largely salvaged at time of loss

75 B4 LA CARAQUENA Sept 4, 1766
SHIP Spanish
LOCATION Galveston Island, Texas, US
ROUTE Veracruz, Mexico, to Spain
CARGO Treasure
SALVAGE Largely salvaged at time of loss

76 C4 EL CAZADOR Jan 1784
SHIP Spanish brigantine-of-war
LOCATION Approximately 50 miles (80 km) off Louisiana, US
ROUTE Veracruz, Mexico, to New Orleans, Louisiana, US
CARGO 450,000 pesos
SALVAGE Discovered Aug 1993. Salvage began Oct 1993. 12,000 silver coins and ship's bell recovered by Dec 1993.

77 A7 NUESTRA SENORA DE LA HABANA 1805
SHIP Spanish frigate, 34 guns
LOCATION Veracruz, Mexico
ROUTE Veracruz, Mexico, to Spain
CARGO Specie

78 G3 GENERAL WELLESLEY 1814
SHIP English East Indiaman
LOCATION Approaching Charleston harbor, South Carolina, US
CARGO Specie

79 F6 SAN FULGENCIO 1814
SHIP Spanish warship, 64 guns
LOCATION Havana harbor, Cuba
CARGO Specie

80 F3 EMPECINADA Jan 3, 1815
SHIP Spanish goleta
LOCATION Amelia Island, Florida, US, 30.36N 81.26W
ROUTE Havana, Cuba, to Spain
CARGO Gold and silver
SALVAGE Salvaged at time of loss

81 L3 CONTEST Apr 1828
SHIP British, 12 guns, 455 tons
LOCATION Near Bermuda
CARGO Valued at £10,000 sterling on board

82 H2 AURORA June 1837
SHIP American schooner
LOCATION 35.07N 75.42W
ROUTE Havana, Cuba, to New York, US
CARGO Gold specie
SALVAGE Plundered at time of loss

83 C3 BEN SHERROD May 8, 1837
SHIP American
LOCATION 10 miles (16 km) north of Fort Adams, Mississippi, US
CARGO Large quantity of specie consigned to banks of Tennessee, US, plus considerable amount of private treasure

84 H2 NORTH CAROLINA July 25, 1840
SHIP American
LOCATION Off Cape Fear, North Carolina, US
ROUTE Wilmington, North Carolina, US, to Charleston, South Carolina, US
CARGO Specie belonging to passenger

85 E3 ORVILLE ST. JOHN 1850
SHIP American river steamboat
LOCATION 4 miles (6 km) south of Montgomery, Alabama River, Alabama, US
CARGO Gold dust valued at US $250,000 belonging to the government, in the care of Colonel Rodman
SALVAGE Attempted recovery at time of loss

86 J1 SALLE FEARN June 1851
LOCATION 36.40N 70.45W
ROUTE New Orleans, Louisiana, US, to Liverpool, England
CARGO Gold valued at US $120,000 and cotton
SALVAGE Some salvage at time of loss
Ship caught fire

87 O5 SANTA RITA June 1851
SHIP American, Grace Line, 8,379 tons
LOCATION 26.11N 55.40W
ROUTE Suez, Egypt, to Philadelphia, Pennsylvania, US
CARGO Gold valued at £20,000 sterling

88 H3 CENTRAL AMERICA Sept 12, 1857
SHIP American mail steamship, G. Law & Co., 1,200 tons
LOCATION Approximately 160 miles (260 km) off Charleston, South Carolina, US, 31.50N 76.15W
ROUTE Havana, Cuba, to New York, US
CARGO Gold valued today at £625 million sterling
SALVAGE In the process of being salvaged
See pp. 94–95

89 E4 HEIDELBERG Nov 14, 1859
LOCATION Florida, US
ROUTE New Orleans, Louisiana, US, to Le Havre, France
CARGO Specie
SALVAGE Some salvage at time of loss

90 H2 REPUBLIC Feb 12, 1871
LOCATION 60 miles (96 km) east of Cape Look Out, North Carolina, US
ROUTE Port-au-Prince, Haiti, to Cape Look Out, North Carolina, US
CARGO Specie

91 H3 BAVARIA Feb 6, 1877
TYPE British steamer, Dominion Line, 2,300 tons
LOCATION 31.14N 78.42W
ROUTE New Orleans, Louisiana, US, to Liverpool, England
CARGO Valued at Mexican $259,000
SALVAGE Possibility of some plundering at time of loss
Ship burned. Some suggestion that fire was deliberate sabotage by crew to enable them to plunder silver.

92 H1 VILLE DE ST. NAZAIRE Mar 8, 1897
SHIP French, Compagnie Générale Transatlantique, 2,640 tons
LOCATION Off Cape Hatteras, North Carolina, US
ROUTE New York, US, to West Indies
CARGO Gold
Capt. Jagueneau

93 H7 NUEVO MORTERA July 27, 1905
SHIP Cuban
LOCATION Off Nuevitas, Cuba
ROUTE Havana, Cuba, to Santiago de Cuba, Cuba
CARGO Specie valued at £30,000 sterling
SALVAGE Largely salvaged at time of loss

94 K1 PIPESTONE COUNTY Mar 19, 1942
SHIP American
LOCATION 37.43N 66.16W
ROUTE Maputo, Mozambique, to Boston, Massachusetts, US
CARGO Gold valued at £17,600 sterling

95 I2 CITY OF NEW YORK Mar 30, 1942
SHIP American, American South African Line, 8,272 tons
LOCATION Approximately 30 miles (50 km) east of Cape Hatteras, North Carolina, US, 35.16N 74.25W
ROUTE Maputo, Mozambique, to US
CARGO Diamonds

THE CARIBBEAN

The map for these listings is on pp. 128–129.

● No known salvage
■ Some salvage history known

1 I3 SANTA MARIA Dec 25, 1492
SHIP Spanish caravel, 100 tons, 85 feet (26 meters) long
LOCATION North of Dominican Republic, 19.47N 72.07W
CARGO Gold, silver, and artifacts
SALVAGE Salvaged by Columbus at time of loss
Columbus's ship, lost on 1st expedition

2 I3 SAN JUAN 1494–1495
SHIP Spanish
LOCATION Port of Isabella, Dominican Republic
CARGO Artifacts
Columbus's ship, lost on 2nd expedition

3 J4 CAPITANA 1502
SHIP Spanish
LOCATION Near Santo Domingo, Dominican Republic
ROUTE Santo Domingo, Dominican Republic, to Spain
CARGO Gold and silver valued at 200,000 castellanos

4 E9 GALLEGA 1503
SHIP Spanish caravel
LOCATION Mouth of Belen River, Santa Maria de Belen, Panama
CARGO Artifacts
One of the ships lost on Columbus's 4th voyage

5 L4 SAN NICOLAS Oct 25, 1515
SHIP Spanish
LOCATION Llamada Island, San Juan, Puerto Rico
ROUTE Spain to Caribbean
CARGO Silver plate and jewelry
Capt. Domingo de Guedin

6 L4 SANTA MARIA 1524
SHIP Spanish, 110 tons
LOCATION Near San Juan, Puerto Rico
ROUTE Spain to Caribbean
CARGO Specie and mercury
SALVAGE Salvaged at time of loss
Capt. Juan Perez de Arrecabal

7 J3 SANTA MARIA 1525
SHIP Spanish, 110 tons
LOCATION Puerto Plata, Dominican Republic
ROUTE Puerto Plata, Dominican Republic, to Spain
CARGO Gold and silver
Capt. Pedro Nunez

8 K4 SAN GERMAN WRECKS Aug 12, 1528
SHIP Spanish
LOCATION Port of San Germán, Puerto Rico
ROUTE Puerto Rico to Spain
CARGO Silver and gold
2 ships were attacked and burned

9 E6 SHIP OF CIFUENTES 1538
SHIP Spanish
LOCATION Serrana Shoals
ROUTE Cartagena, Colombia, to Spain
CARGO Gold and silver

10 J4 SAN JUAN 1549
SHIP Spanish, 200 tons
LOCATION Santo Domingo, Dominican Republic
ROUTE Spain to Caribbean
CARGO Silver plate and personal jewelry
SALVAGE Some salvage at time of loss
Capt. Diego Bernal

11 L4 SANTA MARIA DE JESUS 1550
SHIP Spanish, 625 tons
LOCATION 3 miles (5 km) from port of San Juan, Puerto Rico
ROUTE Spain to Veracruz, Mexico
CARGO Silver plate and jewelry
SALVAGE Some salvage at time of loss

12 J3 SAN MIGUEL 1551
SHIP Spanish, 200 tons
LOCATION 90 miles (145 km) from Puerto Plata, Dominican Republic
ROUTE Veracruz, Mexico, to Spain
CARGO Gold and silver
SALVAGE Largely salvaged at time of loss

13 D5 SANTA CATALINA 1552
SHIP Spanish, 200 tons
LOCATION Between Cartagena, Colombia, and Havana, Cuba
ROUTE Cartagena, Colombia, to Havana, Cuba
CARGO Gold and silver

14 B2 LA MADALENA 1553
SHIP Spanish, 150 tons
LOCATION Coast of Yucatán, Mexico
ROUTE Veracruz, Mexico, to Spain
CARGO Gold and silver
SALVAGE Salvaged at time of loss

15 G8 SAN MARCOS 1553
SHIP Spanish, 600 tons
LOCATION Coast of Cartagena, Colombia
ROUTE Cartagena, Colombia, to Spain
CARGO Gold and silver
SALVAGE Some salvage at time of loss

16 G8 SANTA MARIA DE VILLACELAN 1553
SHIP Spanish, 120 tons
LOCATION Cartagena, Colombia
ROUTE Cartagena, Colombia, to Spain
CARGO Gold and silver
SALVAGE Some salvage at time of loss

17 J4 SAN BARTOLOME 1556
SHIP Spanish, 220 tons
LOCATION Santo Domingo, Dominican Republic
ROUTE Santo Domingo, Dominican Republic, to Spain
CARGO Gold and silver
SALVAGE Some salvage at time of loss
Capt. Blas Alonso

18 L4 SAN ESTEVAN 1562
SHIP Spanish, 120 tons
LOCATION San Juan, Puerto Rico
ROUTE Santo Domingo, Dominican Republic, to Spain
CARGO Gold and silver

19 D2 SAN JUAN BAUTISTA 1563
SHIP Spanish, 150 tons
LOCATION Arrecifes de los Jardines, 24 to 30 miles (39 to 48 km) south of Cuba, and 36 miles (58 km) from Isla de la Juventud (Isle of Pines)
ROUTE Spain to Caribbean
CARGO Large quantities of personal valuables

20 D2 SAN SALVADOR 1563
SHIP Spanish, 350 tons
LOCATION Arrecifes de los Jardines, 24 to 30 miles (39 to 48 km) south of Cuba, and 36 miles (58 km) from Isla de la Juventud (Isle of Pines)
ROUTE Spain to Caribbean
CARGO Mercury, silver plate, and jewelry
Capt. Pedro Menendez Marquez

21 I3 SAN JORGE 1564
SHIP Spanish, 250 tons
LOCATION Port of Montecristi, Dominican Republic
ROUTE Honduras to Spain
CARGO Gold and silver
Capt. Pedro Camina

22 I3 SANTA CATALINA 1564
SHIP Spanish, 250 tons
LOCATION Port of Montecristi, Dominican Republic
ROUTE Veracruz, Mexico, to Spain
CARGO Gold and silver
Capt. Rui Diaz Matamoros

23 I3 SANTA MARIA DE GUADALUPE 1564
SHIP Spanish, 250 tons
LOCATION Near Montecristi, Dominican Republic
ROUTE Honduras to Spain
CARGO Gold and silver
SALVAGE Some salvage at time of loss
Capt. Salvador Gomez

24 B2 SANTA MARIA DE BEGONIA 1586
SHIP Spanish, 140 tons
LOCATION Cape Catoche, Mexico
ROUTE Spain to Campeche, Mexico
CARGO Mercury and specie

25 G8 SPANISH FRIGATE June 20, 1592
SHIP Spanish frigate
LOCATION 25 miles (40 km) north of Cartagena, Colombia
ROUTE Cartagena, Colombia, to Havana, Cuba
CARGO Gold and silver
SALVAGE Largely salvaged at time of loss
The Spanish ship was chased by English privateers. One of the ships belonging to the English privateers was wrecked on a rock and sank within half an hour.

26 I4 EDWARD 1593–1594
SHIP English
LOCATION Unpopulated port of Barahona, Dominican Republic, 50 miles (80 km) from Santo Domingo
CARGO Specie
SALVAGE Some salvage of brass and iron cannons at time of loss

27 H4 NUESTRA SENORA DEL ROSARIO 1595
SHIP Spanish, 150 tons
LOCATION Near Cape Tiburon, western-most point of Haiti
ROUTE Santo Domingo, Dominican Republic, to Spain
CARGO Gold and silver
Capt. Melchor de los Reyes Orne

28 I4 HAITI WRECK c. 1600
SHIP Spanish
LOCATION Off Wahoo beach, NW of Port-au-Prince, Haiti
ROUTE Caribbean to Spain
CARGO Gold valued at US $2 billion according to press reports

29 E5 NUESTRA SENORA DE BEGONA 1605
SHIP Spanish, 500 tons
LOCATION Serranilla Bank, approximately 16.15N 80.45W
ROUTE Cartagena, Colombia, to Havana, Cuba, to Spain
CARGO Jewels, and gold and silver specie
In fleet of Luis Hernandez de Cordoba

30 E5 SAN AMBROSIA 1605
SHIP Spanish, 450 tons
LOCATION Serranilla Bank
ROUTE Cartagena, Colombia, to Havana, Cuba, to Spain
CARGO Gold and silver
In fleet of Luis Hernandez de Cordoba

31 E5 SAN ROQUE Nov 6, 1605
SHIP Spanish, 600 tons
LOCATION Serranilla Bank
ROUTE Cartagena, Colombia, to Havana, Cuba, to Spain
CARGO 300,000 pesos, plus emeralds
In fleet of Luis Hernandez de Cordoba

32 E5 SANTO DOMINGO Nov 6, 1605
SHIP Spanish, 747 tons
LOCATION Serranilla Bank
ROUTE Cartagena, Colombia, to Havana, Cuba, to Spain
CARGO Gold, silver, and jewels
In fleet of Luis Hernandez de Cordoba

33 B2 CAPE CATOCHE WRECKS 1614
SHIP Spanish
LOCATION Cape Catoche, Mexico
ROUTE Cartagena, Colombia, to Havana, Cuba
CARGO Gold and silver
7 ships wrecked

34 B3 LA CANDELARIA 1623
SHIP Spanish, 250 tons
LOCATION Isla de Cozumel, off Yucatán, Mexico
ROUTE Mexico to Spain
CARGO Gold and silver

35 E9 SAN JOSE 1631
SHIP Admiral of the Armada of the South Sea
LOCATION Garachiné island, Panama
ROUTE Callao, Peru, to Panama
CARGO Gold and silver
SALVAGE Some salvage at time of loss

36 G8 LOS TRES REYES Aug 4, 1634
SHIP Spanish
LOCATION Entrance to Cartagena harbor, Colombia
ROUTE Portobelo, Panama, to Cartagena, Colombia
CARGO Pearls, gold, and silver
SALVAGE Salvaged at time of loss

37 M8 SPANISH SHIP 1637
SHIP Spanish
LOCATION Small island near Isla de Margarita
ROUTE South America to Spain
CARGO Pearls, and gold and silver valued at 60,000 to 80,000 ducats
SALVAGE One-third salvaged at time of loss

38 J3 NUESTRA SENORA DE LA CONCEPCION Oct 31, 1641
SHIP Spanish
LOCATION Silver Bank reefs, north of Dominican Republic
ROUTE Havana, Cuba, to Spain
CARGO Large quantity of silver
SALVAGE Salvaged by Phipps in 1680s and rediscovered recently

39 K4 SHIP OF PRINCE MAURICE 1653
SHIP British warship
LOCATION 18 miles (30 km) from Puerto Rico, north of San Germán
CARGO Specie and silver plate
Ship in company with fleet of Prince Rupert

40 L4 SAN MARTIN 1659
SHIP Spanish
LOCATION Los Cayos de Quitasuenos, Puerto Rico
ROUTE Cartagena, Colombia, to Havana, Cuba
CARGO Gold and silver
Galleon belonging to Marques de Villarrubia

41 L4 SANTIAGO 1659
SHIP Spanish
LOCATION Los Cayos de Quitasuenos, Puerto Rico
ROUTE Cartagena, Colombia, to Havana, Cuba
CARGO Gold and silver
Galleon belonging to Marques de Villarrubia

42 I8 MAGDALENA 1669
SHIP Spanish, 26 guns and 12 small guns
LOCATION Isle of Zapan, Bay of Maracaibo, Venezuela
CARGO Silver plate and 40,000 pieces of eight
SALVAGE Partly salvaged at time of loss by Henry Morgan who removed 15,000 pieces of eight and hilts of swords
Spanish fired ship during conflict with Henry Morgan – the Battle of Maracaibo. The ship was also known as the San Felipe.

43 G8 NUESTRA SENORA DEL CARMEN 1669
SHIP Spanish
LOCATION Cartagena, Colombia
CARGO Specie

44 I8 SAN LUIS 1669
SHIP Spanish, 26 guns and 12 small guns
LOCATION Near Maracaibo Castle, Venezuela
Spanish fired ship

45 H4 OXFORD Jan 2, 1669
SHIP English
LOCATION Île-à-Vache, Haiti, 18.10N 73.45W
CARGO Possibility of pirate's loot
Flagship of Henry Morgan. The ship blew up while Morgan was planning his attack on Cartagena, Colombia

46 L4 SHIP OF OGERON 1673
SHIP French
LOCATION West Puerto Rico
CARGO Specie
Ship of M. Ogeron, Governor of Tortugas Island, NW of Hispaniola

47 H4 JAMAICA MERCHANT 1676
SHIP British merchant ship
LOCATION Reef off Île-à-Vache, Haiti
ROUTE London, England, to Port Royal, Jamaica
CARGO Artifacts
SALVAGE Probably salvaged at time of loss
Sir Morgan on board, en route to Jamaica to become deputy governor

48 J4 GOLDEN FLEECE 1686
SHIP Pirate vessel
LOCATION Samaná Bay, Dominican Republic
CARGO Pirate treasure

49 F4 NUESTRA SENORA DE LA CONCEPCION 1691
SHIP Spanish
LOCATION Pedro Bank
ROUTE Veracruz, Mexico, to Havana, Cuba
CARGO Gold and silver

50 F5 NUESTRA SENORA DEL CARMEN 1691
SHIP Spanish
LOCATION Pedro Bank
ROUTE Veracruz, Mexico, to Havana, Cuba
CARGO Gold and silver

51 F5 SANTA CRUZ 1691
SHIP Spanish
LOCATION Pedro Bank
ROUTE Veracruz, Mexico, to Havana, Cuba
CARGO Gold and silver

52 O7 WILLIAM & MARY 1694–1695
SHIP British
LOCATION Near Barbados
ROUTE Windward Islands to UK
CARGO Gold

53 N5 FRENCH PRIVATEER June 4, 1694
SHIP French privateer ship
LOCATION Near Dominica, Windward Islands
CARGO Specie
Ship forced ashore and blown up by Capt. Julius in HMS Chester

54 F9 ST. ANTHONY Dec 25, 1698
SHIP French, 42 guns, with 32 guns mounted
LOCATION 8.50N 77.25W
CARGO 60,000 pieces of eight in gold and silver
SALVAGE Attempted salvage at time of loss, but no success

55 H3 BARBADOES Dec 28, 1705
SHIP English
LOCATION Shoals of Heniagoe, near Great Inagua, Bahamas, approximately 21.04N 73.30W
ROUTE Caribbean to UK
CARGO Specie
SALVAGE Some plundering by French at time of loss

56 F6 NEPTUNE 1707
SHIP British
LOCATION Between Portobelo, Panama, and Jamaica
ROUTE Portobelo, Panama, to Jamaica
CARGO 176,000 pieces of eight

57 G8 SAN JOSE June 8, 1708
SHIP Spanish
LOCATION 12 miles (19 km) south of Cartagena, Colombia, near Isla de Barú
ROUTE Portobelo, Panama, to Cartagena, Colombia
CARGO Emeralds, gold, and silver specie valued today from US $500 million to $10 billion
SALVAGE Several recent claims made that wreck has been found, but no reported salvage because of contractual difficulties with the Colombian Government
Ship sank in 800 feet (250 meters) of water

58 L4 SUCCESS 1716
SHIP English East Indiaman
LOCATION St. Thomas Island, Virgin Islands
ROUTE England to St. Helena to Bengkulu, Sumatra
CARGO Specie

59 J3 NUESTRA SENORA DE GUADALUPE Aug 24, 1724
SHIP Spanish
LOCATION Dominican Republic
ROUTE Spain to Caribbean
CARGO Mercury, glassware, and religious items
SALVAGE Recently rediscovered and excavated
See pp. 60–61

60 J4 CONDE DE TOLOSA Aug 24, 1724
SHIP Spanish
LOCATION NE of Dominican Republic
ROUTE Spain to Caribbean
CARGO Mercury, glassware, and religious items
SALVAGED Recently rediscovered and salvaged
See pp. 60–61

61 M4 SAN IGNACIO 1742
SHIP Spanish
LOCATION Reefs off Anegada, Virgin Islands
ROUTE Caribbean to Spain
CARGO Gold and silver

62 M8 SAN PEDRO 1815
SHIP Spanish, 74 guns
LOCATION 5 miles (8 km) south of the western tip of Isla Coche, Venezuela
ROUTE South America to Spain
CARGO Cargo valued at 800,000 pesos
SALVAGE Extensive salvage carried out at time of loss
All 500 people on board perished

63 K4 PROSERPINA 1821
SHIP Spanish
LOCATION Coast of Aguadilla, Puerto Rico, approximately 18.30N 67.20W
CARGO Specie

64 G3 LIGERA 1822
SHIP Spanish
LOCATION Santiago de Cuba, Cuba
ROUTE Cuba to Spain
CARGO Specie

65 L4 CHARLES CROMWELL July 1, 1853
SHIP British
LOCATION Virgin Passage, off St. Thomas Island, Virgin Islands
ROUTE St. Thomas Island, Virgin Islands, to Turks Head, Turks and Caicos Islands
CARGO Specie

66 K4 HARVEY GALBRAITH Mar 28, 1854
LOCATION Isla Saona, off south coast of Dominican Republic
ROUTE Curaçao, Netherlands Antilles, to Liverpool, England
CARGO Large quantity of specie

67 A4 OSTERVALD May 7, 1858
LOCATION 50 miles (80 km) from Belize
ROUTE New Orleans, Louisiana, US, to Liverpool, England
CARGO Specie valued at US $45,000
SALVAGE Largely salvaged at time of loss

68 L4 WATERWITCH Oct 15, 1858
LOCATION Near St. Thomas Island, Virgin Islands
ROUTE St. Thomas Island, Virgin Islands, to Maracaibo, Venezuela
CARGO Specie

69 A3 MARY Nov 1858
TYPE OF SHIP British
LOCATION 18.45N 87.25W
ROUTE Belize to New Orleans, Louisiana, US
CARGO Specie

70 M4 RHONE Oct 29, 1867
SHIP British Royal Mail steamship, 2,738 tons
LOCATION Salt Island rocks, Virgin Islands, 25 miles (40 km) from St. Thomas Island, Virgin Islands
ROUTE West Indies to UK
CARGO Specie

71 A6 PARKERSBURG Sept 15, 1868
LOCATION Bay of Fonseca, Honduras
ROUTE Panama to Honduras
CARGO Specie
SALVAGE Largely salvaged at time of loss

72 L8 ESTRELLA Dec 21, 1868
SHIP Steamship
LOCATION 16 miles (26 km) north of La Guaira, Venezuela, 10.37N 66.56W
ROUTE St. Thomas Island, Virgin Islands, to Curaçao, Netherlands Antilles
CARGO Specie
SALVAGE Some salvage at time of loss

73 K7 ROSANNA Dec 14, 1871
SHIP Sloop
LOCATION 10 miles (16 km) NW of Bonaire, Netherlands Antilles
ROUTE St. Christopher, St. Christopher and Nevis, to Maracaibo, Venezuela
CARGO Specie valued at US $15,800

74 G4 EMELINE Feb 1, 1881
SHIP Jamaican sailing vessel
LOCATION Off east coast of Jamaica
ROUTE Port Antonio, Jamaica, to Kingston, Jamaica
CARGO Specie

75 J3 TIBER Feb 10, 1882
SHIP British Royal Mail steamship
LOCATION Puerto Plata, Dominican Republic
ROUTE Havana, Cuba, to Southampton, England
CARGO Specie valued at US $160,000
SALVAGE Largely salvaged at time of loss

76 E7 PORT MONTREAL 1942
SHIP British, Port Line, 5,882 tons
LOCATION 12.17N 80.20W
ROUTE Halifax, Nova Scotia, Canada, to Melbourne, Australia
CARGO Diamonds

77 M7 SURINAME Sept 13, 1942
SHIP Dutch
LOCATION 12.07N 63.32W
ROUTE Mombasa, Kenya, to New York, US
CARGO Gold

78 O7 NIDARLAND Nov 11, 1942
SHIP American – but registered in Norway, GM Standifer Construction Corp., 6,076 tons
LOCATION Near Tobago, Trinidad and Tobago, 11.41N 60.42W
CARGO 175 silver bars

79 P8 CITY OF BATH Dec 1, 1942
SHIP British, Ellerman Line, 5,079 tons
LOCATION 09.50N 59.25W
ROUTE Mombasa, Kenya, to Trinidad, Trinidad and Tobago
CARGO Platinum
Ship torpedoed by German submarine and 6 crew members killed

SOUTH AMERICA, WEST AFRICA, AND THE SOUTH ATLANTIC

The map for these listings is on pp. 130–131.
● No known salvage
■ Some salvage history known

1 L1 FRAMENGA 1559
TYPE OF SHIP Portuguese East Indiaman
LOCATION São Tomé, Sao Tome and Principe
ROUTE India to Portugal
CARGO Precious stones and gold

2 I1 MERLIN 1564
LOCATION Off Sierra Leone
ROUTE West Africa to UK
CARGO Gold and ivory
Ship blew up

3 I3 NOSSA SENHORA DA ESTRELLA 1568
SHIP Portuguese East Indiaman
LOCATION NW of Ascension Island
ROUTE Portugal to Far East
CARGO Treasure and silver cruzados

4 I1 WILLIAM & JOHN 1568
SHIP English slaver
LOCATION Coast of Guinea
ROUTE UK to West Africa
CARGO Specie

5 C9 SHIP OF THOMAS CAVENDISH 1592
SHIP English
LOCATION Near Strait of Magellan
ROUTE England too China
CARGO Specie and artifacts
Part of Cavendish's expedition to China via the Strait of Magellan

6 C9 BLACK PINNESSE Oct 2, 1592
SHIP English pinnace
LOCATION Strait of Magellan
ROUTE England to China
CARGO Specie and artifacts
Part of Cavendish's expedition to China via the Strait of Magellan

7 G3 SAN PEDRO Aug 4, 1594
SHIP Portuguese East Indiaman
LOCATION Coast of Brazil
ROUTE India to Portugal
CARGO Gold, jewels, and porcelain
SALVAGE Robbed by English

8 C6 SAN JUAN BAUTISTA 1600
SHIP Spanish
LOCATION Valparaíso, Chile
ROUTE South America to Spain
CARGO Gold and silver
SALVAGE Salvaged at time of loss

9 B6 BUEN JESUS May 15, 1600
SHIP Spanish, 60 tons
LOCATION SW of Valparaíso, Chile
ROUTE South America to Spain
CARGO Gold and silver
Capt. Francisco de Ibarra. Attacked by Oliver Van Noort. The wreck is known locally as Los Picos.

10 J4 WITTE LEEUW 1613
SHIP Dutch East Indiaman
LOCATION Island of St. Helena
ROUTE Banten, Java, to Netherlands
CARGO Chinese porcelain
SALVAGE Salvaged by R. Stenuit in 1976
Sank in engagement with 2 Portuguese ships

11 B4 CANETE WRECKS July 17, 1615
SHIP Spanish
LOCATION Off San Vicente de Cañete, Peru
ROUTE South America to Spain
CARGO Treasure
Ship lost during action with Dutch ships under Spilbergen

12 J4 CONCEICAO 1624
SHIP Portuguese East Indiaman
LOCATION Island of St. Helena
ROUTE Portugal to Goa, India
CARGO Specie

13 J4 MIDDELBURGH 1626
SHIP Dutch East Indiaman
LOCATION Island of St. Helena
ROUTE Jakarta, Java, to Netherlands
CARGO Jewels
Ship lost in fight with Spanish

14 G3 PATER'S FLAGSHIP 1631
SHIP Dutch
LOCATION Off Recife, Brazil
CARGO Specie
Sunk by the Oquendo in battle with Portuguese

15 A2 CHANDUY WRECK 1640s
SHIP Spanish
LOCATION 25 miles (40 km) from Point of Santa Elena, Ecuador, 6 miles (9.5 km) from land
ROUTE Peru to Europe
CARGO Pieces of eight
Ship supposedly en route to assist King Charles I of England

16 C4 SAN NICOLAS May 13, 1647
SHIP Spanish
LOCATION Off Arica, Chile
ROUTE South America to Spain
CARGO Gold

17 A2 CHANDUY WRECK 1654
SHIP Spanish
LOCATION Chanduy Reef, near mouth of Guayaquil River, Ecuador
ROUTE Ecuador to Spain
CARGO Treasure

18 B2 SANTA ELENA WRECK c. 1665
SHIP Spanish
LOCATION Point of Santa Elena, Ecuador
ROUTE Peru to Spain
CARGO Treasure
Mentioned in accounts by Dampier, Capt. John Strong, and Richard Simpson

19 G4 SACRAMENTO 1668
SHIP Portuguese East Indiaman
LOCATION Below Salvador, Brazil
ROUTE Portugal to Brazil
CARGO Majolica plates, religious figures, and brass cannons of Dutch, English, and Portuguese origin
SALVAGE Recently relocated and salvaged

20 B2 SANTA CLARA WRECK 1681
SHIP Spanish
LOCATION Santa Clara, Ecuador, approximately 3.15S 80.23W
ROUTE Lima, Peru, to Guayaquil, Ecuador
CARGO 100,000 pieces of eight in specie

21 B2 ROSARIO Sept 14, 1681
SHIP Spanish
LOCATION 6 miles (9.5 km) from Cape Pasado, Ecuador
ROUTE Lima, Peru, to Panama
CARGO Possibly 700 pigs (lumps) of silver
Pirates set Rosario adrift with pigs of silver still on board, thinking they were pigs of tin. Charts taken from Rosario now in British Library.

22 B3 SAN JOSE 1685
SHIP Spanish
LOCATION Paita, Peru
ROUTE South America to Spain
CARGO Treasure

23 C9 MAGELLAN STRAIT WRECK
c. 1686
SHIP Spanish
LOCATION Strait of Magellan
ROUTE South America to Spain
CARGO Treasure
SALVAGE Partly salvaged
Ship lost after being taken by French buccaneers

24 C9 LA PAVA 1687
SHIP English frigate
LOCATION Strait of Magellan
CARGO Specie

25 G3 VOETBOOG May 29, 1700
SHIP Dutch East Indiaman
LOCATION Recife, Brazil
ROUTE Far East to Netherlands
CARGO Porcelain

26 I3 SHIP OF DAMPIER Feb 1701
SHIP British
LOCATION Ascension Island
CARGO Specie and artifacts, including many of Dampier's books and papers

27 B6 SPEEDWELL 1721
SHIP British
LOCATION Island near Juán Fernandez Islands, Chile
CARGO Gold and silver
SALVAGE Largely salvaged

28 G3 SANTA ROSA 1726
SHIP Portuguese
LOCATION Recife, Brazil
ROUTE Brazil to Portugal
CARGO Gold

29 G3 NOSSA SENHORA DA NAZARETH 1742
SHIP Portuguese East Indiaman
LOCATION Off Salvador, Brazil
ROUTE Portugal to India
CARGO Silver

30 B3 SANTO CRISTO DE LEON 1746
SHIP Spanish
LOCATION Callao harbor, Peru
ROUTE Callao, Peru, to Panama
CARGO Specie

31 J3 PRINCE July 26, 1752
SHIP French East Indiaman
LOCATION 8.30S 5.00W
ROUTE Lorient, France, to Pondicherry, India
CARGO Specie

32 L5 PRINCESSE WILHELMINE CAROLINE 1755
SHIP Danish East Indiaman
LOCATION Between Cape of Good Hope, South Africa, and island of St. Helena
ROUTE Far East to Denmark
CARGO Specie

33 E6 EL PRECIADO 1792
SHIP French
LOCATION Beach of Mulata, near port of Montevideo, Uruguay
ROUTE Argentina to Spain
CARGO Treasure valued at US $1.2 billion
SALVAGE Recently salvaged by Reuben Collado
Ship was chartered by Spanish and was attacked and sunk by English pirates

34 E6 NUESTRA SENORA DE LORETO 1792
SHIP Spanish
LOCATION River Plate, Argentina/Uruguay
ROUTE South America to Spain
CARGO Treasure
Capt. Diego Guinel

35 G4 QUEEN 1800
SHIP English East Indiaman
LOCATION Off Salvador, Brazil
ROUTE UK to India
CARGO Jewels, silver plate, and baggage belonging to General St. John, plus possibility of gold
Capt. Don Antonio Barreda

36 B2 SANTA LEOCADIA Nov 16, 1800
SHIP Spanish, 34 cannons
LOCATION South of Point of Santa Elena, Ecuador
ROUTE Peru to Panama
CARGO Silver valued at 2 million pesos
SALVAGE Largely salvaged

37 G2 BRITANNIA Nov 1, 1805
SHIP English East Indiaman
LOCATION Reef of Rocas island, Brazil
ROUTE UK to Far East
CARGO 550,000 oz (15,592.5 kg) silver
SALVAGE 45,000 oz (1,275.75 kg) removed before ship sank
Ship sank too deep for further salvage at time of loss

38 F5 HMS THETIS Dec 5, 1830
SHIP British warship
LOCATION Cape Frio, Brazil
ROUTE Brazil to UK
CARGO US $810,000
SALVAGE US $586,000 recovered by Capt. Dickinson and US $161,090 by Capt. de Roos

39 I3 ASCENSION ISLAND WRECK
1839
SHIP Dutch merchant ship
LOCATION Off Pyramid Point, Ascension Island
ROUTE Far East to Netherlands
CARGO Specie

40 C9 MANUELA Apr 1850
SHIP English bark
LOCATION Strait of Magellan
CARGO Treasure valued at 46,000 pesos
Captain and crew were picked up by the Taboga

41 F2 MADAGASCAR 1853
SHIP British
LOCATION Thought to be sunk off Bay of Garupy, Brazil
ROUTE Melbourne, Australia, to London, England
CARGO 36,000 oz (1,020.6 kg) gold
Missing ship

42 H3 CONDOR June 10, 1853
SHIP British bark
LOCATION 5.00S 25.00W
CARGO Gold valued at £80,000 sterling
SALVAGE Largely salvaged by the *Charles & Pauline*

43 C4 QUITO July 10, 1853
SHIP British, Pacific Steam Navigation Company
LOCATION Ponta Lobos, Chile
ROUTE Copiapó, Chile, to Huasco, Chile
CARGO Silver and gold bars, and private specie
SALVAGE 24 silver bars and 1 gold bar

44 D1 ORINOCO Jan 19, 1854
SHIP Venezuelan
LOCATION Orinoco River, Venezuela
ROUTE South America to New York, US
CARGO Specie

45 C6 VALDIVIA Dec 11, 1857
SHIP British, Pacific Steam Navigation Company
LOCATION Reef off Llico, Chile
ROUTE Valparaíso, Chile, to Puerto Montt, Chile
CARGO Government treasure valued at 15,000 pesos, plus a considerable quantity of privately owned treasure
SALVAGE 10,000 to 11,000 pesos salvaged

46 B3 J.F.L. Mar 1, 1860
LOCATION Approximately 11.00S 82.00W
ROUTE Callao, Peru, to China
CARGO Specie
SALVAGE 1 box salvaged

47 E6 FILIPPUS CORNELIUS Dec 1862
LOCATION Off Albardão, Brazil, approximately 33.00S 53.00W
ROUTE Montevideo, Uruguay, to Paranagua, Brazil
CARGO Specie
SALVAGE Largely salvaged at time of loss

48 G1 B. F. HOXIE June 14, 1863
SHIP American
LOCATION 10.00N 36.00W
ROUTE US to UK
CARGO Silver valued at US $95,000
SALVAGE Largely salvaged

49 I4 J.E.H. 1864
SHIP Wooden ship, 706 tons
LOCATION South Atlantic
ROUTE Melbourne, Australia, to London, England
CARGO 10,000 oz (283.5 kg) gold
Missing ship

50 D6 OYAPOCK Sept 1866
SHIP Brazilian
LOCATION Off Montevideo, Uruguay
CARGO Specie
SALVAGE Specie valued at US $250,000 saved

51 E9 BLUE JACKET Jan 9, 1869
SHIP American
LOCATION 400 miles (650 km) east of Falkland Islands
ROUTE New Zealand to UK
CARGO Gold

52 C9 SANTIAGO Jan 23, 1869
SHIP British, Pacific Steam Navigation Company, 1,160 tons
LOCATION 2.5 miles (4 km) from Desolación Island, Chile
ROUTE Valparaíso, Chile, to Liverpool, England
CARGO Gold and silver

53 C4 CAPE HORN Sept 9, 1869
SHIP British, W.T. Myers & Sons
LOCATION Off Casualidad Rock, 1.5 miles (2.5 km) NW of Ponta Lobos, Chile
ROUTE Pichidangul, Chile, to Liverpool, England
CARGO Silver
SALVAGE Some salvage at time of loss

54 I1 NIGRETIA June 14, 1873
SHIP British, Elder Dempster Line
LOCATION Carpenter's Rock, 4 miles (6 km) from Freetown, Sierra Leone
ROUTE West Africa to UK
CARGO Specie
SALVAGE Largely salvaged at time of loss

55 J2 GAMBIA May 18, 1877
SHIP British, Elder Dempster Line
LOCATION SE of Cape Palmas, Liberia
ROUTE Calabar, Nigeria, to Liverpool, England
CARGO Specie and ivory
SALVAGE 1 ton ivory recovered in 1889

56 C6 ETEN July 15, 1877
SHIP British, Pacific Steam Navigation Company, 1,853 tons
LOCATION Rocks near Cape Ventanas, 70 miles (115 km) north of Valparaíso, Chile
ROUTE Valparaíso, Chile, to Panama
CARGO Specie

57 F4 PARANA Oct 7, 1877
SHIP French, Messageries Maritimes
LOCATION Abrantes, near Salvador, Brazil
ROUTE Bordeaux, France, to Buenos Aires, Argentina
CARGO Specie
SALVAGE Some salvage at time of loss

58 C5 ATACAMA Nov 30, 1877
SHIP British, Pacific Steam Navigation Company
LOCATION Caja Chica, Copiapó, Chile
ROUTE Carrizal Bajo, Chile, to Caldera, Chile
CARGO Gold and silver

59 D1 SURINAM July 26, 1878
SHIP Dutch
LOCATION River Mahaicony, Guyana, 6.40N 58.00W
ROUTE Georgetown, Guyana, to Surinam
CARGO Specie

60 D9 LUIGIAS 1885
SHIP Italian
LOCATION Falkland Islands
ROUTE Genoa, Italy, to Valparaíso, Chile
CARGO Marble statues
SALVAGE Some statues recovered

61 J2 SENEGAL June 2, 1887
SHIP British, African Steam Navigation Company
LOCATION Tabou, Ivory Coast, 4.25N 7.20W
ROUTE West Africa to UK
CARGO Gold

62 C9 MARLBOROUGH 1890
SHIP British, Shaw, Savill & Albion Company, 1,191 tons
LOCATION South Atlantic
ROUTE New Zealand to UK
CARGO Gold, frozen meat, and wool
Missing ship. Possibly hit icebergs south of Cape Horn, Argentina.

63 J1 SOUDAN July 16, 1891
SHIP African Steamship Company, 2,689 tons
LOCATION 1 mile (1.5 km) from Tabou, Ivory Coast
ROUTE West Africa to Liverpool, England
CARGO Specie and ivory
SALVAGE Largely salvaged at time of loss

64 B6 JOHN ELDER Jan 16, 1892
SHIP British, Pacific Steam Navigation Company, 4,160 tons
LOCATION Cape Humos, NE of Cape Carranza, Chile
ROUTE Valparaíso, Chile, to Liverpool, England
CARGO Gold and silver
SALVAGE Largely salvaged at time of loss by *HMS Melpamere*

65 C6 CHILI May 8, 1892
SHIP French steamer, Compagnie Maritime du Pacific, 2,087 tons
LOCATION Point Tumbez, entrance to harbor of Talcahuano, Chile
ROUTE Guayaquil, Ecuador, to Le Havre, France
CARGO 126 sacks of silver, 1 box of gold and silver, plus silver bars
SALVAGE Some salvage at time of loss

66 C6 LAJA Nov 14, 1893
SHIP Compagna Sud Americana de Vapores, 1,349 tons
LOCATION Port of Valparaíso, Chile
ROUTE From Pimentel, Peru
CARGO Treasure valued at £45,000 sterling
SALVAGE Some salvage at time of loss

67 D9 CITY OF PHILADELPHIA
May 14, 1896
SHIP American merchant ship
LOCATION Off Falkland Islands
CARGO Gold rumored
SALVAGE Attempt at salvage but no results

68 J1 CALABAR II Oct 26, 1898
SHIP British, Elder Dempster Line
LOCATION Yellow Well Reef, Buchanan, Liberia
ROUTE Liberia to Liverpool, England
CARGO Specie

69 B8 SAKKARAH May 13, 1902
SHIP German
LOCATION Guamblin o Socorro Island, Chile
ROUTE Valparaíso, Chile, to Hamburg, Germany
CARGO Gold and specie valued at US $1,500,000
SALVAGE Partly salvaged at time of loss

70 C9 ISIS June 11, 1902
LOCATION Strait of Magellan
CARGO Specie valued at £150,000 sterling
The Isis *had taken specie on board from the wrecked* Sakkarah

71 C6 AREQUIPA June 2, 1903
SHIP British, Pacific Steam Navigation Company, 2,953 tons
LOCATION Port of Valparaíso, Chile
CARGO Gold

72 B3 COLOMBIA Aug 9, 1907
SHIP British, Pacific Steam Navigation Company, 3,335 tons
LOCATION Saenze Point, Lobos de Tierra island, Peru, 6.28S 80.50W
ROUTE Paita, Peru, to Puerto Eten, Peru
CARGO Specie
SALVAGE Partly salvaged

73 B9 HAZEL BRANCH Nov 12, 1907
SHIP British, F. & W. Ritson, 2,623 tons
LOCATION Adelaide Patch, Strait of Magellan, approximately 53.00S 74.50W
ROUTE Antofagasta, Chile, to Liverpool, England
CARGO Silver
SALVAGE Some salvage

74 J4 PAPANEWI 1911
LOCATION Island of St. Helena
ROUTE UK to Australia
CARGO Coronation gifts

75 D9 ORAVIA Nov 12, 1912
SHIP British, Pacific Steam Navigation Company, 5,374 tons
LOCATION Billy Rock, Port Stanley, Falkland Islands
ROUTE Liverpool, England, to Callao, Peru
CARGO Specie

76 F5 PRINCIPE DE ASTURIAS Mar 5, 1916
SHIP Spanish, Pinillos Line
LOCATION 3 miles (5 km) east of Ponta do Boi, Brazil
ROUTE Barcelona, Spain, to Buenos Aires, Argentina
CARGO Gold valued at £1 million sterling, and jewels valued at £500,000 sterling
SALVAGE Various attempts at salvage

77 I1 EMPIRE KOHINOR July 2, 1917
SHIP British, Anchor Line, 5,225 tons
LOCATION 150 miles (240 km) SW of Monrovia, Liberia, 06.20N 16.30W
ROUTE Table Bay, South Africa, to UK
CARGO 2 parcels of diamonds

78 C6 ARAUCANIA Sept 5, 1938
LOCATION Rocks off Quintero Point, Chile
ROUTE Huasco, Chile, to San Antonio, Chile
CARGO Gold

79 I1 BENMOHR Mar 5, 1942
SHIP British merchant ship
LOCATION 6.05N 14.15W
ROUTE Bombay, India, to Freetown, Sierra Leone, and Oban, Scotland
CARGO 1,500,000 oz (42,525 kg) silver bullion

80 I1 CITY OF WELLINGTON Aug 21, 1942
SHIP British steamship, Ellerman Line, 5,733 tons
LOCATION 7.29N 14.40W
ROUTE Mosselbaai, South Africa, to Freetown, Sierra Leone
CARGO Platinum

81 J3 LACONIA Sept 12, 1942
SHIP British, Cunard & White Star Line
LOCATION 5.05S 11.38W
ROUTE Suez, Egypt, to UK, via Cape of Good Hope, South Africa
CARGO Platinum

82 K1 NEW TORONTO Nov 5, 1942
SHIP British, Elder Dempster Line
LOCATION 5.57N 2.30E
ROUTE West Africa to UK
CARGO Gold

83 J5 CITY OF CAIRO Nov 6, 1942
SHIP British steamship, Ellerman Line, 8,034 tons
LOCATION 23.30S 5.30W
ROUTE Bombay, India, to UK
CARGO Over 3 million oz (85,000 kg) silver

84 H1 POLYDORUS Nov 27, 1942
SHIP Dutch
LOCATION 9.01N 25.38W
ROUTE Liverpool, England, to Freetown, Sierra Leone
CARGO Specie

85 J2 EMPRESS OF CANADA Mar 13, 1943
SHIP Canadian Pacific Company, 20,325 tons
LOCATION 1.13S 9.57W
ROUTE South Africa to US
CARGO Gold
1,400 Greek and Polish refugees on board, as well as Italian prisoners of war. Ship sunk by Italian submarine.

86 K1 PHEMIUS Dec 19, 1943
SHIP British, A. Holt
LOCATION 5.01N 00.17W
ROUTE UK to West Africa
CARGO Specie

87 F5 MAGDALENA Apr 26, 1949
SHIP British, Royal Mail Line, 17,500 tons
LOCATION 20 miles (32 km) south of Rio de Janeiro, Brazil, 6 miles (9.5 km) from the coast
ROUTE Buenos Aires, Argentina, to London, England
CARGO Specie
SALVAGE Some salvage at time of loss

EAST COAST OF NORTH AMERICA

The map for these listings is on pp. 132–133.

● No known salvage
■ Some salvage history known

1 H1 DENNIS 1578
LOCATION Mouth of Frobisher Bay, NW Territories, Canada
ROUTE UK to China
CARGO Valuable artifacts and specie

2 J7 DELIGHT 1583
SHIP British
LOCATION Sable Island, Nova Scotia, Canada
ROUTE UK to Canada
CARGO Specie and artifacts
Part of Sir Humphrey Gilbert's expedition

3 I6 CHANCEWEL June 1597
SHIP British
LOCATION St. Ann's Bay, Cape Breton Island, Nova Scotia, Canada
CARGO Specie
SALVAGE Pillaged by French

4 H8 WHYDAH 1717
SHIP Pirate ship
LOCATION 0.25 mile (0.4 km) off Cape Cod, Massachusetts, US
ROUTE Caribbean to Cape Cod, Massachusetts, US
CARGO Specie
SALVAGE Recently located by Barry Clifford of Maritime Explorations
See pp. 68–69

5 E8 LE JEAN FLORIN July 2, 1721
SHIP French frigate
LOCATION 10 miles (16 km) NE of Erie, Pennsylvania, US
CARGO Specie

6 I6 LE CHAMEAU Aug 26, 1725
SHIP French transport, 600 tons
LOCATION Chameau Rock, off Cape Breton Island, Nova Scotia, Canada
ROUTE France to Louisbourg, Nova Scotia, Canada
CARGO Specie valued at 300,000 livres
SALVAGE Salvaged by Alex Storm in 1960s

7 F9 LA GALGA Aug 1750
SHIP Spanish
LOCATION Currituck Inlet, North Carolina, US, 36.29N 75.33W
ROUTE West Indies to Spain
CARGO Gold and silver specie

8 I6 TILBURY June 11, 1757
SHIP British warship
LOCATION Cape Breton Island reef, near Louisbourg, Nova Scotia, Canada
CARGO Specie

9 F8 MERLIN 1777
SHIP British
LOCATION Delaware Channel, Delaware, US
CARGO Rumors of treasure

10 G8 DEFENCE Mar 10, 1779
LOCATION Off Bartlett's Reef, Waterford, near New London, Connecticut, US, 41.21N 72.06W
CARGO Specie valued at US $200,000

11 G8 HUSSAR Sept 13, 1780
SHIP British frigate
LOCATION Top end of East River, Long Island Sound, New York, US
CARGO Rumors of gold valued at many millions of pounds sterling
SALVAGE Repeated plans and attempts at salvage but no significant results

12 G8 LEXINGTON Sept 21, 1780
SHIP British warship
LOCATION Hell's Gate, East River, Long Island Sound, New York, US
CARGO Gold rumored

13 G8 LIVELY July 8, 1781
SHIP American privateer
LOCATION Off Long Island, New York, US
CARGO Gold rumored

14 G8 HERMIONE Nov 1, 1782
SHIP American privateer
LOCATION New London, Connecticut, US
CARGO Rumor of specie valued at US $100,000

15 F7 ONTARIO Nov 23, 1783
SHIP English sloop
LOCATION Lake Ontario, 3 miles (5 km) off Oswego, New York, US
CARGO Specie

16 F9 HMS DE BRAAK May 23, 1798
SHIP British naval sloop
LOCATION Delaware, US
CARGO Possibly treasure
SALVAGE Many attempts at salvage, but no significant results
Rumors of treasure probably ill-founded

17 F9 JUNO Oct 28, 1802
SHIP Spanish
LOCATION Caudales de Indias, near Cape May, off coast of New Jersey, US
ROUTE Veracruz, Mexico, to Cadiz, Spain
CARGO Silver specie

18 F9 MOLLY Nov 26, 1803
LOCATION 3 miles (5 km) south of Currituck Inlet, North Carolina, US
ROUTE Kingston, Jamaica, to New York, US
CARGO Specie

19 I7 BARBADOES Sept 28, 1812
SHIP British warship, 6th rate, 755 tons
LOCATION NW bar of Cape Sable Island, Nova Scotia, Canada
ROUTE Bermuda to St. John's, Newfoundland, Canada
CARGO Specie valued at £60,000 sterling
Capt. T. Huskisson

20 J6 COMUS Nov 4, 1816
SHIP British warship, 6th rate, 522 tons
LOCATION Off Cape Pine, St. Mary's Bay, Newfoundland, Canada
CARGO Specie
SALVAGE Some plundering at time of loss

21 G7 MIDAS Jan 17, 1820
LOCATION Off Boston, Massachusetts, US
ROUTE Santo Domingo, Dominican Republic, to Boston, Massachusetts, US
CARGO Considerable quantity of specie said to be on board

22 G8 CATHARINE 1821
SHIP English Brig
LOCATION Siasconset, south of Nantucket Island, Massachusetts, US, 41.15N 69.58W
ROUTE Montego Bay, Jamaica, to Bermuda
CARGO Specie

23 I6 LEONIDAS Aug 28, 1832
SHIP British
LOCATION Coast of Cape Breton, Scatarie Island, 60 miles (96 km) from Sydney, Nova Scotia, Canada
CARGO 170 boxes of coins
SALVAGE 25 boxes of coins salvaged

24 E7 ERIE 1841
LOCATION Lake Erie, off Silver Creek, 33 miles (53 km) from Buffalo, New York, US
ROUTE Buffalo, New York, US, to Chicago, Illinois, US
CARGO Gold and silver specie
SALVAGE Specie valued at US $200,000 recovered when wreck was raised in 1856
Hull towed to within 4 miles (6 km) of shore, where it sank in 11 fathoms of water

25 H7 COLUMBIA July 1, 1843
SHIP British, Cunard Line, 1,138 tons
LOCATION Lost on Devil's Limb rock, 1 mile (1.5 km) from land, Cape Sable Island, Nova Scotia, Canada
ROUTE Boston, Massachusetts, US, to Halifax, Nova Scotia, Canada
CARGO Specie
SALVAGE Salvaged at time of loss
Loss of ship caused by fog and strong currents in Bay of Fundy, Canada

26 G8 LEXINGTON Nov 19, 1846
SHIP American luxury liner
LOCATION Off Old Field Point, Long Island, 4 miles (6 km) off Point Mouillie, New York, US
ROUTE New York, US, to Stonington, Connecticut, US
CARGO Specie
SALVAGE US $800 recovered at time of loss. Recently rediscovered between Port Jefferson, New York, US, and Stony Brook, New York, US
Ship built by Cornelius Vanderbilt

27 E7 ATLANTIC Aug 19, 1852
SHIP Steam paddleship
LOCATION Lake Erie, 6 miles (9.5 km) east of Long Point Island, Ontario, Canada
ROUTE Buffalo, Michigan, US, to Detroit, US
CARGO Gold, silver, and artifacts recently valued at £150 million sterling
SALVAGE Recently discovered by Mar Dive Corporation, Los Angeles, US

28 I7 HUMBOLDT Dec 5, 1853
SHIP American, New York and Le Havre Steamship Company
LOCATION The Sisters, off Sambro Light, 8 miles (13 km) south of Halifax, Nova Scotia, Canada
ROUTE Le Havre, France, to New York, US
CARGO Specie
SALVAGE Some salvage at time of loss
Ship lost in thick fog

29 D6 SUPERIOR Oct 29, 1856
LOCATION Off Grand Island, Lake Superior, Michigan, US
ROUTE Niagara, Michigan, US, to Lake Michigan, Michigan, US
CARGO Specie

30 G8 BLACK WARRIOR
Feb 20, 1859
SHIP American, 1,556 tons
LOCATION Rockaway Inlet, New York harbour, US
ROUTE Havana, Cuba, to New York, US
CARGO Specie valued at US $208,100
SALVAGE Taken off at time of loss

31 H7 CONNAUGHT Oct 7, 1860
SHIP British, Galway Lines, iron paddlesteamer, 4,400 tons
LOCATION 140 miles (225 km) from Boston, Massachusetts, US, 42.32N 68.14W
ROUTE Galway, Republic of Ireland, to Boston, Massachusetts, US
CARGO Gold valued at £10,000 sterling
SALVAGE Mail saved, but gold lost
Ship caught fire

32 D7 BLACK HAWK Nov 1862
SHIP Brig
LOCATION Lake Michigan, 4 miles (6 km) north of Frankfort, Michigan, US
CARGO Specie and stained glass

33 G7 BOHEMIAN Feb 22, 1864
SHIP Montréal Steamship Company, 2,200 tons
LOCATION Alden's rock, 4 miles (6 km) from Cape Elizabeth, near Portland, Maine, US
ROUTE Liverpool, England, to US
CARGO Gold
SALVAGE 500 sovereigns saved

34 B7 BERTRAND Apr 1, 1865
LOCATION Missouri River, 30 miles (50 km) north of Omaha, Nebraska, US
CARGO Gold
SALVAGE Salvaged, but no gold recovered

35 E7 PEWABIC Aug 12, 1865
SHIP Canadian, 960 tons
LOCATION Lake Huron, 2 miles (3 km) off Thunder Bay Island, Michigan, US
CARGO Specie and copper
SALVAGE Copper salvaged in 1917. Several other attempts, but results not known

36 F8 DE LA MAR June 1866
SHIP Spanish
LOCATION Lower Bay, New York, US
CARGO Gold
SALVAGE Some salvage at time of loss

37 H5 NORTH AMERICAN June 16, 1867
LOCATION Anticosti Island, Québec, Canada
ROUTE Québec, Canada, to Liverpool, England
CARGO Specie
SALVAGE Salvaged at time of loss

38 K5 GERMANIA Aug 7, 1869
SHIP German
LOCATION Cape Race, Newfoundland, Canada
ROUTE New York, US, to Hamburg, Germany
CARGO Specie
SALVAGE Partly salvaged

39 K6 HERDER Oct 10, 1882
SHIP German
LOCATION Off Cape Race, Newfoundland, Canada, 46.39N 53.04W
ROUTE New York, US, to Hamburg, Germany
CARGO Specie
SALVAGE 3 cases of specie saved

40 G8 OREGON Mar 14, 1886
SHIP Cunard Line, 7,375 tons
LOCATION 26 miles (42 km) SE of Fire Island, Long Island, New York, US
ROUTE Liverpool, England, to New York, US
CARGO Diamonds
SALVAGE Some salvage at time of loss

41 J4 LILY Sept 16, 1889
SHIP British Navy gun boat, 720 tons
LOCATION Rocks near Point d'Amour, Strait of Belle Isle, Newfoundland, Canada
ROUTE St. Margaret's Bay, Newfoundland, Canada, to Forteau Bay, Labrador, Newfoundland, Canada
CARGO Specie

42 E7 DEAN RICHMOND Oct 11, 1893
SHIP Western Transportation Company, 1,257 tons
LOCATION 1 mile (1.5 km) off Van Buren Point, near Dunkirk, New York, US
ROUTE Toledo, Ohio, US, to Buffalo, New York, US
CARGO Specie

43 G8 PORTLAND Nov 26, 1898
SHIP American, Portland Steam Packet Company, wooden sidewheel paddle-steamer, 2,284 tons
LOCATION 10 to 15 miles (16 to 24 km) north of Peaked Hill Bars, off Cape Cod, Massachusetts, US
ROUTE Boston, Massachusetts, US, to Portland, Maine, US
CARGO Specie and jewelry

44 G8 HAROLD Sept 27, 1903
SHIP American
LOCATION Off Sewaren, New Jersey, US, 40.33N 75.43W
CARGO Silver
SALVAGE Partly salvaged

45 G8 REPUBLIC Jan 23, 1909
SHIP British, White Star Line, Oceanic Steam Navigation Company, 15,378 tons
LOCATION 20 miles (32 km) south of Nantucket Light Vessel, Massachusetts, US
ROUTE New York, US, to Genoa, Italy, to Alexandria, Egypt
CARGO Gold coins valued at US $3 million
SALVAGE Many attempts without results
Ship collided with the Florida

46 E8 CLARION Dec 8, 1909
SHIP Canadian, Erie & Western Transport Company, 1,712 tons, built 1881
LOCATION Off Point Pelee, Lake Erie, Ontario, Canada
CARGO Gold and silver
Ship destroyed by fire

47 F9 MERIDA May 12, 1911
SHIP American, New York and Cuba Mail Steamship Company
LOCATION Off Virginia Capes, 55 miles (88 km) from Cape Charles, Virginia, US
ROUTE Veracruz, Mexico, to New York, US
CARGO 480,000 oz (13,600 kg) silver
SALVAGE Salvaged in 1930s by Venturi, and salvaged more than once during 1980s but results unclear
Ship collided with the Admiral Farragut

48 H5 EMPRESS OF IRELAND
May 29, 1914
SHIP Canadian Pacific Railway Company, 14,191 tons
LOCATION 5 miles (8 km) east of Father Point, mouth of St. Lawrence River, Québec, Canada
ROUTE Québec, Canada, to Liverpool, England
CARGO Silver
SALVAGE Largely salvaged at time of loss

49 G9 SAMOA June 14, 1918
SHIP Norwegian, 1,137 tons
LOCATION 90 miles (145 km) off coast of Virginia, US, 37.30N 72.10W
ROUTE South Africa to New York, US
CARGO Silver

50 H8 WEST IMBODEN Apr 21, 1942
SHIP American
LOCATION 41.14N 65.55W
ROUTE Durban, South Africa, to Boston, US
CARGO Gold valued at £29,000 sterling

51 K6 EMPIRE MANOR Jan 27, 1944
SHIP British, Ministry of Transport, 7,071 tons
LOCATION 44.05N 52.10W
ROUTE New York, US, to Halifax, Nova Scotia, Canada
CARGO 70 gold bars totaling 28,570 oz (810 kg)
SALVAGE Partially salvaged in the 1970s by Risdon Beazley Marine

52 G8 U8536 May 1945
SHIP German submarine
LOCATION Off Block Island, south of Rhode Island, US
CARGO Rumors of gold

53 G8 ANDREA DORIA
July 25, 1956
SHIP Italian, 29,083 tons
LOCATION Off lightship, Nantucket Island, Massachusetts, US, 40.37N 69.37W
ROUTE Genoa, Italy, to New York, US
CARGO Possibly gold
SALVAGE Salvaged in 1984 by Peter Gimbel, in conjunction with Oceaneering International, but no significant recoveries
See pp. 108–109

NORTHERN EUROPE AND THE NORTH ATLANTIC

The map for these listings is on pp. 134–135.

● No known salvage
■ Some salvage history known

1 J3 OSEBERG BURIAL SHIP 800
SHIP Viking ship
LOCATION Oseberg, Norway
CARGO Valuable carved wooden artifacts
SALVAGE Excavated
Burial ship. See pp. 22–23.

2 J4 GOKSTAD BURIAL SHIP 870
SHIP Viking ship
LOCATION Gokstad, Norway
CARGO Valuable carved wooden artifacts
SALVAGE Excavated
Burial ship

3 E3 FLEET OF ERIK RAUDI 986
SHIP Viking ships
LOCATION East coast of Greenland
ROUTE Iceland to Greenland
CARGO Valuables
Several ships lost on this first colonizing voyage to Greenland

4 E3 SHIP OF ARNBJORN 1125
SHIP Viking ship
LOCATION East coast of Greenland
ROUTE Norway to Greenland
CARGO Large sum of money and other valuables
SALVAGE Money was salvaged at time of loss and found later, by Njalsson, abandoned in an encampment on the shore
The discovery of money led to a family war between rival claimants

5 E3 STANGARFOLI 1189
SHIP Viking ship
LOCATION Coast of Greenland
ROUTE Iceland to Greenland
CARGO Money and artifacts

6 G2 SHIP OF BISHOP OLAF 1266
SHIP Viking knorr
LOCATION Cape Hitarnes, Iceland
ROUTE Igaliku, Greenland, to Iceland
CARGO Valuable cargo of walrus ivory

7 G3 VIKING KNORR 1266
SHIP Viking knorr
LOCATION Between Norway and Greenland
ROUTE To Greenland
CARGO Money and artifacts

8 H3 SHIP OF GUDMUND ORMSSON
c. 14th century
SHIP Viking ship
LOCATION Off Faeroe Islands
CARGO Valuable artifacts

9 J2 VIKING SHIP 1323
SHIP Viking ship
LOCATION West coast of Norway, approximately 65.50N
ROUTE From Iceland
CARGO Large quantity of money
Lord Bishop Elect on board

10 J4 VEJBY COG c. 1380
SHIP Cog
LOCATION Vejby, off north Sjaelland coast, 30 miles (50 km) NW of Copenhagen, Denmark
ROUTE Western Europe to Denmark
CARGO Pewter plate and nobles (gold coins)
SALVAGE Discovered in 1976 and excavated

11 J4 VIGSO WRECK 15th century
LOCATION Sand dunes of Vigsø, Denmark
CARGO Bronze aquamaniles (medieval ewers)
SALVAGE Recently excavated

12 I4 PIERO QUIRINO 1431
LOCATION North Sea, 500 miles (800 km) from Norway
ROUTE Iraklion, Crete, Greece, to Flanders, Belgium
CARGO Spices, cottons, glassware, and silver artifacts
Survivors reached Isle of Saints, Norway

13 J2 BONA CONFIDENTIA 1556
SHIP Part of embassy of Russian Emperor, Ivan Vasilivich
LOCATION 63.26N 10.24E
ROUTE Russian Federation to UK
CARGO Gold and jeweled presents

14 I5 SAN FELIPE Sept 1588
SHIP Spanish
LOCATION Nieuwpoort banks, Netherlands
CARGO Spanish Armada cargo
Capt. Don Francisco de Toledo. Drifted on to Nieuwpoort banks after Armada battle in English Channel

15 G7 SAN LUCAS 1591
SHIP Portuguese East Indiaman
LOCATION Madeira
ROUTE Portugal to India
CARGO Specie

16 I5 GELDERLAND July 20, 1606
SHIP Dutch East Indiaman, 500 tons
LOCATION Flushing harbor, Netherlands
ROUTE Netherlands to Far East
CARGO Specie

17 K4 SOLEN Nov 28, 1627
SHIP Swedish warship
LOCATION Gdansk Bay, Poland
CARGO Bronze cannons, valuable artifacts, and specie
SALVAGE Salvaged from 1969 to 1980
Lost during battle between Poland and Sweden. Excellent artifacts in the Gdansk Maritime Museum, Poland.

18 I4 MORRIS Nov 19, 1628
SHIP English East Indiaman
LOCATION On the flyland near Texel, Netherlands
ROUTE Far East to UK
CARGO Gold and silver presents from King of Bantam, Cocos Island, to King Charles I of England

19 J5 KING OF BOHEMIA WRECK Jan 7, 1629
LOCATION On the Haarlem meer, 0.25 mile (0.4 km) from Amsterdam, Netherlands
CARGO Possessions of the King of Bohemia
Ship was run down by bark that was laden with cargo of beer while en route to view Spanish treasureships captured by Piet Heyn. King of Bohemia's son drowned.

20 G7 SAN JOSEFE 1635
SHIP Spanish, 600 tons
LOCATION Madeira
ROUTE Santo Domingo, Dominican Republic, to Spain
CARGO Gold and silver
Capt. Juan de Aquinaga

21 G8 SANTA CRUZ WRECKS 1657
SHIP Spanish
LOCATION Santa Cruz harbor, Tenerife, Canary Islands
CARGO Specie
2 galleons, 8 merchant ships, and a patache. Sunk by Robert Blake.

22 J4 ISLAND OF VEN WRECK 1658
LOCATION 55.55N 12.45E
CARGO Valuable artifacts
SALVAGE Plundered in 1950s
Artifacts in the Handel-og Sjofartsmuseet, Kronborg, Denmark, and Orlogsmuseet, Copenhagen, Denmark

23 J4 BREDERODE Nov 8, 1658
SHIP Dutch warship
LOCATION Helsingør, Denmark
CARGO Miscellaneous artifacts
SALVAGE Salvaged in 1909
Artifacts in the Historisch Scheepvaart Museum, Amsterdam, Netherlands, and the Tojhus Museum, Copenhagen, Denmark

24 H3 WALCHEREN Sept 1667
SHIP Dutch East Indiaman, 840 tons
LOCATION Near Faeroe Islands
ROUTE Jakarta, Java, to Netherlands
CARGO Porcelain and jewels

25 G3 WAPEN VAN AMSTERDAM Sept 19, 1667
SHIP Dutch East Indiaman, 920 tons
LOCATION South of Iceland
ROUTE Jakarta, Java, to Netherlands
CARGO Porcelain and jewels

26 J4 DEN FORGYLLDA SOLEN 1673
SHIP Swedish merchant ship
LOCATION Tejn, north coast of Bornholm, Denmark
ROUTE Stockholm, Sweden, to UK
CARGO Silver coins
SALVAGE Salvaged in 1969

27 K4 KRONAN 1676
SHIP Swedish warship
LOCATION 4 miles (6 km) off Öland island, Sweden
CARGO Bronze cannons and artifacts
SALVAGE Salvaged in 1980s
Artifacts in the county museum of Kalmar, Sweden

28 I4 STADT HAARLEM 1676
SHIP Dutch
LOCATION Kvitsøy, near Stavanger, Norway
ROUTE Terschelling, Netherlands, to Stavanger, Norway
CARGO Porcelain
SALVAGE Recently excavated by Norsk Sjofartsmuseum, Norway, in conjunction with Stavanger Sjofartsmuseum, Norway

29 J4 SOSEVIG WRECKS 1678
SHIP Swedish
LOCATION Sosevig coast of Bornholm, Denmark
CARGO Gold specie – payroll for the Swedish army
SALVAGE Salvaged in 1978
19 ships sank in total

30 K4 ENIGHED 1679
SHIP Danish warship
LOCATION Kalmar Sound, Sweden
CARGO Artifacts
SALVAGE Salvaged in early 20th century
Artifacts in the Naval Museum, Stockholm, Sweden

31 K4 NYCKELN 1679
SHIP Swedish warship
LOCATION Kalmar Sound, Sweden
CARGO Valuable artifacts
SALVAGE Salvaged in 19th century and again in early 20th century
Some artifacts in the Naval Museum, Stockholm, Sweden

32 I3 KVITSOY WRECK 1692
SHIP Spanish
LOCATION Kvitsøy, near Stavanger, Norway
CARGO Silver
SALVAGE Recently excavated

33 G9 VANSITTART Mar 2, 1719
SHIP English East Indiaman, 480 tons
LOCATION Maio, Cape Verde
ROUTE UK to Madras, India
CARGO 141,031 oz (3,998 kg) silver
SALVAGE Very little salvage at time of loss

34 K3 JOHN BAPTIST c. 1721
SHIP Russian warship
LOCATION Off Helsinki, Finland
CARGO Treasure
SALVAGE Attempted in 19th century

35 I3 AKERENDAM Mar 8, 1725
SHIP Dutch East Indiaman, 850 tons
LOCATION Island of Rundøy, Norway
ROUTE Netherlands to Jakarta, Java
CARGO Specie
SALVAGE Rediscovered in 1970s

36 J4 BUREN Dec 9, 1729
SHIP Dutch East Indiaman, 450 tons
LOCATION Noorderhaaks, near Texel, Netherlands
ROUTE Netherlands to Jakarta, Java
CARGO Specie
SALVAGE English divers managed to bring up some rigging and a cannon, but cargo was lost
Ship foundered in a gale

37 G9 SLOT TER HOGE June 19, 1732
SHIP Dutch East Indiaman, 850 tons
LOCATION Isle of Maio, Cape Verde
ROUTE Netherlands to Jakarta, Java
CARGO Specie

38 I4 ANNA CATHARINA Feb 3, 1735
SHIP Dutch East Indiaman, 600 tons
LOCATION Dorpel sandbank, Deurloo Channel, Texel, Netherlands
ROUTE Netherlands to Jakarta, Java
CARGO Silver specie

39 J4 T. VLIEGEND HART Feb 3, 1735
SHIP Dutch East Indiaman, 850 tons
LOCATION Dorpel sandbank, Deurloo Channel, Texel, Netherlands
ROUTE Netherlands to Jakarta, Java
CARGO Gold and silver valued at 67,000 guilders
SALVAGE Partly salvaged by Rex Cowan

40 G9 PRINCESS LOUISA Apr 18, 1743
SHIP English East Indiaman, 498 tons
LOCATION Reef of rocks near Maio, Cape Verde
ROUTE UK to Iran and Bombay, India
CARGO 69,760 oz (1,977 kg) silver and ivory

41 J4 GOTEBORG 1745
SHIP Swedish East Indiaman
LOCATION Harbor of Gothenburg, Sweden
CARGO Porcelain
SALVAGE Salvaged in early 20th century for its black oak timbers to make furniture
Artifacts in the Gothenburg Historical Museum, Sweden

42 K3 SANKT MIKAEL 1747
SHIP Russian-owned, 3-masted galliot
LOCATION Borsto, Finland
ROUTE Amsterdam, Netherlands, to St. Petersburg, Russian Federation
CARGO Gold and silver jewelry, and other valuable artifacts
SALVAGE Salvaged in 1950s and 1960s
Very interesting drawings in the Maritime Museum of Finland

43 G9 DUKE OF CUMBERLAND Jan 16, 1750
SHIP English East Indiaman
LOCATION Bay of Ayoffe, Cape Verde, Senegal
ROUTE UK to China
CARGO 73 chests of silver specie
SALVAGE Unsuccessful salvage attempt at time of loss but possibility of pillage

44 J4 AMSTELLAND Sept 18, 1751
SHIP Dutch East Indiaman, 850 tons
LOCATION Island of Sylt, Denmark
ROUTE Netherlands to Jakarta, Java
CARGO Silver specie

45 I5 VROUWE ELISABETH DOROTHEA Nov 27, 1767
SHIP Dutch East Indiaman, 600 tons
LOCATION 52.45N 4.40E
ROUTE Jakarta, Java, to Netherlands
CARGO Porcelain

46 G9 LEIMUIDEN Jan 25, 1770
SHIP Dutch East Indiaman, 1,150 tons
LOCATION Cape Verde
ROUTE Netherlands to Jakarta, Java
CARGO 37 gold bars
SALVAGE 21 gold bars recovered

47 K3 VROUW MARIA Oct 4, 1771
SHIP Dutch snow
LOCATION Near Turku, Finland
ROUTE Netherlands to Russian Federation
CARGO Part of the Braamcamp collection of paintings bought by Catherine the Great, Empress of Russia
See pp. 86–87

48 G8 DUIVENBERG May 14–16, 1777
SHIP Dutch East Indiaman, 1,150 tons
LOCATION Canary Islands
ROUTE Jakarta, Java, to Netherlands
CARGO Porcelain

49 F9 HARTWELL May 24, 1787
SHIP English East Indiaman
LOCATION Hartwell Reef, Boa Vista, Cape Verde
ROUTE UK to China
CARGO 209,280 oz (5,933 kg) silver specie
SALVAGE 97,650 oz (2,768 kg) silver specie recovered during the 4 years after loss, then work abandoned
See pp. 76–77

50 G7 SLOT TER HOGE Nov 19, 1794
SHIP Dutch East Indiaman, 850 tons
LOCATION Porto Santo, Madeira
ROUTE Netherlands to Jakarta, Java
CARGO Silver bars and specie
SALVAGE Silver bars, coins, tobacco boxes, pipes, candlesticks, spoons, forks, taps, and stoneware recovered
Artifacts sold at Christie's, Amsterdam

51 I4 LUTINE Oct 7, 1799
SHIP British Navy ship
LOCATION Off Terschelling, Netherlands
ROUTE UK to Netherlands
CARGO Large quantities of silver, gold bullion, and sovereigns
SALVAGE Extensive salvage operations over the years, but 245 gold bars and 79 silver bars still unaccounted for

52 F9 LADY BURGESS Apr 19, 1806
SHIP English East Indiaman
LOCATION Leton Rock, Cape Verde
ROUTE UK to India
CARGO Probably private specie

53 E5 PRESIDENT Mar 11, 1841
SHIP British and American Steam Navigation Company, 1,863 tons
LOCATION Mid-Atlantic
ROUTE New York, US, to Liverpool, England
CARGO Specie valued at US $30,000 on board, belonging to comedian Tyrone Power

54 **J4** BURNHOLM Apr 15, 1850
SHIP Spanish
LOCATION 54.11N 7.53E
CARGO Gold
SALVAGE Largely salvaged at time of loss

55 **G8** NIGER June 12, 1857
SHIP British, Elder Dempster Line
LOCATION Santa Cruz, Tenerife, Canary Islands
ROUTE Sierra Leone to Tenerife, Canary Islands
CARGO Specie
SALVAGE Some salvage at time of loss

56 **J4** LOUISIANA Jan 1868
SHIP German, 1,300 tons
LOCATION 56.29N 8.09E
ROUTE Bremerhaven, Germany, to New York, US
CARGO Porcelain, china dolls, and antique toys
SALVAGE Salvaged in 1980s
Recovered dolls exhibited in Legoland Park, Billund, Denmark

57 **C7** PIZARRO Sept 11, 1878
LOCATION 37.30N 57.00W
ROUTE St. George's Island, Bermuda, to Faial, Azores
CARGO Specie

58 **G8** ALFONSO XII 1885
SHIP Spanish
LOCATION Off Gran Canaria, Canary Islands
ROUTE Cadiz, Spain, to Havana, Cuba
CARGO 10 boxes of gold, each containing 10,000 gold coins
SALVAGE 9 boxes recovered

59 **D6** TITANIC Apr 15, 1912
SHIP White Star Line
LOCATION 41.43.45N 49.56.50W
ROUTE Southampton, England, to New York, US
CARGO Artifacts and personal valuables
SALVAGE Some artifacts recently recovered
See pp. 104–105

60 **G3** BREMEN Oct 1915
SHIP German submarine
LOCATION 300 miles (480 km) south of Iceland
ROUTE Germany to New York, US
CARGO Valuables and precious stones

61 **K4** PRINZ ADALBERT Oct 1915
SHIP German cruiser, 9,050 tons
LOCATION 56.32N 21.01E
CARGO Possibly gold
Sunk by British submarine

62 **I5** TUBANTIA Mar 16, 1916
SHIP Koninklijke Hollandsche Lloyd Line, 13,911 tons
LOCATION 4 miles (6 km) ENE of North Hinder Lightship
ROUTE Netherlands to South America
CARGO Diamonds and rumors of gold
SALVAGE Attempted in 1920s
Famous court case over rights of "salvor in possession"

63 **H5** LACONIA Feb 25, 1917
SHIP British, Cunard Line, 18,099 tons, 17 knots
LOCATION 160 miles (260 km) NW by W of Fastnet, Republic of Ireland
ROUTE US to UK
CARGO 1,060,665 oz (30,070 kg) silver, including 132 boxes of specie
SALVAGE Ship found and partially opened up, but no recoveries made

64 **I5** HEALDTON Mar 21, 1917
SHIP American tanker
LOCATION Off Netherlands
CARGO Rumors of gold valued at US $3 million

65 **N5** ABOSSO Apr 24, 1917
SHIP British, Elder Dempster Line, 7,782 tons, 13 knots
LOCATION 180 miles (290 km) NW of Fastnet, Republic of Ireland
ROUTE Sierra Leone to Liverpool, England
CARGO Gold

66 **I4** RENATE LEONHARDT Aug 1917
SHIP German
LOCATION 5 miles (8 km) off Texel, Netherlands
ROUTE Rotterdam, Netherlands, to northern Germany
CARGO Gold valued at £4–7 million sterling
SALVAGE Various attempts at salvage, but no significant results

67 **H4** ATLANTIAN June 25, 1918
LOCATION 110 miles (177 km) NW by W of Eagle Island, Republic of Ireland
ROUTE Galveston, Texas, US, to Liverpool, England
CARGO Gold and silver

68 **G6** BADAGRI July 13, 1918
SHIP 2,956 tons
LOCATION 425 miles (684 km) WNW of Cape St. Vincent, Portugal
CARGO Gold, silver, and coins

69 **I5** PILOT STEAMER May 11, 1940
LOCATION Off eastern end of Rozenburg Island, Netherlands, between Rotterdam and Hoek van Holland
ROUTE Netherlands to UK
CARGO 200 boxes of gold weighing 125 lb (57 kg) each
SALVAGE Mainly salvaged

70 **G4** APAPA Nov 15, 1940
SHIP British, Elder Dempster Line, 9,333 tons, 14.5 knots
LOCATION 54.34N 16.47W
ROUTE Lagos, Portugal, to Liverpool, England
CARGO Gold valued at £19,188 sterling

71 **G5** GAIRSOPPA Feb 16, 1941
SHIP British India Steam Navigation Company, 5,237 tons, 10.5 knots
LOCATION Approximately 300 miles (500 km) SW of Galway Bay, Republic of Ireland
ROUTE Freetown, Sierra Leone, to UK
CARGO 3 million oz (85,000 kg) gold and silver

72 **H3** BEAVERBRAE Mar 25, 1941
SHIP British
LOCATION 60.12N 9.00W
ROUTE Liverpool, England, to St. John, New Brunswick, Canada
CARGO Gold, 25 boxes of platinum grain, and 1 parcel of rough diamonds

73 **G8** LAFIAN Sept 24, 1941
SHIP British
LOCATION 31.12N 23.32W
ROUTE Port Harcourt, Nigeria, to Liverpool, England
CARGO Bullion

74 **L1** HMS EDINBURGH May 7, 1942
SHIP British Navy warship, 10,000 tons
LOCATION 71.51N 35.10E
ROUTE Russian Federation to UK
CARGO Gold valued at £45 million sterling when salvaged
SALVAGE Salvaged in 1980s by Keith Jessop's consortium
See pp. 112–113

75 **C9** CITY OF MELBOURNE May 13, 1942
SHIP British, Ellerman Line
LOCATION 15.00N 54.40W
ROUTE South Africa to US
CARGO Gold

76 **F8** SIRIS July 12, 1942
SHIP British
LOCATION 31.20N 24.48W
CARGO Gold coins and gold bars

77 **G8** STENTOR Oct 27, 1942
SHIP British, 6,148 tons, China Mutual Steam Navigation Company, 14.5 knots
LOCATION 29.31N 20.55 W
ROUTE Lagos, Nigeria, to Liverpool, England
CARGO 5,000 oz (140 kg) gold

78 **E6** HENRY STANLEY Dec 6, 1942
SHIP British, Elder Dempster Line, 5,026 tons, 13 knots
LOCATION 40.35N 39.40W
CARGO 3 boxes of diamonds

79 **F5** SOEKABOEMI Dec 28, 1942
SHIP Dutch, Rotterdamsche Lloyd Line, 7,051 tons
LOCATION 47.25N 25.20W
ROUTE Glasgow, Scotland, to Salvador, Brazil
CARGO Possibly precious stones

80 **F8** WILLIAM WILBERFORCE Jan 9, 1943
SHIP British, Elder Dempster Line
LOCATION 29.20N 26.53W
ROUTE Africa to UK
CARGO Gold stowed in the strong room in the poop

81 **E9** I-52 June 23, 1944
SHIP Japanese submarine
LOCATION 15.16N 39.55W
ROUTE Singapore to Lorient, France
CARGO Large quantity of gold
See pp. 116–117

82 **F5** U1062 Sept 30, 1944
SHIP German cargo-carrying submarine
LOCATION Mid-Atlantic
ROUTE Far East to Germany
CARGO Gold

83 **J4** U534 May 5, 1945
SHIP German U-boat
LOCATION Island of Anholt, Denmark
CARGO Secret cargo that could include gold or documents
SALVAGE Boat raised Oct 23, 1993

THE UNITED KINGDOM AND REPUBLIC OF IRELAND

The map for these listings is on pp. 136–137.

● No known salvage
■ Some salvage history known

1 **O7** SUTTON HOO BURIAL SHIP 625
SHIP Viking ship
LOCATION Sutton Hoo, England
CARGO Treasures
SALVAGE Excavated in 1939
See pp. 20–21

2 **O8** DRAKAR 851
SHIP Viking ship
LOCATION River Thames, England
CARGO Artifacts

3 **M1** SHIP OF EARL HAKON 1029
SHIP Viking ship
LOCATION Pentland Firth, Scotland
ROUTE Scotland to Norway
CARGO Valuables
Ship returning to Norway after negotiations with King Canute. Lost during a storm.

4 **N3** SHIP OF FLOSSI 12th–13th century
SHIP Viking
LOCATION Westray Sound, Orkney, Scotland
ROUTE Norway to Iceland
CARGO Valuables, including money
Ship sank as a result of being overloaded

5 **K8** SMALLS WRECK 1100
SHIP Viking ship
LOCATION Off the Smalls, west Wales
CARGO Viking sword
SALVAGE Salvaged in 1991

6 **O2** SHIP OF CECILIA 1248
SHIP Viking ship
LOCATION Roost, south of Shetland, Scotland
ROUTE Hebrides, Scotland, to Bergen, Norway
CARGO Valuable presents
Daughter of King Hakon of Norway on board, returning home after marrying King Harald of the Hebrides. Wreckage washed up on the shores of the Shetland and Orkney Islands, Scotland.

7 **K9** ST. ANTHONY Jan 19, 1527
LOCATION Gunwalloe Cove, Cornwall, England
ROUTE Lisbon, Portugal, to Antwerp, Belgium
CARGO Copper and silver ingots
SALVAGE Salvaged at time of loss and recently excavated
Examples of ingots held in the British Museum

8 **O7** LION 1547
SHIP Scottish warship
LOCATION Harwich harbor, England
ROUTE France to Scotland
CARGO Supplies from France to Scotland
Prize of the Pauncye, flagship of Sir Andrew Dudley. Ship lost through negligence.

9 M2 EDWARD BONAVENTURE
Nov 7, 1556
LOCATION Pettislego Bay, near Fraserburgh, Scotland
ROUTE Russian Federation to Scotland
CARGO Jewels, presents, gold, silver, and furs
SALVAGE Some plundering by locals

10 K9 SPANISH SHIP 1557
SHIP Spanish
LOCATION Off Land's End, England
CARGO Specie valued at £10,000 sterling
SALVAGE Specie recovered at time of loss
Ship sunk by Peter Killigrew and specie taken to Isles of Scilly, England

11 N9 MOROSINI E TIEPOLO 1558
SHIP Venetian, 950 tons
LOCATION English Channel
ROUTE Venice, Italy, to England
CARGO Gold and silver ducats, plus spices

12 O3 EL GRAN GRIFON Sept 1588
SHIP Spanish Armada ship
LOCATION Fair Isle, Shetland, Scotland
CARGO Artifacts
SALVAGE Recently found and excavated

13 I7 TRINIDAD Sept 15, 1588
SHIP Spanish Armada ship, Castile squadron, 872 tons, 24 guns, 302 men
LOCATION Valencia Island, County Kerry, Northern Ireland

14 K4 LA TRINIDAD VALENCERA
Sept 16, 1588
SHIP Spanish Armada ship, 1,100 tons, 42 guns, 360 men
LOCATION 600 feet (180 meters) off west end of Kinnagoe Bay, Inishowen Peninsula of County Donegal, Republic of Ireland
CARGO Artifacts
SALVAGE Rediscovered by City of Derry Sub-Aqua Club

15 I7 SANTA MARIA DE LA ROSA
Sept 21, 1588
SHIP Spanish Armada ship, 1,400 tons
LOCATION 600 feet (180 meters) SE of Stromboli Reef, Blasket Sound, County Kerry, Republic of Ireland
CARGO Artifacts
SALVAGE Located by Sydney Wignall
Prince D'Ascoli, son of King Philip II of Spain, on board

16 K3 SAN JUAN DE SICILIA Oct 1588
SHIP Spanish Armada ship
LOCATION Tobermory Bay, Scotland
CARGO Vast wealth rumored to have been aboard
SALVAGE Many attempts at salvage over 400 years, with little success
Ship also known as the Tobermory wreck. See pp. 48–49.

17 K4 GIRONA Oct 28, 1588
SHIP Spanish Armada ship, Naples squadron, 700 tons, 50 guns
LOCATION Off Port na Spaniagh, near Giant's Causeway, Northern Ireland
CARGO Artifacts
SALVAGE 12,000 artifacts recovered by Robert Stenuit in late 1960s, including jewelry and coins
See pp. 50–51.

18 L9 SAN PEDRO MAYOR Oct 28, 1588
SHIP Spanish Armada ship, 580 tons
LOCATION Bolt Tail, Devon, England
ROUTE UK to Spain
CARGO Specie and jewelry. Unlikely to have had very much treasure on board.
SALVAGE Plundered at time of loss

19 O8 GOLDEN LION Dec 1592
SHIP British
LOCATION Goodwin Sands, England
CARGO Silver coins
SALVAGE Partly salvaged at time of loss by Richard Basset of Ramsgate, England

20 P8 RED LION Dec 1592
SHIP British
LOCATION Goodwin Sands, England
CARGO Specie
SALVAGE Partly salvaged by Richard Basset

21 O8 PEGASUS 1598
SHIP British
LOCATION Goodwin Sands, England
ROUTE Puerto Rico to UK
CARGO Treasure
Cumberland's 12th voyage, returning from the sacking of Puerto Rico.

22 L9 LIZARD WRECK 1617
LOCATION Polperro Cove, England
ROUTE Sanlúcar de Barrameda, Spain, to Flushing, Netherlands
CARGO Silver bars and specie
SALVAGE 3 silver bars weighing 1,654 oz (47 kg) recovered in 1620. Ship rediscovered in 1968 and 700 coins recovered.

23 M8 KAMPEN 1627
SHIP Dutch East Indiaman, 300 tons
LOCATION The Needles, Isle of Wight, England
ROUTE Netherlands to Jakarta, Java
CARGO Many chests of silver and other valuable items
SALVAGE Salvaged at time of loss, and rediscovered in 1983 when further artifacts were recovered

24 N8 VLIEGENDE DRAAK Oct 23, 1627
SHIP Dutch East Indiaman, 320 tons
LOCATION The Needles, Isle of Wight, England
ROUTE Netherlands to Far East
CARGO Silver
SALVAGE Salvaged at time of loss and recently rediscovered

25 M4 CHARLES I WRECK 1633
SHIP Scottish ferry
LOCATION Between Burntisland and Leith, Scotland, in 118 feet (36 meters) of water
ROUTE Burntisland, Scotland, to Leith, Scotland
CARGO Presents, including a 280-piece silver and gilt tableware set given to King Charles I of England
SALVAGE Searched for in 1992, but results not yet clear

26 K9 GUAVER'S LAKE WRECK 1634
SHIP Spanish
LOCATION Guaver's Lake, near Penzance, England
ROUTE Caribbean to Spain
CARGO Gold and silver
SALVAGE Pillaged at time of loss
Ship captured by Dutch en route to Spain

27 L9 PALSGRAVE 1637
SHIP English East Indiaman
LOCATION Plymouth Sound, England
ROUTE India to UK
CARGO Gold, jewels, silks, and pepper
SALVAGE Some salvage at time of loss

28 K9 JACKSON WRECK 1643
SHIP Pirate ship
LOCATION Off Land's End, England
CARGO Specie

29 M3 FIRTH OF TAY WRECKS 1651
LOCATION Firth of Tay, Scotland
CARGO Loot from Dundee, Scotland
Retreating fleet of George Monck

30 O1 LASTDRAGER Mar 2, 1655
SHIP Dutch East Indiaman
LOCATION Northern tip of Shetland and Orkney Islands, Scotland
ROUTE Netherlands to Jakarta, Java
CARGO Specie and gold
SALVAGE 2 chests of silver recovered at time of loss, and further recent recoveries
Possibly substantial quantities of silver coins still to be recovered

31 P2 KENNERMERLAND
Dec 20, 1664
SHIP Dutch East Indiaman
LOCATION Stour Stack, Out Skerries, Shetland, Scotland
ROUTE Netherlands to Jakarta, Java
CARGO Silver specie valued at 20,000 florins
SALVAGE Salvaged at time of loss and recently reworked
Some items in the Lerwick Museum, Scotland

32 L9 SANTO CRISTO DE CASTELLO
Oct 7, 1666
SHIP Genoese ship
LOCATION Polperro Cove, England
CARGO Silver coins
SALVAGE Recently excavated
Collection of artifacts at the Royal Institute of Cornwall, England

33 P8 JOHN Jan 25, 1669
SHIP London ship
LOCATION Goodwin Sands, England
ROUTE Canary Islands to UK
CARGO 2 chests of gold dust, elephants' tusks, and other valuable commodities
SALVAGE Some salvage at time of loss. The seamen ventured out in boats and saved most of the elephants' tusks.

34 O7 ROYAL JAMES
May 28, 1672
SHIP English warship
LOCATION Off Aldeburgh, England
CARGO 106 brass cannons, plus silver plate belonging to Lord Sandwich
SALVAGE Recent search attempts, but no salvage to date
Lost during the Battle of Solebay

35 L6 MARY 1675
SHIP Pleasure yacht of King Charles II of England
LOCATION Skerries, Wales
CARGO Gold and silver coins, and jewelry
SALVAGE Rediscovered in 1971
46 passengers including Earl of Meath, Lord Ardee, and the Earl of Ardglass. Artifacts in the Merseyside Museum, England.

36 K9 PHOENIX Jan 11, 1679
SHIP English East Indiaman
LOCATION Approximately 0.25 mile (0.5 km) from Pednathise rock, west side of Broadneck, England
ROUTE Far East to UK
CARGO Diamonds

37 M8 ANNA MARIA
Oct 16, 1682
SHIP Dutch, 400 tons, 32 guns
LOCATION Portland beach, England
ROUTE Venice, Italy, via Cadiz, Spain, to Amsterdam, Netherlands
CARGO Rice, brimstone, and silver
SALVAGE Most of the silver lost except for 7 sows (lumps of silver)
Capt. John Sluymer

38 M6 CHESTER WRECK 1686
LOCATION Near Chester, England
ROUTE Republic of Ireland to UK
CARGO Property of Lord Blessington, rumored to be worth over £12,000 sterling

39 K9 PRINSES MARIA Jan 4, 1686
SHIP Dutch East Indiaman
LOCATION Western Rocks, Isles of Scilly, England
ROUTE Netherlands to Jakarta, Java
CARGO Silver specie
SALVAGE Looted at time of loss and salvaged by Rex Cowan in 1973
Deep layer of sand made excavation difficult

40 N8 GUYNE FRIGATE 1691
SHIP Frigate
LOCATION Near Portsmouth, England
ROUTE West Africa to UK
CARGO Gold
SALVAGE Some salvage at time of loss

41 K9 BERKELEY CASTLE Mar 17, 1694
SHIP English East Indiaman
LOCATION Off Land's End, England
ROUTE Fort St. George, Madras, India, to UK
CARGO Diamonds
SALVAGE Very small quantity of diamonds removed before ship sank
Ship taken by Petit Renau's ship, Le Bon, and sank shortly after being captured

42 I7 HENRY 1695
SHIP English East Indiaman
LOCATION Dingle Bay, Ventry, Republic of Ireland
ROUTE India to UK
CARGO Diamonds valued at £75,000 sterling
SALVAGE Some salvage at time of loss, but no evidence that diamonds were recovered

43 K9 HMS ASSOCIATION Oct 22, 1707
SHIP British warship
LOCATION Gilstone rock, SW edge of Isles of Scilly, England
ROUTE Lisbon, Portugal, to UK
CARGO Specie
SALVAGE Recently found and salvaged by Roland Morris

44 P2 DE LIEFDE Nov 1711
SHIP Dutch East Indiaman
LOCATION Reef of Miouw, Out Skerries, Shetland, Scotland
ROUTE Netherlands to Jakarta, Java
CARGO Silver specie
SALVAGE Worked by scuba-divers in 1960s
Some recovered artifacts in the Lerwick Museum, Scotland

45 P1 RIJNENBURG Mar 15, 1713
SHIP Dutch East Indiaman, 618 tons
LOCATION Ham of Muness, Unst, Shetland, Scotland
ROUTE Netherlands to Jakarta, Java
CARGO Silver
SALVAGE 10 chests of specie and 1 double chest salvaged

46 J2 ADELAAR 1728
SHIP Dutch East Indiaman
LOCATION South Uist, Hebrides, Scotland
ROUTE Netherlands to Far East
CARGO Silver specie
SALVAGE Largely salvaged at time of loss

47 P1 CURACAO 1729
SHIP Portuguese East Indiaman
LOCATION North tip of Shetland, Scotland
ROUTE Far East to Portugal
CARGO Porcelain
SALVAGE Recently located and some salvage of artifacts

48 O7 EGMONT WRECK 1733
LOCATION Outside Harwich, England
ROUTE Harwich, England, to Netherlands
CARGO Gold
SALVAGE 1 chest of gold recovered by Capt. Philips

49 K9 TRIUMPH Oct 9, 1736
LOCATION Western part of St Mary's, Isles of Scilly, England
ROUTE Jamaica to UK
CARGO Gold specie valued at £10,000 sterling
SALVAGE Considerable part of cargo saved, although some people died attempting to bring bags of money ashore

50 P2 VENDELA Dec 18, 1737
SHIP Danish East Indiaman
LOCATION Heilanabretta, East Fetlar, Shetland and Orkney Islands, Scotland
ROUTE Denmark to Far East
CARGO Silver coins and bullion
SALVAGE 75% of cargo recovered at time of loss. Relocated by Robert Stenuit in 1972.
Variety of national coins found, reflecting weakness of Danish currency at time

51 O3 SVECIA Nov 18, 1740
SHIP Swedish East Indiaman, 600 tons, 28 guns
LOCATION Reef Dyke Shoal, 1.5 miles (2.5 km) south of North Ronaldsay, Orkney, Scotland
ROUTE Bengal to Gothenburg, Sweden
CARGO Silk and cotton goods, and some Portuguese coins
SALVAGE Relocated in 1976

52 K9 MARIA ADRIANA 1743
SHIP Dutch East Indiaman, 650 tons
LOCATION Isles of Scilly, England
ROUTE Jakarta, Java, to Netherlands
CARGO Gold bars valued at £12.8 million sterling according to recent newspaper reports, but this sum unlikely
SALVAGE Ship's location is claimed to have been found, but no recoveries made

53 O8 NOTTINGHAM
Feb 25, 1743
SHIP English East Indiaman
LOCATION Lost at Broadstairs, England
ROUTE UK to India
CARGO 1,230 elephants' tusks and privately shipped silver
SALVAGE Silver saved

54 K9 HOLLANDIA
July 13, 1743
SHIP Dutch East Indiaman
LOCATION Off St. Agnes, Isles of Scilly, England
ROUTE Netherlands to Jakarta, Java
CARGO Silver specie
SALVAGE Attempted by John Lethbridge at time of loss without success. Relocated in 1971 and in excess of 35,000 silver coins recovered

55 P8 DOLPHIN 1747
SHIP English East Indiaman
LOCATION Goodwin Sands, England
ROUTE London, England, to Bombay, India
CARGO 40 chests of silver weighing 140,054 oz (3,970 kg)
Ship never heard from after leaving England. Capt. George Newton.

56 N8 LA NYMPHA
Nov 23, 1747
LOCATION Beachy Head, England
ROUTE Veracruz, Mexico, to Cadiz, Spain
CARGO Gold
SALVAGE Recovered at time of loss, and rediscovered in 1974 on the Seven Sisters, near Crow Link Gap, England

57 M9 HOPE Jan 16, 1749
SHIP Dutch, 30 guns
LOCATION Off Weymouth, England
ROUTE Curaçao, Netherlands Antilles, to Amsterdam, Netherlands
CARGO Gold and silver valued at £50,000 sterling
Ship probably called "Hoop" or "Hof"

58 O8 AMSTERDAM Jan 26, 1749
SHIP Dutch East Indiaman, 1,150 tons
LOCATION Hastings, England
ROUTE Netherlands to Far East
CARGO Specie and silver bars valued at 300,104 florins
SALVAGE Salvaged at time of loss
Ship recently excavated

59 N5 BONHOMME RICHARD
Sept 25, 1779
SHIP American, 40 guns, approximately 120 feet (37 meters) long
LOCATION Off Flamborough Head, England
ROUTE France to England
CARGO Money and artifacts belonging to John Paul Jones
SALVAGE Possibly located during 1976 expedition, but no artifacts recovered
See pp. 80–81

60 K9 NANCY Mar 4, 1784
SHIP Packet
LOCATION Rosevear, 4 miles (6 km) south of St. Agnes, Isles of Scilly, England
ROUTE Bombay, India, to UK
CARGO Mail, and the fortune, mainly in cash, of well-known actress, Mrs. Cargill
SALVAGE Mail saved, but very little of cargo salvaged
Ship struck rock

61 L9 GUNWALLOE WRECK c. 1789
SHIP Dutch
LOCATION Under Penguinion Head, near Gunwalloe Cove, Cornwall, England
CARGO 14 tons silver dollars rumored
SALVAGE Numerous salvage attempts since 19th century

62 K9 MERCURY Feb 23, 1791
LOCATION Isles of Scilly, England
ROUTE Virginia, US, to London, England
CARGO Silver
SALVAGE 1,353 oz (38 kg) silver saved

63 K9 ZEELILIE Oct 14, 1795
SHIP Dutch East Indiaman
LOCATION Western Rocks, Isles of Scilly, England
ROUTE Far East to UK
CARGO Tea and porcelain
When the Zeelilie sank it had already been captured by the Sceptre warship. It is likely that the porcelain cargo is broken.

64 L8 JENNY Feb 20, 1797
SHIP English
LOCATION Jenny's Cove, Lundy, England
ROUTE West Africa to UK
CARGO Ivory and gold dust
SALVAGE Salvaged at time of loss

65 N9 HENRY ADDINGTON
Dec 1798
SHIP English East Indiaman
LOCATION Isle of Wight, England
ROUTE UK to India
CARGO 655,744 oz (18,590 kg) silver
SALVAGE Salvaged at time of loss

66 K9 HMS COLOSSUS
Dec 10, 1798
SHIP British warship, 3rd rate, 74 guns
LOCATION Rocks of Southward Well, south of Samson Island, Isles of Scilly, England
ROUTE Mediterranean to UK
CARGO Sir William Hamilton's collection of antiques
SALVAGE Recently rediscovered and salvaged by Roland Morris

67 M2 PHAETON Jan 7, 1800
SHIP Swedish brig
LOCATION Fraserburgh, Scotland
ROUTE Cayenne, French Guiana, to Gothenburg, Sweden
CARGO Gold and precious artifacts

68 O8 HINDOSTAN 1803
SHIP English East Indiaman
LOCATION Wedge Sands, off Margate, England
ROUTE UK to India
CARGO 13 chests of silver on board
SALVAGE 11 chests recovered

69 O8 ACTIVE Jan 10, 1803
SHIP British
LOCATION Margate roads, England
ROUTE West Indies to UK
CARGO Gold valued at £67,000 sterling
SALVAGE Some salvage at time of loss

70 O8 SAN JUAN BAUTISTA
Dec 25, 1803
SHIP Spanish bergantina, 60 tons
LOCATION North Downs, England
ROUTE Spain to UK
CARGO Specie

71 M9 EARL OF ABERGAVENNY
Feb 6, 1805
SHIP English East Indiaman
LOCATION 2 miles (3 km) from Weymouth beach, England, in 12 fathoms water
ROUTE UK to Bengal to China
CARGO US $275,000, earthenware, tin, copper, lead, cloth, and general merchandise
SALVAGE Silver, dollars, and metals largely salvaged at time of loss
Capt. Wordsworth, brother of British poet William Wordsworth, drowned

72 K7 IRLAM 1812
LOCATION Tuskar Rock, Republic of Ireland
ROUTE Barbados to Liverpool, England
CARGO Silver plate and gold guineas

73 L6 PANTHEA Jan 15, 1827
LOCATION East side of Holyhead harbor, England
ROUTE New York, US, to UK
CARGO Specie
SALVAGE Partly salvaged at time of loss

74 K8 HOPE Jan 20, 1830
SHIP Brig
LOCATION St. Martin's, Isles of Scilly, England
CARGO Ivory and gold dust
SALVAGE Largely salvaged at time of loss

75 O8 ROYAL ADELAIDE Mar 30, 1850
SHIP Dublin Steampacket Company, bark, 450 tons
LOCATION Tongue Sands, off Margate, England
ROUTE Cork, Republic of Ireland, to London, England
CARGO Gold valued at £300,000 sterling reported
24 crew and 12 passengers lost

76 L6 ROYAL CHARTER Oct 25, 1859
SHIP British, Liverpool and Australian Steam Navigation Company, 2,719 tons
LOCATION Moelfre Bay, near Point Lynas, Wales
ROUTE Melbourne, Australia, to Liverpool, England
CARGO Gold sovereigns and bars, valued at £321,000 sterling
SALVAGE Largely salvaged at time of loss, and frequently explored since
See pp. 98–99

77 L9 HIOGO Oct 1, 1867
LOCATION Off Eddystone Lighthouse, English Channel
CARGO Specie valued at £20,000 sterling, plus valuable merchandise
SALVAGE Specie recovered

78 J8 CRESCENT CITY Feb 9, 1871
SHIP British, Liverpool and Mississippi Steamship Company, 2,039 tons
LOCATION Dhulic Rock, near Galley Head, Republic of Ireland
ROUTE New Orleans, Louisiana, US, to Liverpool, England
CARGO 40 boxes of specie valued at US $101,402
SALVAGE 20 boxes of specie recovered over the 2 years after the ship went down

79 K9 SCHILLER May 7, 1875
SHIP German, Transatlantic Steam Navigation Company, 3,421 tons
LOCATION Retarrier Ledges, Isles of Scilly, England
ROUTE New York, US, to Hamburg, Germany
CARGO Specie valued at US $300,000
SALVAGE Salvaged at time of loss

80 L9 MOSEL Aug 10, 1882
LOCATION Under signal station at Lizard Point, England
CARGO Large quantity of specie
SALVAGE Salvaged at time of loss

81 N9 EIDER Jan 31, 1892
LOCATION Atherfield, Isle of Wight, England
ROUTE New York, US, to Bremen, Germany
CARGO Gold and silver valued at £300,000 sterling
SALVAGE Salvaged at time of loss

82 L9 JEBBA Mar 18, 1907
SHIP British, Elder Dempster Line, 3,813 tons
LOCATION Near Bolt Tail, Devon, England
ROUTE West Africa to Plymouth, England, and Liverpool, England
CARGO Specie, ivory, palm oil, fruit, and mail, valued at £200,000 sterling in total
SALVAGE Largely salvaged at time of loss

83 N8 OCEANA Mar 16, 1912
SHIP British, P & O Line
LOCATION 50.43N 0.27E
ROUTE London, England, to Bombay, India
CARGO Silver, gold, ivory, and specie valued at £747,610 sterling
SALVAGE Salvaged at time of loss

84 J8 LUSITANIA May 7, 1915
SHIP British, Cunard Line, 30,396 tons
LOCATION 10 miles (16 km) south of Old Head of Kinsale, Republic of Ireland
ROUTE New York, US, to Liverpool, England
CARGO Unconfirmed rumors of bullion and valuables
SALVAGE Salvaged more than once, but only silver teaspoons recovered
The loss of the Lusitania was instrumental in bringing the US into the First World War

85 O7 BATAVIA May 17, 1916
SHIP British
LOCATION Off Great Yarmouth, England
CARGO 14 cases of gold, each valued at £5,000 sterling
SALVAGE Salvaged in 1963 by Hugh Edwards

86 N3 HMS HAMPSHIRE June 5, 1916
SHIP British cruiser
LOCATION 1.5 miles (2.5 km) off shore, between Brough of Bersay and Marwick Head, Orkney, Scotland
ROUTE Scotland to Russian Federation
CARGO Gold valued at £2 million sterling rumored
SALVAGE Salvage attempt in 1930s
Lord Kitchener drowned, along with all but 12 members of crew; 650 drowned in total.

87 J4 LAURENTIC Jan 23, 1917
SHIP British, White Star Line, 14,892 tons
LOCATION 10 miles (16 km) north of Lough Swilly, Republic of Ireland
ROUTE UK to US
CARGO Gold valued at £5 million sterling
SALVAGE All cargo salvaged apart from 20 to 25 gold bars and approximately £60,000 sterling of ship's money. Many recent attempts to salvage remainder.

88 J7 GOLD COAST Apr 19, 1917
SHIP British, Elder Dempster Line
LOCATION 14 miles (23 km) south of Mine Head, Republic of Ireland
ROUTE West Africa to Liverpool, England
CARGO Gold bullion

89 M9 MEDINA Apr 28, 1917
SHIP British, P & O Line, 12,358 tons
LOCATION 2 to 3 miles (3 to 5 km) ENE of Start Point, England
ROUTE India to UK
CARGO Tin, copper, silver, lead, wolfram, and 1 box of silver bullion, as well as jewels belonging to the Viceroy of India, valued at £10 million sterling
SALVAGE Worked on in 1970s and 1980s
Sale of artifacts at recent auction produced disappointing results

90 **I8** **TARQUAH** July 7, 1917
SHIP British, Elder Dempster Line,
3,359 tons
LOCATION 10 miles (16 km) south of Bull
Rock, Republic of Ireland
ROUTE West Africa to Liverpool, England
CARGO Gold
SALVAGE Salvaged in 1980s, but no gold
recovered

91 **P1** **UMGENI** Nov 9, 1917
SHIP British, Bullard, King & Co.,
2,662 tons
LOCATION North of Shetland and Orkney
Islands, Scotland
ROUTE Clyde River, Scotland, to Lagos,
Nigeria
CARGO 12 boxes of silver coins

92 **L6** **APAPA** Nov 28, 1917
SHIP British, Elder Dempster Line,
7,832 tons
LOCATION 3 miles (5 km) NE of Point
Lynas, Wales, 53.26.45N 04.18.50W
ROUTE West Africa to UK
CARGO Silver specie and ivory
SALVAGE Some salvage during 1970s

93 **L7** **AGBERI** Dec 28, 1917
SHIP British, 4,821 tons
LOCATION 18 miles (29 km) NW half W of
Bardsey Island, Wales
ROUTE West Africa to Liverpool, England
CARGO Silver specie and ivory

94 **K4** **ANDANIA** Jan 27, 1918
SHIP British, Cunard Line, 13,405 tons
LOCATION 2 miles (3 km) NE of
Rathlin Island, Northern Ireland
CARGO Silverware and diamonds

95 **N9** **SHIRALA** July 2, 1918
SHIP British India Steam Navigation
Company
LOCATION 4 miles (6 km) NE by E half E
from Owers Light Vessel, England
ROUTE London, England, to India
CARGO Elephants' tusks and 4 packages
of diamonds
SALVAGE Tusks recovered in 1978, but no
record of diamonds being salvaged

96 **O8** **DUNBAR CASTLE** Jan 9, 1940
SHIP British, Union Castle Mail Steamship
Company, built in 1930 by Harland and
Wolff, 10,002 tons
LOCATION 2 miles (3 km) NE by N of
Goodwin's Light, England
ROUTE London, England, to Beira,
Mozambique
CARGO Jewelry
Ship hit mine

97 **I4** **EMPRESS OF BRITAIN**
Oct 26, 1940
SHIP British, Canadian Pacific, 42,348 tons
LOCATION 55.16N 09.50W
ROUTE South Africa to UK
CARGO Gold
SALVAGE Attempted in 1940s according to
newspapers, but no evidence of results

98 **N4** **SOMALI** Mar 26, 1941
SHIP British, P & O Line
LOCATION 1 mile (1.5 km) east of Snoop
Head, Sunderland, England
ROUTE London, England, to Methil,
Scotland
CARGO Gold and precious stones

99 **K7** **DARU** Sept 15, 1941
SHIP British, 3,854 tons
LOCATION Off Waterford, Republic of
Ireland, 51.56N 05.58W
ROUTE West Africa to Liverpool, England
CARGO 50 boxes of coins

THE BAY OF BISCAY TO THE SOUTHERN NORTH SEA

The map for these listings is on pp. 138–139.

● No known salvage
■ Some salvage history known

1 **L3** **BLANCHE NEF** Nov 25, 1120
LOCATION Rock off Barfleur, France
CARGO Specie and valuables
Children of King Henry I of England on board

2 **J4** **CORDELIERE** 1513
SHIP Warship
LOCATION 3 miles (5 km) off Brest, France
CARGO 16 brass cannons, a large sum of
money, and gold chains
Ship blew up during a battle with the Regent

3 **J4** **REGENT** 1513
SHIP Warship
LOCATION 3 miles (5 km) off Brest, France
CARGO Valuables

4 **M2** **LUBECK** c. 1514
LOCATION Off Calais, France
ROUTE UK to France
CARGO Valuables and artifacts
*Lady Mary, sister of King Henry VIII of
England, on board – en route to marry King
Louis XII of France. 400 drowned.*

5 **J7** **SHIP OF KING PHILIP II** 1558
SHIP Spanish
LOCATION Off northern Spain
ROUTE Flanders, Belgium, to Spain
CARGO Valuables and documents
SALVAGE Partly salvaged at time of loss

6 **J8** **DONCELLA** Sept 1588
SHIP Spanish Armada ship
LOCATION Santander harbor, Spain
*Ship foundered after weathering an Atlantic
storm*

7 **K3** **ALDERNEY WRECK**
SHIP Elizabethan warship
LOCATION Alderney, Channel Islands
CARGO Artifacts
SALVAGE Excavation started in 1993 by team
from Oxford University, England

8 **H7** **MERLIN** Oct 21, 1564
SHIP British
LOCATION Bay of Biscay
ROUTE UK to west Africa
CARGO Specie
Ship blew up in a storm

9 **K3** **DELIGHT** Aug 1590
SHIP British
LOCATION Monville de Hage, 8 miles
(13 km) west of Cherbourg, France
ROUTE South America to UK
CARGO Silver

10 **L6** **GIRONDE RIVER WRECKS**
17th century
SHIP French
LOCATION Gironde River, France
CARGO Marble statuary for King Louis XIV
of France

11 **N2** **SAN LUIS** Sept 1615
SHIP Spanish flagship
LOCATION Dunkirk, France
ROUTE Spain to Flanders, Belgium
CARGO Specie for Flanders army
*Flagship of Diego Brochero. Part of a fleet of
15 merchant ships and 4 galleons carrying
troops and supplies.*

12 **H9** **NUESTRA SENORA DEL
SOCORRO** 1619
SHIP Spanish, 120 tons
LOCATION Pontevedra, Galicia, Spain
ROUTE Puerto Rico to Spain
CARGO Specie
SALVAGE Some salvage at time of loss
Capt. Antonio de la Pena

13 **L6** **SANTA ELENA** 1625
SHIP Portuguese East Indiaman
LOCATION Coast of France
ROUTE India to Portugal
CARGO Precious stones

14 **J8** **SANTONA WRECK**
Aug 16, 1639
SHIP Spanish, 40 bronze cannons
LOCATION Santander, Spain
ROUTE Spain to Netherlands
CARGO Specie
Ship sunk by Admiral Monsieur de Bordeaux

15 **F5** **NATHANIEL**
Feb 10, 1685
SHIP English East Indiaman
LOCATION 450 miles (725 km) off Lizard
Point, England
ROUTE India to UK
CARGO Probably included jewels and
porcelain

16 **H7** **WATERLAND** Sept 12, 1692
SHIP Dutch East Indiaman, 1,138 tons
LOCATION Approximately 45.00N
ROUTE Far East to Netherlands
CARGO Precious stones and porcelain
Ship sunk by French

17 **O1** **MAAS WRECK** July 13, 1694
SHIP Dutch frigate, 42 guns
LOCATION Off the mouth of the Mass
River, Netherlands
ROUTE Netherlands to West Indies
CARGO Treasure valued at more than
£100,000 sterling

18 **H9** **SANTO CRISTO DE
MARACAIBO** Oct 1702
SHIP Spanish
LOCATION Entrance to Vigo Bay, Spain
ROUTE Spain to UK
CARGO Specie, plate, and jewels
Prize of English ship, the Monmouth, *after the
Battle of Vigo Bay*

19 **G9** **VIGO BAY WRECKS** Oct 1702
SHIP Spanish
LOCATION Vigo Bay, Spain
ROUTE Havana, Cuba, to Cadiz, Spain
CARGO Silver valued at over 13 million
pesos
SALVAGE Many salvage attempts, but no
significant results
*22 Spanish ships in the fleet, but most of them
were destoyed by the Anglo–Dutch fleet in Vigo
Bay. The bulk of the silver and valuables had
already been unloaded and transported inland.
See pp. 58–59.*

20 **K4** **GRANDE BRETAGNE**
Nov 23, 1711
SHIP French privateer
LOCATION Rocks off St. Malo, France
CARGO Specie

21 **N2** **BARNEVELD** Feb 14, 1724
SHIP Dutch East Indiaman, 1,008 tons
LOCATION Between Grevelingen,
Netherlands, and Dunkirk, France
ROUTE Netherlands to Jakarta, Java
CARGO Specie

22 **N1** **BETHLEHEM** Feb 29, 1741
SHIP Dutch East Indiaman, 850 tons
LOCATION Flemish Sandbanks, off Ostend,
Belgium
ROUTE Netherlands to Sri Lanka
CARGO Silver specie

23 **M2** **WATERVLIET** May 5, 1742
SHIP Dutch East Indiaman, 650 tons
LOCATION Off Calais, France
ROUTE Netherlands to Jakarta, Java
CARGO Specie

24 **K3** **VICTORY** Oct 4 or 5, 1744
SHIP British warship, 1,920 tons
LOCATION Casquets, near Alderney,
Channel Islands
ROUTE Lisbon, Portugal, to UK
CARGO 110 brass cannons and specie
SALVAGE 2 brass cannons possibly looted
from this wreck in 1993

25 **K5** **PRINCE DE CONTY** Dec 1746
SHIP French East Indiaman, 600 tons
LOCATION Cliffs of Port Loscat, off the
southern headland of Belle-Île, France
ROUTE Huang-pu, China, to France
CARGO Porcelain and gold
SALVAGE Surveyed in 1985 and 3 gold
ingots recovered

26 **M2** **ERFPRINS** Oct 16, 1758
SHIP Dutch East Indiaman, 850 tons
LOCATION Near Calais, France
ROUTE Netherlands to Jakarta, Java
CARGO Specie

27 **M2** **LORD CLIVE** Feb 27, 1767
SHIP English East Indiaman
LOCATION 9 miles (14 km) south of
Boulogne, France
ROUTE UK to China
CARGO Specie
SALVAGE Some salvage at time of loss

28 **J4** **WALENBURG** Jan 13, 1770
SHIP Dutch East Indiaman, 880 tons
LOCATION Off Portsall, coast of Brittany,
France, 48.33N 4.42W
ROUTE Netherlands to Jakarta, Java
CARGO Specie

29 **K3** **RESOLUTION'S PRIZE** 1779
SHIP French East Indiaman valued at
approximately £100,000 sterling
LOCATION Coast of Guernsey, Channel
Islands
ROUTE India to France
The Resolution *captured another ship that was
not wrecked and it fetched £106,000 sterling in
London, England*

30 **K3** **VALENTINE** Nov 16, 1779
SHIP English East Indiaman
LOCATION Le Neste Reef, west side of
Brechou, off Sark, Channel Islands
ROUTE China to UK
CARGO Porcelain
SALVAGE Some salvage at time of loss and
worked by local divers in 1975

31 **M2** **BRESLAU** 1783
SHIP Dutch East Indiaman
LOCATION Off Boulogne, France
ROUTE Guangzhou, China, to Netherlands
CARGO Porcelain

32 **M3** **TELEMAQUE** 1790
SHIP French
LOCATION Estuary of River Seine, off
Quillebeuf, France
CARGO Gold and other valuables
SALVAGE Many salvage attempts, but no
significant results
French aristocracy on board, fleeing revolution

33 **L3** **ZAANSTROM** Feb 28, 1791
SHIP Dutch East Indiaman, 564 tons
LOCATION Off Barfleur, France
ROUTE Netherlands to Jakarta, Java
CARGO Specie

34 M2 ZORG Nov 4, 1795
SHIP Dutch East Indiaman, 900 tons
LOCATION Off Boulogne, France
ROUTE Netherlands to Jakarta, Java,
via Plymouth, England
CARGO Specie

35 J5 BETSEY 1799
SHIP English brig
LOCATION Off Pointe de Penmarch, France
ROUTE Santa Cruz, Spain, to Liverpool,
England
CARGO Specie
*Capt. C. Hamilton of the Melpomene was
giving chase when the Betsey ran ashore*

36 L3 BHAVANI Nov 1799
SHIP English East Indiaman
LOCATION Off French coast, opposite
Dunstone Head, England
ROUTE Calcutta, India, to London,
England
CARGO Specie
SALVAGE Some pillaging at time of loss

37 J4 HMS MAGNIFICENT Mar 25, 1804
SHIP British warship, 3rd rate, 74 guns
LOCATION Boufaloe Rock, 7 to 8 miles
(11 to 13 km) from Brest, France
CARGO Valuable silver plate

38 L6 JEUNE HENRI 1820
SHIP French
LOCATION Île d'Oléron, France
ROUTE Venice, Italy, to France
CARGO Gold and jewels
SALVAGE Several unsuccessful attempts at
salvage. Most recent salvage attempt in 1927.

39 L6 LA CONFIDANTE Dec 24, 1821
SHIP English East Indiaman
LOCATION Île de Ré, France, 46.12N 1.25W
CARGO Gold

40 J5 KENT Mar 1, 1825
SHIP English East Indiaman
LOCATION Bay of Biscay
ROUTE UK to India
CARGO Specie
Ship burned at sea

41 H8 SOLWAY Apr 8, 1843
SHIP British, Royal Mail Line
LOCATION 20 miles (32 km) west of La
Coruña, Spain
ROUTE London, England, to West Indies
CARGO Specie
SALVAGE Largely salvaged

42 H3 AMAZON Jan 2, 1852
SHIP British steamer, Royal Mail Line
LOCATION 110 miles (177 km) WSW of
Isles of Scilly, England
ROUTE UK to West Indies
CARGO Coins valued at £20,000 sterling
Ship burned at sea

43 G9 MADRID Feb 20, 1857
SHIP British, P & O Line, 480 tons
LOCATION Near Vigo, Spain
ROUTE Southampton, England, to Cadiz,
Spain
CARGO Specie valued at £26,857 sterling
SALVAGE All specie salvaged
*Ship struck rock when entering Vigo, Spain, and
beached in a small cove. Capt. Bradshaw.*

44 L3 ALABAMA June 19, 1864
SHIP Confederate States Navy cruiser,
1,040 tons
LOCATION 7 to 8 miles (11 to 13 km) off
Cherbourg, France
CARGO Valuable artifacts
Ship lost during naval engagement

45 J4 BOYNE Aug 11, 1875
SHIP British steam packet, Royal Mail Line
LOCATION Rocks off Isle Molène, France
ROUTE Brazil to Southampton, England
CARGO Specie valued at £20,682 sterling
SALVAGE Salvaged by divers at time of loss

46 I4 SARPEDON Sept 4, 1876
SHIP British, Ocean Steamship Company,
1,556 tons, iron construction
LOCATION 70 miles (110 km) SW of
Ushant, France
ROUTE Shanghai, China, to London,
England
CARGO Specie, teas, and silks
SALVAGE Specie saved

47 J4 EUROPEAN Dec 1877
SHIP British, Union Castle Line
LOCATION Barre Meur, west of Ushant,
France
ROUTE South Africa to UK
CARGO Large quantity of diamonds
SALVAGE Mail saved and most of diamonds
recovered loose in mail bags

48 G8 DOURO Apr 1, 1882
SHIP British, Royal Mail Line
LOCATION 45 miles (72 km) north of Cape
Finisterre, Spain
ROUTE Brazil to Southampton, England
CARGO Specie

49 H9 VALPARAISO Feb 28, 1887
SHIP British, Pacific Steam Navigation
Company, 3,575 tons
LOCATION Boneira, Vigo Bay, Spain
ROUTE Liverpool, England, to Valparaíso,
Chile
CARGO Specie and mercury
SALVAGE Specie and 100 bottles of mercury
salvaged

50 I4 PRINS FREDERIK June 25, 1890
SHIP Dutch steamship, Maatschappy
Nederland, 2,997 tons
LOCATION 70 miles (113 km) SW by W of
Ushant, France
ROUTE Netherlands to Jakarta, Java
CARGO 400,000 silver rijksdaalders (coins)
See pp. 102–103.

51 H8 SKYRO Apr 1891
LOCATION Dayo Reef, off Cape Finisterre,
Spain
CARGO 88 silver bars
SALVAGE Partly salvaged. 81 bars had
been recovered when the operation was
abandoned in 1897.

52 J4 DRUMMOND CASTLE
June 16, 1896
SHIP British, Castle Mail Packets
Company, 3,706 tons
LOCATION Reef of rocks, Pierres Vertes,
south entrance to Fronveur Sound, near
Molène island, France
ROUTE Cape Town, South Africa, to
London, England
CARGO Rumors of bullion

53 H8 PALERMO Dec 11, 1910
SHIP German steamer, 1,107 tons
LOCATION Near La Coruña, Spain
ROUTE Hamburg, Germany, to the
Mediterranean
CARGO Gold

54 I4 MADEIRA Nov 17, 1914
SHIP British
LOCATION 47.59N 6.28W
ROUTE West Africa to UK
CARGO Gold

55 H8 HIGHLAND WARRIOR
Oct 3, 1915
SHIP British, Nelson Line, 7,485 tons
LOCATION North of Cape Prior, Spain
ROUTE London, England, to Buenos Aires,
Argentina
CARGO Gold

56 M2 SOCOTRA Nov 30, 1915
SHIP British, P & O Line, 6,009 tons
LOCATION Off Le Touquet, France
ROUTE Brisbane, Australia, to London,
England
CARGO Bullion

57 F3 MANTOLA Feb 9, 1917
SHIP British India Steam Navigation
Company, 8,260 tons, 14.5 knots
LOCATION 49.45N 13.20W
ROUTE UK to India
CARGO 600,000 oz (17,000 kg) silver
Ship floated for a day before it sank

58 F3 ALNWICK CASTLE Mar 19, 1917
SHIP British, Union Castle Line,
5,900 tons, 14 knots
LOCATION 310 miles (500 km) W by S of
Bishop Rock, Isles of Scilly, England
ROUTE Plymouth, England, to South Africa
CARGO Silver

59 G3 GALICIA June 10, 1917
LOCATION 49.00N 10.00W
ROUTE Malaga, Spain, to London, England
CARGO 9 cases of silver, plus ivory

60 K5 ELISABETHVILLE Sept 6, 1917
SHIP Belgian steamship, Cie Belge
Maritime du Congo, 7,017 tons
LOCATION Off Belle-Île, France
CARGO Diamonds valued at £100,000
sterling, plus ivory
SALVAGE Ivory recovered, but not diamonds

61 F4 PRESIDENT LINCOLN
May 31, 1918
SHIP US Government ship, 18,168 tons,
14.5 knots
LOCATION 350 miles (560 km) west of
Brest, France
ROUTE France to US
CARGO Gold

62 I4 ORIGEN June 30, 1918
SHIP British
LOCATION 115 miles (185 km) off Ushant,
France
ROUTE UK to South America
CARGO Specie
SALVAGE Cargo saved at time of loss

63 F3 GALWAY CASTLE Sept 12, 1918
SHIP British, Union Castle Line,
7,988 tons, 14 knots
LOCATION 160 miles (260 km) SW half S of
Fastnet Rock, Republic of Ireland
ROUTE Plymouth, England, to Durban,
South Africa
CARGO Silver
*Ship wrecked in a torpedo position, but floated
for 3 days*

64 J4 EGYPT May 20, 1922
SHIP British steamer, P & O Line,
7,941 tons
LOCATION Near Ushant, France
ROUTE London, England, to Bombay,
India
CARGO Gold and silver valued in excess of
£1 million sterling
SALVAGE 98% of cargo recovered by Italian
company, Sorima
*Gold sovereigns not yet recovered are valued
today at approximately £1 million sterling.
See pp. 106–107.*

65 L6 TANNENFELS Aug 25, 1944
SHIP 7,840 tons
LOCATION Gironde River, 9 miles (15 km)
below Bordeaux, France, 44.57.02N 32.07W
CARGO Gold, silver, and loot
SALVAGE Some salvage at time of loss by
Les Abeilles
Ship scuttled by Germans

ATLANTIC SPAIN, NORTHWEST AFRICA, AND THE AZORES

The map for these listings is on pp. 140–141.

● No known salvage
■ Some salvage history known

1 M4 LA TRINIDAD 1541
SHIP Spanish, 130 tons
LOCATION Bar of Sanlúcar de Barrameda,
Spain
ROUTE Caribbean to Spain
CARGO Gold and silver

2 M4 SAN MEDEL Y CELEDON 1544
SHIP Spanish, 180 tons
LOCATION Port of Huelva, Spain
ROUTE Veracruz, Mexico, to Spain
CARGO Gold and silver

3 K3 LA ASUNCION 1551
SHIP Spanish, 150 tons
LOCATION Near Lisbon, Portugal
ROUTE Caribbean to Spain
CARGO Gold and silver

4 L3 LA PIEDAD 1551
SHIP Spanish, 200 tons
LOCATION Setúbal, Portugal
ROUTE Caribbean to Spain
CARGO Gold, silver, and pearls
Capt. Alonso Martin Escazeria

**5 K3 NUESTRA SENORA DE LA
CONCEPCION** 1551
SHIP Spanish, 120 tons
LOCATION Near Lisbon, Portugal
ROUTE Montecristi, Dominican Republic,
to Spain
CARGO Gold and silver

6 M5 SANTA LUCIA 1551
SHIP Spanish, 200 tons
LOCATION Arenas Gordas, Spain
ROUTE Puerto Plata, Dominican Republic,
to Spain
CARGO Gold and silver

7 M4 ANUNCIADA 1553
SHIP Spanish, 120 tons
LOCATION Chipiona, just north of Rota,
Spain
ROUTE Santiago de Cuba, Cuba, to Spain
CARGO Gold and silver
SALVAGE Some salvage at time of loss
Capt. Pedro Carrino

**8 K4 NUESTRA SENORA DE LA
CONCEPCION** 1553
SHIP Spanish, 200 tons
LOCATION Villanueva, Portugal
ROUTE Puerto Plata, Dominican Republic,
to Spain
CARGO Gold and silver

**9 C7 NUESTRA SENORA DE
GUADALUPE** 1554
SHIP Spanish, 120 tons
LOCATION São Jorge, Azores
ROUTE Santo Domingo, Dominican
Republic, to Spain
CARGO Gold and silver
SALVAGE Largely salvaged at time of loss
Ship attacked by the French

10 M5 SANTA CRUZ Jan 1555
SHIP Spanish
LOCATION Coast of Zahara de los Atunes, Spain, opposite Strait of Gibraltar
ROUTE Cartagena, Colombia, to Spain
CARGO Gold and silver
SALVAGE Most of cargo recovered at time of loss
Capt. Juan de Mondragon

11 K2 SANCT SALBADOR
1556
SHIP Spanish, 120 tons
LOCATION Coast of Portugal
ROUTE San Juan, Puerto Rico, to Spain
CARGO Gold and silver
Capt. Guillen de Lugo

12 K3 NUESTRA SENORA DE LA MERCEDES 1561
SHIP Spanish, 120 tons
LOCATION Cachopos Shoals, near Lisbon, Portugal
ROUTE Santo Domingo, Dominican Republic, to Spain
CARGO Gold and silver
Capt. Domingo de Jarano

13 K3 SAN JUAN 1564
SHIP Spanish, 250 tons
LOCATION Cachopos Shoals, 9 miles (15 km) from Lisbon, Portugal
ROUTE Veracruz, Mexico, to Spain
CARGO Gold and silver
Capt. Francisco Martin

14 L4 NUESTRA SENORA DE LA CONCEPCION 1566
SHIP Spanish, 120 tons
LOCATION Lagos, Portugal
ROUTE Santo Domingo, Dominican Republic, to Spain
CARGO Gold and silver
Capt. Francisco de Morales Carnacho

15 M4 SAN ANTON 1566
SHIP Spanish
LOCATION Port of Sanlúcar de Barrameda, Spain
ROUTE Santo Domingo, Dominican Republic, to Spain
CARGO Gold and silver
Capt. Benito Perez Carrasco

16 M5 SAN ANTONIO 1566
SHIP Spanish, 120 tons
LOCATION Near Arenas Gordas, 21 miles (34 km) north of Cadiz, Spain
ROUTE Puerto Rico to Spain
CARGO Gold and silver
Capt. Juan Arze

17 D8 LA CONCEPCION
1567
SHIP Spanish, 120 tons
LOCATION Near Point Bretanha, São Miguel, Azores
ROUTE Havana, Cuba, to Spain
CARGO Gold and silver
SALVAGE Partly salvaged at time of loss
Capt. Luis de Alcala

18 D8 GUALUA WRECK
Nov 2, 1579
SHIP Spanish
LOCATION Gualua, 6 miles (9.5 km) from Angra do Heroismo, Terceira, Azores
ROUTE Caribbean to Spain
CARGO Treasure
SALVAGE Some cannons raised, but treasure was jettisoned before ship wrecked

19 D7 NUESTRA SENORA DE LA CONCEPCION 1586
SHIP Spanish, 600 tons
LOCATION Terceira, Azores
ROUTE Veracruz, Mexico, to Spain
CARGO Gold and silver
SALVAGE Guns and part of the treasure were recovered the following year
Capt. Martin de Vittoria

20 D8 NUESTRA SENORA DE LOS REMEDIOS 1586
SHIP Spanish, 120 tons
LOCATION Angra do Heroismo, Terceira, Azores
ROUTE Santo Domingo, Dominican Republic, to Spain
CARGO Specie, leathers, and ginger
SALVAGE Salvaged at time of loss
Capt. Francisco Ximenez

21 D8 SANTA MARIA DEL JESUS 1586
SHIP Spanish, 300 tons
LOCATION Angra do Heroismo, Terceira, Azores
ROUTE Veracruz, Mexico, to Spain
CARGO Gold and silver
Capt. Antonio Jorge

22 K4 SAN JUAN 1587
SHIP Spanish, 150 tons
LOCATION Villanueva, Portugal
ROUTE Margarita Island, Venezuela, to Spain
CARGO Gold, silver, and pearls
Capt. Gonzalo Milanes

23 M4 SAN PEDRO 1587
SHIP Spanish
LOCATION Bar of Sanlúcar de Barrameda, Spain
ROUTE Havana, Cuba, to Spain
Cargo Gold and silver
SALVAGE Treasure salvaged

24 M4 SANTA MARIA MADALENA
1587
SHIP Spanish, 300 tons
LOCATION Bar of Sanlúcar de Barrameda, Spain
ROUTE Havana, Cuba, to Spain
CARGO Gold and silver
SALVAGE Treasure salvaged
Capt. Francisco Romero

25 C7 SANTIAGO 1587
SHIP Portuguese East Indiaman
LOCATION Terceira, Azores
ROUTE Melaka, Malaysia, to Portugal
CARGO Jewels, porcelain, and gold

26 M4 TRINIDAD 1587
SHIP Spanish
LOCATION Bar of Sanlúcar de Barrameda, Spain
ROUTE Havana, Cuba, to Spain
CARGO Gold and silver
SALVAGE Treasure salvaged

27 C8 LA TRINIDAD 1589
SHIP Spanish, 350 tons
LOCATION Off south shore of Terceira, Azores
ROUTE Veracruz, Mexico, to Spain
CARGO Treasure
Capt. Martin Monte Bernardo

28 C8 NUESTRA SENORA DE GUIA 1589
SHIP Spanish, 230 tons
LOCATION South of Terceira, Azores
ROUTE Veracruz, Mexico, to Spain
CARGO Treasure
Capt. Francisco Perez Granillo. Ship sunk by English corsairs who were probably part of the Duke of Cumberland's expedition.

29 K3 NUESTRA SENORA DEL ROSARIO 1589
SHIP Spanish, 120 tons
LOCATION Cape Espichel, Portugal
ROUTE Puerto Rico to Spain
CARGO Gold and silver
Capt. Asencio de Vedos

30 C7 SAN CRISTOBAL 1589
SHIP Spanish, 350 tons
LOCATION Off Terceira, Azores
ROUTE Veracruz, Mexico, to Spain
CARGO Treasure
Capt. Francisco Bernal

31 A7 ASCENSION 1591
SHIP Spanish, ship of Seville
LOCATION Off Flores, Azores
ROUTE Havana, Cuba, to Spain
CARGO Gold and silver
Ship sank during fight with the Revenge

32 D7 ESPIRITU SANTO 1591
SHIP Spanish, 150 tons
LOCATION North side of Terceira, Azores
ROUTE Veracruz, Mexico, to Spain
CARGO Treasure
Capt. Pedro Milanes de Mendoza

33 C8 NUESTRA SENORA DEL JUNCAL 1591
SHIP Spanish, 500 tons
LOCATION Near Pico, Azores
ROUTE Cartagena, Colombia, to Spain
CARGO Treasure
Capt. Gaspar Nunez

34 D7 NUESTRA SENORA DEL ROSARIO 1591
SHIP Spanish, 350 tons
LOCATION Terceira, Azores
ROUTE Cartagena, Colombia, to Spain
CARGO Treasure
Capt. Tomas Gallardo

35 E8 SAN BARTOLOME 1591
SHIP Spanish, 200 tons
LOCATION Near Vila Franca do Campo, São Miguel, Azores
ROUTE Veracruz, Mexico, to Spain
CARGO Treasure
Capt. Pedro Martin

36 D7 SAN JUAN 1591
SHIP Spanish, 200 tons
LOCATION Off Terceira, Azores
ROUTE Veracruz, Mexico, to Spain
CARGO Treasure
Capt. Agustin de Paz. Ship attacked by English corsairs.

37 A7 SAN JUAN BAUTISTA
1591
SHIP Spanish, 400 tons
LOCATION Off Flores, Azores
ROUTE Cartagena, Colombia, to Spain
CARGO Treasure
Capt. Rodrigo Gonzalez

38 D8 SAN SALVADOR 1591
SHIP Spanish, 600 tons
LOCATION Near Terceira, Azores
ROUTE Veracruz, Mexico, to Spain
CARGO Treasure
Capt. Juan de Lambarri

39 A7 SANTA CATALINA 1591
SHIP Spanish, 450 tons
LOCATION Off Flores, Azores
ROUTE Cartagena, Colombia, to Spain
CARGO Treasure
Capt. Hernando Guillen

40 C7 SANTA MARIA DE BEGONIA
1591
SHIP Spanish, 200 tons
LOCATION Off Faial, Azores
ROUTE Cartagena, Colombia, to Spain
CARGO Treasure
Capt. Pedro de Fontiduerias

41 C7 SANTA MARIA DEL PUERTO
1591
SHIP Spanish, 300 tons
LOCATION 6 miles (9.5 km) from port of Terceira, Azores
ROUTE Veracruz, Mexico, to Spain
CARGO Treasure
Capt. Melchior Martin

42 C7 LA MADALENA Sept 3, 1591
SHIP Spanish, 650 tons
LOCATION Off Graciosa, Azores
ROUTE Cartagena, Colombia, to Spain
CARGO Treasure
Capt. Antonio Jorge

43 L5 SANTA ANA 1593
SHIP Spanish, 100 tons
LOCATION Lagos, Portugal
ROUTE Honduras to Spain
CARGO Gold and silver
SALVAGE Largely salvaged at time of loss
Capt. Juan Ximenez

44 M5 TOBIE Oct 19, 1593
SHIP English merchant ship
LOCATION 12 miles (19 km) south of Cape Spartel, Morocco
ROUTE UK to Livorno, Italy, Zákinthos, Greece, and Patras, Greece
CARGO Specie, tin, wool, gold, and pearls
SALVAGE Some salvage at time of loss
See pp. 34–35

45 C8 LAS CINQUE CHAGAS
June 23, 1594
SHIP Portuguese East Indiaman
LOCATION 18 miles (29 km) south of Faial, Azores
ROUTE East Indies to Portugal
CARGO Personal jewelry and cargo valued at 2 million ducats
See pp. 64–65

46 L4 LA CONCEPCION 1595
SHIP Spanish, 100 tons
LOCATION Near Ayamonte, Spain
ROUTE Santo Domingo, Dominican Republic, to Spain
CARGO Gold and silver
Ship wrecked while fleeing from the English

47 L5 SAN FRANCISCO 1596
SHIP Spanish, 100 tons
LOCATION Algarve, Portugal
ROUTE Santo Domingo, Dominican Republic, to Spain
CARGO Gold and silver
Capt. Francisco Marquez

48 M4 SANTA MARIA DEL JESUS 1596
SHIP Spanish, 140 tons
LOCATION Bar of Sanlúcar de Barrameda, Spain
ROUTE Santo Domingo, Dominican Republic, to Spain
CARGO Gold and silver

49 M5 PHILIP June 21, 1596
SHIP Spanish
LOCATION Mouth of Cadiz Bay, towards Puente de Suaco, Spain
ROUTE Havana, Cuba, to Spain
CARGO Gold and silver
Ship fired itself during battle

50 K3 SHIP OF AYRES DE SALDANNA 1597
SHIP Portuguese
LOCATION Lisbon, Portugal
CARGO Specie

51 L5 NUESTRA SENORA DEL ROSARIO 1600
SHIP Spanish, 500 tons
LOCATION Faro, Portugal
ROUTE Caribbean to Spain
CARGO Gold and silver
SALVAGE Largely salvaged at time of loss

52 E8 SANTA ANA MARIA
1600
SHIP Spanish, 700 tons
LOCATION São Miguel, Azores
ROUTE Cartagena, Colombia, to Spain
CARGO Treasure
SALVAGE Salvaged at time of loss
Capt. Fermin de Iturnia

53 E8 NUESTRA SENORA DE LOS REYES 1604
SHIP Spanish, 180 tons
LOCATION São Miguel, Azores
ROUTE Havana, Cuba, to Spain
CARGO Treasure
SALVAGE Salvaged at time of loss

54 M4 NUESTRA SENORA DEL ROSARIO 1605
SHIP Spanish, 450 tons
LOCATION Bar of Sanlúcar de Barrameda, Spain
ROUTE Honduras to Spain
CARGO Gold and silver
Capt. Santiago de Arrieta

55 N5 SAN ANTONIO 1609
SHIP Spanish, 200 tons
LOCATION Beach of Jetares, Gibraltar
ROUTE Santo Domingo, Dominican Republic, to Spain
CARGO Gold and silver
Capt. Goncalo de la Rocha

56 K2 NUESTRA SENORA DE AYUDA 1610
SHIP Spanish, 120 tons
LOCATION Cape Mondego, Portugal
ROUTE Cuba to Spain
CARGO Gold and silver
SALVAGE Partly salvaged
Capt. Lucas Correa

57 K3 NUESTRA SENORA DE GRACIA 1610
SHIP Spanish, 100 tons
LOCATION Bar of Setúbal, Portugal
ROUTE Santo Domingo, Dominican Republic, to Spain
CARGO Gold and silver
SALVAGE Some salvage at time of loss
Capt. Sebastian Leyton

58 M4 SAN PEDRO Y LAS ANGUSTIAS 1612
SHIP Spanish, 150 tons
LOCATION Coast of Carbonero, 9 miles (15 km) from Sanlúcar de Barrameda, Spain
ROUTE Puerto Rico to Spain
CARGO Gold and silver
Capt. Francisco de Uncibay

59 K4 LA ENCARNACION 1614
SHIP Spanish, 150 tons
LOCATION Off Cape of Sines, Portugal
ROUTE Santo Domingo, Dominican Republic, to Spain
CARGO Gold and silver
SALVAGE Salvaged at time of loss
Capt. Diego de Vales Ravelo

60 B7 NOSSA SENHORA DA LUZ 1615
SHIP Portuguese East Indiaman
LOCATION Off Faial, Azores
ROUTE India to Portugal
CARGO Jewels, porcelain, and gold

61 M5 LA CARIDAD 1616
SHIP Spanish, 350 tons
LOCATION Chipiona, just north of Rota, Spain
ROUTE Honduras to Spain
CARGO Gold and silver
Capt. Francisco Monte Manzera

62 K3 LAS ANGUSTIAS 1618
SHIP Spanish
LOCATION Lisbon, Portugal
ROUTE Veracruz, Mexico, to Spain
CARGO Gold and silver
Capt. Pedro Diaz Cordero

63 K3 NOSSA SENHORA DA CONCEICAO Oct 1621
SHIP Portuguese East Indiaman
LOCATION In sight of Berlenga island, north of Lisbon, Portugal
ROUTE Goa, India, to Lisbon, Portugal
CARGO Precious stones, gold, and porcelain
Ship burned after conflict with Algerian pirates

64 M5 SAN JUAN BAUTISTA 1623
SHIP Spanish, 600 tons
LOCATION Las Puercas, Cadiz Bay, Spain
ROUTE Havana, Cuba, to Spain
CARGO Gold and silver
Capitana of the fleet of Juan de Benavides Bazan. Capt. Luis Ortiz.

65 K3 FRANCISCO XAVIER Oct 23, 1625
SHIP Portuguese East Indiaman
LOCATION Entrance to Tagus River, Cachopos Shoals, near Lisbon, Portugal
ROUTE India to Portugal
CARGO Jewels and gold
SALVAGE Some salvage at time of loss

66 M4 NUESTRA SENORA DE LA ENCARNACION 1626
SHIP Spanish, 300 tons
LOCATION Sanlúcar de Barrameda, Spain
ROUTE Santo Domingo, Dominican Republic, to Spain
CARGO Gold and silver

67 M4 LA VIZCAINA GRANDE 1629
SHIP Spanish
LOCATION Cazuela Rock, bar of Sanlúcar de Barrameda, Spain
ROUTE Havana, Cuba, to Spain
CARGO Gold and silver

68 K3 SAO IGNACIO 1630
SHIP Portuguese East Indiaman
LOCATION Bar of Tagus River, Portugal
ROUTE Goa, India, to Lisbon, Portugal
CARGO Jewels, gold, and porcelain

69 L4 SAN LUIS Y LA CANDELARIA 1638
SHIP Spanish frigate
LOCATION Tavira, east of Faro, Portugal
CARGO Specie

70 N5 NUESTRA SENORA DE LA CONCEPCION 1648
SHIP Spanish, 100 tons
LOCATION Gibraltar
ROUTE Maracaibo, Venezuela, to Spain
CARGO Gold and silver
SALVAGE Most of the valuables were removed before the ship sank

71 K3 LISBON ROCK WRECK Aug 19, 1650
SHIP Portuguese
LOCATION Lisbon Rock, north of Tagus River, Portugal
CARGO Silver plate valued at £100,000 sterling
Ship sunk by the Constant Warwick

72 M5 SHIP OF JOHN RODRIQUES CALDRON 1656
SHIP Spanish
LOCATION Cadiz Bay, Spain
ROUTE Havana, Cuba, to Spain
CARGO Gold and silver
Ship lost in battle with the English fleet of Capt. Richard Stayner

73 M5 SAN FRANCISCO JAVIER 1656
SHIP Spanish Admiral
LOCATION On shore of Cadiz Bay, Spain
ROUTE Caribbean to Spain
CARGO 600,000 pieces of eight
Ship sunk by the fleet of Capt. Richard Stayner in action at Cadiz Bay, Spain

74 M5 SPANISH VICE ADMIRAL 1656
SHIP Spanish Vice Admiral
LOCATION Within 12 miles (19 km) of Cadiz, Spain
ROUTE Havana, Cuba, to Spain
CARGO 600,000 pieces of eight and the personal fortune of the Marquis de Badex
Ship sunk in the engagement with the English fleet of Capt. Richard Stayner

75 M5 SAN BERNANDO 1660
SHIP Spanish
LOCATION Rota, Spain
ROUTE Havana, Cuba, to Spain
CARGO Gold and silver

76 M5 KING SALAMON 1664
SHIP Dutch
LOCATION Cadiz Bay, Spain
ROUTE Netherlands to Izmir, Turkey
CARGO Large quantity of specie

77 K3 JULES Apr 5, 1673
SHIP Portuguese
LOCATION Cachopos Shoals, near Lisbon, Portugal
ROUTE India to Portugal
CARGO Amber, pearls, and spices, belonging to François Caron

78 M5 SPANISH CAPITANA 1684
SHIP Spanish, 72 brass guns
LOCATION Strait of Gibraltar
ROUTE Havana, Cuba, to Spain
CARGO Gold and silver

79 M5 THOLEN 1687
SHIP Dutch
LOCATION 70 miles (113 km) from Strait of Gibraltar, towards Cadiz, Spain
CARGO Gold

80 K3 SANTA TERESA 1704
SHIP Spanish
LOCATION Bar of Tagus River, Portugal
ROUTE Havana, Cuba, to Spain
CARGO Specie

81 K3 TRINIDAD 1706
SHIP Portuguese
LOCATION Reef off Lisbon harbour, Portugal
ROUTE Lisbon, Portugal, to Goa, India
CARGO Specie

82 M5 SHIP OF SEBASTIAN DE CABRERA, 1707–1708
SHIP Spanish
LOCATION Sanlúcar de Barrameda, Spain
ROUTE Havana, Cuba, to Spain
CARGO Gold and silver

83 K1 PORTUGUESE SHIP Jan 20, 1708
SHIP Portuguese East Indiaman
LOCATION Near Arcos de Vale de Vez, Portugal
ROUTE Macao to Portugal
CARGO Porcelain and gold

84 A7 HILVERSBEEK June 28, 1741
SHIP Dutch East Indiaman, 850 tons
LOCATION Off Flores, Azores
ROUTE Jakarta, Java, to Netherlands
CARGO Porcelain

85 B7 CONCORDIA May 24, 1781
SHIP Dutch East Indiaman
LOCATION Azores
ROUTE Jakarta, Java, to Netherlands
CARGO Porcelain

86 K3 SAN PEDRO ALCANTARA Feb 2, 1786
SHIP Spanish
LOCATION Peniche Bay, north of Tagus River, Portugal
ROUTE Callao, Peru, to Spain
CARGO Immense quantity of gold and silver valued in excess of 7 million pesos
SALVAGE Largely salvaged at time of loss

87 K2 APOLLO Apr 1, 1804
SHIP British warship, 5th rate, 956 tons
LOCATION 9 miles (15 km) north of Cape Mondego, Portugal, 600 feet (180 meters) from the shore, 40.22N
ROUTE Queenstown, Ireland, to West Indies
CARGO Specie
Ship convoying 60 merchant ships, many of which were also lost on the same reef. Deplorable loss of lives and property.

88 L5 MERCEDES Oct 5, 1804
SHIP Spanish galleon
LOCATION Approximately 35 miles (56 km) SW of Cape Santa Maria, Portugal
ROUTE Montevideo, Uruguay, to Cadiz, Spain
CARGO 871,000 silver pesos, plus gold, silver plate, and jewels
SALVAGE Recent salvage attempt might have located wreck

89 M5 BLACK JOKE 1828
SHIP Pirate ship
LOCATION Cadiz, Spain
CARGO Treasure
Ship of pirate Benito de Soto

90 K1 TIBER Feb 21, 1847
SHIP British, P & O Line
LOCATION Vila de Cupa, north of Oporto, Portugal
ROUTE Gibraltar to UK
CARGO Specie

91 G3 CANDACE 1858
SHIP British schooner, African Steam Company
LOCATION 38.38N 15.57W
ROUTE West Africa to UK
CARGO Gold

92 L7 AMAZON Jan 1, 1868
SHIP British, Mersey Steamship Company
LOCATION Off Azemmour, Morocco
ROUTE London, England, to El Jadida, Morocco
CARGO Specie
SALVAGE Some salvage at time of loss

93 K4 MILTON June 15, 1911
SHIP British, Lamport & Holt, 2,679 tons
LOCATION Near Cape Espichel, Portugal
ROUTE London, England, to Santos, Brazil
CARGO Specie

94 M5 DELHI Dec 13, 1911
SHIP British, P & O Line, 8,090 tons
LOCATION 2 miles (3 km) off Cape Spartel, Morocco
ROUTE UK to India
CARGO Gold and silver bullion valued at £295,925 sterling
SALVAGE Salvaged at time of loss
Duke and Duchess of Fife, Scotland, were among the passengers

95 H1 CALIFORNIA July 11, 1943
SHIP British, Anchor Line, 16,792 tons
LOCATION 41.15N 15.24W
ROUTE Freetown, Sierra Leone, to Scotland
CARGO 7 boxes of diamonds valued at £72,250 sterling

THE MEDITERRANEAN

The map for these listings is on pp. 142–143.

● No known salvage
■ Some salvage history known

1 N6 CAPE GELIDONYA WRECK
1200 BC
SHIP Bronze age
LOCATION South coast of Turkey
CARGO Bronze ingots
SALVAGE Recently found and excavated

2 M6 ANATOLIA WRECK BC
LOCATION Near Bodrum, Turkey,
300 feet (90 meters) deep
CARGO Statue of African boy
SALVAGE Discovered in 1962

3 L5 BAY OF MARATHON WRECK BC
SHIP Greek
LOCATION Bay of Marathon, Greece
CARGO Statue of youth
SALVAGE Recovered in 1925

4 L5 CAPE ARTEMISIUM WRECK
Possibly BC
SHIP Greek
LOCATION Cape Artemisium, north end of
island of Euboea, Greece
CARGO Bronze statue of jockey boy
SALVAGE Found in 1927, but wreck now
lost again

5 K5 GULF OF CORINTH WRECK BC
SHIP Greek
LOCATION Gulf of Corinth, Greece
CARGO Statue of Zeus
SALVAGE Recovered in 1809

6 I5 LIPARI WRECK BC
SHIP Greek
LOCATION Lipari Island, Italy
CARGO Bronze statues
SALVAGE Recoveries made in 1927, and
further salvage in 1969

7 J5 LYSIPPOS WRECK BC
SHIP Greek
LOCATION Off Italy
CARGO Sculptures
Relics in J. Paul Getty Museum, California, US

8 H6 MAHDIA WRECK BC
SHIP Greek
LOCATION Off Mahdia, Tunisia, 3 miles
(5 km) from shore
ROUTE Greece to Italy
CARGO 60 marble columns and many
statues
SALVAGE Found and worked between 1907
and 1913
Artifacts in El Alaoui Museum, Tunis, Tunisia

9 M5 MARMARIS BC
SHIP Greek
LOCATION Turkey
CARGO Statue of Demeter
SALVAGE Found in 1953

10 H4 PIOMBINO WRECK BC
SHIP Greek
LOCATION Tuscany, Italy
CARGO Statue of Apollo
SALVAGE Discovered in 1832

11 M6 RHODES WRECK BC
SHIP Greek
LOCATION Rhodes, Greece
CARGO Statue of Aphrodite
SALVAGE Salvaged in 1929

12 L5 SKIATHOS WRECK BC
SHIP Greek
LOCATION Skiathos, Greece
CARGO Statues of gods
SALVAGE Recently excavated

13 H4 GIGLIO WRECK 750–500 BC
SHIP Etruscan
LOCATION Giglio Island, Italy
CARGO Helmets, pottery, and musical
instruments
SALVAGE Excavated by team from Oxford,
England, led by Mensun Bound

14 G3 GRAND CONGLUE WRECK
200–100 BC
SHIP Roman cargo ship of Marcus Sextus
LOCATION Small island SW of Marseille,
France
CARGO Amphorae
SALVAGE Worked by Cousteau and Dumas

15 H4 SPARGI WRECK 170–100 BC
SHIP Greek
LOCATION Between Corsica, France, and
Sardinia, Italy, in 60 feet (18 meters) water
CARGO Amphorae and plates
SALVAGE Partly salvaged

16 L6 ANTIKYTHERA WRECK
120–82 BC
SHIP Roman
LOCATION Midway between Kithira,
Greece, and the tip of Crete, Greece
ROUTE Greece to Rome, Italy
CARGO Statues, glass bowls, and gold
brooches
SALVAGE Recoveries made in early 1900s,
when wreck discovered by sponge divers
See pp. 14–15

17 I6 SHIP OF ST. PAUL 59–60
SHIP Ponto, 300 tons
LOCATION Coast of Malta
ROUTE Caesarea, Israel, to Rome, Italy, via
Myra, Turkey
CARGO Valuable artifacts

18 J5 SAN PIETRO WRECK 200–250
SHIP Roman
LOCATION SE of Taranto, Italy
ROUTE Asia Minor to Rome, Italy
CARGO Marble sarcophagi in unfinished state

19 M6 YASSI ADA WRECK 625
SHIP Byzantine
LOCATION 12 miles (19 km) west of
Bodrum, Turkey
CARGO Valuable artifacts
SALVAGE Excavated by George Bass

20 M6 SERCE LIMANI WRECK
c. 1000
SHIP Byzantine merchantman
LOCATION South coast of Turkey, opposite
Rhodes, Greece
CARGO Gold and silver jewelry, swords,
lances, javelins, and sword blade with
bronze and decorated hilt
SALVAGE Recently salvaged
See pp. 16–17

21 L5 PELAGOS NISOS WRECK
12th century
SHIP 100 tons
LOCATION Sporades, Greece
CARGO 1,200 pieces of colored pottery
SALVAGE Recently excavated

22 I3 KING RICHARD Dec 1, 1192
SHIP English
LOCATION Near head of Adriatic Sea,
coast of Istra, Croatia
ROUTE From Syria
CARGO Valuable personal possessions

23 H5 SHIRKI ROCKS WRECK
13th century
LOCATION Shirki Rocks, Sicily, Italy
CARGO Bronze statues
SALVAGE Recovered in 1960

**24 I4 SHIP OF CHARLES OF
SALERNOS June 5, 1284**
SHIP Flagship
LOCATION Gulf of Naples, Italy
CARGO Valuables

25 N8 CATALAN SHIPS 1411
SHIP Catalan ships
LOCATION Alexandria, Egypt
ROUTE Catalan coast, Spain, to Alexandria,
Egypt
CARGO Cargo valued at 80,000 ducats,
probably including coral

26 N8 ABU QIR WRECK 1415
SHIP Catalan cog
LOCATION Off Abu Qîr, Egypt
ROUTE Catalan coast, Spain, to Damyat,
Egypt
CARGO Saffron, cloth, olive oil, almonds,
and coral

27 I3 SHIP OF NICOLO BARBARIGO
Dec 1417
SHIP Venetian galley
LOCATION Ulbo Island, Italy
ROUTE Alexandria, Egypt, to Venice, Italy
CARGO Porcelain, pearls, precious stones,
spices, and general Middle Eastern cargo
See pp. 32–33

28 K6 ANN Dec 23, 1446
SHIP English cog
LOCATION Modon, south Greece
ROUTE Jaffa, Israel, to England
CARGO Middle Eastern produce, including
pearls, precious stones, wool, and tin
*Ship returning to England having transported
160 pilgrims from England to Jaffa, Israel.
Crew of 37 perished.*

29 M4 VENETIAN SHIP 1452
SHIP Venetian
LOCATION Near Istanbul, Turkey
CARGO Valuables

30 M8 SAN MICHELE 1479
SHIP Italian, ship of Naples
LOCATION Alexandria, Egypt
CARGO Valuables

31 I6 SHIP OF JUAN ANDREA DORIA
1559
SHIP Spanish galera
LOCATION Cape Passero, Sicily, Italy
CARGO Specie

**32 D6 LA TORRE DE VELEZ
MALAGA WRECKS 1562**
SHIP Spanish galleys
LOCATION 36.43N 4.23W
CARGO 80,000 ducats of treasure

33 E6 ESPIRITU SANCTO 1563
SHIP Spanish, 120 tons
LOCATION Cape Palos, near Cartagena, Spain
ROUTE Caribbean to Spain
CARGO Gold and silver

34 F3 RHONE WRECK I 1564
SHIP French
LOCATION Near Arles, France
ROUTE Arles, France, to Paris, France
CARGO Treasures from church of Notre
Dame, Paris, France
SALVAGE Attempted salvage in 1933
without success

35 H3 GALLEY Apr 1582
SHIP Spanish galley
LOCATION Between Barcelona, Spain, and
Genoa, Italy
ROUTE Barcelona, Spain, to Genoa, Italy
CARGO 56 cases of reals, plus a whole case
of escudos, and other gold pieces

**36 G4 COMPAGNO COMPAGNI
WRECK 1592**
SHIP Spanish galley
LOCATION Mediterranean
ROUTE Barcelona, Spain, to Genoa, Italy
CARGO 600,000 to 800,000 crowns and
chests of coins that were carried by the
entire company

37 I3 SAETTIA VIDALA
Feb 1592
SHIP Venetian saettia
LOCATION In a cove, island of Cherso,
Croatia
ROUTE From Venice, Italy
CARGO Merchandise, jewels, and gold
valued at 30,000 ducats
SALVAGE Some looting
Ship plundered by pirates

38 M4 MARTINENGA 1594
SHIP Venetian
LOCATION Istanbul, Turkey
ROUTE Istanbul, Turkey, to Venice, Italy
CARGO Gold, silver, and specie

39 G5 SHIP OF FRANCOIS LULLIER
17th century
SHIP French
LOCATION Mediterranean
ROUTE Egypt to France
CARGO Egyptian curiosities

40 L6 LA COMETE 17th century
SHIP French privateer ship
LOCATION Crete, Greece
CARGO Gold and silver
Ship sailed by the Knights of St. John of Malta

41 M8 PERASTANA 1605
SHIP Venetian
LOCATION Alexandria, Egypt
CARGO Gold

42 L6 MORESINA 1606
SHIP Venetian
LOCATION Milos, Greece
ROUTE Cyprus to Venice, Italy
CARGO Diamonds

43 O6 PIRATE BERTONI 1607
SHIP Pirate ship
LOCATION Saline, Cyprus
CARGO Valuables
Ship sunk while attacking Venetian ship

44 K6 BALBI 1608
SHIP Venetian
LOCATION Port of Pylos, Greece
CARGO Valuables
Ship captured by pirates

45 H6 SHIP OF CAPTAIN BINNY 1608
SHIP Pirate ship
LOCATION Off Carthage, Tunisia
CARGO Pirate loot
*Ship lost in a storm. Capt. Binny was an
associate of Ward.*

46 O7 SALVETTA Jan 1609
SHIP Venetian
LOCATION Outside Acre, Israel
CARGO Valuables
Ship captured by pirates, then lost

47 L6 REINERA E SODERINA 1609
SHIP Venetian
LOCATION Off Kithira, Greece
CARGO Pirate loot
See pp. 66–67

48 H6 TUNIS WRECKS 1609
SHIP Pirate ships
LOCATION Tunis, Tunisia
CARGO Pirate loot
Ship burned in Tunis harbor, Tunisia

49 K6 VENIER 1609
SHIP Venetian
LOCATION Strivadi, Greece
CARGO Silver

50 K5 SANTA MAURA WRECK 1610
LOCATION Entrance to Santa Maura harbor, near Corfu, Greece
CARGO Specie
SALVAGE Some plundering

51 K5 GUIDOTTA E SIMONA 1612
SHIP Venetian
LOCATION Outside Zákinthos, Greece
ROUTE Alexandria, Egypt, to Venice, Italy
CARGO Precious stones and gold
Attacked by Bertoni from Barbary. Crew and cargo all lost. Capt. Alvise di Girolamo.

52 F4 DUKE DORIA'S GOLD 1641
LOCATION Off Perpignan, France
CARGO Gold valued at £1 million sterling
Gold cargo was jettisoned into the sea by Duke Doria shortly before his capture by Marshal De Breze

53 F5 MINORCA WRECKS 1682
SHIP Dutch
LOCATION Minorca, Balearic Islands
CARGO Silver
SALVAGE Some salvage at time of loss

54 H3 ST. GEORGE 1757
SHIP Privateer belonging to Fortunatus Wright of Liverpool, England
LOCATION Off Livorno, Italy, 43.33N 10.20E
CARGO Specie

55 N8 ORIENT Aug 1798
SHIP French warship
LOCATION Abu Qîr Bay, Egypt
CARGO Treasure
SALVAGE Many attempts at salvage
See pp. 82–83

56 F3 RHONE WRECK II c. 1800
LOCATION Arles, France
ROUTE Arles, France, to Paris, France
CARGO Roman statuary and relics collected by Napoleon
SALVAGE Attempted salvage in 1933 without success

57 L6 MENTOR Sept 1802
SHIP British brig
LOCATION St. Nicholas Bay, Kithira harbor, Greece
ROUTE Greece to UK
CARGO Elgin Marbles, 14 pieces of the Parthenon frieze, 4 pieces from the Temple of Athena Nike, and an ancient throne
SALVAGE Mainly salvaged at time of loss
See pp. 88–89

58 H4 POLLUCE 1806
SHIP Spanish sailing ship
LOCATION Portolongone Bay, island of Elba, Italy
ROUTE Italy to France
CARGO Treasures from Royal Palace of King Ferdinand IV of Naples and Sicily, Italy
Treasures supposedly include a complete gold carriage

59 H6 HMS ATHENIENNE Oct 20, 1806
SHIP British warship
LOCATION Keith's reef, off the Esquerques, 80 miles (130 km) west of Sicily, Italy, near Tunis, Tunisia
ROUTE Gibraltar to Malta
CARGO 40,000 pieces of eight and English coins
SALVAGE Salvaged by Robert Stenuit

60 F4 JUSTINA 1822
SHIP Spanish
LOCATION Port of Tarragona, Spain
CARGO Specie

61 K6 NAVARINO WRECK 1827
SHIP Flagship of Turkish fleet
LOCATION Pilos, Greece
CARGO Gold
SALVAGE Many attempts at salvage

62 N3 BLACK PRINCE Nov 14, 1854
SHIP British transport
LOCATION Black Sea, near Sevastopol', Ukraine
ROUTE UK to Crimea, Ukraine
CARGO Gold valued at £500,000 sterling
SALVAGE Attempted in 1899 but results unknown. Many plans for salvage.
Gold possibly unloaded at Istanbul, Turkey

63 J3 BOMBAY Nov 9, 1859
SHIP Austrian
LOCATION Croatia
ROUTE Constantino, Spain, to Trieste, Italy
CARGO Specie
SALVAGE Some salvage at time of loss

64 O7 EUROPA Nov 11, 1863
SHIP Austrian
LOCATION Lanarca, Cyprus
ROUTE Turkey to Cyprus
CARGO Specie
SALVAGE Salvaged at time of loss

65 K6 ITALIA UNA Sept 20, 1865
SHIP Russian
LOCATION 37.47N 20.54E
ROUTE Zákinthos, Greece, to Kalamai, Greece
CARGO Specie valued at US $60,000

66 H4 TASMANIA Mar 17, 1887
SHIP British, P & O Line, 4,488 tons
LOCATION Off Point Roccapina, coast of Corsica, France
ROUTE Bombay, India, to London, England, via Port Said, Egypt, and Marseille, France
CARGO Jewelry in bullion room
SALVAGE Some salvage at time of loss

67 I7 HMS VICTORIA June 22, 1893
SHIP British Navy, 10,470 tons
LOCATION 5 miles (8 km) off Tripoli, Libya
CARGO Army pay rumored to be on board
Ship collided with HMS Camperdown, *resulting in immense loss of life*

68 O7 MABROUK Jan 21, 1895
SHIP Turkish
LOCATION 6 miles (9.5 km) from Beirut, Lebanon
ROUTE Beirut, Lebanon, to Tel Aviv-Yafo, Israel
CARGO Gold valued at £75,000 sterling
Insurance fraud; unlikely that gold was on board

69 G3 MEUSE 1899
LOCATION Off Marseille, France
CARGO Gold
SALVAGE Partly salvaged

70 H5 ANCONA Nov 8, 1915
SHIP Italia Steamship Company, 8,210 tons
LOCATION Off Cape Carbonara, Sardinia, Italy
ROUTE Naples, Italy, to New York, US
CARGO 12 barrels of gold coins
SALVAGE Unsuccessful salvage attempt in 1990
Sunk by German U-boat 38, disguised as an Austrian U-boat – before Italy entered the First World War

71 N8 YASAKA MARU Dec 21, 1915
SHIP Japanese, Nippon Yusen, 10,932 tons
LOCATION 60 miles (96 km) off Port Said, Egypt
ROUTE London, England, to Japan
CARGO Gold sovereigns valued at £200,000 sterling
SALVAGE Some salvage at time of loss

72 M7 PERSIA Dec 30, 1915
SHIP British, P & O Line, 7,974 tons
LOCATION 71 miles (114 km) SE by S of Cape Martello, Crete, Greece
ROUTE London, England, to India, via Marseille, France
CARGO 400,000 oz (11,340 kg) silver bullion, specie, and diamonds

73 J6 MARERE Jan 18, 1916
SHIP British
LOCATION 236 miles (380 km) east of Malta
CARGO Bullion

74 G4 MIRA May 15, 1916
SHIP French, Société Générale de Transports Maritimes
LOCATION Mediterranean
CARGO Large quantity of gold

75 I6 RUPERRA June 20, 1916
SHIP 4,232 tons
LOCATION 20 miles (32 km) E by S from Pantelleria Island, Italy
ROUTE Africa to London, England
CARGO Gold
SALVAGE 1 box of gold removed before ship went down

76 K4 ARABIA Nov 6, 1916
SHIP British, P & O Line, 7,933 tons
LOCATION 35.56N 20.15E
ROUTE Australia to UK
CARGO Silver and jewels

77 J6 CALEDONIA Dec 4, 1916
SHIP British, Anchor Line, 9,223 tons
LOCATION 125 miles (200 km) E by S of Malta
ROUTE Aden, Yemen, to UK
CARGO Silver coins

78 J6 MINAS Feb 15, 1917
SHIP Italian steamship, 2,854 tons
LOCATION 160 miles (260 km) west of Akra Tainaron, Greece
ROUTE Naples, Italy, to Thessaloniki, Greece
CARGO Gold valued at £2 million sterling

79 H5 MOOLTAN July 26, 1917
SHIP British, P & O Line, 9,723 tons
LOCATION 53 miles (85 km) NNW half W of Cape Serrat, Tunisia, 37.56N 08.34E
ROUTE Fremantle, Australia, to Bombay, India, to UK
CARGO Gold

80 D6 NAMUR Oct 29, 1917
SHIP British, P & O Line, 6,701 tons
LOCATION 55 miles (88 km) E by S half S of Gibraltar, 36.05N 4.15W
ROUTE Pinang, Malaysia, to London, England, via Marseille, France
CARGO Gold

81 H4 ROMMEL'S TREASURE Sept 18, 1943
LOCATION 2 to 3 miles (3 to 5 km) offshore from Golo River, east coast of Corsica, France, in 22 fathoms water
CARGO Treasure, valued at £30 million sterling, looted from Bank of Italy
SALVAGE Apparently the French Government financed a search in 1949, but no significant results
Cargo jettisoned from launch

MADAGASCAR AND EAST AFRICA

The map for these listings is on p. 144.

● No known salvage
■ Some salvage history known

1 F5 SHIP OF RUI PEREIRA 1510
SHIP Portuguese
LOCATION Comoros
ROUTE Portugal to India
CARGO Specie

2 C9 GARCA 1559
SHIP Portuguese
LOCATION Off Vila de Joao Belo, Mozambique, 25.00S
ROUTE India to Portugal
CARGO Precious stones and porcelain

3 G6 SANTA MARIA DE BARCA 1559
SHIP Portuguese East Indiaman
LOCATION Off east coast of Madagascar, approximately 18.00S
ROUTE Cochin, India, to Lisbon, Portugal
CARGO Precious stones

4 C7 SAO PEDRO 1582
SHIP Portuguese East Indiaman
LOCATION Reef of Sofala, Mozambique
ROUTE Portugal to India
CARGO Gold and silver
SALVAGE Cargo transferred to the *Chagas*

5 D8 ST. IAGO 1585
SHIP Portuguese East Indiaman
LOCATION Bassas da India, between Madagascar and Africa
ROUTE Portugal to India
CARGO Gold and silver
SALVAGE Relocated by Klaar in 1977
Ship becalmed for 16 days off Guinea due to disagreement over whether to call at Mozambique or sail directly to Cochin, India

6 E6 SAN FRANCISCO DOS ANJOS 1591
SHIP Portuguese East Indiaman
LOCATION Off Mozambique, Mozambique
ROUTE India to Portugal
CARGO Jewels and porcelain

7 C9 PENELOPE Aug 1591
LOCATION Cape Corrontes, Mozambique
ROUTE UK to Far East
CARGO Gold and silver specie

8 C7 NOSSA SENHORA DO CASTELO 1599
SHIP Portuguese East Indiaman
LOCATION Reef of Sofala, Mozambique
ROUTE Portugal to India
CARGO Gold and silver

9 E6 SAO FELIPE 1604
SHIP Portuguese East Indiaman
LOCATION Angoche, Mozambique
ROUTE Portugal to India
CARGO Gold and silver

10 F6 SAO ANTONIO 1607
SHIP Portuguese East Indiaman
LOCATION Coast of Madagascar
CARGO Precious stones
Crew taken off ship by the Mauritius, *which also wrecked*

11 E6 ZIERIKZEE May 26, 1607
SHIP Dutch East Indiaman, 760 tons
LOCATION Off Mozambique, Mozambique
ROUTE Netherlands to Goa, India
CARGO Specie

12 E6 SAO FRANCISCO Sept 1, 1607
SHIP Portuguese East Indiaman
LOCATION Off Mozambique, Mozambique
ROUTE Portugal to India
CARGO Gold and silver
Capt. D. Francisco de Lima

13 E6 NOSSA SENHORA DA PALMA
May 26, 1609
SHIP Portuguese East Indiaman
LOCATION Angoche Islands, Mozambique
ROUTE Portugal to Far East
CARGO Gold and silver

14 F7 SAMARITAN 1615
SHIP English East Indiaman
LOCATION Madagascar
ROUTE UK to India
CARGO Specie
SALVAGE Largely salvaged at time of loss
Part of Middleton's expedition

15 F5 ANGAZIYA WRECK 1616
SHIP Portuguese East Indiaman
LOCATION Island of Angaziya, near
Mayotte, Comoros
ROUTE Portugal to India
CARGO Gold and silver

16 F5 SAN JULIAO 1616
SHIP Portuguese East Indiaman
LOCATION Comoros
ROUTE Portugal to India
CARGO Gold and silver
*Ship fought with 4 English ships and was
wrecked in the battle*

17 D2 SANTO AMARO Dec 10, 1620
SHIP Portuguese East Indiaman
LOCATION Entrance to Mombasa, Kenya
ROUTE Portugal to India
CARGO Gold and silver
Capt. Pedro de Morais Sarmento

18 E6 SANTA TEREZA July 20, 1622
SHIP Portuguese East Indiaman
LOCATION Near rocky islet on which stood
a fort, 1.5 miles (2.5 km) from bar of
Mozambique
ROUTE Portugal to Goa, India
CARGO Gold and silver
SALVAGE Some gold and silver saved at time
of loss; ship burned to prevent plundering
Ship ran aground on a shoal

19 E6 SAO CARLOS July 25, 1622
SHIP Portuguese East Indiaman
LOCATION On rocky inlet, near Fort Santo
Antonio, SW Mozambique
ROUTE Portugal to India
CARGO Gold and silver
SALVAGE Salvaged at time of loss
*Ship lost during engagement with Anglo–Dutch
fleet*

20 E6 SAO JOZEPH July 25, 1622
SHIP Portuguese East Indiaman, carrack
LOCATION Reefs of Mogincali, Mozambique
ROUTE Portugal to India
CARGO Gold and silver
SALVAGE Anglo–Dutch seized 68,553 reals
of eight. 40 chests had already been
removed by the Portuguese.

21 E5 SAO BRAZ Jan 24, 1624
SHIP Portuguese East Indiaman, pinnace
LOCATION Off Mozambique, Mozambique
ROUTE Portugal to India
CARGO Gold and silver

22 E5 SAO SIMAO Jan 24, 1624
SHIP Portuguese East Indiaman
LOCATION Off Mozambique, Mozambique
ROUTE Portugal to India
CARGO Gold and silver

23 E6 SANTA IZABEL Jan 28, 1624
SHIP Portuguese East Indiaman, carrack
LOCATION Monomocaia, Mozambique
ROUTE Portugal to Goa, India
CARGO Gold and silver
*Capt. D. Diego Castelo Branco died near
Mozambique and was succeeded by D. Joao
Coutinho*

24 D6 SANTIAGO 1629
SHIP Portuguese East Indiaman
LOCATION Rocks of Joao da Nova,
Primeira Isles
ROUTE Portugal to Goa, India
CARGO Gold and silver
Capt. Francisco de Sousa de Castro

25 F5 SAMARITAN 1635
SHIP English
LOCATION Comoros
CARGO Loot from rich Mogul ships,
including gold and silver
*Part of a privately sponsored privateering
venture, backed by Endymion Porter*

26 G9 KONING DAVID Mar 29, 1639
SHIP Dutch East Indiaman, 200 tons
LOCATION SE coast of Madagascar
ROUTE Netherlands to East Indies
CARGO Specie

27 E6 SAO BENTO Dec 27, 1642
SHIP Portuguese East Indiaman
LOCATION Off Mozambique, Mozambique
ROUTE Portugal to India
CARGO Gold and silver

28 E6 SANTO ANTONIO 1644
SHIP Portuguese East Indiaman
LOCATION Angoche, Mozambique
ROUTE Portugal to Goa, India
CARGO Gold and silver
Capt. Amador Lousado

29 D6 NOSSA SENHORA DO BOM
Sept 3, 1649
SHIP Portuguese East Indiaman
LOCATION Reefs of Mogincali, between
Angoche Islands and Mozambique,
Mozambique
ROUTE Portugal to Far East
CARGO Gold and silver

30 E6 SAO LOURENCO Sept 3, 1649
SHIP Portuguese East Indiaman
LOCATION Shoals of Mogincali,
Mozambique
ROUTE Lisbon, Portugal, to Goa, India
CARGO Gold and silver
*The mate of the vessel was hanged and the pilot
sentenced to 10 years in the galleys*

31 F9 TULP Dec 2, 1656
SHIP Dutch East Indiaman
LOCATION Off Madagascar
ROUTE Netherlands to Jakarta, Java
CARGO Specie

32 D6 SMYRNA MERCHANT 1660
SHIP English East Indiaman
LOCATION Island of Joao da Nova,
Primeira Isles
ROUTE London, England, to Madras,
India
CARGO Silver specie
SALVAGE 10 chests of silver saved
Survivors rescued by the Mayflower

33 D6 LOVE Nov 28, 1665
SHIP English East Indiaman
LOCATION 60 miles (96 km) from
Mozambique, Mozambique
ROUTE Al Mukha, Yemen, to UK
CARGO Specie
SALVAGE Specie valued at US $12,000 saved
Ship ran on ledge of rocks

34 G5 TAUREAU 1666
SHIP French East Indiaman
LOCATION North coast of Madagascar
CARGO Valuables

35 F9 SOLEIL D'ORIENT 1681
SHIP French East Indiaman
LOCATION Near Fort Dauphin, SE of
Madagascar
ROUTE Thailand to France
CARGO Valuable gold and silver artifacts
from King of Siam to King Louis XIV of
France
SALVAGE Recently searched for but not
found

36 F5 HERBERT July 3, 1690
SHIP English East Indiaman, 750 tons,
54 cannonsmounted
LOCATION Off Anjouan, Comoros
ROUTE UK to India
CARGO Silver specie and bars
Ship blew up during engagement with French

37 D3 SANTO ANTONIO DE TANAH
Oct 20, 1697
SHIP 50-gun frigate, built at Tanah Creek,
near Bassein, Burma, in 1681
LOCATION SE of fort at Mombasa, Kenya
CARGO Specie
SALVAGE Rediscovered by divers in early
1960s

38 F5 RUBY Apr 28, 1699
SHIP English East Indiaman
LOCATION Mayotte, Comoros, 12.47S
45.16E
ROUTE UK to Iran
CARGO 7 chests of silver reals and 11
chests of glassware

39 F9 DEGRAVE 1701
SHIP English East Indiaman, 700 tons
LOCATION South Madagascar
ROUTE India to UK
CARGO Precious stones

40 E6 LIAMPA June 7, 1705
SHIP English East Indiaman
LOCATION Near Mozambique,
Mozambique
ROUTE UK to Iran
CARGO Specie

41 E6 NOSSA SENHORA DA GUIA
Aug 10, 1719
SHIP Portuguese
LOCATION Angoche Islands, approximately
90 miles (145 km) from Mozambique,
Mozambique
ROUTE Portugal to Far East
CARGO Gold and silver

42 D8 SUSSEX 1738
SHIP English East Indiaman
LOCATION Mozambique Channel
ROUTE China to UK
CARGO Porcelain and 53 tons zinc
SALVAGE Some recovery of porcelain
shards. Ship recently located.

43 D6 BREDENHOF 1753
SHIP Dutch East Indiaman
LOCATION 120 miles (190 km) south of
Mozambique, Mozambique, (13 miles)
(21 km) from the coast
ROUTE Netherlands to Jakarta, Java
CARGO 29 chests of silver and 1 chest
of gold
SALVAGE Salvaged by Klaar and
Clackworthy
*Artifacts and bullion were sold at Christie's,
London*

44 H5 AURORA Jan 1770
SHIP English frigate
LOCATION NE Madagascar
ROUTE UK to India
CARGO Specie

45 F5 HUNTINGDON Apr 16, 1774
SHIP English East Indiaman
LOCATION Sands between Anjouan and
Saddle Island, Comoros
ROUTE China to UK
CARGO Porcelain

46 F9 ST. JOHN BAPTISTE 1777
SHIP French East Indiaman
LOCATION Star Bank, west coast of
Madagascar, just west of the southernmost
point of Madagascar
ROUTE France to India
CARGO Specie

47 F5 BRILLIANT Aug 28, 1782
SHIP English East Indiaman
LOCATION On a rock near Saddle Island,
SW of Anjouan, Comoros
ROUTE UK to India
CARGO Specie

48 E7 AURORE Feb 1790
SHIP French, 700 tons
LOCATION Mozambique Channel
ROUTE From Pondicherry, India, via
Mauritius
CARGO Specie

49 E7 WINTERTON Aug 20, 1792
SHIP English East Indiaman, 771 tons
LOCATION 63 miles (101 km) north of
St. Augustin's Bay, Madagascar, 6 miles
(9.5 km) from mainland
ROUTE UK to India
CARGO 75 chests of silver amounting to
261,000 oz (7,400 kg) , plus privately
shipped specie
SALVAGE Approximately half salvaged by
local fishermen

50 D3 JONAS 1857
SHIP French
LOCATION 10 miles (16 km) from bar of
Zanzibar, Tanzania
ROUTE Marseille, France, to Far East
CARGO Specie

51 G5 SALAZIE Nov 21, 1912
SHIP French, Messageries Maritimes,
4,147 tons
LOCATION Nosykomba Reefs, South
Antsiranana, Madagascar
ROUTE Marseille, France, to Mauritius
CARGO Specie

52 G7 AMANDA Mar 4, 1927
SHIP Norwegian, J. P. Pedersen & Son,
1,170 tons
LOCATION Toamasina, Madagascar
CARGO Silver
Ship lost during a cyclone

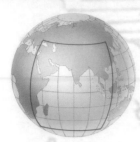

THE INDIAN OCEAN, RED SEA, AND PERSIAN GULF

The map for these listings is on p. 145.

● No known salvage
■ Some salvage history known

1 J4 SHIPS OF PHARAOS 2000 BC
LOCATION Island in the Red Sea, 2 months journey from Thebes, Egypt
ROUTE Ophir, Egypt, to Thebes, Egypt
CARGO Gold, silver, jewels, wood, ivory, apes, and peacocks

2 I3 KING JOSAPHAT WRECKS
873–849 BC
LOCATION Port on most NE point of Red Sea
CARGO Valuable artifacts

3 M5 GOURADOU WRECK
16th century
SHIP Chinese
LOCATION South Male Atoll, Maldives, 3.53N
ROUTE From Sunda, Indonesia
CARGO Porcelain and Chinese merchandise
SALVAGE Some salvage at time of loss

4 K3 SANCTA CRUZ 1510
SHIP Portuguese
LOCATION North coast of Persian Gulf, approximately 27.30N 53.00E
ROUTE Portugal to India
CARGO Specie

5 M6 NOSSA SENHORA DA CONCEICAO 1555
SHIP Portuguese East Indiaman
LOCATION Baixos Pero dos Banhos, Chagos Archipelago
ROUTE Portugal to India
CARGO Royal treasure including gold and silver
SALVAGE Some of the royal treasure salvaged at time of loss

6 K4 ATJEHNESE SHIP
Mar or Apr 1561
SHIP Atjehnese
LOCATION Off Qishn, Yemen
CARGO Gold and jewelry, valued at over 200,000 cruzados, for the Sultan of Turkey
Ship lost during battle with 2 Portuguese galleons; one of the Portuguese galleons also sank.

7 L7 BOM JESUS 1593
SHIP Portuguese East Indiaman
LOCATION Cargados Carajos islands
ROUTE India to Portugal
CARGO Precious stones and porcelain
Manuel de Sousa Coutinho lost on this ship

8 J5 MADRE DE DEUS 1595
SHIP Portuguese East Indiaman
LOCATION Coast of Somalia
ROUTE India to Portugal
CARGO Gold and precious stones

9 K4 SANTO ANTONIO 1601
SHIP Portuguese East Indiaman
LOCATION Socotra
ROUTE Portugal to India
CARGO Gold and silver specie

10 M5 CORBIN June 1602
SHIP French
LOCATION Reef, 15 to 18 miles (24 to 29 km) from Felidu Atoll, Maldives, and south of Maalosmadulu Atoll, Maldives, 4.54N
ROUTE France to India
CARGO Silver
SALVAGE Attempted salvage at time of loss but ship too deep to reach

11 K6 SAINT BOAVENTURA 1615
SHIP Portuguese East Indiaman
LOCATION 25 days from Goa, India
ROUTE Goa, India, to Portugal
CARGO Precious stones and porcelain

12 L8 BANDA Mar 6, 1615
SHIP Dutch East Indiaman, 600 tons
LOCATION Bay of Tombeau, Mauritius
ROUTE Banten, Java, to Netherlands
CARGO Eastern goods valued at 110,370 florins, plus personal fortune of Pieter Both
SALVAGE Some salvage at time of loss. Ship recently rediscovered.

13 K3 SAO PEDRO 1622
SHIP Portuguese
LOCATION Shore near Bandar 'Abbas, Iran
ROUTE Portugal to India
CARGO Specie
Lost during siege of Hormuz Castle, Iran

14 K8 GOUDA Mar 18, 1625
SHIP Dutch East Indiaman, 800 tons
LOCATION Near Madagascar
ROUTE Jakarta, Java, to Netherlands
CARGO Porcelain

15 K3 LION Nov 18, 1625
SHIP English East Indiaman
LOCATION Bandar 'Abbas, Iran
ROUTE UK to Iran
CARGO Specie

16 M4 COMFORT Nov 20, 1638
SHIP English East Indiaman
LOCATION Between Machilipatnam and Surat, India, 11.20N
ROUTE Banten, Java, to Surat, India, via Machilipatnam, India
CARGO Precious stones
Ship blown up in self-defense while being chased by Malabar pirates

17 K7 HENRY BONAVENTURE
c. 1645
SHIP English East Indiaman
LOCATION Mauritius
ROUTE India to UK
CARGO Precious stones

18 L3 ENDEAVOUR Jan 8, 1654
SHIP English East Indiaman
LOCATION Off Sind, Pakistan
ROUTE UK to Iran
CARGO Specie

19 M5 PERSIA MERCHANT
Aug 9, 1658
SHIP English East Indiaman
LOCATION Near the islet of Ingramrudco, Maldives
ROUTE UK to Bengal
CARGO 8 chests of silver, and probably gold from west Africa
SALVAGE Attempted salvage at time of loss, but unsuccessful

20 J4 SHIP OF VINGECLA June 2, 1661
LOCATION Island in mouth of Red Sea
CARGO Jewels, 5 or 6 tons gold, and other valuable commodities
SALVAGE Some salvage at time of loss

21 O4 WEESP Sept 27, 1661
SHIP Dutch East Indiaman, 560 tons
LOCATION Island of Sawalang, near Japara, Andaman Islands, a musket-shot from the shore
ROUTE Thailand to Bengal
CARGO Gold

22 L8 GEKROONDE LEEUW
Feb 10 or 11, 1662
SHIP Dutch East Indiaman, 1,200 tons
LOCATION Indian Ocean, approximately 25.00S
ROUTE Jakarta, Java, to Netherlands
CARGO Porcelain

23 L8 PRINS WILLEM Feb 10 or 11, 1662
SHIP Dutch East Indiaman, 1,100 tons
LOCATION Indian Ocean, approximately 25.00S
ROUTE Jakarta, Java, to Netherlands
CARGO Porcelain

24 L8 WAPEN VAN HOLLAND
Feb 10, 1662
SHIP Dutch East Indiaman, 920 tons
LOCATION Indian Ocean, approximately 25.00S
ROUTE Jakarta, Java, to Netherlands
CARGO Porcelain

25 L7 ARNHEM Mar 12, 1662
SHIP Dutch East Indiaman, 1,000 tons
LOCATION Brandao, an island in the Cargados Shoals, east of Madagascar
ROUTE Jakarta, Java, to Netherlands
CARGO Porcelain and precious stones

26 K4 THOMAS 1698
SHIP Privately owned English trader
LOCATION Off Socotra
ROUTE India to Al Mukha, Yemen
CARGO Precious stones and specie

27 K7 SPEAKER 1702
SHIP Pirate ship
LOCATION Mauritius
CARGO Booty
SALVAGE Salvaged by P. Lize and others

28 K3 HESTOR 1704
SHIP English East Indiaman, 350 tons
LOCATION Persian Gulf
ROUTE UK to Iran
CARGO Specie

29 L8 CONCORDIA 1708
SHIP Dutch East Indiaman, 900 tons
LOCATION Near Mauritius
ROUTE Jakarta, Java, to Netherlands
CARGO Porcelain

30 K7 ZUIDERBURG 1708
SHIP Dutch East Indiaman, 618 tons
LOCATION Near Mauritius
ROUTE Jakarta, Java, to Netherlands
CARGO Porcelain

31 K2 BLENHEIM 1712
SHIP English East Indiaman
LOCATION Euphrates River, Al Basrah, Iraq
ROUTE UK to Iran
CARGO Specie

32 M7 BLEIJENBURG 1722
SHIP Dutch East Indiaman, 1,100 tons
LOCATION Between Jakarta, Java, and Cape of Good Hope, South Africa
ROUTE Jakarta, Java, to Netherlands
CARGO Porcelain

33 L8 HUIS TE FOREEST 1722
SHIP Dutch East Indiaman, 600 tons
LOCATION Near Mauritius
ROUTE Jakarta, Java, to Netherlands
CARGO Porcelain

34 K8 RAADHUIS VAN MIDDELBURG 1722
SHIP Dutch East Indiaman, 890 tons
LOCATION Near Mauritius
ROUTE Jakarta, Java, to Netherlands
CARGO Porcelain

35 K8 RIJNESTEIN 1722
SHIP Dutch East Indiaman, 608 tons
LOCATION Near Mauritius
ROUTE Jakarta, Java, to Netherlands
CARGO Porcelain

36 M5 RAVENSTEIN May 8, 1726
SHIP Dutch East Indiaman, 800 tons
LOCATION Maldives, approximately 5.39N
ROUTE Netherlands to Jakarta, Java
CARGO Gold and silver
SALVAGE 9 chests of silver and 1 chest of gold saved at time of loss

37 K3 RIDDERKERK 1743
SHIP Dutch East Indiaman, 500 tons
LOCATION Iran
ROUTE Jakarta, Java, to Iran
CARGO Specie

38 K7 SAINT GERAN
Aug 18, 1744
SHIP French East Indiaman
LOCATION Reef, 3 miles (5 km) south of Ile d'Ambre, Mauritius
ROUTE Lorient, France, to Mauritius
CARGO 18 chests and 1 barrel of silver
SALVAGE Some looting by local divers at time of loss
Money was stowed in the aft hatch, but ship broke up before it could be saved

39 L6 PRINCE OF ORANGE 1745
SHIP English East Indiaman
LOCATION Indian Ocean
ROUTE India to UK
CARGO Precious stones
Never heard from again after Captain's letter from Anjengo roads, India

40 M7 DRONNINGEN AF DANMARK I
1746
SHIP Danish East Indiaman
LOCATION Indian Ocean
ROUTE Far East to Denmark
CARGO Porcelain

41 K8 NORTHAMPTON
Mar 27, 1746
SHIP English East Indiaman
LOCATION 150 miles (240 km) east of Mauritius
ROUTE Guangzhou, China, to UK
CARGO Porcelain and gold

42 J4 HEATHCOTE June 9, 1747
SHIP English East Indiaman
LOCATION Strait of Bab al Mandab, near Al Mukha, Yemen
ROUTE UK to Iran
CARGO 30 chests of silver

43 K8 VERELST Apr 23, 1771
SHIP English East Indiaman
LOCATION Near Mauritius
ROUTE India to UK
CARGO Precious stones

44 K7 KENT 1800
SHIP English East Indiaman
LOCATION Port Louis, Mauritius
ROUTE UK to India
CARGO Gold
The gold captured from the Kent that did not sink was thrown into the sea at Port Louis by Surcouf as a protest against French Admiralty claims

45 J2 TIGRIS RIVER WRECK
19th century
LOCATION Tigris River, Iraq
ROUTE Iraq to Louvres, France
CARGO Assyrian art treasure

46 K2 ARRAN 1808
LOCATION Island of Karak, Persian Gulf
ROUTE From Persian Gulf
CARGO Copper, drugs, and a large amount of treasure
SALVAGE Some salvage at time of loss

47 K3 DURABLE Aug 21, 1817
LOCATION Durable Shoal, off Bahrain, 26.57N 50.21E
ROUTE Bushehr, Iran, to Bahrain
CARGO Specie

48 L6 RUBY Aug 10, 1838
SHIP British bark, 441 tons
LOCATION 5.43S 64.40E
ROUTE China to Bombay, India
CARGO Gold and silver valued at
US $800,000
SALVAGE Small quantity of gold and
silver removed before ship sank

49 I9 REGULAR Mar 13, 1843
SHIP Dutch East Indiaman, 850 tons
LOCATION 37.30S 36.30E
ROUTE Netherlands to Jakarta, Java
CARGO 22 cases of gold and silver
SALVAGE Some salvage at time of loss

50 M9 JOHN HENDRIK 1845
SHIP Dutch
LOCATION Rocks off St. Paul Island,
38.43S 77.31E
ROUTE Netherlands to Jakarta, Java
CARGO Specie

51 L8 JAMES GIBBON 1857
SHIP Australian
LOCATION 19.40S 63.26E
ROUTE Adelaide, Australia, to Mauritius
CARGO Specie
SALVAGE Some salvage at time of loss

52 L4 SULTAN 1858
SHIP British
LOCATION Reef in Arabian Sea
ROUTE UK to Bombay, India
CARGO Silver

53 I3 ALMA June 12, 1859
SHIP British, P & O Line
LOCATION Red Sea
ROUTE Calcutta, India, to Suez, Egypt
CARGO Specie and mail
SALVAGE Mail saved but specie lost

54 M5 COLOMBO Nov 19, 1862
SHIP British, P & O Line
LOCATION Minicoy, Laccadive Islands,
India
ROUTE Calcutta, India, to Egypt
CARGO Specie
SALVAGE Some salvage at time of loss

55 I3 CARNATIC Sept 13, 1869
SHIP British, P & O Line, 1,776 tons
LOCATION Coral reef, Shadwân, Gulf of
Suez, Egypt
ROUTE UK to Bombay, India
CARGO Specie valued at £40,000 sterling
SALVAGE Partly salvaged. Specie valued at
£8,000 sterling not recovered.

56 J4 HARVESTER Sept 1870
SHIP British
LOCATION 120 miles (190 km) east of
Aden, Yemen
ROUTE Aden, Yemen, to Muscat, Oman
CARGO Specie
SALVAGE Largely salvaged at time of loss

57 I3 PRINCE HENDRIK Oct 1873
SHIP Dutch
LOCATION North of Brothers Islands,
Red Sea
ROUTE Java to Rotterdam, Netherlands
CARGO Specie

58 K5 MEIKONG June 17, 1877
SHIP French, Messageries Maritimes
LOCATION Raas Hafoun, 80 miles (130 km)
south of Cape Gardafui, Somalia
ROUTE Hong Kong to Marseille, France
CARGO 5 cases of treasure

59 K4 CASHMERE July 5, 1877
SHIP British India Steam Navigation
Company, 1,083 tons
LOCATION 6 miles (9.5 km) south of Raas
Asir, Cape Gardafui, Somalia, 11.50N
51.18E
ROUTE Zanzibar, Tanzania, to Aden,
Yemen
CARGO Treasure

60 M4 RAGUDONATHA Apr 26, 1886
SHIP Indian
LOCATION Near Bankot, India, 17.59N
73.03E
ROUTE Bankot, India, to Calicut, India
CARGO Specie

61 J4 HONG KONG Dec 1, 1890
SHIP British, P & O Line, 3,174 tons
LOCATION Azalea Rock, Red Sea
ROUTE Shanghai, China, to UK
CARGO Specie
SALVAGE Some salvage at time of loss

62 K8 WARREN HASTINGS
June 14, 1897
SHIP British
LOCATION SE coast of Réunion
ROUTE Cape Town, South Africa, to
Mauritius
CARGO 7 cases of regimental silver of the
British Army Regiment, Green Jackets
SALVAGE Expedition in 1988 by regimental
divers to recover silver plate unsuccessful

63 J3 EUPHRATES WRECK
Oct 2, 1916
SHIP Shaktur
LOCATION South of Hadethah, Persian
Gulf
CARGO Gold
SALVAGE Attempted by Germans in 1917

64 J4 CEREBOLI Apr 11, 1929
LOCATION 18.00N 37.30E
ROUTE Mits'iwa, Eritrea, to Jedda,
Saudi Arabia
CARGO 17 cases of specie
SALVAGE Specie valued at £3,000 sterling
saved

65 K4 GEORGES PHILIPPAR
May 19, 1932
SHIP French, Messageries Maritimes,
17,000 tons
LOCATION Gulf of Aden, 145 miles (233 km)
NNE of Cape Gardafui, Somalia
ROUTE Yokohama, Japan, to Marseille,
France
CARGO Gold and silver bullion valued at
£30,000 sterling
*Ship caught fire and floated for several days
before foundering*

66 K4 RAHMANIE July 14, 1943
SHIP British, 5,463 tons
LOCATION 14.52N 52.06E
ROUTE Bombay, India, to Saudi Arabia
CARGO Gold sovereigns

67 K4 JOHN BARRY Aug 28, 1944
SHIP American Liberty ship, 7,176 tons
LOCATION 15.10N 55.18E
ROUTE US to India
CARGO 3 million Saudi Arabian silver ryals,
plus possibility of 2,000 tons silver bars
SALVAGE Recently located in 6,000 feet
(1,800 meters) water, and salvage opera-
tions commenced
See pp.118–119

68 M5 LUCONA Jan 23, 1977
SHIP Panamanian
LOCATION 100 miles (160 km) off Minicoy,
Laccadive Islands
ROUTE Chioggia, Italy, to Hong Kong
CARGO Uranium mill valued at £10 million
sterling
SALVAGE Recently located and video taken
*Part of a fraud carried out by Udo Proksch.
Only scrap metal actually found on board.*

69 L4 ALIAKMON RUNNER Feb 1983
LOCATION 10.01N 63.18E
ROUTE Singapore to Piraeus, Greece
CARGO Antique temple artifacts valued at
US $13 million

SOUTHERN AFRICA

The map for these listings is on pp. 146–147.
● No known salvage
■ Some salvage history known

1 H6 SHIP OF BARTOLOMEU DIAS
1500
SHIP Portuguese
LOCATION Agulhas Bank, South Africa
ROUTE Portugal to Far East
CARGO Gold and silver specie
Part of Cabral's fleet

2 G6 BOM JESUS 1533
SHIP Portuguese East Indiaman
LOCATION Off South Africa
ROUTE Lisbon, Portugal, to Goa, India
CARGO Specie

3 L4 SAO JOAO 1552
SHIP Portuguese East Indiaman
LOCATION Just north of Point Edward,
South Africa, approximately 31.00S
ROUTE Cochin, India, to Portugal
CARGO Jewels and porcelain

4 K5 SAO BENTO Apr 22, 1554
SHIP Portuguese East Indiaman
LOCATION Rocks of Pedro dos Parcos,
off east coast of South Africa, 32.19S
ROUTE Portugal to Goa, India
CARGO Gold and silver specie
SALVAGE 5 chests of silver saved

5 H6 BOA VIAGEM 1584
SHIP Portuguese East Indiaman
LOCATION Off Cape of Good Hope,
South Africa
ROUTE Cochin, India, to Portugal
CARGO Porcelain and precious stones

6 M2 SAO THOME 1589
SHIP Portuguese East Indiaman
LOCATION Off Hully Point, near the
border of Mozambique and South Africa,
24 miles (39 km) from land, 27.20S
ROUTE India to Portugal
CARGO Jewels and porcelain
*Dom Paulo de Lima and Bernadim de Carvalho
on board. The pilot, Gaspar Goncalves, had
previously been wrecked in the Santiago.*

7 K4 SAO ALBERTO 1593
SHIP Portuguese East Indiaman
LOCATION 32.02S 29.07E
ROUTE India to Portugal
CARGO Jewels, gold, and porcelain
SALVAGE Chest containing many gold and
silver pieces, plus boxes of crystal rosaries,
salvaged at time of loss. Recently located
by D. R. Wratten.

8 F5 OOSTERLAND May 24, 1607
SHIP Dutch East Indiaman, 1,123 tons
LOCATION Mouth of Salt River, Table Bay,
South Africa
ROUTE Sri Lanka to Netherlands
CARGO Jewels

9 L3 SAO ESPIRITO 1608
SHIP Portuguese East Indiaman
LOCATION Natal coast, South Africa
ROUTE Portugal to India
CARGO Specie

10 J5 SAO JOAO BAPTISTA 1622
SHIP Portuguese East Indiaman
LOCATION Possibly the cannon site,
4 miles (6 km) south of Cape Padrone, near
mouth of Keiskamma River, South Africa,
approximately 33.00S
ROUTE Goa, India, to Portugal
CARGO Jewels, gold, and porcelain
SALVAGE Jewels salvaged at time of loss
*Ship lost after a 19-day battle with Dutch
corsairs*

11 J5 SAO GONCALO 1630
SHIP Portuguese East Indiaman
LOCATION Algoa Bay, South Africa
ROUTE India to Portugal
CARGO Porcelain and jewels

12 K4 SAO JOAO BAPTISTA 1634
SHIP Portuguese East Indiaman
LOCATION North of Port St. Johns,
South Africa
ROUTE India to Portugal
CARGO Precious stones and porcelain
SALVAGE Salvaged at time of loss

13 K5 NOSSA SENHORA DE BELEM
1635
SHIP Portuguese East Indiaman
LOCATION Near mouth of Umzimvubu
River, 130 miles (210 km) south of Durban,
South Africa, approximately 32.00S
ROUTE Goa, India, to Portugal
CARGO Jewels, porcelain, and gold
SALVAGE Some salvage at time of loss
*Capt. Joseph de Cabreira. Survivors made
their way up the west coast of Africa to
Luanda, Angola.*

14 K5 SANTA MARIA DE DEUS
1643
SHIP Portuguese East Indiaman
LOCATION Bonza Bay, 5 miles (8 km)
north of East London, South Africa
ROUTE India to Portugal
CARGO Jewels, porcelain, and gold
*Chinese porcelain found at Bonza Bay,
South Africa*

15 G5 MAURITIUS EILAND
Feb 7, 1644
SHIP Dutch East Indiaman
LOCATION Reef off Saldanha Bay,
South Africa
ROUTE Netherlands to Jakarta, Java
CARGO Specie
SALVAGE Money saved at time of loss

16 G5 HAARLEM Apr 6, 1647
SHIP Dutch East Indiaman, 500 tons
LOCATION On a sandy beach opposite
Table Bay, between Robben Island and
mainland South Africa
ROUTE Jakarta, Java, to Netherlands
CARGO Porcelain and precious stones
SALVAGE Some salvage at time of loss

17 J5 SACRAMENTO
June 30, 1647
SHIP Portuguese East Indiaman
LOCATION Sardinie Bay, near south
point of Algoa Bay, South Africa,
approximately 34.00S
ROUTE Goa, India, to Portugal
CARGO Jewels, china, and gold
SALVAGE Recently rediscovered by Dave
Allan and Gerry van Niekerk. Ming china
and 26 bronze cannons raised.
*Location shown on chart by Robert Jacob
Gordon, 1778*

**18 K5 NOSSA SENHORA DE
ATALAIA** July 4, 1647
SHIP Portuguese East Indiaman
LOCATION Off Cintsa Bay, south of the
Great Kei River, South Africa, 33.20S
ROUTE Portugal to Goa, India
CARGO Gold and silver specie
*Ship went aground on the Rijbank, Algoa Bay,
South Africa, was refloated, and wrecked off
Cintsa Bay*

19 M2 JOHANNA 1682
SHIP English East Indiaman
LOCATION Cape of Good Hope,
South Africa
ROUTE UK to India
CARGO 70 chests of treasure
SALVAGE Recently relocated

20 L4 GOOD HOPE May 1685
SHIP English East Indiaman
LOCATION Durban harbor, South Africa
ROUTE UK to India
CARGO Specie

21 L4 STAVERNISSE
Feb 16, 1686
SHIP Dutch East Indiaman, 544 tons
LOCATION Ifafa beach, 40 miles (64 km)
south of Durban, South Africa,
approximately 30.28S
ROUTE Bengal to Netherlands
CARGO Precious stones

22 F5 MILAGRES Apr 18, 1686
SHIP Portuguese East Indiaman
LOCATION Cape of Good Hope,
South Africa
ROUTE Goa, India, to Portugal
CARGO Precious stones, porcelain,
and gold

23 G5 GOEDE HOOP
June 5, 1692
SHIP Dutch East Indiaman, 1,177 tons
LOCATION Near Salt River, Table Bay,
South Africa
ROUTE Jakarta, Java, to Netherlands
CARGO Precious stones and porcelain
SALVAGE Considerable salvage at time
of loss

24 G5 HOGERGEEST
June 10, 1692
SHIP Dutch East Indiaman, 222 tons
LOCATION Salt River, Table Bay,
South Africa
ROUTE Jakarta, Java, to Netherlands
CARGO Porcelain and precious stones

25 G6 ORANGE 1693
SHIP English East Indiaman
LOCATION Mouth of Salt River, Table
Bay, South Africa
ROUTE India to UK
CARGO Diamonds
SALVAGE 10 bags of diamonds salvaged

26 G5 GOUDE BUYS Oct 1693
SHIP Dutch East Indiaman
LOCATION 24 miles (39 km) north of
St. Helena Bay, South Africa
ROUTE Netherlands to Jakarta, Java
CARGO 17 chests of treasure
SALVAGE Treasure transferred to
the *Dageraad*

27 G5 DAGERAAD
Dec 1693
SHIP Dutch East Indiaman, 140 tons
LOCATION Rocks on the west side of
Robben Island, South Africa
ROUTE Netherlands to Jakarta, Java
CARGO 17 chests of treasure transferred
from the *Goude Buys*

28 G6 WADDRINXVEEN
May 1697
SHIP Dutch East Indiaman
LOCATION Mouth of Salt River, Table
Bay, South Africa
ROUTE Sri Lanka to Netherlands
CARGO Precious stones

29 G6 L'HUIS TE KAIJENSTEIN
May 27, 1698
SHIP Dutch East Indiaman, 1,154 tons
LOCATION Oudekraal, Camps Bay, 3 miles
(5 km) from Cape Town, South Africa
ROUTE Netherlands to Jakarta, Java
CARGO 19 chests of money
SALVAGE 17 chests of money salvaged

30 G5 MERESTEIN Apr 3, 1702
SHIP Dutch East Indiaman
LOCATION Jutten Eiland, Saldanha Bay,
South Africa
ROUTE Netherlands to Jakarta, Java
CARGO 16 chests of specie
SALVAGE Attempted salvage by John
Lethbridge in 1728 without much success.
Further salvage in the 1970s and sale of
artifacts in London, England.

31 H6 BENNEBROEK 1711
SHIP Dutch East Indiaman, 800 tons
LOCATION Struys Bay, east of Cape
Agulhas, South Africa
ROUTE Sri Lanka to Netherlands
CARGO Precious stones

32 G6 CHANDOS 1719
SHIP English East Indiaman
LOCATION Cape of Good Hope,
South Africa
ROUTE UK to Bombay, India
CARGO Specie
SALVAGE Capt. Samuel Brathwait of
HMS Salisbury involved in salvage

33 H6 ADDISON Nov 5, 1720
SHIP English East Indiaman
LOCATION Cape of Good Hope,
South Africa
ROUTE UK to India
CARGO Silver specie
SALVAGE Capt. Samuel Brathwait of
HMS Salisbury involved in salvage

34 G6 NIGHTINGALE
Feb 26, 1721
SHIP English East Indiaman
LOCATION Cape of Good Hope,
South Africa
ROUTE UK to Madras, India
CARGO Silver specie
SALVAGE Silver valued at £65,051 sterling
recovered. Capt. Samuel Brathwait of
HMS Salisbury involved in salvage.

35 G6 ROTTERDAM
June 15, 1722
SHIP Dutch East Indiaman, 800 tons
LOCATION Cape of Good Hope,
South Africa
ROUTE Netherlands to Jakarta, Java
CARGO Silver specie
SALVAGE Attempted salvage by
Lethbridge in 1727

36 G6 STANDVASTIGHEID
June 15, 1722
SHIP Dutch East Indiaman, 888 tons
LOCATION Cape of Good Hope,
South Africa
ROUTE Netherlands to Jakarta, Java
CARGO Specie
SALVAGE Attempted by Lethbridge but
silver not recovered

37 G4 METEREN Nov 7, 1723
SHIP Dutch East Indiaman
LOCATION West coast of South Africa,
approximately 31.20S
ROUTE Netherlands to Jakarta, Java
CARGO Silver

38 G5 MIDDENRAK
July 3, 1728
SHIP Dutch East Indiaman
LOCATION Salt River, Table Bay,
South Africa
ROUTE Netherlands to Jakarta, Java
CARGO Specie
*Ship wrecked in same area and same year as
the* Haarlem

39 G5 HAARLEM Dec 4, 1728
SHIP Dutch East Indiaman, 850 tons
LOCATION Salt River, Table Bay,
South Africa
ROUTE Netherlands to Jakarta, Java
CARGO Silver specie
2 chests of money washed up on shore

40 H6 SAKSENBURG Jan 8, 1730
SHIP Dutch East Indiaman, 610 tons
LOCATION Near Cape Agulhas,
South Africa
ROUTE Netherlands to Jakarta, Java
CARGO Specie

41 G5 REIJGERSDAAL
Oct 25, 1747
SHIP Dutch East Indiaman, 850 tons
LOCATION On mainland, near Dassen
Island, South Africa
ROUTE Netherlands to Jakarta, Java
CARGO Silver specie
SALVAGE Some salvage at time of loss

42 J5 DODDINGTON
July 17, 1754
SHIP English East Indiaman
LOCATION Bird Island, off Port Elizabeth,
South Africa
ROUTE India to UK
CARGO Gold coins and silver specie
SALVAGE Some salvage at time of loss.
Ship was recently rediscovered by Dave
Allan. Coins, glasses, and tortoiseshell
combs were found.
*Cargo supposedly included lost treasure of Clive
of India*

43 G6 VOORZICHTIGHEID
June 8, 1757
SHIP Dutch East Indiaman, 850 tons
LOCATION Cape of Good Hope,
South Africa
ROUTE Far East to Netherlands
CARGO Rice and porcelain

44 G5 JONGE THOMAS
June 2, 1773
SHIP Dutch East Indiaman 1,150 tons
LOCATION Sands near Salt River, Cape of
Good Hope, South Africa
ROUTE Netherlands to Jakarta, Java
CARGO Silver

45 G6 NIEUW RHOON
Feb 5, 1776
SHIP Dutch East Indiaman, 1,150 tons
LOCATION Cape of Good Hope,
South Africa
ROUTE Jakarta, Java, to Netherlands
CARGO Porcelain
SALVAGE Recently rediscovered and
some porcelain recovered

46 G5 COLEBROOKE Aug 1778
SHIP English East Indiaman
LOCATION Eastern shore of Kogel Bay,
South Africa
ROUTE UK to India
CARGO Small quantity of coins
SALVAGE Relocated in 1986
*Ship struck Anvil Rock in False Bay,
South Africa*

47 H6 MENTOR Jan 5, 1780
SHIP Dutch East Indiaman
LOCATION Reef off Cape Agulhas,
South Africa
ROUTE Jakarta, Java, to Netherlands
CARGO Porcelain

48 G5 MIDDELBURG
July 21, 1781
SHIP Dutch East Indiaman
LOCATION Saldanha Bay, South Africa
ROUTE China to Netherlands
CARGO Porcelain
SALVAGE Recently salvaged by Bill Dodds

49 K4 GROSVENOR Aug 4, 1782
SHIP English East Indiaman
LOCATION Mouth of Tezani River,
20 miles (32 km) north of Port St. Johns,
South Africa
ROUTE India to UK
CARGO Gold, jewels, and peacock thrones
rumored. In fact, it was only carrying a
relatively small quantity of precious stones.
SALVAGE Many unsuccessful attempts

50 G6 NICOBAR 1783
SHIP Danish East Indiaman
LOCATION Near Cape of Good Hope,
South Africa
ROUTE Denmark to Far East
CARGO Specie

51 F6 HOOP June 30, 1784
SHIP Dutch East Indiaman, 800 tons
LOCATION Mouille Point, Table Bay,
South Africa
ROUTE Jakarta, Java, to Netherlands
CARGO Porcelain

52 H6 BREDERODE
May 4, 1785
SHIP Dutch East Indiaman, 1,150 tons
LOCATION Off Cape Agulhas, South
Africa
ROUTE China to Netherlands
CARGO Porcelain

53 F6 AVENHORN Jan 22, 1788
SHIP Dutch East Indiaman, 880 tons
LOCATION Table Bay, South Africa
ROUTE Jakarta, Java, to Netherlands
CARGO Porcelain

54 G6 STERRESCHANS
May 20, 1793
SHIP Dutch East Indiaman, 850 tons
LOCATION Off rocks, south of castle,
Table Bay, South Africa
ROUTE Netherlands to Jakarta, Java
CARGO Specie

55 H7 GANGES May 29, 1807
SHIP English East Indiaman
LOCATION Off Laccam's Channel,
38.22S 19.50E
ROUTE China to UK
CARGO Porcelain
Ship burned

56 J5 WILLIAM PITT Dec 16, 1814
SHIP English East Indiaman
LOCATION East of Algoa Bay, South
Africa
ROUTE UK to India
CARGO Specie

57 G5 BIRKENHEAD Jan 7, 1852
SHIP British, Paddle Transport,
1,400 tons
LOCATION 2 miles (3 km) from shore,
pinnacle of rock off Danger Point, False
Bay, South Africa
ROUTE Cape Town, South Africa, to Port
Elizabeth, South Africa
CARGO Supposedly gold coins valued at
£240,000 sterling for the army payroll
SALVAGE Salvaged from 1986 to 1988, but
recoveries of gold sovereigns minimal

58 H6 QUEEN OF THE THAMES
Mar 18, 1871
SHIP Devitt & Moore steamer
LOCATION Spit of sand near Cape Agulhas,
South Africa
ROUTE Melbourne, Australia, to London,
England
CARGO Gold dust valued at £7,000 sterling

59 G5 THERMOPYLAE
Sept 11, 1899
SHIP British, Henderson Line
LOCATION Green Point Lighthouse, Table
Bay, South Africa
ROUTE Australia to UK
CARGO Gold
SALVAGE Some salvage at time of loss

60 I6 WARATAH 1909
SHIP British, Blue Anchor Line,
9,339 tons
LOCATION Between Durban and Cape
Town, South Africa
ROUTE Sydney, Australia, to London,
England
CARGO Rumors of gold
Missing ship

61 **E4** KALEWA Aug 1, 1942
SHIP British, Burma Line
LOCATION 30.16S 13.39E
ROUTE Glasgow, Scotland, to South Africa
CARGO Specie

62 **F6** COLORADAN Oct 9, 1942
SHIP American, Hawaiian Steamship
Company, 6,557 tons
LOCATION 35.47S 14.34E
ROUTE South Africa to US
CARGO Gold

63 **F6** ORCADES Oct 10, 1942
SHIP British, Orient Steam Navigation
Company, 23,456 tons
LOCATION 35.51S 14.40E
ROUTE South Africa to UK
CARGO Platinum

64 **K4** MELISKERK Jan 8, 1943
SHIP Dutch
LOCATION Port St. Johns, South Africa
CARGO Bullion
SALVAGE Salvaged at time of loss

INDIA, SRI LANKA, AND THE BAY OF BENGAL

The map for these listings is on pp. 148–149.

● No known salvage
■ Some salvage history known

1 **J3** PERSIAN SHIPS 10th century
SHIP Persian ships
LOCATION Bay of Bengal
ROUTE Sri Lanka to Palembang, Sumatra
CARGO Linen, cotton, wool, rugs, metal-
work, and bullion

2 **B3** SHIP OF AHMAD 919
SHIP Arabian
LOCATION Off Saymur, west coast of India
ROUTE Persian Gulf to India
CARGO Enormous wealth including bullion
2 other ships in same convoy also lost

3 **D8** ARRELIKIAS 16th century
SHIP Portuguese
ROUTE India to Portugal
LOCATION Outside Cochin, India
CARGO Gold and jewels
SALVAGE Divers only recovered a few
chests

4 **K8** PORTUGUESE WRECKS 1592
SHIP Portuguese East Indiaman
LOCATION Nicobar Islands
ROUTE Portugal to China
CARGO Reals of silver
SALVAGE Partly salvaged by natives
*James Lancaster obtained some of these salvaged
reals on his journey in 1592*

5 **C6** PORTUGUESE SHIP
Apr 1594
SHIP Portuguese
LOCATION Outside Goa, India
ROUTE China to Goa, India
CARGO Gold and porcelain
Ship destroyed during 3-day fight

6 **D7** NOSSA SENHORA DE
GUADALUPE 1598
SHIP Portuguese East Indiaman
LOCATION Cochin, India
CARGO Jewels and porcelain
Ship burned while loading at Cochin, India

7 **D7** COCHIN WRECK 1600
SHIP Portuguese East Indiaman
LOCATION Cochin, India
ROUTE India to Portugal
CARGO Precious stones, gold, and porcelain
*Ship burned. Contained riches valued at
£1.5 million sterling at time of loss.*

8 **E8** DON ANTONIO DE MENESEZ
1607
SHIP Portuguese East Indiaman
LOCATION Off Cape Comorin, India
ROUTE Goa, India, to China
CARGO Specie
Many merchants and passengers on board

9 **F8** SAN MARTINHO 1607
SHIP Portuguese, 27 brass guns
LOCATION Off Manaar, Sri Lanka
ROUTE Goa, India, to Melaka, Malaysia
CARGO Specie

10 **C6** SANTO ANDRE
May 27, 1608
SHIP Portuguese
LOCATION Bar of Goa, India
ROUTE Portugal to Goa, India
CARGO Specie
Capt. Luis de Brito de Melo

11 **C3** ASCENSION Sept 2, 1609
SHIP English East Indiaman
LOCATION 60 miles (96 km) from Chaul
coast, leaving Mua canal, east of Diu, India
ROUTE Red Sea to India
CARGO Specie valued at £10,000 sterling

12 **E8** SANTO ANTONIO 1610
SHIP Portuguese
LOCATION Cape Comorin, India
ROUTE Goa, India, to Macao
CARGO Specie

13 **C6** NOSSA SENHORA DE
GUADALUPE 1615
SHIP Portuguese East Indiaman
LOCATION Melinde, India
ROUTE Portugal to India
CARGO Specie
SALVAGE Specie partly saved

14 **C4** BASSEIN WRECK
May 16, 1618
SHIP Portuguese
LOCATION Bassein River, near Bombay,
India
ROUTE Hormuz, Iran, to India
CARGO Gold and specie

15 **C3** WHALE 1623–24
SHIP English East Indiaman, 700 tons
LOCATION 30 miles (48 km) from Surat
roads, India
ROUTE Iran to Surat, India
CARGO Gold and specie

16 **C4** MISERICORDIA 1625
SHIP Portuguese
LOCATION Sanjan, near Bombay, India
ROUTE Muscat, Oman, to Suvali, India
CARGO Specie
SALVAGE Artillery saved

17 **C4** SANCTO ANTONIO 1625
SHIP Portuguese galleon
LOCATION Bombay, India
ROUTE Muscat, Oman, to Suvali, India
CARGO Gold and valuables
SALVAGE Artillery recovered

18 **F5** ROSE July 21, 1627
SHIP English East Indiaman
LOCATION Coast of Machilipatnam, India
ROUTE UK to Bengal
CARGO Specie
SALVAGE Ordnance saved at time of loss

19 **C5** MADRE DE DEUS
Aug 4, 1635
SHIP Portuguese
LOCATION Panaji, India
ROUTE Portugal to India
CARGO Specie
Ship burned

20 **F6** EAGLE 1638
SHIP English East Indiaman
LOCATION Madraspatnam roads, India
ROUTE UK to Bengal
CARGO Specie

21 **C5** MADRE DE DEUS 1638
SHIP Portuguese
LOCATION Goa, India
ROUTE Portugal to India
CARGO Specie
Ship blew up during fight with Dutch

22 **F6** UNITY 1640
SHIP English East Indiaman
LOCATION Madras, India
ROUTE UK to India
CARGO Gold

23 **E9** DRAGON 1641
SHIP English East Indiaman
LOCATION 120 miles (190 km) from Sri
Lanka, towards Cape of Good Hope,
South Africa
ROUTE Far East to UK
CARGO Jewels and gold
*One of Captain Weddel's ships. Captured and
plundered by the Dutch and sunk.*

24 **F6** JOHN 1641
SHIP English East Indiaman
LOCATION Armagon, India, 13.55N 80.14E
ROUTE UK to India
CARGO Specie

25 **E9** KATHERINE 1641
SHIP English East Indiaman
LOCATION 120 miles (190 km) from Sri
Lanka, towards Cape of Good Hope,
South Africa
ROUTE Far East to UK
CARGO Jewels and gold
*One of Capt. Weddel's ships. Captured and
plundered by the Dutch and sunk.*

26 **F5** SAMARITAN 1659
SHIP English East Indiaman
LOCATION Between Machilipatnam and
Narasapur, India
ROUTE UK to India
CARGO Gold valued at £5,000 sterling
Ship ran ashore

27 **F9** HERCULES May 21, 1661
SHIP Dutch East Indiaman, 540 tons
LOCATION Point de Galle, Sri Lanka
ROUTE Netherlands to Jakarta, Java
CARGO Gold and silver

28 **H3** JAMES AND HENRY 1663
SHIP English East Indiaman
LOCATION 18 to 24 miles (29 to 39 km)
west of bar of Baleshwar, towards Palmyras
Point, India
ROUTE UK to Bengal
CARGO 70,000 reals of eight

29 **C3** VINE Apr 29, 1664
SHIP English East Indiaman
LOCATION 4 miles (6 km) from Surat, India
ROUTE Surat, India, to Sumatra
CARGO Gold
SALVAGE Attempt at salvage unsuccessful

30 **I3** HAPPY ENTRANCE
Nov 1670
SHIP English East Indiaman
LOCATION Bay of Bengal, India
ROUTE Bengal to UK
CARGO Precious stones

31 **E8** GEORGE 1673
SHIP English East Indiaman
LOCATION Off reef near Tuticorin, India,
8.48N 78.10E
ROUTE To Surat, India
CARGO Specie
Ship captured by Dutch before it struck reef

32 **F5** ANTELOPE Aug 22, 1673
SHIP English East Indiaman
LOCATION Pettipollee Bay, off
Machilipatnam, India, 16.10N 81.11E
ROUTE UK to India
CARGO Specie
Ship captured by Dutch and sank the next day

33 **C3** REVENGE Jan 21, 1682
SHIP English East Indiaman
LOCATION 4 miles (6 km) from Daman,
India
ROUTE UK to India
CARGO Specie
SALVAGE Some salvage at time of loss

34 **F6** ADVENTURE Dec 7, 1684
SHIP English East Indiaman
LOCATION Madras, India
ROUTE UK to India
CARGO Specie

35 F6 BORNEO MERCHANT
Oct 4, 1687
SHIP English East Indiaman
LOCATION Fort St. George, Madras, India
ROUTE Bengal to UK
CARGO Precious stones

36 F6 LOYAL ADVENTURE Oct 8, 1687
SHIP English East Indiaman
LOCATION Near south end of Mucquaw Town, a village just south of White Town, India
ROUTE Bengal to UK
CARGO Included presents from King of Siam, including porcelain and gold caskets

37 F7 MADRAS FRIGATE 1688
SHIP English East Indiaman
LOCATION Off Tranquebar, India
ROUTE UK to India
CARGO Specie

38 I3 JAMES AND MARY 1694
SHIP English East Indiaman
LOCATION James and Mary Shoal, near Tunbolee Point, Hugli River, India
ROUTE UK to Bengal
CARGO Treasure

39 F5 GINGERLEE 1696
SHIP English East Indiaman
LOCATION Pettipollee, India
ROUTE India to UK
CARGO Precious stones

40 I3 GRACEDIEU Dec 3, 1698
SHIP English East Indiaman
LOCATION Bay of Bengal, India
ROUTE UK to Bengal
CARGO 73,294 reals of eight

41 E8 PRINCESS LOUISE 1699
SHIP Danish East Indiaman
LOCATION Manapaer, near Tuticorin, India
ROUTE Denmark to Bengal
CARGO Specie
SALVAGE Some salvage at time of loss

42 F9 RAN MUTHU WRECK
late 17th century
SHIP Possibly Dutch
LOCATION Off Sri Lanka
CARGO Silver coins
SALVAGE Recently worked by Arthur C. Clarke and P. Throckmorton

43 C4 SOLDAET 1700
SHIP Dutch East Indiaman
LOCATION Cliffs of Tarrapour, west coast of India
ROUTE Netherlands to Far East
CARGO Gold and silver specie
SALVAGE Some salvage at time of loss

44 C4 WIJCK OP ZEE 1700
LOCATION Cliffs of Tarrapour, west coast of India
ROUTE Netherlands to Far East
CARGO Gold and silver valued at 204,236 rijksdaalders (coins)
SALVAGE Partly salvaged at time of loss

45 D7 BOMBAY FRIGO Oct 18, 1706
SHIP English East Indiaman
LOCATION Coast of Malabar, India
ROUTE St. Helena to Al Mukha, Yemen, to India
CARGO Specie

46 C4 GODOLPHIN Apr 9, 1709
SHIP English East Indiaman
LOCATION Island off Bombay, India
ROUTE Plymouth, England, to Al Mukha, Yemen, to Bombay, India
CARGO Coffee and specie

47 E8 PHOENIX Apr 15, 1710
SHIP English East Indiaman
LOCATION Near Cape Comorin, India
ROUTE UK to India
CARGO Specie

48 F6 KING GEORGE Feb 28, 1719
SHIP English East Indiaman
LOCATION Fort St. George, Madras, India
ROUTE Bengal to UK
CARGO Precious stones

49 C4 ST. GEORGE Dec 8, 1719
SHIP English East Indiaman
LOCATION Bombay, India
ROUTE UK to India
CARGO Specie

50 F6 DARTMOUTH Nov 14, 1721
SHIP English East Indiaman
LOCATION Madras, India
ROUTE UK to Bengal
CARGO 20 chests of silver

51 C3 SURAT ROADS WRECK
Apr 29, 1725
LOCATION Surat roads, India, 1 mile (1.5 km) from shore
CARGO Spanish dollars, silver ingots, and other treasure
SALVAGE About £5,000 sterling salvaged at time of loss by British ship, *Monmouth*

52 C4 BERRINGTON Dec 13, 1729
SHIP English East Indiaman, 440 tons
LOCATION Bombay, India
ROUTE Al Mukha, Yemen, to Bombay, India
CARGO Gold and specie

53 C5 ANGLESEA July 23, 1738
SHIP English East Indiaman, 490 tons
LOCATION Wallwan's country, north of Goa, India
ROUTE UK to Madras, India, via Bombay, India
CARGO Specie

54 F7 LINCOLN Apr 14, 1749
SHIP English East Indiaman
LOCATION Near Fort St. David, India, 11.46N 79.46E
ROUTE UK to Bengal
CARGO 28 chests of specie
Ship driven ashore by a violent storm

55 D7 WIMMENUM Jan 1754
SHIP Dutch East Indiaman, 1,150 tons
LOCATION Off Malabar coast, India
ROUTE Jakarta, Java, to Netherlands
CARGO Porcelain
Ship attacked by Angrias and blew up

56 C3 BLOEMENDAAL 1756
SHIP Dutch East Indiaman, 1,150 tons
LOCATION Off Surat, India
ROUTE Netherlands to Jakarta, Java
CARGO Specie valued at 215,629 florins

57 I3 LORD HOLLAND 1769
SHIP English East Indiaman
LOCATION Mouth of Hugli River, India
ROUTE Bengal to UK
CARGO 13 tons of gold according to contemporary Dutch source, although this seems unlikely

58 I3 DUKE OF ALBANY July 26, 1772
SHIP English East Indiaman
LOCATION Hugli River, India
ROUTE UK to Bengal
CARGO Specie

59 F6 MARQUIS OF ROCKINGHAM
May 20, 1777
SHIP English East Indiaman
LOCATION Rock near Madras, India
ROUTE Bombay, India, to Madras, India
CARGO 23 chests of company treasure
SALVAGE 22 chests salvaged

60 C3 FATTY BUMBARASH
Apr 20, 1782
SHIP Indian
LOCATION Surat roads, India
ROUTE Surat, India, to Basrah, Iraq
CARGO Jewels and specie

61 F6 EARL OF HERTFORD
Oct 15, 1782
SHIP English East Indiaman
LOCATION Madras, India
ROUTE China to UK
CARGO Porcelain
Ship lost in the surf

62 F6 DUKE OF ATHOLL Apr 19, 1783
SHIP English East Indiaman
LOCATION Madras, India
ROUTE UK to Bengal
CARGO Specie
Ship blew up

63 C4 FAIRFORD June 5, 1783
SHIP English East Indiaman
LOCATION Bombay, India
ROUTE UK to India
CARGO Specie
Ship blew up

64 F9 DUKE OF KINGSTON
Aug 20, 1783
SHIP English East Indiaman
LOCATION Off Sri Lanka
ROUTE UK to India
CARGO Specie

65 I3 MAJOR Apr 23, 1784
SHIP English East Indiaman
LOCATION Culpee, Hugli River, India
ROUTE UK to Bengal
CARGO Specie

66 I2 ROYAL CHARLOTTE Oct 8, 1797
SHIP English East Indiaman
LOCATION Kedgeree, at entrance to Hugli River, India
ROUTE UK to India
CARGO Specie
Ship blew up

67 D7 PRINCESS AMELIA Apr 5, 1798
SHIP English East Indiaman
LOCATION Burned off Pigeon Island, near Cannanore, India
ROUTE Bombay, India, to Tellicherry, India
CARGO Treasure or specie for payment of troops at Malabar, India

68 D7 MARQUIS OF WELLESLEY
Apr 2, 1806
SHIP English East Indiaman
LOCATION Off Calicut, India
ROUTE UK to India
CARGO Specie

69 F8 PUTTALAM WRECK 1807
SHIP Pirate ship
LOCATION Puttalam Fort, Sri Lanka
CARGO Specie valued at 20,000 rupees

70 D6 CEYLON 1808
SHIP Portuguese register ship
LOCATION 15 miles (24 km) north of Mangalore, India
ROUTE Portugal to India
CARGO Specie valued at 600,000 rupees

71 K5 TRAVERS Nov 7, 1808
SHIP English East Indiaman
LOCATION On a rock, NE by N of Drowned Island, Burma, 15.28N 94. 20E
ROUTE UK to Bengal
CARGO Copper and specie

72 I3 ASIA June 1, 1809
SHIP English East Indiaman
LOCATION Hugli River, near Mud Point, Diamond harbor, India
ROUTE UK to Calcutta, India
CARGO £10,000 sterling, woolens, madeira wine, and copper
SALVAGE Very little saved

73 D8 NANCY GRAB 1810
SHIP Grab
LOCATION India
CARGO 230,000 star pagodas (coins)
SALVAGE Some salvage at time of loss

74 C4 EARL CAMDEN July 24, 1810
SHIP English East Indiaman
LOCATION Bombay harbor, India
ROUTE UK to India
CARGO Specie

75 C4 MARQUIS OF WELLESLEY 1813
SHIP English East Indiaman
LOCATION Bombay, India
ROUTE UK to India
CARGO Specie

76 I3 SUROJPOOR WRECKS
May 24, 1815
SHIP Pinnaces and budgerows
LOCATION On rocky bank of Surojpoor, near Monghyr, India
ROUTE To Calcutta, India
CARGO 2.5 million rupees
SALVAGE Largely salvaged at time of loss
13 out of 15 boats carrying treasure were lost

77 F7 LALLA ROOKH 1828
LOCATION Near Pondicherry, India, 11.56N 79.50E
ROUTE UK to India
CARGO Silver

78 G5 PERSEVERANCE May 1829
LOCATION Coromandel Coast, 40 miles (64 km) south of Coringa, India, 16.21N
ROUTE England to Singapore
CARGO Specie

79 H4 POOREE WRECK 1838
SHIP Small boat unloading treasure from larger ship
LOCATION Puri, India, 19.48N 85.49E
CARGO Treasure
SALVAGE Salvage attempted, but it was unsuccessful owing to heavy surf

80 C4 CANDAHAR 1844
LOCATION Coast of Janjira, India
ROUTE From Bombay, India
CARGO Gold dust insured for US $50,000

81 I3 COLUMBINE Mar 8, 1844
LOCATION Sagar sands, India
CARGO Treasure
SALVAGE Some of the treasure saved

82 I3 HARLEQUIN 1845
LOCATION Sandheads, Hugli River, India
ROUTE China to England
CARGO Specie valued at US $750,000
SALVAGE Divers attempted to salvage ship, but unsuccessful because of strong current

83 G9 ERIN June 6, 1857
SHIP British, P & O Line, 850 tons
LOCATION East coast of Sri Lanka
ROUTE Bombay, India, to China
CARGO Specie, treasure, and opium
SALVAGE Some salvage at time of loss

84 L6 CORNELIA Feb 1858
SHIP Sailing bark
LOCATION 1 or 2 days' distance from Rangoon, Burma
ROUTE Singapore to Rangoon, Burma
CARGO Silver valued at 22,000 reals
Ship capsized on a sandbank

85 F8 AVA Feb 16, 1858
SHIP British, P & O Line
LOCATION Pigeon Island, off Trincomalee, Sri Lanka
ROUTE Calcutta, India, to Suez, Egypt, to London, England
CARGO Specie valued at £250,000 sterling
SALVAGE Salvaged at time of loss

86 F9 MALABAR June 1860
SHIP British, P & O Line
LOCATION Point de Galle, Sri Lanka
ROUTE Hong Kong to India
CARGO 1,080 boxes of bullion valued at £300,000 sterling
SALVAGE Bullion valued at £280,000 sterling recovered by Siebe

87 **J3** THUNDER 1867
SHIP Steamer
LOCATION Bay of Bengal, India
ROUTE Hong Kong to Calcutta, India
CARGO Treasure valued at more than
£50,000 sterling
*Left Pinang, Malaysia, on October 27, 1867,
and not heard from since*

88 **F9** RANGOON Nov 1, 1871
SHIP British, P & O Line
LOCATION Kadir Rock, 1 mile (1.5 km)
from Point de Galle harbor, Sri Lanka
ROUTE China to UK
CARGO Specie

89 **C5** CHALDEA Mar 22, 1874
SHIP British
LOCATION 10 miles (16 km) from
Vengurla, India
ROUTE Bombay, India, to Calcutta, India
CARGO Specie
SALVAGE Ship beached and cargo salvaged
at time of loss
Ship struck a rock

90 **F8** INDUS Nov 8, 1885
SHIP British, P & O Line
LOCATION Sandbank Muliavatti, 60 miles
(96 km) north of Trincomalee, Sri Lanka
ROUTE Calcutta, India, to London, England
CARGO Specie
SALVAGE Some salvage at time of loss.
Specie valued at £2,750 sterling recovered and
possibly specie on board valued at £40,000.

91 **C4** MONGOLIA June 23, 1917
SHIP British, P & O Line, 9,505 tons
LOCATION 50 miles (80 km) S by W of
Bombay, India
ROUTE London, England, to Australia,
via India
CARGO Large quantity of paper money

92 **B4** FORT STIKINE Apr 14, 1944
SHIP British, Ministry of War transport
ship, 7,142 tons
LOCATION Bombay harbor, India
ROUTE UK to India
CARGO Gold valued at £1 million sterling
SALVAGE About 50% of gold recovered
*Ship blew up and scattered gold ingots over a
wide area*

AUSTRALIA AND NEW ZEALAND

The map for these listings is on pp. 150–151.

● No known salvage
■ Some salvage history known

1 **B3** TRYAL WRECK 1622
SHIP English East Indiaman
LOCATION Tryal Rocks, Monte Bello
Islands, Australia, 20.16S 115.23E
ROUTE UK to Far East
CARGO Silver specie, plus gold ornaments
for the King of Siam
SALVAGE Site recently rediscovered,
although some doubts about this

2 **B5** BATAVIA June 4, 1629
SHIP Dutch East Indiaman
LOCATION Morning Reef, East Wallabi
Island, Houtman Abrolhos, Australia
ROUTE Netherlands to Jakarta, Java
CARGO Silver specie, and silverware for
Mogul Emperor Janghir
SALVAGE Rediscovered and excavated
in 1970s
See pp. 72–73

3 **B5** VERGULDE DRAECK
1656
SHIP Dutch East Indiaman
LOCATION Reef off Western Australia,
31.16S
ROUTE Netherlands to Jakarta, Java
CARGO 8 chests of silver coins valued at
78,600 guilders
SALVAGE Some salvage at time of loss, and
rediscovered in 1963. Lead, ivory, amber,
and coral recovered, as well as 10,000 coins.
*Artifacts in the Fremantle Maritime Museum,
Australia*

4 **A5** DE RIDDERSCHAP VAN
HOLLAND 1684
SHIP Dutch East Indiaman
LOCATION Possibly Western Australia
ROUTE Netherlands to Jakarta, Java
CARGO Silver specie
*Ship may have been captured by pirates and
taken to Madagascar*

5 **A4** ZUYTDORP 1712
SHIP Dutch East Indiaman
LOCATION 500 miles (800 km) NW of
Perth, 37 miles (60 km) north of mouth of
Murchison River, Australia
ROUTE Netherlands to Jakarta, Java
CARGO Silver and possibly gold specie
estimated at 250,000 guilders
SALVAGE Recently rediscovered, but
difficult site to excavate

6 **B3** FORTUYN 1724
SHIP Dutch East Indiaman
LOCATION Possibly Western Australia
ROUTE Netherlands to Jakarta, Java
CARGO Silver specie
Missing ship

7 **A5** AAGTERKERKE 1726
SHIP Dutch East Indiaman
LOCATION Probably a reef off Houtman
Abrolhos, Australia
ROUTE Netherlands to Jakarta, Java
CARGO Silver specie and bullion valued at
200,000 guilders

8 **B5** ZEEWYK 1727
SHIP Dutch East Indiaman
LOCATION Half Moon Reef, Houtman
Abrolhos, Australia, 28.50S
ROUTE Netherlands to Jakarta, Java
CARGO 10 chests of specie valued at
315,836 guilders
SALVAGE Recently excavated. Chinese
porcelain and German and SE Asian
stoneware recovered. Silver probably
recovered at time of loss.

9 **J2** ASTROLABE 1788
SHIP French
LOCATION Reefs of Vanikoro Island,
Santa Cruz Islands
CARGO Artifacts
SALVAGE Rediscovered in 1826 by Capt.
Peter Dillon
Ship belonging to French explorer, de la Perouse

10 **J2** BOUSSOLE 1788
SHIP French
LOCATION Reefs of Vanikoro Island,
Santa Cruz Islands
CARGO Artifacts
SALVAGE Rediscovered in 1826 by Capt.
Peter Dillon
Ship belonging to French explorer, De la Perouse

11 **L3** ELIZA June 1808
SHIP American brig
LOCATION Reef east of Viti Levu, Fiji
ROUTE Sydney, Australia, to Norfolk
Island and Fiji
CARGO Specie valued at US $60,000
SALVAGE Largely salvaged at time of loss

12 **A4** POINT CLOATES WRECK
c. 1809
SHIP Portuguese
LOCATION Point Cloates, North West Cape,
Australia
ROUTE Lisbon, Portugal, to Macao
CARGO 20,000 Spanish and US dollars
SALVAGE Recovered in 1978

13 **K6** BOYD Dec 1809
SHIP British, 500 tons
LOCATION Whangaroa harbor, New
Zealand
ROUTE New Zealand to UK
CARGO £30,000 sterling, the personal
fortune of Capt. Burnsides
SALVAGE Possibility of looting

14 **A3** RAPID Jan 7, 1811
SHIP 367 tons
LOCATION Ningaloo Reef, near Point
Cloates, Western Australia, 22.43S 113.41E
ROUTE Boston, Massachusetts, US, to
Guangzhou, China
CARGO Cargo valued at US $330,000
SALVAGE Largely salvaged at time of loss,
and relocated in 1981

15 **G1** SUN 1826
SHIP Brig, 185 tons
LOCATION Eastern Fields, 192 miles
(309 km) E by N of Thursday Island,
Australia
ROUTE Sydney, Australia, to Jakarta, Java,
to Singapore
CARGO Spanish $40,000

16 **G8** HOPE Apr 29, 1827
LOCATION Hope Beach, near River
Derwent, Tasmania, Australia
CARGO Gold

17 **I5** GEORGE 1830
SHIP Whaler
LOCATION Lord Howe Island
CARGO 5,000 sovereigns
SALVAGE Salvaged at time of loss

18 **B5** CUMBERLAND Aug 28, 1834
SHIP Cutter, 16 tons
LOCATION Between Cape Peron and
Penguin Island, Australia, approximately
32.10S 115.40E

ROUTE Fremantle, Australia, to Port
Augusta, Australia
CARGO Jewelry and silverware belonging to
the Bussell family
SALVAGE Pillaged at time of loss

19 **B5** LANCIER Sept 28, 1839
SHIP Bark, 285 tons
LOCATION Off Fremantle, Australia
ROUTE Port Louis, Mauritius, to Hobart,
Australia
CARGO Supposedly carrying a considerable
quantity of gold sovereigns.

20 **K8** MAGNET Sept 3, 1844
SHIP New Zealand bark, 148 tons
LOCATION Ickolaki, south of Akaroa, New
Zealand
ROUTE Wellington, New Zealand, to
Waikouaiti, New Zealand
CARGO Specie

21 **K7** TYNE July 4, 1845
SHIP Bark
LOCATION Rimarapa Rocks, close to Sin-
clair Head, New Zealand, 41.22S 174.43E
ROUTE London, England, to New Zealand
CARGO Specie
SALVAGE Salvaged at time of loss

22 **J3** PATAGONIA Feb 4, 1851
SHIP British
LOCATION New Caledonia, Pacific Ocean
ROUTE Sydney, Australia, to Manila,
Philippines
CARGO Specie

23 **H6** FAVORITE 1852
LOCATION Ten Mile Beach, near Cape
Howe, Australia
ROUTE Melbourne, Australia, to Sydney,
Australia
CARGO 2,000 oz (57 kg) gold, plus large
quantity of private gold shipped by Capt.
Kersopp, Mr. Smyth, and Mr. Peppers

24 **G7** UNION Mar 1852
LOCATION 1.5 miles (2.5 km) NW of Swan
Island, Australia
ROUTE Geelong, Australia, to Hobart,
Australia
CARGO gold

25 **H4** THOMAS KING Apr 17, 1852
SHIP Bark, 346 tons
LOCATION 17 miles (27 km) east of Cato
Reef, Coral Sea
ROUTE Sydney, Australia, to Manila,
Philippines
CARGO Specie valued at £3,500 sterling
and gold dust valued at £8,000 sterling

26 **G6** NELSON June 1, 1852
SHIP Sailing vessel
LOCATION Melbourne, Australia
ROUTE Melbourne, Australia, to London,
England
CARGO Gold valued at £25,000 sterling
SALVAGE Ship plundered

27 **G2** ROYAL PACKET July 1852
SHIP British
LOCATION Great Barrier Reef, Australia
ROUTE Sydney, Australia, to Java
CARGO Gold
SALVAGE Some salvage at time of loss

28 **B5** EGLINTON Sept 3, 1852
SHIP British bark, 462 tons
LOCATION North Beach, 20 miles (32 km)
north of Fremantle, Australia
ROUTE London, England, to Australia
CARGO 65,000 gold sovereigns in the
aft hold
SALVAGE Some salvage at time of loss

29 **G7** CONSIDE Sept 14, 1852
LOCATION Port Phillip Heads, Victoria,
Australia
CARGO Specie
SALVAGE Salvaged at time of loss

30 G7 MAHOMED SHAH 1853
LOCATION Tasmania, Australia
ROUTE UK to New Zealand
CARGO Specie
SALVAGE Salvaged at time of loss

31 G6 SACRAMENTO Apr 27, 1853
SHIP 447 tons
LOCATION Point Lonsdale, Port Phillip
Heads, Victoria, Australia
ROUTE London, England, to Melbourne,
Australia
CARGO Specie valued at £60,000 sterling
SALVAGE Salvaged at time of loss

32 G7 PRINCE OF WALES May 30, 1853
LOCATION Bass Strait, Australia
ROUTE Melbourne, Australia, to Sydney,
Australia
CARGO Gold dust

33 F7 WATERWITCH Sept 20, 1854
SHIP Sailing ship
LOCATION West side of King Island, Bass
Strait, Australia
ROUTE Melbourne, Australia, to Mauritius
CARGO Gold valued at £20,000 sterling
SALVAGE Salvaged at time of loss

34 G7 EMPRESS OF THE SEA
Dec 19, 1861
SHIP 2,200 tons
LOCATION Queenscliff, Australia
CARGO Gold
SALVAGE 20,612 oz (584 kg) gold removed
at time of loss
Ship destroyed by fire

35 J9 GENERAL GRANT May 14, 1866
SHIP American clipper, 1,103 tons
LOCATION Near Disappointment Island,
Auckland Islands, New Zealand
ROUTE Melbourne, Australia, to London,
England
CARGO 2,576 oz (73 kg) gold on manifest,
but reputedly much more on board
SALVAGE Many unsuccessful salvage
attempts
See pp. 96–97

36 J8 SOUTH AUSTRALIAN
Apr 2, 1867
LOCATION Coal Point, South Island, New
Zealand, approximately 46.07S 166.38E
ROUTE Dunedin, New Zealand, to
Melbourne, Australia
CARGO Gold
SALVAGE Largely salvaged at time of loss

37 L8 MATOAKA 1869
SHIP British, Shaw, Savill & Albion Line
LOCATION Off New Zealand
ROUTE Lyttelton, New Zealand, to
London, England
CARGO Gold
Missing ship

38 M7 GLENMARK 1872
SHIP 953 tons
LOCATION Pacific Ocean
ROUTE Lyttelton, New Zealand, to
London, England
CARGO Gold valued at £80,000 sterling
Missing ship

39 G3 GOTHENBURG Feb 24, 1875
SHIP McMeckan, Blackwood & Co.,
501 tons
LOCATION 24 miles (39 km) off Cape
Upstart, Flinders Passage, Great Barrier
Reef, Australia
ROUTE Port Darwin, Australia, to Adelaide,
Australia
CARGO Gold valued at £43,000 sterling
SALVAGE Salvaged at time of loss

40 F2 HEROINE Apr 24, 1846
LOCATION McKenzie Shoal, Endeavour
Strait, NE tip of Australia
ROUTE Sydney, Australia, to Singapore
CARGO Gold sovereigns

41 J8 TARANUA Apr 29, 1881
SHIP Steamer, 692 tons
LOCATION Otara Reef, near Waipapa Point,
between Dunedin and Bluff, New Zealand
ROUTE Port Chalmers, New Zealand, to
Bluff, New Zealand
CARGO Gold

42 J7 TAKARNA 1884
LOCATION Between New Zealand and
Australia
ROUTE New Zealand to Australia
CARGO Silver

43 H5 CATTERTHUN Aug 8, 1895
SHIP Australian, Eastern and Australian
Steamship Company, 2,179 tons
LOCATION Seal Rocks, near Sugarloaf
Point, New South Wales, Australia, in
30 fathoms water
ROUTE Sydney, Australia, to Hong Kong
CARGO 11,000 gold sovereigns
SALVAGE Gold sovereigns valued at £8,000
sterling recovered
*2,000 sovereigns buried when wreck fell to pieces.
Gold stowed in tank beneath floor of chart room.*

44 K6 ELINGAMITE Nov 9, 1902
SHIP Huddart, Parker & Co., 2,585 tons
LOCATION West Island, Three Kings
Islands, New Zealand
ROUTE Sydney, Australia, to Auckland,
New Zealand
CARGO 1 box of gold and 49 boxes of silver
SALVAGE Approximately 25% of gold and
silver recovered in 1907 by Capt. Willis

45 G6 BEGA Mar 29, 1908
SHIP Australian, Illawarra Shipping
Company, 567 tons
LOCATION Tanga Point, near Bermagui,
160 miles (257 km) south of Sydney,
Australia
ROUTE Tathra, Australia, to Sydney,
Australia
CARGO 561 oz (16 kg) gold, and presentation
silver plate belonging to Reverend Briscombe
SALVAGE Some salvage at time of loss, but
results unknown

46 K6 NIAGARA June 18, 1940
SHIP British, Canadian Australian Line,
13,415 tons
LOCATION 35.53S 174.54E
ROUTE Auckland, New Zealand, to
Vancouver, British Columbia, Canada
CARGO Gold valued at £2.5 million sterling
SALVAGE £2,379,000 sterling recovered in
1942 and £120,000 sterling in 1953, the
latter by Risdon Beazley

47 M6 RANGETANE Nov 26, 1940
SHIP British, New Zealand Shipping
Company, 16,712 tons
LOCATION 36.58S 175.22W
ROUTE New Zealand to Panama
CARGO Silver

48 M6 PEARY Feb 19, 1942
SHIP US destroyer
LOCATION Darwin, Australia
CARGO Reports of gold bullion valued at
£1 million sterling
No foundation for newspaper reports of bullion

ISLAND ASIA

The map for these listings is on pp. 152–153.

● No known salvage
■ Some salvage history known

1 I6 SHIP OF FRANCISCO SERRAO
1512
SHIP Portuguese
LOCATION Isle of Luco Pino, south of
Ambon, Moluccas
ROUTE Melaka, Malaysia, to Moluccas
CARGO Specie

**2 I5 SHIP OF SANCHO DE
VASCONCELOS** 1571
SHIP Portuguese
LOCATION Cape Nousanive, 36 miles
(58 km) from Tidore, Halmahera,
Moluccas
ROUTE Goa, India, to Ambon, Moluccas
CARGO Specie

3 I5 HENDRIK FREDERIK
Feb or Mar 1601
SHIP Dutch East Indiaman, 350 tons
LOCATION Ternate, Halmahera,
Moluccas
ROUTE Netherlands to Ternate,
Halmahera, Moluccas
CARGO Specie

4 E6 SHIP OF PEREIRA DE SANDE
Feb 3, 1601
SHIP Portuguese
LOCATION Rocks of Peressada,
NE Java
ROUTE Melaka, Malaysia, to Ambon,
Moluccas
CARGO Gold and silver specie

5 I5 ENKHUIZEN 1607
SHIP Dutch East Indiaman, 300 tons
LOCATION Halmahera, Moluccas
1.00N 127.00W
ROUTE Local trading
CARGO Specie

6 I4 WALCHEREN 1608
SHIP Dutch East Indiaman, 700 tons
LOCATION Off Ternate, Halmahera,
Moluccas
ROUTE Local trading
CARGO Specie

7 I4 CHINA July 1608
SHIP Dutch East Indiaman, 420 tons
LOCATION Off Ternate, Halmahera,
Moluccas
ROUTE Netherlands to Far East
CARGO Specie
Ship lost riding at anchor

8 I5 GROTE AEOLUS
Jan 31, 1613
SHIP Dutch East Indiaman, 300 tons
LOCATION Near Makian, Halmahera,
Moluccas
ROUTE Local trading
CARGO Specie

9 G6 THOMAS c. 1618
SHIP English East Indiaman
LOCATION Strait of Desalon, 66 miles
(106 km) off Ujung Pandang, Celebes
CARGO Specie
SALVAGE Some salvage at time of loss

10 D6 ZWARTE LEEUW 1619
SHIP Dutch East Indiaman
LOCATION Jakarta, Java
ROUTE Jakarta, Java, to Netherlands
CARGO Gold

11 I6 EENDRACHT May 13, 1622
SHIP Dutch East Indiaman, 700 tons
LOCATION West coast of Ambon, Moluccas
ROUTE Local trading
CARGO Specie

12 E6 REFUGE 1623
SHIP English East Indiaman
LOCATION Java
ROUTE UK to Far East
CARGO Specie

13 D6 BANTAM Mar 24, 1627
SHIP Dutch East Indiaman, 800 tons
LOCATION Jakarta, Java
ROUTE Netherlands to Jakarta, Java
CARGO Specie
SALVAGE Probably salvaged
Ship burned at the quay wall

14 D6 KAMEEL Feb 17, 1630
SHIP Dutch East Indiaman, 500 tons
LOCATION Boompjes Island, off Java
CARGO Specie

15 D6 NIJMEGEN Aug 1632
SHIP Dutch East Indiaman
LOCATION Near Jakarta, Java
ROUTE Jakarta, Java, to Netherlands
CARGO Porcelain

16 E6 GOUDEN LEEUW 1634
SHIP Dutch East Indiaman, 550 tons
LOCATION Reef near Borneo
ROUTE Local trading
CARGO Silver

17 G7 AAGTERKERKE Mar 4, 1650
SHIP Dutch East Indiaman
LOCATION Reef south of Celebes
ROUTE Local trading
CARGO Specie

18 G7 BERGEN OP ZOOM Mar 4, 1650
SHIP Dutch East Indiaman, 300 tons
LOCATION Reef south of Celebes
ROUTE Local trading
CARGO Specie

19 G7 JUFFER Mar 4, 1650
SHIP Dutch East Indiaman, 480 tons
LOCATION Reef south of Celebes
CARGO Specie

20 G7 LUIPAARD Mar 4, 1650
SHIP Dutch East Indiaman, 320 tons
LOCATION Reef south of Celebes
CARGO Specie

21 H7 TIJGER Mar 4, 1650
SHIP Dutch East Indiaman, 1,000 tons
LOCATION South of Celebes
ROUTE Jakarta, Java, to Ambon, Moluccas
CARGO Specie

22 I6 GOEDE HOOP July 13, 1654
SHIP Dutch East Indiaman
LOCATION Near Ambon, Moluccas
CARGO Specie
ROUTE Jakarta, Java, to Ambon, Moluccas

23 D6 WINDHOND May 30, 1658
SHIP Dutch East Indiaman, 360 tons
LOCATION Boompjes Island, off Java
ROUTE Local trading
CARGO Specie

**24 G6 FRANCISCO VIERA DE
FIGUEIREDO** May 29, 1660
SHIP Portuguese
LOCATION Ujung Pandang harbor,
Celebes
ROUTE Ujung Pandang, Celebes, to Goa,
India
CARGO Gold

㉕ G6 MACASSAR WRECKS
June 8, 1660
SHIP Portuguese ship, plus another wreck
LOCATION Ujung Pandang harbor, Celebes
ROUTE Ujung Pandang, Celebes, to Jakarta, Java
CARGO Gold and silver
Ship lost during battle with Dutch

㉖ G6 WALVIS Jan 7, 1663
SHIP Dutch East Indiaman, 1,000 tons
LOCATION Salayar Island, Celebes
ROUTE Local trading
CARGO Specie

㉗ G6 ZIERIKZEE 1668
SHIP Dutch East Indiaman, 400 tons
LOCATION Off Ujung Pandang, Celebes
ROUTE Local trading
CARGO Specie

㉘ G6 NIEUWENDAM
Oct 2, 1670
SHIP Dutch East Indiaman, 210 tons
LOCATION Between Bima, Sumbawa, and Ujung Pandang, Celebes
ROUTE Ujung Pandang, Celebes, to Ambon, Moluccas
CARGO Specie

㉙ I7 HUIS TE NOORDWIJK
Jan 24, 1687
SHIP Dutch East Indiaman, 506 tons
LOCATION Damar Island, approximately 7.30S 128.00E
CARGO Specie

㉚ H6 NOORDBECK
July 9, 1730
SHIP Dutch East Indiaman, 858 tons
LOCATION Cliffs of Lapando, just south of Buton Island, Celebes
ROUTE Jakarta, Java, to Ternate, Halmahera, Moluccas
CARGO Specie

㉛ H6 DELFT 1731
SHIP Dutch East Indiaman, 600 tons
LOCATION Just west of Buton Island, Celebes
ROUTE Local trading
CARGO Specie

㉜ G6 RIJKSDORP
June 1, 1734
SHIP Dutch East Indiaman, 792 tons
LOCATION Bay of Bone, Celebes
CARGO Specie

㉝ J6 SPIERING Mar 10, 1740
SHIP Dutch East Indiaman, 810 tons
LOCATION Island of Watubela, near Banda islands, Indonesia
ROUTE Local trading
CARGO Specie

㉞ D6 KASTEEL VAN WOERDEN
1744
SHIP Dutch East Indiaman, 850 tons
LOCATION Off rock, 9 miles (14 km) from Pamanukan, Java
CARGO Specie

㉟ G6 MAARSSEVEEN 1748
SHIP Dutch East Indiaman, 850 tons
LOCATION Just east of Salayar Island, Celebes
ROUTE Banda islands, Indonesia, to Jakarta, Java
CARGO Gold
Ship blew up

㊱ H6 NIEUWERKERK 1748
SHIP Dutch East Indiaman, 1,135 tons
LOCATION East of Binongko Island, Celebes
ROUTE Jakarta, Java, to Banda islands, Indonesia
CARGO Specie

㊲ H6 SCHELLAG 1748
SHIP Dutch East Indiaman, 850 tons
LOCATION Just east of Binongko Island, Celebes
ROUTE Japan to Jakarta, Java
CARGO Silver and porcelain

㊳ I6 SCHAKENBOS Feb 17, 1752
SHIP Dutch East Indiaman, 850 tons
LOCATION Manipa Strait, between Buru and Seram, Moluccas
ROUTE Jakarta, Java, to Ambon, Moluccas
CARGO Specie

㊴ F6 KLEVERSKERKE 1761
SHIP Dutch East Indiaman, 850 tons
LOCATION Between Jakarta, Java, and Ujung Pandang, Celebes
ROUTE Jakarta, Java, to Ujung Pandang, Celebes
CARGO Specie

㊵ D6 PIJLSWAART Feb 24, 1765
SHIP Dutch East Indiaman, 880 tons
LOCATION Near Jakarta, Java
ROUTE Netherlands to Jakarta, Java
CARGO Specie

㊶ H6 GIESSENBERG 1766
SHIP Dutch East Indiaman, 1,150 tons
LOCATION Just north of Buton Island, Celebes
ROUTE Jakarta, Java, to Banda islands, Indonesia
CARGO Specie

㊷ D6 EUROPA July 23, 1784
SHIP Dutch East Indiaman, 1,200 tons
LOCATION Rock of Indramajoe, a few miles (km) east of Jakarta, Java
ROUTE Local trading
CARGO Specie

㊸ H7 OCEAN Feb 1, 1797
SHIP English East Indiaman
LOCATION Island of Kalaotoa, Indonesia
ROUTE UK to China
CARGO Specie

㊹ G7 ALICE 1817
LOCATION Sumba Island, south of Flores
ROUTE Port Louis, Mauritius, to Surabaya, Java
CARGO Specie
SALVAGE 820 sovereigns recovered at time of loss

㊺ D6 JOANNA MARIA WILHELMINA 1831
LOCATION Java
CARGO Specie valued at 130,000 guilders

㊻ G5 PREMIER July 27, 1844
LOCATION Panjang Island, Borneo
ROUTE Hong Kong to Bali
CARGO Specie and jewels
SALVAGE Looted

㊼ D6 WENA Dec 26, 1852
SHIP Dutch
LOCATION Near Jakarta, Java
ROUTE Rotterdam, Netherlands, to Jakarta, Java
CARGO Specie
SALVAGE Some salvage at time of loss

㊽ C6 ROBERTUS HENDRIKUS
June 10, 1856
SHIP Dutch
LOCATION Jakarta roads, Java
ROUTE Netherlands to Jakarta, Java
CARGO Government specie valued at 80,000 florins

㊾ E6 LIEUTENANT ADMIRAL STELLINGWERF 1857
SHIP Dutch schooner
LOCATION 7.01S 110.27E
ROUTE Semarang, Java, to Singapore
CARGO Treasure valued at US $20,000 to $30,000

㊿ D7 AGATHA MARIA June 17, 1861
SHIP Dutch sailing ship
LOCATION Reef near Cilacap, Java, approximately 7.41S 109.05E
ROUTE Cilacap, Java, to Amsterdam, Netherlands
CARGO Coins
SALVAGE Salvage attempt at time of loss, but results unknown

51 G6 FRANKFORT OLD Feb 19, 1863
SHIP British bark
LOCATION Reef near Ujung Pandang, Celebes
ROUTE Cardiff, Wales, to Shanghai, China
CARGO Gold and silver specie valued at £50,000 sterling
Capt. Hicks

52 C7 NEVA Aug 7, 1875
SHIP French, Messageries Maritimes
LOCATION 8 miles (13 km) from Jakarta, Java
ROUTE Singapore to Jakarta, Java
CARGO Specie
SALVAGE Some salvage at time of loss

53 N6 NEW GUINEA WRECK 1943
SHIP Japanese
LOCATION Off Sepik, Papua New Guinea
CARGO Gold valued at US $1.68 billion
SALVAGE Attempted by Singapore-based group
Ship supposedly sunk by British submarine

54 E6 ITSUKISHIMA Oct 17, 1944
SHIP Japanese minelayer, 1,970 tons
LOCATION 5.27S 112.43E
ROUTE Indonesia to Japan
CARGO 2 tons gold

55 D7 BARENTSZ 1945
SHIP Japanese
LOCATION Cilacap harbor, Java
ROUTE Indonesia to Japan
CARGO Possibly 20 tons gold
SALVAGE Probably salvaged

56 D7 PASIR 1945
SHIP Japanese, 1,187 tons
LOCATION Cilacap harbour, Java
ROUTE Indonesia to Japan
CARGO 5 tons gold
SALVAGE Probably salvaged

THE PHILIPPINES

The map for these listings is on p. 154
● No known salvage
■ Some salvage history known

❶ F5 SAN JUANILLO 1575
SHIP Spanish
LOCATION San Bernardino Strait, Philippines
ROUTE Manila, Philippines, to Acapulco, Mexico
CARGO Gold and porcelain
Capt. Juan de Ribera

❷ E5 MARINDUQUE WRECK
1590
SHIP Spanish almiranta
LOCATION Island of Marinduque, between Mindoro and Luzon, Philippines
ROUTE Acapulco, Mexico, to Manila, Philippines
CARGO Silver specie

❸ F5 SAN JERONIMO June 1596
SHIP Spanish
LOCATION Reefs of Catanduanes, Philippines
ROUTE Acapulco, Mexico, to Manila, Philippines
CARGO Silver specie
Capt. Fernando de Castro

❹ D6 CHINESE JUNK c. 1600
SHIP Chinese
LOCATION Royal Captain Shoal, 47 miles (76 km) west of Palawan, Philippines
CARGO Porcelain
SALVAGE Located and salvaged by Frank Goddio in late 1980s

❺ D7 ROYAL CAPTAIN SHOAL
WRECK 16th–17th century
SHIP Chinese junk
LOCATION Royal Captain Shoal, 47 miles (76 km) west of Palawan, Philippines
ROUTE China to Manila, Philippines, to Borneo
CARGO Porcelain, trade-wind beads (used as currency), and brass gongs
SALVAGE Salvaged by Frank Goddio and Wild West First
Wreck was found during the search for the Royal Captain

❻ E5 SAN DIEGO Dec 12, 1600
SHIP Spanish
LOCATION Isle of Fortune, Manila Bay, Philippines
CARGO Porcelain and other artifacts
SALVAGE Recently discovered by Frank Goddio's team
Ship lost during battle with Dutchman Oliver van Noort

❼ F5 SANTO TOMAS May 1601
SHIP Spanish
LOCATION Catamban Bay, Catanduanes, Philippines
ROUTE Acapulco, Mexico, to Manila, Philippines
CARGO Silver specie valued at 2.5 million pesos
SALVAGE Partly salvaged at time of loss

8 E5 NUESTRA SENORA DE LOS REMEDIOS 1603
SHIP Spanish
LOCATION Manila, Philippines
ROUTE Acapulco, Mexico, to Manila, Philippines
CARGO Silver specie

9 G7 JESUS MARIA 1606
SHIP Spanish
LOCATION Mindanao, Philippines
ROUTE Acapulco, Mexico, to Manila, Philippines
CARGO Silver specie
SALVAGE Largely salvaged at time of loss

10 D5 AEOLUS GROTE
Apr 16, 1617
SHIP Dutch East Indiaman, 320 tons
LOCATION Near Wittert's Island, north of Manila Bay, Philippines
CARGO Loot from 2 Chinese junks
Ship blew up during Battle of Manila

11 E4 GROTE ZON
Apr 16, 1617
SHIP Dutch East Indiaman, 600 tons
LOCATION Manila Bay, Philippines
CARGO Loot from 2 Chinese junks
Ship blew up during Battle of Manila

12 E5 NIEUWE SONNE
Apr 16, 1617
SHIP Dutch East Indiaman, 320 tons
LOCATION Near Wittert's Island, north of Manila Bay, Philippines
CARGO Loot from Chinese junks
Ship burned

13 E4 TER VEERE
Apr 16, 1617
SHIP Dutch East Indiaman, 320 tons
LOCATION Near Wittert's Island, north of Manila Bay, Philippines
CARGO Loot from Chinese junks
Ship blew up during Battle of Manila

14 G7 SANTA ANA 1620
SHIP Spanish
LOCATION Mindanao, Philippines
ROUTE Acapulco, Mexico, to Manila, Philippines
CARGO Silver specie
SALVAGE Largely salvaged at time of loss

15 E5 SANTA MARIA MAGDALENA 1631
SHIP Spanish
LOCATION Port of Cavite, Manila, Philippines
ROUTE Manila, Philippines, to Acapulco, Mexico
CARGO Porcelain and gold

16 E5 CHAMPAN 1639
SHIP Spanish
LOCATION 12 miles (19 km) from Manila, Philippines
ROUTE Manila, Philippines, to China
CARGO Silver specie

17 F4 SAN AMBROSIO 1639
SHIP Spanish
LOCATION East coast of Luzon, Philippines
ROUTE Acapulco, Mexico, to Manila, Philippines
CARGO Silver specie
SALVAGE Private cargo valued at 550,000 pesos not recovered, but cargo belonging to the King was saved

18 E3 SAN LUIS 1646
SHIP Spanish
LOCATION Philippines
ROUTE Acapulco, Mexico, to Manila, Philippines
CARGO Silver specie
SALVAGE Silver specie saved

19 E5 SAN DIEGO June 1654
SHIP Spanish
LOCATION Near Balaian, Manila Bay, Philippines
ROUTE Acapulco, Mexico, to Manila, Philippines
CARGO Silver specie
SALVAGE Some salvage at time of loss

20 E5 WILLIAM 1658
SHIP English East Indiaman
LOCATION In sight of Manila port, Philippines
ROUTE India to Manila, Philippines
CARGO Specie

21 G6 SAN FRANCISCO JAVIER c. 1659
SHIP Spanish
LOCATION Port of Borongan, Samar, Philippines
ROUTE Acapulco, Mexico, to Manila, Philippines
CARGO Silver specie
SALVAGE Looting at time of loss and some salvage

22 F8 TREVITORE Sept 4, 1678
SHIP English East Indiaman
LOCATION Mindanao, Philippines
ROUTE Madras, India, to Manila, Philippines
CARGO Specie

23 E5 SAN JOSE 1694
SHIP Spanish
LOCATION Lubang Island, Philippines
ROUTE Manila, Philippines, to Acapulco, Mexico
CARGO Porcelain and gold
SALVAGE Excavated by Frank Goddio's team in 1990s

24 F5 SANTO CRISTO DE BURGOS 1726
SHIP Spanish
LOCATION Ticao Island, Philippines
ROUTE Manila, Philippines, to Acapulco, Mexico
CARGO Porcelain and gold

25 G7 NUESTRA SENORA DE LOS DOLORES 1729
SHIP Spanish patache
LOCATION Near town of Abulu, north Mindanao, Philippines
ROUTE Manila, Philippines, to Acapulco, Mexico
CARGO Porcelain and gold

26 F6 SACRA FAMILIA 1730
SHIP Spanish
LOCATION Embocadero, San Bernardino Strait, Philippines
ROUTE Acapulco, Mexico, to Manila, Philippines
CARGO Specie

27 D6 PATACHE 1735
SHIP Spanish
LOCATION Rocks off Calamian Group, Philippines
ROUTE Acapulco, Mexico, to Manila, Philippines
CARGO Silver specie
SALVAGE Over 1.5 million pesos salvaged at time of loss

28 G5 CAPITANA 1756
SHIP Spanish
LOCATION Off Catanduanes, Philippines
ROUTE Acapulco, Mexico, to Manila, Philippines
CARGO Silver specie

29 F5 LA GALERA 1756
SHIP Spanish
LOCATION Catanduanes, Philippines
ROUTE Acapulco, Mexico, to Manila, Philippines
CARGO Silver specie

30 E8 GRIFFIN June 20, 1761
SHIP English East Indiaman
LOCATION Griffin Rocks, north of Jolo, Philippines
ROUTE China to UK, via Philippines
CARGO Porcelain
SALVAGE Recently relocated and partly salvaged

31 D7 ROYAL CAPTAIN Dec 17, 1773
SHIP English East Indiaman, 499 tons
LOCATION Royal Captain Shoal, 47 miles (76 km) west of Palawan, Philippines
ROUTE Manila, Philippines, to UK
CARGO Porcelain, glass beads, and gold
Ship was searched for by Frank Goddio, but not found

32 F6 SAN ANDRES Oct 1797
SHIP Spanish
LOCATION Naranjos Shoals, near Ticao Island, San Bernardino Strait, Philippines
ROUTE Acapulco, Mexico, to Manila, Philippines
CARGO Silver specie

33 E5 TELLICHERRY 1808
SHIP Botany Bay ship
LOCATION Apo Shoal, Mindoro, Philippines
ROUTE Australia to China
CARGO Specie

34 E5 FIDELIDAD 1821
SHIP Spanish
LOCATION Off Lubang Island, Philippines
CARGO Specie

35 D5 REGENT Nov 3, 1822
SHIP English East Indiaman
LOCATION Near Manila, Philippines
ROUTE London, England, to Manila, Philippines
CARGO Specie

36 E5 ASIA Oct 24, 1827
LOCATION Off Lubang Island, Philippines
CARGO Specie
SALVAGE Capt. Campbell of *HMS Cyrene* involved in salvage attempt

37 D6 SULTANA Jan 4, 1841
LOCATION 30 miles (50 km) NE of Bombay Shoal, coast of Palawan, Philippines
CARGO Specie and jewels
SALVAGE Partly salvaged

38 G5 OHIO Nov 1852
SHIP German
LOCATION Philippines
ROUTE Lima, Peru, to China
CARGO Specie
SALVAGE Some salvage at time of loss

39 D4 REINDEER Feb 12, 1859
SHIP American clipper
LOCATION Coral reef, near Iba, Luzon, Philippines
ROUTE Manila, Philippines, to San Francisco, California, US
CARGO Gold

40 E4 CHINA PACKET Aug 4, 1868
SHIP American
LOCATION Philippines
ROUTE California, US, to Hong Kong
CARGO Specie

41 D6 QUEEN July 27, 1878
LOCATION 24 hours' sailing from Palaos, Palawan, Philippines
ROUTE Singapore to Manila, Philippines
CARGO Large quantity of specie

42 E2 RAINBOW Oct 31, 1891
SHIP British
LOCATION Approximately 20.00N 120.00E
CARGO Specie

43 E5 CORREGIDOR 1942
LOCATION Corregidor Island, Manila Bay, Philippines
CARGO 15,792,000 silver pesos
SALVAGE Largely salvaged during the Second World War, but it has been estimated that in excess of 1 million pesos remain unsalvaged
Ship dumped by US minelayer, Harrison, *to avoid seizure by Japanese*

44 D4 HOSPITAL SHIP 1945
SHIP Japanese hospital ship
LOCATION 16.22N 119.49E
ROUTE Philippines to Japan
CARGO Rumors of bullion

MALAYA AND SUMATRA

The map for these listings is on p. 155.

● No known salvage
■ Some salvage history known

❶ I3 SHIP OF TU YUAN c. 1400
SHIP Chinese junk
LOCATION Chi Shui Lian, Surat Passage, off promontory of Aceh, Sumatra
ROUTE China to India
Chinese junk of the Cheng Ho era

❷ M6 SHIPS OF CH'EN TSU-I 1407
SHIP Chinese pirate ships
LOCATION Palembang, Sumatra
CARGO Treasure
Ship sunk and burned by Cheng Ho during the return voyage of his first expedition

❸ K4 SANTA CLARA 1508
SHIP Portuguese
LOCATION Polveira Island, off coast of east Sumatra
CARGO Silver

❹ K4 FLOR DE LA MAR 1511
SHIP Portuguese
LOCATION Polveira Island, off coast of east Sumatra
ROUTE Melaka, Malaysia, to Goa, India
CARGO Loot from the sacking of Melaka, including jeweled and gold artifacts, 4 ornate lions, 2 daggers, and a royal throne
Recent newspaper claims that the wreck has been found are not proven. See pp. 38–39.

❺ J3 SHIP OF ANTONIO PACHECO 1516
SHIP Portuguese
LOCATION NE of Sumatra, approximately 5.20N 97.00E
ROUTE India to China
CARGO Specie

❻ I3 SHIP OF FRANCISCO DE MELO 1527
SHIP Portuguese
LOCATION Near Aceh, Sumatra
ROUTE Aceh, Sumatra, to Goa, India
CARGO Gold

❼ K5 SAO PAULO Jan 1561
SHIP Portuguese East Indiaman
LOCATION Off west coast of Sumatra
ROUTE Portugal to India
CARGO Specie and armaments
SALVAGE Some cargo washed ashore
See pp. 40–41

❽ J3 ATJEHNESE SHIP Mar 1565
SHIP Atjehnese
LOCATION Off northern Sumatra
ROUTE Iran to Aceh, Sumatra
CARGO Silver, gold, and jewels
Ship lost during battle with Portuguese galleon, Sao Sebastiao. Both ships caught fire and were destroyed.

❾ L5 SHIP OF COUTINHO 1583
SHIP Portuguese
LOCATION Off Melaka, Malaysia
ROUTE Goa, India, to China
CARGO Specie
Ship blew up in battle with Atjehnese

❿ L5 JOHOR WRECK 1583
SHIP Portuguese
LOCATION Rock off Johor, near Melaka, Malaysia
ROUTE Goa, India, to Macao
CARGO 1 million silver cruzados for the Chinese silk trade

⓫ I3 SHIP OF SIMAO FERREIRA Jan 1583
SHIP Portuguese
LOCATION Between Changi Point and Bedok, SE Singapore
ROUTE Melaka, Malaysia, to China
CARGO Large quantity of silver cruzados
SALVAGE Some salvage at time of loss

⓬ I3 SHIP OF LEONARDO DA SA 1588
SHIP Portuguese carrack
LOCATION Aceh, Sumatra
ROUTE Goa, India, to China
CARGO Specie for purchase of copper

⓭ L5 DON DUARTE DE GUERRA Aug 16, 1607
SHIP Portuguese
LOCATION Off Cape Tuan, Malaysia
CARGO Specie
SALVAGE Located in 1993 by Malaysian-based company, Transea sdn, and bronze cannons were recovered
Ship destroyed by fire during Battle of Malacca

⓮ L4 NOSSA SENHORA DE CONCEPCION Oct 29, 1607
SHIP Portuguese, 1,000 tons
LOCATION Off Melaka, Malaysia
CARGO Specie
Ship destroyed by fire during Battle of Malacca

⓯ L4 SHIP OF PAULO DE PORTUGAL Oct 29, 1607
SHIP Portuguese carrack
LOCATION Off Melaka, Malaysia
ROUTE Goa, India, to China
CARGO 200,000 cruzados plus considerable private merchandise
Ship lost during Battle of Malacca

⓰ L5 JOHOR STRAIT WRECK 1615
SHIP Portuguese carrack
LOCATION 1.27N 103.46E
ROUTE India to China
CARGO Silver
1,000 people on board ship at time of loss

⓱ L8 AEOLUS KLEINE Aug 25, 1616
SHIP Dutch East Indiaman, 240 tons
LOCATION Rocks of Enggano, Indonesia
ROUTE Coromandel, India, to Banten, Java
CARGO Merchandise and possibly silver
SALVAGE Very little cargo saved at time of loss

⓲ L8 SUN Nov 1618
SHIP English East Indiaman, 700 tons
LOCATION Rocks of Enggano, Indonesia
ROUTE UK to China
CARGO Treasure of English East India Company and Sir Thomas Dale's private treasure, plus 80,000 reals captured from Portuguese ships en route
SALVAGE Attempted at time of loss but largely unsuccessful

⓳ L7 HOORN Dec 14, 1619
SHIP Dutch East Indiaman, 700 tons
LOCATION 80 miles (130 km) west of Sumatra, 5.00S
ROUTE Netherlands to Banten, Java
CARGO Specie
Bontekoe, Dutch author of early travel book, on board

⓴ L5 CONCEICAO 1620
SHIP Portuguese East Indiaman
LOCATION Island near Melaka Fortress, Malaysia
ROUTE Goa, India, to Macao
CARGO Silver coins

㉑ L5 WIERINGEN June 2, 1636
SHIP Dutch East Indiaman
LOCATION Outside Melaka, Malaysia
CARGO Specie

㉒ M8 PRINS WILLEM Jan 2, 1637
SHIP Dutch East Indiaman, 500 tons
LOCATION Sunda Strait
ROUTE Jakarta, Java, to Netherlands
CARGO Porcelain
SALVAGE Some salvage at time of loss

㉓ M5 ADMIRAL STELLINGWERF REEF WRECK 1643
SHIP Chinese junk
LOCATION Admiral Stellingwerf Reef, east of Bintan, Indonesia
ROUTE China to Indonesia
CARGO 17th-century Ming porcelain
SALVAGE Salvaged by Michael Hatcher
Hatcher found the Geldermalsen after finding this wreck about 1 mile (1.5 km) away

㉔ M6 FREDERIK HENDRIK 1646
SHIP Dutch East Indiaman, 1,100 tons
LOCATION Reef in Bangka Strait
ROUTE Jakarta, Java, to China
CARGO Gold and silver specie

㉕ M7 SCHERMER June 4, 1671
SHIP Dutch East Indiaman, 636 tons
LOCATION Bangka Strait
ROUTE Jakarta, Java, to China
CARGO Silver

㉖ N6 PRINS WILLEM HENDRIK Sept 18, 1686
SHIP Dutch East Indiaman, 1,094 tons
LOCATION Bangka Strait
ROUTE Jakarta, Java, to Thailand
CARGO Specie

㉗ L5 SPEEDWELL Feb 1702
SHIP Scottish East Indiaman
LOCATION On rock, Melaka roads, Malaysia
ROUTE UK to China
CARGO Specie
SALVAGE Largely salvaged at time of loss

㉘ M8 KATTENDIJK Apr 1709
SHIP Dutch East Indiaman, 759 tons
LOCATION Sunda Strait
ROUTE Local trading
CARGO Specie

㉙ N7 CATHERINE Sept 20, 1716
SHIP English East Indiaman
LOCATION Catherine Rock, east of Belitung, Indonesia
ROUTE UK to Bengkulu, Sumatra
CARGO Silver specie
SALVAGE Some salvage at time of loss

㉚ L5 JOHOR RIVER WRECKS Mar 1718
SHIP 2 sloops
LOCATION Johor River, near Pancor, Malaysia
CARGO 200 peculs (27,000 lb/12,000 kg) gold and many other valuable items belonging to King Raiamuda of Johor

㉛ M5 RISDAM 1726
SHIP Dutch East Indiaman, 520 tons
LOCATION Near Setindam Island, Malaysia, 2.30N 103.52E
ROUTE Thailand to Jakarta, Java
CARGO Ivory
SALVAGE Recently salvaged

㉜ M5 GELDERMALSEN Jan 3, 1752
SHIP Dutch East Indiaman, 1,150 tons
LOCATION Admiral Stellingwerf Reef, east of Bintan, Indonesia
ROUTE China to Netherlands
CARGO Porcelain and gold
SALVAGE Salvaged by Michael Hatcher and Max de Rham. Cargo sold for £10 million sterling at Christie's, Amsterdam.
See pp. 74–75.

㉝ L7 DENHAM 1758
SHIP English East Indiaman
LOCATION Bengkulu roads, Sumatra, 3.47S 102.15E
ROUTE UK to Bengkulu, Sumatra
CARGO Silver specie
Ship burned to avoid capture by French

㉞ M7 LINDENHOF May 15, 1766
SHIP Dutch East Indiaman, 1,150 tons
LOCATION Tree Island, Indonesia, approximately 4.10S 106.00E
ROUTE Jakarta, Java, to China
CARGO 10,000 silver guilders

㉟ M8 ZEEPLOEG 1779
SHIP Dutch East Indiaman, 1,150 tons
LOCATION Sunda Strait
ROUTE China to Netherlands
CARGO Porcelain

㊱ L4 OVERDUIN June 27, 1784
SHIP Dutch East Indiaman, 1,150 tons
LOCATION Melaka roads, Malaysia
ROUTE Jakarta, Java, to Netherlands
CARGO Porcelain

㊲ K4 MALACCA STRAIT WRECK 1787
SHIP Portuguese carrack
LOCATION Strait of Malacca
ROUTE Goa, India, to Macao
CARGO Silver, plus valuable personal possessions

㊳ M6 VANSITTART Aug 24, 1789
SHIP English East Indiaman, 828 tons
LOCATION Bangka, Indonesia
ROUTE UK to China
CARGO 45 chests of silver, each containing 156,960 oz (4,450 kg)
SALVAGE Only 3 of the 13 chests thrown overboard were recovered; the 6 left in the ship's hold were too deep to recover.

㊴ M6 HMS RESISTANCE July 24, 1798
SHIP British warship
LOCATION Near Palembang, Sumatra, 9 miles (14 km) off the coast
ROUTE To China
CARGO Specie
The HMS Resistance had seized several Dutch prizes

㊵ O6 ONTARIO Jan 4, 1799
SHIP American East Indiaman
LOCATION Ontario Reef, Karimata Strait
ROUTE China to US
CARGO Porcelain for the New York market, US
SALVAGE Part of the wreck found in 1992, but no recoveries made

㊶ N7 FORBES Nov 11, 1806
SHIP English country trader
LOCATION South end of Strait of Belitung
ROUTE China to India
CARGO Gold and porcelain

㊷ L8 UNION 1815
SHIP English East Indiaman
LOCATION Enggano, Indonesia
ROUTE UK to Far East
CARGO Specie

㊸ L5 DIANA 1817
SHIP British
LOCATION Off Melaka, Malaysia
ROUTE China to UK
CARGO Porcelain
Wreck being searched for at present

㊹ N7 HMS ALCESTE Feb 18, 1817
SHIP British frigate
LOCATION Rock in the Gaspar Strait, 3 to 4 miles (5 to 6 km) from Liat Island, Indonesia
ROUTE China to UK
CARGO Dr. Abel's entire collection of plants, minerals, and other objects lost
SALVAGE Some plundering by pirates

45 L7 FAME Feb 2, 1824
SHIP English East Indiaman
LOCATION 50 miles (80 km) SW of Bengkulu, Sumatra
ROUTE Sumatra to UK
CARGO Raffles's entire collection of books and other valuables were lost, as well as gold, jewels, and a silver plate service presented to Raffles by the Javanese
See pp. 90–91

46 M5 DOURADO Jan 25, 1829
SHIP Portuguese brig
LOCATION Coast of Bintan, Indonesia, near Pedra Branca rock
ROUTE Macao to Bombay, India
CARGO US $500,000 plus valuable artifacts and antiques
SALVAGE Possibility of some plundering
Archaeologist Domenic de Rienzi on board with his collection of rare astronomical instruments. See pp. 44–45.

47 M5 PEDRA BRANCA WRECK
July 1830
SHIP Chinese junk
LOCATION Near Pedra Branca rock, Strait of Singapore
ROUTE Singapore to Shanghai, China
CARGO Singapore $22,016

48 M5 PARSEE Nov 1845
SHIP British bark, 390 tons
LOCATION NE point of Bintan, Indonesia
CARGO Very valuable cargo, including specie
SALVAGE Partly salvaged at time of loss

49 M5 FREDERICK VI
July 6, 1846
SHIP British mailship, P & O Line
LOCATION 0.36N 105.17E
CARGO Specie

50 J2 ARDASEER Apr 17, 1851
SHIP British
LOCATION Approximately 9.00N 97.30E
ROUTE China to Singapore to Calcutta, India
CARGO Large quantity of specie
SALVAGE Some treasure removed before ship sank

51 L5 PACHA July 22, 1851
SHIP British paddlesteamer, P & O Line
LOCATION Mount Formosa, 8 miles (13 km) NE half E of Strait of Malacca
ROUTE Hong Kong to Calcutta, India
CARGO Cargo valued at US $600,000 originally on board, including 42 boxes of gold bars, 47 boxes of gold dollars, 9 boxes of gold dust, 6 boxes of sycee, 1 case of diamonds, and 1 case of silverware
SALVAGE Cargo valued at US $300,000 to $350,000 recovered

52 M7 WILLEM KRONPRINS
Nov 9, 1878
SHIP Dutch steamship
LOCATION Bangka Strait
CARGO Specie
SALVAGE Attempted at time of loss, but results unknown
Collision with the Atjeh caused the ship to sink in 13 fathoms water

53 M5 LA SEYNE Nov 14, 1909
SHIP French mail steamship, Messageries Maritimes
LOCATION Near Singapore, 1.01N 104.12.10E
ROUTE Jakarta, Java, to Europe
CARGO Diamonds
Ship collided with the Onda

54 M6 VYNER BROOKE
Feb 13, 1942
SHIP Sarawak Steamship Company
LOCATION 15 miles (24 km) north of Mentok, Bangka, Indonesia
CARGO Jewelry

55 K4 I34 Nov 12, 1943
SHIP Japanese submarine
LOCATION 5.17N 100.05E
ROUTE Japan to Germany
CARGO Half a ton gold
SALVAGE Salvaged, but no reports that gold was found

56 K4 HAGURA May 16, 1945
SHIP Japanese heavy cruiser
LOCATION 30 miles (50 km) SW of Pinang, Malaysia
ROUTE Malaysia to Japan
CARGO Gold

57 M6 ASHIGARA June 8, 1945
SHIP Japanese heavy cruiser, 12,700 tons
LOCATION North entrance to Bangka Strait, 1.59S 104.57E
ROUTE Indonesia to Japan
CARGO Gold
SALVAGE Worked by joint Japanese and Indonesian salvage venture in 1988
Ship sunk by British submarine

THE SOUTH CHINA SEA AND GULF OF THAILAND

The map for these listings is on pp. 156–157.

● No known salvage
■ Some salvage history known

1 H1 WU WRECKS 233
SHIP Warships
LOCATION Yellow Sea
CARGO Artifacts
Lost in a storm. Ships from state of Wu.

2 D8 DRAGON JUNK 1069
SHIP Dragon junk
LOCATION Rocks near port of Bo Chanh, probably near Vung Tau, Vietnam
CARGO Treasure

3 G4 QUANZHOU WRECK
12th century
SHIP Chinese
LOCATION Quanzhou, China
CARGO Artifacts
SALVAGE Recently excavated
Sung dynasty ship

4 F5 MANDARIN'S CAP WRECK
12th–13th century
SHIP Chinese junk
LOCATION Close to Mandarin's Cap, approximately 60 miles (96 km) SW of Macao
ROUTE Possibly China to Indonesia
CARGO Porcelain, silver ingots, and gold chains
SALVAGE Partly salvaged in the late 1980s by Roy Martin and Lyle Craigie Halkett who were working on a joint venture with the Chinese

5 F4 SUNG WRECKS 1279
SHIP Chinese
LOCATION Near Guangzhou, China
CARGO Artifacts
Ship lost in battle between Sung troops and Mongols

6 C9 THAILAND WRECK
14th century
LOCATION 60 miles (96 km) off coast of Thailand
CARGO Porcelain valued at £2.8 million sterling
SALVAGE Salvaged by Michael Hatcher in 1992. Cargo seized by Thai Government.

7 E7 SHIP OF ANTONIO DE FARIA
16th century
SHIP Portuguese
LOCATION South China Sea
ROUTE Hainan, China, to Goa, India
CARGO Loot from the royal tombs in Hainan, China

8 C8 KO CHANG WRECK
16th century
LOCATION Near Ko Chang, Thailand
CARGO Porcelain
SALVAGE Recently excavated

9 F5 4 SHIPS OF FARIA 1540
LOCATION Wanshan Islands, China
CARGO Looted treasure

10 E6 SHIP OF EMMANUEL DE MENDOZA Oct 1561
SHIP Spanish
LOCATION Haikou harbor, Hainan, China
ROUTE China to Melaka, Malaysia
CARGO Porcelain and gold

11 E6 SHIP OF ALFARO 1580
SHIP Portuguese
LOCATION Haikou, Hainan, China
ROUTE Macao to Goa, India
CARGO Specie

12 F5 SAN MARTIN 1587
SHIP Spanish
LOCATION Macao
ROUTE Manila, Philippines, to Macao
CARGO Specie
SALVAGE Mostly salvaged at time of loss
Ship wrecked and burned. Capt. D. Lopez de Palaios.

13 F6 SHIP OF JOHN CAVADO DE GAMBOA 1595
SHIP Portuguese
LOCATION 180 miles (290 km) from Macao
ROUTE Goa, India, to Macao
CARGO Silver

14 F5 ALMIRANTA 1598
SHIP Spanish
LOCATION Uninhabited island south of Macao
ROUTE Manila, Philippines, to Macao
CARGO Silver
Ship belonging to Spanish sea captain Dasmarinas

15 D9 VUNG TAU WRECK
17th century
SHIP Chinese junk
LOCATION 18.5 miles (30 km) east of Condor Island, ESE of island of Hon Bay Canh, Vietnam, 8.38N 106.48E
ROUTE From China
CARGO Porcelain
SALVAGE Salvaged in 1991 by Sverker Hallstrom and sold at Christie's, Amsterdam, for £4 million sterling
See pp. 28–29

16 F5 GUANGDONG COAST WRECK
1601
SHIP Portuguese
LOCATION Guangdong coast, China
ROUTE Goa, India, to Macao
CARGO 400,000 pardoes of reals of eight

17 G6 PORTUGUESE SHIP 1609
SHIP Portuguese
LOCATION Uninhabited island between Macao and Manila, Philippines, probably Dongsha Qundao, China
ROUTE Macao to Manila, Philippines
CARGO Amber, musk, pearls, and precious stones

18 F5 SHANGCHUAN WRECK
1613
SHIP Portuguese
LOCATION Near Shangchuan, China, 180 miles (290 km) from Macao
ROUTE Goa, India, to Macao
CARGO Silver
Ship lost in a typhoon

19 E5 UNICORN 1619
SHIP English East Indiaman
LOCATION Near Macao
ROUTE Banten, Java, to Japan
CARGO Specie
Crew survived

20 E5 HOPE 1622
SHIP Dutch East Indiaman
LOCATION Near Macao
ROUTE Jakarta, Java, to Guangzhou, China
CARGO Specie

21 G7 SHIP OF ANTONIO SOARES VIVAS 1630
SHIP Portuguese
LOCATION South China Sea
ROUTE China to India
CARGO 150,000 xerafins of silver

22 F5 SHIP OF ANTONIO PINTO 1636
SHIP Portuguese, Captain General of Fleet of Japan
LOCATION Macao
ROUTE Macao to Japan
CARGO Gold

23 D6 KEIZERIN Oct 29, 1636
SHIP Dutch East Indiaman, 200 tons
LOCATION Bay of Padaran, coast of Champa, Vietnam
ROUTE Taiwan to Vietnam
CARGO Porcelain
SALVAGE Recent attempts to relocate wreck not successful

24 G5 JONKER Oct 21, 1647
SHIP Dutch East Indiaman
LOCATION Near Guangzhou, China, 23.14N 118.16E
ROUTE Jakarta, Java, to Guangzhou, China
CARGO 75,000 taels of silver
SALVAGE 52 chests salvaged by Chinese

25 G5 UTRECHT June 22, 1654
SHIP Dutch East Indiaman
LOCATION Reef off Dongsha Qundao, China
ROUTE Jakarta, Java, to China
CARGO Silver
SALVAGE 1 chest of silver saved

26 F6 GEELMUIDEN 1659
SHIP Dutch East Indiaman, 202 tons
LOCATION South China Sea
ROUTE Jakarta, Java, to Guangzhou, China
CARGO Silver

27 F9 ZWARTE BUL 1659
SHIP Dutch East Indiaman, 400 tons
LOCATION South China Sea
ROUTE Jakarta, Java, to Japan
CARGO Specie

28 E8 WAPEN VAN ZEELAND Sept 16, 1663
SHIP Dutch East Indiaman
LOCATION South China Sea
ROUTE Jakarta, Java, to China
CARGO Silver

29 F5 SHIP OF PENHA DE FRACA 1668
SHIP Portuguese
LOCATION Wanshan Islands, China
ROUTE Goa, India, to Macao
CARGO Silver specie

30 F5 SAN MIGUEL 1668
SHIP Spanish
LOCATION Wanshan Islands, China
ROUTE Manila, Philippines, to Macao
CARGO Specie

31 F6 HOOGKARSPEL 1670
SHIP Dutch East Indiaman, 212 tons
LOCATION South China Sea, between Vietnam and Japan
ROUTE Vietnam to Japan
CARGO Specie

32 C8 LANTHAM Feb 16, 1680
SHIP English trader
LOCATION Coast of Cambodia
ROUTE China to India
CARGO Porcelain and gold

33 D6 IMYRNASTE Feb 25, 1683
SHIP English East Indiaman
LOCATION Bar of Tongking, Vietnam
ROUTE UK to China
CARGO Specie

34 F5 MONSARATE 1686
SHIP Portuguese
LOCATION Near Macao
ROUTE Goa, India, to Macao
CARGO Silver

35 F6 PORTUGUESE WRECK 1690
SHIP Portuguese
LOCATION North Paracel Islands
ROUTE Goa, India, to Macao
CARGO Specie

36 F7 ARION 1714
SHIP Dutch East Indiaman, 630 tons
LOCATION Paracel Islands
ROUTE Jakarta, Java, to Japan
CARGO Specie

37 E5 NUESTRA SENORA DE LORETO 1719
SHIP Spanish
LOCATION Coast of Vietnam
ROUTE India to Thailand
CARGO Specie

38 E6 ALBLASSERDAM 1735
SHIP Dutch East Indiaman
LOCATION Off coast of China
ROUTE Guangzhou, China, to Netherlands
CARGO Porcelain

39 F5 DEN DAM July 3, 1735
SHIP Dutch East Indiaman
LOCATION Near Guangzhou, China
ROUTE Jakarta, Java, to Guangzhou, China
CARGO Silver
SALVAGE Small quantity of silver removed before ship foundered

40 F8 VERWACHTING 1744
SHIP Dutch East Indiaman, 850 tons
LOCATION South China Sea
ROUTE China to Surat, India
CARGO Porcelain and gold

41 E7 EARL TEMPLE 1759
SHIP British
LOCATION South of Paracel Islands
ROUTE Jakarta, Java, to Manila, Philippines
CARGO Specie

42 G5 FREDERIK ADOLPHUS Sept 4, 1761
SHIP Swedish East Indiaman
LOCATION East Dongsha Qundao, China
CARGO Silver
SALVAGE 39 boxes of silver salvaged

43 F5 ELIZABETH Jan 8, 1763
SHIP English East Indiaman
LOCATION Peak of Lintin, SE by E and 6 or 7 miles (10 or 11 km) from Canton River, China
ROUTE UK to China
CARGO Silver
Ship blew up. The fire was started by 2 French prisoners and the sailmaker smoking in the cable tier.

44 F6 RIJNSBURG July 17, 1772
SHIP Dutch East Indiaman, 850 tons
LOCATION Near Mandarin's Cap, China, approximately 60 miles (96 km) SW of Macao
ROUTE Jakarta, Java, to Guangzhou, China
CARGO 43,168.96 oz (1,223.84 kg) silver and 850,000 lb (385,560 kg) tin
SALVAGE Most of silver saved at time of loss
8 Chinese divers were eaten by sharks while salvaging silver

45 F4 PRINCESS SOPHIE FREDERICK 1781
SHIP Danish East Indiaman
LOCATION Huang-pu, China
ROUTE Denmark to China
CARGO Silver specie valued at £60,000 sterling
SALVAGE Some salvage thought to have taken place

46 F7 ADMIRAAL DE SUFFREN 1787
SHIP Dutch East Indiaman, 1,300 tons
LOCATION Rocks off Lincoln Island, Paracel Islands, 16.40N
ROUTE China to Netherlands
CARGO Porcelain and silk
SALVAGE Silk looted by pirates, but unlikely that porcelain was removed

47 E8 HASTINGS 1787
SHIP English country trader
LOCATION Between Poulo Sapate and Macclesfield Bank
ROUTE Guangzhou, China, to Bombay, India
CARGO Porcelain

48 F9 MIDDELWIJK 1788
SHIP Dutch East Indiaman, 800 tons
LOCATION South China Sea
ROUTE Jakarta, Java, to China
CARGO Silver

49 F7 CANTON 1790
SHIP Dutch East Indiaman, 1,150 tons
LOCATION South China Sea
ROUTE Jakarta, Java, to Guangzhou, China
CARGO Silver

50 F5 SANTA CLARA Aug 18, 1799
SHIP Portuguese
LOCATION West of Guangzhou roads, China
ROUTE Goa, India, to Macao
CARGO Silver

51 F7 EARL TALBOT c. Aug 16, 1800
SHIP English East Indiaman, 1,500 tons
LOCATION Paracel Islands
ROUTE Bombay, India, to China
CARGO Specie

52 E6 GENEROUS FRIENDS Nov 1801
LOCATION On a reef, Paracel Islands, 2 days' distance SW by S from Macao
ROUTE From Macao
CARGO Gold and US dollars
SALVAGE Plundered

53 F5 FERROLENA URCA Sept 15, 1802
SHIP Spanish
LOCATION Brandons Bay, near Pedro Branco, off China, 22.50N 113.42E
ROUTE Manila, Philippines, to Guangzhou, China
CARGO Silver
SALVAGE Extensive salvage at time of loss and some looting. Cargo valued at US $1,800,000 lost.
Total quantity of silver unknown because large quantity of unofficial cargo on board

54 F7 ST. ANTONIO July 22, 1804
SHIP Portuguese
LOCATION On high sandbank, Paracel Islands, 16.45N
ROUTE Ho Chi Minh City, Vietnam, to Guangzhou, China
CARGO Specie

55 F4 ALBION Dec 1807
SHIP English East Indiaman
LOCATION Huang-pu, China
ROUTE UK to China
CARGO Cargo valued at US $1.5 million
SALVAGE Most of cargo recovered

56 E9 TRUE BRITON Oct 13, 1809
SHIP English East Indiaman
LOCATION South China Sea
ROUTE Bombay, India, to Guangzhou, China
CARGO Specie
Ship missing

57 E8 OCEAN Sept 1810
SHIP English East Indiaman
LOCATION Off Poulo Sapate
ROUTE China to UK
CARGO Porcelain
Parted from the frigate Modeste *and not heard from since*

58 E6 PRESIDENT ADAMS 1813
SHIP American
LOCATION St. John's Island, SW of Guangzhou, China
ROUTE Boston, Massachusetts, US, to Guangzhou, China
CARGO Silver specie and Turkish opium valued at US $170,000
SALVAGE Plundered

59 F5 ELPHINSTONE 1817
SHIP English East Indiaman
LOCATION Guangzhou, China
ROUTE UK to Guangzhou, China
CARGO Specie

60 F4 ROYAL GEORGE Dec 24, 1825
SHIP English East Indiaman
LOCATION Huang-pu, China
ROUTE UK to China
CARGO Specie

61 G6 MATADOR Oct 1835
SHIP Danish
LOCATION 18.00N 117.00E
CARGO Silver dollars
Boxes of dollars put on deck, but the ship collided with the Golconda *and sank before they could be removed*

62 E6 SUNDA Oct 1840
LOCATION Off Taya Islands, near Hainan, China, 19.55N 111.20E
CARGO Treasure
SALVAGE Possibility of pillage

63 G5 SINGULAR 1842
SHIP Spanish brig
LOCATION Dongsha Qundao, China
ROUTE Manila, Philippines, to China
CARGO Gold valued at US $50,000

64 E7 CHRISTINA July 1, 1842
SHIP English East Indiaman
LOCATION Vietnam
ROUTE Macao to Bombay, India
CARGO Large quantity of treasure
SALVAGE Some salvage by fishermen 1 or 2 years after loss. Recent attempt to relocate ship was not successful.

65 F5 MAVIS Aug 29, 1842
LOCATION Bearing east from Wanshan Islands, China
CARGO Specie valued at US $20,000
Ship struck by lightning and blew up. Capt. Cow of British Sovereign picked up survivors.

66 G6 CITY OF SHIREZ 1845
LOCATION Reef off Dongsha Qundao, China
ROUTE Huang-pu, China, to Bombay, India
CARGO Specie
SALVAGE Salvage attempt in 1846, but results unclear

67 F7 CASTLE HUNTLEY Oct 27, 1845
SHIP British
LOCATION Lincoln's Shoal, Paracel Islands
ROUTE Bombay, India, to Guangzhou, China
CARGO Treasure valued at US $15,000

68 F5 PARADOX 1848
SHIP Small schooner
LOCATION Entrance to Hong Kong harbor from Cap Sing Moon Passage
ROUTE Guangzhou, China, to Hong Kong
CARGO Specie
SALVAGE Salvage attempted, but not successful
Ship capsized and sank

69 D6 SHAP'NG TSAI'S FLEET 1850
SHIP Vietnamese pirate ship
LOCATION Gulf of Tongking, Vietnam
CARGO Treasure

70 E5 DONNA MARIA 2
Oct 29, 1851
SHIP Portuguese
LOCATION Macao
CARGO Considerable quantity of money
on board

71 E7 DOURO May 24, 1853
SHIP British, P & O Line
LOCATION Paracel Islands
CARGO Specie

72 G5 ELIZA THORNTON
Sept 30, 1854
SHIP American brig
LOCATION Pedro Branco, off China,
approximately 22.50N 115.20E
ROUTE San Francisco, California, US,
to Hong Kong
CARGO Gold
SALVAGE Passengers tried in vain to swim
with gold-dust belts

73 B8 NEPTUNE Feb 26, 1856
SHIP 1,000 tons
LOCATION Barat Menam, Thailand
CARGO Gold bars, gold leaf, and sycee
silver
Ship blew up and was on fire for 28 hours

74 F5 JAMES HARTLEY
Oct 29, 1859
SHIP British
LOCATION Near Hong Kong
CARGO Treasure
SALVAGE Salvaged at time of loss

75 C8 CONDOR Feb 3, 1860
SHIP German
LOCATION Off Thailand, approximately
11.00N 103.00E
ROUTE Macao to Bangkok, Thailand
CARGO Treasure
SALVAGE Salvaged at time of loss

76 G8 BALD EAGLE 1861
SHIP American clipper
LOCATION South China Sea
ROUTE Hong Kong to San Francisco,
California, US
CARGO Specie valued at US $100,000

77 G6 BELLA CARMEN
Mar 26, 1861
LOCATION South China Sea
ROUTE Manila, Philippines, to Xiamen,
China
CARGO Specie valued at US $30,000

78 G5 PHANTOM July 12, 1862
SHIP American clipper
LOCATION North Dongsha Qundao,
China
ROUTE San Francisco, California, US,
to Hong Kong
CARGO Treasure valued at US $50,576
SALVAGE Most of treasure saved

79 G6 GEORGES SAND Aug 1863
SHIP American
LOCATION Reef off Dongsha Qundao,
China
ROUTE San Francisco, California, US,
to Hong Kong
CARGO Gold, rumored to be valued in
excess of £2 million sterling, but actual
quantity thought to be much less

80 F5 DOUGLAS 1870
SHIP British
LOCATION Hong Kong
CARGO Treasure
SALVAGE Treasure valued at US $450,000
salvaged

81 E7 YANGTZE 1871
SHIP American tea-clipper
LOCATION Paracel Islands
ROUTE New York, US, to Fuzhou,
China
CARGO Specie

82 G5 MARS June 14, 1871
SHIP British, iron steamship, 1,021 tons
LOCATION Reef near Cupchi Point, off
Brewers Point, China
ROUTE Hong Kong to Xiamen, China
CARGO Treasure valued at US $7,000

83 G5 JAPAN Dec 18, 1874
SHIP American sidewheel paddlesteamer
LOCATION Approximately 22.50N
113.42E
ROUTE San Francisco, California, US, to
Hong Kong
CARGO Treasure valued at US $365,000,
plus gold and gold dust
SALVAGE Attempt at salvage continued for
some years. By 1878, treasure valued at
US $183,000 had been recovered. Further
attempts were then abandoned.

84 F5 SHIROGANE MARU
Mar 14, 1945
SHIP Japanese
LOCATION Off Hong Kong, approximately
22.18N 114.10E
ROUTE Malaysia to Japan
CARGO Gold and silver
SALVAGE Several salvage attempts

JAPAN, KOREA, AND EASTERN CHINA

The map for these listings is on pp. 158–159.

● No known salvage
■ Some salvage history known

1 D4 WU WRECKS 233
SHIP Warships
LOCATION Yellow Sea, China
CARGO Artifacts
Lost in a storm. Ships from state of Wu.

2 D6 SHIP OF ENNIN 838
SHIP Japanese
LOCATION Entrance to Yangtze River,
China
ROUTE Kyoto, Japan, to China
CARGO Presents for the Emperor of
China including silks, sabres studded with
jewels, and precious metals
*Ship was carrying a group of Japanese monks
and was wrecked after a 15-day journey*

3 D8 T'AI PING WRECK 1056
SHIP Chinese
LOCATION T'ai Ping, near mouth of River
Min, China
CARGO Presents
Ambassador to Court of China on board

4 F5 KUBLAI KHAN FLEET 1281
SHIP Chinese invasion fleet
LOCATION Off north Kyushu, Japan
ROUTE China to Japan
CARGO Rare and valuable artifacts

5 F5 SINAN WRECK 1323
SHIP Chinese junk
LOCATION 35.01.15N 126.05.06E
ROUTE China to Japan
CARGO 28 tons coins and artifacts
SALVAGE Recently excavated
See pp. 26–27

6 G6 PORTUGUESE SHIP 1573
LOCATION Off Amakusa Island, near
Nagasaki, Japan
ROUTE China to Japan
CARGO Gold and porcelain

**7 G7 ILHAS DOS LEQUIOS REEF
WRECK** 1583
SHIP Portuguese
LOCATION Ilhas dos Lequios Reef,
Ryukyu Islands, Japan
ROUTE Macao to Japan
CARGO Gold and porcelain

8 D9 SPANISH SHIP 1583
SHIP Spanish
LOCATION Taiwan
ROUTE China to Manila, Philippines
CARGO Porcelain
P. Alonso Sanchez on board

9 H5 SAN FELIPE Oct 19, 1596
SHIP Spanish
LOCATION Off Tosa, Shikoku, 100 miles
(160 km) from port of Nagasaki, Japan
ROUTE Manila, Philippines, to Acapulco,
Mexico
CARGO 30,000 pesos of gold and porcelain
SALVAGE Some salvage at time of loss

10 G6 JUNK 1599
SHIP Chinese
LOCATION Outside Nagasaki, Japan
ROUTE Nagasaki, Japan, to Macao
CARGO Silver valued at 400,000 cruzados

11 J5 SAN ANTONIO June 1603
SHIP Spanish
LOCATION Approximately 34.00N
ROUTE Manila, Philippines, to Mexico
CARGO Gold and porcelain
Capt. D. Diego de Mendoza

12 G5 SPANISH FRIGATE 1605
SHIP Spanish frigate
LOCATION Off Nagasaki, Japan
ROUTE Manila, Philippines, to Japan
CARGO Specie valued at 50,000 cruzados

13 G5 SANTA ANNA 1609
SHIP Spanish
LOCATION Bungo Strait, Japan
ROUTE Manila, Philippines, to Acapulco,
Mexico
CARGO Gold and porcelain
Ship driven ashore by bad weather conditions

14 I5 SAN FRANCISCO 1609
SHIP Spanish
LOCATION 120 miles (190 km) from
Tokyo, Japan
ROUTE Manila, Philippines, to Acapulco,
Mexico
CARGO Gold and porcelain

15 G6 MADRE DE DEUS
July 9, 1609
SHIP Portuguese
LOCATION Fukunda, Nagasaki Bay, Japan
ROUTE Macao to Nagasaki, Japan
CARGO Gold and treasure. Value in 1980s
estimated at 300 – 400 million yen.
SALVAGE Attempted by Japanese Maritime
Development Company in 1980s, but
results not known
*Ship scuttled by Portuguese captain during sea
battle with Japanese. See pp. 42–43.*

16 D8 JUNK 1611
SHIP Chinese junk
LOCATION Fujian coast, China
ROUTE Macao to Japan
CARGO Gold

17 D8 MACAO SHIP 1611
SHIP Portuguese
LOCATION Fujian coast, China
ROUTE Macao to Nagasaki, Japan
CARGO Gold specie

18 F6 RODE LEEUW Jan 31, 1613
SHIP Dutch East Indiaman, 400 tons
LOCATION Near Japan
ROUTE Manila, Philippines, to Japan
CARGO Specie

19 G6 SPANISH SHIP 1616–1617
SHIP Spanish
LOCATION South Japan
ROUTE Manila, Philippines, to Japan
CARGO Large quantity of treasure

20 F5 EXPEDITION 1620
SHIP English East Indiaman
LOCATION Firando, NW Kyushu, Japan
ROUTE UK to Japan
CARGO Specie

21 F5 HOWND 1622
SHIP Dutch East Indiaman
LOCATION Cochie roads, port of Firando,
NW Kyushu, Japan
ROUTE Banten, Java, to Japan
CARGO Specie

22 G5 MAAN 1622
SHIP Dutch East Indiaman
LOCATION Cochie roads, port of Firando,
NW Kyushu, Japan
ROUTE Indonesia to Japan
CARGO Specie

㉓ E7 SANTA CROIX 1622
SHIP Dutch
LOCATION Between Japan and P'eng-hu Lieh-tao, Taiwan
ROUTE Japan to Taiwan
CARGO Silver and porcelain

㉔ D8 TIJGER Sept 1622
SHIP Dutch East Indiaman, 140 tons
LOCATION River Chincheu, near Xiamen, China
CARGO Specie
SALVAGE Salvaged by Chinese

㉕ C8 MUIDEN 1623
SHIP Dutch East Indiaman, 160 tons
LOCATION Off Kolongsoe Island, near Xiamen, China
ROUTE China to Japan
CARGO Specie
Ship ran aground and burned completely. Wrecked on island of Glan Fau according to Astley.

㉖ C8 OUDERKERK Oct 12, 1627
SHIP Dutch East Indiaman, 100 tons
LOCATION Near Xiamen, China
CARGO Specie
Ship lost in battle with Portuguese

㉗ C8 SLOTEN Oct 7, 1633
SHIP Dutch East Indiaman, 100 tons
LOCATION River Chincheu, near coast of China
CARGO Specie

㉘ D9 VLIEGENDE HERTE 1643
SHIP Dutch East Indiaman
LOCATION Rovers Island, P'eng-hu Lieh-tao, Taiwan, 23.31N 119.33E
ROUTE China to Jakarta, Java
CARGO Porcelain

㉚ E8 VREDE Oct 28, 1654
SHIP Dutch East Indiaman
LOCATION North coast of Taiwan
ROUTE Jakarta, Java, to Taiwan
CARGO Specie

㉛ D8 VLEERMUIS Sept 26, 1655
SHIP Dutch East Indiaman, 150 tons
LOCATION Reefs of Vuile Island, P'eng-hu Lieh-tao, Taiwan
ROUTE China to Japan
CARGO Silver valued at 25,773.2 florins

㉜ D9 MAARSSEN Sept 11, 1656
SHIP Dutch East Indiaman
LOCATION Taiwan roads
ROUTE Jakarta, Java, to Taiwan
CARGO Specie

㉝ D8 KORTENHOF Sept 16, 1661
SHIP Dutch East Indiaman, 216 tons
LOCATION Fort Zeelandia, Taiwan
ROUTE Jakarta, Java, to Fort Zeelandia, Taiwan
CARGO Specie

㉞ F6 PEPERBAL Aug 26, 1663
SHIP Dutch East Indiaman
LOCATION Off Mishima Islands, SW of Japan, approximately 32.00N 128.30E
ROUTE Jakarta, Java, to Japan
CARGO Specie

㉟ F6 VOLLENHOVEN Aug 26, 1663
SHIP Dutch East Indiaman
LOCATION Off Mishima Islands, SW of Japan, approximately 32.00N 128.30E
CARGO Specie

㊱ G5 RODE HERT July 7, 1665
SHIP Dutch East Indiaman, 340 tons
LOCATION Off Nagasaki Bay, Japan
ROUTE Jakarta, Java, to Japan
CARGO Specie

㊲ D8 HMS HARWICH 1698
SHIP British
LOCATION Xiamen, China
CARGO Silver

㊳ I5 VALKENBOS Aug 1722
SHIP Dutch East Indiaman
LOCATION Near Japan
CARGO Specie

㊴ C8 AMOY WRECK 1749
SHIP Chinese ship
LOCATION Near Xiamen, China
ROUTE Luzon, Philippines, to China
CARGO Silver dollars

㊵ E8 ANN 1841
SHIP British
LOCATION Taiwan
CARGO Silver
SALVAGE Ship pillaged

㊶ C8 PIRATE SHIP May 31, 1848
SHIP Pirate ship
LOCATION Chimmo Island, near Fuzhou, China
CARGO Looted treasure
Ship sunk by Commander Frederick Johnston in the Scout

㊷ D8 BEN AVON 1856
SHIP British
LOCATION Rock off Hoe Tow Point, 20 miles (32 km) north of Xiamen, China
ROUTE London, England, to Shanghai, China
CARGO Specie

㊸ C8 MAZEPPA 1857
SHIP Opium schooner
LOCATION Near Shantou, China
CARGO Treasure
SALVAGE Searched for by Capt. Tucker, but although he eventually located the wreck, there are no reports of any recovery

㊹ E6 CAIRNSMORE 1858
SHIP British
LOCATION Approximately 30.45N 122.20E
ROUTE Hong Kong to Shanghai, China
CARGO Specie
SALVAGE Some salvage

㊺ J4 LOCH LOMOND July 5, 1859
LOCATION Tokyo Bay, Japan
ROUTE Nagasaki, Japan, to Kanagaiva, Japan
CARGO Specie
SALVAGE Some salvage at time of loss

㊻ D6 SANTA CRUZ Mar 14, 1862
LOCATION Yangtze River, China
ROUTE Shanghai, China, to Hankou, China
CARGO Treasure

㊼ J2 ASHMORE Nov 24, 1864
LOCATION Benten Sama, Tsugaru Strait, near Hakodate, Japan
ROUTE Yokohama, Japan, to Hakodate, Japan
CARGO Treasure
SALVAGE Treasure salvaged at time of loss

㊽ J4 ONWARD Dec 29, 1865
SHIP British bark
LOCATION Kashima, east coast of Japan, 250 miles (400 km) from Yokohama
ROUTE Yokohama, Japan, to Hakodate, Japan
CARGO Specie
SALVAGE Salvaged at time of loss

㊾ J2 SINGAPORE Aug 20, 1867
SHIP British, P & O Line
LOCATION 8 miles (13 km) off Hakodate, Japan
CARGO Specie
SALVAGE Specie only partly salvaged

㊿ C8 NIPHON Jan 23, 1868
SHIP British steamship, P & O Line
LOCATION Reef of House Hill, near Xiamen, China
ROUTE Hong Kong to Shanghai, China
CARGO Specie

51 E6 BENARES May 23, 1868
SHIP British, P & O Line
LOCATION Shanghai, China,
ROUTE Shanghai, China, to Hong Kong
CARGO Specie
SALVAGE Specie later recovered by divers

52 E6 HAMILLA MITCHELL
Aug 11, 1869
LOCATION Leuconna Rocks, 120 miles (190 km) SE of Shanghai, China
ROUTE London, England, to Shanghai, China
CARGO Treasure
SALVAGE Treasure valued at US $17,000 recovered. 2 separate salvage operations took place before salvors gave up.

53 J4 ONEIDA Jan 24, 1870
SHIP US Navy corvette
LOCATION Off Saratoga Spit, Tokyo Bay, Japan, 5 miles (8 km) from shore
ROUTE Yokohama, Japan, to Hong Kong
CARGO Gold valued at US $400,000 rumored, but small quantity of silver definitely on board

54 D6 TONBRIDGE 1872
SHIP British
LOCATION Near Gutzlaff, China, approximately 30.48N
CARGO Treasure
SALVAGE Salvaged by divers from *HMS Cadmus*

55 I5 AMERICA Aug 24, 1872
SHIP American paddlesteamer, Pacific Mail Line, 4,560 tons
LOCATION Yokohama harbor, Japan
ROUTE California, US, to Yokohama, Japan
CARGO Gold and Mexican $1,600,000
SALVAGE Largely salvaged at time of loss

56 D8 GLENGYLE Dec 30, 1875
SHIP British
LOCATION Rock in Three Chimneys Passage, off China, approximately 25.10N 119.58E
ROUTE Shanghai, China, to Shantou, China
CARGO Treasure
SALVAGE Plans for salvage attempt 3 years later, but results unknown

57 D8 TAIWAN Feb 14, 1879
LOCATION NW P'eng-hu Lieh-tao, Taiwan
CARGO Large quantity of treasure
SALVAGE Wreck bought by Chinese salvagers

58 C9 YESSO Mar 17, 1879
LOCATION Off Lamock Island, China, 23.05N 117.18E
ROUTE Shantou, China, to Xiamen, China
CARGO Treasure valued at US $100,000

59 D8 KWANGTUNG Dec 5, 1884
SHIP British, Douglas Steamship Company
LOCATION River Min, near Fuzhou, China
CARGO Specie

60 D8 BOKHARA Oct 10, 1892
SHIP British, P & O Line, 2,944 tons
LOCATION P'eng-hu Lieh-tao, Taiwan
ROUTE Shanghai, China, to Hong Kong
CARGO Specie valued at US $200,000
SALVAGE Specie valued at US $90,000 salvaged

61 G5 ADMIRAL NAKHIMOFF
May 28, 1905
SHIP Russian cruiser, 8,524 tons
LOCATION Off Tsushima Island, Japan
ROUTE Sunk during Russian–Japanese war
CARGO Included gold and platinum. Recent newspaper reports estimate the value of the cargo at US $3.774 billion.
SALVAGE Many salvage plans. The most recent salvage was by the Nippon Marine Development Company in the 1980s, although the results were disputed.

62 E4 TOONAN July 10, 1933
SHIP China Merchants' Steam Navigation Company, 1,482 tons
LOCATION 36.52.30N 122.47.30E
ROUTE Yingkou, China, to Shanghai, China
CARGO Sycee silver valued at US $1.5 million
SALVAGE Salvaged by Tokyo Salvage Company
Ship collided with Chosun Maru

63 F5 TOYOURA MARU May 6, 1944
SHIP Japanese, Nippon Yusen Company, 2,510 tons
LOCATION 32.18N 127.11E
CARGO Gold
Sunk by US submarine, Spearfish

64 G5 SANSEI MARU June 28, 1944
SHIP Japanese, Yamashita Kisen Company, 2,386 tons
LOCATION 33.53N 129.01E
ROUTE Indonesia to Japan
CARGO Large quantity of coins supposedly on board
SALVAGE Disappointing salvage results

65 D8 AWA MARU Apr 1, 1945
SHIP Japanese, Nippon Yusen Company, 11,249 tons
LOCATION 24.40N 119.45E
ROUTE Singapore to Japan
CARGO Gold and treasure
SALVAGE Only tin and rubber recovered by Chinese salvage company
Rumored to be one of the richest treasureships in the world

66 H4 HIKAWA MARU 2
Aug 19, 1945
SHIP Previously Dutch hospital ship, *Op Ten Noort*, 6,076 tons
LOCATION Entrance to Wakasa Bay, north of Kammuri Island, Japan, 35.45N 135.30E
ROUTE To Japan
CARGO Gold, treasure, and war booty
SALVAGE Supposedly located by Japanese salvage company in 1980s, but results unknown
Ship was returning to Japan at the end of the Second World War

GLOSSARY

ADMIRAL Commander of a fleet or part of a fleet; can refer to a ship or a person.

AFT HATCH Entrance to the cargo holds or lower decks at the rear of the ship.

AFT HOLD Compartment below the lower rear deck for storing cargo or provisions.

ARGOSY A large pre-eighteenth-century trading ship.

ASTROLABE Navigational aid that measures the positions of the stars or sun.

AZOGUE Spanish ship carrying mercury.

BARK (BARQUE) Three-masted, square-rigged sailing ship.

THE "BENDS" A sudden decompression of nitrogen in the bloodstream that can affect deep-sea divers as they surface.

BERGANTINA Small ship powered by oars and sails, used by sailors in the Mediterranean between the fourteenth and sixteenth centuries.

BLOCKADE-RUNNER Ship that attempts to enter blockaded ports during wartime, carrying essential supplies.

BRIG Two-masted, square-rigged ship.

BRIGANTINE-OF-WAR Two-masted ship with a square-rigged foremast and a fore-and-aft rigged mainmast.

BUDGEROW A cabined passage boat, used particularly on rivers in India.

BULKHEAD An upright partition that divides a ship's hull into separate (often watertight) sections.

BULLION Precious metal, such as gold or silver, before conversion into coins or bars.

BURDEN Measurement defining the capacity of a ship by the number of casks of wine it could carry in its holds.

CARAVEL Small, light sailing ship, popular in Spain and Portugal between the fifteenth and seventeenth centuries.

CAREENING Method of cleaning or repairing a ship by turning it onto one side at a time.

CARRACK Large merchant ship with a high forecastle, popular in Europe from the sixteenth to the seventeenth centuries. Usually square-rigged on the fore- and mainmast, and lateen-rigged on the mizzen mast.

CLIPPER Very fast nineteenth-century sailing ship.

COG Broad-beamed trading ship, popular in Europe between the thirteenth and fifteenth centuries.

CORSAIR Term used to describe privateers and their ships that operated in the Mediterranean.

CRUZADO Portuguese monetary unit.

DESTROYER Fast light warship developed in the late nineteenth century, mainly used to protect merchant shipping from enemy submarines.

DHOW Small lateen-rigged sailing ship, common in the Indian Ocean

DOUBLOON Spanish gold coin.

DUCAT Gold or silver coin of differing values used in Europe.

FLORIN (1) Thirteenth-century gold coin issued in Florence; (2) Dutch currency from the seventeenth to the nineteenth century, worth about one guilder.

FORECASTLE Raised section at the bow of a ship, used by artillery.

FREEBOARD The part of a ship's side between the upper deck and the waterline.

FRIGATE Small warship, often used for special or independent missions.

GALERA Spanish galley-type warship.

GALLEASS Long narrow ship with oars and sails, popular in the Mediterranean in the sixteenth century.

GALLEON Large sailing ship developed around the sixteenth century from the carrack but with a lower forecastle. Used initially as a warship, but was also used for trading purposes.

GALLEY Fighting ship propelled by oars and sail-power.

GRAB Mechanical tool, sometimes used by salvors for lifting heavy objects.

GROSS TONNAGE Cubic capacity of a ship below deck, calculated in cubic feet divided by one hundred.

GUNWALE Plank forming the upper edge of the side of a ship.

HULK Large and bulky trading ship.

JUNK Far Eastern sailing vessel, with a flat bottom, high stern, and square bows; particularly used by the Chinese.

LATEEN-RIGGED A ship rigged with triangular fore-and-aft sails.

LONGBOAT The largest boat carried on a sailing ship.

LONGSHIP (LANGSKIP) Oar-powered Viking ship with one square sail, constructed for speed and lightness.

LORCHA Sailing ship with a Western-style hull and Chinese-style rigging.

MAGNOMETER Salvage equipment used to detect and locate iron at a wreck site.

MAIL SHIP Used from the nineteenth century to carry mail and packages.

MANNED SUBMERSIBLES Small manned submarines, used in salvage operations, which operate at different depths according to their design.

MINELAYER Fast warship converted or built to lay mines, first used substantially in the First World War.

MIZZEN MAST Third mast of a sailing ship.

NO CURE, NO PAY Traditional and modern-day universal code of salvage. If no salvage takes place, then the salvors do not receive any payment.

PACKET A boat carrying mail between two ports, sometimes used to carry passengers.

PADDLESTEAMER Vessel propelled by paddlewheels at the rear or the side that are driven by steam engines.

PIECES OF EIGHT Old Spanish coin worth eight reals or one Spanish dollar, also known as reals of eight.

PINK Small, square-rigged ship.

PINNACE Small, two-masted ship often used for carrying messages between large ships of the fleet.

PIRATE Person or ship that unlawfully robs and plunders on the sea.

PONTO A derivation of pontoon or punt, a raftlike vessel.

PRIVATEER Person or ship licensed by the government to carry out hostilities against enemy merchant shipping, or the ship itself.

QUARTERDECK Part of the upper deck at the ship's stern.

REGISTER SHIP Spanish galleon carrying treasure from South or Central America to Spain. Also describes ships carrying treasure.

ROADS Area of water just outside a main harbor where ships can anchor.

ROV (REMOTE-OPERATED VEHICLE) Unmanned piece of machinery used in salvage investigation, and controlled from the ship.

SAETTIA Small lateen-rigged Venetian sailing ship.

SATURATION DIVING A form of diving whereby the diver remains under pressure for long periods of time; used in time-sensitive salvage operations.

SCHOONER Sailing vessel introduced in the early eighteenth century, usually with two masts carrying fore-and-aft sails and topsails on the foremast.

SHIPS OF THE LINE Main battle fleet during the eighteenth and nineteenth centuries. The term describes the strategy of the fleet lining up in a bow-to-stern position, facing the enemy broadside on.

SIDE-SCAN SONAR Salvage equipment that is normally used to survey the seabed by emitting soundwaves.

SKIFF Small, light rowing boat with one or two sets of oars.

SLOOP Small, single-masted sailing boat with fore-and aft-rigging.

SNOW European two-masted merchant ships, popular between the sixteenth and nineteenth centuries. The term derives from the Dutch word "snaauw," meaning snout and referring to the shape of the bow.

SPAR Strong support that is used in the rigging of a ship.

SPECIE Coin money.

SQUARE-RIGGED A ship rigged with square sails.

STEAMER Ship propelled by steam.

SUPERCARGO Person appointed by the owners of a merchant ship to supervise the trading aspects of a voyage.

TAEL A money unit (not a coin) in China, originally a silver weight.

TENDER Small boat usually used to take stores or passengers to a larger ship when in harbor.

TRANSPORT Troop-carrying ship.

U-BOAT German submarine.

VIKING KNORR Old Norse merchant ship, similar to a longship, used for trading rather than war, with one mast and a square sail.

XEBEC Small three-masted vessel used from the sixteenth to nineteenth century, exclusively in the Mediterranean.

XERAFIN/XERAPHIM A silver coin from Goa, India.

BIBLIOGRAPHY

Andrews, Kenneth R. *Trade, Plunder & Settlement: Maritime Enterprise & the Genesis of the British Empire, 1480-1630*. New York: Cambridge University Press, 1984.

Ballard, Robert D. *The Discovery of the Titanic*. Avenel, New Jersey: Outlet Book Co., 1990.

Barker, Ralph. *Goodnight, Sorry for Sinking You: The Story of the SS City of Cairo*. London: Collins, 1984.

Bass, George F., ed. *Ships & Shipwrecks of the Americas: A History Based on Underwater Archaeology*. New York: Thames & Hudson, 1988.

Bastin, John, ed. *Memoir of Sir T.S. Raffles by Sophia*. London: Oxford University Press, 1991.

Blair, E.H., & J.A. Robertson, eds. *The Philippine Islands, 1493-1898*, 55 vols. Cleveland, Ohio: A.H. Clark & Co., 1903-1909.

Bonsor, N.R.P. *North Atlantic Seaway*. Lancashire, England: T. Stephenson & Sons, 1955.

Bonsor, N.R.P. *South Atlantic Seaway*. Cambridge, England: Patrick Stephens, 1983.

Boxer, C.R. *The Affair of the Madre Deus*. London: Kegan Paul & Co., 1929.

Boxer, C.R. *Further Selections from the Tragic History of the Sea*. Cambridge, England: Cambridge University Press, 1969.

Boxer, C.R. *The Portuguese Seaborn Empire 1415-1825*. London: Hutchinson & Co., 1969.

Boxer, C.R. ed. *The Tragic History of the Sea, 1589-1622*. Millwood, New York: Kraus, 1959.

Braudel, Fernand. *The Mediterranean & the Mediterranean World in the Age of Philip 2nd*. New York: HarperCollins, 1977. Revised in 1992.

Brogger, A.W., & H. Shetelig. *The Viking Ships*. Oslo: Dreyers Forlag, 1953.

Bruin, J.R., et al., ed. *Dutch Asiatic Shipping in the 17th and 18th Centuries*. 3 vols. The Hague, the Netherlands: Martinus Nijhoff, 1987.

Burney, James. *A Chronological History of Voyages*. 5 vols. London: G. & W. Nicol, 1803–1817.

Campbell, John. *Lives of the Admirals*. 4 vols. London: 1750.

Cederlund, Carl. *The Old Wrecks of the Baltic Sea*. Oxford, England: Oxford University Press, 1983.

Chaudhuri, K.N. *Trade and Civilisation in the Indian Ocean: An Economic History from the Rise of Islam to 1750*. New York: Cambridge University Press, 1985.

Chaunu, H., and P. Chaunu. *Seville et l'Atlantique*. 8 vols. Paris: (Ecole Pratique des hautes etudes, vie section, centre de recherches hist. ports, routes, trafics, 6.), 1955-56.

Clowes, William L., ed. *The Royal Navy, A History from the Earliest Times to the Present*. 7 vols. New York: AMS Press, reprint of 1903 edition.

Cowden, James, and John Duffy. *The Elder Dempster Fleet History*. Mallet & Bell, 1986.

Cruikshank, E.A. *The Life of Sir Henry Morgan*. Toronto, Canada: Macmillan Co., 1935.

D'alboquerque, Afonso. *The Commentaries*. 4 vols. Cambridge, England: Cambridge University Press, 1880 (translated from the Portuguese edition of 1774).

Duffy, James. *Shipwreck and Empire*. Cambridge, Massachusetts: Harvard University Press, 1955.

Duncan, A. *The Mariner's Chronicle*. 6 vols. London, 1810.

Duro, C. Fernandez. *Armada Española desde la union de los reinos de Castillay de Aragon*. 9 vols. Madrid: Museo Naval, 1873.

Earle, P. *Corsairs of Malta & Barbary*. London: Sidgwick & Jackson, 1970.

Earle, P. *The Wreck of the Almiranta, Sir William Phips and the Hispaniola Treasure*. London: Macmillan, 1979.

Edwards, Hugh. *Islands of Angry Ghosts*. London: Hodder & Stoughton, 1966.

Esquemeling, J. *Buccaneers of America*. New York: Dorset Press, 1988 (originally published 1684).

Eunson, Keith. *The Wreck of the General Grant*. Wellington, New Zealand: Reed, 1974.

Evans, Angela Care. *The Sutton Hoo Ship Burial*. London: British Museum Publications, 1986.

Fallon, Niall. *The Armada in Ireland*. Ann Arbor, Michigan: Books on Demand, 1978.

Fernandez, Armesto Felipe. *The Spanish Armada*. Oxford, England: Oxford University Press, 1988.

Gibbs, Jr., James. *Shipwrecks of the Pacific Coast*. Portland, Oregon: Binford & Mort Publishing, 1989.

Gilly, W.O.S. *Narratives of Shipwrecks of the Royal Navy*. London: John Parker, 1851.

Glamann, K. *Dutch Asiatic Trade 1620-1750*. Copenhagen, Denmark: Danish Science Press and The Hague, the Netherlands: Martinus Niyhoff, 1958.

Gores, J.N. *Marine Salvage: The Unforgiving Business of No Cure, No Pay*. Garden City, New Jersey: Doubleday, 1971.

Gosse, Philip. *The History of Piracy*. Detroit, Michigan: Omnigraphics, 1992 (reprint of 1934 edition).

Gosset, W.P. *The Lost Ships of the Royal Navy 1793-1900*. London: Mansell Publishing Ltd., 1986.

H.M.S.O. *British Vessels Lost at Sea 1939-1945*. London: H.M.S.O., 1947.

Hakluyt, Richard. *The Principal Navigations, Voyages, Traffiques & Discoveries of the English Nation*. 12 vols. New York: AMS Press, reprint of 1903 edition.

Haring, C.H. *The Buccaneers in the West Indies in the Seventeenth Century*. London: Methuen & Co., 1910.

Haring, C.H. *Trade and Navigation between Spain and the Indies in the Time of the Hapsburgs*. Cambridge, Massachusetts: 1918 (1906 edition: Harvard University).

Hatcher, Michael. *The Nanking Cargo*. London: Hamish Hamilton, 1987.

Henderson, Graeme, and Kandy-Jane Henderson. *Unfinished Voyages: Western Australian Shipwrecks, 1851-1880*. Perth: University of Western Australia Press (International Specialized Book Services), 1988.

Hocking, Charles. *Dictionary of Disasters at Sea During the Age of Steam, 1824-1962*. 2 vols. London: Lloyds Register of Shipping, 1969.

Hoffer, William. *Saved: The Story of the Andrea Doria*. London: Macmillan, 1980.

Horner, D. *The Treasure Galleons*. London: Hale, 1973.

Hourani, G. F. *Arab Seafaring in the Indian Ocean in Ancient and Early Medieval Times*. Princeton, New Jersey: Princeton University Press, 1951.

Ingram, W.N., & P. Owen Wheatley. *Shipwrecks, New Zealand Disasters, 1795-1950*. Wellington, New Zealand: Reed, 1951.

James, W. *The Naval History of Great Britain*. 5 vols. London: Richard Bentley, 1822-1824.

Kirby, P.R. *The True Story of the Wreck of the Grosvenor*. Oxford, England: Oxford University Press, 1960.

Knox-Johnston, Robin. *The Cape of Good Hope*. London: Hodder & Stoughton, 1989.

Lane, Frederic. *Venetian Ships and Shipbuilders of the Renaissance*. Baltimore: John Hopkins University Press, 1934.

Lane, Frederic. *Venice & History*. Baltimore: John Hopkins University Press, 1960.

Larn, Richard. *Shipwrecks of Great Britain & Ireland*. Newton Abbott, England: David & Charles, 1981.

de Latil, Pierre, & Jean Rivoire. *Man and the Underwater World*. London: Jarrolds, 1956.

Lloyd, Chris. *English Corsairs on the Barbary Coast*. London: Collins, 1981.

Loney, J.K. *Victorian Shipwrecks*. Melbourne: Hawthorn Press, 1971.

Lucie-Smith, E. *Outcasts of the Sea*. London: Paddington Press, 1978.

McKee, Alexander. *The Golden Wreck: The Tragedy of the Royal Charter*. London: Souvenir Press (International Specialized Book Services), 1987.

McLeay, Alison. *The Tobermory Treasure*. London: Conway Maritime Press, 1986.

Marcus, G.J. *The Conquest of the North Atlantic*. Suffolk, England: Boydell Press, 1980.

Martin, Colin, & Geoffrey Parker. *The Spanish Armada*. New York: Norton, 1992.

Marx, Robert. *Shipwrecks in the Americas*. New York: Dover Books, 1971.

May, R. *The Gold Rushes*. London: Luscombe, 1977.

Mills, J.V.G., ed. *The Overall Survey of the Ocean's Shores*. Cambridge, England: Cambridge University Press, 1980.

de Morga, Antonia. *The Philippine Islands*. Cambridge, England: Cambridge University Press, 1868 (translation of the 1609 Spanish edition).

Navarrete, Domingo. *The Travels and Controversies 1618-86*. 2 vols. Cambridge, England: Cambridge University Press, 1962 (translation of the 1609 Spanish edition).

de Navarette, M. Fernandez. *Coleccion de los Viages y Descubrimientos que Bicieron por Mar los Espanoles desde Fines del Siglo XV*. 5 vols. Madrid: Imprenta Real, 1825-1829.

Needham, Joseph. *Science & Civilisation in China*, vol. 4 part III. New York: Cambridge University Press, 1984.

Parry, J.H. *The Spanish Seaborne Empire*. Berkeley, California: University of California Press, 1990.

Penrose, Barrie. *Stalin's Gold* (HMS Edinburgh). London: Granada Publishing Ltd., 1982.

Pope, Dudley. *Harry Morgan's Way*. London: Secker & Warburg, 1977.

Potter, Jr., John S. *The Treasure Diver's Guide*. Port Salerno, Florida: Florida Classics, 1988.

Rohwer, Jurgen. *Axis Submarine Successes 1939-1945*. Annapolis, Maryland: Naval Institute Press, 1983 (translated from the German edition).

de la Roncière, C.B. *Histoire de la Marine Française*. Paris: 1932.

Schaeper, Thomas J. *John Paul Jones & the Battle of Flamborough Head: A Reconsideration*. New York: Peter Lang Publishing, 1990.

Schurz, W.L. *The Manila Galleon*. New York: 1939.

Scott, David. *The Egypt's Gold*. London: Faber & Faber, 1932.

Sergeant, R.B. *The Portuguese off the South Arabian Coast*. Oxford, England: Oxford University Press, 1963.

Simkin, C.G.F. *The Traditional Trade of Asia*. London: Oxford University Press, 1968.

Snow, E.R. *Pirates and Buccaneers*. Boston: Hankee Publishing Co., 1944.

Stenuit, Robert. *Treasures of the Armada* (Girona). New York: E.P. Dutton & Co., 1973.

Sue, E. *Histoire de la Marine Française*. 5 vols. Paris: 1835-1837.

Tavernier, Bruno. *Great Maritime Routes*. New York: Viking, 1972.

Tenenti, Alberto. *Piracy and the Decline of Venice*. Ann Arbor, Michigan: Books on Demand, 1967.

Throckmorton, P., ed. *The Sea Remembers: Shipwrecks and Archaeology*. New York: Grove Press, 1987.

Valentyn, François. *Oud en Nieuw Oost-Indien*. 5 vols. Dordrecht, Amsterdam, 1724-1726.

Wright, I.A., ed. *Spanish Documents Concerning English Voyages to the Caribbean, 1527-1568*. London: Hakluyt Society, 1929.

Wurtzburg, C.E. *Raffles of the Eastern Isles*. London: Hodder & Stoughton, 1954.

PERIODICALS:
International Journal of Nautical Archaeology
National Geographic

INDEX

Page numbers in bold refer to the illustrations

A

Aasa, Queen, 22
Abu Qîr bay:
  Catalan cog wrecked in, 31
  Orient blown up in, 79, 82
Abyssinia, 44
Acapulco:
  Manila–Acapulco route, 52, **52-53**, 56
  Nuestra Señora de la Concepción, 56
  Spanish plate ships, 52, **52**
Acre, 31
  Venetian traders to, 30, 32
Adams, Robert, **47**
Aden:
  early traders, 17
  Roman traders, 12
  Second World War, 118
  trade with China, 24
Admiral Stellingwerf Reef:
  Chinese junk, **25**
  Geldermalsen, 75
Adriatic Sea:
  Ulbo Island wreck, 33
  Venice controls, 30
Aegean Sea:
  Antikythera wreck, 14
  trade routes, 17
Africa:
  map **146-147**
  pirates, 62
  Portuguese traders, **36**
  Roman traders, 12
  trade with China, **24**
  triangular Atlantic trade, 68
Aghulas Reefs, **101**
Aguadilla, 60
aircraft carriers, **117**
aircraft, reconnaissance, **113**
Alaska, 92
Albuquerque, Alfonso de, 38-39
Alceste, HMS, **85**
Alexandria:
  early traders, 12, 17
  glassware, 15
  Napoleonic Wars, 82
  Pharos (lighthouse), 33
  Roman traders, 12
  Venetian traders, 30, 31
    and Ulbo Island wreck, 32
Algiers, pirates, 63, 66
Allemand, 79
Alliance, **80-81**
Als Efferne wreck, **62**
Amazon, **101**
America, **93**
American Revolution, 78
  Bonhomme Richard, 80-81
Amherst, 97
Amherst, Lord, **85**
Amoy, see Xiamen
Andrea Doria, **100**, 108-109, **108-109**
Angola, 64
Anna Maria, 30
Ansaldo shipyards, **108**
anti-aircraft guns, **116**
Antikythera ship, **13**, 14-15
Apulia, 33
Arabia, 12, 44
Arabian Sea, 118
Arabs:
  dhows, 17
  glassware, 16, **16**

archaeology, underwater, 8-9
Arctic Circle, 112
Argyll, seventh earl of, 48
Argyll, eleventh duke of, 49
Arima, 42
Arles wreck, 84
Armada, 46-51, **46-51**
Armada de Barlovento, 58
Arnauld, George, **83**
Arnbjorn, ship of, 18
Ashworth, David, **97**
Asia, map, **152-153**
Asia Minor, 15
Asiatic Prince, **101**
Aspinwall, 94
Assab, 44
Athenienne, 79
Athens:
  Elgin marbles, 88-89
  General Sulla loots, 15
Atlantic Charter Maritime
  Archaeological Foundation, 81
Atlantic Ocean:
  Liberty ships, 118
  mail ships, 133
  maps:
    South Atlantic **130-131**
    North Atlantic **134-135**
  Spanish Armada, 46
  triangular Atlantic trade, 68
Atlantic Salvage Company, 58
Atocha, **53**
Auckland Island, 96
Australia:
  and the *Batavia*, **71**, 72- 73
  in early maps, **37**
  immigrants, 100
  map, **150-151**
  ownership of wrecks, 9
  rush for gold, 92, **93**, 98
Awa Maru, **111**
azogues, 60
Azores:
  map, **140-141**
  privateers, 64, **65**

B

Bacaim wreck, **37**
Bahamas, 68
Bahrain, 118
Balkans, 16
Ballard, Robert, 105
Baltic fleet, 80
Baltic Sea, *Vrouw Maria* sunk in, 84, 86
Banks, Joseph, 84
Banten, 41
Barbarigo, Nicolo, 32-33
Barbarossa, brothers, 63, 66, 67
Barbary pirates, 63, 66
  and Levantine trade 31
Barents Sea:
  HMS *Edinburgh*, 112
  I-52, 116
Bass, George, 16
Batavia, see Jakarta
Batavia, **71**, 72-73, **72-73**
Bay of Raging Waters, **25**
Belfast, HMS, **112**
Belgium, 47, 67
Bellamy, Sam, **62**, 68-69
Bellini, School of, **32**
Bencoolen, see Bengkulu
Bendoran, SS, 115
Bengal, **25**, 70
Bengal, Bay of, **148-149**
Bengkulu, 90-91
Benjamin Bourne, 118
Berlenga island 64, **65**
Bermudas, map **126-127**
Billingsgate, Massachusetts, 69
Billingsgate wharf, London, **35**
Bintan, 45
bireme galleys, 32

Biscay, Bay of:
  Amazon sunk in, **101**
  I-52 lost in, 117
  loss of the *Prins Frederik*, **100**, 102-103
  map, **138-139**
Black Sea:
  early traders, 13
  and the Serçe Limani wreck, 16-17
  trade routes, 31
  Vikings in, 18, 19
Black Ships, 43
Blacksod Bay, 50
blanc-de-chine porcelain, 29
Blaues, 41
Block Island, 69
blue and white porcelain, 27, 29
blunderbuss, 78
Boa Vista, island of, 76
Bogor, 90
Bogue, USS, 116, **117**
Bom Jesus, 37
Bombay, **71**, 114
Bonhomme Richard, **79**, 80-81, **80-81**
Borneo, **25**, 90
Borneo, 90
Boston, 69
Botany Bay, 91
Bowden, Captain Tracy, **60**
Bowen, John, 63
Braamcamp collection, 87
Braithwaite, William and John, 77
Brazil, 36
Brest, 79
brigs, 88
Britain:
  and the American Revolution, 78, 80-81
  East India Company, 70, 76-77
  Elgin marbles, 88-89
  and the French Revolution, 78
  loss of *HMS Edinburgh*, 112-113
  Napoleonic Wars, 82-83
  ownership of wrecks, 9
  pirates, 66-67
  privateers, 64-65
  Second World War, 110
  shipping companies, 100
  Spanish Armada, 46-51, **46-47**
  Sutton Hoo burial ship, 20-21, **20-21**
  Tobie, 34, **34**
  trade with Venice, 30
  Vikings, 18
  War of the Spanish Succession, 58, **59**
  Whydah, **68-69**
Britannia, **70**
British Columbian gold, 93
British Museum, 84
Britt, Sidney, 115
bronze sculpture, 15, **15**
Broom Hall, Fifeshire, 88
Brother Jonathan, **93**
Brown, Basil, 20
Brueys, Vice Admiral, 82-83
buccaneers, 129
Buddha, 23
buoys, sonar, 116
burial ships:
  Oseberg, 22-23, **22-23**
  Sutton Hoo, 20-1, **20-1**
Burke, Richard, 50
Byron, Lord, 45
Byzantine empire, 16

C

Cadiz, **53**
  Napoleonic Wars, 82
  War of the Spanish Succession, 58
Caesarea, 16
Cairo, 31

Calais, 46
Calamai, Peter, 108
Calcutta, 71
Calicut:
  Chinese traders, 24
  early traders, 17
California:
  rush for gold, 92, 94-95
Californian, SS, 104
Camoens, 44
Campbell, Nina, 29
Canada:
  fogs, 133
  immigrants, 100
  Second World War, 110
  and the *Titanic*, 105
Canadian–Australian Line, 111
cannons:
  East Indiamen, 76
  Spanish, **50**
Canton, see Guangzhou
Cape Artemesium ship, **13**
Cape Bojador, **36**
Cape Cod, 69
Cape Finisterre, 138
Cape Gelidonya ship, **13**
Cape of Good Hope:
  Aghulas Reefs, **101**
  Las Cinque Chagas, 64
  City of Cairo, 114
  East Indiamen, **70**
  iron steamships, 92
  supply station, 72
  trade routes, 40
  Vasco da Gama, 36
Cape Horn:
  General Grant, 96
  Royal Charter, 98
  weather, 131
Cape Passero, 82
Cape San Raphael, 61
Cape Spartel, 34
Cape St. Vincent, Battle
  of (1797), 79
Cape Town, *City of Cairo*, 114, 115
Cape Verde islands, 76-77
Capuchin monks:
  Central America, 94-95,
  Egypt, 107
Caravellas, 115
caravels:
  Portuguese, 36, **38-39**
  privateers, 62
  Spanish, **49**
  Tortugas wreck, **54**
careening, 39
Caribbean:
  American Revolutionary wars, 78, **78**
  map, **128-129**
  pirates,
    Hartwell, 77
    Whydah, 68
Caribe Salvage, 60, 61
Cariboo goldfields, 93
Carnatic, **101**
Carpathia, 105
carracks:
  Portuguese, 36-45, **36-45**
  Spanish, **49**
Carreira da India, 36
Cartagena, 129
carvings, Oseberg ship, 23, **23**
castaways:
  City of Cairo, 114-115, **115**
  General Grant, 96-97, 96
  São Paulo, 40-41
  Tobie, 35
Catalonia, 31
Catherine the Great, Empress
  of Russia:
  art collection, 84, 87
  loss of *Vrouw Maria*, 86-87
  portrait, **86**
  Winter Palace, 84

Catholic Church, Spanish
  Armada, 46
cat, stowaway on *City of
  Cairo*, 114
Cattherthun, **101**
caulking, 39
Cecilia, ship of, **19**
celadon pottery, 26-27, **27**
Celebes, 90
Central America, **92-93**, 94-95
ceramics:
  Chinamania, 29
  Chinese, **6, 25**
  Geldermalsen cargo, 74, **75**
  Shinan cargo 27, **27**
  Vung Tau wreck, 28-29, **28-29**
Cerigo, see Kithira
Ceylon, **37**
Chanduy Reef wrecks, **53**
Charlestown Ferry, Boston, 69
Charlotte, Queen of Great
  Britain, 90
Châteaurenault, 58
Ch'en Tsu-i, ship of, 63
Cheng Ho, 24, **25**,
  and pirates, **63**
Cherbourg, 104
China:
  early traders, 13
  East India trade, 70, 76
  Geldermalsen cargo, 74, **75**
  ginseng, **25**
  gold trade, 92
  junks, 24-29, **24-29**
  map, **158-159**
  porcelain exports, **6, 25**, 27
  Roman traders, 12
  Silk route, 31
  Sinan wreck, 26-27, **26-27**
  tea trade, **71**, 74, **74-75**
  territorial waters, 9
  trade routes, 17
  Vung Tau wreck, 28-29, **28-29**
Chinamania, 29
Christianity, 16, **67**
Christie's:
  Admiral Stellingwerf Reef
    porcelain, **25**
  Geldermalsen porcelain, 74
  Vung Tau wreck, 29, **29**
Las Cinque Chagas, 62, 64-65, **64-65**
City of Cairo, **110-111**, 114-115, **114-115**
Civitavecchia, 82
Clan Alpine, SS, 115
Clifford, Barry, 69
clippers, 124
  General Grant, **97**
  Royal Charter, 98
cloves, **71**
Clowes, W.L., 58
clyster pump, 8
Cochin, 24
Coedyk, 87
coins:
  American, 94
  Australian, 99
  Chinese, 26
  Saudi ryals, 118, 119
  Spanish, **68**
    escudos **53**
Coleman, George, **44**
collectors, 84-91
Collyer, Captain, 106
Colossus, HMS, **84**, **85**
Columbia University, 94-95
Columbus America Discovery
  Group, 94-95
compasses:
  Chinese, **25**
  lodestone, **24**
Conde de Tolosa, see *Tolosa*
conning towers, 116
Constantinople, see Istanbul

Convention on the Law
    of the Sea, 9
    and the *Titanic*, 105
convoys, Second World War, 112
Cook, Captain James, 84
Copenhagen, Battle of (1801), **79**
Cornelisz, 73
Cornwall, 34
    pirate ships **62**
Coromandel Peninsula, 93
corsairs, French, 78, **79**
Coruña, La, 46
Countess of Scarborough, 80
Crabb, Commander, 49
Crete, 82
    Napoleon's fleet near, 82
    trade with Venice, 30, **32**
Cuba, 61
    gold trade, 94
    Spanish plate ships, 54-55
    Whydah, 68
cultural heritage, 9
Cumberland, duke of, **62**
Cumberland, George Clifford,
    third earl of, 64-65, **65**
Cunard Line, 100
Cyprus:
    Roman traders, 12
    trade with Venice, 33

D

Dakar, 110
Dalmatia:
    Ulbo Island wreck, 33
    Venetian traders, 30
Dammtor, 112
Dartmouth, 64
Darwin, Charles, 84, **85**
D'Ascoli, Prince, **46**
Davis, Thomas, 69
De Braak, 78
Dean, James, 99
Debden, River, 21
Decca Recorder, 81
Defoe, Daniel, 29
Delaware, **78**
Denmark:
    East India Company, 70
    Vikings, 18
    Vrouw Maria and, 86
depth charges, 116, **117**
dhows, 17
diamonds, 92
Diane, La, HMS, 88
Diderot, Denis, 84
dividers, navigational, **50**
diving:
    diving bells, **77**
    helmets, **8**
    moon pool, **112**
    Rowe's diving engine, 48, **48**
Dnieper, River, **19**
doldrums, 36
    detours around, 40
    Las Cinque Chagas caught in, 64
Dominican Republic, 60-61
Dorinda, 88
Dou, Gerard, 87, **87**
Dourado, **37**, 44-45
Drake, Sir Francis, **47**, 62
Duc de Duras, 80
Dunkirk, 46
Duquesa Santa Ana, 50-51
Dutch East India Company
    (VOC), 70, 72-75, **72-75**

E

Eannes, Captain Gil, 36
East Indiamen, 70-77, **70-77**
    Batavia, 72-73, **72-73**
    Geldermalsen, 71, 74-75
    Hartwell, 70, 76-77, **76-77**
    ownership of wrecks, 9

East Wallabi Island, 73
Eastport International, 119
Edinburgh, HMS, 8, **111**, 112-113,
    112-113
Egypt:
    early traders, 12, 16
    looting of antiquities, 84, **84**
    Napoleonic Wars, 82-83
    Second World War, 118
    Venetian traders, 30
Egypt, 106-107, **106-107**
Elba, **79**
Elgin, Lord, **84**, 88-89, **89**
Elingamite, 93
Elizabeth I, Queen of
    England:
    and the earl of
        Cumberland, **65**
    Minerva Medal, **46**
    Spanish Armada, 46
Ellerman Lines, 114
Ellerwald, Joseph, 118
Elout, Colonel, 45
Empire Manor, **110**
England, see Britain
English Channel:
    Spanish Armada, 46, **47**
    voyage of the *Tobie*, 34
English East India
    Company, 70
    Hartwell, 76-77
    Raffles and, 90
Europe, map, **134-135**
execution for piracy, 69
    for mutineering, 73

F

Faeroe Islands, 22
Faial, 64, **65**
Fakunda, 42
Fame, 85, 90-91, **91**
Farid, Sheikh Ahmed, 119
Farouk, King of Egypt, 83
Ferrolena, 52
Fes, 35
figureheads, **88**
Fiott, John, 76
First World War, 104
Fisher, Mel, **53**
Fishmongers' Hall,
    London, **35**
Flamborough Head, Battle
    of, 80-81, **80**
Flanders, 67
Flor de la Mar, **37**, 38-39
Florence, **32**
Florida:
    Spanish treasure ships
        wrecked off, 68
    Tortugas wreck, 54-55,
        54-55
Flossi, ship of, **19**
Formosa, Mount, 44
Foss, Colonel, 48, **49**
Foster, Mrs., 98
Fowliang, porcelain, **25**
    on *Geldermalsen*, 74
    on Sinan ship, 27
    on Vung Tau wreck, 29
Framengo, 36
France:
    American Revolution, 78, 80
    East India Company, 70
    Napoleonic Wars, 82-83
    ownership of wrecks, 9
    Second World War, 110
    trade routes, 17
    trade with Venice, 30, 32
    Vikings, 18
    War of the Spanish Succession,
        58, 59
Francisca, Doña, 41
Frederick Adolphus, **71**
French Revolution, 78
frigates, 78, **82**

G

Gairsoppa, **110**
galleasses, 49, 50, **50**
galleons:
    English, **49**
    Guadalupe, **53**, 60-61
    *Nuestra Señora de la
        Concepción*, 56-57, **57**
    Spanish Armada, 49
    Spanish plate fleets, 52, **52-53**
    Tobermory galleon, 48-49
    Tolosa, 53, 60-61, **60-61**
galleys:
    pirates: 62, 66
    Venetian, 32, **32-33**
Gama, Vasco da, 36
Ganges, River, 71
Gaul, 21
Geary, Captain, 102
Geldermalsen, **71**, 74-75
General Barker, 84
General Grant, 92-93, 96-97, **96**
Genoa:
    Andrea Doria sails from, 108
    Levantine trade, 30
    rivalry with Venice, 32
Germany:
    cargo-carrying submarines,
        116-117, **116-117**
    Second World War, 110
    shipping companies, 100
    sinks the *City of Cairo*, 114
    sinks the *John Barry*, 118
    U-boats, 112
Gibraltar, Strait of:
    trade routes, 17
    wreck of the *Tobie*, 34
Giglio ship, 12
Gimbel, Peter, 109
ginger, **32**
ginseng, **25**
Girona, 46, 50-51, **50-51**
glassware:
    Serçe Limani wreck, 16-17,
        16-17
    Viking, **19**
Glenmark, 93
globes, **7**
Goa, Portuguese traders, 36
    treasure from, 39
Gokstad ship, 18, **19**
gold:
    Central America, 94-95
    Edinburgh, HMS, 112-113, **113**
    Egypt, 106-107, **107**
    Girona, 51
    Guangzhou–Jakarta trade, 75
    I-52, 116
    Nuestra Señora de la Concepción,
        56-57, **57**
    Rand gold-fields, 92
    rush for gold, 92-93, **92-93**
    in Second World War, 110
    Spanish plate fleets, 52
Golden Gate, 93
Goodlay, George, 34-35
El Gran Grifon, 47
Graveleines, Battle of (1588), 46
graves, see war graves
Greece:
    Antikythera wreck, 14-15
    early traders, 12
    Elgin marbles, 89
    ownership of wrecks, 9
    Tobie bound for, 34
Greenland, Vikings, 18, **18**
Grimm, Jack, 95
Grosvenor, 71
Guadalupe, **53**, 60-61
Guam, 56
Guangzhou (Canton):
    early traders, 27
    East India trade, 74-75
    tea trade, 92
Guardi, Giacomo, **82**

Gudrod the Hunter, 22
Guidotta e Simona, **31**
Guinea, 40
Gulf Stream, 108
guns:
    Liberty ships, **118**
    submarines, **116**
    see also cannon
Guzman, Doña Catalina de, **57**

H

hafskips, 18
Hakluyt, Richard, 34
Hallstrom, Sverker, 28, **28**
Hamilton, Sir William, **82**, **85**
Hampton roads, Norfolk, 118
hanging for piracy, 69
Gama, Vasco da, 36
Harald Granraude, King of
    Agder, 22
Harding, Samuel, 69
Harland and Wolff, 104
Hartwell, 70, 76-77, **76-77**
Hasegawa, 42
Hatcher, Michael, **25**, 75
Havana, 61
    gold trade, 94
    Spanish plate ships, 54-55, 68
Haverfield, USS, 117
Hayes, 73
Hellespont, 13
Helsingør, 86
Henry, Samuel, 98
Herbert, **63**
Hickory, **60**
Hilliard, Nicholas, **65**
Hispaniola, 60
Ho Chi Minh City, 28
Holland, see Netherlands
Holy Roman Empire, 30
Holyhead, 98
Hon Bay Canh, 28
Hong Kong, 28
Hormuz:
    early traders, 17
    Portuguese traders, 36
    Roman traders, 12
Hornigold, Benjamin, 68
Horsbrough, James, 45
Horsbrough Lighthouse, 45
Hosia, William, 71
Houtman Abrolhos Islands, 73, **73**
Hull, 114
Hunt, Lord, 88
Hussar, 78

I

I-8, **116**
I-29, 116
I-52, 116-117
icebergs, 104-105
Iceland, Vikings, 18, **19**
Ifremer:
    and the *John Barry*, 119
    and the *Titanic*, 105
Île de France, **109**
India:
    Chinese traders, 24
    early traders, 13
    East Indiamen, 70
    map, **148-149**
    Portuguese traders, 36
    Roman traders, 12
    silver imports, 119
    spice trade, 71
    trade routes, 17, 40
Indian Ocean:
    Arab traders, 17
    Greek traders, 12
    map, **8**
    pirates, **63**
    privateers, **63**
    Second World War, 116
    trade routes, 70

Indonesia:
    East Indiamen, 70
    and the *Flor de la Mar*, 39
    map, **152-153**
    pirates, **63**
international waters, 9
Iran (Persia):
    East Indiamen, 70
    lead production, 16
    Portuguese traders, 36
Ireland:
    Girona, 50-51, **50-51**
    map, **136-137**
    Spanish Armada, 46, 50-51, **51**
    Vikings, 18
Irish Sea, 98
iron ships, 100
Islam, see Muslims
Isle of Wight, 34
Israel:
    and the Serçe Limani
        wreck, 16
    Venetian traders, 30
Istanbul (Constantinople): 16
    Byzantine empire, 16
    English ambassadors, 34
    trade routes, 19
    Venetian traders, 30, **31**, 32
Italian careening, **39**
Italy:
    and the Antikythera wreck, 15
    Tobie bound for, 34
    trade routes, 17
Itsukishima, **111**
Iyeyasu, Shogun, 42

J

Jacobsz, 72-73
Jakarta:
    and the *Batavia*, 72
    gift of diamonds to Raffles, 90
    gold trade, 75
    porcelain trade, **25**, 29
    tea trade, 75
Jamaica:
    American Revolution, **78**
    pirates, **62**
    triangular Atlantic trade, 68
James I, King of England, 66
Janssen, USS, 117
Japan:
    East Indiamen, 70
    and the *Madre de Deus*, 42-43
    map, **158-159**
    recovery of Second World War
        losses, 8
    Second World War, 116
    trade with China, 27
Japan, 93
Japanese Maritime Development
    Company, 43
Java:
    East Indiamen, 70
    Raffles and, 90, **90**
Jayatama Istikacipta, 39
Jessop, Keith
    and the *HMS Edinburgh*,
        113, **117**
    and the *John Barry*, 119
Jessop Marine, 112, 113
Jesuits, 42
*Jesus y Nuestra Señora del
    Rosario*, 55
Jewell, Joseph and Ann, 96
jewelry:
    on *Las Cinque Chagas*, 64
    Spanish, **52**
    on *Tolosa* wreck, 61
Jedda, 24
Jingdezhen, see Fowliang
Johanna, 70
John Barry, **111**, 118-119
John Elder, **100**
John, Harry, 94-95
John L. Stephens, 94

Jones, John Paul, 80-81, **81**
Jules, 36
Julian, John, 69
junks, 24-29, **24-29**
   Cheng Ho's voyages, 24
   Sinan wreck, 26-27
   Vung Tau wreck, 28-29, **28-29**

K

Kalgoorlie, 93
Kangxi, Emperor of China, 28
Kensington Palace, London, 29
Kimberley, 92
Kitchen Quing, 29
Kithira, (Cerigo) 67, 88-89
knarr (knorr) ships, 18
Knights of St. John, 63
Kondos, Captain Dimitrios, 14
Korea:
   map, **158-159**
   Sinan wreck, 26
   trade with China, 27
Kos, 15
Kronborg Castle, 86, **87**
Ksar el Kebir, 35
Kuantung wreck, **37**
Kublai Khan, 27
Kure Navy Yard, 116

L

La Rochelle, 106
Lagos, 58
Landais, Captain, **81**
Languedoc, 30
Laqui, **87**
lateen sails, **66**
law, 9
Le Havre, 106
Lebanon, trade routes, 17
Lebous, Louis, 68
Leiva, Don Alonso de, 50-51
Leptis Magna, 12
letters of marque, 62, **63**
Levant Company, 34
Levantine trade, 30-35, **30-31**
Liberty ships, 118-119, **118-119**
lighthouse, Pharos, **33**
liners, 100-109, **100-101**
   Andrea Doria, **100**, 108-109, **108-109**
   Egypt, 106-107, **106-107**
   Titanic, 104-105, **104-105**
Lisbon, 37
   East Indiamen, 70
   Spanish Armada, 46, **46**
   trade with England, 84
   wrecks, 36
Liverpool Bay, 98
Livorno, 34
Llanallgo, 99
lodestone, **24**
logbooks, 7
London:
   gold market, 110
   River Thames, 34, **34-35**
London Bridge, **35**
London Salvage Association, 95
Long Island, Bahamas, 68
longships, Viking, 18
lorcha, 28
Lorentz, Reinhold, 86
Lorient, 116, 116
Louis XIV, King of France, 71
Lucian, 15
Lysippos ship, **12**

M

Maatschappy Nederland, **102**
Macao:
   Andre Pessoa in, 43
   Dourado, 44

Maclean of Duart Castle, 48
Madagascar:
   map, 144
   pirates, 63
   São Paulo's voyage, 40
   Winterton wrecked off, 71
Madagascar, 93
Madre de Deus, **37**, 42-43
Madre de Dios, 64, 65
Magdalena, **62**
Magellan, Strait of, 131
Mahdia ship, **12**
mail ships, 100-109; see also liners
Malabar, **101**
Malacca *see* Melaka
Malaya:
   map, **155**
   Second World War, 116
Malaysia, 39
Malea, 15
Malta, 82
Manchus, 29
Mandarin's Cap wreck, **25**
Manila:
   Spanish plate ships, 56
   Spanish traders, 52
Manila Bay, 111
MARAD (US Department of Maritime Administration), 9
Marine, 94
Marine Salvage Services, 103
Mariner, 91
Maritime Explorations, North America, 69
Marmara, Sea of, 16
Marpessa, 102-103
Mary, 58
Mary Ann, 69
Massachusetts, 69
masts:
   Chinese junks, **26-27**, 27
   galleys, **33**
   mizzen:
      Hartwell, **76**
      Sinan wreck, 26
      Spanish galleons, **57**
      Viking ships, 22, **23**
Matsuura, Lieutenant Commander Shin-ichi, 116
May, E.C., 97
Mayflower, 64-65
medicine chests, **40**
Medina Sidonia, Duke of, 46
Mediterranean:
   Antikythera wreck, 14-15
   Barbary pirates, 66
   early traders, 17
   Liberty ships, 118
   map, **142-143**
   Napoleonic Wars, 82-83
   Roman ships, 12
   Serçe Limani wreck, 16-17
   Venetian traders, 30
   Vikings, 18
Mehmed II, Sultan, **31**
Melaka:
   Albuquerque captures, 38, 39
   early traders 17
   importance of, 39
   map, **39**
   Portuguese traders, 36
   São Paulo survivors reach, 41, **41**
   trade with China, 24
Melbourne, 96, 98
Mello, Don Francisco de, 64
Melo, Dona Louisa de, 65
Menachini, Basilio, 89
Menencabo River, 41, **41**
Mentor, **84**, 88-89, **89**
Mercedes, **79**
mercury carriers, 60-61, **60**
Merlin (remote-operated vehicle), 55, **55**
Merten, Karl-Friedrich, 114
Messina, 82
Metsu, Gabriel, 87

Mexico:
   gold-rushes, 92
   silver mines, 60
Mexico, Gulf of, map, **126-127**
microscope, 85
Minas Gerais, 36
Minerva Medal, 46
Ming Empire, 24, 29
Mingzhou, 27
mizzen masts:
   Sinan wreck, **26**
   Hartwell, **76**
Moluccas (Spice Islands), 90
   East Indiamen, 70
   spice trade, 71
   trade with Melaka, 39
Mongols, 27
Monomatapa, 36
moon pool, **112**
Moors, 35
Morea, 82
Morel, Jan, 74
Morgan, Henry, **62**
Morning Reef, 73
Morocco, 30, 35
Morse, Jacob, 97
Mozambique, 64
Mull, Isle of, 48
Murchison, K., 45
Murmansk, 112
Musée du Louvre, Paris, 84
Muslims:
   influence in the Mediterranean, 16
   pirates, 62, 66-67
Mutine, HMS, 88

N

Nagasaki Bay, 42-43
Nanhai trade, 26
Nanking porcelain, 74
Nantucket lightship, 108
Naples, Bay of, 82, **82**
Napoleon I, Emperor, 78
   Battle of the Nile, 82-83
   collections of antiquities, 84, **84**
Napoleonic Wars, 82-83
National Ocean Industries Association, 81
navigation:
   Chinese, **25**
   compasses, 24, **25**
   dividers, **50**
   instruments, **7**
   lodestone, **24**
   sextants, 76
   Venetian traders, 30
   Vikings, 18
Nelson, Horatio:
   Battle of Copenhagen, **79**
   Battle of the Nile, 82-83
   dress coat, **79**
   and the Elgin marbles, 89
Netherlands:
   Batavia, 72-73, **72-73**
   East India Company, 70, 72-75
   Geldermalsen, 74-75
   loss of the *Prins Frederik*, 102
   and the Spanish Armada, 46
   trade with Venice, 30, 32
   War of the Spanish Succession, 58, **59**
New York:
   Andrea Doria lost off, **100**, 108
   Hussar wrecked off, **78**
New Zealand:
   map, **150-151**
   rush for gold, 92-93
Newton, Isaac, 59
Niagara, **111**
Nile, Battle of the (1798), 82-83, **83**
Noord Island, 75

North Africa:
   pirates, 63, 66-67
   trade with Venice, 30
North America:
   maps:
      Eastern coast of, **124-125**
      Western coast of, **132-133**
      Vikings, 18
   see also Canada; United States of America
North Sea, 136
   map, **138-139**
Northern Mariana Islands, 56
Norway:
   Oseberg burial ship, 22-23, **22-23**
   Vikings, 18
Nuestra Señora de Guadalupe, see *Guadalupe*
Nuestra Señora de Guia, 62
Nuestra Señora de la Concepción (wrecked 1638), **52**, 56-57, **57**
Nuestra Señora de la Concepción (wrecked 1641), **53**
Nuestra Señora de la Consolación, 55
Nuestra Señora de los Reyes, 55

O

oarsmen:
   galleys, 32-33, **32**
   Girona, **51**
   pirate ships, 62, **66-67**
   Venetian galleys, 32, **32**
   Viking ships, 18, 20-21
Olaf, Bishop, **19**
Old Head of Kinsale, 98
Ophir, 12
Order of the Knights of St. John, 67
Order of the Knights of Santiago, **61**
Orient, **79**, 82-83, **83**
Ortelius, Abraham, **120-121**
Oseberg burial ship, 18, **19**, 22-23, **22-23**
Oslo Fjord, 22
Ostade, Adriaan van, 87
Ottoman Empire, 30, **31**
ownership of wrecks, 9
Oxford, **62**

P

Pacific Mail Steamship Company, 92
Pacific Ocean, maps, **124-125**
Pacific Steam Navigation Company, **100**
paddlesteamers, 100
   gold shipments, 92, **95**
Pallas, **80**
Palmer, William, 35
Panama, 94
Panin, Count, 86-87
parallel rulers, **7**
Parma, Duke of, 46
Parthenon, Athens, 88-89
Patras, 34
pearls, 71
Pearson, Captain, 80-81
Pedra Branca, 45
Pelsaert, Captain, 72-73
Peninsular and Oriental (P & O), 100, 106
pepper, 71
Persia, see Iran
Persian Gulf:
   John Barry's route, 118
   map, **145**
   trade routes, 17
Pessoa, Andre, 42-43
Petra, 44, **45**
Phantom DHD2, 54, **54**

Pharos of Alexandria, 33
Philip II, King of Spain: 46, **46**
   Armada, **46**, 47
   Tobermory galleon, 49
Philip V, King of Spain, 58
Philippines:
   map, **154**
   Spanish plate ships, 56
   Spanish traders, 52
   territorial waters, 9
   trade with China, 27
Phocaeans, 12
Phoenicians, 12
Piercy, Captain, 80
pilgrims, 32
pincer tools, **107**
Pine, John, 47
Piraeus, 88
pirates, 62-69, **62-63**
   Barbary, **63**
   Caribbean:
      Hartwell, **77**
      Reinera e Soderina captured by, 66-67
      Whydah captured by, 68-69
Plantain, James, **63**
plate fleets, Spanish, 52-61, **52-61**
Plymouth:
   Armada, 46
   privateers, 64, **65**
   Royal Charter sails from, 98
Point Romania, 44, 45
Polluce, **79**
porcelain:
   Chinamania, 29
   Chinese, 6, **25**
   Geldermalsen cargo, 74, **75**
   Vung Tau wreck, 28-29, **28-29**
Port na Spaniagh, 50
Port Royal, 62
Port Said, 118
Portland, Oregon, 118
Portsmouth, 34
Portugal:
   caravels, **38-39**
   carracks, 36-45, **36-45**
   East India Company, 70
   English privateers and, 64
   ownership of wrecks, 9
Poseidon, statue of, **13**
Postboy, 58
Potosi, **53**
Potter, John, 58
Pratas Reef wreck, **37**
Pretty, Mrs., 20
Prince de Conty, **70**
Prins Alexander, **103**
Prins Frederik, **100**, 102-103, **102-103**
privateers:
   American, 78
   English, 64-65
   letters of marque, 62, **63**
   sponsors, 62
Puerto Rico, 60, 68
Punt, 12

Q

Quaglia, Commendatore, 107, **107**
Quanzhou, 27
Québec, 78
Queen, **70**
Queen of the Thames, **92**
Queenstown, 104

R

Raedwald, King, 21
Raffles, Lady Sophia, 90-91, **91**
Raffles, Sir Thomas Stamford:
   establishes settlement at Singapore, 44
   loss of the *Fame*, **85**, 90-91
   portrait, **91**

Ragusa, 30, 49
Raphael, 33
Ras Tannurah, 118
La Rata Encoronada, **46**
Ravenstein, 71
Recife, 36, 114
Red Sea:
  Chinese traders, 24
  map, **145**
  trade routes, 17
  Venetian traders, **31**
  wreck of *Carnatic*, **101**
Redondela, 58, 59
Reinera e Soderina, **63**, 66-67
remote-operated vehicles (ROV),
  54-55, **55**
Revolution, age of, **78-79**, 78-83
Reynolds, Sir Joshua, 85
Rhakotis, 115
Rham, Max de, 75
Rhode Island, 68-69
Rhodes:
  early traders, 15
  Knights of St. John, **63**
  trade with Ottoman
    Empire, **31**
Rienzi, Louis Domenic de,
  44-45, **45**
Risdon Beazley Ltd, 6-7, 113
RMS Titanic Inc., 105
Rodgers, Joseph, 98
Rogerson, Captain, 114
Roman Empire, 12
  Antikythera wreck, 15
  merchant ships, **14-15**
Rooke, Admiral Sir George,
  58, **58**
Rosario, 62
round ships, 33
Rowe, Jacob, 48, **48**
Royal Captain Shoal wreck, **25**
Royal Charter, **92**, 98-99, **98-99**
Royal Exchange, 64-65
Royal Mail, 100
Royal Mint, 59
Royal Navy:
  American Revolution, 78
  Baltic fleet, 80
  war graves, 8
rulers, parallel, **7**
Russia:
  the *John Barry's* cargo, 118-119
  loss of *HMS Edinburgh*, 112-113
  loss of the *Vrouw Maria*, 86-87
ryals, Saudi, 118, 119
Rynsburgh, 71

S

Sable Island, 133
Sacramento, 36
sails:
  caravels, **39**
  Chinese junks, **26-27**
  lateen, 66
  Oseberg burial ship, **22**
  Spanish galleons, **57**
  studding, **88**
Saint Geran, 71
St. Helena, 114-115
St. Petersburg, Winter Palace,
  84, 86
St. Vincent, Earl of, 82
Saints, Battle of (1782), 78
Saipan, 56
Salé, 35
  pirates, 62
Salvador, 40
Salvage Association, 9
salvage operations, controversy,
  8-9
Samaná Bay, 60-61
Samaritan, 63
Sampson, 64-65
San Agustin, 53
San Bernardino Strait, 56

San Felipe, **47**, **52**
San Francisco, **94-95**
  gold shipments, 92, 94
San José, **56**
San Juan de Sicilia, 49
San Michele, 31
San Pedro, **53**
San Pedro de Alcantara, 53
San Pedro Mayor, 47
San Pietro ship, **12**
sandbanks, 70
Sandberg, Peter, 106-107, **106**
Santa Margherita, **52**
Santa Maria de la Rosa, 46
Santa Maria Encoronada, 50-51
Santa Rosa, 36
Santo Alberto, 36, 64
Santo Cristo de Castello, 30
Santo Cristo de Maracaibo, 59
Santo Domingo, 61
São Paulo, **37**, 40-41, **41**
São Thome, 37
Sardam, 73
Sarpedon, 103
Saudi ryals, 118-119
Scaleby Castle, 76
Scandinavia, Vikings, 18
scientific voyages, 84
Scotland:
  Spanish Armada, 48-49, **51**
  Tobermory Galleon, 48-49
sculpture, bronze, 15, **15**
Seahawk Deep Ocean
  Technology Inc., 54-55
Second World War, 110-119,
  110-111
  City of Cairo, 114-115,
    114-115
  HMS Edinburgh, 112-113,
    112-113,
  I-52, 116-117
  John Barry, 118-119
  war graves, 8
Seine, 71
Selim I, Sultan, 66
Sensible, 83
Serapis, 80-81, **80-81**
Serçe Limani wreck, 9, **12-13**,
  16-17
Serrao's ship, 37
Seville, 58
sextants, 76
Shakespeare, William, 11, 121
Shap'ng Tsai, **24**
ships of the line, 78
Shoemaker, Captain, 119
silk, 42-43, **42**
Silk route, 31
silver:
  from the *Batavia*, 72
  on the *City of Cairo*, 114
  on the *Egypt*, 106-107
  on the *Hartwell*, 77
  on the *John Barry*, 118-119
  Manila Bay treasure, 111
  Mexican mines, 60
  on the *Prins Frederik*, 102
  South American mines,
    52, **53**
  Vigo Bay wrecks, 58-59
Sinan ship, **25**, 26-27
Singapore, 28
  I-52 in, 116
  importance of, 44, **44**
  wreck of the *Dourado*,
    44-45
Singapore Strait, 29
Skagen, 86
Sluttsbush, Massachusetts, 69
Smallett, 48
Smit, 119
Smith, Captain, 104
Smith, Mr., 99
snows, 86-87, **86-87**
Soleil d'Orient, 71
sonar buoys, 116
Sorima, 106, 107

South Africa:
  immigrants, 100
  rush for gold, 92
  Second World War, 114
South America:
  silver mines, 52, **53**
South China Sea, 74
  map, **156-157**
Southack, Captain, 69
Southampton:
  Prins Frederik calls at, 102
  Titanic leaves from, 104
Spain:
  Armada, **7**, 46-51, **46-47**
  English privateers and, 64
  map, **140-141**
  ownership of wrecks, 9
  plate fleets, 52-61, **52-61**
  Roman traders, 12
  trade with Venice, 30, 32
  Vikings, 18
  War of the Spanish Succession,
    58, **59**
Speaker, 63
Spice Islands, see Moluccas
spice trade:
  and the Levant, **31**
  and East Indiamen, **71**
sponge diving, 14, 15
Sri Lanka (Ceylon):
  East Indiamen, 70
  Malabar, **101**
  map, 148-149
  Roman traders, 12
  trade with China, 24
Stadiatos, Elias, 14
Stalin, Joseph, 112
Stangarfoli, **18**
steamships, 98, 100
Stenuit, Robert, 50
Stephaniturm, 112
Stockholm, 108-109
Stoller, Mike, 108
studding sails, **88**
submarines:
  German Biber, **111**
  I-52, **110**, 116-117, **116-117**
  sink the *City of Cairo*, 114
  sink the *John Barry*, 118
  U-boats, 112
Suez, 118
Sulla, General, 15
sultanas, 32
sultans, **32**
Sumatra, 90
  East Indiamen, 70
  Flor de la Mar wrecked off, 38
  map, **155**
  São Paulo wrecked off, 40, **41**
  spice trade, 71
  trade routes, 29
  trade with China, 24
Sunda, Strait of, 75
Sunetta, 118
Sung dynasty, 27
Supreme Court (US), 95
Sutton Hoo, 20-21, **20-21**
Sweden:
  East India Company, 70
  Vikings, 18
swords, Viking, **18**
Syracuse, 82
Syre, 44
Syria:
  Muslims control, 16
  trade with Venice, 33

T

Table Mountain, **115**
T'ai Ping, **25**
Tauro, 58
Taylor, Captain, 98-99
Taylor, Lieutenant
  Commander, 116
tea trade, 71, 74-75, **74-75**
Teer, James, 96-97

Telemaque, 79
Tengah reef, 39
territorial waters, 9
textiles:
  silk, 42-43, **42**
  wool, 34, **34**
Thailand, 9
  map, **156-157**
Thames, River, 34, **34-35**
tin trade, 34, **34**
Titanic, 8, **100**, 104-105, **104-105**
Tobermory galleon, 47, 48-49
Tobie, 30, 34-35, **34-35**
Tolosa, 53, 60-61, **60-61**
torpedoes, 118
Tortugas wreck, **53**, 54-55, **54-55**
Toulon, 82
trade routes:
  Acapulco–Manila, 52, **52-53**, 56
  of East Indiamen, 70
  to India, 40
  Mediterranean, 17
  trade winds, 71
La Trinidad Valencera, 46
Tripoli:
  Levantine trade, 30
  pirates, 63, 66
  trireme galleys, 32
Tu Yuan, ship of, **25**
Tunis:
  Levantine trade, 30
  pirates, 63, 66-67
Turkey:
  Serçe Limani wreck, 16-17
  trade routes, 17
  Venetian traders, 30
Turkey Company, 34
*Twenty Thousand Leagues Under
  the Sea*, 59, **59**

U

U-boats, 112
  sink the *City of Cairo*, 114
  sink the *John Barry*, 118
U530, 116
Ulbo Island, 32-33, **32-33**
underwater archaeology, 8-9
United Kingdom, see Britain
United Nations, Convention of
  the Sea, 9
  and the *Titanic*, 105
United States of America:
  immigrants, 100
  Liberty ships, 118-19, **118-119**
  ownership of wrecks, 9
  Revolution, 78, 80-81
  rush for gold, 92, 94
  Second World War, 110
  and the *Titanic*, 105
  Tortugas wreck, 54-55, **54-55**
United States Maritime
  Commission, 118
Uno, Kameo, 116
Urca Doncella, La, 46
Ushant:
  wreck of the *Egypt*, 106
  wreck of the *Prins Frederik*,
    102-103

V

Van der Mylen, Lucretia, 72-73
Van Dijk, 75
Vanguard, 82
Velasco, Manuel de, 58
Vendela, **70**
Vengeance, **80**
Venice:
  Levantine trade, 30-33, **30-31**
  Reinera e Soderina, 67
Veracruz, 60
Verne, Jules, 59
Versailles, Peace of (1783), 78
Vicar of Bray, **95**

La Victorieuse, HMS, 89
Vidala, 30
Vietnam:
  Vung Tau wreck, 28-29
Vigo Bay wrecks, 53, 58-59, **58-59**
Viking Ship Museum, Oslo, 22
Vikings, 18
  Oseberg burial ship, 22-23,
    22-23
  Sutton Hoo burial, 20-21, **20-21**
Violet, 64
Visal, 28
Visman, Captain Klaus, 102-103
VOC, see Dutch East India
  Company
Voltaire, 84
Vroom, Henrik Cornelisz, **10-11**
Vrouw Maria, 84, 86-87, **87**
Vung Tau wreck, **25**, 28-29, **28-29**

W

Wapping, 69
war graves:
  HMS Edinburgh, 113
  shipwrecks as, 8
War of the Spanish Succession, 58
War Risk Insurance Office, 9
Ward, John, 66-67
Warley, 76
warships:
  Armada, 46-51, **46-49**
  Bonhomme Richard, 80-81, **80-81**
  Orient, 82-83, **83**
  ships of the line, 78
  see also U-boats
Wellington, 91
Wells Fargo American Exchange
  Bank, 94, **95**
West Indies, 68
West of Scotland Syndicate, 49
Western Australia, 93
Western Australian Museum, 72
White Star Line, 104
Whydah, **62**, 68-69
Williams, Paul, 68-69
winds:
  Roaring Forties, 71
  trade winds, 71
Windward Passage, 68
Winterton, 71
Witte Leeuw, **70**
wood carvings, Oseberg ship,
  23, **23**
Woods Hole Institute, 105
wool, Elizabethan trade, 34, **34**
Wouverman, Philip, 87
Wright, Edward, **65**

X

xebecs, 62
Xiamen (Amoy), 29

Y

Yankee Blade, **93**
Yassi Ada ship, **13**
Yuan dynasty, 27
Yung Lo, Emperor of China, 24

Z

Zákinthos, 31, 34
Zoffany, John, 88

ACKNOWLEDGMENTS

Special thanks to: Christian Ahlstrom for information on the *Vrouw Maria*, Sverker Hallstrom for information on the Vung Tau wreck, George Bass for information on the Serçe Limani wreck, and Ralph Barker for information on the *City of Cairo*

Additional editorial assistance:
Lorna Damms, Elise Bradbury, Roderick Craig, Debra Clapson, Francis Dunne, Ray Rogers

Additional design assistance:
Ursula Dawson, Robyn Tomlinson, Nathalie Godwin, Glenda Tyrell, Steve Painter, Steve Josland

DTP designer: Karen Ruane

Additional picture research assistance: Fiona Watson

Index: Hilary Bird

Dorling Kindersley would like to thank the following for their kind permission to reproduce the photographs:
Ancient Art and Architecture Collection: 56-57; John Bastin 91cl; Battye Library: 72-73t, 73cl; Bibliothèque Nationale de France: 32tr; Bodrum Museum: 16r, 17cl, 17cr; Tracy Bowden/Pedro Borrell: 9tc, 60r, 61cr, 61c, 61br, front jacket tl, clb, back jacket cr, bl; Bridgeman Art Library: 86cl, 88br, 92tr, 120-121; British Library: 45crb, 63tl, 76bl, 86-87; British Library Oriental and India Office Collections: 90bl, 91t; British Museum: 6b, 20b, 21tr, 21cr, 34-35t, 59t, 89cl; Bill Buckhart : 57cr, 57tr; Christies: 29r, 75tl, 75bl; David G. Crawford: 112-113b; E.T. Archive: 10/11, 31tl, 32cr, 53br, 71cl; Mary Evans Picture Library: 36br, 37tl, 44-45, 59br, 61tr, 67br, 68r, 74-75c, 87cla, 102-103b, 104tr; Florida Division of Historical Research: 52br, 53tl, 56cr, 56br, 56cb, 68br; Gemeentearchief, Amsterdam: 103c; Giraudon: 84cr; Sverker Hallstrom: 28bl, 28cb, 28tr; Michael Holford: 15br; Hulton Deutsch Collection: 34bc, 108-109b, 108-109t, 109tr, 109br; The Mansell Collection: 33c, 81cr; Maritime Heritage, Boston: 94-95t; Mull Museum: 49tr; Museum of Athens: 13t, 15tl, 15tr; Museum of the History of Science, Oxford: 40br; Museum of the Order of Saint John: 67crb; Museum of Saint Malo: 63tr; National Archives: 117t, 117b; National Geographic /Edward. H. Kim: 27c, National Maritime Museum: 2, 4c, 4br, 7c, 38bl, 38-39b, 39cr, 41t, 41cl, 46clb, 46cla, 47cr, 48c, 49br, 50-51c, 51br, 58cb, 62bl, 65t, 65r, 67tl, 68cr, 76tr, 77cr, 76-77b, 79cr, 79br, 80-81b, 81tl, 82tr, 83tc, 83bl, 88-89, 89bl, 96-97, 101tl,118-119b; National Museums of Merseyside: 98cr; National Portrait Gallery, *Hamilton* by J. Reynolds: 85tl, *Raffles* by George Francis Joseph 91br; Peter Newarks Western Americana: 92bl 94ca; Christine Osbourne: 45cb; Otago Witness: 96b, 97tr; Douglas Quantrill: 115cr; Rijksmuseum, Amsterdam: 87br; Rigsarkivet (Danish Archives): 87tl; Royal Charter Salvage Operation/Peter Day/Jack Smart/Ken Jones: 3br, 99cr, 99br; The Royal Navy Submarine Museum: 116c; Scala: 33tr; Science Museum: 66-67; Scottish Records Office: 102-3; Seahawk Deep Ocean Technology/Greg Stemm: 54tr, 55tl, 55tr, 55cr; Southland Museum: 96tr; Sunday Times/Ian Yeomans: 112tr, 113tl, 113c, 113ca, front jacket tc; Ulster Museum Belfast : 3c, 50bl, 51c, 51tr, 51cr, front jacket bl; University of Glasgow: 114-115t; University of Wales Museum: 18cl; Louis Vuitton: 101ca; Wallace Collection: 31bl; Wells Fargo Historical Service: 94br; Werner Forman Archives/H.M. de Young Memorial Museum, San Francisco: 42-43; Western Australian Maritime Museum: 72bl, 72br; Worlds End Picture Library 99tl, endpaper

Every effort has been made to trace the copyright holders. However, Dorling Kindersley apologizes for unintentional omissions and would be pleased in such cases to add an acknowledgment in future editions.